What is
Cultural Studies?

What is
Cultural Studies?

A Reader

Edited by

John Storey

Reader in Cultural Studies
University of Sunderland

A member of the Hodder Headline Group
LONDON • NEW YORK • SYDNEY • AUCKLAND

First published in Great Britain in 1996 by
Arnold, a member of the Hodder Headline Group
338 Euston Road, London NW1 3BH
175 Fifth Avenue, New York, NY 10010

Second impression 1997

Distributed exclusively in the USA by
St Martin's Press Inc.,
175 Fifth Avenue,
New York, NY 10010

British Library Cataloguing in Publication Data
A catalogue entry for this book is available from the British Library

Library of Congress Cataloging-in-Publication Data
What is cultural studies?: a reader/edited by John Storey.
    p. cm.
  Includes bibliographical references and index.
  ISBN 0–340–65239–X. – ISBN 0–340–65240–3 (pbk.)
  1. Culture–Study and teaching. I. Storey, John, 1950–
HM101.W439   1996
306'.07–dc20   95–25445
                                                                                CIP

ISBN 0 340 65240 3 (Pb)
ISBN 0 340 65239 X (Hb)

Composition by J&L Composition Ltd, Filey, North Yorkshire
Printed and bound in Great Britain by J.W. Arrowsmith Ltd, Bristol

For Kate and Jenny

Contents

Preface

This is not a 'Cultural Studies Reader'. That is, it is not a collection of essays from and about cultural studies, demonstrating the range, the diversity and the infectious excitment of the field. Instead, the concerns of this volume are far more modest, far more specific. The aim is to collect together for the first time a group of essays from Australia, Britain and the USA, which attempt, sometimes directly, sometimes indirectly, to define the project of cultural studies. The title is intended to be taken quite literally: 'what *is* cultural studies?' Definitions range from the explicit to the implicit, from historical cartographies of its past to claims made on its future.

Of course, it might be argued that all cultural studies readers address this question implicitly, through the bringing together of significant work in the field. What makes this volume different is its self-imposed concentration of focus. It is an introduction to cultural studies through a series of attempts to define cultural studies. It does not offer examples of work in the field, but collects together work which attempts to define it. The essays are collected in chronological order to allow the reader to map the development of the field. Together the 22 essays provide a perspective on the past, present and possible future(s) of cultural studies. Together they make fascinating and indispensable reading for the student of cultural studies.

I would like to take this opportunity to thank all those who have contributed, knowingly and unknowingly, to the writing of this book, especially family, friends, colleagues and students (past and present). I would also like to thank the School of Arts, Design and Communications, University of Sunderland, for lightening my teaching load during the course of writing this book. Finally, I would especially like to thank Paul Marris, Lesley Riddle, Jannette Storey, Jenny Storey, Kate Storey and Sue Thornham, for their support and encouragement throughout.

Acknowledgements

The editor and publishers would like to thank the following for permission to use copyright material in this book:

Screen and the author for Colin Sparks, 'The evolution of cultural studies', *Screen Education* 22, 16–30; Sage Publications for Stuart Hall, 'Cultural studies: two paradigms', *Media, Culture and Society* 2, 57–72; Methuen & Co. for Michael Green, 'The Centre for Contemporary Cultural Studies', reprinted from Peter Widdowson (ed.), *Re-Reading English* (London: Methuen & Co.); Sage Publications for James W. Carey, 'Overcoming resistance to cultural studies', *Mass Communication Yearbook* 5 (1985); Duke University Press for Richard Johnson, 'What is cultural studies anyway?' *Social Text* 16 (1986–87) 38–80, © Duke University Press, 1990; the University of North Carolina Press and Routledge for John Fiske, 'British cultural studies and television', reprinted from Robert Allen (ed.), *Channels of Discourse* (University of North Carolina Press, 1987); Indiana University Press and the author for Meaghan Morris, 'Banality in cultural studies', *Discourse: Journal for Theoretical Studies in Media and Culture* X.2 (spring–summer, 1988), 3–29; Verso for Raymond Williams, 'The future of cultural studies', reprinted from Raymond Williams, *The Politics of Modernism* (London: Verso, 1989), 151–62; SCA Publications for Lawrence Grossberg, 'The circulation of cultural studies', Alan O'Connor, 'The problem of American cultural studies' and Elizabeth Long, 'Feminism and cultural studies', from *Critical Studies in Mass Communication* 6 (1989); Pembroke Center for Teaching and Research on Women for Ellen Rooney, 'Discipline and vanish: feminism, the resistance to theory, and the politics of cultural studies', *Differences: A Journal of Feminist Cultural studies* 2 (1990); the author for Duncan Webster, 'Pessimism, optimism, pleasure: the future of cultural studies', *News From Nowhere* 8 (1990); Sage Publications for Ien Ang, 'Culture and communication: towards an ethnographic critique of media consumption in the transnational media system', *European Journal of Communication* 5 239–60, © 1990 Sage Publications Ltd; Routledge and the authors for Sarah Franklin, Celia Lury and Jackie Stacey, 'Feminism and cultural studies: pasts, presents, futures', *Off-Centre* (1991); the Midwest

Modern Language Association and the author for Cary Nelson, 'Always already cultural studies: academic conferences and a manifesto', *The Journal of the Midwest Modern Language Association* 24 (1991); the Johns Hopkins University Press for Joel Pfister, 'The Americanization of cultural studies', *Yale Journal of Criticism* 4 (1991); Afterimage and the author for Manthia Diawara, 'Black studies, cultural studies: performative acts', *Afterimage* October (1992); Tony Bennett, 'Putting policy into cultural studies', reprinted from *Cultural Studies* (1992), by permission of the publisher, Routledge, New York; Graeme Turner, '"It works for me": British cultural studies, Australian cultural studies, Australian film', reprinted from *Cultural Studies* (1992), by permission of the publisher, Routledge, New York; Guilford Publications for Stuart Hall, 'Race, culture and communications: looking backward and forward at cultural studies', *Rethinking Marxism* 5 (1992); Allen & Unwin for John Frow and Meaghan Morris, 'Australian cultural studies', reprinted from John Frow and Meaghan Morris (eds), *Australian Cultural Studies: A Reader* (Allen and Unwin, 1993).

Every effort has been made to trace copyright holders of material produced in this book. Any rights not acknowledged here will be acknowledged in subsequent printings if notice is given to the publisher.

Cultural studies: an introduction

John Storey

Preliminary definitions

Colin Sparks (Chapter 1) highlights the difficulties involved in trying to define cultural studies with any degree of precision:

> It is not possible to draw a sharp line and say that on one side of it we can find the proper province of cultural studies. Neither is it possible to point to a unified theory or methodology which are characteristic to it or of it. A veritable rag-bag of ideas, methods and concerns from literary criticism, sociology, history, media studies, etc., are lumped together under the convenient label of cultural studies.

Although Sparks's essay dates from 1977, problems of definition still remain for an author writing almost 20 years later. Therefore, although it is possible to point to degree programmes, to journals, to conferences and to associations, there is no simple answer to the question, 'what is cultural studies?' ... Traditionally, an academic discipline is defined by three criteria: first, there is the object of study; secondly, there are the basic assumptions which underpin the method(s) of approach to the object of study; and thirdly, there is the history of the discipline itself.

John Fiske (Chapter 6), maintains that 'culture' in cultural studies 'is neither aesthetic nor humanist in emphasis, but political'. What he means by this is that the object of study in cultural studies is not culture defined in the narrow sense, as the objects of aesthetic excellence ('high art'); nor culture defined in an equally narrow sense, as a process of aesthetic, intellectual and spiritual development; but culture understood, in Raymond Williams's famous appropriation from anthropology, as 'a particular way of life, whether of a people, a period or a group' (1976, 90). This is a definition of culture which can embrace the first two definitions but also, and crucially, it can range beyond the social exclusivity and narrowness of these to include the study of popular culture. Although cultural studies cannot (or should not) be reduced to the study of popular culture, it is certainly the case that the study of popular culture is central to the project of cultural studies. As Cary Nelson

(Chapter 16) points out, 'people with ingrained contempt for popular culture can never fully understand the cultural studies project'. But it is also the case, as argued by Richard Johnson (Chapter 5), that 'all social practices can be looked at from a cultural point of view, for the work they do, subjectively'. Johnson defines cultural studies as the study of 'historical forms of consciousness or subjectivity'. Defined in this way, it must

> decentre 'the text' as an object of study. 'The text' is no longer studied for its own sake, nor even for the social effects it may be thought to produce, but rather for the subjective or cultural forms which it realises and makes available. The text is only a means in cultural studies; strictly, perhaps, it is a raw material from which certain forms (e.g. of narrative, ideological problematic, mode of address, subject position, etc.) may be abstracted. . . . But the ultimate object of cultural studies is not . . . the text, but the social life of subjective forms at each moment of their circulation, including their textual embodiments.

John Frow and Meaghan Morris (Chapter 22) take a slightly different view:

> There is a precise sense in which cultural studies uses the concept of *text* as its fundamental model. . . . Rather than designating a place where meanings are constructed in a single level of inscription (writing, speech, film, dress . . .), it works as an interleaving of 'levels'. If a shopping mall [for example] is conceived on the model of textuality, then this 'text' involves practices, institutional structures and the complex forms of agency they entail, legal, political, and financial conditions of existence, and particular flows of power and knowledge, as well as a particular multilayered semantic organisation; it is an ontologically mixed entity, and one for which there can be no privileged or 'correct' reading. It is this, more than anything else, that forces cultural studies' attention to the diversity of audiences for or users of the structures of textuality it analyses – that is, to the open-ended social life of texts – and that forces it, thereby, to question the authority or finality of its own readings.

Moreover, as Frow and Morris make clear, texts exist only within networks of intertextual relations. To study a 'text' means to locate it across a range of competing moments of inscription, representation and struggle. In other words, cultural studies seeks to keep in equilibrium the different moments of cultural production – material production, symbolic production, textual production, and the 'production in use' of consumption. To narrow one's focus to one moment only, and think this will adequately account for the others, is to think and act (to borrow a phrase from the good old days of certainty) 'ideologically'.

Cultural studies also regards culture as political in a quite specific sense, one which reveals the dominant political position within cultural studies. Typically, Frow and Morris (Chapter 22) conceive of culture 'not as organic expression of a community, nor as an autonomous sphere of aesthetic forms, but as a contested and conflictual set of practices of representation bound up with the processes of formation and re-formation of social groups'. Perhaps the best-known elaboration of this conception of culture comes from Stuart Hall (1981, 239). He describes popular culture, for example, as 'an arena of consent and resistance. It is partly where hegemony arises, and where it is secured. It is not a sphere where socialism, a socialist culture – already fully formed – might be simply "expressed". But it is one of the places where socialism might be constituted. That is why "popular culture matters".' Others within cultural studies might not express their attitude to popular culture quite in these terms, but they would certainly share Hall's concern to think culture politically. Johnson (Chapter 5) explains this in terms of three main premisses regarding culture:

> The first is that cultural processes are intimately connected with social relations, especially with class relations and class formations, with sexual divisions, with the racial structuring of social relations and with age oppressions as a form of dependency. The second is that culture involves power and helps to produce asymmetries in the abilities of individuals and social groups to define and realise their needs. And third, which follows the other two, is that culture is neither an autonomous nor an externally determined field, but a site of social differences and struggles.

Tony Bennett (Chapter 19) makes the case for cultural studies to change its understanding of culture. Central to his argument for the introduction of 'policy' into cultural studies is a changed definition of culture, from one which defines it in semantic terms to one that sees it as a governmental practice for transforming both mental and physical behaviour.

All the basic assumptions of cultural studies are Marxist. This is not to say that all practitioners of cultural studies are Marxists, but that cultural studies is itself grounded in Marxism. Marxism informs cultural studies in two fundamental ways. First, to understand the meanings of culture we must analyse it in relation to the social structure and its historical contingency. Although constituted by a particular social structure with a particular history, culture is not studied as a reflection of this structure and history. As Williams (Chapter 8) makes clear, history and culture are not separate entities. It is never a question of reading a text against its historical background or using the text to illustrate an already-formulated account of a historical moment – history and text are inscribed in each other and are embedded together as a part of the same process. Cultural studies insists that culture's importance derives from the fact that it helps constitute the structure and shape the history. As Hall (Chapter 21) explains, 'what cultural studies has helped me to understand is that the media [for example] play a part in the formation, in the constitution, of the things that they reflect. It is not that there is a world outside, "out there", which exists free of the discourses of representation. What is "out there" is, in part, constituted by how it is represented'. Second, cultural studies assumes that capitalist industrial societies are societies divided unequally along ethnic, gender, generational and class lines. It contends that culture is one of the principal sites where this division is established and contested: culture is a terrain on which takes place a continual struggle over meaning, in which subordinate groups attempt to resist the imposition of meanings which bear the interests of dominant groups. It is this which makes culture ideological.

Ideology is without doubt the central concept in cultural studies. James W. Carey (Chapter 4) even suggests that 'British cultural studies could be described just as easily and perhaps more accurately as ideological studies'. There are many competing definitions of ideology, but it is the formulation established by Hall (1982) which is generally accepted as the dominant definition within cultural studies. Working within a framework of Antonio Gramsci's concept of hegemony, Hall developed a theory of 'articulation' to explain the processes of ideological struggle (Hall's use of 'articulation' plays on the term's double meaning: to express and to join together). He argues that cultural texts and practices are not inscribed with meaning, guaranteed once and for all by the intentions of production; meaning is always the result of an act of 'articulation' (an active process of 'production in use'). The process is called 'articulation' because meaning has to be expressed, but it is always expressed in a specific context, a specific historical moment, within a specific discourse(s). Thus expression is always connected (articulated) to and conditioned by context. Hall also draws on the work of the Russian theorist Valentin Volosinov. Volosinov (1973) argues that meaning is always determined by context of articulation. Cultural texts and practices are 'multiaccentual'; that is, they can be articualted with different 'accents' by different people in different contexts for different politics. Meaning is therefore a social production; the world has to be made to mean. A text or practice or event is not the issuing source of meaning, but a site where the articulation of meaning – variable meaning(s) – can take place. And because different meanings can be ascribed to the same text or practice or event, meaning is always a potential site of conflict. Thus the field of culture is for cultural studies a major site of ideological struggle; a terrain of 'incorporation' and 'resistance'; one of the sites where hegemony is to be won or lost.

According to Hall's influential account (Chapter 2) of the formation and development of British cultural studies, the key point to understand is that 'there are no "absolute beginnings" and few unbroken continuities. . . . What is important are the significant *breaks* – where old lines of thought are disrupted, older constellations displaced, and elements, old and new, are regrouped around a different set of premises and themes'. Hall charts the history of cultural studies from its 'founding' in the late 1950s, through its institutionalization at the Birmingham Centre for Contemporary Cultural Studies (CCCS) in 1964, and the subsequent theoretical moments of culturalism, structuralism and Gramscian Marxism.[1] Other essays collected here elaborate and extend this history to include the moments of poststructuralism and postmodernism (see, for example, Franklin *et al.*, Chapter 15). Others extend the account geographically, charting the movement of cultural studies from Birmingham to Australia and the USA.

Cultural studies: a political project

Johnson (Chapter 5) argues that cultural studies is political, 'but not in an immediate pragmatic sense'. Nelson (Chapter 16) makes a similar point: although 'cultural studies allies itself with and helps theorize political action . . . political action and cultural studies are not interchangeable'. Nevertheless, as Alan O'Connor (Chapter 10) contends, 'The tradition of

cultural studies is not one of value-free scholarship but of political commitment'. Frow and Morris (Chapter 22) make a similar point: 'cultural studies
. . . is partisan in its insistence on the political dimension of knowledge. . . .
[T]he intellectual project of cultural studies is always at some level marked
. . . by a discourse of social *involvement*'.

In the early days of the Birmingham CCCS, cultural studies was
regarded, at least by Hall (1990a, 12), as 'politics by other means'. Part
of, or perhaps central to, the project of cultural studies (at least from the
1970s) was the production of what Gramsci (1971) calls 'organic intellectuals'. According to Hall (1992, 281), 'there is no doubt in my mind that we
[at the CCCS] were trying to find an institutional practice in cultural
studies that might produce an organic intellectual'.

Bennett (Chapter 19) is more than a little sceptical of Hall's reading of
cultural studies as a political project to establish organic intellectuals.
According to Bennett, 'to attribute such a function to an intellectual project
which has and continues to be based primarily in the academy suggests a
degree of misrecognition of its relations to the real conditions of its
existence that can only be described as ideological'. Frow and Morris
(Chapter 22) suggest that 'In Australian conditions . . . Bennett's judgment
may be too harsh'. Nevertheless, the change in cultural studies from post-
graduate area of research to undergraduate teaching (students take undergraduate degrees in cultural studies – are taught cultural studies) may mean
that many of the grander claims made in the 1970s are no longer applicable
or relevant in the 1990s. Rather than ask 'what is cultural studies?' perhaps
the more pressing question is 'whom is cultural studies for?'

According to Michael Green (Chapter 3), it is a question of locating the
nearest appropriate constituency:

> Inside the the Centre [for Contemporary Cultural Studies], groups attempted to
> think of their work in relation to the problems of the nearest appropriate
> constituency, which might not always be that of teachers in higher or second-
> ary education. For example, there could be a connection between media
> research and the interests of media workers; between research on popular
> literature and alternative publishers and bookshops, or the Federation of
> Worker Writers; between studies of the cultural formation of teenage work-
> ing-class girls and strategies of feminist 'youth work'.

In a response to a paper by Hall (1992, 294), bell hooks argued that,
ultimately, the politics of cultural studies are to be found in its pedagogy:

> Really responding to students who go see *Do the Right Thing* and come back
> and say 'Look, we took your class, we understand this feminist standpoint, but
> we also think Spike Lee is a down brother so how do we deal with what we feel
> we saw in this particular cultural production?' To me, that's the exciting
> dimension of cultural studies, that it can take place, not as me writing a
> privatized article, but as a response to students asking what type of critical
> thinking allows them to engage this cultural production in a way that informs
> our political practice.

Williams (Chapter 8) contends that the future of cultural studies (at least in
Britain) should be to intervene in 16–18 education to challenge 'a definition
of industrial training which would have sounded crude in the 1860s'.

Henry A. Giroux (1994), however, argues that cultural studies needs to rethink the practice of pedagogy; to engage in what he calls 'critical pedagogy'. Giroux's point is that cultural studies frequently fails to take seriously questions of pedagogy. Too often, according to Giroux, those working in the field of cultural studies adhere to 'the notion of pedagogy as a transparent vehicle for transmitting truth and knowledge' (1994, 130). But pedagogy does not represent a neutral site, free from the operations of power and politics. Far from being the simple transmission of ready-made information, pedagogy is for Giroux a site of struggle, a terrain where the complex relations between knowledge and power are worked over.

As part of his project, Giroux distinguishes between a pedagogy of theory and a pedagogy of theorizing. Put simply, this is the difference between theory as a body of knowledge to be learnt and theory as an activity to be practised. In the former, theory is taught as a means of understanding the world; in the latter, theorizing is encouraged as a pedagogical practice in which students become actual participants in the use of theory. Although both are crucial to the production of 'critical pedagogy', too often it is only the former which actually happens.

Post-Marxism: a crisis in cultural studies?

'Crisis', as Lidia Curti (1992, 134) points out, 'has been the password of the field from Hoggart to . . . Hebdige'. Angela McRobbie (1992, 719) agrees: 'The word crisis is one which appears with alarming regularity in the discourses of cultural studies'. For McRobbie (*ibid.*), the current crisis is perhaps better understood as a 'panic' engendered by an undermining of the Marxist paradigm:

> Marxism, a major point of reference for the whole cultural studies project in the UK, has been undermined not just from the viewpoint of the postmodern critics who attack its teleological propositions, its meta-narrative status, its essential-ism, economism, Eurocentrism, and its place within the whole Enlightenment project, but also, of course, as a result of the events in Eastern Europe, with the discrediting of much of the socialist project.

As McRobbie points out (*ibid.*), the debate about Marxism in cultural studies has yet to take place. The role of Marxism in cultural studies is still uncertain, but what does seem to be the case

> is that the return to a pre-postmodern Marxism as marked out by critics like Fredric Jameson (1984) and David Harvey (1989) is untenable because the terms of that return are predicated on prioritizing economic relations and economic determinations over cultural and political relations by positioning these latter in a mechanical and reflectionist role.

However, there is a sense in which cultural studies was always-already post-Marxist. As Hall (1992, 279) makes clear,

> There was never a prior moment when cultural studies and Marxism repre-sented a perfect theoretical fit. From the beginning . . . there was always-already the question of the great inadequacies, theoretically and politically,

the resounding silences, the great evasions of Marxism – the things that Marx did not talk about or seem to understand which were our privileged object of study: culture, ideology, language, the symbolic. These were always-already, instead, the things which had imprisoned Marxism as a mode of thought, as an activity of critical practice – its orthodoxy, its doctrinal character, its determinism, its reductionism, its immutable law of history, its status as a metanarrative. That is to say, the encounter between British cultural studies and Marxism has first to be understood as the engagement with a problem – not a theory, not even a problematic.

Therefore, although speaking of cultural studies as a political project is to articulate, sooner or later, its relationship with Marxism, and while it is clear that virtually all its founding assumptions are Marxist, it is not the case that cultural studies is 'simply' Marxism in disguise – what Green (Chapter 3) calls 'a "cover" for a revised and qualified marxism'. Marxism was one of the things it struggled against. As Green points out, cultural studies was born in a double refusal. On the one hand, it 'refused the elitism of high culture and the great tradition' and, on the other, 'it was equally opposed to the reductions of marxism understood as a hard determinism of the economic'.

Uses and abuses of cultural studies

Jim McGuigan (1992) claims that the real 'crisis' in cultural studies is that it has narrowed its focus to questions of consumption without situating such questions within the context of the material relations of production. To reverse the trend, he advocates a dialogue between cultural studies and the political economy of culture. He fears that for cultural studies to remain separate is for it to remain politically ineffective as a mode of explanation, and to risk becoming complicit with the prevailing forces of exploitation and oppression.[2]

McGuigan (*ibid.*, 85) identifies Fiske's work as 'indicative of the critical decline of British cultural studies'. Now McGuigan may be right about Fiske, but this does not make him right about cultural studies. Put simply, Fiske is not cultural studies (and nor would he claim to be). Others, from *within* cultural studies, have made similar criticisms of Fiske's work – for example, Ien Ang (Chapter 14), Martin Barker (1990), Martin Barker and Anne Beezer (1992), Lawrence Grossberg (1992) and Morris (Chapter 7). To establish Fiske as cultural studies requires their exclusion – it requires a reified and reduced field of study. David Harris's (1992) critique of cultural studies operates in much the same way. For example, in his discussion of what he regards as the inadequacies of youth studies at the CCCS, he uses the contributions of Jenny Garber and McRobbie to highlight the gender-blindness of much of this early work. But he conveniently fails to acknowledge, for the telling moment of his critique, that both Garber and McRobbie make their criticisms not only from within cultural studies but also in one of the Birmingham Centre's own publications. In other words, the fact that their argument (their work) is also cultural studies is bracketed out of the argument in order for it to function as a critique of cultural studies.

Whatever else cultural studies is, it is certainly not the monolithic unity conjured up by both McGuigan and Harris. As Green (Chapter 3) points out, 'cultural studies has been resolutely "impure"'. Frow and Morris (Chapter 22) also refer to the 'methodological impurity' of cultural studies. Hall (1992, 278) makes this very clear:

> Cultural Studies has multiple discourses; it has a number of different histories. It is a whole set of formations; it has its own different conjunctures and moments in the past. It included many different kinds of work. I want to insist on that! It always was a set of unstable formations. It was 'centred' only in quotation marks. . . . It had many trajectories; many people had and have different theoretical positions, all of them in contention. Theoretical work at the Centre for Contemporary Cultural Studies was more appropriately called theoretical noise. It was accompanied by a great deal of bad feeling, argument, unstable anxieties, and angry silences.

For example, the centrality of class in cultural studies was disrupted first by feminism's insistence on the importance of gender, and then by black students raising questions about the invisibility of race in much cultural studies analysis. *Women Take Issue* (Women's Studies Group, 1978, 15) is a telling example: 'Our initial reason for wanting to produce the book was fundamental: the continued absence from CCCS of a visible concern with feminist issues.' *The Empire Strikes Back* (Centre for Contemporary Cultural Studies, 1982, 7) announces:

> There are many reasons why the issues raised by the study of 'races' and racisms should be central to the concerns of cultural studies. Yet racist ideologies and racial conflicts have been ignored, both in historical writing and in accounts of the present. If nothing else, this book should be taken as a signal that this marginalization cannot continue.

Paul Gilroy (1987, 12) makes a similar point in *There Ain't No Black In The Union Jack*: 'The book . . . related to its origins in cultural studies . . . seeks to provide . . . a corrective to the more ethnocentric dimensions of that discipline.'

Cultural studies has always been an unfolding discourse, responding to changing historical and political conditions and always marked by debate, disagreement and intervention. Now this does not mean that cultural studies is a completely open disciplinary field. One cannot simply rename as cultural studies what one already does in order to impress publishers or to salvage a declining area of academic work. Cultural studies does mean something.

There can be no doubt that cultural studies has been experiencing great success recently. While success is to be welcomed, there are suspicions that it might not be all that it seems. Nelson *et al.* (1992, 10–11), for example, claim that 'Too many people simply rename what they were already doing to take advantage of the cultural studies boom'. Grossberg (1992, 404) makes a similar point: 'Many of those now describing their work as cultural studies were attacking cultural studies only a few years ago although they have not changed their project in the interim. Many of those who now appropriate the term want to read only very selectively in the tradition.'

Hegemony theory revisited

McRobbie's (1994) response to the so-called 'crisis' in cultural studies is to argue for a return to neo-Gramscian hegemony theory. McRobbie accepts that cultural studies has been radically transformed as debates about postmodernism and postmodernity have replaced the more familiar debates about ideology and hegemony. Cultural studies, she claims, has responded in two ways. On the one hand, it has prompted a return to economic reductive forms of analysis; and on the other, it has given rise to an uncritical celebration of consumerism, in which consumption is understood *too* exclusively in terms of pleasure and meaning-making. McRobbie argues for a return to the concept of 'reproduction' to enable consumption to be seen in its broader context of political and social relations. She rejects a return 'to a crude and mechanical base-superstructure model, and also the dangers of pursuing a kind of cultural populism to a point at which anything which is consumed and is popular is also seen as oppositional' (*ibid.*, 39). Instead, she calls for 'an extension of Gramscian cultural analysis' (*ibid.*) and for a return to ethnographic cultural analysis which takes as its object of study '[t]he lived experience which breathes life into [the] . . . inanimate objects [of popular culture]' (*ibid.*, 27). Such work would be situated in a context of reproduction.

Ang (Chapter 14) also calls for 'a return to the problematic of hegemony':

> To avoid the 'banality' in cultural studies that Morris [Chapter 7] points to . . . the ethnographic perspective on audiences needs to be placed in a broader theoretical framework, so that it ceases to be just a sophisticated empirical audience research, but becomes part of a more encompassing understanding, both structural and historical, of our contemporary cultural condition.

Neo-Gramscian hegemony theory at its best insists that there is a dialectic between the processes of production and the activities of consumption. The consumer always confronts a text or practice in its material existence as a result of determinate conditions of production. But in the same way, the text or practice is confronted by a consumer who in effect *produces in use* the range of possible meaning(s) – these cannot just be read off from the materiality of the text or practice, or the means or relations of its production.

Cultural studies would also insist that making popular culture ('production in use') can be empowering to subordinate and resistant to dominant understandings of the world. But this is not to say that popular culture is always empowering and resistant. To deny the passivity of consumption is not to deny that sometimes consumption is passive; to deny that the consumers of popular culture are not cultural dupes is not to deny that the culture industries seek to manipulate. But it is to deny that popular culture is little more than a degraded landscape of commercial and idealogical manipulation, successfully imposed from above, to make profit and secure social control. The best of cultural studies insists that to decide these matters requires vigilance and attention to the details of the production, distribution and consumption of culture. These are not matters that can be decided once and for all (outside the contingencies of history and politics) with an élitist glance and a condescending sneer. Nor can they be read off from the moment of production (locating meaning, pleasure, ideological effect, etc., in, variously, the intention, the means of production or the production itself): these are only aspects of the contexts for 'production in use', and it is, ultimately, in 'production in use' that questions of meaning, pleasure, ideological effect, etc., can be (contingently) decided. Moreover, it is important to distinguish between the power of the culture industries and the power of their influence. Too often the two are conflated, but they are not necessarily the same. The trouble with the political economy approach is that too often it is assumed that they are the same.

While it is clearly important to locate the texts and practices of popular culture within the field of their economic determinations, it is clearly insufficient to do this and think you have also analysed important questions of audience appropriation and use. As Hall (Chapter 2) points out, the problem with the political economy of culture approach is that 'It tends to conceive the economic level as not only a "necessary" but a "sufficient" explanation of cultural and ideological effects'.

There are different ways of thinking, different ways of using what Hall calls 'the enormously productive metaphor of hegemony' (1992, 280). Hegemony theory in cultural studies operates not always quite as formulated by Gramsci. The concept has been expanded and elaborated to take into account other areas of struggle. Whereas for Gramsci the concept is used to explain and explore relations of power articulated in terms of class, recent formulations in cultural studies have extended the concept to include, for example, gender, race, meaning and pleasure. What has remained constant (or relatively constant under the impact of political and theoretical change, from the left-Leavisism of Richard Hoggart to the postmodernism of, for example, McRobbie, Fiske and Grossberg) is a particular guiding principle of cultural analysis. It is first found in what Green (Chapter 3) quite rightly calls 'Hoggart's remarkably enduring formulation': 'Against this background may be seen how much the more generally diffused appeals of the mass publications connect with commonly accepted attitudes, *how they are altering those attitudes and how they are meeting resistance*' (my italics, Hoggart, 1957, 19). In the 1960s it is given a culturalist accent by Hall and Whannel: 'Teenage culture is a contradictory mixture of the authentic and the manufactured: it is *an area of self-expression for the young and a lush grazing pasture for the commercial providers*' (my italics, 1964, 276). In the 1970s it is found in the Gramscian tones of John Clarke *et al.*: 'Men and women are . . . formed, and form themselves through society, culture and history. So the existing cultural patterns form a sort of historical reservoir – a pre-constituted "field of possibilities" – which groups take up, transform, develop. Each group *makes something* of its *starting conditions* – and through this "making", through this practice, culture is reproduced and transmitted' (my italics, 1976, 11). In the 1980s we hear it in the Foucauldian analysis of Mica Nava: 'Consumerism is far more than just economic activity: it is also about dream and consolation, communication and confrontation, image and identity. . . . Consumerism is a discourse through which *disciplinary power is both exercised and contested*' (my italics, 1987, 209–10). In the 1990s it is located by Angela McRobbie in the 'new times' of postmodernism: 'Finally we need a mode of analysis which is connective and integrative and which tracks the social and ideological relations which prevail at every level between cultural production and consumption . . . *from where it is socially constructed to where it is socially deconstructed and contested*, in the institutions, practices and relationships of everyday life' (my italics, 1994, 41). In every decade in the history of cultural studies, the point has been made and repeated. It is the 'Gramscian insistence' (before, with and after Gramsci), learnt from Marx, that we make culture and we are made by culture; there is agency and there is structure. It is not enough to celebrate agency; nor is it enough to detail the structure(s) of power – we must always keep in mind the dialectical play between resistance and incorporation. The best of cultural studies has always been mindful of this.

Where is cultural studies?

Things have certainly changed a great deal since the early days of cultural studies. Hall (Chapter 21) remembers: 'When I first went to the University of Birmingham in 1964 to help Professor Richard Hoggart found the Centre for Contemporary Cultural Studies, no such thing as cultural studies yet existed. . . . Today cultural studies programs exist everywhere, especially in the United States.'

During the course of the last 15–20 years, the location of cultural studies has shifted from Britain to Australia, the USA and beyond.[3] The internationalization of cultural studies can be easily demonstrated by an examination of the editorial board of the journal, *Cultural Studies*. Of its 47 members, 19 are from the USA, nine from Australia, nine from the UK, five from Canada, two from Italy, and one each from Germany, Finland and Taiwan.[4]

Morris (Chapter 7) tells us that 'cultural studies in Australia has been for some time in the state that the Japanese call a *boom*'. What she means by this is not just that cultural studies is developing quickly in Australia but 'that the marketing of cultural studies is beginning to define and restrict what it is possible to do and say in its name'. Graeme Turner (Chapter 20) makes a similar point:

In Australia . . . the influence of British cultural studies has been profound. Most of us are aware that, as it establishes itself ever more securely within the academy, and as it becomes increasingly comfortable in its relations with the disciplines it originally interrogated, British cultural studies is in danger of becoming a pedagogic rather than a critical or poltiical enterprise.

Hall (1992, 285) also speaks of danger. It is the USA rather than Australia which is his concern. His focus is what he calls

the enormous explosion of cultural studies in the US, its rapid professionalization and institutionalization, is not a moment which any of us who tried to set up a marginalized Centre in a university like Birmingham could, in any simple way, regret. And yet I have to say, in the strongest sense, that it reminds me of the ways in which, in Britain, we are always aware of institutionalization as a moment of profound danger.

What concerns Hall is that the institutionalization of cultural studies in America will follow the same pattern as the institutionalization of French deconstruction; it will 'formalize out of existence the critical questions of power, history, and politics' by reducing them to 'exclusively matters of language and textuality' (*ibid.*, 286). But Hall does not advocate the cultural studies equivalent of a 'back to basics' policy (in this instance, a return to British origins). As he explains, 'It has nothing to do with [American] cultural studies making itself more like British cultural studies, which is I think, an entirely false and empty cause to try to propound' (*ibid.*).

O'Connor's (Chapter 10) worry is slightly different. He contends that in the USA cultural studies is in danger of becoming 'synonymous with various types of postmodern theorizing'. But worse still, 'Cultural studies in the United States is being sponsored by scholars who rarely have any connection to existing political and cultural movements and are somewhat surprised that this might even be possible'. Nelson (Chapter 16) is concerned that 'Of all the intellectual movements that have swept the humanities in America since the seventies, none will be taken up so shallowly, so opportunistically, so unreflectively, and so ahistorically as cultural studies'. In a Gramscian move ('pessimism of the intellect, optimism of the will'), Nelson, on the one hand, wishes to encourage other academics to help 'make American institutions nervous about cultural studies' while, on the other, remaining resigned to the fact that 'The depoliticizing of cultural studies will no doubt pay off, making it more palatable at once to granting agencies and to conservative colleagues, administrators, and politicians, but only at the cost of blocking cultural studies from having any critical purchase on this nation's social life'.

Elizabeth Long (Chapter 11) argues for the need to prevent the marginalization of British feminist cultural studies (an 'exclusion' she already detects taking place) as it is this tradition that has 'the best chance of maintaining a critical stance in its appropriation by feminist scholars in America, both because of their connections with a broad social movement and because of the nature of their practices within the academy'. For these reasons 'feminism is central for developing the critical potential of cultural studies'. Ellen Rooney (Chapter 12) makes much the same argument, pointing to the fact that the absence of a political constituency outside the university (unlike, say, women's studies or African-American studies) makes cultural studies 'peculiarly vulnerable to political neutralization *within the university*'.

Manthia Diawara (Chapter 18) focuses on the way African-American studies should respond to the import of cultural studies. He distinguishes between two traditions in British cultural studies, the Birmingham School (CCCS) and what he calls the 'Black British School', consisting of London-based black artists and writers. In the USA, African-American studies must embrace both schools, not in order to replicate what they have already done but to make a cultural studies grounded in the material conditions of American life, to produce what he calls 'performance studies', 'the study of ways in which black people, through communicative action, created and continue to create themselves within the American experience'.

Finally, it seems appropriate to close with Hall's demand (Chapter 21) for a deeper commitment within cultural studies (regardless of its geographic location) to the analysis of racism:

> the work that cultural studies has to do is to mobilize everything that it can find in terms of intellectual resources in order to understand what keeps making the lives we live, and the societies we live in, profoundly and deeply antihumane in their capacity to live with difference. Cultural Studies' message is a message for academics and intellectuals but, fortunately, for many other people as well. In that sense, I have tried to hold together in my own intellectual life, on the one hand, the conviction and passion and the devotion to objective interpretation, to analysis, to rigorous analysis and understanding, to the passion to find out, and to the production of knowledge that we did not know before. But, on the other, I am convinced that no intellectual worth his or her salt, and no university that wants to hold up its head in the face of the twenty-first century, can afford to turn dispassionate eyes away from the problems of race and ethnicity that beset our world.

It is not possible to be *in* cultural studies and to not agree with Hall's claim on the future of cultural studies.

Notes

1. For another version of this history, with particular reference to popular culture, see Storey (1993) and Storey (1994).
2. For an informed and polemical debate between cultural studies and the political economy of culture, see *Critical Studies in Mass Communication* 12 (1995).
3. See Bill Schwarz's essay, 'Where is cultural studies?' (1994). The essay ·has a double focus: on the one hand, it poses the question in the sense that cultural studies has gone missing and, on the other, in terms of the new geographic locations of cultural studies.
4. The readings collected here are divided among Australia (Chapters 7, 14, 19, 20 and 22), Britain (Chapters 1, 2, 3, 5, 8, 13, 15 and 21) and the USA (Chapters 4, 6, 9, 10, 11, 12, 16, 17 and 18).

1

The evolution of cultural studies . . .

Colin Sparks

It is extremely difficult to define 'Cultural Studies' with any degree of precision. It is not possible to draw a sharp line and say that on one side of it we can find the proper province of cultural studies. Neither is it possible to point to a unified theory or methodology which are character-istic to it or of it. A veritable rag-bag of ideas, methods and concerns from literary criticism, sociology, history, media studies, etc., are lumped together under the convenient label of cultural studies.

The intellectual problem is compounded by an institutional difficulty. While it is possible to locate literary criticism, sociology, even media studies, at a number of levels from the learned journals through higher education and the school curriculum down to the publishing policy of Penguin Books, it is not possible to perform the same operation for cultural studies. There is one institution, the Centre for Contemporary Cultural Studies at University of Birmingham. There are the spasmodic publica-tions of its journal, *Working Papers in Cultural Studies*. There are a number of emerging undergraduate courses. But at the same time there are people beavering away at very similar problems, writing and researching and teaching, often in considerable isolation.

In this paper I intend to look at a very limited part of this complex whole: the work of the Birmingham Centre. There are three reasons for this. The first and simplest is the sheer biographical accident of having spent two years as a member which has given me a rather greater familiarity with its concerns than I can claim for other areas. The second is exogenous to the centre: its work, and in particular its publications, have a wide and growing influence in the circles which discuss these issues.[1] The third is endogenous: as a result of its unique institutional position the Birmingham Centre has, in its own internal development, confronted the dilemmas of the project of cultural studies with a particular intensity. I believe that this self-imposed restriction allows for the understanding of much, but not all, of the advances made in cultural studies.

The origins of cultural studies lie in two books published in the 1950s: *The Uses of Literacy* by Richard Hoggart and *Culture and Society* by Raymond

Williams.[2] Both of these writers emerged out of the academic study of English Literature and the two books bear considerable evidence of that. This is particularly true of *Culture and Society*. Twenty years later, it is possible to read the book as consisting of two separate and unequal moments. The first is a protracted and painful settling of accounts with the literary tradition which not only makes up the bulk of the material of the book but pervades its whole, and very peculiar, style. The second is concentrated in the 'Introduction' and 'Conclusion' and begins to consider the implications of the now-famous reformulation of the scope of culture.[3] This second moment is developed in some of Williams' later work, in particular in *The Long Revolution*.[4]

The advantages of this restrospective reading are evident: in the case of Williams, in particular, it is possible to locate the origins of cultural studies in a rejection of a particular dominant notion of culture.[5] It is out of that rejection, with all its hesitations and evasions, that cultural studies issued. However, the limitations of the historical reading are considerable. The implications of the equally-famous 'shift from the aesthetic to the anthropological definition of culture' were indeed profound but the rupture was a complex process and at least three features of cultural studies – its omnivorous concerns, its populism and its relative institutional marginality – are marked by the continuities and discontinuities of the rupture itself.

The crisis of literary criticism was not, as is sometimes supposed, that it gave exclusive attention to 'great writers' and 'great works of art', and that this provided no basis for the study of 'popular culture'. This is simply not true of Arnold, Eliot or Leavis, although the charge may have some justice when directed against their epigones. All of these writers were concerned precisely with the relationship between culture, and in particular the high art of Literature, and general social organisation. *Culture and Anarchy* is an obvious example; so is *Notes towards a Definition of Culture*. Leavis too, although professionally concerned with high art, had more far-reaching aims which are often expressed in surprising terms:

> [Cecil Sharp] discovered that the traditions of song and dance . . . had persisted so vigorously because the whole context to which folk-song and folk-dance belong was there too: he discovered, in fact, a civilisation or 'way of life' (in our democratic parlance) that was truly an art of social living.[6]

The real origins of the crisis were quite precisely political.[7] The dominant tradition was openly unashamedly and profoundly anti-democratic; cultural studies, from its inception, was a champion of democracy.[8] But democracy was championed by a simple reversal of terms. The plus and minus signs on 'elite' and 'popular' reversed: the same fundamental notions of culture were set in motion once again. Cultural studies took over the total project of Literary Criticism but defined its separation from its parent by its populism. It thus consigned itself to institutional marginality in a way that sociology did not – the intellectual space which it proposed to fill was already dominated by its hostile parent, which had powerful institutional motives for a little quiet infanticide.[9]

Certain other features of cultural studies reveal the extent to which the structure of the dominant model of the cultural was directly inherited.

This dominant model seems to me to be a peculiarly British version of the development of an affirmative culture.[10] This may seem at first sight to contradict what was argued above but the opposition of the two positions is in fact the condition for their unity. The dominant model began with a radical separation between 'work' and 'culture' and in place of that material determination introduced the empty and non-contradictory notion of 'community' or 'whole way of life'. That false resolution, which ignored the critiques of Ruskin and Morris – not to mention Marx – was in fact taken over wholesale by cultural studies.[11] Within that fundamental separation the conception of culture was once again reified to exclude any reference to social antagonism. Thus a non-antagonistic culture could be re-introduced as a healing balm for social antagonisms; that too was taken over wholesale. In the developing model of cultural studies the operative notion of culture was one in which culture arose from a whole way of life and was a means by which those within that pre-given structure gave meaning to their experiences. Those deep-lying contradictions gave rise to the surface oddities of cultural studies: in particular its combination of historic nostalgia and radical ahistoricity; its combination of democratic aspirations and fundamental conservatism; its combination of political intentions, and neglect of politics.

However, since the work of the founding fathers and their immediate disciples, there has been a further rupture – that occasioned by the Centre's encounter with Marxism. In theory at least this should have led to a clarification of the problems and opened the way to their resolution. The body of this paper will argue that this second encounter has been as problematic as the first and that, although at the surface level this has led to marked changes in the work produced, at the fundamental level the transformation has been as yet incomplete. Some of the current developments indicate that this is developing towards a crisis whose outcome is unpredictable.

The encounter with Marxism clearly cannot be discussed with reference to the Birmingham Centre alone: that development is part of the transformation which has occurred in British intellectual life in the last ten years. The average social science undergraduate today is probably more familiar with the work of Marx than the average professor of sociology was ten years ago. We are not, of course, speaking of a purely intellectual movement. The roots of this problem are undoubtedly social and clearly extend much further than the narrowly-defined 'intellectual' milieu itself. The immediate cause of the concern with Marxism can be located in 1968 and its aftermath – the simple temporal fact that the members of the RSSF are now, rather more soberly, members of NATFHE, the NUT, the AUT, ASTMS, or whatever. Both the events of that period and the nature of their persistent effect require explanation in their turn.

The explanation which ran along the lines of the failures of the Wilson Government, the impact of the Vietnam War and the impact of the French events no longer seems adequate. All of those factors undoubtedly played a role but none of them can account for the persistence of the issues, and indeed of the personnel. Any adequate explanation of the phenomenon has to be located in the structure of British society. We have to distinguish between the conjunctural factors underlying the new mood of 1968 – and to a large extent it was precisely a mood – and the historical forces which have determined the trajectory of the British intelligentsia for the last decade.

The bureaucratic rationalisation of intellectual life has been a persistent tendency of the bourgeois epoch[12] although this process has taken place extremely unevenly both between and within various national states. To restrict our analysis simply to British capitalism, it is my contention that the last 30 years have seen a qualitative acceleration of this process and that certain internal features of the development itself have assumed a decisive role. The state machine has been expanded considerably within the last 30 years and the range of its interventions in social life increased. This is particularly true of education and, more recently, of higher education.

This extension of state organisation to a range of intellectual functions has meant that the notorious label 'petit-bourgeois intellectual' has lost a great deal of its objective validity – the world of *New Grub Street* or *Point Counter Point* has almost disappeared. The general tendency of modern capitalism is to reduce the intellectual not merely to the role of bureaucratic functionary but increasingly to that of wage worker. At the same time both the conditions and rewards of 'mental labour' have approximated more and more closely to those of 'manual labour'. The process of the division of labour, as a general feature of capitalist society, has extended ever more sharply inside the world of 'mental labour'.[13]

In this sense the rupture of 1968 was not simply a response to a series of events presenting themselves at the political level, nor a mere reflection of the beginning of general crisis of advanced capitalist societies. Both of these factors were undoubtedly present, but there was also a third important feature: the initial and confused subjective recognition of an objective change in the position of the intelligentsia. The subsequent evolution of the intelligentsia is, at least in part, an attempt to work out the consequences of that change.

That evolution has been a complex and contradictory one. If we take a broad definition of 'intelligentsia' we can see that the tendency towards wage work proceeds at an uneven pace for various sections. At the same time, it is not simply a 'proletarianisation' or the construction of a 'new working class': it is also a tendency towards the creation of a *new labour aristocracy structurally dependent upon the state machine*. But that change, both in its subjective and objective aspects, took place within a general evolution of the working class in which the major political and economic institutions of the class presented an archaic and impenetrable facade while the self-proclaimed alternatives to these institutions remained trapped within an objective impotence resulting from their extreme marginality. Hence the initial and fairly persistent form taken by this subjective movement of an intense politicisation coupled with an apparently contradictory rejection of existing political organisations. It required some years of experience, and important theoretical changes on the part of the major political institutions, before there was any substantial organisational influx of the new forces into the appropriate organs of reformist and statist socialism.

There remains, however, the important problem of why this evolution should be argued out in the terminology of Marxism. That this should occur in Britain, of all places, is, on the face of it, extremely unusual. In the first place, there is a long tradition of reformist and statist socialism reaching back at least to the Fabians which is articulated in specifically anti-Marxist terms. Secondly, the Marxist tradition in Britain, both practically and theoretically, has always occupied an extremely marginal position. The first question is fairly easily answered in that the political conjuncture in which this movement began was precisely one in which the Fabian tradition had transparently failed to realise its own reforming pretensions. The second is more complex and requires attention to the narrow definition of 'intellectuals'.

Given that the problem was first posed among students in higher education the internal contradictions of those institutions played a major role. At the heart of the massive expansion of higher education in the sixties there was a contradiction between the humane liberal-conservative ortho-doxy which formed both the historical legacy of higher education and its current institutional pinnacle on the one hand, and the narrow 'techno-cratic' protagonists of expansion on the other. Neither of these forces was able to provide any serious critical perspective on British society – one seeking its values from its own comfortable insertion into the most archaic features of British capitalism, the other seeks to destroy those archaic features in order to salvage capitalism as a whole. Thus British intellectual life was unable to reproduce itself from inside, but the two forces in conflict barred certain options and opened others. The humane tradition could be used to counter the specialism and the ruthless and valueless social engineering of the modernisers. The technocratic critique of the old tradi-tion could be used to block off the escape route into the archaic. Both together were united in their muted insistence that there was something wrong with British society. Thus any critical perspective had to come from outside British intellectual life. In fact a whole range of alternatives were taken up and tried on for size. Many of these had a much greater immedi-ate attraction that Marxism but, unlike the others, it provided an activist perspective which, over time, was bound to win out against the funda-mental tendencies towards quietistic individualism which lay at the root of the competitors.

Marxism, therefore, has come to dominate the critical areas of British intellectual life. But we have been using the term very loosely and it is now necessary to be critical of the critics. There was, of course, a fundamental problem which confronted new discoverers of Marxism and which gave the early phase of the movement so much of the character of a Children's Crusade. The most obvious feature of Marxism is that it gives the working class, and in particular the industrial proletariat, an absolute role as the bearers of socialism. Unfortunately in Britain in 1968 this was patently not a very useful statement. It therefore proved necessary to make a number of adjustments, not to say revisions, to the original theory. *Both the original encounter with Marxism and the subsequent evolution in Britain have been marked by a struggle to resolve this problem.*

If we examine some of the original texts through which Marxism was encountered, we confront this problem very sharply. At its crudest it was formulated in these terms:

> . . . the traditional critical structures, that is, the left political parties and, above all, the workers' movement have stopped playing their role of radical opposition to the existing society . . . [14]

There were other, perhaps more influential and certainly more honest, attempts to confront the problem. Marcuse provides the best example, not only arguing that the practical problem was capable of resolution because:

> . . . underneath the conservative popular base is the substratum of the outcasts and outsiders, the exploited and persecuted of other races and other colours, the unemployed and the unemployable . . . their opposition is revolutionary even if their consciousness is not. [15]

but also recognising and confronting the theoretical problem posed by this social reality:

> At its origins in the first half of the nineteenth century, when it elaborated the first concepts of the alternatives, the critique of industrial society attained concreteness in a historical mediation between theory and practice, values and facts, needs and goals. This historical mediation occurred in the consciousness and in the political action of the two great classes which faced each other in society: the bourgeoisie and the proletariat. In the capitalist world they are still the basic classes. However, the capitalist development has altered the structure and function of these two classes in such a way that they no longer appear to be agents of historical transformation. . . . In the absence of demonstrable agents and agencies of social change, the critique is thus thrown back to a high level of abstraction. There is no ground on which theory and practice, thought and action meet. [16]

There were, fundamentally, two alternative resolutions to these problems. The first was to accept, more or less, the outlines of Marcuse's analysis and to construct, a mixture of practical activity which lay outside, or at the margins, orthodox working-class political activity, and at the same time continue an almost independent critical activity, at a high level of abstraction. The other was to reject the original analysis and to enter what is fashionably termed the 'world of the left sects'.

The second alternative was, given the marginality of the groups and the powerful institutional pressures of the hierarchical employment structure, a minority choice, particularly among intellectuals. The first alternative appeared very much more attractive. Initially, an attempt was made to provide a justification for this; the most revealing set of documents are the debate around 'Red Bases'. In particular, James Wilcox attempted to theorise a new practice:

> In all repressive societies the masses will discover their own discrete and individual forms of resistance to the established system. The pseudo-left only recognises those forms of resistance which have the blessing of the ruling order (orderly demonstrations, trade unionism, etc.). It is not prepared to consider the testimony of other popular acts of resistance (industrial sabotage, absenteeism, fiddles, delinquency, shop-lifting, 'madness', etc.). For the philistines these are

'symptoms' of capitalist decadence not tributes to the healthy instincts of the masses. Of course on a purely individual plane such activities get nowhere, but the bien pensant band-aid revolutionaries are no happier when such resistance erupts on a mass scale (black loot-ins, students on the barricades, factory mass occupations, etc.). For them a Black uprising is just an understandable excess committed by the oppressed Black people: they do not see that it has many very positive aspects (e.g. it constitutes a strain on the stretched resources of the repressive power, it involves a direct re-appropriation of surplus value, etc.).[17]

From the beginning, the possibilities of political action were located out-side, and to a considerable extent in opposition to, the concerns and organisations which had long characterised Marxist politics. These forms of political activity are, however, notoriously unstable and, being periph-eral to capitalist production, equally notoriously ineffectual on their own. There was, therefore, an inbuilt tendency in the vision of Marxism adopted by this current to theoreticism, which was once again reinforced by the very real pressures of earning one's living. The ground was well-prepared for a Marxism which systematically evaded the squalid concerns of political parties, trade unions, and all the rest of the baggage of Marxist ortho-doxy, and which elevated debates on culture, epistemology, etc., to the centre of theoretical concern.[18]

This development was facilitated by the confusions of the main channel for the introduction of these ideas, the magazine *New Left Review*. This journal has always been characterised by an extreme lack of theoretical rigour.[19] In this it was not exceptional – confusion over the elementary categories of Marxism seems to have been endemic on a world scale since about 1923. It was rather the scholarship than the theory of *New Left Review* which gave it its attraction, while its occasional lapses into mere politics, like the one quoted above, have been uniformly unfortunate.

Given this political and intellectual impasse the popularity of Louis Althusser in Britain was, one might say, overdetermined. A writer who could speak with regret of the fact that: 'we spent the best part of our time in agitation when we would have been better employed in the defence of our right and duty to know, and in study for production as such' and could resolve the central problem with the neat formulation of 'theoretical practice' was bound to gain a big audience.[20] The problem is not simply that there was and is, as Althusser was later to recognise,[21] a danger of this theoreticist reading, but that a number of central formulations – in parti-cular the notion of a 'structure in dominance' and the critique of the 'expressive totality' – appear to have been precisely designed to circum-vent a number of very directly political problems. These ambiguities persist even in the development of his work up to the recent piece on Lysenko.[22] In fact, together with an interpretation of Gramsci designed to deny the decisions of Livorno, they have provided the intellectual bridge over which a portion of the intellectuals have now passed in their search for an organised political expression.[23]

The Birmingham Centre reflected this development.[24] The series of *Working Papers* demonstrates an increasing concern with the assimilation of the newly developed variants of Marxism. This concern was mediated by way of a series of confrontations not only with the newly available texts but also with a number of previously established traditions of analysis and subjects of research. The most developed aspect of this phase of the Centre's work is the study of sub-cultures, brought together in *Resistance through Rituals*. This work, which is very impressively realised and has an obvious teaching use, focusses more of the internal problems of cultural studies than, for example, the developing work on conventional art objects, and is less readily fitted to the category of 'Media Studies' than the work on television or the press.[25] The formative text for the study of sub-cultures is undoubtedly Phil Cohen's justly famous article 'Subcultural conflict and working class community'.[26] The arguments put forward there set the parameters for a great deal of the work of the next three years.[27] Although the paper lacks the normal scholarly apparatus of references which facilitate the task of tracing the intellectual heritage it is possible to indicate the general features of the mental universe in which it was written.

Cohen's basic argument is that the relatively stable East London working class community he was writing about was in the throes of a major structural crisis. This was based on changes in the patterns of employment and housing which led to the destruction of the cultural patterns of the community, in particular the extended family but also the controlled social space within which the community defined itself. These tensions were severe among adults, who were denied both the supportive structures of the previous community and full access to the alleged new world of satisfaction through consumption, but found their external expression in the activities of (male) youth. In place of the old structures of the 'democratic' community, new externally directed bureaucratic agencies – the police and social workers – attempted to control and support the disoriented population. But because of their class character, their external motives and their symptomatic concerns these agencies proved inadequate. While the social worker labelled the adults as 'inadequate' the police defined the youth as 'deviant'. As an alternative to this impasse Cohen proposed the development of 'community action'.[28] Within this framework Cohen developed a number of very influential ideas. In particular, the formulation of the function of subcultures proved singularly effective:

> It seems to me that the latent function of sub-culture is this – to express and resolve, albeit 'magically', the contradictions which remain hidden or unresolved in the parent culture. The succession of sub-cultures which this parent culture generated can thus all be considered as so many variations on a central theme – the contradiction, at an ideological level, between traditional working class puritanism, and the new hedonism of consumption; at an economic level between a future as part of the socially mobile elite, or as part of the new lumpen. Mods, Parkers, skinheads, crombies, all represent, in their different ways, an attempt to retrieve some of the socially cohesive elements destroyed in their parent culture, and to combine these with elements selected from other class fractions symbolising one or other of the options confronting it.[29]

The working out of the strengths of that formulation provides the bulk of the concrete 'ethnography' of *Resistance through Rituals*. Furthermore, the subsequent formulation of 'the original mod life style could be interpreted as an attempt to real-ise, *but in an imaginary relation* the conditions of existence of the socially mobile white collar workers' (original emphasis)[30] bears a distinct resemblance to Althusser's famous formulation: 'Ideology represents the imaginary relationship of individuals to their real conditions of existence.'[31]

Despite its positive aspects, this tradition suffers from very severe limitations. Cohen, despite his attempt to integrate the problem of production, undoubtedly reproduces the old cultural emphasis on the importance of 'community', but this is articulated precisely in the terms of the political debate outlined above. The difficulty is twofold. In the first place 'community' is the classic site of the defensive and 'corporate' characteristics of the culture of a subordinate class: it is production which defines the class as such and which determines its possibility for historical action.[32] Secondly, it is obvious that Cohen's model depends on an accurate reading of the parent culture for its efficacy in understanding the youth culture. However, here the general rejection of production as a determinate is joined by a very specific rejection of 'orthodox' political analysis which places Cohen squarely in the first phase of intellectual revolt. The consequence is that Cohen gives a very curious account of the history of the parent culture. He writes of 'political' activity that:

> The Labour party and CP do occasionally attempt to mobilise local people on community issues, but only in so far as this serves the national electoral interests of their respective organisations. . . . *The only historical exception to this rule was possibly the early period of George Lansbury's career in the* East End . . . (my emphasis).[33]

Whatever truth the contemporary statement may have, one is stunned by the inadequacy of the historical account. Cohen has simply omitted the fact that the very area of which he is writing was, in the 1930s the site of one of the most protracted attempts at the political mobilisation of the community and that Mile End has been remarkable in formal political terms in that it has returned a member of the Communist Party as its MP.[34] This particular oversight could be dismissed as an individual eccentricity, or Cohen could have argued that the whole affair was the product of a particular conjuncture with no lasting significance. Neither of these explanations would account for the *pervasive* neglect of traditional structures and political forms in development of sub-cultural theory, nor for the attempt to theorise that neglect. This attempt was not specific to work on sub-cultures, as the following quotation, editorialised as 'one of the clearest public statements of our position',[35] shows:

> The context of this sketch of culture, is then, political, not artistic, and it is necessary to continue to insist [*sic*] this as we move closer to the present day. Whereas the stress previously was on the need to control the *activity*, the behaviour of the working class, the site has now definitely shifted more to their consciousness which may be produced by a change in the political and economic structure in which the structures have become voluntarist: formal political democracy, and consumerism, themselves negotiated responses to changing general political and economic changes. The dominant group now requires the assent of the subordinate group, an affirmation especially in this continuing development of the political and cultural class struggle; not in terms of

immediate opinion formation, but of long-term development of life-styles, and ideologies.[36]

We are here clearly confronted with a position which seeks to define its practice precisely in terms of some radical change in the structure of society which has rendered the older models obsolete and which thus prioritises the conflicts at the level of cultures and sub-cultures.[37]

The appropriation of particular readings of Gramsci and Althusser began to alter this early formation and by the time of *Resistance through Rituals* there is an attempt to use the categories of these thinkers to embed the study of sub-cultures in a more sophisticated account of social development. In the work in question, however, this account remains substantially underdeveloped and schematic and constitutes the weakest link in the general theoretical statement while, at the same time, having only a very shadowy presence in the ethnographic work. This work is, despite its finished form, very much a product of a transition from a mode of thought which selected sub-cultures for their oppositional content to one which saw them as incapable of expressing more than a confused and marginal response to the fact of domination.

I have already indicated some features of the specificity of the development which permitted this ambivalence to arise but it is necessary to say a few words as to its concrete form. It seems to me that there was a double movement. In the first place the notions of 'relative autonomy', 'determination in the last instance' and 'structure in dominance' were initially used to provide a set of defences for the reading of culture as an *effectively* autonomous practice in which determination was very much a distant term which barely penetrated concrete analysis. Further, the capital/labour contradiction was seen as one among several contradictions, others of which were then regarded as currently 'dominant'. This allowed a relatively unproblematic assumption of Marxist vocabulary into concerns which went back to Hoggart. However, once inside that mode of discourse the notion of the 'ISA' provided a powerful attraction, given that this directed attention precisely at *structures*. However, the crucial formulation that the 'Ideological State Apparatuses may not be only the *stake*, but also the *site* of class struggle',[38] together with the failure to differentiate between the significance of the various Apparatuses themselves, meant that, while it was now necessary to admit structures like trade unions, these were merely one instance among many, without any particular priority. Indeed, the notion that ideology 'interpellates individuals as subjects'[39] seems to me to negate the possibility of any prioritisation. It may be that I have misunderstood the sense of this passage, but it seems that trade unions in particular interpellate *collectives* as partial and limited subjects and that this, indeed, is the source of their profoundly contradictory role in a capitalist society. It constitutes the core of the reason why the Marxist tradition has always considered these institutions distinct from the 'private' institutions (e.g. the family) on the one hand, the state institutions (e.g. the BBC) on the other, and further distinct from the institution of revolutionary leadership (the political party).

The dubious distinction between state power and state apparatus furthered this tendency.[40] At the same time it allowed an approach to Gramsci, in particular the famous statement:

> In Russia the State was everything, civil society was primordial and gelatinous; in the West, there was a proper relation between State and civil society; and when the State trembled a sturdy structure of civil society was at once revealed. The State was only an outer ditch, behind which there stood a powerful system of fortresses and earthworks.[41]

Which has, of course under contemporary Italian influence, been read as a rejection of what are termed 'Russian models'.[42]

This relocation of cultural studies within a framework which recognised the traditional structural concerns of Marxism with state and class domination (hegemony) redirected attention to a more adequate reading of the historical trajectory of British society and a re-discovery of the productive definition of the working class. A new problematic was being born.

The next issue of *Working Papers* (No 9) relfected this even in its title: 'Culture and domination'. It also contained reports on the progress of two new areas of work – the study of work and the study of history.[43] However, both of these reports demonstrate the incompleteness of the absorption of the new problematic together with the internal strains and tensions which this has meant for the Centre as a collective grouping. The report of the 'Culture History Group' puts the problem very clearly:

> The existence and importance of historical work in this Centre was acknowledged in 1973–74, with the formation of a 'period' sub-group for two main reasons. First, work on problems in contemporary culture was increasingly being grounded in an analysis of British capitalism since the nineteenth century; second, and more urgently, we lacked an adequate working account, for reference, and revision, of basic themes in that development . . .[44]

The article goes on to outline some features of the decade from 1935 to 1945. In particular there is an examination of the problem of 'war radicalism' based largely on ideas suggested by Calder's book *The People's War*. Not surprisingly, given this source, recognition is granted to the importance of 'the involvement of the unions in meeting production targets'[45] but the epochal significance of Bevin's famous statement that 'I shall be Minister of Labour for the next 50 years' remains unappreciated. In fact, the confusion with regard to the limit and extent of war-radicalism among the working class, which the authors note, was not simply a result of the ideological ambivalences of Cassandra or Priestley. Rather the space within which it was possible for this vague and ill-defined mood to obscure class issues was the consequence of structural factors – in particular the massive collapse of the trade union bureaucracy into class-collaboration *and*, after 1941, the lack of any organised alternative mode of action.

> The political situation in the 1939–1945 war was much more settled and it was difficult to impute strikes to political motives. The Labour Party was a full coalition partner; a trade union leader, Ernest Bevin, held a Cabinet post which in terms of power was second only to that of the Prime Minister; and, after Russia entered the war in 1941, Communists in industry who would have been the natural leaders of unofficial movements lent all their energies to supporting

the war. The Gallachers and the Kirkwoods of the Second World War were preventing strikes and were pressing Joint Production Committees for still greater production. It is significant that the only political strike worth recording in World War II was attributed to Trotskyists, a Communist splinter group.[46]

There remains, then, in the attempt to construct an historical perspective for cultural studies an inadequate recognition of the significance of organised structures in determining the limits of political action.

In the discussions on work, the problem is even more acute. Paul Willis recognises that trade unions are 'by far the most important working-class institution'.[47] This statement marks an important advance for an institution which, while dedicated to the study of working-class culture has not, as yet, produced any major study, either theoretical or empirical, of the trade union movement.[48] However, he immediately goes on to down-grade the importance of these institutions:

> . . . trade unionism has many failings. By being, in its own right, a formal structure with narrowly defined ends, it has excluded, to an ever greater degree, the actual informal sturcture and culture of the work place from which it grew.[49]

In part, Willis's reservations are grounded in an embryonic theory of trade union bureaucracy, which is certainly an important feature of the British movement and undoubtedly does play, in part, the role of what he describes as 'another authority structure over the worker'.[50] There is, however, another element of hostility to formal structures *as such*, which are seen as inimicable to the 'rich dense texture' of experienced culture.

Reading between the lines of this contribution and Andrew Tolson's response to a paper origianting outside of the Centre – Charles Woolfson's 'The semiotics of working class speech' – one can detect the symptoms of a profound crisis in the Centre's evolution.[51] It would seem that at least one tendency in the Centre has made, or is making, a passage to that organised expression of reformist and statist socialism which is ambivalent on the question of the state, locates the working class as one force among several in the transformation of society, encourages discrete practices (particularly at the academic level) and is relatively uncritical of contradictions within the trade union movement. This tendency moves increasingly towards propagandist interpretations of political activity. Against this current, characteristic of the broader movement of the intelligentsia, are a number of confused alternative positions, some of which represent a definite retreat from the current positions.

It is important that the hard-won gains of the last few years are not abandoned. However, no further substantial advance can be expected from a tendency which refuses to recognise the socially contradictory nature of the major working class institutions. If it is agreed that the culture which we are studying is that of a subordinate class, and that this subordination is something which can be ended, then it follows that a great deal of contemporary working-class culture is an historically transient formation. If it is further agreed that this gap between potential and actual is crucially determined by the structures of formal organisations then those structures, and the political and cultural positions which accompany them, need to be recognised as contradictory.

In fact, the study of formal structures needs to be extended rather than limited. Owing to the peculiar historical formation of the British working class, there has been a tendency to consider the formal organisations as distinct from other organised forms of cultural activity, due to the generally 'low visibility' of the determinations. The classic period of the German labour movement provides a salutary contrast. German Social Democracy developed as the classic 'state within a state' in which the determination of the organisation of culture by the aims of a political organisation is well-known. After 1919 there were two competing organisations within the working class each trying to construct its own cultural definitions. The clash between the two was frequently fairly sharp. Clearly, this type of organisation has never existed in Britain. No organisation or apparatus – in the political, cultural or informational field – has ever had the resources of the KPD, let alone the SPD. Labour historians have paid some attention to the material there is, but a great deal needs to be done before we have any real picture of the extent of the differences. It is not in dispute that the links between cultural activity and the historic structures of the working class are marginal compared with those cultural practices which are radically corporate. What is important in the past, and is clearly central to the development of any Marxist version of cultural studies is the mode of relation between the 'corporate' and 'historic' aspects of working-class culture. As I have shown above, the study of popular culture as developed by the Birmingham Centre has proposed a model of this relationship which began by ignoring these 'historic' structures and locating 'corporate' activities as the source of a transcendence of corporatism. The subsequent partial recognition of the historic structures has not, as yet, succeeded in re-thinking that relationship.

The question is, therefore; what lines of development can assist in this change? I must stress the tentative nature of what follows, in that it is not based on any body of substantial work and remains at the level of suggested projects. Paradoxically, those areas which have remained unintegrated into the work on sub-cultures – the media and the problems of 'high' cultural analysis – provide the most fruitful source of alternatives. To consider here only the study of the media, a number of areas suggest themselves. Since the last third of the nineteenth century the production of newspapers has been dominated by the 'commodity form'. This is predicated upon an atomised audience of discrete individuals. The form taken by the dominant institutions of the electronic media clearly reproduces this on an extended scale. It is fairly well-established that this hypothesised audience does not exist in a pure form, but it is equally clear that both the mode of social organisation and the special features of the mass media themselves represent a constant *tendency* in this direction. There is, however, a constant contra-tendency which produces and utilises the media as an element in radical social organisation. One of the key areas in which this exists, and the crucial one for the study of working-class culture, is precisely the link between the media and the historic structures of the working class. There are a number of fairly obvious examples of this. *The Clarion*, with its concomitant range of activities, is the best known, but the same process can be seen at work in a number of newspapers from the *Daily Herald* and *Daily Worker* down to more modest contemporary examples. Sectoral, and in particular local, research would undoubtedly reveal a much wider range. Such studies do not need massive resources and can be conducted quite easily on the basis of, for example, a school teaching project.

With regard to the electronic media, the control of airwaves, the scale of the investment required, and the domination of expectations by massive and highly professionalised bureaucracies, make the amount of historical material fairly small. There are, however, signs that certain small contemporary developments represent a break in this dominance. At the Polytechnic of Central London, for example, there have been very tentative attempts to find a structured and differentiated 'audience' for student-produced television documentaries. Other, more ambitious, attempts have been made elsewhere. The extent of the experience is perhaps too small to allow any serious generalisations about the problems involved but there are a number of hints as to the theoretical and practical problems involved in this sort of project. For example, it seems that both the levels of technical expertise and the formal rhetoric of professional television production for an undifferentiated and seralised audience determine in significant ways the reception of material produced with other purposes in mind. Secondly, the technical mode of presentation is qualitatively different from that of a newspaper in that it cannot be inserted 'immediately' into, for example, a work situation. It seems likely, therefore, that any such use of this medium as a social organiser will stand in a different relationship to formal organisation. It will necessarily be dependent upon a pre-existing organisation and require for its utilisation a higher threshold of involvement. Given the type of existing formations which can command both the material resources and the level of commitment it is likely that developments in this area will rapidly encounter the internal contradictions of these structures in a particularly sharp form. To take the trade union situation as an example, it is likely that the technical equipment will remain in the hands of the bureaucracy and that it will be utilised in various formal training schools. Given the current formation of the bureaucracy and the mode of its insertion into capitalist society it is probable that ideological questions will figure very prominently in any such development. It is precisely in this area, I have argued, that there is a marked weakness in the way in which the notions of 'popular culture' and 'cultural studies' have been developed. The path which has been followed by cultural studies up until now has enabled it to avoid coming to terms with these difficulties. Future practical and theoretical developments are, in my opinion, impossible without a fairly fundamental questioning of some basic assumptions.

Notes

1. The most obvious example of a positive evaluation of this work is the fact that the Open University has reprinted *Working Papers in Cultural Studies 7/8*

(hereafter *WPCS* as Hall and Jefferson (eds) *Resistance through Rituals* (Hutchinson/OU, 1976). Attention of a less favourable kind is the F. Inglis' 'Cant and culture' in *Universities Quarterly* Autumn (1975).

2. Hoggart's work first appeared in 1957, Williams' in 1958.
3. The implications of 'a whole way of life' were sufficiently apparent at the time for Williams to return to the question in answer to critics in *The Long Revolution*. My point is rather that it is today the dis-unity, rather than the unity, of the book which strikes us. This is, in my experience, particularly true when attempting to use the book in teaching students coming from a 'non-literary' background.
4. Stuart Hall, who knows much better than I do, argues that the first section of *The Long Revolution* was the crucial text in the evolution of the Centre in the late 1960s.
5. Williams points to this in a lecture re-printed in C.W.E. Bigsby (ed.), *Approaches to Popular Culture* (Arnold, 1976), pp. 27–38.
6. *The Common Pursuit* (Penguin, 1962), p. 190. Leavis quotes without comment Sharp's attribution of the homogeneity of Appalachian culture to its 'racial inheritance'.
7. Bigsby's essay 'The politics of popular culture' in Bigsby, *op. cit.* outlines this.
8. The social roots of this development require a detailed analysis. I find the sketch in the 'Introduction' to *WPCS* 6, focusing on the position of secondary teachers, attractive but, without a more substantial investigation, it is impossible to reach a conclusion.
9. The English Department at Birmingham University has in fact attempted this exercise quite directly at least once in the last five years.
10. Although Marcuse's famous essay appears to have been written without any knowledge of British developments, it does display a striking familiarity. For example the passage: 'Culture should ennoble the given by permeating it, rather than putting something new in its place. It thus exalts the individual without freeing him from his factual debasement. Culture speaks of the dignity of "man" without concerning itself with a concretely more dignified status for men. The beauty of culture is above all an inner beauty and can only reach the external world from within. Its realm is essentially a realm of the *soul*' (*Negations*, trans. J.J. Shapiro, Penguin, 1972, p. 103) is a remarkable parallel to *Culture and Anarchy*, although the verbal similarity may be an accident of translation.
11. I have developed this point in 'The abuses of literacy' published in *WPCS* 6.
12. See F.L. Neumann, 'The intelligentsia in exile' in P. Connerton (ed.), *Critical Sociology* (Penguin, 1976).
13. This theme has been developed at length by H. Braverman in *Labor and Monopoly Capital*. New York (1975).
14. E. Mandel, 'The changing role of the bourgeois university', in T. Pateman (ed.), *Counter Course* (Penguin, 1972), p. 18.
15. *One Dimensional Man* (Sphere, 1968), p. 200.
16. *Ibid.*, pp. 11–12.
17. From 'Two tactics' in *New Left Review* 53 (January–February 1969), p. 28.
18. A similar point is made at considerable length by P. Anderson in his *Considerations on Western Marxism* NLB (1976). It seems to me that the obvious internal contradictions of this book, some of which Anderson himself notes, make my point for me. The book combines a detailed and sophisticated knowledge of a range of academic thinkers together with a patchy, innaccurate and self-contradictory account of the European labour movement – it is, not surprisingly, a simple reflection of the problem it tries to analyse.
19. The early history of the journal is outlined by P. Sedgewick in 'The two new lefts' printed D. Widgery (ed.), *The Left in Britain* (Penguin, 1976).

20. The above applies to a specific French situation (see *For Marx*, trans. B. Brewster, Penguin, 1968) but the cast of that 'Introduction' undoubtedly influenced formulations adopted in Britain.
21. It had also been recognised by one of his pupils, Regis Debray (whose subsequent evolution makes an interesting comparison) who wrote: '. . . all we had to do to become good theoreticians was to be lazy bastards' (quoted in A. Callinicoss, *Althusser's Marxism*, Pluto Press, 1976, p. 60).
22. Translated in the February 1977 *Marxism Today*.
23. The publishing history of Gramsci is a minor confirmation of my argument in that the understandably evasive *Prison Notebooks* appeared in English some six years before the *Political Writings*.
24. Biographical accident played some role here in that Richard Hoggart, an avowed opponent of Marxism, left the Centre at this point, first for UNESCO and then Goldsmith's College. How important the change in Directorship was is impossible to say exactly.
25. There has, of course been a strong relationship between the study of subcultures and some aspects of media studies.
26. Published in *WPCS* 2.
27. A fact which is evident from the central place occupied by a disucssion of this paper in the long theoretical piece by Hall, Clarke, Jefferson and Roberts, 'Subcultures, cultures and class' which opens *Resistance through Rituals*. This essay traces in considerable detail the various contributory strands in the development of the position and provides a great deal of the detailed sourcing which is absent from P. Cohen's paper.
28. According to Cohen's own account, the paper originated as a proposal to fund just such a project.
29. P. Cohen, *op cit.*, p. 23.
30. *Ibid.*, p. 24.
31. From the essay 'Ideology and ideological state apparatuses' in *Lenin and Philosophy* (trans. B. Brewster, NLB, 1971, p. 153). The publishing history makes it unlikely that the relation was direct. The authors of 'Subcultures, cultures, and class' draw the source from the earlier essay 'Marxism and humanism' in *For Marx*, pp. 233–34. The later essay, with its notion of Ideological State Apparatuses, provided the framework for subsequent developments.
32. F. Parkin, *Class Inequality and Political Order* (Paladin, 1972), pp. 89–90.
33. P. Cohen *op cit.*, p. 39.
34. Phil Piratin was elected MP in 1945. He recorded a somewhat evasive account of the proceeding twenty years in *Our Flag Stays Red* (Thames, 1948). The most significant of these, about Cable street, I have examined in my article 'Fighting the beast' (a title for which I apologise and over which I had no control) in *International Socialism* 94.
35. Editorial note, *WPCS* 6, p. 25.
36. Bryn Jones, 'The politics of popular culture' in *WPCS* 6, p. 29.
37. *WPCS* 9, p. 123.
38. *Lenin and Philosophy*, p. 140.
39. *Ibid.*, p. 160.
40. Althusser's distinction (*Ibid.*, pp. 134–35) is considerably more ambiguous than Poulantzas' (in 'The problem of the capitalist state' printed in R. Blackburn (ed.), *Ideology in Social Science* (Fontana, 1972), pp. 252–53).
41. In *Prison Notebooks* (trans. Hoare and Nowell-Smith, Lawrence & Wishart, 1971, p. 238).
42. Comparisons with Section VI of *Political Writings 1910–20* (trans. Mathews, ed.

Hoare, Lawrence & Wishart, 1977) are essential for understanding the limits of this interpretation.

43. *WPCS* also contains a report on the Women's Studies Group. The absence of this area from cultural studies had been sharply noted in *Resistance through Rituals*. I have omitted consideration of this development for three reasons: lack of personal knowledge; the embryonic state of the material; its real absence from the development until very recently. I am very conscious of participating in one of the major errors of the tradition I am criticising.
44. *WPCS* 9, p. 29. This issue also contains an interesting overview of the development of British society by Richard Johnson.
45. *WPCS* 9, p. 35.
46. V.L. Allen, *Trade Unions and Government*, Longman (1960), p. 143. It should be added that one of the leaders of this strike was a certain T. Dan Smith.
47. *WPCS* 9, p. 159.
48. When I wrote the article in *WPCS* 6, I was able to claim that no attention had ever been payed to trade unions. This has clearly changed, although from the texts cited the study is still in its initial stages.
49. *WPCS*, p. 159.
50. *Ibid.*
51. *WPCS* 9, p. 202.

2

Cultural studies: two paradigms

Stuart Hall

In serious, critical intellectual work, there are no 'absolute beginnings' and few unbroken continuities. Neither the endless unwinding of 'tradition', so beloved of the History of Ideas, nor the absolutism of the 'epistemological rupture', punctuating Thought into its 'false' and 'correct' parts, once favoured by the Althussereans, will do. What we find, instead, is an untidy but characteristic unevenness of development. What is important are the significant *breaks* – where old lines of thought are disrupted, older constellations displaced, and elements, old and new, are regrouped around a different set of premises and themes. Changes in a problematic do significantly transform the nature of the questions asked, the forms in which they are proposed, and the manner in which they can be adequately answered. Such shifts in perspective reflect, not only the results of an internal intellectual labour, but the manner in which real historical developments and transformations are appropriated in thought, and provide Thought, not with its guarantee of 'correctness' but with its fundamental orientations, its conditions of existence. It is because of this complex articulation between thinking and historical reality, reflected in the social categories of thought, and the continuous dialectic between 'knowledge' and 'power', that the breaks are worth recording.

Cultural Studies, as a distinctive problematic, emerges from one such moment, in the mid-1950s. It was certainly not the first time that its characteristic questions had been put on the table. Quite the contrary. The two books which helped to stake out the new terrain – Hoggart's *Uses of Literacy* and Williams's *Culture and Society* – were both, in different ways, works (in part) of recovery. Hoggart's book took its reference from the 'cultural debate', long sustained in the arguments around 'mass society' and in the tradition of work identified with Leavis and *Scrutiny*. *Culture and Society* reconstructed a long tradition which Williams defined as consisting, in sum, of 'a record of a number of important and continuing reactions to ... changes in our social, economic and political life' and offering 'a special kind of map by means of which the nature of the changes can be explored' (p. 16). The books looked, at first, simply like updating of these earlier concerns, with reference to the post-war world. Retrospectively, their 'breaks' with the traditions of thinking in which they were situated seem as important, if not more so, than their continuity with them. The *Uses of Literacy* did set out – much in the spirit of 'practical criticism' – to 'read' working class culture for the values and meanings embodied in its patterns and arrangements: as if they were certain kinds of 'texts'. But the application of this method to a living culture, and the rejection of the terms of the 'cultural debate' (polarized around the high/low culture distinction) was a thorough-going departure. *Culture and Society* – in one and the same movement – constituted a tradition (*the* 'culture-and-society' tradition), defined its 'unity' (not in terms of common positions but in its character-istic concerns and the idiom of its inquiry), itself made a distinctive modern contribution to it – *and* wrote its epitaph. The Williams book which succeeded it – *The Long Revolution* – clearly indicated that the 'culture-and-society' mode of reflection could only be completed and developed by moving somewhere else – to a significantly different kind of analysis. The very difficulty of some of the writing in *The Long Revolution* – with its attempt to 'theorize' on the back of a tradition resolutely empirical and particularist in its idiom of thought, the experiential 'thickness' of its concepts, and the generalizing movement of argument in it – stems, in part, from this determination to *move on* (Williams's work, right through to the most recent *Politics and Letters*, is exemplary precisely in its sustained developmentalism). The 'good' and the 'bad' parts of *The Long Revolution* both arise from its status as a work 'of the break'. The same could be said of E.P. Thompson's *Making of the English Working Class*, which belongs decisi-vely to this 'moment', even though, chronologically it appeared somewhat later. It, too, had been 'thought' within certain distinctive historical tradi-tions: English marxist historiography, Economic and 'Labour' History. But in its foregrounding of the questions of culture, consciousness and experi-ence, and its accent on agency, it also made a decisive break: with a certain kind of technological evolutionism, with a reductive economism and an organizational determinism. Between them, these three books constituted the *caesura* out of which – among other things – 'Cultural Studies' emerged.

They were, of course, seminal and formative texts. They were not, in any sense, 'text-books' for the founding of a new academic sub-discipline: nothing could have been farther from their intrinsic impulse. Whether historical or contemporary in focus, they were, themselves, focused *by*, organized through and constituted responses to, the immediate pressures of the time and society in which they were written. They not only took 'culture' seriously – as a dimension without which historical transforma-tions, past and present, simply could not adequately be thought. They were, themselves, 'cultural' in the *Culture and Society* sense. They forced on their readers' attention the proposition that 'concentrated in the word *culture* are questions directly raised by the great historical changes which the changes in industry, democracy and class, in their own way, represent, and to which the changes in art are a closely related response' (p. 16). This was a question for the 1960s and 70s, as well as the 1860s and 70s. And this is perhaps the point to note that this line of thinking was roughly cotermi-nous with what has been called the 'agenda' of the early New Left, to which these writers, in one sense or another, belonged, and whose texts these were. This connection placed the 'politics of intellectual work' squarely at the centre of Cultural Studies from the beginning – a concern from which, fortunately, it has never been, and can never be, freed. In a deep sense, the 'settling of accounts' in *Culture and Society*, the first part of *The Long Revolution*, Hoggart's densely particular, concrete study of some aspects of working-class culture and Thompson's historical reconstruction of the formation of a class culture and popular traditions in the 1790–1830 period formed, between them, the break, and defined the space from which a new area of study and practice opened. In terms of intellectual bearings and emphases, this was – if ever such a thing can be found – Cultural Studies moment of 're-founding'. The institutionalization of Cultural Studies – first, in the Centre at Birmingham, and then in courses and publications from a variety of sources and places – with its characteristic gains and losses, belongs to the 1960s and later.

'Culture' was the site of the convergence. But what definitions of this core concept emerged from this body of work? And, since this line of thinking has decisively shaped Cultural Studies, and represents the most formative *indigenous* or 'native' tradition, around what space was its concerns and concepts unified? The fact is that no single, unproblematic definition of 'culture' is to be found here. The concept remains a complex one – a site of convergent interests, rather than a logically or conceptually clarified idea. This 'richness' is an area of continuing tension and difficulty in the field. It might be useful, therefore, briefly to resume the characteristic stresses and emphases through which the concept has arrived at its present state of (in)-determinacy. (The characterizations which follow are, necessarily crude and over-simplified, synthesizing rather than carefully analytic.) Two main problematics only are discussed.

Two rather different ways of conceptualizing 'culture' can be drawn out of the many suggestive formulations in Raymond Williams's *Long Revolution*. The first relates 'culture' to the sum of the available descriptions through which societies make sense of and reflect their common experiences. This definition takes up the earlier stress on 'ideas', but subjects it to a thorough reworking. The conception of 'culture' is itself democratized and socialized. It no longer consists of the sum of the 'best that has been thought and said', regarded as the summits of an achieved civilization – that ideal of perfection to which, in earlier usage, all aspired. Even 'art' – assigned in the earlier framework a privileged position, as touchstone of the highest values of civilization – is now redefined as only one, special, form of a general social process: the giving and taking of meanings, and the slow development of 'common' meanings – a common culture: 'culture', in this special sense, 'is ordinary' (to borrow the title of one of Williams's earliest attempts to make his general position more widely accessible). If even the highest, most refined of descriptions offered in works of literature are also 'part of the general process which creates conventions and institutions, through which the meanings that are valued by the community are shared and made active' (p. 55), then there is no way in which this process can be hived off or distinguished or set apart from the other practices of the historical process: 'Since our way of seeing things is literally our way of living, the process of communication is in fact the process of community:

the sharing of common meanings, and thence common activities and purposes; the offering, reception and comparison of new meanings, leading to tensions and achievements of growth and change' (p. 55). Accordingly, there is no way in which the communication of descriptions, understood in this way, can be set aside and compared externally with other things. 'If the art is part of society, there is no solid whole, outside it, to which, by the form of our question, we concede priority. The art is there, as an activity, with the production, the trading, the politics, the raising of families. To study the relations adequately we must study them actively, seeing all activities as particular and contemporary forms of human energy.'

If this first emphasis takes up and re-works the connotation of the term 'culture' with the domain of 'ideas', the second emphasis is more deliberately anthropological, and emphasizes that aspect of 'culture' which refers to social *practices*. It is from this second emphasis that the somewhat simplified definition – 'culture is a whole way of life' – has been rather too neatly abstracted. Williams did relate this aspect of the concept to the more 'documentary' – that is, descriptive, even ethnographic – usage of the term. But the earlier definition seems to me the more central one, into which 'way of life' is integrated. The important point in the argument rests on the active and indissoluble relationships between elements or social practices normally separated out. It is in *this* context that the 'theory of culture' is defined as 'the study of relationships between elements in a whole way of life'. 'Culture' is not *a* practice; nor is it simply the descriptive sum of the 'mores and folkways' of societies – as it tended to become in certain kinds of anthropology. It is threaded through *all* social practices, and is the sum of their inter-relationship. The question of what, then, is studied, and how, resolves itself. The 'culture' is those patterns of organization, those characteristic forms of human energy which can be discovered as revealing themselves – in 'unexpected identities and correspondences' as well as in 'discontinuities of an unexpected kind' (p. 63) – within or underlying *all* social practices. The analysis of culture is, then, 'the attempt to discover the nature of the organization which is the complex of these relationships'. It begins with 'the discovery of patterns of a characteristic kind'. One will discover them, not in the art, production, trading, politics, the raising of families, treated as separate activities, but through 'studying a general organization in a particular example' (p. 61). Analytically, one must study 'the relationships between all these patterns'. The purpose of the analysis is to grasp how the interactions between these practices and patterns are lived and experienced as a whole, in any particular period. This is its 'structure of feeling'.

It is easier to see what Williams was getting at, and why he was pushed along this path, if we understand what were the problems he addressed, and what pitfalls he was trying to avoid. This is particularly necessary because *The Long Revolution* (like many of Williams's works) carries on a submerged, almost 'silent' dialogue with alternative positions, which are not always as clearly identified as one would wish. There is a clear engagement with the 'idealist' and 'civilizing' definitions of culture – both the equation of 'culture' with *ideas*, in the idealist tradition; and the assimilation of culture to an *ideal*, prevalent in the elitist terms of the 'cultural debate'. But there is also a more extended engagement with certain kinds of Marxism, against which Williams's definitions are consciously pitched. He is arguing against the literal operations of the base/superstructure metaphor, which in classical Marxism ascribed to domain of ideas and of meanings to the 'superstructures', themselves conceived as merely reflective of and determined in some simple fashion by 'the base'; without a social effectivity of their own. That is to say, his argument is constructed against a vulgar materialism and an economic determinism. He offers, instead, a radical interactionism: in effect, the interaction of all practices in and with one another, skirting the problem of determinacy. The distinctions between practices is overcome by seeing them all as variant forms of *praxis* – of a general human activity and energy. The underlying patterns which distinguish the complex of practices in any specific society at any specific time are the characteristic 'forms of its organization' which underlie them all, and which can therefore be traced in each.

There have been several, radical revisions of this early position: and each has contributed much to the redefinition of what Cultural Studies is and should be. We have acknowledged already the exemplary nature of Williams's project, in constantly rethinking and revising older arguments – in going on thinking. Nevertheless, one is struck by a marked line of continuity through these seminal revisions. One such moment is the occasion of his recognition of Lucien Goldmann's work, and through him, of the array of Marxist thinkers who had given particular attention to superstructural forms and whose work began, for the first time, to appear in English translation in the mid-1960s. The contrast between the alternative Marxist traditions which sustained writers like Goldman and Lukacs, as compared with Williams's isolated position and the impoverished Marxist tradition he had to draw on, is sharply delineated. But the points of convergence – both what they are against, and what they are about – are identified in ways which are not altogether out of line with his earlier arguments. Here is the negative, which he sees as linking his work to Goldmann's: 'I came to believe that I had to give up, or at least to leave aside, what I knew as the Marxist tradition: to attempt to develop a theory of social totality; to see the study of culture as the study of relations between elements in a whole way of life; to find ways of studying structure . . . which could stay in touch with and illuminate particular art works and forms, but also forms and relations of more general social life; to replace the formula of base and superstructure with the more active idea of a field of mutually if also unevenly determining forces' (*NLR* 67, May–June 1971). And here is the positive – the point where the convergence is marked between Williams's 'structure of feeling' and Goldmann's 'genetic structuralism': 'I found in my own work that I had to develop the idea of a structure of feeling. . . . But then I found Goldmann beginning . . . from a concept of structure which contained, in itself, a relation between social and literary facts. This relation, he insisted, was not a matter of content, but of mental structures: "categories which simultaneously organize the empirical consciousness of a particular social group, and the imaginative world created by the writer". By definition, these structures are not individually but collectively created.' The stress there on the interactivity of practices and on the underlying totalities, and the homologies between them, is characteristic and significant. 'A correspondence of content between a writer and his world is less significant than this correspondence or organization, of structure.'

A second such 'moment' is the point where Williams really takes on board E.P. Thompson's critique of *The Long Revolution* (cf. the review in *NLR* 9 and 10) – that no 'whole way of life' is without its dimension of struggle and confrontation between opposed *ways* of life – and attempts to rethink the key issues of determination and domination via Gramsci's concept of 'hegemony'. This essay ('Base and superstructure', *NLR* 82, 1973) is a seminal one, especially in its elaboration of dominant, residual and emergent cultural practices, and its return to the problematic of determinacy as 'limits and pressures'. None the less, the earlier emphases recur, with force: 'we cannot separate literature and art from other kinds of social practice, in such a way as to make them subject to quite special and distinct laws'. And, 'no mode of production, and therefore no dominant society or order of society, and therefore no dominant culture, in reality exhausts human practice, human energy, human intention'. And this note is carried forward – indeed, it is radically accented – in Williams's most sustained and succinct recent statement of his position: the masterly condensations of *Marxism and Literature*. Against the structuralist emphasis on the specificty and 'autonomy' of practices, and their analytic separation of societies into their discrete instances, Williams's stress is on 'constitutive activity' in general, on 'sensuous human activity, as practice', from Marx's first 'thesis' on Feuerbach; on different practices conceived as a 'whole indissoluble practice'; on totality. 'Thus, contrary to one development in Marxism, it is not "the base" and "the superstructure" that need to be studied, but specific and indissoluble real processes, within which the decisive relationship, from a Marxist point of view, is that expressed by the complex idea of "determination"' (1977, pp. 30–31, 82).

At one level, Williams's and Thompson's work can only be said to converge around the terms of the same problematic through the operation of a violent and schematically dichotomous theorization. The organizing terrain of Thompson's work – classes as relations, popular struggle, and historical forms of consciousness, class cultures in their historical particularity – is foreign to the more reflective and 'generalizing' mode in which Williams typically works. And the dialogue between them begins with a very sharp encounter. The review of *The Long Revolution*, which Thompson undertook, took Williams sharply to task for the evolutionary way in which culture as a 'whole way of life' had been conceptualized; for his tendency to absorb conflicts between class cultures into the terms of an extended 'conversation'; for his impersonal tone – above the contending classes, as it were; and for the imperializing sweep of his concept of 'culture' (which, heterogeneously, swept everything into its orbit because it was the study of the interrelationships between the forms of energy and organization underlying *all* practices. But wasn't this – Thompson asked – where History came in?). Progressively, we can see how Williams has persistently rethought the terms of his original paradigm to take these criticisms into account –

though this is accomplished (as it so frequently is in Williams) obliquely: via a particular appropriation of Gramsci, rather than in a more direct modification.

Thompson also operates with a more 'classical' distinction than Williams, between 'social being' and 'social consciousness' (the terms he infinitely prefers, from Marx, to the more fashionable 'base and superstructure'). Thus, where Williams insists on the absorption of all practices into the totality of 'real, indissoluble practice', Thompson does deploy an older distinction between what is 'culture' and what is 'not culture'.'Any theory of culture must include the concept of the dialectical interaction between culture and something that is *not* culture.' Yet the definition of culture is not, after all, so far removed from Williams's: 'We must suppose the raw material of life experience to be at one pole, and all the infinitely complex human disciplines and systems, articulate and inarticulate, formalised in institutions or dispersed in the least formal ways, which "handle", transmit or distort this raw material to be at the other.' Similarly, with respect to the commonality of 'practice' which underlies all the distinct practices: 'It is the active process – which is at the same time the process through which men make their history – that I am insisting upon' (*NLR* 9, p. 33, 1961). And the two positions come close together around – again – certain distinctive negatives and positives. Negatively, against the 'base/superstructure' metaphor, and a reductionist or 'economistic' definition of determinacy. On the first: 'The dialectical intercourse between social being and social consciousness – or between "culture" and "*not* culture" – is at the heart of any comprehension of the historical process within the Marxist tradition. . . . The tradition inherits a dialectic that is right, but the particular mechanical metaphor through which it is expressed is wrong. This metaphor from constructional engineering . . . must in any case be inadequate to describe the flux of conflict, the dialectic of a changing social process. . . . All the metaphors which are commonly offered have a tendency to lead the mind into schematic modes and away from the interaction of being-consciousness.' And on 'reductionism': 'Reductionism is a lapse in historical logic by which political or cultural events are "explained" in terms of the class affiliations of the actors. . . . But the mediation between "interest" and "belief " was not through Nairn's "complex of superstructures" but through the people themselves' ('Peculiarities of the English', *Socialist Register*, 1965, pp. 351–52). And, more positively – a simple statement which may be taken as defining virtually the whole of Thompson's historical work, from *The Making* to *Whigs and Hunters*, *The Poverty of Theory* and beyond – 'capitalist society was founded upon forms of exploitation which are simultaneously economic, moral and cultural. Take up the essential defining productive relationship . . . and turn it round, and it reveals itself now in one aspect (wage-labour), now in another (an acquisitive ethos), and now in another (the alienation of such intellectual faculties as are not required by the worker in his productive role)' (*ibid.*, p. 356).

Here, then, despite the many significant differences, is the outline of one significant line of thinking in Cultural Studies – some would say, *the* dominant paradigm. It stands opposed to the residual and merely-reflective rôle assigned to 'the cultural'. In its different ways, it conceptualizes culture as interwoven with all social practices; and those practices, in turn, as a common form of human activity: sensuous human praxis, the activity through which men and women make history. It is opposed to the base–superstructure way of formulating the relationship between ideal and material forces, especially where the 'base' is defined as the determination by 'the economic' in any simple sense. It prefes the wider formulation – the dialectic between social being and social consciousness: neither separable into its distinct poles (in some alternative formulations, the dialectic between 'culture' and 'non-culture'). It defines 'culture' as *both* the meanings and values which arise amongst distinctive social groups and classes, on the basis of their given historical conditions and relationships, through which they 'handle' and respond to the conditions of existence; *and* as the lived traditions and practices through which those 'understandings' are expressed and in which they are embodied. Williams brings together these two aspects – definitions and ways of life – around the concept of 'culture' itself. Thompson brings the two elements – consciousness and conditions – around the concept of 'experience'. Both positions entail certain difficult fluctuations around these key terms. Williams so totally absorbs 'definitions of experience' into our 'ways of living', and both into an indissoluble real material practice-in-general, as to obviate any distinction between 'culture' and 'not-culture'. Thompson sometimes uses 'experience' in the more usual sense of consciousness, as the collective ways in which men 'handle, transmit or distort' their given conditions, the raw materials of life; sometimes as the domain of the 'lived', the mid-term *between* 'conditions' and 'culture'; and sometimes as the objective conditions themselves – against which particular modes of consciousness are counterposed. But, whatever the terms, both positions tend to read structures of relations in terms of how they are 'lived' and 'experienced'. Williams's 'structure of feeling' – with its deliberate condensation of apparently incompatible elements – is characteristic. But the same is true of Thompson, despite his far fuller historical grasp of the 'given-ness' or structuredness of the relations and conditions into which men and women necessarily and involuntarily enter, and his clearer attention to the determinacy of productive and exploitative relations under capitalism. This is a consequence of giving culture-consciousness and experience so pivotal a place in the analysis. The *experiential pull* in this paradigm, and the emphasis on the creative and on historical agency, constitutes the two key elements in the *humanism* of the position outlined. Each consequently accords 'experience' an authenticating position in any cultural analysis. It is, ultimately, where and how people experience their conditions of life, define them and respond to them, which, for Thompson defines why every mode of production is also a culture, and every struggle between classes is always also a struggle between cultural modalities; and which, for Williams, is what a 'cultural analysis', in the final instance, should deliver. In 'experience', all the different practices intersect; within 'culture' the different practices interact – even if on an uneven and mutually determining basis. This sense of cultural totality – of *the whole* historical process – over-rides any effort to keep the instances and elements distinct. Their real interconnection, under given historical conditions, must be matched by a totalizing movement 'in thought', in the analysis. It establishes for both the strongest protocols against any form of analytic abstraction which distinguishes practices, or which sets out to test the 'actual historical movement' in all its intertwined complexity and particularity by any more sustained logical or analytical operation. These positions, especially in their more concrete historical rendering (*The Making, The Country and the City*) are the very opposite of a Hegelian search for underlying Essences. Yet, in their tendency to reduce practices to *praxis* and to find common and homologous 'forms' underlying the most apparently differentiated areas, their movement is 'essentializing'. They have a particular way of understanding the totality – though it is with a small 't', concrete and historically determinate, uneven in its correspondences. They understand it 'expressively'. And since they constantly inflect the more traditional analysis towards the experiential level, or read the other structures and relations downwards from the vantage point of how they are 'lived', they are properly (even if not adequately or fully) characterized as 'culturalist' in their emphasis: even when all the caveats and qualifications against a too rapid 'dichotomous theorizing' have been entered. (Cf. for 'culturalism', Richard Johnson's two seminal articles on the operation of the paradigm: in 'Histories of culture/theories of ideology', *Ideology and Cultural Production*, eds M. Barrett, P. Corrigan *et al.*, Croom Helm, 1979; and 'Three problematics' in *Working Class Culture*, Clarke, Critcher and Johnson, Hutchinson and CCCS, 1979. For the dangers in 'dichotomous theorizing', cf. the Introduction, 'Representation and cultural production', to Barrett, Corrigan *et al.*.)

The 'culturalist' strand in Cultural Studies was interrupted by the arrival on the intellectual scene of the 'structuralisms'. These, possibly more varied than the 'culturalisms', nevertheless shared certain positions and orientations in common which makes their designation under a single title not altogether misleading. It has been remarked that whereas the 'culturalist' paradigm can be defined without requiring a conceptual reference to the term 'ideology' (the *word*, of course, does appear: but it is not a key concept), the 'structuralist' interventions have been largely articulated around the concept of 'ideology': in keeping with its more impeccably Marxist lineage, 'culture' does not figure so prominently. Whilst this may be true of the Marxist structuralists, it is at best less than half the truth about the structuralist enterprise as such. But it is now a common error to condense the latter exclusively around the impact of Althusser and all that has followed in the wake of his interventions – where 'ideology' has played a seminal, but modulated rôle: and to omit the significance of Lévi-Strauss. Yet, in strict historical terms, it was Lévi-Strauss, and the early semiotics, which made the first break. And though the Marxist structuralisms have superseded the latter, they owed, and continue to owe, an immense theoretical debt (often fended off or down-graded into footnotes, in the search for a retrospective orthodoxy) to his work. It was Lévi-Strauss's structuralism which, in its appropriation of the linguistic paradigm, after Saussure, offered the promise to the 'human sciences of culture' of a paradigm capable of rendering them scientific and rigorous in a thoroughly new way. And when, in Althusser's work, the more classical Marxist themes were recovered, it remained the case that Marx was 'read' – and reconstituted – through the terms of the linguistic paradigm. In *Reading Capital*, for example, the case is made that the mode of production – to coin a phrase – could best be understood as if 'structured like a language' (through the selective combination of invariant elements). The a-historical and synchronic stress, against the historical emphases of 'culturalism', derived from a similar source. So did a pre-occupation with 'the social, *sui generis*' – used not adjectivally but substantively: a usage Lévi-Strauss derived, not from Marx, but from Durkheim (the Durkheim who analysed the social categories of thought – e.g. in *Primitive Classification* – rather than the Durkheim of *The Division of Labour*, who became the founding father of American structural-functionalism).

Lévi-Strauss did, on occasion, toy with certain Marxist formulations. Thus, 'Marixism, if not Marx himself, has too commonly reasoned as though practices followed directly from praxis. Without questioning the undoubted primacy of infrastructures, I believe that there is always a mediator between praxis and practices, namely, the conceptual scheme by the operation of which matter and form, neither with any independent existence, are realized as structures, that is as entities which are both empirical and intelligible'. But this – to coin another phrase – was largely 'gestural'. This structuralism shared with culturalism a radical break with the terms of the base/superstructure metaphor, as derived from the simpler parts of *The German Ideology*. And, though 'It is to this theory of the super-structures, scarcely touched on by Marx' to which Lévi-Strauss aspired to contribute, his contribution was such as to break in a radical way with its whole terms of reference, as finally and irrevocably as the 'culturalists' did. Here – and we must include Althusser in this characterization – culturalists and structuralists alike ascribed to the domains hitherto defined as 'super-structural' a specificity and effectivity, a constitutive primacy, which pushed them beyond the terms of reference of 'base' and 'superstruc-ture'. Lévi-Strauss and Althusser, too, were anti-reductionist and anti-economist in their very cast of thought, and critically attacked that transi-tive causality which, for so long, had passed itself off as 'classical Marxism'.

Lévi-Strauss worked consistently with the term 'culture'. He regarded 'ideologies' as of much lesser importance: mere 'secondary rationaliza-tions'. Like Williams and Goldmann, he worked, not at the level of correspondences between the *content* of a practice, but at the level of their forms and structures. But the manner in which these were conceptualized were altogether at variance with either the 'culturalism' of Williams or Goldmann's 'genetic structuralism'. This divergence can be identified in three distinct ways. First, he conceptualized 'culture' as the categories and frameworks in thought and language through which different societies classified out their conditions of existence – above all (since Lévi-Strauss was an anthropologist), the relations between the human and the natural worlds. Second, he thought of the manner and practice through which these categories and mental frameworks were produced and trans-formed, largely on an analogy with the ways in which language itself – the principal medium of 'culture' – operated. He identified what was specific to them and their operation as the 'production of meaning': they were, above all, *signifying* practices. Third, after some early flirtations with Durkheim and Mauss's social categories of thought, he largely gave up the question of the relation *between* signifying and non-signifying practices – between 'culture' and 'not-culture', to use other terms – for the sake of concentrating on the *internal* relations within signifying practices by means of which the categories of meaning were produced. This left the question of determinacy, of totality, largely in abeyance. The causal logic of determinacy was abandoned in favour of a structuralist causality – a logic of *arrangement*, of internal relations, of articulation of parts within a structure. Each of these aspects is also positively present in Althusser's work and that of the Marxist structuralists, even when the terms of reference had been regrounded in Marx's 'immense theoretical revolution'. In one of Althusser's seminal formulations about ideology – defined as the themes, concepts and representations through which men and women 'live', in an imaginary relation, their relation to their real conditions of existence – we can see the skeleton outline of Lévi-Strauss's 'conceptual schemes between praxis and practices'. 'Ideologies' are here being conceptualized, not as the contents and surface forms of ideas, but as the unconscious categories through which conditions are represented and lived. We have already commented on the active presence in Althusser's thinking of the linguistic paradigm – the second element identified above. And though, in the concept of 'over-determination' – one of his most seminal and fruitful contributions – Althusser did return to the problems of the relations *between* practices and the question of determinacy (proposing, incidentally, a thoroughly novel and highly suggestive reformulation, which has received far too little subsequent attention), he did tend to reinforce the 'relative autonomy' of different practices, and their internal specificities, conditions and effects at the expense of an 'expressive' conception of the totality, with its typical homologies and correspondences.

Aside from the wholly distinct intellectual and conceptual universes within which these alternative paradigms developed, there were certain points where, despite their apparent overlaps, culturalism and structuralism were starkly counterposed. We can identify this counterposition at one of its sharpest points precisely around the concept of 'experience', and the rôle the term played in each perspective. Whereas, in 'culturalism', experience was the ground – the terrain of 'the lived' – where consciousness and conditions intersected, structuralism insisted that 'experience' could not, by definition, be the ground of anything, since one could only 'live' and experience one's conditions *in and through* the categories, classifications and frameworks of the culture. These categories, however, did not arise from or in experience: rather, experience was their 'effect'. The culturalists had defined the forms of consciousness and culture as collective. But they had stopped far short of the radical proposition that, in culture and in language, the subject was 'spoken by' the categories of culture in which he/she thought, rather than 'speaking them'. These categories were, however, not merely collective rather than individual productions: they were *unconscious* structures. That is why, though Lévi-Strauss spoke only of 'Culture', his concept provided the basis for an easy translation, by Althusser, into the conceptual framework of ideology: 'Ideology is indeed a system of "representations", but in the majority of cases these representations have nothing to do with "consciousness" . . . : it is above all as structures that they impose on the vast majority of men, not via their "consciousness" . . . it is within this ideological unconsciousness that men succeed in altering the "lived" relation between them and the world and acquiring that new form of specific unconsciousness called "consciousness"' (*For Marx*, p. 233). It was, in this sense, that 'experience' was conceived, not as an authenticating source but as an effect: not as a reflection of the real but as an 'imaginary relation'. It was only a short step – the one which separates *For Marx* from the 'Ideological State Apparatuses' essay – to the development of an account of how this 'imaginary relation' served, not simply the dominance of a ruling class over a dominated one, but (through the reproduction of the relations of production, and the constitution of labour-power in a form fit for capitalist exploitation) the expanded reproduction of the mode of production itself. Many of the other lines of divergence between the two paradigms flow from this point: the conception of 'men' as bearers of the structures that speak and place them, rather than as active agents in the making of their own history; the emphasis on a structural rather than a historical 'logic'; the preoccupation with the constitution – in 'theory' – of a non-ideological, scientific discourse; and hence the privileging of conceptual work and of Theory as guaranteed; the recasting of history as a march of the structures (cf. passim, *The Poverty of Theory*): the structuralist 'machine'. . . .

There is no space in which to follow through the many ramifications which have followed from the development of one or other of these 'master paradigms' in Cultural Studies. Though they by no means acount for all, or even nearly all, of the many strategies adopted, it is fair to say that, between them, they have defined the principal lines of development in the field. The seminal debates have been polarized around their thematics; some of the best concrete work has flowed from the efforts to set one or other of these paradigms to work on particular problems and materials. Characteristically – the sectarian and self-righteous climate of critical intellectual work in England being what it is, and its dependency being so marked – the arguments and debates have most frequently been over-polarized into their extremes. At these extremities, they frequently appear only as mirror-reflections or inversions of one another. Here, the broad typologies we have been working with – for the sake of convenient exposition – become the prison-house of thought.

Without suggesting that there can be any easy synthesis between them, it might usefully be said at this point that neither 'culturalism' nor 'structuralism' is, in its present manifestation, adequate to the task of constructing the study of culture as a conceptually clarified and theoretically informed domain of study. Nevertheless, something fundamental to it emerges from a rough comparison of their respective strengths and limitations.

The great strength of the structuralisms is their stress on 'determinate conditions'. They remind us that, unless the dialectic really can be held, in any particular analysis, between both halves of the proposition – that 'men make history . . . on the basis of conditions which are not of their making' – the result will inevitably be a naïve humanism, with its necessary consequence: a voluntarist and populist political practice. The fact that 'men' can become conscious of their conditions, organize to struggle against them and in fact transform them – without which no active politics can even be conceived, let alone practised – must not be allowed to override the awareness of the fact that, in capitalist relations, men and women are placed and positioned in relations which constitute them as agents. 'Pessimism of the intellect, optimism of the will' is a better starting point than a simple heroic affirmation. Structuralism does enable us to begin to think – as Marx insisted – of the *relations* of a structure on the basis of something other than their reduction to relationships between 'people'. This was Marx's privileged level of abstraction: that which enabled him to break with the obvious but incorrect starting point of 'political economy' – bare individuals.

But this connects with a second strength: the recognition by structuralism not only of the necessity of abstraction as the instrument of thought through which 'real relations' are appropriated, but also of the presence, in Marx's work, of a continuous and complex movement *between different levels of abstraction*. It is, of course, the case – as 'culturalism' argues – that, in historical reality, practices do not appear neatly distinguished out into their respective instances. However, to think about or to analyse the complexity of the real, the act of the practice of thinking is required; and this necessitates the use of the power of abstraction and analysis, the formation of concepts with which to cut into the complexity of the real, in order precisely to reveal and bring to light relationships and structures which cannot be visible to the naïve naked eye, and which can neither present nor authenticate themselves: 'In the analysis of economic forms, neither microscopes nor chemical reagents are of assistance. The power of abstraction must replace both.' Of course, structuralism has frequently taken this proposition to its extreme. Because thought is impossible without 'the power of abstraction', it has confused this with giving an absolute primacy to the level of the formation of concepts – and at the highest, most abstract level of abstraction only: Theory with a capital 'T' then becomes judge and jury. But this is precisely to lose the insight just won from Marx's own practice. For it is clear in, for example, *Capital*, that the *method* – whilst, of course, taking place 'in thought' (as Marx asked in the 1857 Introduction, where else?) – rests, not on the simple exercise of abstraction but on the movement and relations which the argument is constantly establishing between *different levels* of abstraction: at each, the premises in play must be distinguished from those which – for the sake of the argument – have to be held constant. The movement to another level of magnification (to deploy the microscope metaphor) requires the specifying of further conditions of existence not supplied at a previous, more abstract level: in this way, by successive abstractions of different magnitudes, to *move towards* the constitution, the *reproduction*, of 'the concrete in thought' as an effect of a certain kind of thinking. This method is adequately represented in *neither* the absolutism of Theoretical Practice, in structuralism, nor in the anti-abstraction 'Poverty of Theory' position into which, in reaction, culturalism appears to have been driven or driven itself. Nevertheless it is intrinsically *theoretical*, and must be. Here, structuralism's insistence that thought does not reflect reality, but is articulated on and appropriates it, is a necessary starting point. An adequate *working through* of the consequences of this argument might begin to produce a method which takes us outside the permanent oscillations between abstraction/anti-abstraction and the false dichotomies of Theoreticism *vs.* Empiricism which have both marked and disfigured the structuralism/culturalism encounter to date.

Structuralism has another strength, in its conception of 'the whole'. There is a sense in which, though culturalism constantly insists on the radical particularity of its practices, its mode of conceptualizing the 'totality' has something of the complex simplicity of an expressive totality behind it. Its complexity is constituted by the fluidity with which practices move into and out of one another: but this complexity is reducible, conceptually, to the 'simplicity' of praxis – human activity, as such – in which the same contradictions constantly appear, homologously reflected in each. Structuralism goes too far in erecting the machine of a 'Structure', with its self-generating propensities (a 'Spinozean eternity', whose function is only the sum of its effects: a truly structural*ist* deviation), equipped with its distinctive instances. Yet it represents an advance over culturalism in the conception it has of the necessary *complexity* of the unity of a structure (over-determination being a more successful way of thinking this complexity than the combinatory invariance of structuralist causality). Moreover, it has the conceptual ability to think of a unity which is constructed through the *differences* between, rather than the homology of, practices. Here, again, it has won a critical insight about Marx's method: one thinks of the complex passages of the 1857 Introduction to the *Grundrisse* where Marx demonstrates how it is possible to think of the 'unity' of a social formation as constructed, not out of identity but out of *difference*. Of course, the stress on difference can – and has – led the structuralisms into a fundamental conceptual heterogeneity, in which all sense of structure and totality is lost. Foucault and other post-Althussereans have taken this devious path into the absolute, not the relative, autonomy of practices, via their necessary heterogeneity and 'necessary non-correspondence'. But the emphasis on unity-in-difference, on complex unity – Marx's concrete as the 'unity of many determinations' – can be worked in another, and ultimately more fruitful direction: towards the problematic of relative autonomy and 'over-determination', and the study of *articulation*. Again, articulation contains the danger of a high formalism. But it also has the considerable advantage of enabling us to think of how specific practices (articulated around contradictions which do not all arise in the same way, at the same point, in the same moment), can nevertheless be thought *together*. The structuralist paradigm thus does – if properly developed – enable us to begin really to *conceptualize* the specificity of different practices (analytically distinguished, abstracted out), without losing its grip on the ensemble which they constitute. Culturalism constantly affirms the specificity of different practices – 'culture' must not be absorbed into 'the economic': but it lacks an adequate way of establishing this specificity theoretically.

The third strength which structuralism exhibits lies in its decentring of 'experience' and its seminal work in elaborating the neglected category of 'ideology'. It is difficult to conceive of a Cultural Studies thought within a

Marxist paradigm which is innocent of the category of 'ideology'. Of course, culturalism constantly make reference to this concept: but it does not in fact lie at the centre of its conceptual universe. The authenticating power and reference of 'experience' imposes a barrier between culturalism and a proper conception of 'ideology'. Yet, without it, the effectivity of 'culture' for the reproduction of a particular mode of production cannot be grasped. It is true that there is a marked tendency in the more recent structuralist conceptualizations of 'ideology' to give it a functionalist reading – as the necessary cement of the social formation. From this position, it is indeed impossible – as culturalism would correctly argue – to conceive either of ideologies which are not, by definition, 'dominant': or of the concept of struggle (the latter's appearance in Althusser's famous ISA's article being – to coin yet another phrase – largely 'gestural'). Nevertheless, work is already being done which suggests ways in which the field of ideology may be adequately conceptualized as a terrain of struggle (through the work of Gramsci, and more recently, of Laclau), and these have structuralist rather than culturalist bearings.

Culturalism's strengths can almost be derived from the weaknesses of the structuralist position already noted, and from the latter's strategic absences and silences. It has insisted, correctly, on the affirmative moment of the development of conscious struggle and organization as a necessary element in the analysis of history, ideology and consciousness: against its persistent down-grading in the structuralist paradigm. Here, again, it is largely Gramsci who has provided us with a set of more refined terms through which to link the largely 'unconscious' and given cultural categories of 'common sense' with the formation of more active and organic ideologies, which have the capacity to intervene in the ground of common sense and popular traditions and, through such interventions, to organize masses of men and women. In this sense, culturalism *properly* restores the dialectic between the unconsciousness of cultural categories and the moment of conscious organization: even if, in its characteristic movement, it has tended to match structuralism's over-emphasis on 'conditions' with an altogether too-inclusive emphasis on 'consciousness'. It therefore not only recovers – as the necessary moment of any analysis – the process by means of which classes-in-themselves, defined primarily by the way in which economic relations position 'men' as agents – become active historical and political forces – for-themselves: it also – against its own anti-theoretical good sense – *requires* that, when properly developed, each moment must be understood in terms of the level of abstraction at which the analysis is operating. Again, Gramsci has begun to point a way through this false polarization in his discussion of 'the passage between the structure and the sphere of the complex superstructures', and its distinct forms and moments.

We have concentrated in this argument largely on a characterization of what seem to us to be the two seminal paradigms at work in Cultural Studies. Of course, they are by no means the only active ones. New developments and lines of thinking are by no means adequately netted with reference to them. Nevertheless, these paradigms can, in a sense, be deployed to measure what appear to us to be the radical weaknesses or inadequacies of those which offer themselves as alternative rallying-points. Here, briefly, we identify three.

The first is that which follows on from Lévi-Strauss, early semiotics and the terms of the linguistic paradigm, and the centring on 'signifying practices', moving by way of psychoanalytic concepts and Lacan to a radical recentring of virtually the whole terrain of Cultural Studies around the terms 'discourse' and 'the subject'. One way of understanding this line of thinking is to see it as an attempt to fill that empty space in early structuralism (of both the Marxist and non-Marxist varieties) where, in earlier discourses, 'the subject' and subjectivity might have been expected to appear but did not. This is, of course, precisely one of the key points where culturalism brings its pointed criticisms to bear on structuralism's 'process without a subject'. The difference is that, whereas culturalism would correct for the hyper-structuralism of earlier models by restoring the unified subject (collective or individual) of consciousness at the centre of 'the Structure', discourse theory, by way of the Freudian concepts of the unconscious and the Lacanian concepts of how subjects are constituted in language (through the entry into the Symbolic and the Law of Culture), restores the *decentred* subject, the contradictory subject, as a set of positions in language and knowledge, from which culture can appear to be enunciated. This approach clearly identifies a gap, not only in structuralism but in Marxism itself. The problem is that the manner in which this 'subject' of culture is conceptualized is of a trans-historical and 'universal' character: it addresses the subject-in-general, not historically-determinate social subjects, or socially determinate particular languages. Thus it is incapable, so far, of moving its in-general propositions to the level of concrete historical analysis. The second difficulty is that the processes of contradiction and struggle – lodged by early structuralism wholly at the level of 'the structure' – are now, by one of those persistent mirror-inversions, lodged exclusively at the level of the unconscious processes of the subject. It may be, as culturalism often argues, that the 'subjective' is a necessary moment of any such analysis. But this is a very different proposition from dismantling the whole of the social processes of particular modes of production and social formations, and reconstituting them exclusively at the level of unconscious psychoanalytic processes. Though important work has been done, both within this paradigm and to define and develop it, its claims to have replaced *all* the terms of the earlier paradigms with a more adequate set of concepts seems wildly over-ambitious. Its claims to have integrated Marxism into a more adequate materialism is, largely, a semantic rather than a conceptual claim.

A second development is the attempt to return to the terms of a more classical 'political economy' of culture. This position argues that the concentration on the cultural and ideological aspects has been wildly overdone. It would restore the older terms of 'base/superstructure', finding, in the last-instance determination of the cultural-ideological by the economic, that hierarchy of determinations which both alternatives appear to lack. This position insists that the economic processes and structures of cultural production are more significant than their cultural-ideological aspect: and that these are quite adequately caught in the more classical terminology of profit, exploitation, surplus-value and the analysis of culture as commodity. It retains a notion of ideology as 'false consciousness'.

There is, of course, some strength to the claim that both structuralism and culturalism, in their different ways, have neglected the economic analysis of cultural and ideological production. All the same, with the return to this more 'classical' terrain, many of the problems which originally beset it also reappear. The specificity of the effect of the cultural and ideological dimension once more tends to disappear. It tends to conceive the economic level as not only a 'necessary' but a 'sufficient' explanation of cultural and ideological effects. Its focus on the analysis of the commodity-form, similarly, blurs all the carefully established distinctions between different practices, since it is the most *generic* aspects of the commodity-form which attract attention. Its deductions are therefore, largely, confined to an epochal level of abstraction: the generalizations about the commodity-form hold true throughout the capitalist epoch as a whole. Very little by way of concrete and conjunctural analysis can be derived at this high-level 'logic of capital' form of abstraction. It also tends to its own kind of functionalism – a functionalism of 'logic' rather than of 'structure' or history. This approach, too, has insights which are well worth following through. But it sacrifices too much of what has been painfully secured, without a compensating gain in explanatory power.

The third position is closely related to the structuralist enterprise, but has followed the path of 'difference' through into a radical heterogeneity. Foucault's work currently enjoying another of those uncritical periods of discipleship through which British intellectuals reproduce today their dependency on yesterday's French ideas – has had an exceedingly positive effect: above all because – in suspending the nearly-insoluble problems of determination Foucault has made possible a welcome return to the concrete analysis of particular ideological and discursive formations, and the sites of their elaboration. Foucault and Gramsci between them account for much of the most productive work on *concrete analysis* now being undertaken in the field: thereby reinforcing and – paradoxically – supporting the sense of the concrete historical instance which has always been one of culturalism's principal strengths. But, again, Foucault's example is positive only if his general epistemological position is not swallowed whole. For in fact Foucault so resolutely suspends judgment, and adopts so thoroughgoing a scepticism about any determinacy or relationship between practices, other than the largely contingent, that we are entitled to see him, not as an agnostic on these questions, but as deeply committed to the necessary non-correspondence of all practices to one another. From such a position neither a social formation, nor the State, can be adequately thought. And indeed Foucault is constantly falling into the pit which he has dug for himself. For when – against his well-defended epistemological positions – he stumbles across certain 'correspondences' (for example, the simple fact that all the major moments of transition he has traced in each of his studies – on the prison, sexuality, medicine, the asylum, language and political economy – all appear to converge around exactly that point where industrial capitalism and the bourgeoisie make their fateful, historical rendez-vous), he lapses into a vulgar reductionism, which thoroughly belies the sophisticated positions he has elsewhere advanced.[1]

I have said enough to indicate that, in my view, the line in Cultural Studies which has attempted to *think forwards* from the best elements in the structuralist and culturalist enterprises, by way of some of the concepts elaborated in Gramsci's work, comes closest to meeting the requirements of the field of study. And the reason for that should by now also be obvious. Though neither structuralism nor culturalism will do, as self-sufficient paradigms of study, they have a centrality to the field which all the other contenders lack because, between them (in their divergences as well as their convergences) they address what must be the *core problem* of Cultural Studies. They constantly return us to the terrain marked out by those strongly coupled but not mutually exclusive concepts culture/ideology. They pose, together, the problems consequent on trying to think *both* the specificity of different practices and the forms of the articulated unity they constitute. They make a constant, if flawed, return to the base/superstructure metaphor. They are correct in insisting that this question – which resumes all the problems of a non-reductive determinacy – is the heart of the matter: and that, on the solution of this problem will turn the capacity of Cultural Studies to supersede the endless oscillations between idealism and reductionism. They confront – even if in radically opposed ways – the dialectic between conditions and consciousness. At another level, they pose the question of the relation between the logic of thinking and the 'logic' of historical process. They continue to hold out the promise of a properly materialist theory of culture. In their sustained and mutually reinforcing antagonisms they hold out no promise of an easy synthesis. But, between them, they define where, if at all, is the space, and what are the limits, within which such a synthesis might be constituted. In Cultural Studies, theirs are the 'names of the game'.

Note

1. He is quite capable of wheeling in through the back door the classes he recently expelled from the front.

3

The Centre for Contemporary Cultural Studies

Michael Green

Though cultural studies was substantially pioneered at the Centre for Contemporary Cultural Studies in Birmingham University, these notes attempt neither a history of significant intellectual developments there, nor a consideration of the distinctive relations between cultural studies and the analysis of literary texts.[1] They are concerned instead with some aspects (productive and also problematic) of marginality in a set of new intellectual endeavours: the relation of cultural studies to the established 'disciplines'; to some received working practices of higher education; and to the purposes and possibilities of intellectual work from such a location. This has involved continual excitements and difficulties hardly mentioned here: difficulties of institutional continuity (particularly of funding), and excitements of comradeship in the complex relations of research and 'teaching'. The main questions concern the breaking of frames and boundaries. In particular, the brief history is of necessity caught in the specific, and rapidly shifting conditions of the politics of intellectual work in Britain between the early 1960s and the early 1980s: from Hoggart to Gramsci, but also from Macmillan to Thatcher.

Cultural studies and the disciplines

> When the most basic concepts . . . from which we begin, are seen to be not concepts but problems, not analytic problems either but historical movements that are still unresolved . . . we have, if we can, to recover the substance from which their forms were cast. (Raymond Williams)

Cultural studies began as the outcrop of an English Department. What became known as its founding texts were ambitious, brave, but lonely ventures, whose premises were largely given by their common foundation in 'Left-Leavisism'. In them *Scrutiny*'s concerns were sustained, extended and re-thought, even as the journal itself began to consolidate inwards to a pessimistic retrenchment in higher education. Leavis and colleagues had attempted to unite a close, though untheorised, attention to texts with a wide-ranging social criticism: the projected idea for an English School (in

Education and the University, 1943) is still worth reading for its scope. A dissenting stance (alternately self-conscious and paranoid) was taken towards the fashionable and the routinely academic, while new forms of educational organisation, journals and networks were set up in a cultural politics whose lines of development, after the war, became badly blocked. The founding texts in question here were both a diagnosis of those blocks and a set of moves beyond them. Williams's *Culture and Society* (1958) tried to locate and understand Leavis's dissent, while *The Long Revolution* (1961) put together many of *Scrutiny*'s concerns (art, education, politics, communication) in an optimistic view of the future, free of *Scrutiny*'s contempt for the present. Hoggart's *The Uses of Literacy* (1957) sought to describe the containment and resistance of a class through a reading of its texts: 'listening to the voices' at all levels from idioms and common sense through to magazines and newspapers. If this work refused the élitism of high culture and the great tradition, it was equally opposed to the reductions of marxism understood as a hard determinism of the economic. The aim was not, as it later in part became, to put new questions to a marxist agenda.

These themes took their meaning and force from the political abyss of the left in the 1950s, and from the decade's central (and now ever more powerfully communicated) myths of affluence and embourgeoisement. The much-discussed, highly visible crisis of the interwar economy was superseded by the reconstruction of a capitalist prosperity with a quite fresh kind of 'glossy futurism against the hard, rationed, sharing world of the war' (Williams, 1976–7, p. 87). In the 1950s the forms of domestic consumer production which had been only patchily visible between the wars became more fully developed in the enormous extension of the home market. The mass media, Enzensberger's 'consciousness industries' (and television in particular), constructed a new place for women as at once consumers, symbols and spectators of commodities – ITV born next to *Woman* and *Woman's Own.* At the same time the confrontation of 'the people' with a visibly ruling class was replaced by the longer lines of intermediary managerial groupings necessary to more concentrated production and to the enhanced role and protection of a 'welfare' state. The expanded state education system displaced class differences in the apparent mobility of a 'meritocracy' open to all the talents, with its new rhetoric of intelligence and ability. On top of this, replacing fascism, 'the old gang' and an oppositional popular radicalism, there developed a consensus politics of the centre, the 'Butskellite' convergence. The domestic programme to deliver full employment and low inflation raised doubts whether Labour would ever return to office. In foreign policy, Britain's special relationship with the United States, Europe and the new Commonwealth locked it securely in alliance against the 'god that failed' of the USSR. The discrediting of hope in 'science' was surpassed only by the attempted discrediting of the left and the 1930s together, as an anachronism in which class was an archaic British residuum, a dwindling or removable variable.

The texts in question here were a series of counter-statements to this formation, around four themes. *One,* the demonstration of strong, persistent and complex cultural differences: E.P. Thompson's early industrial working class and its active self-making, Hoggart's resilient near-contemporary northern working-class culture, Williams's working-class achievements of collectivism in the institutions of the labour movement. This emphasis continued in the attention given to the inflections of class and culture inside education (Hoggart, Williams, Jackson and Marsden (1962), later Willis (1977)), and to the highly public and stigmatised symbolic forms of youth sub-cultures, read as the condensed exploration of routes and pressures inside the class or 'parent' culture. *Two*, the account of culture as 'ordinary', as the making and taking of meanings in everyday life. This was put against the strong postwar investment in versions of heritage, tradition and monarchy (Labour's 'people's' Festival of Britain replaced by the spectacle of the Coronation), themselves linked with the conservatism of Reith's BBC, the Arts and British Councils, and much English publishing in the 1940s and 1950s with its refusal of foreign and difficult work. *Three*, the argument that the new forms of education and communication were profoundly undemocratic: Williams's 'third revolution' or the 'aspiration to extend active processes of learning to all people rather than to limited groups' (1965, p. xi) his strongly (and morally) evaluative critique (as Hoggart's of ITV) of the deformations of contemporary communications and the concern with opportunities for democratic modes of representation, secured in non-capitalist forms of production and distribution. *Four*, the debate around the condition of England and 'decency': the refusal of imperial Englishness, but also of the future as American (and brashly commercial) or Swedish (and mutedly social democratic) – the attempt to prefigure another society (variously through 'community', through Morris and Blake, through the blocked forms of return to the country or region, to another Englishness – or Welshness).

What then started to give such ideas their distinctive 'set' was not an agreed programme of work, even less 'culturalism', but a political condensation around these shared and new themes as they converged with the emergent moments of a 'new' Left. As the 1950s ended, a 'moral' cause became political in both the British CND marches and the American Black Rights campaigns. The issues themselves, and the improvised and original forms of spontaneous tactics employed, were outside the agendas (and imaginations) of the main political parties in both countries. It seemed now, also, that an important agency of change could be found outside the labour movement, in the college-educated, middle-class children of liberal professional parents: 'the ideological dimensions of the revolution are likely to come initially from within the ideologically dominant class', as Juliet Mitchell put it in *Woman's Estate* (1971) – with its symptomatic claim that blacks, students and women were together significant sources of dissent from the management of production and consumption, production and reproduction. The crisis of Stalinism and, to a lesser extent and with many differences of perspective, of the postwar Labour Party was simultaneously the possibility of a new political constituency, with a new political agenda. High on that agenda would be the refusal of academic 'neutrality', exemplified in Williams and Thompson, powerfully by the Wright Mills of *The Power Elite* (1956) and *Listen, Yankee!* (1961) (on Cuba), and later amplified through studies of academic involvement in research support for the 'military-industrial complex'.

There were thus very strong connections between the work on culture and some new forms of politics. Both saw the 'mass' circulation of media images and languages as the treacherous representation of groups and classes to themselves – but also as a site of refusals, of values *not* shared, and as one site of a politics adequate to conflicts in the spheres of reproduction and consumption. In Hoggart's remarkably enduring formulation:

> I have therefore taken one fairly homogeneous group of working-class people, have tried to evoke the atmosphere, the quality of their lives by describing their setting and their attitudes. Against this background may be seen how much the more generally diffused appeals of the mass publications connect with commonly accepted attitudes, how they are altering those attitudes and how they are meeting resistance. (1957, p. 19)

Both, too, saw in strategies of cultural and community politics – the self-making of classes and fractions – the 'speaking' of values inimical to capitalism. Both were concerned not so much with classes or parties but with *cultures* – of resistance. To put it another way, an adequate political understanding, for both would require a knowledge of the values and motifs and knowledges generated through the forms of everyday life. The strategies of a politics of experience, in a full and ambitious sense, needed to understand and to articulate the 'maps of meaning' of subordinate groups. Those maps lay at once in the media, in the ways the media were received, understood, used and 'handled', and in the informal understandings, the common senses, the lived experience of work, household and street.

To speak of 'both' is to address the tensions between kinds and occasions of knowledge of cultures, and of the sites and forms of such knowledge's production. These tensions form a set of links between cultural studies, the New Left, and the women's movement. The sites of cultural knowledges, or reflexive understandings, have in this period included the shared experience of community or of sexual politics: or shared consciousness of a job (as in the rich range of teachers' journals); or the problem-oriented forms of action-research (as in the Community Development Projects). Only by one route and set of choices did such knowledge become theoretical work, produced within an intellectual field of higher education and at times producing in its turn a mirror-opposite revulsion from 'theory'. Williams's own account of the New Left's formation describes disagreement between the aim for '20 or 30 good socialist books' linked to a publishing and discussion programme and the 'big goal' of 'the germs of a new kind of political movement' (adding that he was wrong to 'assume that cultural and educational programmes alone could revitalise the left or alter areas of popular opinion sufficiently to change the traditional institutions of the labour movement' (1979, pp. 363–64).

From this point on cultural studies could reproduce, inside higher education, the simultaneous concern with forms of knowledge and the forms of their politics, or sometimes (with conviction or regret) allow the one to stand in for, stand as, the other – at some moments with energy, at others ambiguity or antagonism. The tension was stretched further and re-cast by the appearance of forms of structuralism diminishing the importance of experience and meaning; re-cast again by its generation in the women's movement (and later women's studies). It has remained, and it must remain, at the centre of the enterprise. Meanwhile the 'field' was established, not in the political affiliations conjured up by hostile fantasy, but in disciplinary recruitment – in the meeting of three routes out from English, Sociology and History.

The stress lies on routes out, on absences and dissatisfactions and exasperations and dissent within the well-established boundaries of knowledge. The route from English concerned popular cultural forms, along with an interest in texts and textuality outside the 'language and literature' couplet, and/or a challenge to the very construction of 'the literary' and its various exclusions of class and gender. The route from History included in the broadest sense history 'from below', but also oral histories (a re-cast 'listening to the voices') and popular memory (the daily, informally exchanged, construction of a past). The route from Sociology involved ethnomethodologies, interests in meaning-construction, the examination of the structural reproduction of subordination.

There have from the start been rough connections between these disciplinary 'ways out' and the three different levels which any developed version of cultural studies has, from *The Uses of Literacy* on, attempted to think together: that of *lived experience*, requiring attention to the maps of *meanings* in the daily life of particular cultures and sub-cultures; that of *texts*, requiring a close attention to symbolic forms; that of larger determining *social structures*, requiring a specific historical account of the formation as a whole. Clearly the three can be thought in very different ways (for instance in one view the first two are elided, while in another the specific differences between 'common-sense' understandings and fully worked-up and often substantially ideological representations are stressed). But the strands and the connections between them have recurrently been extremely important – it seems that when any one is lost, or when the question of 'meanings' is no longer central, then what we have is no longer distinctively 'cultural' studies.

In these two senses, then – in the double academic/political insertion and in the mixed encounter of issues – cultural studies has been resolutely 'impure'. In consequence it has neither claimed nor been accorded (any more than has women's studies or indeed marxism) 'disciplinary' status. For that reason it has remained a thorn in the side, grit in the harmony. At all events, it has found only an uneasy lodgement in the academy.

Yet in any case, none of the surrounding 'subjects' could be readily shown to have been either coherent or stable bodies of work. 'English' displayed not only the rift between language and literature, but also that between scholarship and moral/aesthetic evaluation. 'History' subordinated its 'economic' and 'social' concerns to sub-divisions, often separate departments, within the dominant (and unnamed) 'political'. 'Sociology' yoked an English tradition of social policy/research/work to theoretical work where larger tensions between (at their most general) conflict and consensus models went unresolved. From the middle of the 1960s – from the moment of the academic development of cultural studies – the 'crisis' in these subjects was continually discussed and protested. (See, for example, Pateman, 1972, Roszak, 1968.)

Two points might be made here. One, that in each subject area the 'crisis' has been contained more readily than then seemed possible. Despite very important new bodies of work in each case, including new kinds of relation to intellectual work itself (feminist writing and criticism, the National Deviancy Conference, the Ruskin historians), the 1970s in many ways witnessed a reconsolidation rather than a re-thinking, or disarray. The university 'apex' of higher education remained almost immune to the changes seen in some CNAA degrees at polytechnics or in mode 3 CSE English. This alone gave the 'break' of cultural studies a high visibility. Two, a materialist explanation of the organisation and continual re-organisation of academic disciplines would need an account related at once to the changing class-composition of postwar education (where the university/polytechnic and grammar/comprehensive contrasts would be salient), and to the social changes of which disciplines are complexly articulated mediations. In both respects the issue is the constant re-composition of the legitimated ('academic') forms of knowledge – in which (whether or not we still speak of 'bourgeois' disciplines) the disciplinary form of knowledge production is itself a sophisticated ideology.

Cultural studies has thus not become a new form of 'discipline'. Attempts to 'unify' the field as the analysis of signifying practices, or as the study of forms of symbolic production, distribution and consumption ('cultural materialism'), are premature or unsatisfactory beneath a very high level of abstraction – though preferable to the view that cultural studies is merely one way of studying communications, or just a 'cover' for a revised and qualified marxism. Equally, the notion of interdisciplinarity no longer seems forceful – not so much because marxism itself has superseded its ambitions (though that is substantially true), but because 'specialist skills' do not just lie ready to collaborate together: the presence of other questions requires the disciplinary knowledges to address their object in quite unfamiliar ways. The relation of cultural studies to the disciplines is rather one of critique: of their historical construction, of their claims, of their omissions, and particularly of the forms of their separation. At the same time, a critical relationship to the disciplines is also a critical stance to their forms of knowledge production – to the prevalent social relations of research, the labour process of higher education.

Group work

It would be possible to look in some detail at academic modes of production and to note their own variety in detail, and of kind. Basil Bernstein (1975) has commented extensively on the tendency of primary schools, particularly those with a strong middle-class intake, to replace formal by informal pedagogy. In this process the relation of teacher to taught was in some substantial ways made less formal, while group work and group projects were encouraged. At the other end of the education system, graduate research work remains notoriously solitary – a long grind, formed in a supervisor/student, guru/apprentice relation of unequal power, infinitely compounded and further distorted when the tenured academic is male, the researcher female. It would be hard to think of a working situation at once so privatised and so necessarily caught up in defensive anxiety. Ironically its outcome ('the thesis') typically bears little relation to later modes of writing and teaching, and may itself be unpublishable until rewritten in an entirely new form. This relation has remained at the centre of humanities research, and almost no challenge to it has been admitted. Certainly a joint thesis is unheard of.

From an early stage the Centre in Birmingham attempted to develop other forms of work, and of necessity – given the already mentioned levels of the work in hand – the primacy of the unexplored 'contemporary', and the project to democratise academic knowledge forms. Its working groups (usually of six to ten members) began as forums for the discussion of individual thesis projects in the main areas of cultural studies, of which media studies has been of longest standing, followed by that of work/fieldwork/ethnographies of work. Weekly sessons would typically alternate between exploration of a central text and individual presentations of work-in-progress, some of which were later put together in the cheap typescript form of working-papers with a view to sharing issues and problems as they were appearing in the projects. These groups were, and are, the working mainstay of the unit. Formally, they lie between a full seminar on problems of theory or studies in cultural history, to which their work may contribute, and the individual thesis project by which their knowledge is advanced. Informally, the friendships and collaborations made have generated new enterprises and altered the direction of others. Typically, such groups have had a three- or four-year lifespan: moving from a preliminary review of an area to a full-scale 'mapping' of the field, then developing a distinctive purchase (through critique) and a particular set of concerns. These have been carried further in both group and individual work, and have usually issued in the Centre's self-published *Working Papers*, later in the series of books published by Hutchinson. In turn this project will often have led to group and individual papers at conferences, and later (often, it must be said, much later) to theses drawing further on particular strands.[2]

This rather formal account is both accurate and highly concealing. Progress in such groups has often been a painful series of pauses, doubts, changes of tack and irruptions. The conditions of graduate work remain almost uniformly insecure – substantially unrecognised and unsupported, uncertainly transitional. To that has been added the relentless procession of new paradigms and bodies of work inside the field, often in a highly combative and polemical mode, crossed by further and often conflicting political imperatives and doubts. It has been difficult for groups so constituted to develop modes of serious intellectual and political disagreement, even more of detailed sustained and supportive mutual criticisms of work in progress – or of work not realised. To all these has been added a further set of challenges from feminism, not to be accommodated comfortably (important as this move has been) by the making of gender central to all groups (and no longer ghettoised in a separate 'women's studies'). At the same time collective work sits in uneasy relation to individual theses, as do the social relations of the group to the traditional and privatised relation of adviser and advisee which has remained the most unexamined and impregnably traditional area of practice. And if the work of groups has sometimes been so organised as to produce the theoreticism endemic to a review of intellectual 'prolematics', so these have sometimes involved an inversely exclusive attention to empirical detail. Above all, whilst the excitement of group work has been in the opening-up of a connecting, and often proliferating, series of projects, it has also invited and colluded in over-extension to produce a situation in which no piece of work or undertaking can be fully thought out or completed.

The other side of that collusion, another way of understanding it, would be to connect it with the difficulties of assessing priorities. In another form, these are the difficulties of a 'politics of publication'. If one internal aim for group research has been to make it more complexly engaged with particular concrete historical moments, and less a theoretical 'mapping', the other more urgent struggle has been to find forms of writing and forms of making knowledge which do not endlessly reproduce themselves inside the boundaries of higher education. To that extent important distinctions can be made (very roughly) between decades in the intellectual/political relations of cultural studies and of similar ventures.

The constituencies of intellectual work

There were two characteristic modes of 'critical' research in the 1960s. One was the advisory relation to political parties or to semi-autonomous state bodies or enquiries: for instance policy research for the Labour Party, of which the most famous case was the connection, in the campaign to abolish the 'eleven-plus' and later to establish comprehensive schools, between academic sociologists of education, reforming teachers and Labour leaders (see CCCS, *Unpopular Education* . . . , 1981). There have also continually been 'researched' arguments submitted to government review bodies or investigations. The other strategy was that of the 'non-aligned' grouping of independent researchers, loosely linked (as in the New Left case) to political and cultural groups, working generally through educational forms, though by no means always those of the state (Penguin Specials, WEA dayschools). In addition, as suggested, a wide range of cultural 'inquiry' could be found in the working practice of political groupings and of teams dealing with particular situations and problems.

In the 1970s the consolidation of cultural studies as such around some key themes coincided with and helped to shape the opening-up of new syllabi in polytechnics and secondary schools. It relates also to the astonishing proliferation of radical journals and their accompanying left and feminist distribution network. Whether or not reinforced and consolidated by forms of Althusserian marxism (or by a faith in 'science'), this new higher education 'movement' developed an important confidence in its own distinctive intellectual production, support networks, and even in its forms of insertion into political groups and parties – though the near-absence from this picture of a radical/critical/marxist English Studies, and the possible reasons for it, will be of interest to readers of this book. One leading version of intellectual work, in this period, amounted to a fairly unspecified 'making available' of new work: not necessarily in crude forms of translation or handing-down, but in writing of some difficulty making considerable demands of a (usually graduate) reader. Work was often a 'ground-clearing', both conceptually and in opposition to dominant intellectual and political forms. Its typical form was that of critique: the 'interrogation' of dominant practices, and particularly doubts about liberal-humanist and social-democratic orthodoxies and their various disciplinary supports.

Within cultural studies, at least at the Centre, these forms were already being doubted and found insufficient, even before the populist conservative onslaught (at the end of the 1970s) on the left and on its by now quite developed sites of intellectual production. If a key 'model' at the beginning had been Williams, and later (with all kinds of doubts and modifications) Althusser, now Gramsci's work (1971) was both fertile and exemplary. The problem had already become one of 'organic' connections to be made in and through intellectual work, particularly as some men discovered their own distance from the confidence and shared purposes in phases of the women's movement: the connections made between analysis and 'experience', and made also across the division of labour. Inside the Centre, groups attempted to think of their work in relation to the problems of the nearest appropriate constitutency, which might not always be that of teachers in higher or secondary education. For example, there could be a connection between media research and the interests of media workers; between research on popular literature and alternative publishers and bookshops, or the Federation of Worker Writers; between studies of the cultural formation of teenage working-class girls and strategies of feminist 'youth work'. More generally, the issue turned from the 'independent critic' of the culture/society 'tradition', through notions of 'science' and rigour, to the classic marxist problem of intermediate class locations and strategies. Where attention had from the beginning been given to cultural forms which were then shown (often without much specificity) to have a class-belonging or class-location, and later (in no simple 'addition'!) a belonging to gender, there had now, in reverse, to be questions about the cultural forms of intermediate groupings in developed capitalism, including those of the 'academic' (or paid) intellectuals whose forms of production arguably confirmed their own knowledge and power, their own 'cultural capital'.

In theoretical terms this involved at once and chiefly Gramsci for his work on the relations of 'common sense' to 'good sense' and on the need for organic connections with popular attitudes and for organic intellectuals of popular classes. It also implied a particular engagement with the various neo-marxist theorisations of 'new middle class' or 'contradictory' or 'professional managerial' class relations – of who or indeed what the 'popular classes' in the 1980s might be. (See, for instance, Carchedi, 1977, Poulantzas, 1978, Olin Wright, 1979 and Walker, 1979.) In practical terms it meant attempts to move through and beyond a politics of publication based in the crucial support networks of higher education (and their defence and redefinition in the early 1980s), to the formation of work with other groups. For the future, it must involve simultaneously the protection of spaces already won (but now rapidly being clawed back); close study of the relations of classes (including political relations) where 'intermediary' groups are ever more prominent (but where classes are no longer thought solely through masculine relations to production); and the development of cultural forms in a 'political' mode (which is not necessarily the same as 'cultural politics').

If cultural studies has become a set of knowledges, or at least an agenda for knowledges, that is not its sufficient goal.

Notes

1. For the first, see Stuart Hall's long essay on 'Cultural studies and the centre: some problematics and problems' in Hall, Hobson, Lowe and Willis (eds), *Culture, Media, Language* (Hutchinson, 1980). Other versions of this account were published in *Media, Culture and Society* 2 (1) (January 1980) and in *Annali-Anglistica* (Naples, 1978), no. 3. See also Richard Johnson's important 'Three problematics: elements of a theory of working-class culture' in Clarke, Critcher and Johnson (eds), *Working-Class Culture* (Hutchinson, 1979). For the second, see work in *Culture, Media, Language* and in the Essex conference proceedings, *1936: The Sociology of Literature*, two vols (Colchester: University of Essex Press, 1979) – though the whole issue has scarcely been broached as yet. Much depends on the view taken both of the 'text' and of the 'literary'.
2. The Centre publishes pamphlets, stencilled papers in typescript, a series of books through Hutchinson and individual books through other houses. Pamphlets and stencilled papers can be bought through the Centre, which also distributes lists of all its Centre publications and an annual report on the Centre's activities. (Centre for Contemporary Cultural Studies, University of Birmingham, Birmingham B15 2TT.)

References

BERNSTEIN, B. (1975) 'Class and pedagogies: visible and invisible' in *Class, Codes and Control* (revised 2nd edn), Routledge and Kegan Paul.
CARCHEDI, G. (1977) *On the Economic Identification of Social Classes*. Routledge and Kegan Paul.
Centre for Contemporary Cultural Studies (1981) *Unpopular Education: Schooling and Social Democracy in England since 1944*. Hutchinson.
GRAMSCI, A. (1971) 'The philosophy of praxis'. In *The Prison Notebooks*, Lawrence and Wishart.
HOGGART, R. (1957) *The Uses of Literacy*. Penguin Books.
JACKSON, B. and MARSDEN, D. (1962) *Education and the Working Class*. Routledge and Kegan Paul.
MILLS, C.W. (1956) *The Power Elite*. New York: Oxford University Press; (1961) *Listen, Yankee!* New York: Oxford University Press.
MITCHELL, J. (1971) *Woman's Estate*. Penguin Books.
PATEMAN, T. (ed.), (1972) *Counter-Course*. Penguin Books.
POULANTZAS, N. (1978) *Classes in Contemporary Capitalism*. New Left Books.

ROSZAK, T. (ed.), (1968) *The Dissenting Academy*. Penguin Books (1969).
THOMPSON, E.P. (1963) *The Making of the English Working Class*. Penguin Books (1968).
WALKER, P. (ed.), (1979) *Between Labour and Capital*. Harvester.
WILLIAMS, R. (1958) *Culture and Society 1780–1950*. Penguin Books; (1965) *The Long Revolution*. Penguin Books; 'Notes on British Marxism since the war', *New Left Review* 100 (November 1976–January 1977); (1979) *Politics and Letters*. New Left Books.
WRIGHT, E.O. (1979) *Class, Crisis and the State*. New Left Books.

Postscript (1995)

The CCCS which this article described is now itself history in two ways. First, as cultural studies developed and gained recognition through a proliferation of stimulating publications and degree programmes, histories have been written around 'the Birmingham School' and its influence. These accounts vary greatly, ranging from the insights of John Clarke (in his *New Times and Old Enemies*, 1991), who was himself involved at Birmingham, to Ben Agger's ambitious and invigorating overview in *Cultural Studies as Critical Theory* (1992). Second, the pioneering group which had developed out of English at Birmingham was too small a unit to survive in the harsh conditions of the later 1980s. Instead it became a Department of Cultural Studies, moving from Arts to Social Science, fusing interests from cultural studies and from sociology with a larger staff and a more stable position. The Centre was typically postgraduate, many of its members going on to publish widely and start programmes elsewhere. Now the new Department has added a major undergraduate programme which retains some collaborative work and emphasises investigative project-based research in connection with groups and activities outside education. Through a technology now needing a footnote, the Centre produced a series of 'stencilled' papers, which are still selling through the Department because they articulate early and tentative work-in-progress. Now the Department publishes its own journal with staff and student contributors, *Cultural Studies from Birmingham*. The Centre attempted in its time to connect its work with 'some new forms of politics'. Now, political and intellectual changes have occurred on a huge scale, in conjunction with a drastic restructuring (though also enlargement) of higher education itself, such that the 'political' effects of cultural studies work need rethinking. Work in the field still attempts, more modestly perhaps, to provide insights into culture, to do research, some of which may be useful off campus, to construct a challenging syllabus and to provide forms of support for different kinds of people entering higher education. More generally, cultural studies 15 years on looks very different. No longer does it chiefly address forms of popular culture which other academic disciplines typically excluded: its range is wider, its problematics still more varied. No longer does cultural studies fight for institutional existence (at least in Britain), however uneven and under-resourced its academic lodgements. Other disciplines, of which some such as geography would never have been mentioned in previous accounts, converge in the empirical and theoretical study of meanings and culture. Nor does cultural studies any longer feel so English (so Welsh?), not because it is now North American (despite striking developments, see for instance Valda Blundell, John Shepherd and Ian Taylor's collection *Relocating Cultural Studies*, 1993), but because there are cultural studies from and about Latin America (see the journal *Travesia*), North Africa and South Korea. Cultural studies is more about migrations of labour, of capital, of cultural forms, and it itself migrates. It is trying, in Birmingham, to be less West-centred, to be more global and also to be more local and conscious of links with a wider world.

Michael Green

4

Overcoming resistance to cultural studies

James W. Carey

The major issues that face students of mass communications, the macro issues, have been the same for the past 15 years. They concern the entire framework within which our studies proceed and, therefore, the nature, purpose, and pertinence of the knowledge we profess. In order to reorient this framework, I have been making an argument for a particular and distinctive point of view toward the mass media, for something I call, without originality, cultural studies. Much of that argument has been made by indirection, suggesting that the study of the mass media would be better served if we pretty much abandoned our commitments to certain forms of explanation that have dominated the enterprise over the last 50 years or so. We have had our equivalent of the quest for the Holy Grail: the search for a positive science of communications, one that elucidates the laws of human behavior and the universal and univocal functions of the mass media. It is time to give it up, to relinquish happily what John Dewey called a couple of generations back the 'neurotic quest for certainty'. To abandon the traditional framework would not only invigorate our studies, it would liberate us as well from a series of bad and crippling ideas, particularly from a model of social order implicit in this framework, a twisted version of utilitarianism, and form a rhetoric of motives that I have elsewhere called a power and anxiety model of communications.[1] I am suggesting that we unload, in a common phrase, the 'effects tradition'.

There is now, I believe, a large and compelling literature, one written from every point on the compass of knowledge, ethics, and beauty, attacking the behavioral and functional sciences on both epistemological and ethicopolitical grounds. Idealism and pragmatism have undermined the notions of objectivity and objective truth that ground the explanatory apparatus of such sciences. Marxism, existentialism, and a variety of continental philosophies have elucidated the baleful consequences of such sciences for politics and morals, for conduct and practice. However, it is not necessary to be either so contentious or so philosophical about the entire business. The argument can be made in the small rather than the large. Contrary to Bernard Berelson's dire prediction of 25 years ago, the field of mass communication has not withered away. In fact, it is a successful, growing, highly institutionalized academic enterprise. But, despite its academic success, as measured by courses, students, journals, and faculty, it is intellectually stagnant and increasingly uninteresting. It is also crippled by a widening gap between the ambitions of the students and the intellectual and ideological poses of the faculty. Part of the problem, although only part, is that the central tradition of effects research has been a failure on its own terms, and where it is not a failure, it is patently antidemocratic and at odds with the professed beliefs of its practitioners.[2] In political terms, it would be a greater failure if it were more of a success.

The effects tradition has not generated any agreement on the laws of behavior or the functions of communications of sufficient power and pertinence to signal to us that success has been achieved. The entire enterprise has degenerated into mere academicism: the solemn repetition of the indubitable. Our commitments are no longer advancing but imped- ing inquiry, reproducing results of such studied vagueness and predict- ability that we threaten to bore one another to death. The surest sign of this state of affairs is the long-term retreat into method at the expense of substance, as if doing it right guarantees getting it right. The sharpest criticism of the behavioral and functional sciences ushering forth from philosophical quarters are now dealt with by silence. Under these circum- stances, we can continue to wait for our Newton to arise within the traditional framework, but that increasingly feels like waiting for Godot. Or, we can try to shift the framework and hold on to what is valuable in the tradition, even as we recast it in an alternative conceptual vocabulary.

Let me be clear on one point the speed readers always seem to miss. To abandon the effects tradition does not entail doing away with research methods – including the higher and more arcane forms of counting – that take up so much time in our seminars. Nor does it require turning up the academic temperature to 451 Fahrenheit and indulging in wholesale book burning. No one, except the congenitally out of touch, suggests we have to stop counting or that we can afford to stop reading the 'classics' in the effects literature. However, this literature will have to be deconstructed and reinterpreted and the methods and techniques of the craft redeployed. I am trying to be ecumenical about this – not solely for reasons of decency, although that would be sufficient, but for a serious philosophical purpose. There will be no progress in this field that does not seriously articulate with, engage, and build upon the effects tradition we have inherited. A wholesale evacuation or diremption of the theories, methods, insights, and techniques so painfully wrought in the last half-century would be a sure invitation to failure. This is true if only because intelligence continually overflows the constrictions provided by paradigms and methods. But more to the point, the effects tradition attempted to deal with serious problems of American politics and culture, at least on the part of its major practitioners, and it is now part of that culture. Any attempt to avoid it will only consign one to irrelevancy.

However, to reorient the study of mass communication, we will have to change the self-image, self-consciousness, and self-reflection we have of the enterprise: our view of what we are up to, the history we share in common, how we are situated in the societies in which we work, and the claims we make for the knowledge we profess. This is both a little easier and much more painful a surrender than changing a reading list or substituting participant observation or close reading for factor analysis and linear regression equations. If we make the shift I have been recommending, we would, to borrow some observations from Richard Rorty (1984a), talk much less about paradigms and methods and much more about certain concrete achievements. There would be less talk about rigor and more about originality. We would draw more on the vocabulary of poetry and politics and less on the vocabulary of metaphysics and determinism. And we would have more of a sense of solidarity with both the society we study and our fellow students than we now have. Above all, we would see more clearly the reflexive relationship of scholarship to society and be rid of the curse of intellectual humanity: the alternating belief that we are either a neutral class of discoverers of the laws of society or a new priesthood endowed by credentials with the right to run the social machinery. We would, finally, see truth and knowledge not as some objective map of the social order, nature speaking through us, but, in the lovely phrase of William James, as that which is good by way of belief, that which will get us to where we want to go.

Cultural studies is a vehicle that can alter our self-image and carry forward the intellectual attitudes noted above. At the very least, this position entails recentering and thinking through the concept of culture relative to the mass media and disposing of the concepts of effect and function. Now I realize that only the excessively adventurous, consistently unhappy, or perpetually foolhardy are going to leave the cozy (if not very interesting) village of effects research for the uncharted but surprising savannah of cultural studies without a better map of the territory than I or anyone else has been able to provide. Filling that gap is a major task of the future. The best I can do at the moment is to encourage people to circle within an alternative conceptual vocabulary and an alternative body of literature that will assist in marking out this unclaimed territory. To make things familiar, if not exactly precise, this means connecting media studies to the debate over mass culture and popular culture, which was a modest but important moment in the general argument over the effects of the mass media in the 1950s. The debate itself will have to be reconstructed, of course. The basic lines of such reconstruction were set out in the early work of Raymond Williams and Richard Hoggart in England when they attempted to apply the anthropological or primitive society conception of culture to the life and peoples of industrial society: to the language, work, community life, and media of those living through what Williams called 'the long revolution'.

The connection of cultural studies to the work of Max Weber is more important yet, for Weber attempted to provide both a phenomenology of industrial societies – that is, a description of the subjective life or conscious-ness of industrial peoples, including the ends or purposes of their char-acteristic actions – and an analysis of the patterns of dominance and authority typical of such societies. Weber described this enterprise as 'cultural science' during the interminable argument over *Naturwis-senschaft* and *Kulturwissenschaft*. I much prefer cultural studies to cultural science because I abhor the honorific sense that has accumulated around the word 'science'. As Thomas Kuhn has recently remarked, the term 'science' emerged at the end of the eighteenth century to name a set of still forming disciplines that were simply to be contrasted with medicine, law, engineering, philosophy, theology, and other areas of study (Kuhn, 1983). To this taxonomic sense was quickly added the honorific one: the distinction between science and nonscience was the same as the Platonic distinction between knowledge and opinion. This latter distinction, along with the correlative distinctions between the objective and the subjective, primary and secondary, is precisely the distinction cultural studies seeks, as a first order of business, to dissolve. More than that, I rather like the modest, even self-deprecating, connotation of the word 'studies': It keeps us from confusing the fish story with the fish. It might even engender a genuinely humble attitude toward our subject and a sense of solidarity with our fellow citizens who are outside the formal study of the mass media while, like us, inside the phenomenon to be studied.

Cultural studies, on an American terrain, has been given its most powerful expression by John Dewey and in the tradition of symbolic interactionism, which developed out of American pragmatism generally. It was Dewey's student, Robert Park, who provided the most powerful analysis of mass culture (although he did not call it that) that was adapted to the circumstances of the country. Dewey, Park, and others in the Chicago School transplanted, without attempting to do so, Weberian sociology to American soil, although happily within the pragmatist attempt to dissolve the distinction between the natural and cultural sciences. Not so happily, although understandably, they also lost the sharper edges of Weberian sociology, particularly its emphasis on authority, conflict, and domination, and that will have to be restored to the tradition.

Names solve nothing, I realize, but they begin to suggest at the very least a series of concepts and notions within which media studies might fruitfully circle: experience, subjectivity, interaction, conflict, authority, domination, class, status, and power, to state but part of the catalogue. As I have earlier argued, it was precisely these connections and issues that formed scholars striking a minor but enduring theme of media studies during the ferment in the 1940s and 1950s: David Riesman, C. Wright Mills, Harold Innis and Kenneth Burke (Carey, 1983). Cultural studies, in an American context, is an attempt to reclaim and reconstruct this tradition.

I realize that, in an age of internationalism, I have set this argument out ethnocentrically. I do so to make a philosophical point and not a nationalist one. Since the advent of the printing press, at least, the arguments that comprise social analysis have been ethnocentrically formulated. To try to escape these formulations, to try to import wholesale from somewhere else an analysis that does not develop roots on native grounds, is simply a pose, another way of being an observer. This is not to say that other voices from other valleys cannot make a major contribution. Weber has been mentioned; Marx cannot for long be avoided; and I have paid homage to Williams and Hoggart. On the contemporary scene one thinks of four foreign voices that have something of the right spirit to them: Habermas, Foucault, Giddens, and Bourdieu. But such voices must be embedded in, deeply connected with, the lines of discourse and the canons of evidence and argument that are only decipherable within the social, political, and intellectual traditions of given national, social formations.

The issues surrounding cultural studies have been very much complicated, as well as enormously enriched, by the increasing prominence in the United States of the work of the Center for the Study of Contemporary Culture [sic] at the University of Birmingham, and, in particular, that portion of the center's activity identified with Stuart Hall. Hall's work is theoretically, historically, and, often, empirically elegant and very much deserves the influence it has acquired. The center's research, while distinctively English in orientation and therefore in its limitations, draws heavily on certain traditions of continental theory and politics, particularly Marxism and structuralism, although interestingly enough not on critical theory of the Frankfurt School variety.

British cultural studies could be described just as easily and perhaps more accurately as ideological studies in that it assimilates, in a variety of complex ways, culture to ideology. More accurately, it makes ideology synecdochal of culture as a whole. Ideological studies, in Stuart Hall's lovely phrase, represent 'the return of the repressed in media studies'. Ideology, on this reading, was always the unacknowledged subtext of effects research. Differences of opinion described by psychological scales masked structural fault lines along which ran vital political divisions. The 'consensus' achieved by the mass media was only achieved by reading the 'deviants' out of the social formation: political difference reduced to normlessness. The positive sciences did not provide an analysis of ideology (or of culture) but rather were part of the actual social process by which ideological forms masked and sustained the social order.

This analysis, while radically undersketched, has had a rejuvenating effect on a variety of Marxist and neo-Marxist analyses of capitalist societies by North American scholars. Unfortunately, the ferment this rejuvenation has provided in the field is often described by the stale and unproductive contrast between administrative and critical research, a legacy left over from the years the Frankfurt School was in exile and, in truth, in hiding. But the difference between cultural studies and the positive sciences is not in any simple sense a mere difference between supporting or criticizing the status quo, although I suppose it is comforting for some to think so.

There are gross and important similarities between British and American cultural studies that derive from certain common origins and influences. Both trace their founding to the early 1950s and both have been influenced, to a greater or lesser degree, by the debate over mass culture and the work of Williams, Hoggart, and E.P. Thompson. Both have drawn extensively on symbolic interactionism, although in somewhat different ways. In the British case symbolic interactionism has been limited to providing an approach to the analysis of subcultures and the 'problem of deviance', whereas it has provided a much more generalized model of social action in the American case. Similarly, both traditions have been influenced by Max Weber. The principal concept of Weber that has worked its way into British studies is that of legitimation, while the rest of Weber's analysis of class, status, and authority – important as that has been to American scholars – has largely been shorn away. Finally, British cultural studies has circled within a variety of meanings of ideology, meanings provided by the wider debate within Marxism, particularly by the encounter of Marxism and French structuralism. In fact, beginning from the work of Williams, Hoggart, and Thompson, British cultural studies have made a long detour through French structuralism and, like everything else these days, have been deeply divided over the encounter. Structuralism, in turn, has made little headway in the United States, where it must contend with the far more powerful formalisms provided by information theory and transformational linguistics.

These wide-ranging and often contradictory influences have been held in remarkable equipoise by Stuart Hall. He has shown an exceptional capacity to be open and generous in absorbing currents of thought while firmly fixed on centering cultural studies on ideological analysis within a neo-Marxist framework. However, despite the power and elegance of this analysis, I think it is likely to increase rather than reduce resistance to cultural studies in the United States. That resistance, however understandable, is, I believe, shortsighted.

The two dominant types of resistance to cultural studies take a positivist and a phenomenological form, although the labels – like all labels – are not quite adequate. As forms of resistance they overlap and have something important in common; however, they proceed from different origins and therefore end up in different dilemmas.

The positivist resistance to cultural studies, beyond the ever-present desire to maintain a distinction between hard science and soft scholarship, between knowledge and opinion, is grounded in a deep political instinct. The positive sciences, of which physics is the model and psychology the pretender, grew up in a distinct historical relation not only to capitalism but to parliamentary democracy. These sciences are the crowning achievement of Western civilization, far less ambiguous in many ways than either capitalism or democracy. Indeed, the positive sciences epistemologically grounded democracy, provided some guarantee that opinion could be transcended by truth, and, most of all, provided a model of uncoerced communication in terms of which to judge and modify political practice. In short, the positive sciences are historically linked to certain valuable practices that no one particularly wants to surrender. Therefore, cultural studies, in its attack on the self-understanding of the positive sciences, seems to buy into a moral and political vocabulary that is, if not antidemocratic, at least insufficiently sensitive to the ways in which valued political practices intertwine with certain intellectual habits. More than that, few can completely forget that the positive sciences shored up parliamentary democracy at a particularly perilous moment in its history – during the Depression and World War II. Positive science, anchored as it was in a notion of truth independent of politics, arrived at by open communication and in the doctrine of natural rights, was one means of withstanding the totalitarian temptation.

I think it is important to be sympathetic to this form of resistance to cultural studies, but in the end it is misplaced and counterproductive.

Because the positive sciences shored up democracy at one bad moment, it is not necessary to conclude they can or will do it permanently. I have already suggested, in fact, that in the post-World War II phase, the positive sciences increasingly assumed an antidemocratic character that was implicit in the commitments of the behavioral and functional sciences. Notions of laws of behavior and functions of society pretty much obliterate the entire legacy of democracy; they substitute ideological and coercive practice for the process of consensus formation via uncoerced conversation.[3] The suggestion that positive science be substituted for uncoerced communication was first put forward, within our tradition, by Walter Lippmann in *Public Opinion*. John Dewey instantly responded to the book, describing it as the greatest indictment of democracy yet written. By the time of the Vietnam war, Dewey proved prophetic, for the behavioral sciences were central to that intellectual, moral, and political disaster.

Democracy may be damaged by the positive sciences but it does not need to be buttressed by them or defended and justified in terms of them. The valued practices and habits of the intellectual and political enlightenment can be better defended by what Richard Rorty (1984b) has called a 'criterionless muddling through', by comparing those societies that exhibit qualities of tolerance, free inquiry, and a quest for undistorted communication with those that do not. We do not need to buttress this comparison by designating certain methods and theories as guarantors of the truth.

Of course, cultural studies consists of a thinly disguised moral and political vocabulary. But that is true of all intellectual vocabularies, including the vocabulary of the positive sciences. If students in this field have not learned it from Kenneth Burke perhaps they are no longer capable of learning, but conceptual vocabularies always contain a rhetoric of attitudes and a rhetoric of motives. There is no way of doing intellectual work without adopting a language that simultaneously defines, describes, evaluates, and acts toward the phenomena in question. Therefore, resistance to centering the question of ideology or of adopting cultural studies as a point of view toward the mass media is that it seems to commit oneself in advance to a moral evaluation of modern society – American in particular, the Western democracies in general, the mass media above all – that is wholly negative and condemnatory. It seems, therefore, to commit one to a revolutionary line of political action or, at the least, a major project of social reconstruction. The fear is real but it is a little silly, if only for the reason that there aren't any revolutionaries anywhere these days.

If the behavioral and functional sciences contain a moral and political vocabulary, then the problem is not to undertake the hapless task of sundering science from morals and politics but rather to recognize the inevitable interconnection of these forms of activity and to make them ever more explicit and defensible. The behavioral and cultural sciences should contain an analysis of ideology beyond the crude and reductive one they now have but they should also make explicit their own ideological implications and persuasions and defend them on their own ground, not by pretending that 'science says' is an adequate defense. (A paradoxical fact of our times is that right-wing scholarship, as represented by neoconservatism, does not have much of an analysis of ideology; it just has an ideology. The Left has a dozen different analyses of ideology; it just does not have an ideology in the sense of a plan for political action.)

Cultural studies looks at ideology and theory as varying forms of expression within the same culture. They differ semantically, stylistically, and in terms of their conditions of expression and reception. They do not differ because one contains truth and one error, one knowledge and one opinion, one fact and one fancy, in some a priori way. The task is to see the characteristic kinds of difficulties our ideologies and our theories (and our culture) get us into and then to try to devise ways of getting out of those difficulties.[4] However, getting out will not be accomplished by getting rid of or devaluing ideology and culture in the name of science but by plunging the latter more deeply into the former. All forms of practice and expression, including science, are cultural forms and can only be understood in that light.

An instructive lesson here, although I am hardly in the business of extolling or applauding positivists and neoconservatives, was provided by Daniel Bell and Irving Kristol when they founded *The Public Interest*. The journal was established in 1965 at a moment when the orthodox (as opposed to the radical) Left was in control of American politics. Bell and Kristol felt the American society had been badly damaged by the social programs as well as the cultural and foreign policy initiatives of those in charge. *The Public Interest* was designed as a place for like-minded persons to work out a broad social program to change the direction of American life. They did not waste their time, I can assure you, on defending or explaining the theories and methods of the positive sciences. It was not for them to chase metaphysical bats around intellectual belfries. They simply gathered up a group of social scientists and left the church. They disappeared down the street. They didn't even leave a forwarding address or a note in the pew saying regards. They went off and built a different church on a different intellectual site, on a site that was not as easily shaken by an antipositivist critique. They systematically went about the task of using intelligence, irrespective of method and theory, to reground the social order, undertaking what Stuart Hall would call a hegemonic project but which we might more evenhandedly call a project of social reconstruction. They did not need an outmoded philosophy of science to ground their own image of democracy and intellectual work. Despite having written essays on the 'end of ideology', they unabashedly admitted the interconnection between ideology and science and made a case, a remarkably successful case as it has turned out, for their own way of viewing the world and proceeding within it. The task for those who believe that current versions of cultural studies corrupt or compromise democratic practice is not a retreat into value-free objectivist science but to unearth, make explicit, and critique the moral and political commitments in their own contingent work.[5] In short, the answer is to move toward, not away from, a cultural studies viewpoint.

The phenomenological resistance to cultural studies is more difficult to characterize because it otherwise shares so much in common with cultural studies. Phenomenologists are quite willing to give up the entire positivist framework of the science of human communication or, at a minimum, to settle for a bargain in which the labor is divided between the sciences and humanities. They are willing to follow or work out a parallel path to cultural studies up to the point of using the mass media as a context within which to write a phenomenology of modern experience and consciousness: to describe the subjective life – the modern 'structure of feeling' in Raymond Williams's arch but useful phrase – in relation to the media of communication, *one* of the paramount forms of experience in relation to which consciousness is formed. In practice, this means only going as far as the early work of Williams and Hoggart and particularly not into the intellectual, moral, and political quicksand one encounters when one starts romancing French structuralism. Phenomenologists, in the restricted sense I am using the term, are willing to commit themselves to a reconstruction of consciousness through methods as simple as *verstehen* or as complex as hermeneutics. While recognizing that modern consciousness is riddled by antinomy and contradictions formed in relation to and exacerbated by the mass media, and while standing in firm opposition to many forms of life in modern capitalist societies, phenomenologists resist moving power, conflict, domination, or any given set of sociostructural elements to the center of analysis.

Again, I am not at all unsympathetic to this resistance, but I think it is misplaced. It is clear, however, that ideological and cultural analysis can be simply another entry of the Platonic: The distinction between knowledge and opinion is simply replaced by a distinction between knowledge and ideology. The only gain here is the more explicit political reference of the word 'ideology'. But what, then, is one buying into by centering the ideological and political? When 'ideology' becomes a term to describe an entire way of life or just another name for what is going on, then the rich phenomenological diversity of modern societies is reduced to a flattened analysis of conflict between classes and factions. Cultural – or ideological – studies replaces economics as the dismal science.[6]

Phenomenologists of all stripes are committed to the *varieties* of human experience as providing the deepest pleasure, the wasting resource, and the most complex explanatory problems in modern society. To strip away this diversity, even if it is described as relatively autonomous diversity, in order to reveal a deep and univocal structure of ideology and politics, is to steamroller subjective consciousness just as effectively as the behaviorists and functionalists did. One does not, on this reading, wish to trade the well-known evils of the Skinner box for the less well-known, but just as real, evils of the Althusserian box. Any movement, therefore, toward encompassing elements of social structure – class, power, authority – which explain away the diversity of consciousness is to head one down a road just as self-enclosing as the behaviorist terrain phenomenologists have been trying in one way or another to evacuate for most of this century. To put the matter differently, phenomenologists just cannot take seriously the claim they sense in ideological studies that, in Otto Neurath's (1935) familiar analogy, we cannot make a sailable boat out of the planks of the ship on which we are currently sailing but rather we must abandon ship altogether and start anew. Why abandon something of rich diversity in order to build something of self-enclosing monotony? It is precisely the phenomenological diversity of modern society and the extraordinary tensions of consciousness this produces, particularly in relation to the mass media, that is the most compelling problem, however critical or skeptical phenomenologists may be about the actual experience in modern Western societies.

I believe that both of these forms of resistance to cultural studies are of real significance and genuine importance – neither can be easily or summarily dismissed. I disagree with them, however. I have already said that I do not believe that social democracy needs to be propped up with the objectivist grounding of the positive sciences, that the latter are a weakness of the former. We can get along quite nicely by looking at intellectual work, including science, as a muddling through of the dilemmas that history, tradition, and contemporary life have placed before us. Neither do I think it is necessary to abandon the notion of ideology or to close our eyes to the forms of power, authority, and domination characteristic of the modern world in order to do justice to its phenomenological diversity. Conflicts and contradictions are as typical and often irremovable a part of our society as any other.[7] Ideology does, after all, play a larger role in modern life because coercion plays a much smaller role. Ideological state apparatuses have significantly displaced repressive state apparatuses, if that is what we wish to call them, and that is not necessarily a bad thing. No one has, as yet, doped out an adequate analysis of power, conflict, contradiction, and authority. That task remains. The problem was absolutely central to the rich, diverse, and melancholy work of Max Weber. In fact, part of the phenomenological resistance to cultural studies stems from the simple fact that notions of power and authority that were firmly attached in Weber to matters of action and subjectivity are now more often derived from Durkheim, the social integrationist, in whose work power and authority were invisible and unnoted. As a result, the analysis is constantly slipping into a functionalism, despite the most heroic attempts to prevent it from doing so. It is not absolutely given that the forms of inequality and domination typical of modern society are so odious that they can only be maintained by the silent and invisible agency of cultural reproduction, behind the backs, as it were, of its 'subjects'.[8]

In short, it is possible, I believe, to press forward with a form of cultural studies that does not perforce reduce culture to ideology, social conflict to class conflict, consent to compliance, action to reproduction, or communication to coercion. More than that, despite the dangers and reservations acknowledged herein, cultural studies, in whatever form it survives, offers the real advantage of abandoning an outmoded philosophy of science (maybe even getting rid of the philosophy of science altogether) and centering the mass media as a *site* (not a subject or a discipline) on which to engage the general question of social theory: How is it, through all sorts of change and diversity, through all sorts of conflicts and contradictions, that the miracle of social life is pulled off, that societies manage to produce and reproduce themselves? Put in a slightly different way, how is it through communication, through the

integraded relations of symbols and social structure, that societies are
created, maintained, and transformed?

Notes

1. Utilitarianism has historically provided the basic model and explanation of social
    order in Western democracies and utility theory; therefore, it is the most influen-
    tial form of social theory. Utilitarianism starts from the assumption that the
    desires that motivate human action are individual and subjective and are, there-
    fore, either unknowable to the observer or purely exogenous. These subjective
    desires, these given and individual preferences, are expressed in human action as
    an attempt to maximize utility or the pleasure or happiness that the satisfaction
    of desire brings. Economic theory and capitalist economies are built upon this
    principle of the maximization of utility. The rest of the social sciences, generally
    unhappy because utility theory tends to skirt or assume away the problem of
    social order, desubjectivize utility, drive it outside of the head and into the
    objective world. But, the social sciences then relocate utility in our genes or in
    our environment or in our society. Social Darwinism and its latter day embodi-
    ment, sociobiology, are examples of the first strategy whereas behaviorism and
    sociological functionalism are examples of the second and third. It is these later
    positions, both particularly behaviorism and functionalism, that provide the
    underpinning for mass communication research. Indeed, communications
    research has been little touched by utility theory in either its economic or
    biological form except, and it is a big exception, that certain assumptions about
    language and communication (the theory of representation, the self-righting
    process in the free market of ideas) have undergirded economists' notions of
    the ways in which the quest for utility can also produce a progressive social
    order. The utilitarian conception of human conduct and society, then, is the
    implicit subtext of communication research, but it has been twisted out of its
    originally subjective framework and resituated in the objective world of envir-
    onment and social structure. It is a form of utilitarianism nonetheless: the
    objective utilities of natural ecology, the utilities that promote the survival of
    the human population or the given social order. Now, it would be comforting to
    think that our small-scale empirical investigations are detached from these
    overarching solutions to the problem of social order but they are not. Our
    studies inevitably articulate 'into' and 'out of' these wider theories. They
    articulate out because they inevitably borrow language, concepts, and assump-
    tions from the more encompassing intellectual environment; they articulate into
    the wider theories in that they provide evidence or they are used as evidence for
    and against the soundness of these social theories. Concepts such as attitude,
    effect, uses, and gratifications are borrowed from utility theory; evidence from
    effects studies are used to support one or another theory of mass society, usually
    the liberal, utilitarian, or pluralist theory. Indeed, the study of communication
    effects makes sense and has pertinence only insofar as it actively articulates with
    these larger positions. Unfortunately, there are no neutral positions on the
    questions that vex society.
2. Utility theory, as practiced by economists, produces the classic dilemma for
    democracy. If human agents are driven by subjective desire disconnected from
    the feelings of others, how do they manage to create and sustain the associated,
    cooperative form of social life we call democracy? Why don't people always
    gouge one another to the limit, as they often do even in the best of times? No one
    has produced an adequate answer to that problem and it is usually dismissed

with one or another metaphysical concept, such as the invisible hand of the market. The objective utility theorists give us an answer: Our genes, or our environment, or the norms of society, make us democrats, although I am here engaging in a bit of burlesque. Besides being a little too optimistic, objective utility theorists achieve an image of democracy at an enormous price: the surrender of any notion of a self-activating, autonomous, self-governing subject. The 'new' subject is one controlled or constrained by the laws of biology, or nature, or society – laws to which he or she submits because he or she can hardly do otherwise. This is the image of humanity and the dilemma of democracy with which the entire tradition of mass communication research struggles. It is at the heart of our founding book, Lippman's *Public Opinion*. It is the reason why Paul Lazarsfeld's work was so important. *The People's Choice* turns out not to be the people's choice but the choice of an index of socioeconomic status. Such laws of behavior are antidemocratic either because they reveal a subject who is not fit for democracy or they can be used to control the subjects of a mere presumptive democracy. As so often happens in intellectual work, the answers we give become disconnected from the questions we are asking, or, better, they become actively suppressed.

3. If behind our subjective notions of what we are up to there lie in wait our genes, our conditioning history, or the functions of society exacting their due, then our subjective life, our intentions and purposes, are just so many illusions, mere epiphenomena. The only people who grasp the distinction between reality and appearance, who grasp the laws of conduct and society, are the ruling groups and those that do their bidding: scientific, technical elites who elucidate the laws of behavior and the functions of society so that people might be more effectively, albeit unconsciously, governed.

4. I have already suggested how it is that utility theory, the social sciences, and liberal ideology get us into a series of difficulties. How do we reconcile the individual desires unleased by capitalism with the demands of associated life, with the justice, equality, and mutual concern necessary for democracy? That dilemma is bad enough but as soon as we resolve it by the route open through the objective sciences (don't worry, justice is in our genes or in our institutions), we end up in a worse dilemma, a dilemma the Left has critiqued with precision. We have, then, a ruling class of social scientists – disinterested, of course – managing the social order on the basis of uncontaminated truth. We are entitled to be skeptical about such a priesthood. Once social scientists adopt the role of seers, we should entertain the notion that their position is not based on their knowledge but on their ability to monopolize positions of power and influence in the social structure. Again, it was Max Weber, who looked at intellectual credentials as a device of class closure, who was most trenchant on this point. The supply of valued things in a society, including valued occupations, is strictly limited. Work in industrial societies is hierarchically organized so that valued occupations can be identified and showered with income, amenities, and prestige. Preferred jobs are positional goods, as opposed to material goods, in the well-known distinction of the late British economist Fred Hirsch, and they are valued because they are in short supply. They are valued also because power attaches to them, the power to monopolize valued cultural resources – to monopolize objective knowledge, uncontaminated by ideology, knowledge only the social scientist can grasp. This is not a healthy climate for democracy. Forgive me if I don't announce how to get out of this fix, but we don't have a chance until we recognize the fix we are in.

5. Intellectual work, then, is contingent upon the entire framework of articulated social order – and the ideologies that articulate it – and does not usher forth from

some Archimedean point in the universe – from some observer 'out there', where, as Gertrude Stein said of Oakland, California, 'there is no there there'. If one objects to current versions of cultural studies, then the only answer is to analyze the articulations between theory, practice, and ideology present within the effects traditions: to give up, in short, the pose of the observer and to undertake, explicitly, the task of using intelligence to change, modify, or reconstruct the social order.

6. Economics became the 'dismal science' for two interrelated reasons. First, utility theory reduced social life to the flywheel of acquisitiveness and accumulation. Economic man became the whole man, the only man. However, the repetitive dullness of acquisition was not the only dismal prospect economics held out. Society became a 'world without end, amen!' where the acquisitive itch could never be adequately scratched because of the Malthusian spectre. Every gain was balanced off by a rise in population, and the children that we love became merely the tyrants who turn the wheel of gain. Cultural studies can also turn into a dismal science if the phenomenological diversity of society is reduced to the single quest for power and domination. We are again laced to Axion's wheel. By evacuating diversity in the prerevolutionary era, we are left with only one motive with which to run the postrevolutionary society. But the pursuit of power will prove as exhausting and inexhaustible as the pursuit of wealth. The pursuit of power, and theories that rationalize it, nonetheless catches something of the predicament we are in. Power, and the prestige that goes with it, is as archetypal of a bureaucratic age as wealth was of the era of penny capitalism. There is no reason, however, except a positivist one, why a phenomenology of communications must avoid the phenomena of power and domination, lest all human relations and all symbols be reduced to the terms of power and politics alone. I support the phenomenological enterprise because I believe any healthy society will possess that part of its spirit that admits to the inevitable and desirable pluralizing of the varieties of experience. Just because you admit power to the household of consciousness and conduct, you do not have to let it occupy every room, although I admit that, like many an unwanted guest, you will have to struggle to prevent it from taking over the entire domicile.

7. We live in the lap of a vast series of contradictions. There is, for example, the contradiction of the employment market referred to earlier, a contradiction relevant to our experience in education. We observe in the swings of student interest among college majors a wholesale competition for positions in the occupational structure and, increasingly, attempts by parents to purchase with the tuition paid to prestige universities a place for their children in the occupational structure. This is an old story that federal aid and loan programs have more or less (largely less) democratized. That these occupational niches are thought to be entitlements, rewards for education virtue, disconnected from conduct or self-worth, presents one kind of contradiction. That such competition for jobs in an age in which automation widens the gulf between mechanical and immiserating work and the presumed glamour of the professions presents another kind of contradiction. Both of them exist in our classrooms every day, and we have no answer to them. If we remove those contradictions, we will have others, equally difficult and punishing, with which to replace them. This is not a call for resignation but just an admission that life goes on.

8. I suppose it would be nice if the social order worked by the silent reproduction of cultures and structures. It would spare us from all the misery that conflict and antagonism brings. Unfortunately, they do not work in this way. We live this reproduction in all its turmoil and ambiguity. In contrast to the Marxist tradition, Durkheim, the theorist of social integration, deliberately downplayed elements

of power and conflict. Inspired by the complexity of anthropological studies of social reproduction, he invented notions of 'collective representation' and 'collective conscience' to explain how societies were held intact in the midst of conflict and strain. Although my chronology is off here, when he applied this analysis to modern societies he tried to show how capitalist societies depended for their very existence and stability on an inherited precapitalist society – the so-called precontractual elements of contract. *Gesellschaft* society, the society regulated by utility and contract, could not work without the integrative mechanisms of *Gemeinschaft* society: nonutilitarian values, beliefs, traditions, and the like. To the old slogan that money is to the West what kinship is to the rest, he added that kinship performs a continuing integrative function in advanced societies. In a sense, Durkheim inverts the relations of base and superstructure: The capitalist economy thrives on the root system of traditional society. This aspect of Durkheim has been of signal importance and usefulness. But just because culture provides the supportive background to contract, it is not necessary to argue that culture is unconscious, irrational, coercive, or automatic. To make this argument is to become either an objective utility theorist or a mechanical Marxist. This leap to culture as unconscious or part of the deep structure makes it difficult to distinguish Marxism from functionalism, except – and it is an important exception – that they make quite different evaluations of the social order that is being silently, automatically integrated.

References

CAREY, J.W. (1983) 'The origins of radical discourse on communications in the United States', *Journal of Communication* 33, 311–13.

KUHN, T. (1983) 'Rationality and theory choice', *Journal of Philosophy* 80, 567.

LIPPMANN, W. (1922) *Public Opinion*. New York: Harcourt Brace.

NEURATH, O. (1935) 'Pseudorationalismus der Falsifikation', *Erkenntnis*, 5, 353–65.

RORTY, R. (1984a) 'Science as solidarity.' Paper presented to the symposium on the Rhetoric of the Human Sciences, University of Iowa, March.

RORTY, R. (1984b) 'Solidarity or objectivity.' Paper presented to the symposium on the Rhetoric of the Human Sciences, University of Iowa, March.

5

What is cultural studies anyway?

Richard Johnson

Cultural studies is now a movement or a network. It has its own degrees in several colleges and universities and its own journals and meetings. It exercises a large influence on academic disciplines, especially on English studies, sociology, media and communication studies, linguistics and history. In the first part of the article,[1] I want to consider some of the arguments for and against the academic codification of cultural studies. To put the question most sharply: should cultural studies aspire to be an academic discipline? In the second part, I'll look at some strategies of definition short of codification, because a lot hangs, I think, on the *kind* of unity or coherence we seek. Finally, I want to try out some of my own preferred definitions and arguments.

The importance of critique

A codification of methods or knowledges (instituting them, for example, in formal curricula or in courses on 'methodology') runs against some main features of cultural studies as a tradition: its openness and theoretical versatility, its reflexive even self-conscious mood, and, especially, the importance of critique. I mean critique in the fullest sense: not criticism merely, nor even polemic, but procedures by which other traditions are approached both for what they may yield and for what they inhibit. Critique involves stealing away the more useful elements and rejecting the rest. From this point of view cultural studies is a process, a kind of alchemy for producing useful knowledge; codify it and you might halt its reactions.

In the history of cultural studies, the earliest encounters were with literary criticism. Raymond Williams and Richard Hoggart, in their different ways, developed the Leavisite stress on literary-social evaluation, but turned the assessments from literature to everyday life.[2] Similar appropriations have been made from history. The first important moment here was the development of the post-war traditions of social history with their focus on popular culture, or the culture of 'the people' especially in its political forms. The Communist Party Historians' Group was central here, with its 1940s and early 1950s project of anglicising and historicising old marxism. In a way this influence was paradoxical; for the historians were less concerned with contemporary culture or even with the twentieth century, putting energies instead into understanding the long British transition from feudalism to capitalism and the popular struggles and traditions of dissent associated with it. It was this work which became a second matrix for cultural studies.

Central in both literary and historical strands was the critique of old marxism. The recovery of 'values' against Stalinism was a leading impulse of the first new left, but the critique of economism has been the continuous thread through the whole 'crisis of marxism' which has followed. Certainly cultural studies has been formed on this side of what we can call, paradoxically, a modern marxist revival, and in the cross-national borrowings that were so marked a feature of the 1970s. It is important to note what different places the same figures have occupied in different national routes. The take-up of Althusserianism is incomprehensible outside the background of the dominant empiricism of British intellectual traditions. This feature helps to explain the appeal of philosophy, not as a technical pursuit, but as a generalised rationalism and excitement with abstract ideas.[3] Similarly, it is important to note how Gramsci, a version of whose work occupies a place of orthodoxy in Italy, was appropriated by us as a critical, heterodox figure. He provided mighty reinforcements to an already partly-formed cultural studies project, as late as the 1970s.[4]

Some students of culture remain 'marxist' in name (despite the 'crisis' and all that). It is more interesting, however, to note where cultural studies has been Marx-influenced. Everyone will have their own checklist. My own, which is not intended to sketch an orthodoxy, includes three main premises. The first is that cultural processes are intimately connected with social relations, especially with class relations and class formations, with sexual divisions, with the racial structuring of social relations and with age oppressions as a form of dependency. The second is that culture involves power and helps to produce asymmetries in the abilities of individuals and social groups to define and realise their needs. And the third, which follows the other two, is that culture is neither an autonomous nor an externally determined field, but a site of social differences and struggles. This by no means exhausts the elements of marxism that remain active and alive and resourceful in the existing circumstances, provided only they, too, are critiqued, and developed in detailed studies.

Other critiques have been distinctly philosophical. Cultural studies has been marked out, in the British context, for its concern with 'theory', but the intimacy of the connection with philosophy has not been obvious until recently. Yet there is a very close cousinhood between epistemological problems and positions (e.g. empiricism, realism and idealism) and the key questions of 'cultural theory' (e.g. economism, materialism, or the problem of culture's specific effects). Again, for me, a lot of roads lead back to Marx, but the appropriations need to be wider ones. Lately there have been attempts to go beyond the rather sterile opposition of rationalism and empiricism in search of a more productive formulation of the relation between theory (or 'abstraction' as I now prefer) and 'concrete studies'.[5]

More important in our recent history have been the critiques deriving from the women's movement and from the struggles against racism.[6] These have deepened and extended the democratic and socialist commitments that were the leading principles of the first new left. If the personal was already political in the first phase of the Campaign for Nuclear Disarmament (CND), it was oddly ungendered. The democratic foundations of the early movements were therefore insecurely based as a new form of politics. Similarly there were (and are) deep problems about the ethno- and anglo-centricity of key texts and themes in our tradition.[7] The contemporary salience in Britain of a conservative-nationalist and racist politics means these flaws are all the more serious. It is incorrect therefore to see feminism or anti-racism as some kind of interruption or diversion from an original class politics and its associated research programme. On the contrary, it is these movements that have kept the new left new.

The specific results for cultural studies have been no less important.[8] Much more has been involved than the original question: 'what about women?' Feminism has influenced everyday ways of working and brought a greater recognition of the way that productive results depend upon supportive relationships. It has uncovered some unacknowledged premises of 'left' intellectual work and the masculine interests that held them in place. It has produced new objects of study and forced a rethinking of old ones. In media studies, for example, it has shifted attention from the 'masculine' genre of news and current affairs to the importance of 'light entertainment'. It has aided a more general turn from older kinds of ideology critique (which centred on maps of meaning or versions of reality) to approaches that centre on social identities, subjectivities, popularity and pleasure. Feminists also seem to have made a particular contribution to bridging the humanities/social science divide by bringing literary categories and 'aesthetic' concerns to bear on social issues.

I hope these cases show how central critique has been and how connected it is with political causes in the broader sense. A number of questions follow. If we have progressed by critique, are there not dangers that codifications will involve systematic closure? If the momentum is to strive for really useful knowledge, will academic codification help this? Is not the priority to become more 'popular' rather than more academic? These questions gain further force from immediate contexts. Cultural studies is now a widely taught subject, thus, unless we are very careful, students will encounter it as an orthodoxy. In any case, students now have lectures, courses and examinations in the study of culture. In these circumstances, how can they occupy a critical tradition culturally?

This is reinforced by what we know – or are learning – about academic and other disciplinary dispositions of knowledge. Recognition of the forms of power associated with knowledge may turn out to be one of the leading insights of the 1970. It is a very general theme: in the work of Pierre Bourdieu and Michel Foucault, in the radical philosophers' and radical scientists' critiques of science or scientism, in radical educational philosophy and sociology and in feminist critiques of the dominant academic forms. There has been a marked change from the singular affirmation of science in the early 1970s (with Althusser as one main figure) to the dissolution of such certainties (with Foucault as one point of reference) in our own times. Academic knowledge-forms (or some aspects of them) now look like part of the problem, rather that part of the solution. In fact, the problem remains much as it has always been – what can be won from the academic concerns and skills to provide elements of useful knowledge.

Pressures to define

Yet there are important pressures to define. There is the little daily politics of the college or the school – not so little since jobs, resources and opportunities for useful work are involved. Cultural studies has won real spaces here and they have to be maintained and extended. The context of ('big') politics makes this still more important. We also have a Conservative Counter-Reformation in Britain and the US. One manifestation is a vigorous assault on public educational institutions, both by cutting finance and by defining usefulness in strictly capitalist terms. We need definitions of cultural studies to struggle effectively in these contexts, to make claims for resources, to clarify our minds in the rush and muddle of everyday work, and to decide priorities for teaching and research.

Most decisively, perhaps, we need ways of viewing a vigorous but fragmented field of study, if not as a *unity* at least as a *whole*. If we do not discuss central directions of our own, we will be pulled hither and thither by the demands of academic self-production and by the academic disciplines from which our subject, in part, grows. Academic tendencies, then, tend to be reproduced on the new ground: there are distinctively literary and distinctively sociological or historical versions of cultural studies, just as there are approaches distinguished by theoretical partisanship. This would not matter if any one discipline or problematic could grasp the objects of culture as a whole, but this is not, in my opinion, the case. Each approach tells us about a tiny aspect. If this is right, we need a particular kind of defining activity: one which reviews existing approaches, identifies their characteristic objects and their good sense, but also the limits of their competence. Actually it is not definition or codification that we need, but *pointers* to further transformations. This is not a question of aggregating existing approaches (a bit of sociology here, a spot of linguistics there) but of reforming the elements of different approaches in their relations to each other.

Strategies of definition

There are several different starting-points. Cultural studies can be defined as an intellectual and political tradition, in its relations to the academic disciplines, in terms of theoretical paradigms, or by its characteristic objects of study. The last starting-point now interests me most; but first a word about the others.

We need histories of cultural studies to trace the recurrent dilemmas and to give perspective to our current projects. But the informed sense of a 'tradition' also works in a more 'mythical' mode to produce a collective identity and a shared sense of purpose. To me, a lot of powerful continuities are wrapped up in the single term 'culture', which remains useful not as a rigorous category, but as a kind of summation of a history. It references in particular the effort to heave the study of culture from its inegalitarian anchorages in high-artistic connoisseurship and in discourses, of enormous condescension, on the not-culture of the masses. Behind this intellectual redefinition there is a somewhat less consistent *political* pattern, a continuity that runs from the first new left and the first Campaign for Nuclear Disarmament to the post-1968 currents. Of course there have been marked political antagonisms within the new left and between new left politics and the intellectual tendencies it has produced. The intellectual detours have often seemed politically self-indulgent. Yet what unites this sequence is the struggle to reform 'old left' politics. This includes the critique of old marxism but also of old social-democracy too. It involves a constructive quarrel with dominant styles within the Labor Movement, especially the neglect of cultural conditions of politics, and a mechanical narrowing of politics itself.

This sense of an intellectual-political connection has been important for cultural studies. It has meant that the research and the writing has been political, but not in any immediate pragmatic sense. Cultural studies is not a research programme for a particular party or tendency. Still less does it subordinate intellectual energies to any established doctrines. This political-intellectual stance is possible because the politics which we aim to create is not yet fully formed. Just as the politics involves a long haul, so the research must be as wide-ranging and a profound, but also as politically-directed, as we can make it. Above all, perhaps, we have to fight against the disconnection that occurs when cultural studies is inhabited for merely academic purposes or when enthusiasm for (say) popular cultural forms is divorced from the analysis of power and of social possibilities.

I have said a lot already about the second definitional strategy – charting our negative/positive relation to the academic disciplines. Cultural processes do not correspond to the contours of academic knowledges, as they are. No one academic discipline grasps the full complexity (or seriousness) of the study. Cultural studies must be inter-disciplinary (and sometimes anti-disciplinary) in its tendency. I find it hard, for example, to think of myself as an historian now, though perhaps historian-of-the-contemporary is a rough approximation in some contexts. Yet some historian's virtues seem useful for cultural studies – concerns for movement, particularity, complexity and context, for instance. I still love that combination of dense description, complex explanation and subjective even romantic evocation, which I find in the best historical writing. I still find most sociological description thin and obvious and much literary discourse clever but superficial! On the other hand, the rooted empiricism of historical practice is a real liability often blocking a properly cultural reading. I am sure it is the same for other disciplines too. Of course, there are lots of half-way houses, many of them serviceable workshops for cultural study, but the *direction* of movement, to my mind, has to be out, and away, and into more dangerous places!

Our third definitional strategy – the analysis and comparison of theoretical problematics – was, until recently, the favorite one.[9] I still see this as an essential component in all cultural study, but its main difficulty is that abstract forms of discourse disconnect ideas from the social complexities that first produced them, or to which they originally referred. Unless these are continuously reconstructed and held in the mind as a reference point, theoretical clarification acquires an independent momentum. In teaching situations or similar interchanges, theoretical discourse may seem, to the hearer, a form of intellectual gymnastics. The point appears to be to learn a new language, which takes time and much effort, in order, merely, to feel at ease with it. In the meantime there is something very silencing and perhaps oppressive about new forms of discourse. I think that this has been a fairly common experience, for students, even where, eventually, 'theory' has conferred new powers of understanding and articulation. This is one set of reasons why many of us now find it useful to start from concrete cases, either to teach theory historically, as a continuing, contextualised debate about cultural issues, or to hook up theoretical points and contemporary experiences.

This leads me to my preferred definitional strategy. The key questions are: what is the characteristic *object* of cultural studies? What is cultural studies *about*?

Simple abstractions: consciousness, subjectivity

I have suggested already that 'culture' has value as a reminder but not as a precise category; Raymond Williams has excavated its immense historical repertoire.[10] There is no solution to this polysemy: it is a rationalist illusion to think we can say 'henceforth this term will mean . . .' and expect a whole history of connotations (not to say a whole future) to fall smartly into line. So although I fly culture's flag anyway, and continue to use the word where imprecision matters, definitionally I seek other terms.

My key terms instead are 'consciousness' and 'subjectivity' with the key problems now lying somewhere in the relation between the two. For me cultural studies is about the historical forms of consciousness or subjectivity, or the subjective forms we live by, or, in a rather perilous compression, perhaps a reduction, the subjective side of social relations. These definitions adopt and gloss some of Marx's simple abstractions, but value them also for their contemporary resonance. I think of consciousness, first, in the sense in which it appears in *The German Ideology*. As a (fifth) premise for understanding human history, Marx and Engels add that human beings 'also possess consciousness'. This usage is echoed in later works too. Marx implies it when in *Capital*, volume I, he distinguishes the worst architect from the best bee by the fact that the architect's product has 'already existed ideally' before it is produced. It has existed in the consciousness, the imagination. In other words, human beings are characterised by an ideal or imaginary life, where will is cultivated, dreams dreamt, and categories developed. In his *1844 Manuscripts* Marx called this a feature of 'species being', later he would have called it a 'general-historical' category, true of all history, a simple or universal abstraction'. Although the usage is less clear Marx also habitually refers to the 'subjective side' or 'subjective aspect' of social processes.[11]

In marxist discourse (I am less sure of Marx) consciousness has overwhelmingly cognitive connotations: it has to do with knowledge (especially correct knowledge?) of the social and the natural worlds. I think Marx's consciousness was wider than this! It embraced the notion of a consciousness of self and an *active mental and moral self-production*. There is no doubt, however, that he was especially interested in conceptually-organised knowledge, especially in his discussions of particular ideological forms (e.g. political economy, Hegelian idealism, etc.) In his most interesting text on the character of thinking (the 1857 Introduction to the *Grundrisse*) other modes of consciousness, the aesthetic, the religious, etc., were bracketed out.

'Subjectivity' is especially important here, challenging the absences in consciousness. Subjectivity includes the possibility, for example, that some elements or impulses are subjectively active – they *move* us – without being consciously known. It highlights elements ascribed (in the misleading conventional distinction) to aesthetic or emotional life and to conventionally 'feminine' codes. It focuses on the 'who I am' or, as important, the 'who we are' of culture, on individual and collective identities. It connects with the most important structuralist insight: that subjectivities are produced, not given, and are therefore the objects of inquiry, not the premises or starting-point.

In all my thinking about cultural studies I find the notion of 'forms' also repeatedly recurs. Lying behind the usage are two major influences. Marx continuously uses the terms 'forms' or 'social forms' or 'historical forms' when he is examining in *Capital* (but especially in the *Grundrisse*) the various moments of economic circulation: he analyses the money form, the commodity form, the form of abstract labour, etc. Less often he used the same language in writing of consciousness or subjectivity. The most famous instance is from the 1859 *Preface*:

> a distinction should always be made between the material transformation of the economic conditions of production, which can be determined with the precision of natural science, and the legal, political, religious, aesthetic or philosophic – in short, ideological *forms* in which men become conscious of this conflict and fight it out (emphasis added).

What interests *me* about this passage is the implication of a different parallel project to Marx's own. His preoccupation was with those social forms through which human beings produce and reproduce their material life. He abstracted, analysed and sometimes reconstituted in more concrete accounts the economic forms and tendencies of social life. It seems to me that cultural studies too is concerned with whole societies (or broader social formations) and how they move. But it looks at social processes from another complimentary point of view. *Our* project is to abstract, describe and reconstitute in concrete studies forms through which human beings 'live', become conscious, sustain themselves subjectively.

The stress on forms is reinforced by some broad structuralist insights. These have drawn out the structured character of the forms we inhabit subjectively: language, signs, ideologies, discourses, myths. They have pointed to regularities and principles of organisation – of form-ful-ness if you like. Though often pitched at too high a level of abstraction (e.g. language in general rather than language in particular) they have strengthened our sense of the hardness, determinancy and, indeed, actual existence of social forms which exercise their pressures through the subjective side of social life. This is not to say that the description of form, in this sense, is enough. It is important to see the historical nature of subjective forms too. Historical in this context means two rather different things. First, we need to look at forms of subjectivity from the point of view of their pressures or tendencies, especially their contradictory sides. Even in abstract analysis, in other words, we should look for principles of movement as well as combination. Second, we need histories of the forms of subjectivity where we can see how tendencies are modified by the other social determinations, including those at work through material needs.

As soon as we pose this as a project, we can see how the simple abstractions which we have thus far used, do not take us very far. Where are all the intermediate categories that would allow us to start to specify the subjective social forms and the different moments of their existence? Given our defini-tion of culture, we cannot limit the field to specialised practices, particular genres, or popular leisure pursuits. *All social practices* can be looked at from a cultural point of view, for the work they do, subjectively. This goes, for instance, for factory work, for trade union organisation, for life in and around the supermarket, as well as for obvious targets like 'the media' (misleading unity!) and its (mainly domestic) modes of consumption.

Circuits of capital – circuits of culture?

So we need, first, a much more complex model, with rich intermediate categories, more layered than the existing general theories. It is here that I find it helpful to pose a kind of realist hypothesis about the existing state of theories. What if existing theories – and the modes of research associated with them – actually express different sides of the same complex process? What if they are all true, but only as far as they go, true for those parts of the process which they have most clearly in view? What if they are all false or incomplete, liable to mislead, in that they are only partial, and therefore cannot grasp the process as a whole? What if attempts to 'stretch' this competence (without modifying the theory) lead to really gross and dan-gerous (ideological?) conclusions?

I certainly do not expect immediate assent to the epistemological premises of this argument. I hope it will be judged in the light of its results. But its immediate merit is that it helps to explain one key feature: the theoretical and disciplinary fragmentations we have already noted. Of course these could be explained by the political social and discursive differences we have also considered: especially the intellectual and academic divisions of labour and the social reproduction of specialist forms of cultural capital. Yet I find it more satisfactory to relate these manifest differences to the very processes they seek to describe. Maybe academic divisions also correspond to rather different social positions and viewpoints from which different aspects of cultural circuits acquire the greatest salience. This would explain not merely the fact of different theories, but the *recurrence* and *persistence* of differences, especially between large *clusters* of approaches with certain affinities.

The best way to take such an argument further would be to hazard some provisional description of the different aspects or moments of cultural processes to which we could then relate the different theoretical problematics. Such a model could not be a finished abstraction or theory, if such can exist. Its value would have to be heuristic or illustrative. It might help to explain why theories differ, but would not, in itself, sketch the ideal approach. At most it might serve as a guide to the desirable directions of future approaches, or to the way in which they might be modified or combined. It is important to bear these caveats in mind in what follows. I find it easiest (in a long CCCS tradition) to present a model diagrammatically (see p. 84). The diagram is intended to represent a circuit of the production, circulation and consumption of cultural products. Each box represents a moment in this circuit. Each moment or aspect depends upon the others and is indispensable to the whole. Each, however, is distinct and involves characteristic changes of form. It follows that if we are placed at one point of the circuit, we do not necessarily see what is happening at others. The forms that have most significance for us at one point may be very different from those at another. Processes disappear in results.[12] All cultural products, for example, require to be produced, but the conditions of their production cannot be inferred by scrutinising them as 'texts'. Similarly all cultural products are 'read' by persons other than professional analysts (if they weren't there would be little profit in their production), but we cannot predict these uses from our own analysis, or, indeed, from the conditions of production. As anyone knows, all our communications are liable to return to us in unrecognisable or at least transformed terms. We often call this *mis*understanding or, if we are being very academic, *mis*-readings. But these 'misses' are so common (across the range of a whole society) that we might well call them normal. To understand the transformations, then, we have to understand specific conditions of consumption or reading. These include asymmetries of resources and power, material and cultural. They also include the existing ensembles of cultural elements already active within particular social *milieux* ('lived cultures' in the diagram) and the social relations on which these combinations depend. These reservoirs of discourses and meanings are in turn raw material for fresh cultural production. They are indeed among the specifically cultural *conditions* of production.

In our societies, many forms of cultural production also take the form of capitalist commodities. In this case we have to supply specifically capitalist conditions of production (see the arrow pointing to moment 1) and specifically capitalist conditions of consumption (see the arrow pointing to moment 3). Of course this does not tell us all there is to know about these moments, which may be structured on other principles as well, but in these cases the circuit is, at one and the same time, a circuit of capital and its expanded reproduction *and* a circuit of the production and circulation of subjective forms.

Some implications of the circuit may be clearer if we take a particular case. We can, for example, whiz a Mini-Metro car around it. I choose the Mini-Metro because it is a pretty standard late twentieth-century capitalist commodity that happened to carry a particularly rich accumulation of meanings. The Metro was the car that was going to save the British car industry, by beating rivals from the market and by solving British Leyland's acute problems of industrial discipline. It came to signify solutions to

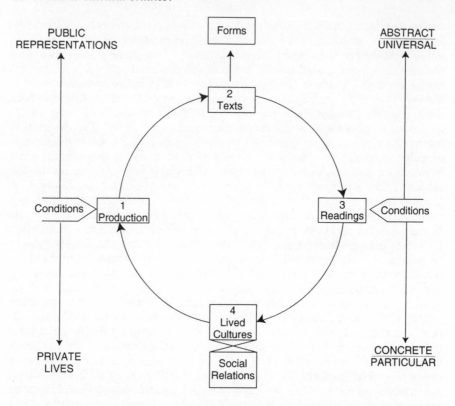

internal and external national threats. The advertising campaigns around its launching were remarkable. In one television ad, a band of Mini-Metros pursued a gang of foreign imports up to (and apparently over) the White Cliffs of Dover, whence they fled in what looked remarkably like landing-craft. This was a Dunkirk in reverse with the Metro as nationalist hero. Certainly these are some of the forms – nationalist epic, popular memory of World War II, internal/external threat – that I would want to abstract for further formal scrutiny. But this raises interesting questions too about what constitutes the 'text' (or raw material for such abstractions) in these cases. Would it be enough to analyse the design of the Metro itself as Barthes once analysed the lines of a Citreon? How could we exclude ads and garage showroom displays? Shouldn't we include, indeed, the Metro's place in discourses upon national economic recovery and moral renaissance?

Supposing that we answered these questions affirmatively (and gave ourselves a lot more work) there would still be some unposed questions. What was *made* of the Metro phenomenon, more privately, by particular groups of consumers and readers? We would expect great diversity of response. Leyland workers, for example, were likely to view the car differently from those who only bought it. Beyond this, the Metro (and its transformed meanings) became a way of getting to work or picking the kids up from school. It may also have helped to produce, for example, orientations towards working life, connecting industrial 'peace' with national prosperity. Then, of course, the products of this whole circuit returned once more to the moment of production – as profits for fresh investment, but also as market researcher's findings on 'popularity' (capital's own 'cultural studies'). The subsequent use, by British Leyland management, of similar strategies for selling cars and weakening workers suggests considerable accumulations (of both kinds) from this episode. Indeed the Metro became a little paradigm, though not the first, for a much more diffused ideological form, which we might term, with some compression, 'the nationalist sell'.

Publication and abstraction

So far I have talked rather generally about the transformations that occur around the circuit without specifying any. In so brief a discussion, I will specify two related changes of form indicated on the left and right hand sides of the circuit. The circuit involves movements between the public and the private but also movements between more abstract and more concrete forms. These two poles are quite closely related: private forms are more concrete, and more particular in their scope of reference; public forms are more abstract but also apply over a more general range. This may be clearer if we return to the Metro and, thence to different traditions of cultural study.

As a designer's idea, as a manager's 'concept', the Metro remained private.[13] It may even have been conceived in secret. It was known to a chosen few. At this stage, indeed, it would have been hard to separate it out from the social occasions at which it was discussed: board-room meetings, chats at the bar, Saturday's game of golf? But as ideas were 'put on paper' it started to take a more objective and more public form. The crunch came when decisions were made to go ahead with 'the concept' and, then again, to 'go public'. Finally, the Metro-idea, shortly followed by the Metro-car, moved into 'the full glare of publicity'. It acquired a more general significance, gathering around it, in fact, some pretty portentious notions. It became, in fact, a great public issue, or a symbol for such. It also took shape as an actual product and set of texts. In one obvious sense it was made 'concrete': not only could you kick it, you could drive it. But in another sense, this Metro was rather abstract. There it stood, in the showroom, surrounded by its texts of Britishness, a shiny, zippy thing. Yet who would know, from this display, who conceived it, how it was made, who suffered for it, or indeed what possible use it was going to have for the harassed-looking woman with two children in tow, who has just walked into the showroom. To draw out more general points, three things occurred in the process of public-ation. First, the car (and its texts) became *public* in the obvious sense: it acquired if not a *universal* at least a more *general* significance. Its messages too were generalised, ranging rather freely across the social surface. Second, at the level of *meaning*, publication involved *abstraction*. The car and its messages could now be viewed in relative isolation from the social conditions that formed it. Thirdly, it was subjected to a process of public *evaluation* (great public issue) on many different scales: as a technical-social instrument, as a national symbol, as a stake in class war, in relation to competing models, etc. It became a site of formidable struggles over meaning. In this process it was made to 'speak', evaluatively, for 'us (British) all'. Note, however, in the moment of consumption or reading, represented here by the woman and her children (who have decided views about cars), we are forced back again to the private, the particular and concrete, however publicly displayed the raw materials for their readings may be.

I want to suggest that these processes are intrinsic to cultural circuits under modern social conditions, and that they are produced by, and are productive of, *relations of power*. But the most germane evidence for this lies in some repeated differences in the forms of cultural study.

Forms of culture – forms of study

One major division, theoretical and methodological, runs right through cultural studies. On the one side there are those who insist that 'cultures' must be studied as a whole, and *in situ*, located, in their material context. Suspicious of abstractions and of 'theory', their practical theory is in fact 'culturalist'. They are often attracted to those formulations in Williams or E.P. Thompson that speak of cultures as whole ways of life or whole ways of struggle. Methodologically, they stress the importance of complex, concrete descriptions, which grasps, particularly, the unity or homology of cultural forms and material life. Their preferences are therefore for social-historical recreations of cultures or cultural movements, or for ethnographic cultural description, or for those kinds of writing (e.g. autobiography, oral history, or realist forms of fiction) which recreate socially-located 'experience'.

On the other side, there are those who stress the relative independence or effective autonomy of subjective forms and means of signification. The practical theory here is usually structuralist, but in a form which privileges the discursive construction of situations and subjects. The preferred method is to treat the forms abstractly, sometimes quite formalistically, uncovering the mechanisms by which meaning is produced in language, narrative or other kinds of sign-system. If the first set of methods are usually derived from sociological, anthropological or social-historical roots, the second set owe most to literary criticism, and especially the traditions of literary modernism and linguistic formalism.[14]

In the long run, this division is, in my opinion, a sure impediment to the development of cultural studies. But it is important first to note the logic of such a division in relation to our sketch of cultural processes as a whole. If we compare, in more detail, what we have called the public and private forms of culture, the relation may be clearer.[15]

Private forms are not necessarily private in the usual sense of personal or individual, though they may be both. They may also be shared, communal and social in ways that public forms are not. It is their particularity or concreteness that marks them as private. They relate to the characteristic life experiences and historically-constructed needs of particular social categories. They do not pretend to define the world for those in other social groups. They are limited, local, modest. They do not aspire to universality. They are also deeply embedded in everyday social intercourse. In the course of their daily lives, women go shopping and meet and discuss the various doings of themselves, their families and their neighbours. Gossip is a private form deeply connected with the occasions and relations of being a woman in our society. Of course, it is *possible* to describe the discursive forms of gossip abstractly, stressing for instance the forms of reciprocity in speech, but this does seem to do a particular violence to the material, ripping it from the immediate and visible context in which these texts of talk arose.

An even more striking case is the working-class culture of the shop floor. As Paul Willis has shown there is a particularly close relationship here between the physical action of labour and the practical jokes and common sense of the workplace.[16] The whole discursive mode of the culture is to refuse the separation of manual practice and mental theory characteristic of public and especially academic knowledge forms. In neither case - gossip and shop-floor culture - is there a marked division of labour in cultural production. Nor are there technical instruments of production of any great complexity, though forms of speech and the symbolic uses of the human body are complex enough. Nor are the consumers of cultural forms formally or regularly distinguished from their producers, or far removed from them, in time or space.

I would argue that particular forms of inquiry and of representation have been developed to handle these features of private forms. Researchers, writers and all kinds of rapporteurs have adjusted their methods to what have seemed the most evident features of culture in this moment. They have sought to hold together the subjective and more objective moments, often not distinguishing them theoretically, or, in practice, refusing the distinction altogether. It is this stress of 'experience' (the term that perfectly captures this conflation or identity) that has united the practical procedures of social historians, ethnographers and those interested, say, in 'working-class writing'.

Compared with the thick, conjoined tissue of face-to-face encounters, the television programme 'going out on the air' seems a very abstracted, even ethereal product. For one thing it is so much more plainly a *re*presentation of 'real life' (at best) than the (equally constructed) narratives of everyday life. It takes a separated, abstracted or objective form, in the shape of the programme/text. It comes at us from a special, fixed place, a box of standardised shape and size in the corner of our sitting room. Of course, we apprehend it socially, culturally, communally, but it still has this separated moment, much more obviously than the private text of speech. This separated existence is certainly associated with an intricate division of labour in production and distribution and with the physical and temporal distance between the moment of production and that of consumption, characteristic of public knowledge forms in general. Public media of this kind, indeed, permit quite extraordinary manipulations of space and time as, for example, in the television revival of old movies.

I would argue that this apparent abstraction in the actual forms of public communication underlies the whole range of methods that focus on the construction of reality through symbolic forms themselves - with language as the first model, but the key moment as the objectification of language in text. It would be fascinating to pursue an historical inquiry linked to this hypothesis which would attempt to unravel the relationship between the real abstractions of communicative forms and the mental abstractions of cultural theorists. I do not suppose that the two processes go easily hand in hand or that changes occur synchronously. But I am sure that the notion of text - as something we can isolate, fix, pin down and scrutinise - depends upon the extensive circulation of cultural products which have been divorced from the immediate conditions of their production and have a moment of suspension, so to speak, before they are consumed.

Publication and power

The public and private forms of culture are not sealed against each other. There is a real circulation of forms. Cultural production often involves public-ation, the making public of private forms. On the other side, public texts are consumed or read in private. A girls' magazine, like *Jackie* for instance, picks up and represents some elements of the private cultures of feminity by which young girls live their lives. It instantaneously renders these elements open to public evaluation - as for example, 'girls stuff', 'silly' or 'trivial'. It also generalises these elements within the scope of the particular readership, creating a little public of its own. The magazine is then a raw material for thousands of girl-readers who make their own *re*-appropriations of the elements first borrowed from their lived culture and forms of subjectivity.

It is important not to assume that public-ation only and always works in dominating or in demeaning ways. We need careful analyses of where and how public representations work to seal social groups into the existing relations of dependence and where and how they have some emancipatory tendency. Short of this detail, we can nonetheless insist on the importance of *power* as an element in an analysis , by suggesting the main ways it is active in the public-private relationship.

Of course there are profound differences in terms of access to the public sphere. Many social concerns may not acquire publicity at all. It is not merely that they remain private, but that they are actively privatised, *held* at the level of the private. Here, so far as formal politics and state actions are concerned, they are invisible, without public remedy. This means not only that they have to be borne, but that a consciousness of them, as evils, is held at a level of implicit or communal meanings. Within the group a knowledge of such sufferings may be profound, but not of such a kind that expects relief, or finds the sufferings strange.

As often, perhaps, such private concerns do appear publicly, but only on certain terms, and therefore transformed and framed in particular ways. The concerns of gossip, for example, do appear publicly in a wide variety of forms, but usually in the guise of 'entertainment'. They appear, for instance, in soap opera, or are 'dignified' only by their connection with the private lives of royalty, stars or politicians. Similarly, elements of shop-floor culture may be staged as comedy or variety acts. Such framings in terms of code or genre may not, as some theorists believe, altogether vitiate these elements as the basis of a social alternative, but they certainly work to contain them within the dominant public definitions of significance.

Public representations may also act in more openly punitive or stigmatising ways. In these forms the elements of private culture are robbed of authenticity or rationality, and constructed as dangerous, deviant, or dotty.[17] Similarly the experiences of subordinated social groups are presented as pathological, problems for intervention not in the organisation of society as a whole, but in the attitudes or behaviour of the suffering group itself. This is representation with a vengeance: representation not as subjects demanding redress, but at objects of external intervention.

If space allowed it would be important to compare the different ways in which these processes may occur across the major relationships of class, gender, race and age-dependence. One further general mechanism is the construction, in the public sphere, of definitions of the public/private division itself. Of course, these sound quite neutral definitions: 'everyone' agrees that the most important public issues are the economy, defence, law and order and, perhaps, welfare questions, and that other issues - family life, sexuality for example - are essentially private. The snag is that the dominant definitions of significance are quite socially specific and, in particular, tend to correspond to masculine and middle-class structures of 'interest' (in both the meanings of this term). It is partly because they start fundamentally to challenge these dispositions that some feminisms, the peace movements and the Green parties are amongst the most subversive of modern developments.

I have stressed these elements of power, at the risk of some diversion from the main argument, because cultural studies practices must be viewed within this context. Whether it takes as its main object the more abstracted public knowledges and their underlying logics and definitions, or it searches out the private domains of culture, cultural studies is necessarily and deeply implicated in relations of power. It forms a part of the very circuits which it seeks to describe. It may, like the academic and the professional knowledges, police the public-private relation, or it may critique it. It may be involved in the surveillance of the subjectivities of subordinated groups, or in struggles to represent them more adequately than before. It may become part of the problem, or a part of the solution. That is why as we turn to the particular forms of cultural study, we need to ask not only about objects, theories and methods, but also about the political limits and potentials of different standpoints around the circuit.

From the perspective of production

This is a particularly wide and heterogeneous set of approaches. For I include under this head, approaches with very different political tendencies, from the theoretical knowledges of advertisers, persons involved in public relations for large organisations, many liberal-pluralist theorists of public communication and the larger part of writings on culture within the marxist and other critical traditions. As between disciplines, it is sociologists or social historians or political economists, or those concerned with the political organisation of culture, who have most commonly taken this viewpoint.

A more systematic approach to cultural production has been a relatively recent feature of the sociology of literature, art or popular cultural forms. These concerns parallel debates about the mass media and were originally deeply influenced by the early experiences of state propaganda under the conditions of the modern media, especially in Nazi Germany. Crossing the more aesthetic and political debates has been the pervasive concern with the influence of capitalist conditions of production and the mass market in cultural commodities on the 'authenticity' of culture, including the popular arts. Studies of production within these traditions have been equally varied: from grandiose critiques of the political economy and cultural pathology of mass communications (e.g. the early Frankfurt School) to close empirical inspections of the production of news or particular documentary series or soap operas on television.[18] In a very different way still, much modern history has been concerned with 'cultural production', though this time the cultural production of social movements or even whole social classes. It is important to accept E.P. Thompson's invitation to read *The Making of the English Working Class* from this cultural standpoint; Paul Willis's work, especially *Learning to Labour*, represents in many ways the sociological equivalent of this historiographical tradition.

What unites these diverse works, however, is that they all take, if not the viewpoint of cultural producers, at least the *theoretical* standpoint of production. They are interested, first and foremost, in the production and the social organisation of cultural forms. Of course, it is here that marxist paradigms have occupied a very central place, even when continuously argued against. Early marxist accounts asserted the primacy of production conditions and often reduced these to some narrowly-conceived version of 'the forces and the relations of production'. Even such reductive analysis had a certain value: culture was understood as a social product, not a matter of individual creativity only. It was therefore subject to political organisation, whether by the capitalist state or by parties of social opposition.[19] In later marxist accounts, the historical forms of the production and organisation of culture – 'the superstructures' – have begun to be elaborated.

In Gramsci's writing the study of culture from the viewpoint of production becomes a more general interest with the cultural dimensions of struggles and strategies as a whole. The longstanding and baneful influence of 'high-cultural' or specialist definitions of 'Culture' *within* marxism was also definitively challenged.[20] Gramsci was, perhaps, the first major marxist theorist and communist leader to take the cultures of the popular classes as a serious object of study and of political practice. All the more modern features of culture organisation also start to appear in his work: he writes of cultural organisers/producers not just as little knots of 'intellectuals' on the old revolutionary or Bolshevik model but as whole social strata concentrated around particular institutions – schools, colleges, the law, the press, the state bureaucracies and the political parties. Gramsci's work is the most sophisticated and fertile development of a traditional marxist approach via cultural production. Yet I think that Gramsci remains much more the 'Leninist' than is sometimes appreciated in new left or academic debates in Britain.[21] From the work available in English, it seems to be he was less interested in how cultural forms work, subjectively, than in how to 'organise' them, externally.

Limits of the viewpoint of production

I find two recurrent limits to looking at culture from this viewpoint. The first difficulty is the familiar one of 'economism', though it is useful, I hope, to restate the problem in a different way. There is a tendency to neglect what is specific to *cultural* production in this model. Cultural production is assimilated to the model of capitalist (usually) production in general, without sufficient attention to the *dual* nature of the circuit of cultural commodities. The conditions of production include not merely the material means of production and the capitalist organisation of labour, but a stock of already existing *cultural* elements drawn from the reservoirs of lived culture or from the already public fields of discourse. This raw material is structured not only by capitalist production imperatives (i.e. commodified) but also by the indirect results of capitalist and other social relations on the existing rules of language and discourse, especially, class and gender-based struggles in their effects on different social symbols and signs. As against this, marxist political economy still goes for the more brutally-obvious 'determinations' – especially mechanisms like competition, monopolistic control, and imperial expansion.[22] This is why the claim of some semiologies to provide an alternative materialist analysis does have some force.[23] Many approaches to production, in other words, can be faulted on their chosen grounds: as accounts of *cultural* production, of the production of *subjective* forms, they tell us at most about some 'objective' conditions and the work of some social sites – typically the ideological work of capitalist business (e.g. advertising, the work of commercial media) rather than that of political parties, schools, or the apparatuses of 'high culture'.

The second difficulty is not economism but what we might call 'productivism'. The two are often combined but are analytically distinct. Gramsci's marxism, for instance, is certainly not economistic, but it is, arguably, productivist. The problem here is the tendency to infer the character of a cultural product and its social use from the conditions of its production, as though, in cultural matters, production determines all. The common sense forms of this inference are familiar: we need only trace an idea to its source to declare it 'bourgeois' or 'ideological' – hence 'the bourgeois novel', 'bourgeois science', 'bourgeoise ideology' and, of course, all the 'proletarian' equivalents. Most critics of this reduction attack it by denying the connection between conditions of origin and political tendency.[24] I do not myself wish to deny that conditions of origin (including the class or gender position of producers) exercise a profound influence on the nature of the product. I find it more useful to question such identifications not as 'wrong' but as *premature*. They may be true as far as they go, according to the logics of that moment, but they neglect the range of possibilities in cultural forms especially as these are realised in consumption or 'readership'. I do not see how any cultural form can be dubbed 'ideological' (in the usual marxist critical sense) until we have examined not only its origin in the primary production process, but also carefully analysed its textual forms *and* the modes of its reception. 'Ideological', unless deployed as a neutral term, is the *last* term to use in such analysis, certainly not the first.[25]

I still find the debate between Walter Benjamin and Theodor Adorno about the tendency of mass culture a very instructive example.[26] Adorno swept on in his majectic polemic identifying capitalist production conditions, tracing effects in the 'fetishised' form of the cultural commodity and finding its perfect compliment in the 'regressive listening' of fans for popular music. There is a highly deductive or inferential element in his reasoning, often resting on some giant theoretical strides, plotted first by Lukacs. The conflations and reductions that result are well illustrated in one of his (few) concrete examples: his analysis of the British brewer's slogan – 'What We Want is Watneys'.

> The brand of the beer was presented like a political slogan. Not only does this billboard give an insight into the nature of the up to date propaganda, which sells its slogans as well as its wares . . . the type of relationship which is suggested by the billboard, by which the masses make a commodity recommended to them the object of their own action, is in fact found again in the pattern of reception of light music. They need and demand what has been palmed off on them.[27]

The first four lines of this are fine. I like the insight about the parallel courses of political propaganda and commercial advertising, forced on as it was by the German situation. The reading of the slogan is also quite interesting, showing how advertising works to produce an *active* identification. But the analysis goes awry as soon as we get to 'the masses'. The actual differentiated drinkers of Watneys and readers of the slogan are assumed to act also as the brewer's ventriloquists' dummy, without any other determinations intervening. Everything specific to the enjoyment of slogans or the drinking of beer is abstracted away. Adorno is uninterested, for example, in the meaning of Watneys (or any other tipple) in the context of pub sociability, indexed by the 'we'. The possibility that drinkers may have their own reasons for consuming a given product and that drinking has a social use value is overlooked.[28]

This is quite an extreme case of productivism but the pressure to infer effects or readings from an analysis of production is a constant one. It is a feature, for example, of a rich vein of work in cultural studies which has mainly been concerned to analyse particular fields of public discourse. Among CCCS publications, *Policing the Crisis* and *Unpopular Education*[29] both were analyses of our first two moments – of texts, in this case the fields of discourse about law and order and about public education – and of their conditions and histories of production – law and order campaigns, media *cause celebre*, the work of 'primary definers' like judges and the police, the role of a new political tendency, 'Thatcherism', etc. Both studies proved to have considerable predictive value, showing the strengths and the popularity of new right politics before, in the case of *Policing*, Mrs

Thatcher's first electoral victory in 1979.[30] Similarly, I believe that *Unpopular Education* contained what has turned out to be a percipient analysis of the fundamental contradictions of social-democratic politics in Britain and therefore of some of the agonies of the Labour Party. Yet, as political guides both studies are incomplete: they lack an account of the crisis of '1945-ism' in the lived culture of, especially, working-class groups, or a really concrete rendering of the popular purchase of new right ideologies. They are limited, in other words, by reliance upon, for the most part, the 'public' knowledges of the media and of formal politics. Something more is required than this, especially if we are to go beyond critique to help in producing new political programmes and movements.

This argument may be capped if we turn to Walter Benjamin. Benjamin certainly took a more open view of the potentialities of mass cultural forms than Adorno. He was excited by their technical and educational possibilities. He urged cultural producers to transform not only their works, but also their ways of working. He described the techniques of a new form of cultural production: Brecht's 'epic theatre'. Yet we can see that all of these insights are primarily the comments of a critic upon the theories of producers, or take the standpoint of production. It is here, still with the creator, that the really revolutionary moves are to be made. It is true that Benjamin also had interesting ideas about the potentiality of modern forms to produce a new and more detached relationship between reader and text, but this insight remained abstract, as optimistic, in the same rather *a priori* way, as Adorno's pessimism. It was not rooted in any extended analysis of the larger experience of particular groups of readers.

Our first case (production) turns out to be an interesting instance of an argument the general form of which will recur. Of course, we must look at cultural forms from the viewpoint of their production. This must include the conditions and the means of production, especially in their cultural or subjective aspects. In my opinion it must include accounts and understandings too of the actual moment of production itself – the labour, and its subjective and objective aspects. We cannot be perpetually discussing 'conditions' and never discussing acts! At the same time, we must avoid the temptation, signalled in marxist discussions of determination, to subsume all other aspects of culture under the categories of production-studies. This suggests two stages in a more sensible approach. The first is to grant independence and particularity to a distinct production moment – and to do the same for other moments. This is a necessary, negative, holding of the line against reductionisms of all kinds. But once the line is held in our analysis, another stage becomes quite evident. The different moments or aspects are not in fact distinct. There is, for instance, a sense in which (rather carefully) we can speak of texts as 'productive' and a much stronger case for viewing reading or cultural consumption as a production process in which the first product becomes a material for fresh labour. The text-as-produced is a different object from the text-as-read. The problem with Adorno's analysis and perhaps with productivist approaches in general is not only that they infer the text-as-read from the text-as-produced, but that also, in doing this, they ignore the elements of production in other moments, concentrating 'creativity' in producer or critic. Perhaps this is the deepest prejudice of all among the writers, the artists, the teachers, the educators, the communicators and the agitators within the intellectual divisions of labour!

Text-based studies

A second whole cluster of approaches are primarily concerned with cultural products. Most commonly these products are treated as 'texts'; the point is to provide more or less definitive 'readings' of them. Two developments seem especially important: the separation between specialist critics and ordinary readers, and the division between cultural practitioners and those who practise, primarily, by commenting on the works of others. Both developments have much to do with the growth and elaboration of educational and especially academic institutions, but it is interesting that the 'modernisms' which have so deeply influenced cultural studies, had their origins as producer's theories, but are now discussed most intensively in academic and educational contexts. I am thinking particularly of the theories associated with Cubism and Constructivism, Russian formalism and film-making, and, of course, Brecht on theatre.[31]

Much of what is known about the textual organisation of cultural forms is now carried in the academic disciplines conventionally grouped together as the humanities or the arts. The major humanities disciplines, but especially linguistic and literary studies, have developed means of formal description which are indispensable for cultural analysis. I am thinking, for example, of the literary analysis of forms of narrative, the identification of different, *genre*, but also of whole families of genre categories, the analysis of syntactical forms, possibilities and transformations in linguistics, the formal analysis of acts and exchanges in speech, the analysis of some elementary forms of cultural theory by philosophers, and the common borrowings, by criticism and cultural studies, from semiology and other structuralisms.

Looking at it from outside, the situation in the humanities and especially in literature seems to me very paradoxical: on the one hand, the development of immensely powerful tools of analysis and description, on the other hand, rather meagre ambitions in terms of applications and objects of analysis. There is a tendency for the tools to remain obstinately technical or formal. The example I find most striking at the moment is linguistics, which seems a positive treasure-chest for cultural analysis but is buried in a heightened technical mystique and academic professionalism, from which, fortunately, it is beginning to emerge.[32] Other possibilities seem perpetually cooped up in the 'need' to say something new about some well-thumbed text or much disputed author. This sometimes encompasses a free-ranging amateurism whose general cultural credentials apparently sanction the liberal application of some pretty common sense judgments to almost everything. Yet the paradox is that humanities disciplines, which are preeminently concerned with identifying the subjective forms of life, are already cultural studies in embryo!

Forms, regularities and conventions first identified in literature (or certain kinds of music or visual art) often turn out to have a much wider social currency. Feminists working on romance, for example, have traced the correspondences between the narrative forms of popular romantic fiction, the public rituals of marriage (e.g. the Royal Wedding) and, if only through their own experience, the subjective tug of the symbolic resolutions of romantic love.[33] Provoked by this still-developing model, a similar set of arguments and researchers are developing around conventional masculinity, the fighting fantasies of boy-culture, and the narrative forms of epic.[34] As if on a prompter's cue, the Falklands/Malvinas conflict crystallised both of these forms (and conjoined them) in a particularly dramatic and real public spectacle. There is no better instance, perhaps, of the limits of treating forms like romance or epic as merely *literary* constructions. On the contrary, they are among the most powerful and ubiquitous of *social* categories or *subjective* forms, especially in their constructions of conventional feminity and masculinity. Human beings live, love, suffer bereavement and go off and fight and die by them.

As usual, then, the problem is to appropriate methods that are often locked into narrow disciplinary channels and use their real insights more widely, freely. What kinds of text-based methods, then, are most useful? And what problems should we look for and try to overcome?

The importance of being formal

Especially important are all the modernist and post-modernist influences, particularly those assocaited with structuralism and post-Saussurean linguistics. I include the developments in semiology here, but would also want to include, as a kind of cousinhood, once-removed, some strands in 'Anglo-American' linguistics.[35] Cultural studies has often approached these strands quite gingerly, with heated battles, in particular, with those kinds of text-analysis informed by psycho-analysis,[36] but the fresh modernist infusions continue to be a source of developments. As someone coming from the other historical/sociological side, I am often surprised and uncritically entranced by the possibilities here.

Modern formal analysis promises a really careful and systematic description of subjective forms, and of their tendencies and pressures. It has enabled us to identify, for example, narrativity as a basic form of organisation of subjectivities.[37] It also gives us leads – or more – on the repertoire of narrative forms existing contemporaneously, the actual story-forms characteristic of different ways of life. If we treat these not as archetypes but as historically-produced constructions, the possibilities for fruitful concrete study on a wide range of materials is immense. For stories obviously come not merely in the form of bookish or filmic fictions but also in everyday conversation, in everyone's imagined futures and daily projections, and in the construction of identities, individual and collective, through memories and histories. What are the recurrent patterns here? What forms can we abstract from these texts most commonly? It seems to me that in the study of subjective forms, we are at the stage in political economy which Marx, in the *Grundrisse*, saw as necessary but primitive: 'when the forms had still to be laboriously peeled out from the material'.

There are a number of inhibitions here. One powerful one is an opposition to abstract categories and a terror of formalism. I think that this is often quite misplaced. We need to abstract forms in order to describe them carefully, clearly, noting the variations and combinations. I am sure that Roland Barthes was right when he argued against the quixotic rejection of 'the artifice of analysis':

> Less terrorised by the spectre of 'formalism', historical criticism might have been less sterile; it would have understood that the specific study of forms does not in any way contradict the necessary principles of totality and History. On the contrary: the more a system is specifically defined in its forms, the more amenable it is to historical criticism. To parody a well-known saying, I shall say that a little formalism turns one away from History, but that a lot brings one back to it.[38]

Admittedly Barthes' 'History' is suspiciously capitalised and emptied of content: unlike marxism, semiology does not present us with a practice (unless it be Barthes' little essays) for reconstituting a complex whole from the different forms. But I am sure we do end up with better, more explanatory, histories, if we have comprehended, more abstractedly, some of the forms and relations which constitute them. In some ways, indeed, I find Barthes' work not formal enough. The level of elaboration in his later work sometimes seems gratuitous: too complex for clarity, insufficiently concrete as a substantive account. In these and other semiological endeavours do we mainly hear the busy whir of self-generating intellectual systems rapidly slipping out of control? If so, this is a different noise from the satisfying buzz of a really 'historical' abstraction!

Radical structuralisms excite me for another reason.[39] They are the furthest reach of the criticism of empiricism which, as I suggested earlier, founds cultural studies philosophically. This radical constructivism – nothing in culture taken as given, everything produced – is a leading insight we cannot fall behind. Of course, these two excitements are closely related, the second as a premise of the first. It is because we know we are not in control of our own subjectivities, that we need so badly to identify their forms and trace their histories and future possibilities.

What is a text anyway?

But if text analysis is indispensable, what is a text? Remember the Mini-Metro as an example of the tendency of 'texts' to a polymorphous growth: Tony Bennett's example of the James Bond genres is an even better case.[40] The proliferation of allied representations in the field of public discourses poses large problems for any practitioner of contemporary cultural studies. There are, however, better and worse ways of coping with them. Often, I think, it is a traditional literary solution that is reached for: we plump for an 'author' (so far as this is possible), a single work or series, perhaps a distinctive genre. Our choices may now be popular texts and perhaps a filmic or electronic medium, yet there are still limits in such quasi-literary criteria.

If, for example, we are really interested in how conventions and the technical means available within a particular medium structure representations, we need to work *across* genre and media, comparatively. We need to trace the differences as well as the similarities, for example, between literary romance, romantic love as public spectacle and love as a private form or narrative. It is only in this way that we can resolve some of the most important evaluative questions here: how far, for instance, romance acts merely to seal women into oppressive social conditions, and how far ideologies of love may nonetheless express utopian conceptions of personal relations. We certainly do not *have* to bound our research by literary criteria; other choices are available. It is possible for instance to take 'issues' or periods as the main criterion. Though restricted by their choice of rather 'masculine' genre and media, *Policing the Crisis* and *Unpopular Education* are studies of this kind. They hinge around a basically historical definition, examining aspects of the rise of the new right mainly from the early 1970s. The logic of this approach has been extended in recent CCCS media-based studies: a study of a wide range of media representations of the Campaign for Nuclear Disarmament in October 1981[41] and a study of the media in a post-Falklands' holiday period, from Christmas 1982 to New Year 1983.[42] This last approach is especially fruitful since it allows us to examine the construction of a holiday (and especially the play around the public/ private division) according to the possibilities of different media and genre, for example, television soap opera and the popular daily press. By capturing something of the contemporaneity and combined 'effects' of different systems of representations, we also hope to get nearer to the commoner experience of listening, reading and viewing. This form of study, based upon a conjuncture which in this case is both historical (the post-Falklands moment of December 1982) and seasonal (the Christmas holiday), is premised on the belief that context is crucial in the production of meaning.

More generally, the aim is to decentre 'the text' as an object of study. 'The text' is no longer studied for its own sake, nor even for the social effects it may be thought to produce, but rather for the subjective or cultural forms which it realises and makes available. The text is only a *means* in cultural study; strictly, perhaps, it is a raw material from which certain forms (e.g. of narrative, ideological problematic, mode of address, subject position, etc.) may be abstracted. It may also form *part* of a larger discursive field or *combination* of forms occurring in other social spaces with some regularity. But the ultimate object of cultural studies is not, in my view, the text, but *the social life of subjective forms* at each moment of their circulation, including their textual embodiments. This is a long way from a literary valuing of texts for themselves, though, of course, the modes in which some textual embodiments of subjective forms come to be valued over others, especially by critics or educators – the problem especially of 'high' and 'low' in culture – is a central question, especially in theories of culture and class. But this is a problem which subsumes 'literary' concerns, rather than reproducing them. A key issue is how criteria of 'literariness' themselves come to be formulated and installed in academic, educational and other regulative practices.

Structuralist foreshortenings

How to constitute the text is one problem; another is the tendency of other moments, especially of cultural production and reading, but more generally of the more concrete, private aspects of culture, to disappear into a reading of the text. Around this tendency, we might write a whole complicated history of formalisms, using the term now in its more familiar critical sense. I understand formalism negatively, not as abstraction of forms from texts, but as the abstraction of texts from the other moments. For me this distinction is critical, marking the legitimate and excessive concerns with form. I would explain formalism in the negative sense in terms of two main sets of determinations: those that derive from the social location of 'critic' and the limits of a particular practice, and those that derive from particular theoretical problematics, the tools of different critical schools. Although there is a clear historical association, especially in the twentieth century, between 'criticism' and formalism, there is no necessary connection.

The particular formalisms that interest me most – because there is the most to rescue – are those associated with the various structuralist and post-structuralist discussions of text, narrative, subject positions, discourses and so on. I include here, in a necessarily compressed way, the whole sequence that runs from Saussure's linguistics and Lévi-Strauss' anthropology to early Barthes and what is sometimes called 'semiology mark 1'[43] to the developments set in train by May 1968 in film criticism, semiology and narrative theory, including the complicated intersection of Althusserian marxism, later semiologies and psycho-analysis. Despite their variations, these approaches to 'signifying practices' share certain paradigmatic limits which I term the 'structuralist foreshortening'.

They are limited, in a very fundamental way, by staying within the terms of textual analysis. In so far as they go beyond it, they subordinate other moments *to* textual analysis. In particular they tend to neglect questions of the production of cultural forms or their larger social organisation, or reduce questions of production to the 'productivity' (I would say 'capacity to produce') of the already existing systems of signification, that is the formal languages or codes. They also tend to neglect questions of readership, or subordinate them to the competencies of a textual form of analysis. They tend to derive an 'account' of readership, in fact, from the critic's own textual readings. I want to suggest that the common element in both these limits is a major theoretical lack – the absence of an adequate post-structuralist (or should I say post-post-structuralist) *theory of subjectivity*. This absence is one that is stressed within these approaches themselves; in fact, it is a major charge against old marxisms that they lacked 'a theory of the subject'. But the absence is supplied most unsatisfactorily by twinning textual analysis and psycho-analysis in an account of subjectivity which remains very abstract, 'thin' and un-historical and also, in my opinion, overly 'objective'. To sum up the limitations, there is not really an account or accounts here, of the *genesis* of subjective forms and the different ways in which human beings *inhibit* them.

The neglect of production

This is the easier point to illustrate. It is the difference, for example, between cultural studies in the CCCS tradition, and especially the CCCS appropriation of Gramsci's accounts of hegemony and, say, the main theoretical tendency in the magazine of film criticism associated with the British Film Institute, *Screen*. In the Italian context the comparison might be between the 'pure' semiological and cultural studies traditions. While cultural studies at Birmingham has tended to become *more* historical, more concerned with particular conjunctures and institutional locations, the tendency of film criticism in Britain has been, rather, the other way. Initially, an older marxist concern with cultural production, and, in particular with cinema as industry and with conjunctures in cinematic production was common both in Britain and France. But like the French film magazines, *Screen* became in the 1970s, increasingly pre-occupied less with production as a social and historical process, and more with the 'productivity' of signifying systems themselves, in particular, with the means of representation of the cinematographic medium. This move was very explicitly argued for, not only in the critiques of realist theories of the cinema and of the realist structures of conventional film itself, but also in the critique of the 'super-realism' of (honoured) marxist practitioners like Eisenstein and Brecht.[44] It formed part of a larger movement which placed increasing emphasis on the means of representation in general and argued that we had to choose between the virtual autonomy and absolute determinancy of 'signification' or return to the consistency of orthodox marxism. As the elegant one-sided exaggeration put it, it is the myths that speak the myth-maker, the language which speaks the speaker, the texts which read the reader, the theoretical problematic which produces 'science', and ideology or discourse that produces 'the subject'.

There *was an* account of production in this work, but a very attenuated one. If we think of production as involving raw materials, tools or means of production, and socially-organised forms of human labour, *Screen*'s accounts of film, for instance, focussed narrowly on some of the tools or means of production/representation. I say 'some' because semiologically-influenced theories have tended to invert the priorities of older marxist approaches to production, focussing only on some of the cultural means, those, in fact, which political economy neglects. Film theory in the 1970s acknowledged the 'dual' nature of the cinematic circuit, but was mainly concerned to elaborate cinema as 'mental machinery'.[45] This was an understandable choice of *priorities*, but often pursued in a hyper-critical and non-accumulative way. More serious was the neglect of labour, of the actual human activity of producing. Again this may itself have been an exaggerated reaction against older fashions, especially, in this case *auteur* theory, itself an attenuated conception of labour! The neglect of (structured) human activity and especially of conflicts over all kinds of production seems in retrospect the most glaring absence. Thus, although the conception of 'practice' was much invoked (e.g. 'signifying practice') it was practice quite without 'praxis' in the older marxist sense. The effects of this were especially important in the debates, which we shall come to, about texts and subjects.

This criticism can be pushed, however, one stage further: a very limited conception of 'means'. In *Screen's* theory there was a tendency to look only at the specifically cinematographic 'means' – the codes of cinema. The relations between these means and other cultural resources or conditions were not examined: for example, the relation between codes of realism and the professionalism of film-makers or the relation between media more generally and the state and formal political system. If these elements might be counted as means (they might also be thought of as social relations of production), the raw materials of production were also largely absent, especially in their cultural forms. For cinema, like other public media, takes its raw materials from the pre-existing field of public discourses – the whole field that is, not just from the bit called 'cinema' – and, under the kind of conditions we have examined, from private knowledges too. A critique of the very notion of representation (seen as indispensable to the critique of realism) made it hard for these theorists to pull into their accounts of film any very elaborate recognition of what an older, fuller theory might have called 'content'. Cinema (and then television) were treated as though they were, so to speak, only 'about' cinema or television, only reproducing or transforming the cinematographic or televisual forms, not pulling in and transforming discourses first produced elsewhere. In this way the cinematic text was abstracted from the whole ensemble of discourses and social relations which surrounded and formed it.

One further major limitation in much of this work was a tendency to refuse any explanatory move that went behind the existing means of representation, whether this was the language system, a particular 'signifying practice' or, indeed, the political system. The account was foreshortened to textual means and (just) textual 'effects'. The means were not conceived historically, as having their own moment of production. This was not a local difficulty in particular analyses, but a general theoretical absence, to be found in the earliest influential models of the theory. The same difficulty haunts Saussurean linguistics. Although the rules of language systems determine speech acts, the everyday deployment of linguistic forms appears not to touch the language system itself. This is partly because its principles are conceived so abstractly that historical change or social variation escapes detection, but it is also because there is no true production moment of the language system itself. Crucial insights into language and other systems of signification are therefore foreclosed: namely, that languages are produced (or differentiated), reproduced and modified by socially-organised human practice, that there can be no language (except a dead one) without speakers, and that language is continually fought over in its words, syntax and discursive deployments. In order to recover these insights, students of culture who are interested in language have had to go outside the predominantly French semiological traditions, back to the marxist philosopher of language Voloshinov or across to particular researches influenced by the work of Bernstein or Halliday.

Readers in texts; readers in society

The most characteristic feature of later semiologies has been the claim to advance a theory of the production of subjects. Initially, the claim was based on a general philosophical opposition to humanist conceptions of a simple, unified 'I' or subject, standing unproblematically at the centre of thought or moral or aesthetic evaluation. This feature of structuralism had affinities with similar arguments in Marx about the subjects of bourgeois ideologies, especially about the premises of political economy, and with Freud's anatomisation of the contradiction of human personality.

'Advanced semiology' presents several layers of theorisation of subjectivity which are difficult to unravel.[46] This complicated set of fusions and tangles combined fine leading insights with theoretical disasters. The key insight, for me, is that narratives or images always imply or construct a position or positions from which they are to be read or viewed. Although 'position' remains problematic (is it a set of cultural competences or, as the term implies, some necessary 'subjection' to the text?), the insight is dazzling, especially when applied to visual images and to film. We cannot perceive the work which cameras do from a new aspect, not merely presenting an object, but putting us in place before it. If we add to this the argument that certain kinds of texts ('realism') naturalise the means by which positioning is achieved, we have a dual insight of great force. The particular promise is to render processes hitherto unconsciously suffered (and enjoyed) open to explicit analysis.

Within the context of my own argument, the importance of these insights is that they provide a way of *connecting* the account of textual forms with an exploration of intersections with readers' subjectivities. A careful, elaborated and hierarchised account of the reading positions offered in a text (in narrative structure or modes of address for instance) seems to me the most developed method we have so far within the limits of text analysis. Of course, such readings should not be taken to negate other methods: the reconstruction of the manifest and latent themes of a text, its denotative and connotative moments, its ideological problematic or limiting assumptions, its metaphorical or linguistic strategies. The legitimate object of an identification of 'positions' is the *pressures* or *tendencies* of subjective forms, the *directions* in which they move us, their *force* – once inhabited. *The difficulties arise* – and they are very numerous – *if such tendencies are held to be realised in the subjectivities of readers, without additional and different forms of inquiry.*

The intoxications of the theory make such a move very tempting. But to slip from 'reader in the text' to 'reader in society' is to slide from the most abstract moment (the analysis of forms) to the most concrete object (actual readers, as they are constituted, socially, historically, culturally). This is conveniently to miss – but not explicitly as a rational abstraction – the huge number of fresh determinations or pressures of which we must now take account. In disciplinary terms we move from a ground usually covered by literary approaches to one more familiar to historical or sociological competences, but the common new element here is the ability to handle a mass of co-existing determinations, operating at many different levels.

It would take us into a long and complicated exploration of 'reading' to try and gauge the full enormity of the leap.[47] There is only room to stress a few difficulties in treating reading, not as reception or assimilation, but as itself an act of production. If the text is the raw material of this practice, we encounter, once again, all the problems of textual boundaries. The isolation of a text for academic scrutiny is a very specific form of reading. More commonly texts are encountered promiscuously; they pour in on us from all directions in diverse, coexisting media, and differently-paced flows. In everyday life, textual materials are complex, multiple, overlapping, coexistent, juxta-posed, in a word, 'inter-textual'. If we use a more agile category like discourse, indicating *elements* that cut across different texts, we can say that all readings are also 'inter-discursive'. No subjective form ever acts on its own. Nor can the *combinations* be predicted by formal or logical means, nor even from empirical analysis of the field of public discourse, though of course this may suggest hypotheses. The combinations stem, rather, from more particular logics – the structured life-activity in its objective and subjective sides, of readers or groups of readers: their social locations, their histories, their subjective interests, their private worlds.

The same problem arises if we consider the tools of this practice, or the codes, competences and orientations already present within a particular social *milieu*. Again these are not predictable from public texts. They belong to private *cultures*, in the way that term has usually been used in cultural studies. They are grouped according to 'ways of life'. They exist in the chaotic and historically-sedimented *ensembles* which Gramsci referred to as common sense. Yet these must determine the longer and shorter-range results of particular interpellative moments, or, as I prefer, the forms of cultural transformations which always occur in readings.

All this points to the centrality of what is usually called 'context'. Context determines the meaning, transformations or salience of a particular subjective form as much as the form itself. Context includes the cultural features described above, but also the contexts of immediate situations (e.g. the domestic context of the household) and the larger historical context or conjuncture.

Yet an account would remain incomplete without some attention to the act of reading itself and an attempt to theorise its products. The absence of action by the reader is characteristic of formalist accounts. Even those theorists (e.g. Brecht, *Tel Quel*, Barthes in *S/Z*) who are concerned with productive, deconstructive or critical reading ascribe this capacity to types of text (e.g. 'writable' rather than 'readable' in Barthes's terminology) and not at all to a history of real readers. This absence of production in reading parallels the ascription of productivity to signifying systems which we have already noted. At best particular acts of reading are understood as a replaying of primary human experiences. Just as an older literary criticism sought universal values and human emotions in the text, so the new formalisms understand reading as the reliving of psycho-analytically-defined mechanisms. Analysis of the spectator's gaze, based on Lacanian accounts of the mirror phase, identify *some* of the motions of the way men use images of women and relate to heroes.[48] Such analyses *do* bridge text and reader. There is a huge potentiality, for cultural studies, in the critical use of Freudian categories, as critical that is, as the use of marxist categories has become or is becoming. Yet present uses often bridge text and reader at a cost: the radical simplification of the social subject, reducing him or her to the original, naked, infant needs. It is difficult on this basis to specify all the realms of difference which one wishes to grasp, even, surprisingly, gender. At worst the imputations about real subjects come down to a few universals, just as it is now only a few basic features of the text which interest us. There are distinct limits to a procedure which discovers, in otherwise varied phenomena, the same old mechanisms producing the same old effects.

One lack in these accounts is an attempt to describe more elaborately the surface forms – the flows of inner speech and narrative – which are the most empirically obvious aspect of subjectivity. Perhaps it is thought humanist to pay attention to consciousness in this way? But we all are (aren't we?) continuous, resourceful and absolutely frenetic users of narrative and image? And these uses occur, in part, inside the head, in the imaginative or ideal world which accompanies us in every action. We are not merely positioned by stories about ourselves, stories about others. We use realist stories about the future to prepare or plan, acting out scenarios of dangerous or pleasurable events. We use fictional or fantastical forms to escape or divert. We tell stories about the past in the form of memory which construct versions of who we presently are. Perhaps all this is simply presupposed in formalist analysis, yet to draw it into the foreground seems to have important implications.[49] It makes it possible to recover the elements of self-production in theories of subjectivity. It suggests that before we can gauge the productivity of new interpellations, or anticipate their popularity, we need to know what stories are already in place.

All this involves a move beyond what seems to be an underlying formalist assumption: that real readers are 'wiped clean' at each textual encounter to be positioned (or liberated) anew by the next interpellation. Post-structuralist revisions, stressing the continuous productivity of language or discourse as *process*, do not necessarily help here, because it is not at all clear what all this productivity actually produces. There is no real theory of subjectivity here, partly because the *explanandum*, the 'object' of such a theory, remains to be specified. In particular there is no account of the carry-over or continuity of self-identities from one discursive moment to the next, such as a re-theorisation of memory in discursive terms might permit. Since there is no account of continuities or of what remains constant or accumulative, there is no account of structural shifts or major re-arrangements of a sense of self, especially in adult life. Such transformations are always, implicitly, referred to 'external' text-forms, for example revolutionary or poetic texts, usually forms of literature. There is no account of what predisposes the reader to use such texts productively or what conditions, other than the text-forms themselves, contribute to revolutionary conjunctures in their subjective dimensions. Similarly, with such a weight on the text, there is no account of how some readers (including, presumably, the analysts) can use conventional or realist texts critically. Above all, there is no account of what I would call *the subjective aspects of struggle*, no account of how there is a moment in subjective flux when social subjects (individual or collective) produce accounts of who they are, as conscious political agents, that is, constitute themselves, politically. To ask for such a theory is not to deny the major structuralist or post-structuralist insights: subjects *are* contradictory, 'in process', fragmented, produced. But human beings and social movements also strive to produce some coherence and continuity, and through this, exercise some control over feelings, conditions and destinies.

This is what I mean by a 'post-post-structuralist' account of subjectivity. It involves returning to some older but reformulated questions – about struggle, 'unity', and the production of a political will. It involves accepting structuralist insights as a statement of the problem, whether we are speaking of our own fragmented selves or the objective and subjective fragmentation of possible political constituencies. But it also involves taking seriously what seems to me the most interesting theoretical lead: the notion of a discursive self-production of subjects, especially in the form of histories and memories.[50]

Social inquiries – logic and history

I hope that the logic of our third cluster of approaches, which focus on 'lived culture', is already clear. To recapitulate, the problem is how to grasp the more *concrete* and more *private* moments of cultural circulation. This sets up two kinds of pressures. The first is towards methods which can detail, recompose and represent complex ensembles of discursive and non-discursive features as they appear in the life of particular social groups. The second is towards 'social inquiry' or an active seeking out of cultural elements which do not appear in the public sphere, or only appear abstracted and transformed. Of course, students of culture have access to private forms through their own experiences and social worlds. This is a continuous resource, the more so if it is consciously specified and if its relativity is recognised. Indeed, a cultural self-criticism of this kind is *the* indispensable condition for avoiding the more grossly ideological forms of cultural study.[51] But the first lesson here is the recognition of *major cultural differences*, especially across those social relationships where power, dependence and inequality are most at stake. There are perils, then, in the use of a (limited) individual or collective self-knowledge where the limits of its representativeness are uncharted and its other sides – usually the sides of powerlessness – are simply unknown. This remains a justification for forms of cultural study which take the cultural worlds of others (often reverse sides of one's own) as the main object.

We have to keep a discomforted eye on the historical pedigrees and current orthodoxies of what is sometimes called 'ethnography', a practice of representing the cultures of others. The practice, like the word, already extends social distance and constructs relations of knowledge-as-power. To 'study' culture forms is already to differ from a more implicit inhabitation of culture which is the main 'common-sense' mode in *all* social groups. (And I mean *all* social groups – 'intellectuals' may be great at describing *other* people's implicit assumptions, but are as 'implicit' as anyone when it comes to their own.)

The early years of new left research in particular – the 1940s, 50s and early 60s – involved a new set of relations between the subjects and objects of research, especially across class relations.[52] Intellectual movements associated with feminism and the work of some black intellectuals have transformed (but not abolished) these social divisions too. Experiments in community-based authorship have also, within limits, achieved new social relations of cultural production and publication.[53] Even so it seems wise to be suspicious, not necessarily of these practices themselves, but of all accounts of them that try to minimise the political risks and responsibilities involved, or to resolve magically the remaining social divisions. Since fundamental social relations have not been transformed, social inquiry tends constantly to return to its old anchorages, pathologising subordinated cultures, normalising the dominant modes, helping at best to build academic reputations without proportionate returns to those who are represented. Apart from the basic political standpoint – whose side the researchers are on – much depends on the specific theoretical forms of the work, the *kind* of ethnography.

Limits of 'experience'

There seems to be a close association between ethnographies (or histories) based on sympathetic identification and empiricist or 'expressive' models of culture. The pressure is to represent lived cultures as authentic ways of life and to uphold them against ridicule or condescension. Research of this kind has often been used to criticise the dominant representations, especially those influencing state policies. Researchers have often mediated a private working-class world (often the world of their own childhood) and the definitions of the public sphere with its middle-class weighting. A very common way of upholding subordinated cultures has been to stress the bonds between the subjective and objective sides of popular practices. Working-class culture has been seen as the authentic expression of proletarian conditions, perhaps the only expression possible. This relation or identity has sometimes been cemented by 'old marxist' assumptions about the proper state of consciousness of the working-class. A similar set of assumptions can be traced in some feminist writings about culture which portray and celebrate a distinct feminine cultural world reflective of woman's condition. The term which most commonly indexes this theoretical framework is 'experience', with its characteristic fusing of objective and subjective aspects.

Such frameworks produce major difficulties, not least for researchers themselves. Secondary analysis and re-presentation must always be problematic or intrusive if 'spontaneous' cultural forms are seen as a completed or necessary form of social knowledge. The only legitimate practice, in this framework, is to represent an unmediated chunk of authentic life experience itself, in something like its own terms. This form of cultural empiricism is a dead hand on the most important of cultural studies practices, and is one of the reasons why it is also the most difficult to deliver at all.

There is also a systematic pressure towards presenting lived cultures primarily in terms of their homogeneity and distinctiveness. This theoretical pressure, in conceptions like 'whole way of life', becomes startingly clear when issues of nationalism and racism are taken into account. There is a discomforting convergence between 'radical' but romantic versions of 'working-class culture' and notions of a shared Englishness or white ethnicity. Here too one finds the term 'way of life' used as though 'cultures' were slabs of significance always humped around by the same set of people. In left ethnography the term has often been associated with an under-representation of non-class relations and of fragmentations within social classes.[54]

The main lack within expressive theories is attention to the means of signification as a specific cultural determination. There is no better instance of the divorce between formal analysis and 'concrete studies' than the rarity of linguistic analysis in historical or ethnographic work. Like much structuralist analysis, then, ethnographies often work with a foreshortened version of our circuit, only here it is the whole arc of 'public' forms which is often missing. Thus the creativity of private forms is stressed, the continuous cultural productivity of everyday life, but not its dependence on the materials and modes of public production. Methodologically, the virtues of abstraction are eschewed so that the separate (or separable) elements of lived cultures are not unravelled, and their real complexity (rather than their essential unity) is not recognised.

Best ethnography

I do not wish to imply that this form of cultural study is intrinsically compromised. On the contrary, I tend to see it as the privileged form of analysis, both intellectually and politically. Perhaps this will be clear if I briefly review some aspects of the best ethnographic studies at Birmingham.[55]

These studies have used abstraction and formal description to identify key elements in a lived cultural ensemble. Cultures are read 'textually'. But they have also been viewed alongside a reconstruction of the social position of the users. There is a large difference here between a 'structural ethnography' and a more ethnomethodological approach concerned exclusively with the level of meaning and usually within an individualistic framework. This is one reason, for instance, why feminist work in the Centre has been as much preoccupied with theorising the position of women as with 'talking to girls'. We have tried to ally cultural analysis with a (sometimes too generalised) structural sociology, centring upon gender, class and race.

Perhaps the most distinctive feature has been the connections made between lived cultural ensembles and public forms. Typically, studies have concerned the appropriation of elements of mass culture and their transformation according to the needs and cultural logics of social groups. Studies of the contribution of mass cultural forms (popular music, fashion, drugs or motor bikes) to sub-cultural styles, of girls' use of popular cultural forms, and of the lads' resistance to the knowledge and authority of school are cases in point. In other words the best studies of lived culture are also, necessarily, studies of 'reading'. It is from this point of view – the intersection of public and private forms – that we have the best chance of answering the two key sets of questions to which cultural studies – rightly – continually returns.

The first set concerns 'popularity' pleasure and the *use value* of cultural forms. Why do some subjective forms acquire a popular force, become principles of living? What are the *different* ways in which subjective forms are inhabited – playfully or in deep seriousness, in fantasy or by rational agreement, because it is the thing to do or the thing *not* to do?

The second set of questions concerns the *outcomes* of cultural forms. Do these forms tend to reproduce existing forms of subordination or oppression? Do they hold down or contain social ambitions, defining wants too modestly? Or are they forms which permit a questioning of existing relations or a running beyond them in terms of desire? Do they point to alternative social arrangements? Judgments like these cannot be made on the basis of the analysis of production conditions or texts alone; they can best be answered once we have traced a social form right through the circuit of its transformations and made some attempt to place it within the whole context of relations of hegemony within the society.

Future shapes of cultural studies: directions

My argument has been that there are three main models of cultural studies research: production-based studies, text-based studies, and studies of lived cultures. This division conforms to the main appearances of cultural circuits, but inhibits the development of our understandings in important ways. Each approach has a rationality in relation to that moment it has most closely in view, but is quite evidently inadequate, even 'ideological', as an account of the whole. Yet each approach also implies a different view of the politics of culture. Production-related studies imply a struggle to control or transform the most powerful means of cultural production, or to throw up alternative means by which a counter-hegemonic strategy may be pursued. Such discourses are usually addressed to institutional reformers or to radical political parties. Text-based studies, focussing on the forms of cultural products, have usually concerned the possibilities of a transformative cultural practice. They have been addressed most often to *avant-garde* practitioners, critics and teachers. These approaches have appealed especially to professional educators, in colleges or schools, because knowledges appropriate to radical practice have been adapted (not without problems) to a knowledge appropriate to critical readers. Finally, research into lived cultures has been closely associated with a politics of 'representation' upholding the ways of life of subordinated social groups and criticising the dominant public forms in the light of hidden wisdoms. Such work may even aspire to help to give hegemonic or non-corporate turns to cultures that are usually privatised, stigmatised or silenced.

It is important to stress that the circuit has not been presented as an adequate account of cultural processes or even of elementary forms. It is not a completed set of abstractions against which every partial approach can be judged. It is not therefore an adequate strategy for the future just to add together the three sets of approaches, using each for its appropriate moment. This would not work without transformations of each approach and, perhaps, our thinking about 'moments'. For one thing there are some real theoretical incompatibilities between approaches; for another, the ambitions of many projects are already large enough! It is important to recognise that each aspect has a life of its own in order to avoid reductions, but, after that, it may be more transformative to rethink each moment in the light of the others, importing objects and methods of study usually developed in relation to one moment into the next. The moments, though separable, are not in fact discrete, therefore we need to trace what Marx would have called 'the inner connections' and 'real identities' between them.

Those concerned with production studies need to look more closely, for example, at the specifically cultural conditions of production. This would include the more formal semiological questions about the codes and conventions on which a television programme, say, draws, and the ways in which it reworks them. It would also have to include a wider range of discursive materials – ideological themes and problematics – that belong to a wider social and political conjuncture. But already, in the production moment, we would expect to find more or less intimate relations with the lived culture of particular social groups, if only that of the producers. Discursive and ideological elements would be used and transformed from there too. 'Already' then, in the study of the production moment, we can anticipate the other aspects of the larger process and prepare the ground for a more adequate account. Similarly we need to develop, further, forms of text-based study which hook up with the production and readership perspectives. It may well be, in the Italian context, where semiological and literary traditions are so strong, that those are the most important transformations. It *is* possible to look for the signs of the production process in a text: this is one useful way of transforming the very unproductive concern with 'bias' that still dominated discussion of 'factual' media. It *is* also possible to read texts as forms of representation, provided it is realised that we are always analysing a representation of a representation. The first object, that which is represented in the text, is not an objective event or fact, but has already been given meanings in some other social practice. In this way it is possible to consider the relationship, if any, between the characteristic codes and conventions of a social group and the forms in which they are represented in a soap opera or comedy. This is not merely an academic exercise, since it is essential to have such an account to help establish the text's salience for this group or others. There is no question of abandoning existing forms of text analysis, but these have to be adapted to, rather than superseding, the study of actual readerships. There seem to be two main requirements here. First, the formal reading of a text has to be as open or as multi-layered as possible, identifying preferred positions or frameworks certainly, but also alternative readings and subordinated frameworks, even if these can only be discerned as fragments, or as contradictions in the dominant forms. Second, analysts need to abandon once and for all, both of the two main models of the critical reader: the primarily evaluative reading (is this a good/bad text?) and the aspiration to text-analysis as an 'objective science'. The problem with both models is that by de-relativising our acts of reading they remove from self-conscious consideration (but not as an active presence) our common sense knowledge of the larger cultural contexts and possible readings. I have already noted the difficulties here, but want also to stress the indispensability of this resource. The difficulties are met best, but not wholly overcome, when 'the analyst' is a group. Many of my most educative moments in cultural studies have come from these internal group dialogues about the readings of texts across, for example, gendered experiences. This is not to deny the real disciplines of 'close' reading, in the sense of *careful*, but not in the sense of *confined*.

Finally, those concerned with 'concrete' cultural description cannot afford to ignore the presence of text-like structures and particular forms of discursive organisation. In particular we need to know what distinguishes private cultural forms, in their basic modes of organisation, from the public forms. In this way we might be able to specify, linguistically for example, the differential relation of social groups to different media forms, and the real processes of reading that are involved.

Of course, the transformation of particular approaches will have effects on others. If linguistic analysis takes account of historical determinations, for example, or provides us with ways of analysing the operations of power, the division between language studies and concrete accounts will break down. This goes for the associated politics too. At the moment there are few areas so blocked by disagreement and incomprehension as the relationship between *avant-garde* theorists and practitioners of the arts and those interested in a more grass-roots entry through community arts, working-class writing, women's writing and so on. Similarly, it is hard to convey, just how mechanical, how unaware of cultural dimensions, the politics of most left fractions remain. If I am right that theories are related to viewpoints, we are talking not just of theoretical developments, but about some of the conditions for effective political alliances as well.

Notes

1. This paper is a revised and expanded version of talks given at the Department of English at Istituto Universitario Orientale in Naples and at the University of Palermo in April 1983. I am grateful to colleagues at Naples, Palermo, Pescara and from Bari for fruitful discussions around the themes raised here. In revising this paper, I have tried to respond to some comments, especially those concerning questions about consciousness and unconsciousness. I am grateful to Lidia Curti, Laura di Michele and Marina Vitale for encouraging the production of this paper and advising on its form, to the British Council for funding my visit, and to friends and students (not mutually exclusive categories) at Birmingham for bearing with very many different versions of 'the circuit'.
2. The key texts are Richard Hoggart, *The Uses of Literacy* (Penguin Books, 1958); Raymond Williams, *Culture and Society* (Penguin Books, 1958); Raymond Williams, *The Long Revolution* (Penguin Books, 1961).
3. For a still useful summary of CCCS responses to Althusser, see McLennan, Molina and Peters, 'Althusser's theory of ideology' in CCCS, *On Ideology* (Hutchinson, 1978).
4. See, for example, Hall, Lumley and McLennan, 'Politics and ideology: Gramsci' in *On Ideology*. But Gramsci's theorisations are a main presence in much of the empirical work from the Centre from the mid-1970s.
5. See McLennan, *Methodologies* and Richard Johnson, 'Reading for the best Marx: history-writing and historical abstraction' in CCCS, *Making Histories: Studies in History-Writing and Politics* (Hutchinson, 1982).
6. These are difficult to represent bibliographically, but key points are marked by

CCCS Women's Study Group, *Women Take Issue* (Hutchinson, 1978); CCCS, *The Empire Strikes Back* (Hutchinson, 1982). See also the series on women and on race in CCCS stencilled papers.

7. This is not a new criticism but given fresh force by the 1970s salience of race. See Paul Gilroy, 'Police and thieves' in *Empire Strikes Back*, esp. pp. 147–51.

8. Some of these, at an early stage, are discussed in *Women Take Issue*, but there is need for a really full and consolidated account of the transformations in cultural studies stemming from feminist work and criticism. See also Angela McRobbie, 'Settling accounts with sub-cultures', *Screen Education* 34 (Spring, 1980) and the articles by Hazel Carby and Pratibha Parmar in *Empire Strikes Back*.

9. See, for example, Stuart Hall, 'Some paradigms in cultural studies', *Anglistica* (1978); Stuart Hall, 'Cultural studies: two paradigms', *Media, Culture and Society* 2 (1980) (reprinted here as Chapter 2 and reprinted in part in Tony Bennett *et al.* (eds), *Culture, Ideology and Social Process* [Open University and Batsford, 1981]), and the introductory essays in Hall, Hobson, Lowe and Willis (eds), *Culture, Media and Language* (Hutchinson, 1980). These essays are highly compressed versions of the MA Theory Course at CCCS which Stuart Hall taught and which comprised a comprehensive theoretical mapping of the field. See also my own attempts at theoretical clarification, much influenced by Stuart's, especially in Clark, Critcher and Johnson (eds), *Working Class Culture* (Hutchinson, 1979).

10. Raymond Williams, *Culture and Society* and the entry in *Keywords* (Fontana, 1976).

11. For a discussion of 'general-historical' abstraction in Marx, see Johnson, 'Best Marx', p. 172.

12. The diagram is based, in its *general* forms, on a reading of Marx's account of the circuit of capital and its metamorphoses. For an important and original account of this, and of related questions (e.g. fetishism) see Victor Molina, 'Marx's arguments about ideology', MLitt Thesis (University of Birmingham, 1982). This thesis is currently being revised for submission as a PhD. Also important is Stuart Hall, 'Encoding/decoding' in *Culture, Media, Language*.

13. I am afraid this illustrative case is largely hypothetical since I have no contacts inside British Leyland management. Any resemblance to persons living or dead is entirely fortuitous and a pure instance of the power of theory!

14. This is the division between 'structuralist' and 'culturalist' approaches Stuart Hall and I, among others, have already discussed, but now in the form of 'objects' and methods, rather than 'paradigms'. See sources listed in note 9 above and add Richard Johnson, 'Histories of culture/theories of ideology: notes on an impasse', in Barrett *et al.* (eds), *Ideology and Cultural Production* (Croom Helm, 1979).

15. My thinking on 'the public and the private' is much influenced by certain German traditions, especially discussions around Jürgen Habermas' work on 'the public sphere'. This is now being interestingly picked up and used in some American work. See Jürgen Habermas, *Strukturwandel der Öffentlichkeit* (Neuweid, Berlin, 1962); Oskar Negt and Alexander Kluge, *Öffentlichkeit und Erfahrung: Zur Organisationsanalyse von Burgerlicher und proletarischer Öffentlichkeit* (Frankfurst am Main, 1972). For an extract of Negt and Kluge's work, see A. Matterlart and S. Siegelaub (eds), *Communication and Class Struggle*, Vol. 2.

16. Paul Willis, 'Shop-floor culture, masculinity and the wage form' in Clarke, Critcher and Johnson (eds), *Working Class Culture*.

17. There is a very large sociological literature on these forms of stigmatisation, especially of the deviant young. For a cultural development of this work, see Stuart Hall *et al.*, *Policing the Crisis: 'Mugging', the State and Law and Order* (Macmillan, 1978). For more subtle forms of marginalisation, see CCCS Media

Group, 'Fighting over peace: representations of the Campaign for Nuclear Disarmament in the media', *CCCS Steniclled Paper* 72. For current treatment of the left and the trade unions in the British media, see the sequence of studies by the Glasgow Media Group, starting with Glasgow University Media Group, *Bad News* (Routledge & Kegan Paul, 1976). Stanley Cohen and Jock Young (eds), *The Manufacture of News* (Constable, 1973) was a pioneer collection.

18. Among the best close studies of this kind are Philip Elliott, *The Making of a Television Series: A Case Study in the Sociology of Culture* (Constable/Sage, 1972); Philip Schlesinger, *Putting 'Reality' Together: BBC News* (Constable/Sage, 1978); Jeremy Tunstall, *Journalists at Work* (Constable, 1971); Dorothy Hobson, *Crossroads* Methuen, 1982).

19. The forms of 'political organisation' were often not specified in Marx or in the theorists who followed him, up to and including, in my view, Lenin. For Lenin, it seems to me, cultural politics remained a matter of organisation and 'propaganda' in quite narrow senses.

20. Althusser's exceptions of 'art' from ideology are an instance of the persistance of this view within marxism. It is interesting to compare Althusser's and Gramsci's views of 'philosophy' here too, Althusser tending to the specialist academic or 'high cultural' definition, Gramsci to the popular.

21. I think the predominant reception of Gramsci in Britain is 'anti-Leninist', especially among those interested in discourse theory. But it may be that CCCS appropriation underestimates Gramsci's Leninism too. I am grateful to Victor Molina for discussions on this issue.

22. See, for instance, the work of Graham Murdock and Peter Golding on the political economy of the mass media: e.g. 'Capitalism, communication and class relations' in Curran *et al.* (eds), *Mass Communication and Society* (Arnold, 1977); Graham Murdock, 'Large corporations and the control of the communications industries' in Gurevitch *et al.* (eds), *Culture, Society and the Media* (Methuen, 1982); for a more explicitly polemical engagement with CCCS work, see Golding and Murdock, 'Ideology and the mass media: the question of determination' in Barratt *et al.* (eds), *Ideology and Cultural Production*. For a reply, see I. Connell, 'Monopoly capitalism and the media: definitions and struggles' in S. Hibbin (ed.), *Politics, Ideology and the State* (Lawrence & Wishart, 1978).

23. These claims have their proximate origin in Althusser's statement that ideologies have a material existence. For a classic English statement of this kind of 'materialism', see Rosalind Coward and John Ellis, *Language and Materialism: Developments in Semiology and the Theory of the Subject* (Routledge and Kegan Paul, 1977). This is rather different from Marx's argument that under particular conditions ideologies acquire a 'material force' or Gramsci's elaboration of this in terms of the conditions of popularity.

24. This applies to a wide range of structuralist and post-structuralist theories from Poulantzas's arguments against class reductionist notions of ideology to the more radical positions of Barry Hindess and Paul Hirst and other theorists of 'discourse'.

25. In this respect I find myself at odds with many strands in cultural studies, including some influential ones, which opt for an expanded use of ideology rather in the Bolshevik sense or in the more Leninist of Althusser's (several) uses. Ideology is applied, in Oxford's important popular culture course, for instance, to the formation of subjectivities as such. If stretched thus, I would argue that the term loses its usefulness – 'discourse', 'cultural form', etc., would do quite as well. On the whole, I wish to retain the 'negative' or 'critical' connotations of the term 'ideology' in classic marxist discourse, though not,

as it happens, the usual accompaniment, a 'hard' notion of marxism-as-science. It may well be that all our knowledge of the world and all our conceptions of the self are 'ideological', or more or less ideological, in that they are rendered partial by the operation of interests and of power. But this seems to me a proposition that has to be plausibly argued in particular cases rather than assumed at the beginning of every analysis. The expanded, 'neutral' sense of the term cannot altogether lay to rest the older negative connotations. The issues are interestingly stated in the work of Jorge Larrain. See *Marxism and Ideology* (Macmillan, 1983) and *The Concept of Ideology* (Hutchinson, 1979).

26. See especially Theodore Adorno, 'On the fetish character of music and the regression of listening' in A. Arato and E. Gebhardt (eds), *Frankfurt School Reader* (Blackwell, 1978); T.W. Adorno and M. Horkheimer, *Dialects of Enlightenment* (Allen Lane, 1973); Walter Benjamin, 'The work of art in an age of mechanical reproduction' in *Illuminations* (Fontana, 1973).
27. 'Fetish character of music', pp. 287–88. Later he gives slightly more rounded pictures of types of consumption of popular music, but even his fans' dancing resembles 'the reflexes of mutilated animals' (p. 292).
28. For more developed critiques, see Dick Bradley, 'Introduction to the cultural study of music', *CCCS Stencilled Paper* 61; Richard Middleton, 'Reading popular music', *Oxford Popular Culture Course Unit*, Unit 16, Block 4 (Open University Press, 1981).
29. CCCS Education Group, *Unpopular Education: Schooling and Social Democracy in England since 1944* (Hutchinson, 1981).
30. The analysis of Thatcherism has continued to be one of Stuart Hall's major concerns. See the very important essays republished in Stuart Hall and Martin Jacques (eds), *The Politics of Thatcherism* (Lawrence & Wishart/Marxism Today, 1983). 'The Great Moving Right Show', written before the 1979 election, proved to be especially perceptive.
31. Particularly useful introductions in English to these combined impacts are Sylvia Harvey, *May 1968 and Film Culture* (BFI, 1980); Tony Bennett, *Formalism and Marxism* (New Accents, Methuen, 1979).
32. See, for instance, the work of a group of 'critical linguists' initially based on the University of East Anglia, especially: R. Fowler *et al.*, *Language and Control* (Routledge and Kegan Paul, 1979). I am especially grateful to Gunther Kress, who spent some months at the Centre, and to Utz Maas of Osnabruck University for very fruitful discussions on the relationship of language studies and cultural studies. See also Utz Maas, 'Language studies and cultural analysis', paper for a Conference on Language and Cultural Studies at CCCS, December 1982.
33. Much of this work remains unpublished. I very much hope that one of the next CCCS books will be a collection on romance. In the meantime, see English Studies Group, 'Recent developments' in *Culture, Media, Language*', Rachel Harrison, 'Shirley: romance and relations of dependence' in CCCS Women's Studies Group, *Women Take Issue*; Angela McRobbie, 'Working-class girls and feminity'. *ibid.*; Myra Connell, 'Reading and romance', unpublished MA dissertation (University of Birmingham, 1981); Christine Griffin, 'Cultures of feminity: romance revisited', *CCCS Stencilled Paper* 69; Janice Winship, 'Woman becomes an individual: feminity and consumption in women's magazines', *CCCS Stencilled Paper* 65; Laura di Michele, 'The Royal Wedding', *CCCS Stencilled Paper*, forthcoming.
34. Much of this work is in connection with the work of the Popular Memory Group in CCCS towards a book on the popularity of Conservative nationalism. I am especially grateful to Laura di Michele for her contribution in opening up these

questions in relation to 'epic', and to Graham Dawson for discussions on masculinity, war, and boy culture.

35. Especially those developing out of the work of M.A.K. Halliday which includes the 'critical linguistics' group. For Halliday, see Gunther Kress (ed.), *Halliday: System and Function in Language* (Oxford University Press, 1976).

36. See especially the long, largely unpublished critique of *Screen* by the CCCS Media Group, 1977–78. Parts of this appear in Stuart Hall *et al.* (eds), *Culture, Media, Language*, 157–73.

37. I take this to be the common message of a great range of work, some of it quite critical of structuralist formalism, on the subject of narrative in literature, film, television, folk tale, myth, history and political theory. I am in the middle of my own reading list, delving into this material from a quite unliterary background. My starting points are theories of narrative in general – compare Roland Barthes, 'Introduction to the structural analysis of narratives' in Stephen Heath (ed.), *Barthes on Image, Music, Text* (Fontana, 1977) and Fredric Jameson, *The Political Unconscious: Narrative as a Socially-Symbolic Act* (Methuen, 1981), but I am most interested in work, at a lesser level of generality, that specifies the types of *genres* of narrative. Here I have found much stimulus in work on filmic or televisual narratives, see especially the texts collected in Tony Bennett *et al.* (eds), *Popular Television and Film* (BFI/Open University, 1981), but also on 'archetypal' genre forms – epic, romance, tragedy, etc. – as in Northrop Frye, *Anatomy of Criticism* (Princeton University Press, 1957). My particular concern is with the stories we tell ourselves individually and collectively. In this respect the existing literature is, so far, disappointing.

38. Roland Barthes, *Mythologies* (Paladin, 1973), p. 112.

39. By which I mean 'post-structuralism' in the usual designation. This seems to be a rather misleading tag since it is hard to conceive of late semiology without early, or even Foucault without Althusser.

40. Tony Bennett, 'James Bond as popular Hero', *Oxford Popular Culture Course Unit*, Unit 21, Block 5; 'Text and social process: the case of James Bond', *Screen Education* 41 (Winter/Spring, 1982).

41. 'Fighting over peace: representations of CND in the media', *CCCS Stencilled Paper* 72.

42. This project is not yet completed; provisional title: 'Jingo Bells: the public and the private in Christmas media 1982'.

43. This term has been used to distinguish 'structuralist' and 'post-structuralist' semiologies, with the incorporation of emphases from Lacanian psycho-analysis as an important watershed.

44. The relation of *Screen*'s theory to Brecht and Eisenstein is rather odd. Characteristically, quotations from Brecht were taken as starting-points for adventures which led to quite other destinations than Brecht's own thinking. See, for example, Colin MacCabe, 'Realism and the cinema: notes on some Brechtian theses' in Bennett *et al.* (eds), *Popular Television and Film*.

45. 'The cinematic institution is not just the cinema industry (which works to fill cinemas, not to empty them), it is also the mental machinery – another industry – which spectators "accustomed to the cinema" have internalised historically and which has adapted them to the consumption of films.' C. Metz, 'The imaginary signifier', *Screen* 16 (2) (Summer, 1975), p. 18.

46. What follows owes much to the CCCS *Screen* critique cited above (note 36).

47. There seem to be two rather distinct approaches to reading or 'audiences', the one an extension of literary concerns, the other more sociological in approach and often growing out of media studies. I find David Morley's work in this area consistently interesting as an attempt to combine some elements from both sets

of preoccupations, though I agree with his own assessment that the Centre's early starting-points, especially the notions of 'hegemonic', 'negotiated' and 'alternative' readings were exceedingly crude. See David Morley, *The Nationwide Audience* (BFI, 1980); 'The Nationwide audience: a postcript', *Screen Education* 39 (Summer, 1981).

48. See the famous analysis in terms of 'scopophilia' in Laura Mulvey, 'Visual pleasure and narrative cinema', *Screen* 16 (3) (Autumn, 1975).

49. Is it significant, for instance, that Barthes does not mention 'internal' narrative in his view of the omnipresence of the narrative form, *Image-Music-Text* (Routledge, 1977), p. 79. Does this absence suggest a larger structuralist difficulty with inner speech?

50. The ideas of the last few paragraphs are still in the process of being worked out in the CCCS Popular Memory Group. For some preliminary considerations about the character of oral-historical texts, see Popular Memory Group, 'Popular memory: theory, politics, method' in CCCS, *Making Histories*. I have found some of the essays in Daniel Bertaux, *Biography and Society: The Life History Approach in the Social Sciences* (Sage, 1981) useful to argue with, especially Agnes Hankiss, 'Ontologies of the self: on the mythological rearranging of one's life history'.

51. Some of the best and most influential work in cultural studies has been based on personal experience and private memory. Richard Hoggart's *The Uses of Literacy* is the most celebrated example, but, in general, students of culture should have the courage to use their personal experience more, more explicitly and more systematically. In this sense cultural studies is a heightened, differentiated form of everyday activities and living. Collective activities of this kind, attempting to understand not just 'common' experiences but real diversities and antagonisms, are especially important, if they can be managed, and subject to the caveats which follow.

52. This is forcefully argued by Paul Jones in '"Organic" Intellectuals and the Generation of English Cultural Studies', *Thesis Eleven* 5/6, 1982, 85–124.

53. See Dave Morley and Ken Worpole (eds), *The Republic of Letters: Working Class Writing and Local Publishing* (Comedia, 1982). For a more external and critical view, see 'Popular memory' in *Making Histories*. Also instructive is the debate between Ken Worpole, Stephen Yeo and Gerry White in Raphael Samuel (ed.), *People's History and Socialist Theory* (Routledge and Kegan Paul, 1981).

54. Some CCCS work is not exempt from this difficulty. Some of these criticisms apply, for instance, to *Resistance through Rituals*, especially parts of the theoretical overviews.

55. What follows is based, in rather too composite a way perhaps, on the work of Paul Willis, Angela McRobbie, Dick Hebdige, Christine Griffin, and Dorothy Hobson and on discussions with other ethnographic researchers in the Centre. See especially Paul Willis, *Learning to Labour*, Paul Willis, *Profane Culture* (Routledge and Kegan Paul, 1978); Angela McRobbie, 'Working-class girls and femininity' and Dorothy Hobson, 'Housewives: isolation as oppression', in *Women Take Issue*: Dick Hebdige, *Subculture* Routledge, 1979); Christine Griffin, CCCS Stencilled Papers 69 and 70. For an all-too-rare discussion of method in this area, see Paul Willis, 'Notes on method' in Hall *et al.*, *Culture, Media, Language*.

6

British cultural studies and television

John Fiske

The term *culture*, as used in the phrase 'cultural studies', is neither aesthetic nor humanist in emphasis, but political. Culture is not conceived of as the aesthetic ideals of form and beauty found in great art, or in more humanist terms as the voice of the 'human spirit' that transcends boundaries of time and nation to speak to a hypothetical universal man (the gender is deliberate – women play little or no role in this conception of culture). Culture is not, then, the aesthetic products of the human spirit acting as a bulwark against the tide of grubby industrial materialism and vulgarity, but rather a way of living within an industrial society that encompasses all the meanings of that social experience.

Cultural studies is concerned with the generation and circulation of meanings in industrial societies. (The study of culture in nonindustrial societies may well require a different theoretical base, though Claude Lévi-Strauss's work has proved of value in studying the culture of both types of society). But the tradition developed in Britain in the 1970s necessarily focused on culture in industrial societies. In this chapter I shall draw largely upon the work done at the University of Birmingham's Centre for Contemporary Cultural Studies (CCCS) under Stuart Hall, with some references to the works of Raymond Williams and those appearing in the journal *Screen*. The cultural studies developed at the CCCS is essentially Marxist in the traditions of Louis Althusser and Antonio Gramsci, though this Marxism is inflected sometimes with a structuralist accent, sometimes with an ethnographic one.

Some basic Marxist assumptions underlie all British works in cultural studies. As Mimi White (1992) notes, they start with the belief that meanings and the making of them (which together constitute culture) are indivisibly linked to social structure and can only be explained in terms of that structure and its history. Correlatively, the social structure is held in place by, among other forces, the meanings that culture produces; as Stuart Hall says, 'A set of social relations obviously requires meanings and frameworks which underpin them and hold them in place'.[1] These meanings are not only meanings of social experience, but also meanings of self, that is, constructions of social identity that enable people living in industrial capitalist societies to make sense of themselves and their social relations. Meanings of experience and meanings of the subject (or self) who has that experience are finally part of the same cultural process.

Also underlying this work is the assumption that capitalist societies are divided societies. The primary axis of division was originally thought to be class, though gender and race have now joined it as equally significant producers of social difference. Other axes of division are nation, age group, religion, occupation, education, political allegiance, and so on. Society, then, is not an organic whole but a complex network of groups, each with different interests and related to each other in terms of their power relationship with the dominant classes. Social relations are understood in terms of social power, in terms of a structure of domination and subordination that is never static but is always the site of contestation and struggle. Social power is the power to get one's class or group interest served by the social structure as a whole, and social struggle – or, in traditional Marxist terms, the class struggle – is the contestation of this power by the subordinate groups. In the domain of culture, this contestation takes the form of the struggle for meaning, in which the dominant classes attempt to 'naturalize' the meanings that serve their interests into the 'common sense' of society as a whole, whereas subordinate classes resist this process in various ways and to varying degrees and try to make meanings that serve their own interests. Some feminist work provides a clear example of this cultural struggle and contestation. Angela McRobbie and Lisa Lewis, for instance, both show how young girls are able to contest the patriarchal ideology structured into such films as *Flashdance* or the pop stars Madonna and Cindy Lauper and produce feminine readings of them.[2]

The attempt of the dominant classes to naturalize their meanings rarely, if ever, results from the conscious intention of individual members of those classes (though resistance to it is often, though not always, both conscious and intentional). Rather, it must be understood as the work of an ideology inscribed in the cultural and social practices of a class and therefore of the members of that class. And this brings us to another basic assumption: culture is ideological.

The cultural studies tradition does not view ideology in its vulgar Marxist sense of 'false consciousness', for that has built into it the assumption that a true consciousness is not only possible but will actually occur when history brings about a proletarian society. This sort of idealism seems inappropriate to the late twentieth century, which appears to have demonstrated not the inevitable self-destruction of capitalism but its unpredicted (by Marx) ability to reproduce itself and to incorporate into itself the forces of resistance and opposition. History casts doubts on the possibility of a society without ideology, in which people have a true consciousness of their social relations.

Structuralism, another important influence on British cultural studies, also denies the possibility of a true consciousness, for it argues that reality can only be comprehended through language or other cultural meaning systems. Thus the idea of an objective, empirical 'truth' is untenable. Truth must always be understood in terms of how it is made, for whom, and at what time it is 'true'. Consciousness is never the product of truth or reality but rather of culture, society, and history.

Althusser and Gramsci were the theorists who offered a way of accommodating both structuralism (and, incidentally, Freudianism) and the history of capitalism in the twentieth century with Marxism. For Althusser, ideology is not a static set of ideas imposed upon the subordinate by the dominant classes but rather a dynamic process constantly reproduced and reconstituted in practice – that is, in the ways that people think, act, and understand themselves and their relationship to society.[3] He rejects the old idea that the economic base of society determines the entire cultural superstructure. He replaces this base/superstructure model with his theory of overdetermination, which not only allows the superstructure to influence the base but also produces a model of the relationship between ideology and culture that is not determined solely by economic relations. At the heart of this theory is the notion of ideological state apparatuses (ISAs), by which he means social institutions such as the family, the educational system, language, the media, the political system, and so on. These institutions produce in people the tendency to behave and think in socially acceptable ways (as opposed to repressive state apparatuses such as the police force or the law, which coerce people into behaving according to the social norms). The social norms, or that which is socially acceptable, are of course neither neutral nor objective; they have developed in the interests of those with social power, and they work to maintain their sites of power by naturalizing them into the commonsense – the only – social positions for power. Social norms are ideologically slanted in favor of a particular class or group of classes but are accepted as natural by other classes, even when the interests of those other classes are directly opposed by the ideology reproduced by living life according to those norms.

Social norms are realized in the day-to-day workings of the ideological state apparatuses. Each one of these institutions is 'relatively autonomous', according to Althusser, and there are no overt connections between it and any of the others – the legal system is not explicitly connected to the school system nor to the media, for example – yet they all perform similar ideological work. They are all patriarchal; they are all concerned with the getting and keeping of wealth and possessions; and they all endorse the individualism and competition between individuals. But the most significant feature of ISAs is that they all present themselves as socially neutral, as not favoring one particular class over any other. Each presents itself as a principled institutionalization of equality: the law, the media, and education all claim, loudly and often, to treat all individuals equally and fairly. The fact that the norms used to define equality and fairness are those derived from the interests of the white, male, middle classes is more or less adequately disguised by these claims of principle, though feminists and those working for racial and class harmony may claim that this disguise can be torn off with relative ease.

Althusser's theory of overdetermination explains this congruence between the 'relatively autonomous' institutions by looking not to their roots in a common, determining economic base but to an overdetermining network of ideological interrelationships among all of them. The institutions appear autonomous only at the official level of stated policy, though the belief in this 'autonomy' is essential for their ideological work. At the unstated level of ideology, however, each institution is related to all the others by an unspoken web of ideological interconnections, so that the operation of any one of them is 'overdetermined' by its complex, invisible network of interrelationships with all the others. Thus the educational system, for example, cannot tell a story about the nature of the individual different from those told by the legal system, the political system, the family, and so on.

Ideology is not, then, a static set of ideas through which we view the world but a dynamic social practice, constantly in process, constantly reproducing itself in the ordinary workings of these apparatuses. It also works at the micro-level of the individual. To understand this we need to replace the idea of the individual with that of the subject. The individual is produced by nature, the subject by culture. Theories of the individual concentrate on differences between people and explain these differences as natural. Theories of the subject, on the other hand, concentrate on people's common experiences in a society as being the most productive way of explaining who (we think) we are. Althusser believes that we are all constituted as subjects-in-ideology by the ISAs, that the ideological norms naturalized in their practices constitute not only the sense of the world for us, but also our sense of ourselves, our sense of identity, and our sense of our relations to other people and to society in general. Thus we are each of us constituted as a subject in, and subject to, ideology. The subject, there-fore, is a social construction, not a natural one. A biological female can have a masculine subjectivity (that is, she can make sense of the world and of her self and her place in that world through patriarchal ideology). Similarly, a black person can have a white subjectivity and a member of the working classes a middle-class one.

The ideology theory of the subject differs in emphasis, though not fundamentally, from that developed in psychoanalysis by placing greater emphasis on social and historical conditions, particularly those of class. Althusser drew upon Freudian theory to develop his idea of the subject: As Ann Kaplan notes, feminists too have used psychoanalytic theory, though much more sophisticatedly, to theorize the gendered subject. This gendered subject is more rooted in psychological processes, the ideological subject of Althusser in historical and social ones.

But both theories stress the role played by the media and language in this constant construction of the subject, by which we mean the constant reproduction of ideology in people. Althusser uses the words *interpella-tion* and *hailing* to describe this work of the media. These terms derive from the idea that any language, whether it be verbal, visual, tactile, or whatever, is part of social relations and that in communicating with someone we are reproducing social relationships.

In communicating with people, our first job is to 'hail' them, almost as if hailing a cab. To answer, they have to recognize that it is to them, and not to someone else, that we are talking. This recognition derives from signs, carried in our language, of whom we think they are. We will hail a child differently from an adult, a male differently from a female, someone whose status is lower than ours differently from someone in a higher social position. In responding to our hail, the addressees recognize the social position our language has constructed, and if their response is cooperative, they adopt this same position. Hailing is the process by which language identifies and constructs a social position for the addressee. Interpellation is the larger process whereby language constructs social relations for both parties in an act of communication and thus locates them in the broader map of social relations in general.

Hailing is obviously crucial at the start of a 'conversation', though its ideological work continues throughout. Look, for instance, at the opening statements of the anchor and reporter on a US network news report in April 1991:

> *Anchor*: There is growing concern tonight about the possible economic impact that a nationwide railroad strike set for midnight tonight poses. The unions and the railroads remain deadlocked. Wyatt Andrews brings us up to date on what President Bush and Congress may do about it.

> *Reporter*: By morning 230 000 rail workers might not be working on the railroad and the strike threatens millions of Americans. Just as thousands of commuters may find no train leaving the station beginning tonight at midnight.

The word *strike* hails us an antiunion, for 'striking' is constructed as a negative action by labor unions that 'threatens' the nation. By ascribing responsibility to the unions, the word hides the fact that management plays some role, possibly even a greater one, in the dispute. The report opposes the unions not to management but to 'the railroads' and thus excludes the unions from them. This exclusion of the unions from the railroads allows the unspoken management to become synonymous with them, and ideology continues its work by constructing the railroads not as an industry but as a national resource and so uses them as a metonym for the nation and, by extension, of 'us'. Recognizing ourselves in the national 'us' interpellated here, we participate in the work of ideology by adopting the antiunion subject position proposed for us. This subject-as-ideology is developed as the item progresses:

> *Passenger A*: Gas, miles, time. The highways are going to be packed. Not much we can do, though.

> *Passenger B*: I'm going to stay home. I've got an office in my home and I'm going to just stay there and work.

> *Reporter*: But the commuter inconvenience is nothing compared to the impact on freight trains. Up to half a million industrial jobs may be at stake. Whether it's cars in the heartland or chemicals in Kansas City, the railroads still carry more freight than either trucks or airplanes, meaning that the strike would threaten the heart of industrial America in the heart of this recession.

> *Railroad Official*: If we don't get this strike settled quickly a lot more people are going to be out of work, a lot more product is not going to be shipped and this economy's recovery is going to be set back immensely.

> *Reporter*: Negotiations meanwhile seem to be at bedrock bottom, on wages, on health care, and the number of workers per train. Both sides even late today

were on opposite tracks. The unions complain the railroad blocked raises and stonewalled the negotiations for three years. The railroads accuse the unions of protecting legions of workers who essentially do nothing.

Railroad Official: The issue with our union is between who works and who watches. That's the issue of whether we have excess people in the cab who don't have anything to do.

The national 'we' is constructed as hardworking producers at the personal level by the passengers and at the industrial level by the reporter. The repeated use of the 'heart' metaphor not only makes 'America' into a living, breathing body (like the one 'we' inhabit), but it constructs the unions as a potentially lethal disease, if not a stiletto-wielding assassin! The railroad official continues to conflate 'the railroads' (by which he means 'the management') with the national subject of the hard-working producer.

So far, the dispute has been cast solely in terms of the bad effects the unions have upon this national 'us', and only in the reporter's next segment do we receive a hint that there are causes of the dispute that may both justify it and implicate management in it. These hints are left floating, so we have no way of assessing the reasonableness of the wage claims, for instance. The generalized terms – 'on wages, on health care, on the number of workers per train' – contrast with the concrete realities of 230 000 unionists not working and of the millions of Americans, thousands of commuters, and up to half a million jobs that are threatened. We might like to think about the ideological practice of not allowing the unions to speak for themselves 'live', but of putting their case into the words of the reporter-management-'us'. Unionists would not, for instance, describe their negotiating opponents as 'the railroads', not would they categorize their arguments as mere 'complaints' while according management's the stronger status of 'accusations'.

The news item concludes by continuing the ideological practice that by now seems so natural and familiar:

Reporter: What exactly happens in the morning? If you are a commuter, check locally. Some Amtrak and commuter trains will be operating and some of the unions say they will strike only freight lines and not passenger trains. In Washington, watch Capitol Hill. Tomorrow President Bush is likely to ask Congress to impose a solution: the move, the unions say, plays right into the railroad's hands. The unions have all along warned the railroads would stall the negotiations and force tonight's strike all in the snug belief that Congress would bail them out.

As Mimi White (1992) points out, this view of ideology as a process constantly at work, constructing people as subjects in an ideology that always serves the interests of the dominant classes, found powerful theoretical support in Gramsci's theory of hegemony. Originally, *hegemony* referred to the way that one nation could exert ideological and social, rather than military or coercive, power over another. However, cultural theorists tend to use the term to describe the process by which a dominant class wins the willing consent of the subordinate classes to the system that ensures their subordination. This consent must be constantly won and rewon, for people's material social experience constantly reminds them of the disadvantages of subordination and thus poses a constant threat to the dominant class. Like Althusser's theory of ideology, hegemony does not denote a static power relationship but a constant process of struggle in which the big guns belong to the side of those with social power, but in which victory does not necessarily go to the big guns – or, at least, in which that victory is not necessarily total. Indeed, the theory of hegemony foregrounds the notion of ideological struggle much more than does Althusser's ideological theory, which at times tends to imply that the power of ideology and the ISAs to form the subject in ways that suit the interests of the dominant class is almost irresistible. Hegemony, on the other hand, posits a constant contradiction between ideology and the social experience of the subordinate that makes this interface into an inevitable site of ideological struggle. In hegemonic theory, ideology is constantly up against forces of resistance. Consequently it is engaged in a constant struggle not just to extend its power but to hold on to the territory it has already colonized.

This definition of culture as a constant site of struggle between those with and those without power underpins the most interesting current work in cultural studies. Earlier work in the tradition tended to show how the dominant ideology reproduced itself invisibly and inevitably in the forms of popular television.[4] Hall's influential essay 'Encoding/decoding' is often seen as a turning point in British cultural studies, for it introduces the idea that television programs do not have a single meaning but are relatively open texts, capable of being read in different ways by different people.[5] Hall also suggests that there is a necessary correlation between people's social situations and the meanings that they may generate from a television program. He thus postulates a possible tension between the structure of the text, which necessarily bears the dominant ideology, and the social situations of the viewers, which may position them at odds with that ideology. Reading or viewing television, then, becomes a process of negotiation between the viewer and the text. Use of the word *negotiation* is significant, for it implies both that there is a conflict of interests that needs to be reconciled in some way and that the process of reading television is one in which the reader is an active maker of meanings from the text, not a passive recipient of already constructed ones.

Hall developed his theory of the 'preferred reading' to account for this conflict of interests. He postulates three broad reading strategies produced by three generalized, not material, social positions that people may occupy in relation to the dominant ideology. These are the *dominant*, the *negotiated*, and the *oppositional*. The dominant reading is produced by a viewer situated to agree with and accept the dominant ideology and the subjectivity that it produces. A negotiated reading is one produced by a viewer who fits into the dominant ideology in general but who needs to inflect it locally to take account of his or her social position. This inflection may contain elements of resistance deriving from the perception of areas of conflict between the constructions of the dominant ideology and the viewer's more materially based construction of social experience. And finally there are readings produced by those whose social situation puts them into direct

opposition with the dominant ideology – these readings are termed oppositional.

The preferred reading theory proposes that TV programs generally prefer
a set of meanings that work to maintain the dominant ideologies but that
these meanings cannot be imposed, only preferred. Readers whose social
situations lead them to reject all or some constructions of the dominant
ideology will necessarily bring this social orientation to their reading of the
program.

Such negotiations of meaning occur not only with specific programs but
also with genres, for example that of the action-detective show (for decades
common on US television), which I propose to call 'muscle drama'. I would
include in this genre such hits of the 1970s and 1980s as *Starsky and Hutch*,
The A-Team, and *Magnum, P.I.*, as well as more recent variants, such as
Simon and Simon, Hunter, and *Jake and the Fatman*. A dominant reader of the
genre would find pleasure in it because it reproduces in him/her a subject
position that fits easily into the dominant ideology, bolsters that ideology as
an adequate way of making sense of the world, and therefore affirms the
subject position as the natural one from which to view the world. The
typical male hero can be seen as literally embodying patriarchal capitalism. The ideology works both through the progress and resolution of each
week's narrative and through the frame of that narrative – that is, those
elements of the program that are consistent from week to week. They are
not part of the conflict to be resolved in each episode and therefore form the
basic, uninspected assumptions, or common sense, through and in which
the dominant ideology naturalizes itself. The dominant ideology works in a
number of overlapping specific ideologies: masculinity, individualism,
competition, all merge 'naturally' into the general (that is, the dominant)
ideology of patriarchal capitalism.

This is a masculine genre, dominated by male heroes. Maleness is a fact
of nature, but masculinity is a cultural constraint that gives meaning to
maleness by opposing it to femininity. Shere Hite investigated men's
opinions of what makes a man a man. The list of characteristics she
generated began with such qualities as self-assurance, lack of fear, the
ability to take control, autonomy and self-sufficiency, leadership, depend-
ability, and achievement. These qualities work along two main avenues:
self-sufficiency, which stresses the absence of a need to depend on others;
and assertiveness, expressed as the ability to lead others and to influence
events and most readily experienced in performance and achievement.[6]
Freudian explanations of how masculinity is achieved in childhood point
to the boy's rejection of his desire for his mother because it puts him in a
position of rivalry with his father. He then identifies with his father in order
to gain access to masculine power and authority. The price he pays,
however, is the guilt-producing rejection of his mother and the consequent
suppression in himself of the feminine characteristics that threaten male
power and independence. These characteristics are essentially ones of
nurturing and of intimacy. The absence of women from significant roles
in most muscle drama represents the suppression and devaluation of
feminine characteristics in patriarchal constructions of masculinity.

Like all ideological constructs, masculinity is constantly under threat – it can never rest on its laurels. The threats come internally from its insecure bases in the rejection of the mother (and the guilt that this inspires) and the suppression of the feminine, and externally from social forces, which may vary from the rise of the women's movement to the way that the organization of work denies many men the independence and power that their masculinity requires. Thus masculinity constantly has to be reachieved, rewon. This constant need to reachieve masculinity is one of the underlying reasons for the popularity of the frequent television display of male performance. Masculinity forms a link between muscle drama and pornography. For, as Andrew Moye points out, pornography reduces masculinity to performance – in this case, the performance of the penis.[7] In a patriarchy, masculinity must be able to cope with any situation; it becomes less a construction of man than of superman. It is the perpetual gap between the actual male performance and the supermale performance proposed by patriarchy that these programs are striving to close. Similarly, it is the gap between the penis and the phallus that pornography strives to close. The penis is the natural sign of maleness; the phallus is the cultural sign of masculinity – the totality of meanings, rights, and power that a culture ascribes to maleness. Hence these shows, in their role as 'masculine definers', are full of phallic symbols, particularly guns as agents of male power (think how rare it is for a female on TV to use a gun successfully, particularly to kill a male). They are also full of machinery, particularly cars, as extensions of the masculine body in powerful, spectacular action.

This male power must be tempered with notions of duty and service; it must be used in the interest of the weak or of the nation. If used for personal gain, it becomes the mark of the villain. So masculine power involves both exerting and submitting to authority. This is one of the reasons why the male team or duo is such a popular formation of the masculine hero, and why this hero formation so commonly works on the side of, but in tension with, an institution of official authority. Another reason is that the male bonding inherent in such a formation allows for an intimacy that excludes the threat of the feminine. Feminine intimacy centers on the relationship itself and produces a dependence on the other that threatens masculine independence – consequently, any woman who attracts a hero has to be rejected at the end of the episode. Male bonding, on the other hand, allows an interpersonal dependency that is goal-centered, not relationship-centered, and thus serves masculine performance instead of threatening it. The hero team also compensates for male insecurity: any inadequacies of one team member are compensated by the strengths of another, so the teams become composite constructions of masculinity. All the traits embodied in one man would make him into an unbelievable superman, and ideology – closely connected to fantasy though it be – has to be grounded in credibility, that is, in a conventional construction of the realistic. If it were not, it would be unable to work on, and be put to work by, the viewers.

I have concentrated on how the ideology of masculinity is actively at work in the muscle drama. It is comparatively easy to see how this merges indistinguishably into the overlapping ideologies of individualism, competition, and a form of 'social Darwinism' that proposes that morality is always on the side of eventual winners. These ideologies, in turn, merge into a particular construction of American and Western nationalism – a right-wing version of the nation that sees it as masculine (exerting in the international sphere power over others in the service of the weak or of a higher morality), based on competitive individualism and social Darwinism. Such an ideology serves, at the broader level, to link this genre with the rehabilitation of the Vietnam war that occurred during the 1980s. Heroes like Magnum, T.J. Hooker, one of the Simon brothers, and the whole A-Team developed their masculinity in Vietnam. Their popularity was part of the remasculinization of Reagan's America after its 'softness' under Carter and served to underwrite ideologically Reagan's Grenada 'rescue' and, more recently, Bush's invasions of Panama and Iraq. Ideologically, this genre as it developed in the 1980s worked to ground problematic political acts in the much-less-questioned and therefore more natural-seeming construction of masculinity.

The generic hero team is conventionally constructed to embody, not just the ideologies of masculinity and nation, but also the overlapping ones of race. In *Magnum, P.I.*, for instance, T.C., the driver/pilot and engineering expert, represented masculinity as physical power and its mechanical extensions. His blackness (like that of B.A. in *The A-Team*, who performed a similar ideological role) introduces the racial dimension: physical power may be the basis of masculinity, but because it needs leadership and social control to be acceptable, it therefore ranks low in the hierarchy of masculine traits. It is noticeable how often the hero team contains a nonwhite in a subordinate position, from Ahab and Queequeg in *Moby Dick*, through the Lone Ranger and Tonto, to the television hero teams of *Ironside*, *The A-Team*, and *Magnum, P.I.* In *Starsky and Hutch*, Starsky, the dark Jewish one, was the driver; Hutch, the blond, college-educated Aryan, was the leader. Their superior officer may have been black, but, as is often the case, the role of the official superior was narratively subordinated to the hero team. In *Miami Vice* Crocket was blond and white, while his partner Tubbs was a black-looking cocktail of nonwhite races.

The reader whose social position is one of ease with the dominant ideology, who works *with* the genre, will use its foregrounded ideology to reaffirm his (gender deliberate) ideological frame, through which he views the world and makes sense of both himself and his social experience. In responding to the program's interpellation, he adopts the subject position it constructs for him. Althusser's account of the power of the dominant ideology working through language and texts to construct the reader as a subject in ideology can really only account for Hall's 'dominant reading'. Gramsci's notion of hegemony, with its emphasis on the dominant ideology's constant struggle to win the consent of the subordinate and to incorporate or diffuse oppositional forces, underlies Hall's next two reading strategies – those that produce negotiated and oppositional readings.

A negotiated reading is one that inflects the dominant ideology toward the social experience of a particular viewing group. Thus, boys watching a muscle drama might concentrate on the performance side. Their social situation denies them the ability to exert the power (either physically, because their bodies are still immature, or socially, because of their low hierarchical position in the family or school) that society tells them they should if they are to be 'masculine'. We know that B.A., the muscular black driver and mechanic in *The A-Team*, was particularly popular with white youths. Presumably they foregrounded his strength, engineering expertise, and low rank in the hero team over his race and therefore made sense of his subordinate position as a way of articulating their subordination in society, not the powerlessness of blacks in a white hegemony. Black youths, however, would have been more likely to use B.A.'s blackness, his strengths, and the gold chains he always wore (which Mr T said were symbols of his people's slavery) to make sense of their constant struggle to assert and extend their own position in society.

Female viewers of the genre will also negotiate it toward their interests. The physical attractiveness of Hunter, Jake, Magnum, or Crockett may be read as an integral part of their protection of the weak. Their rejection of intimacy with any one woman would not be seen as a latent recognition of women's threat to masculinity, nor as a representation of the suppression of the feminine in the masculine psyche and therefore of the subordination of women in a patriarchal society (for the two are structural reflections of each other). It would rather be seen as a means of maintaining their masculine freedom to serve all women and provide them with the security and justice that their material social position may deny them. Masculinity in heroes like these can be read, then, not as the embodiment of masculine oppression in patriarchy, but as the patriarchal agent that rights the wrongs and corrects the deficiencies of the system in practice.

These sorts of negotiated readings are ones produced by ideologically cooperative readers who read 'with' the structures of the text and seek to match their social experiences with the ideology-in-the-text. Actually, they produce almost dominant readings, which may lead us to speculate whether the 'pure' dominant reading is ever achieved. There is probably no one audience group positioned in perfect ideological centrality. All groups will need to 'shift' the text slightly to fit their social positions, in which case all readings become, as Horace Newcomb suggests, negotiated ones.[8] But if this is so, it is still valuable to recognize that negotiated readings can occur on a scale stretching from the ideologically central to the deviant. Thus a macho teenager, at the point of maximum opposition to authority, may read the violence in the genre as justified masculinity that overrides the 'weakness' of its use in the service of the weak or of 'natural justice'. Such a reading may see the failure of the police or official authorities as a criticism of them and of the society they stand for, and in this way may veer toward the oppositional because it plays down the contextual ideologies within which that of masculinity operates and from which it acquires its social and moral acceptability.

Readings at this end of the scale stop being negotiated and become oppositional when they go 'against' the text to deconstruct the dominant ideology. Thus, a feminist could read the genre as a blatant display of patriarchal chauvinism and how it sells itself to society. This reading would produce, not pleasure (except the wry pleasure of recognizing that patriarchy is up to its tricks yet again), but annoyance. That annoyance could be used to incite political action, either in the form of consciousness-raising or more directly. Similarly, a black activist could find the subordinate position of T.C., B.A., and Tubbs in the hero formation a perfect example of white hegemony at work and a spur to further oppositional practice.

We have already traced the dominant or preferred reading of the TV news report on the railroad dispute. An oppositional reading, possibly by an Amtrak blue-collar worker, might read in the mediated versions of the union case what has been repressed or distorted and would thus make sense of the story not as an account of the dispute but as a representation of 'what we unionists are always up against in this society'.

A negotiated reading, however, might pick up the same hints but would use them to mean something like, 'I bet there's more to this than they're telling us here: Amtrak management is not exactly the most efficient or progressive in the country'. Although such a reading does not accept the preferred reading of the story, neither does it challenge the dominant ideology that such a reading prefers. It negotiates a position for this specific occasion.

The typical reading of television is probably, as Newcomb argues, a negotiated one.[9] This is an underlying assumption of the cultural studies approach. For if our society is seen not as homogeneous but as a structure of different interest groups, and if television is to appeal to a large number of people in our society, then it follows that the television audience must not be seen as a homogeneous mass but as a mix of social groups, each in a different relationship to the dominant ideology. However complex and difficult it might be to describe these relationships, they can always be placed on a scale that ranges from *acceptance* to *opposition to* the dominant ideology. The television text can only be popular if it is open enough to admit a range of negotiated readings through which various social groups can find meaningful articulations of their own relationships to the dominant ideology. Any television text must, then, be polysemic to a certain extent, for the structured heterogeneity of the audience requires a correspondingly structured heterogeneity of meanings in the text. The hero team is a significant ideological formation here, as it provides for a greater 'openness' than the single hero. Its greater variety of opportunities for identification enables various social groups to negotiate appropriate points of entry into the dominant ideology.

This polysemy is never free but is constrained and structured, for it exists always against the dominant ideology, which works to close off alternate or resisting meanings and to homogenize the preferred ones around its own interests. Mikhail Bakhtin's theory of heteroglossia is an attempt to explain this process.[10] Bakhtin analyzes the difference between heteroglossic or multitongued texts, which contain the many voices of subordinated groups, and monoglossic or more homogeneous ones, which carry only the voice of the dominant. He uses the metaphor of a spinning wheel to illustrate the difference: at the center is a relatively homogeneous hub of domination and control, and around the circumference are multiple, heterogeneous points of subordination that form potential points of resistance. Centripetal forces, those tending toward the center, are ones of hegemony and domination working through homogenization, whereas centrifugal forces, those tending toward the circumference, are ones of resistance and difference working through heterogeneity. The two are always opposed to each other, and television texts are held in an unstable tension between them.

An earlier version of this theory, and one that has been very influential in British cultural studies, is Valentin N. Volosinov's account of 'multiaccentuality'.[11] This theory proposes that the prime determinant of the meaning of a sign is the social context of its use and not, as structuralism argues, its relationship to other signs in the structure of a sign system.

In capitalism the social context of a sign's use is typically one of social struggle, so the meaning of the sign becomes part of that social struggle. The same word can be spoken in different 'accents' according to who is using it, and thus to 'accent' a word is to inflect its meaning with the social interests of a particular group against those of others. When the word *nigger* is accented by contemporary black rap artists in their music videos, to take an example, they are giving it *their* meanings of blackness, racial subordination, and prejudice against the historically dominant white ones. In doing so, they are exploiting the multiaccentuality of the sign 'nigger' and are thus politically engaging in racial relations. (They are also, incidentally, engaging in another struggle for meaning, this time within race relations but across class relations, with those who prefer to be called 'African American' and those who prefer to be called 'black'). The struggle over the sign 'nigger' – and thus over the racial identities and politics of those categorized by it – is a more confrontational version of the racial struggle engaged in by the previous generation over the multiaccentuality of 'black' in the 'black is beautiful' movement. It is not just a struggle over the meanings of a word but over who has the power to control those meanings. This is important, for the power to control the meaning of social experience is a crucial part of controlling the social relations, identities, and behaviors of those (both blacks and whites) involved in that experience. The semiotic struggle does not reflect the social struggle but is part of it.

The interests of the socially dominant are served by 'uniaccentuality', that is, by limiting the meanings of a sign to those that it bears when spoken with the dominant accent, thereby taking it out of the realm of struggle. The TV news report analyzed above, for instance, spoke the word *railroads* with a managerial accent and thus excluded the different and contradictory meanings that a union accent would have given it. Again, social and ideological domination is seen to work through homogeneity and the construction of social difference within this unity. So it is in the interests of dominant whites to construct both the blue-collar classes and other races as different from and subordinate to them and to contain this difference within a homogeneous ideology. The interests of subordinate groups, however, are served by exploiting multiaccentuality or heteroglossia, for this enables them to 'speak' their difference from the dominant position in *their* accents and to engage in the struggle to make sense of social difference in their own terms rather than submitting to those proposed and preferred by the dominant group.

An important body of cultural studies work has derived from the recognition of the heteroglossia or multiaccentuality of TV texts and the heterogeneity of audiences. Such scholars as David Morley, John Corner and his colleagues, Angela McRobbie, and Robert Hodge and David Tripp have set out to discover how actual audience groups actively use television as part of their own cultures – that is, use it to make meanings that are useful to them in making sense of their own social experiences and therefore of themselves.[12] These scholars are in opposition to the other main strand of British (and European) study of culture, which is centered around the journal *Screen* and has come to be known as Screen Theory. Screen Theory draws on a combination of structuralism and semiotics with psychoanalysis and Marxism to argue the power of the text over the viewing subject and to analyze, with great theoretical sophistication, the textual strategies that operate to position the viewing subject within dominant ideology. David Morley has clearly elaborated the theoretical and methodological differences between the two schools.[13]

Morley tested Hall's preferred reading theory in the field. He took a television program that he and Charlotte Brunsdon had previously subjected to detailed cultural analysis, showed it to groups of people, and then held discussions on their reactions to the program and its meanings for them.[14] He turned to groups rather than individuals because he was interested in the shared, and therefore social, dimensions of reading. The groups were defined largely by occupation – bank managers, apprentices, students, trade unionists, and so on – because occupation is a prime definer of social class, and class was, in Hall's theory, the prime producer of social difference and therefore of different readings. (A few of Morley's groups, however, were defined by gender or race – black unemployed women, for example.) What Morley found was that the preferred reading theory overemphasized the role of class in the production of semiotic differences and underestimated the variety of readings that could be made. Thus the readings showed some interesting and unexpected cross-class similarities: bank managers and apprentices, for example, produced broadly similar readings despite their class differences; so, too, did some university students and shop stewards. We could explain these apparent anomalies by suggesting that the apprentices and bank managers were similarly constructed as subjects of a capitalist ideology, in that both were inserting themselves into the dominant system (albeit at different points) and thus had a shared interest in its survival and success. Some university students (not all, by any means) and trade union officials, however, were in institutions that provided them with ways of criticizing the dominant system and they thus produced more oppositional readings.

Another interesting example of class difference emerged as one of the findings in a recent study by John Corner, Kay Richardson, and Natalie Fenton on the ways in which different audiences read different British TV programs dealing with nuclear power in the wake of the Chernobyl explosion in the Soviet Union.[15] The most 'mainstream' of the programs contained reassurances by white-coated scientists as to the high safety standards of British installations. Middle-class and educated viewers tended to accept these assurances at face value: some working-class viewers, however, were much more skeptical and produced readings along the lines of, 'Well, they would say that, wouldn't they?' This skepticism is a product of the constant experience of class difference in their workaday lives and was brought from there to contradict a TV text with a strongly preferred meaning. It was a social discourse in negotiation with a televisual one.

Morley's study led him to develop a theory of discourse rather than one of class to account for the different readings of television. A discourse is a socially produced way of talking or thinking about a topic. It is defined by reference to the area of social experience that it makes sense of, to the social location from which that sense is made, and to the linguistic or signifying system by which that sense is both made and circulated. When the media report, as they typically do, that management 'offers' but trade unions 'demand', they are using the mass media discourse of industrial relations, which is located in a middle-class position. They could equally well report (but never do) that the unions 'offered' to work for an extra five percent, but management 'demanded' that they work for two percent. The consistent ascription of the generous 'offer' and the grasping 'demand' to management and unions, respectively, is clear evidence of the social location of this particular discourse. A discourse, then, is a socially located way of making sense of an important area of social experience.

A television text is, therefore, a discourse (or a number of discourses if it contains contradictions), and the reader's consciousness is similarly made up of a number of discourses through which she/he makes sense of his/her social experience. Morley defines reading a television text as that moment when the discourses of the reader meet the discourses of the text. Reading becomes a negotiation between the social sense inscribed in the program and the meanings of social experience made by its wide variety of viewers; this negotiation is a discursive one.

But not all TV audiences read all the discourses in a TV text. For instance, a study in which I was recently involved showed how homeless men watched television in their church shelter.[16] They rarely watched broadcast television because the norms of domestic life and of work and leisure that were structured into the regular broadcast schedule were irrelevant to them; they expressed their opposition to the dominant ideology by avoiding expressions of it. Instead, they preferred to watch movies – almost always violent ones – on the VCR. In viewing these, they opposed the dominant ideology, or preferred reading, by avoiding those parts of the text that worked actively to promote it and by paying greater attention to those parts that opposed it. So, while watching *Die Hard*, they cheered enthusiastically when the villains killed the company's chief executive officer and when they destroyed a police armored vehicle and its occupants, but they switched off the tape before the end, when the hero and the police force restored law and order and reconfirmed the dominant ideology.

A later study by David Morley found that the way in which TV was watched was as significant as the readings made from it.[17] In the lower-class household he studied, Morley found that the process of watching TV was a key site for the struggles of gender politics. The male of the household tended to dominate the selection of viewing and, in particular, to monopolize the remote control. He employed masculine values in this selection, so that programs appealing to masculine tastes (ones that showed 'real life' outside the home – news, documentaries, sports, or the masculine muscle drama) were seen as 'better' than ones appealing to feminine tastes (those concerned with people and relationships, such as soap operas). He also attempted to control the conditions of viewing and would shush his wife or children if they distracted him with noise or conversation.

Cultural studies sees the television experience (that is, the entity constituted by the text and the activity of viewing it) as a constant dynamic movement between similarity and difference. The dimension of similarity is that of the dominant ideology that is structured into the forms of program and is common to all the viewers from whom that program is popular. The dimension of difference, however, accounts for the wide variety of groups who must be reached if the program is to be popular with a large audience. These groups will be positioned to the dominant ideology in different ways, and these ways will be paralleled in the different readings they make of the program and the different ways in which they watch it. The play between similarity and difference is one way of experiencing the struggle between hegemony and resistance.

This emphasis on the reader and the struggle for meaning necessarily reduces the prime position granted to the text by the cultural theorists of the 1970s. The text can no longer be seen as a self-sufficient entity that bears either the dominant ideology or its own meaning and exerts a similar influence on all its readers. Rather, it is seen as a potential of meanings that can be activated in a number of ways. Of course, this potential is proscribed and is thus neither infinite nor free; the text does not determine its meaning so much as delimit the arena of the struggle for that meaning by marking the terrain within which its variety of readings can be negotiated. This discursive negotiation that we now understand reading to be also means that the boundaries of the text are fluid and unstable. Raymond Williams suggested in the early seventies that television was not a discrete series of programs or texts but a 'flow' in which programs, commercials, newsbreaks, and promotional spots all merged into a continuous cultural experience. More recently, John Hartley has suggested that television is a 'leaky' medium whose meanings constantly spill over into other areas of life.[18]

Angela McRobbie has also explored the permeability of the boundary between television and other forms of cultural experience. Her study of girls and dance shows that girls derive similar pleasure and meanings from dancing in discos and from viewing films and television programs such as *Flashdance* or *Fame*.[19] On one level of reading, the narrative form and pleasure of *Flashdance* clearly work hegemonically – the female factory worker uses her dancing skills to win a place in a ballet company and marry the boss's son. In the process she displays her body for patriarchal pleasure; indeed, her beautiful body is crucial to her successful move up the social hierarchy (from breakdancing to ballet and marrying into management). Women, so the hegemonic reading would go, are rewarded for their ability to use their beauty and talents to give pleasure to men. But McRobbie has shown that this is not the only reading. She has found among teenage girls a set of meanings for dance and female sexuality that contest and struggle against the patriarchal hegemony. For these girls, dance is a form of autoeroticism, a pleasure in their own bodies and sexuality that gives them an identity not dependent upon the male gaze of approval. *Their* discourse of dance gives a coherent meaning to dancing in discos or to watching filmic and televisual representations of dance that asserts their subcultural identity and difference from the rest of society. This meaning is one that they have made out of the cultural forms provided for them by patriarchy.

McRobbie's study preceded the movie and TV series *Dirty Dancing* by some years, but her findings and analysis still apply if one major difference is taken into account. *Dirty Dancing* reverses the gender politics of the class relations between hero and heroine. In this scenario, the hero is of a lower class than the heroine, but it is still the socially subordinate person who uses the control of his body in dance not only to assert his own social worth but also to overcome his subordination. The upper-middle-class heroine finds, through dancing and through her relations with the working-class hero, an authenticity of identity and experience that is lacking in the masquerade necessary for her to conform to the version of femininity proposed by a patriarchial, bourgeois society. Exploring the strategies by which subordinate subcultures make their own meanings in resistance to the dominant is currently one of the most productive strands of cultural studies.

Madonna, who has been a major phenomenon of popular culture for almost a decade, can provide us with a good case study. Her success has arguably been due largely to television and to her music videos; most critics have nothing good to say about her music, but they have a lot to say about her image – 'the Madonna look'. The simple view of her success would attribute it to her skill in manipulating her sexuality to make as much money as possible, largely from one of the most powerless and exploitable sections of the community – young girls.

But such an account is inadequate (though not necessarily inaccurate as far as it goes) because it assumes that Madonna fans are, in Stuart Hall's phrase, 'cultural dupes', able to be manipulated at will and against their own interests by the moguls of the culture industry.[20] Such a manipulation is not only economic but also ideological, because the economic system requires the ideology of patriarchal capitalism to underpin and naturalize it; economics and ideology can never be separated. There is plenty of evidence to support this view, too. Madonna's videos exploit the sexuality of her face and body and frequently show her in postures of submission ('Burning Up') or subordination to men. As Ann Kaplan points out (Kaplan, 1992) Madonna's physical similarity to Marilyn Monroe is stressed (particularly in the video of 'Material Girl'), an intertextual reference to another star commonly thought to owe her success to her ability to embody masculine fantasies. All this would suggest that she is teaching her young female fans to see themselves as men would see them – that is, she is hailing them as feminine subjects within patriarchy and as such is an agent of patriarchal hegemony.

But if her fans are not 'cultural dupes' – if, rather, they actively choose to watch, listen to, and imitate Madonna rather than anyone else – there must be some gaps or spaces in her image that escape ideological control and allow her audiences to make meanings that connect with *their* social experience. For many of her audiences, this social experience is one of powerlessness and subordination, and if Madonna as a site of meaning is not to naturalize this, she must offer opportunities for resisting it. Her image becomes, then, not an ideological role model for young girls in patriarchy, but a site of semiotic struggle between the forces of patriarchal control and feminine resistance, of capitalism and the subordinate, of the adult and the young.

Cultural studies, in its current state of development, offers two over-lapping methodological strategies that can usefully be combined to help us understand how this cultural struggle operates. One derives from ethno-graphy and encourages us to study the meanings that the fans of Madonna actually *do* (or appear to) make of her. This involves listening to them, reading the letters they write to fan magazines, or observing their beha-viour at home or in public. The fans' words or behaviour are not, of course, empirical facts that speak for themselves; they are, rather, texts that need 'reading' theoretically in just the same way as the 'texts of Madonna' do.

The other strategy derives from semiotic and structuralist textual analy-sis. This strategy involves a close reading of the signifiers of the text – that is, its physical presence – but recognizes that the signifieds exist not in the text itself but extratextually, in the myths, countermyths, and ideologies of their culture.[21] It recognizes that the distribution of power in society is paralleled by the distribution of meanings in texts, and that struggles for social power are paralleled by semiotic struggles for meanings. Every text and every reading has a social and therefore a political dimension, which is to be found partly in the structure of the text itself and partly in the relation of the reading subject to that text.

It follows that the theory informing any anlaysis also has a social dimension, which is a necessary part of the 'meanings' that analysis reveals. Meanings, therefore, are relative and change according to histor-ical and social conditions. What is constant is the ways in which texts relate to the social system. A cultural analysis, then, will reveal the way in which the dominant ideology is structured into the text and into the reading subject and those textual features that enable negotiated, resisting, or oppositional readings to be made. Cultural analysis reaches a satisfactory conclusion when the ethnographic studies of the historically and socially located meanings that *are* made are related to the semiotic analysis of the text. Semiotic relates the structure of the text to the social system to explore how the economic and ideological system is reproduced in the text but also how the polysemy of the text exceeds this reproduction. Ethnographic studies show us how this semiotic excess is exploited by specific audiences in specific social conditions as they struggle to make their meanings in relationship to those that work to reproduce the patriarchal capitalist system encompassing both the text and its readers.

Thus Lucy, then a 14-year-old Australian fan, said of an early Madonna poster: 'She's tarty and seductive . . . but it looks alright when she does it, you know, what I mean, if anyone else did it it would look right tarty, a right tart you know, but with her it's OK, it's acceptable. . . . With anyone else it would be absolutely outrageous, it sounds silly, but it's OK with her, you know what I mean.'[22] We can note a number of points here. Lucy could find only patriarchal words to describe Madonna's sexuality – 'tarty' and 'seductive' – but she struggled against the patriarchy inscribed in them. At the same time she struggled against the patriarchy inscribed in her own subjectivity. The opposition between 'acceptable' and 'absolutely outrageous' refers not only to representations of female sexuality but is also an externalization of the tension felt by adolescent girls trying to come to terms with the contradictions between a positive feminine view of their sexuality and the alien patriarchal one that appears to be the only one offered by the available linguistic and symbolic systems. Madonna's 'tarty' sexuality is 'acceptable' – but to whom? Certainly to her young female fans who are experiencing the problems of establishing a satisfactory sexual identity within an opposing ideology: at the moment when girls become aware of their potential as women, patriarchy rushes in to assert its control over their identities and social relations. At this moment, Madonna intervenes, for, as Judith Williamson points out, she 'retains all the bravado and exhibitionism that most girls start off with, or feel inside, until the onset of "womanhood" knocks it out of them'.[23]

Further evidence to support the empowerment that Madonna can offer to girls comes from the reactions to her of some boys. Matthew, aged 15 and not a particular fan of Madonna, commented that he wouldn't like to be married to her 'because she'd give any guy a hard time'. Matthew is not untypical in his opinion, for a 1990 poll showed that, when asked if they would like to sleep with Madonna, 60 percent of the boys questioned declined. Not surprisingly, a powerful female in control of her own sexuality appeals more strongly to girls than to boys. As we shall see later, Madonna often denies or mocks patriarchy's conventions for representing women. This might well be why, according to *Time*, many boys find her sexiness difficult to handle and 'suspect that they are being kidded'.[24] Lucy and Matthew both recognize, in different ways and from different social positions, that Madonna's sexuality can offer a challenge or a threat to dominant definitions of femininity and masculinity.

'Madonna's Best Friend', writing to the music magazine *Countdown*, also recognized Madonna's resistance to patriarchy:

> I'm writing to complain about all the people who write in and say what a tart and a slut Madonna is because she talks openly about sex and she shows her belly button and she's not ashamed to say she thinks she's pretty. Well I admire her and I think she has a lot of courage just to be herself. All you girls out there! Do you think you have nice eyes or pretty hair or a nice figure? Do you ever talk about boys or sex with friends? Do you wear a bikini? Well according to you, you're a slut and a tart!! So have you judged Madonna fairly? – Madonna's Best Friend, Wahroonga, New South Wales.[25]

This praise for Madonna's 'courage just to be herself' is further evidence of the difficulty girls feel in finding a sexual identity that appears to be formed in their interests rather than in those of the dominant male. Madonna recognizes – some might say overemphasizes – the importance of sexual identity in determining the sort of social relations we enter into and thus the social experience we undergo:

> People's sexuality and the way they relate to the world is very important. . . . It's so much more than just fornication. Your sexual identity is so important. The more you pay attention to it, the more you realize that just about every- thing in the world is centered around sexual attraction and sexual power. You also become aware of people who are not in touch with their own, or have the wrong idea about it or abuse it.[26]

If some girls feel that patriarchy promotes the 'wrong idea' of their sexuality and leads them to 'abuse it', then Madonna's invitation to them to get 'in touch with their own' and to construct a gender identity (and the social relations that go with it) in their own interests is a politically positive one. Her fans are aware that she does indeed offer them this invitation: 'She's sexy but she doesn't need men. . . . She's kind of there all by herself'; or 'She gives us ideas. It's really women's lib, not being afraid of what guys think.'[27]

This sense of their own identity is never, of course, constructed freely by the girls, for it can be achieved only by struggling against the identity proposed by patriarchy. This struggle, this fighting back, can be enjoy- able, as evidenced by a student fan in an essay:

> There is also a sense of pleasure, at least for me and perhaps a large number of other women, in Madonna's defiant look or gaze. In 'Lucky Star' at one point in the dance sequence Madonna dances side on to the camera, looking provoca- tive. For an instant we glimpse her tongue: the expectation is that she is about to lick her lips in a sexual invitation. The expectation is denied and Madonna appears to tuck her tongue back into her cheek. This, it seems, is how most of her dancing and grovelling in front of the camera is meant to be taken. She is setting up the sexual idolization of women. For a woman who has experienced this victimization, this setup is most enjoyable and pleasurable, while the male position of voyeur is displaced into uncertainty.[28]

But, like all pop stars, Madonna has her 'haters' as well as her fans: 'When I sit down on a Saturday and Sunday night I always hear the word Madonna and it makes me sick, all she's worried about is her bloody looks. She must spend hours putting on that stuff and why does she always show her belly button? We all know she's got one. My whole family thinks she's pathetic and that she loves herself. – Paul Young's sexy sneakers.'[29] Here again, the 'hate' centers on her sexuality and her painting and displaying herself to arouse the baser side of man – expressed by detractors as her presenting herself in whorelike terms. But the sting comes in the last sentence, when the writer recognizes Madonna's apparent enjoyment of her own sexuality, which he (the letter is clearly from a masculine subject, if not an actual male) ascribes to egocentricity and thus condemns.

Madonna's love of herself, however, is not seen as selfish and egocentric by girls; rather, it is the root of her appeal, and its significance becomes clear in the context of the way they are addressed by the rest of the media. McRobbie has shown how the 'teenage press' typically constructs a girl's body, and therefore her sexuality, as a series of problems: breasts the wrong size or shape, spotty skin, lifeless hair, fatty thighs, problem periods. The list is endless, of course, and the advertisers, the ones who really benefit from these magazines, always have a product that promises – at a price – to solve the problem.

Madonna is much loved or much hated, a not-untypical position for woman to occupy in patriarchy, whose inability to understand women in their own terms is evidenced by the way it polarizes femininity into the opposing concepts of Virgin-Angel and Whore-Devil.

Madonna consciously and parodically exploits these contradictions: 'When I was tiny', she recalls, 'my grandmother used to beg me not to go with men, to love Jesus and be a good girl. I grew up with two images of women: the virgin and the whore. It was a little scary.' She consistently refers to these contradictory meanings of women in patriarchy. Her video of 'Like a Virgin' alternates the white dress of Madonna the bride with the black, slinky garb of Madonna the singer; the name Madonna (the virgin mother) is borne by a sexually active female; the crucifixes adopted from nuns' habits are worn on a barely concealed bosom or in a sexually gyrating navel. 'Growing up I thought nuns were beautiful. . . . They never wore any make-up and they just had these really serene faces. Nuns are sexy.'[30]

But the effect of working these opposite meanings into her texts is not just to call attention to their role in male hegemony: woman may either be worshiped and adored by man or used and despised by him, but she has meaning only from a masculine subject position. Rather, Madonna calls into question the validity of these binary oppositions as a way of conceptualizing woman. Her use of religious iconography is neither religious nor sacrilegious. She intends to free it from this ideological opposition and to enjoy it, use it, for the meanings and pleasure it has for *her* and not for those of the dominant ideology and its simplistic binary thinking:

> I have always carried around a few rosaries with me. One day I decided to wear [one] as a necklace. Everything I do is sort of tongue in cheek. It's a strange blend – a beautiful sort of symbolism, the idea of someone suffering, which is what Jesus Christ on a crucifix stands for, and then not taking it seriously. Seeing it as an icon with no religiousness attached. It isn't sacrilegious for me.[31]

The crucifix is neither religious nor sacrilegious, but beautiful: 'When I went to Catholic schools I thought the huge crucifixes nuns wore were really beautiful'. In the same way, her adolescent fans find in Madonna meanings of femininity that have broken free from the ideological binary opposition of virgin/whore. They find in her image positive feminine-centered representations of sexuality that are expressed in their constant references to her independence, her being herself. This apparently independent, self-defining sexuality is only as significant as it is because it is working within and against a patriarchal ideology.

As Ann Kaplan argues (Kaplan, 1992) Madonna's image is based in part on that of Marilyn Monroe, the great sex symbol of an earlier generation. But the differences between the two 'blond bombshells' are more instructive than the similarities. In the video 'Material Girl', Madonna goes through a dance routine with tuxedo-clad young men in a parody of Monroe's number 'Diamonds Are a Girl's Best Friend' from *Gentlemen*

Prefer Blondes. During the number, she collects jewelry from the men as she sings the refrain, 'Cause we're living in a material world, and I am a material girl'. But despite her whorelike gathering of riches from men and her singing that only boys with money have any chance with her (which is close to Monroe's performance in 'Diamonds Are a Girl's Best Friend'), she toys with the boys, showing that their jewelry has bought them no power over her, but instead that extracting it is an expression of her power over them. This quite contradicts Monroe's performance. Madonna says about her image's more general reference: 'I don't see myself as Marilyn Monroe, I'm almost playing with her image, turning it around. I don't claim to know her and can barely believe most of what's written about her. The impression I get is, she didn't know her own strength and didn't know how to nurture it.'[32] Madonna clearly does know where her own strength lies and how to use it. Her accumulation of material goodies is not mere capitalist greed but a way of exerting power over men.

But even the materialist reading of the video is contradicted. The stage performance is embedded in a mininarrative in which she rejects a rich suitor and accepts a poor one. The conclusion of the video shows her driving off with him in an old workman's truck, in which they make love during a rainstorm. The material girl has fallen for the nonmaterial values of love after all. The undermining of the song by the mininarrative may not seem to offer much of a resistance; after all, the main narrative is a conventional romance in which the poor, sensitive man is finally preferred to the apparently more attractive rich one. The 'true love' that triumphs is as much a part of patriarchal capitalism as the materialism it defeats. But this contradiction does not work alone – it is supported by parody, by puns, and by Madonna's awareness of *how* she is making an image, not just of *what* her image is.

Some of the parody is subtle and hard to tie down for textual analysis, but some, such as the references to Marilyn Monroe and the musicals she often starred in, is more obvious. The subtler parody lies in the knowing way in which Madonna uses the camera, mocking the conventional representations of female sexuality at the same time she conforms to them. Even *Playboy* recognizes her self-parody: 'The voice and the body are her bona fides, but Madonna's secret may be her satirical bite. She knows a lot of this image stuff is bullshit: she knows that *you* know. So long as we're all in on the act together, let's enjoy it.'[33] One of her former lovers supports this: 'Her image is that of a tart, but I believe it's all contrived. She only pretends to be a gold digger. Remember, I have seen the other side of Madonna.'[34]

Madonna knows she is putting on a performance. The fact that this knowingness is part of the performance enables the viewer to respond to a different interpellation from that proposed by the dominant ideology and thus to occupy a resisting subject position. The sensitive man watching her material girl performance knows as she does – as we might also – that this is only a performance. Those who take the performance at face value, who miss its self-parody, are hailed as ideological subjects in patriarchy or else they reject the hailing, deny the pleasure, and refuse the communication:

The *National Enquirer*, a weekly magazine devoted to prurient gossip, quotes two academic psychiatrists denouncing her for advocating teenage promiscuity, promoting a lust for money and materialism, and contributing to the deterioration of the family. Feminists accuse her of revisionism, of resurrecting the manipulative female who survives by coquetry and artifice. 'Tell Gloria [Steinem] and the gang', she retorts, 'to lighten up, get a sense of humour. And look at my video that goes with Material Girl. The guy who gets me in the end is the sensitive one with no money.'[35]

Madonna consistently parodies conventional representations of women, and parody can be an effective device for interrogating the dominant ideology. It takes the defining features of its object, exaggerates and mocks them, and thus mocks those who 'fall' for its ideological effect. But Madonna's parody goes further than this: she parodies, not just the stereotypes, but the way in which they are made. She represents herself as one who is in control of her own image and of the process of making it. This, at the reading end of the semiotic process, allows the reader similar control over her own meanings. Madonna's excess of jewelry, of makeup, of trashy style, offer similar scope to the reader. Excessiveness invites the reader to question ideology; too much lipstick interrogates the tastefully made-up mouth, too much jewelry questions the role of female decorations in patriarchy. Excess overspills ideological control and offers scope for resistance. Thus Madonna's excessively sexual pouting and overdone lipstick can be read to mean that she looks like that not because patriarchy determines that she should but because she knowingly chooses to. She wears religious icons (and uses a religious name) not to support or attack Christianity's role in patriarchy (and capitalism) but because she chooses to see them as beautiful, sexy ornaments. She constantly takes items of urban living, prizes them free from their original social, and therefore signifying, context, and combines them in new ways and in a new context that denies their original meaning. Thus the crucifix is torn from its religious context and lacy gloves from their context of bourgeois respectability – or, conversely, of the brothel. By wearing underwear as outerwear and taking it out of the boudoir and into the street (or even into church), she reconfigures it. With her, dyed blond hair and with the dark roots deliberately displayed is no longer the sign of the tarty slut, and the garter belt and stockings no longer signify soft porn or male kinkiness.

This wrenching of the products of capitalism from their original context and recycling them into a new style is, as Iain Chambers has pointed out, a typical practice of urban popular culture.[36] The products are purified into signifiers; their ideological signifieds are dumped and left behind in their original context. These freed signifiers do not necessarily mean *something*, they do not necessarily acquire new signifieds. Rather, the act of freeing them from their ideological context signifies their users' freedom from that context. It signifies the power (however hard the struggle to attain it) of the subordinate to exert some control process of making meanings.

Madonna's videos constantly refer to the production of the image, and they make her control over its production part of the image itself. This emphasis on the making of the image allows, or even invites, an equivalent control by the reader over its reception. It enables girls to see that the meanings of feminine sexuality *can* be in their control, *can* be made in their interests, and that their subjectivities are not necessarily totally determined by the dominant patriarchy.

The constant puns in Madonna lyrics work in a similar way. Puns arise when one word occurs in two discourses – in the case of 'Material Girl', those of economics and sexuality: one signifier has simultaneous but different signifieds according to its discourse. The most obvious puns are 'give me proper credit', 'raise my interest', 'experience has made me rich'. Less obvious ones are 'the boy with the cold hard cash' or 'only boys that save their pennies make my rainy day' ('make' has only vestigial sexual meanings, and the homonym between 'pennies' and 'penis' is only faint). The puns perform typical ideological work by equating economic with sexual success, a common strategy of popular culture in patriarchal capitalism. But puns demand active readers and can never fully control the meanings that are provoked by the yoking of disparate discourses. These puns can expose and thus reject, or at least resist, the economic and sexual subordination of women and the way that each is conventionally used to naturalize the other. The first and last verses of the song are:

Some boys kiss me some boys hug me
I think they're OK
If they don't give me proper credit
I just walk away

Boys may come and boys may go
And that's all right you see
Experience has made me rich
And now they're after me.[37]

The puns here can be used, not to naturalize the dual subordination of woman, but to assert woman's ability to achieve sexual-economic independence. If a body is all that patriarchy allows a woman to be, then at least she can use it in *her* interests, not in men's.

The pun always resists final ideological closure: the potential meanings provoked by the collision of different discourses is always greater than that proposed by the dominant ideology. Thus 'Boy Toy', the name that Madonna has given to her range of products and that the media apply to her, can be read as *Playboy* does when it calls her the 'world's number one Boy Toy' or 'the compleat Boy Toy'.[38] In this reading, Madonna is the toy for boys, but the pun can also mean that the boy is her toy – as she toys with the boys in 'Material Girl'.

Puns are also at work in the word 'material', which is located in the discourse of the economic capitalism but which is often used to criticize that discourse either from a religious viewpoint or from one of a 'finer sensibility'. In rejecting the materialism of the song, Madonna may be read as proposing the values of a finer sensitivity and a more spiritual love, either secular-erotic or religious-erotic. Madonna's combining of secular and religious love makes explicit a powerful undercurrent of patriarchal Christianity in general – and Catholicism in particular – that traditionally has tried to mogilize man's lustful love for Mary Magdalene, displace it onto Mary the Virgin, and spiritualize it in the process. With Madonna, however, the dualism of the love is denied; it does not fit an either/or dichotomy in which one sort of love is morally superior to the other. By denying the opposition and the moral hierarchy inscribed in it, she rejects the traditional patriarchal Christian evaluation of love and allows sexual or sentimental love to appear on the same level as religious love – certainly not as inferior to it. Her use of the cross as a beautiful ornament for the female body and her characterization of nuns as sexy are all part of her critical interrogation of a patriarchal Christian tradition that makes sense of love by means of a moralistic opposition between the spirituality of the virgin and the lust and the love of the whore. Similarly, the video of 'Like a Virgin' refuses to allow the viewer a moral choice between the white-robed, virginal Madonna bride and the black-clad, sexy Madonna singer. As she says, referring to the video: 'Passion and sexuality and religion all bleed into each other for me. I think you can be a very sexual person and also a very religious and spiritual person. . . . I'm a very sexual, very spiritual person. What's the problem?'[39]

In 'Like a Prayer' this spirituality and passion are brought together in a way so explicit as to have caused Pepsi to withdraw their TV commercial based on the video. The video consists of a complex montage that juxta-poses images of Madonna in her underwear in a black church, kissing the icon of a black saint and bringing him to life, with a narrative in which she secures the release of a young black man jailed for a crime he did not commit. Although there may be no preferred meaning to the video, its use of provocative images organized around the themes of sexuality, religion, race, gender, and justice offended many of the dominant groups in society. But whereas mainstream religious groups condemned the video as blas-phemous, two students of mine could find no evidence of black churches that were offended.[40]

Madonna's ability to offend the socially dominant while appealing to the subordinate reached its peak (so far at least) at the end of 1990 with the release of her video 'Justify My Love' (see below). The music television channel (MTV) refused to screen it, and a hostile, sexist interview on NBC's *Nightline* accused Madonna of overstepping acceptable limits of sexual representation. Her response was that, in her view, these conventional limits allow the degradation and humiliation of women and tolerate violence toward them, but do not allow two or more people, regardless of gender, to enter into a mutual exchange of the sensual pleasures of touching and looking. The conventional limits confine sexuality to patri-archal dominance, and by rejecting them and replacing them with ones of her own, Madonna was asserting her control over her own sexual politics, however offensive they might be to other people. The fact that the group offended was, again, the socially dominant one is a good indicator of the politics of this control.

An earlier video, 'Open Your Heart', also centered its images around the control of sexuality. In it, Madonna plays a striptease dancer in a peep show. As her sexual and revealing dance progresses, we gradually realize that she is subverting the conventions of striptease by making her parody of it muscular, assertive, and sexually challenging instead of supplicating and appealing. She uses this 'turned' striptease not to allure the male voyeurs watching her but to control them, and in doing so she reverses the power relations in Freud's theory of voyeurism.

The video explicitly shows us a number of voyeurs, whereas, according to Freud, voyeuristic power depends upon a voyeur's invisibility. But these men are not only pulled into the light and made visible, they are mocked, parodied, and exaggerated. They are represented by a series of disempowering images such as a coke-bottle spectacles or cardboard cutouts (which Madonna kicks over); some are shown groveling downward to catch a final glimpse of her under the descending shutter of the booth. Outside, by the box office, is a young boy trying to get in – possibly to 'become a man' in the conventional sense. Madonna 'rescues' him from this fate, and in the final shot the two of them, androgynously dressed alike, dance away in a nonsexual, gender-equal dance of joy while the peep-show owner desperately begs Madonna to return to her role as sexual lure. The irony, of course, is that, in controlling the look of those she entices, she was never the lure he thought she was.

Madonna knows well the importance of the look. This is a complex concept, for it includes how she *looks* (what she looks like), how *she* looks (how she gazes at others – the camera in particular), and how others look at her. Traditionally, looking has been in the control of men, and the male look has, following Freud's theory of voyeurism, been a central element in patriarchal control over women. But Madonna appropriates this control for herself and shows that women's control of the look (in all three senses) is crucial to their gaining control over their meanings within patriarchy.

One of the ways in which she gains this control is paradoxically, by relinquishing it. She does not wish to restrict and tie down the meanings of gender and the identities that go with them, for to do so would be merely to reproduce the worst of patriarchal politics. Her aim is to open them up, to give those who are subordinated or marginalized by patriarchy – that is, those who are not heterosexual men – greater control over their own sexuality and thus to diversify sexual identities and sexual relations in our society.

Semiotic power is exerted by controlling the categorizations used to make sense of the world, and patriarchy constantly attempts to control sexual categories and their meanings. So Madonna's consistent refusal to accept or fit into these categories is a strategy of resistance. She deliberately promotes ambiguity and androgyny in her songs and videos, and her 1990 video 'Justify My Love' is the most explicit of all her work in its refusal of conventional sexual categories.[41] Its sensuous, erotic representation of mutual love moves easily across the categories of the clearly heterosexual, the clearly homosexual, and the androgynous: it shows highly feminine women and men, as well as masculine men and women; its pleasures are extended beyond the confines of the traditional couple and include those of looking as well as those of touching. No wonder MTV refused to show it. The video became, for a short time, a *cause célèbre* of gender politics and was accused, predictably, of promoting pornography, perversion, and promiscuity while being defended, equally predictably, for being emancipatory, honest, and erotic. One of its defenders summed up the controversy thus:

There's no mistaking this piece of porn, because it carries such a firm point of view. Madonna uses her portrayal of blurred genders to amuse and liberate, as well as to exploit. Her cheeky S&M fantasies wind up asserting the independence of the individual, and to make sure we don't miss the point, she spells out with the lyrics printed on-screen at the clip's close: 'Poor is the man whose pleasures depend on the permission of another'.[42]

So far in this chapter I have focused on young girls as a typical subcultural audience of Madonna. But they are far from the only one. Madonna is also highly significant in gay culture.[43] A disc jockey at a gay bar in Madison, Wisconsin, calls her 'an equalist who speaks to a generation who thirsts for diversity'. For him Madonna's diversification of patriarchy's restricted sexual categories is appealingly progressive. Other members of Madison's gay community find a real attraction in her campy, playful control over her own image and in her ability to change that image at will. There is little explicit evidence that her image control appealed to the need experienced by some gay people to masquerade in order to reduce the problems of living in a heterosexual society; rather, the appeal lay in her honesty and power in rejecting sexual stereotyping. Her emphasis that 'Justify My Love' is about 'being truthful and honest with our partners' carries the implications that conventional sexuality often involves dishonesty and the attempt to fit one's own sexuality into a category already constructed, thereby submitting oneself to the control inherent in that categorization.[44] As one gay magazine puts it:

> She helps us confront religious guilt, purges us of libidinal inhibitions and forces us to rethink the limitations of gender, intercourse and responsibility – all with a good beat that you can dance to. . . . Her pride, flamboyance and glamour reach out to gay guys as much as her butch/fem dichotomy and her refusal to be victimized strikes a chord in lesbians.[45]

Madonna herself justifies her video by saying: 'It's a celebration of sex. It is about two people regardless of gender displaying affection for each other, there's nothing wrong with that.' To those who claim she is demeaning herself and women in her work, she replies confidently that they 'are missing a few things. I am the one in charge. I put myself in these situations. There isn't a man making me do these things. I am in charge'.[46]

This sense of power and control in sexual relations appeals equally, if differently, to both young girls and to the gay and lesbian communities. A final, if extreme, endorsement of this appeal is provided by Michael Musto of *Outweek*: 'Despite the government's attempt to render some of Madonna's themes invisible, as a role model and evocator of change, Madonna is right now more powerful than the government'.[47]

Cultural studies does not try to understand Madonna simply either as a bearer of meanings and ideology or as an agent of commodification and profit making, though she is clearly both of these. By stressing her multi-accentuality, it reveals her as a terrain of struggle upon which various social formations engage in relations with the dominant social order. Her meanings and their politics cannot be evaluated in terms of what she *is*, but only in terms of what people make of her in their social contexts. The controversy she provokes is evidence not only of how open a terrain she is for this struggle over meaning, but also of people's desire to seize what opportunities they can find to engage in it.

What I have tried to do in this chapter is to demonstrate some of the methodology and theoretical implications of British cultural studies. I shall now try to summarize these.

The television text is a potential of meanings. These meanings are activated by different readers in their different social situations. Because the television text is produced by a capitalist institution, it necessarily bears that ideology. Any subcultural or resistant meanings that are made from it are not 'independent' but are made in relation to the dominant ideology. Because subcultures are related in various ways to the social system, they will produce an equivalent variety of ways in which to relate their subcultural readings of television to those preferred by the dominant ideology. Social relations in capitalism always involve a political dimension (because all such relations are determined more or less directly by the unequal distribution of power), and so all meanings arise, in part, from a political base. For some, the politics will be those of acceptance, for others, those of rejection or opposition, but for most the politics will be a base for the negotiation of meaning or for resistance.

Cultural analysis can help us to reveal how the television text serves as an arena for this struggle over meanings. It treats television as part of the total cultural experience of its viewers; the meanings of television are always intertextual, for it is always read in the context of the other texts that make up this cultural experience. These intertextual relations may be explicit and close or implicit and tenuous. All muscle dramas share many generic characteristics, but they also bear less obvious – though not necessarily less significant – relations with the Vietnam veterans' parade held in New York ten years after the war ended and with the unveiling of the Vietnam Memorial in Washington, DC.

Critical and journalistic comments on television programs, fan magazines, and gossip publications are examples of other types of significant intertextuality. Criticism is, according to Tony Bennett, a series of ideological bids for the meaning of a text, and studying which interpretations are preferred in which publications and for which audiences can help us to understand why and how certain meanings of the text are activated rather than others.[48] We must be able to understand how that bundle of meanings that we call 'Madonna' allows a *Playboy* reader to activate meanings of 'the compleat Boy Toy' at the same time that a female fan sees her as sexy but not needing men, as being there 'all by herself'. Publications reflect the meanings circulating in the culture, and these meanings will be read back into the television text as an inevitable part of the assimilation of that text into the total cultural experience of the reader.

For culture is a process of making meanings in which people actively participate; it is not a set of preformed meanings handed down to and imposed upon the people. Of course, our 'freedom' to make meanings that suit our interests is as circumscribed as any other 'freedom' in society. The mass-produced text is produced and circulated by capitalist institutions for economic gain and is therefore imprinted with capitalist ideology. But the mass-produced text can only be made into a *popular* text by the people, and this transformation occurs when the various subcultures can activate sets of meanings and insert those meanings into their daily cultural experience. They take mass-produced signifiers and, by a process of 'excorporation', use them to articulate and circulate subcultural meanings.[49]

Gossip is one important means of this active circulation of meanings. The 'uses and gratifications' theorists of the 1970s recognized how commonly television was used as a 'coin of social exchange', that is, as something to talk about in schoolyards, suburban coffee mornings, coffee breaks at work, and the family living room.[50] Dorothy Hobson has shown the importance of gossip among soap opera fans, and Christine Geraghty has called it the 'social cement' that binds the narrative strands of soap opera together and that binds fans to each other and to the television text.[51] This use of television as a cultural enabler, a means of participating in the circulation of meanings, is only just becoming clear, and gossip or talk about television is no longer seen as the end in itself (as it was in the 'uses and gratifications' approach), but rather as a way of participating actively in that process of the production and circulation of meanings that constitutes culture.

The cultural analysis of television, then, requires us to study three levels of 'texts' and the relations between them. First, there is the primary text on the television screen, which is produced by the culture industry and needs to be seen in its context as part of that industry's total production. Second, there is a sublevel of texts, also produced by the culture industry, though sometimes by different parts of it. These include studio publicity, television criticism and comment, feature articles about shows and their stars, gossip columns, fan magazines, and so on. They can provide evidence of the ways in which the potential meanings of the primary text are activated and taken into their culture by various audiences or subcultures. On the third level of textuality lie those texts that the viewers produce themselves: their talk about television; their letters to papers or magazines; and their adoption of television-introduced styles of dress, speech, behavior, or even thought into their lives.

These three levels leak into one another. Some secondary texts, such as those of official publicity and public relations, are very close to primary texts; others, such as independent criticism and comment, attempt to 'speak for' the third level. Underlying all this, we can, I think, see an oral popular culture adapting its earlier role to one that fits within a mass society.

This social circulation of meanings always entails struggle and contestation, for those with social power constantly attempt to repress, invalidate, or marginalize meanings that are produced by and serve the interests of subordinate groups and that therefore conflict with their own. This foregrounding of conflict, which informs the realm of culture just as it does that of social relations, is the key difference between the development of cultural studies in Britain and in the United States. Britain, like most of continental Europe, has never doubted that it is a society structured around class conflict; as a result, Marxist modes of analysis, which developed to explain capitalist societies as necessarily ones of conflicting social interests and therefore of constant social struggle, were particularly pertinent to cultural studies as it developed in Britain in the 1970s and 1980s.

Cultural criticism in the United States, however, has quite a different history. Its major concern has been to forge a national unity or consensus out of widely differing immigrant, enslaved, and native social groups. Its industrialization did not grow from a society of agrarian capitalism with an already politicized peasant class – which is one root reason for both the instability of the labor movement and the invisibility of the class system in the United States compared with Britain. US cultural studies, then, tended toward liberal pluralist theories in which different social groups were seen to live together in relative harmony and stability. The models to which US cultural theory turned were ones derived not from Marxism and the analysis of social conflict but from anthropology and the analysis of social consensus. Drawing on notions of ritual and mythology, they stressed what different social groups had in common, which was a form of *communitas* produced by a shared language and culture into which all entered freely and from which all derived equal benefits. The dominant ideology thesis, of course, differs diametrically while still stressing what people have in common: in its case, what is common to all is the dominant ideology, which is far from equal in the distribution of its benefits.

The growth of interest in British cultural studies in the United States during the 1980s may well be related to the rise of Reaganism. Reaganism rolled back the progress made during the 1960s and 1970s toward reducing inequalities in gender, race, and class; it widened the gap between the privileged and the deprived and concentrated power in the white, male, upper middle classes. Under such conditions, models of cultural consensus proved less convincing than ones of cultural conflict. British cultural studies, with its focus on struggle and its commitment to promoting the interests of the subordinate and critiquing the operations of the dominant, seemed to be tailor made for importation. But the theory should not be allowed to emerge unchanged from its transatlantic crossing. The different histories of the United States and Britain, particularly in race and class relations, require its models to be modified. Such differences, though, significant as they are, are still differences within the commonality of a white, patriarchal capitalism whose enormous benefits, rewards, and resources are unfairly distributed among its members. If an American adaptation of British cultural studies can provide a critically engaged theory that critiques the culture of domination and endorses those cultures of the subordinate that work against social inequality, and if by so doing it contributes to a more equal but diverse society, its importation will have been well justified. If it doesn't, the sooner it's dumped the better.

Notes

1. Stuart Hall, 'The narrative construction of reality', *Southern Review* 17 (1984): 1–17.
2. Angela McRobbie, 'Dance and social fantasy', in Angela McRobbie and Mica Nava (eds), *Gender and Generation* (London: Macmillan, 1984), pp. 130–61; Lisa Lewis, *Gender Politics and MTV: Voicing the Difference* (Philadelphia: Temple University Press, 1990).

3. Louis Althusser, 'Ideology and ideological state apparatuses', in *Lenin and Philosophy and Other Essays* (London: New Left Books, 1971), pp. 127–86.
4. Stuart Hall *et al.* 'The unity of current affairs television', in Tony Bennett *et al.* (eds), *Popular Television and Film: A Reader* (London: British Film Institute/Open University Press, 1981), pp. 88–117; Stephen Heath and Gillian Skirrow, 'Television: a world in action', *Screen* 18, no. 2 (1977): 7–59; John Fiske, 'Television and popular culture: reflections on British and Australian critical practice', *Critical Studies in Mass Communication* 3 (September 1986): 200–16.
5. Stuart Hall, 'Encoding/decoding', in Stuart Hall *et al.* (eds), *Culture, Media, Language* (London: Hutchinson, 1980), pp. 128–39.
6. Shere Hite, *The Hite Report on Male Sexuality* (London: Macdonald, 1981).
7. Andrew Moye, 'Pornography', in Adrian Metcalf and Martin Humphries (eds), *The Sexuality of Men* (London: Macmillan, 1985), pp. 44–69.
8. Horace Newcomb, 'On the dialogue aspect of mass communication', *Critical Studies in Mass Communication* 1 (March 1984): 34–50.
9. *Ibid.*
10. Mikhail Bakhtin, *The Dialogic Imagination* (Austin: University of Texas Press, 1981).
11. Valentin N. Volosinov, *Marxism and the Philosophy of Language* (New York: Seminar Press, 1973). There is a well-grounded theory that Volosinov and Bakhtin were the same writer.
12. David Morley, *The 'Nationwide' Audience: Structure and Decoding* (London: British Film Institute, 1980); McRobbie, 'Dance and social fantasy'; Robert Hodge and David Tripp, *Children and Television* (Cambridge: Polity, 1986).
13. Morley, *The 'Nationwide' Audience.*
14. *Ibid.* See also Charlotte Brunsdon and David Morley, *Everyday Television: 'Nationwide'* (London: British Film Institute, 1978).
15. John Corner, Kay Richardson, and Natalie Fenton, *Nuclear Reactions: Form and Response in Public Issue Television* (London: John Libbey, 1990).
16. See Robert Dawson, 'Culture and deprivation: ethnography and everyday life'. Paper presented at the International Communication Association Conference, Dublin, Ireland, July 1990; John Fiske, 'For cultural interpretation: a study of the culture of homelessness', *Critical Studies in Mass Communication* (forthcoming); John Fiske and Robert Dawson, 'Audiencing violence', in Lawrence Grossberg and Ellen Wartella (eds), *Toward a Comprehensive Theory of the Audience* (Champaign: University of Illinois Press, 1992).
17. David Morley, *Family Television: Cultural Power and Domestic Leisure* (London: Comedia, 1986).
18. Raymond Williams, *Television: Technology and Cultural Form* (London: Fontana, 1974); John Hartley, 'Television and the power of dirt', *Australian Journal of Cultural Studies* 1, no. 2 (1983): 68–82.
19. McRobbie, 'Dance and social fantasy', see note 2.
20. Stuart Hall, 'Notes on deconstructing the popular', in Raphael Samuel (ed.), *People's History and Socialist Theory* (London: Routledge and Kegan Paul, 1981).
21. See Roland Barthes, *Mythologies* (London: Paladin, 1973); John Fiske, *Introduction to Communication Studies* (London: Methuen, 1982); John Fiske and John Hartley, *Reading Television* (London: Methuen, 1978).
22. Interview by John Fiske, December 1985.
23. Judith Williamson, 'The making of a material girl', *New Socialist*, October 1986, pp. 46–47.
24. *Time,* 27 May 1985, p. 47.
25. *Countdown,* December 1985, p. 70.
26. *US,* 13 June 1991, p. 23.

27. *Time*, 27 May 1985, p. 47.
28. Robyn Blair, student paper, School of Communication and Cultural Studies, Curtin University, November 1985.
29. *Countdown Annual*, 1985, p. 109.
30. Madonna, quoted in *National Times*, 23/29 August 1985, p. 9.
31. *Ibid.*, p. 10.
32. *Star*, 7 May 1991, p. 7.
33. *Ibid.*, p. 127.
34. Professor Chris Flynn, quoted in *New Idea*, 11 January 1986, p. 4.
35. *National Times*, 23/29 August 1985, p. 10.
36. Iain Chambers, *Popular Culture: The Metropolitan Experience* (London: Methuen, 1986), pp. 7–13.
37. From 'Material Girl', lyrics by Peter Brown and Robert Raus (Minong Publishing Company, BMI, 1985).
38. *Playboy*, September 1985, pp. 122, 127.
39. *US*, 13 June 1991, p. 23.
40. David Brean and Chad Dell, 'Like a prayer'. Unpublished paper, University of Wisconsin-Madison, April 1989.
41. *US*, 13 June 1991, pp. 20–23.
42. Jim Farber in *Entertainment Weekly*, 14 December 1990, p. 19.
43. The research into Madonna's appeal to Madison's gay and lesbian communities was conducted by a student of mine, Jennifer Alterman. For a fuller account, see her 'Madonna: a visual illusion'. Unpublished paper, University of Wisconsin-Madison, May 1991.
44. Madonna, speaking on *Nightline*, NBC, 3 December 1990.
45. *Outweek*, March 1991, pp. 35–41.
46. *Nightline*, NBC, 3 December 1990.
47. *Outweek*, March 1991, p. 62.
48. Tony Bennett, 'The Bond phenomenon: theorizing a popular hero', *Southern Review* 16, no. 2 (1983): 195–225.
49. Lawrence Grossberg, 'Another boring day in paradise: rock and roll and the empowerment of everyday life', *Popular Music* 4 (1984): 225–57.
50. Denis McQuail *et al.*, 'The television audience: a revised perspective', in Denis McQuail (ed.), *The Sociology of Mass Communications* (Harmondsworth: Penguin, 1972), pp. 135–65.
51. Dorothy Hobson, *'Crossroads': The Drama of a Soap Opera* (London: Methuen, 1982); Christine Geraghty, 'The continuous serial – a definition', in *Coronation Street*, by Richard Dyer *et al.* (London: British Film Institute, 1981), pp. 9–26.

7

Banality in cultural studies

Meaghan Morris

What goes around, comes around.
– Patrice Petro

This paper takes a rather circuitous route to get to the point. I'm not sure that banality can have a point, any more than cultural studies can properly constitute its theoretical object. My argument does have a point, but one that takes the form of pursuing an aim rather than reaching a conclusion. Quite simply, I wanted to come to terms with my own irritation about two developments in recent cultural studies.

One was Jean Buadrillard's revival of the term 'banality' to frame a theory of media. It is an interesting theory that deals in part with the tele-visual relationship between everyday life and catastrophic events. Yet why should such a classically dismisive term as 'banality' re-appear, yet again, as a point of departure for discussing popular culture?

The other development occurs in the quite different context that John Fiske calls 'British cultural studies',[1] and is much more difficult to specify. Judith Williamson, however, has bluntly described something that also bothers me: 'left-wing academics . . . picking out strands of 'subversion' in every piece of pop culture from Street Style to Soap Opera'.[2] In this kind of analysis of everyday life, it seems to be criticism that actively strives to achieve 'banality', rather than investing it negatively in the object of study.

These developments are not *a priori* related, let alone opposed (as, say, pessimistic and optimistic approaches to popular culture). They also involve different kinds of events. 'Baudrillard' is an author, British Cultural Studies is a complex historical and political movement as well as a library of texts. But irritation may create relations where none need necessarily exist. To attempt to do so is the real point of this paper.

First, I want to define the position of 'cultural studies' in the cultural context in which I study it. In a small way, cultural studies in Australia has been for some time in the state that the Japanese call a *boom*.

This is not merely to say that it's 'booming' in the innocuous and exciting sense that lots of people are doing it or talking about it. It is also to say that the marketing of cultural studies is beginning to define and restrict what it is possible to do and say in its name. Fortunately for the future of cultural studies, a 'boom' in this sense is not a reflection of broader economic conditions at any given time. It is a massive *wave* of collective, but culturally localized, passion – for a musician, a film star, an intellectual topic or figure – which is as emphemeral as it is absolute for participants while it happens. Japanese booms may generate a great deal of money, and the art of predicting and second-guessing them becomes the basis of a whole new industry of expertise.

There is a difference between the Japanese concept of cultural boom, and the older European notion of 'fashion' (which is often still what we think we mean by 'boom' in intellectual or cultural activity). I prefer 'boom' to 'fashion' because it admits greater frankness in discussion about the politics of intellectual work as it relates to, and moves in and out of, commodity circulation. I once saw a TV documentary about booms in Japan, and how useful they could be to Australian bands which couldn't get a hearing anywhere else without Americanizing their music. The program warned that 'no future' is allowed in the mythology of boom – at least, not for the stars. Time is on the side of the promoters only. Next season, instead of a return tour of Japan, the bands would probably get the apologetic refusal, *'very sorry, boom over'*. But if it is impossible for stars to sustain a condition of boom, it is very difficult for anyone to achieve it in the first place. New players would also be rejected: 'Very sorry, no boom'.

This Catch-22 principle was explained on the show by a cartoon-Japanese businessman, who spoke cartoon-Japanese English. This is a way of saying that my notion of Japanese boom is a creation of Australian TV. But shortly after seeing this program, I discussed a translation project with a real Japanese media analyst. When he saw that the Australian collection contained several essays on Foucault, he said, 'Ah Foucault . . . I'm very sorry, but there's no boom'.

So what I'm calling 'frankness' is an admission that cultural boom involves a pre-emptive prohibition and limitation of activity, as well as passion and enthusiasm. The notion of 'intellectual fashion', in contrast, is usually used to denigrate passion and enthusiasm as 'fickle' – in order to imply that real, solid scholarship is going on somewhere in spite of the market, within which it will nonetheless find its true place of recognition once the fuss of fashion subsides. A boom, however, overtly defines and directs what can be done at a given moment. Once it is conceded that booms positively shape the possible, by stabilizing a temporary horizon in relation to which one cannot claim a position of definite exteriority, then it also becomes possible to think more carefully the politics of one's own participation and complicity.

To frame cultural studies as a boom of this kind – in however small a way – may seem excessively cynical, especially to those for whom 'cultural studies' means the rigorous pedagogical and political program of the Birmingham school in England. So I'll complete these preliminary remarks with a comment on how I see the institutional status of cultural studies in Australia. As a constituted discipline, it has a fragile to non-existent academic status. It isn't really a subject area, or a school project in its own right as it can be in the UK. But it has a strong practical force, mostly in media, art, and journalism schools with an associated production unit (for film/radio/TV trainees), or through the work of individuals dispersed in a number of subject areas in universities and colleges.

That means two things. First, cultural studies increasingly has a weak degree of proximity to institutionalized literary criticism, although many individual practitioners may still have received their own first training in English (or French). One immediate consequence is that certain inherited problems – like the high art/mass culture dichotomy, for example, or the debate about the necessity for canons – need not *necessarily* be posed as defining frameworks of argument and research, though they can recur as questions about the history of the present.

A second consequence of a strong or strengthening relation between cultural studies and media production is that our students are likely to be dreaming of a career in the culture industries (including art). This means that as participants in cultural studies as boom, we are helping to train students in the commodification skills that we are also, hopefully, claiming to teach them to criticize. This can create a very complex situation, especially since there is a booming magazine and paperback market for popular essays in cultural studies. Recently, a Sydney gig guide which is handed out free at venues and has a street circulation of 20 000 copies a week had an item under a simulated screaming banner-headline: 'THE CULT DIS-COVER SEMIOTICS! LIVE EQUIPMENT DECONSTRUCTION.'[3] The article never referred back to semiotics or deconstruction. It was in fact a friendly but patronizing review of a Brisbane (i.e. in this code, 'provincial') band called The Cult, which had re-invented the smashing-equipment-on-stage routine. So the gist of the review was : 'cults/semiotics/ deconstruction/Hendrix/The Who/punk/post-punk . . . snooze, snooze, cliché, cliché, very sorry, boom over'.

This sort of thing happens all the time in most places. However, rather than appearing as an amusing side-effect, this defines for me the basic context of my own activity as a writer in Australia, and I take its problems as well as its amusements into serious account when formulating theoretical, as well as pedagogical, problems in practicing cultural studies.

The seriousness of booms for intellectual work can be gauged by comparing the old slogan 'publish or perish' with the newer version, 'commodify or die'. 'Publish or perish' still suggests that it doesn't matter *what* you publish (and of course a lot of academic production still obeys that principle). 'Commodify or die' defines a scarier, if perhaps less hypocritical, principle for academic practice. It also defines the context in which I want to consider 'banality' as a problem in and for cultural theory. For what I see emerging from the recent cultural studies boom is the beginning of a move to 'commodify' an appropriate theoretical *style* for analyzing everyday life – and consequently a proper (and in my view, 'banal') speaking-position for the theorist of popular culture.

I want to begin with a couple of anecdotes about banality, fatality, and television. But since story-telling itself is a popular practice that varies from culture to culture, I shall again define my terms. My impression is that American culture easily encourages people to assume that a first person anecdote is primarily oriented towards the emotive and conative functions, in Jakobson's terms, of communication: that is, towards speaker-expressive and addressee-connective activity, or an I/you axis in discourse. However, I take anecdotes, or yarns, to be primarily referential. They are oriented futuristically towards the construction of a precise, local, and *social* discursive context, of which the anecdote then functions as a *mise en abyme*. That is to say, anecdotes for me are not expressions of personal experience, but allegorical expositions of a model of the way the world can be said to be working. So anecdotes need not be true stories, but they must be functional in a given exchange. Most of my anecdotes in this paper are proposed in that spirit.

It's also in what I take to be an American sense that these (mostly true) stories are offered as a personal response to Patricia Mellencamp's article, 'Situation comedy, feminism and Freud: discourses of Gracie and Lucy'.[4] I discovered this article after thinking for some time about banality and fatality and what these terms had to do with each other, and with my own feeling that there is something both 'fatal' and 'banal' about British Cultural Studies.

Mellencamp's article clarifies the problem for me in two ways. First, it discusses the 'pacification' of women in American situation comedy between 1950 and 1960 by developing a metaphor that *entangles* military and domestic scenes, catastrophic and everyday scenarios: 'foreign policy of "containment"'. It does this not to retrieve a presupposed sociological or historical model of the past, but in order to question the rhetoric of liberation through comedy and pleasure used in theoretical debates in the present. Second, it also analyzes the contradiction in specific Gracie and Lucy programs, not simply to prove the resistant possibilities of female comedians 'being out of control via language (Gracie) or body (Lucy)', but in order to define, in the 'double bind' of the female spectator and comedian, 'dilemmas which . . . no modern critical model can resolve' (81, 87). It is to the difficulty of maintaining and articulating that sense of *dilemma* in cultural studies today that my anecdotes are also addressed.

The first is a fable of origin about situation comedy, foreign policy, and domestic catastrophe.

TV came rather late to Australia: 1956 in the cities, later still in country regions where the distance between towns was immense for the technology of that time. So it was in the early 1960s that in a remote mountain village – where few sounds disturbed the peace except for the mist rolling down to the valley, the murmur of the wireless, the laugh of the kookaburra, the call of the bellbird, the humming of chainsaws and lawnmowers, and the occasional rustle of a snake in the grass – the pervasive silence was shattered by the voice of Lucille Ball.

In the memory of many Australians, television came as Lucy, and Lucy was television. There's a joke in *Crocodile Dundee* where the last white frontiersman is making first contact with modernity in his New York hotel, and he's introduced to the TV set. But he already knows TV: 'I saw that twenty years ago at so-and-so's place'. He sees the title 'I LOVE LUCY', and quips 'yeah, that's what I saw'. It's a throwaway line that at one level works as a formal definition of the 'media-recycle' genre of the film itself. But in terms of the dense cultural punning that characterizes the film, it's also, for Australians, a precise historical joke. It's the more dense in that Paul Hogan was himself one of the first major Australian TV stars, finding an instant stardom in the late 1960s (since Australian-made TV *precedes* postwar Australian cinema) by faking his way on to a talent-quest show, and then abusing the judges. Subsequently, he took on the Marlboro Man in a massive cigarette-advertising battle that lasted long enough to convert the slogan of Hogan's commercials ('Anyhow, have a Winfield') into a proverb inscrutable to foreigners. So Hogan's persona already incarnates a populist myth of indigenous Australian response to 'Lucy' as synecdoche of all American media culture.

But in the beginning was Lucy, and I think she is singled out in memory – since obviously hers was not the only available program – because of the impact of her voice. The introduction of TV in Australia led not only to the usual debates about the restructuring of family life and domestic space, and to predictable fears that the Australian 'accent' in language and culture might be abolished, but also to a specific local version of anxiety about the effects of TV on children. Lucy was heard by many Australians as a screaming hysteric: as 'voice', she was 'seen' to be a woman out of control in both language *and* body. So there was concern that Lucy-television would, by some mimesis or contagion of the voice, metabolically trans- form Australian children from the cheeky little larrikins we were expected to be, into ragingly hyperactive little psychopaths.

My own memory of this lived theoretical debate goes something like this. My mother and I loved Lucy, my father loathed 'that noise'. So once a week, there would be a small scale domestic catastrophe, which soon became routinized, repetitive, banal. I'd turn Lucy on, my father would start grumbling, Mum would be washing dishes in the next room, ask me to raise the volume, I'd do it, Dad would start yelling, Mum would yell back, I'd creep closer to the screen to hear, until Lucy couldn't make herself heard, and I'd retire in disgust to my bedroom, to the second-best of reading a novel. On one of the rare occasions when all this noise had led to a serious quarrel, I went up later as the timid little voice of reason, asking my father why, since it was only half an hour, did he make such a lot of noise. He said that the American voices (never then heard 'live' in our small town) reminded him of the Pacific war. And that surely, after all these years, there were some things that, in the quiet of his own home, a man had a right to try to forget.

Looking back from the contradictions of the present – a locus of concerns which I share with Patricia Mellencamp – I can define from this story a dilemma which persists in different forms today. On the one hand, Lucy had a galvanizing and emancipating effect because of her loquacity, and her relentless tonal insistence. Especially for Australian women and chil- dren, in a society where women were talkative with each other and laconic with men, men were laconic with each other and catatonic with women, and children were seen but not heard. Lucy was one of the first signs of a growing sense that women making a lot of noise did not need to be confined to the harem-like rituals of morning and afternoon tea, or the washing up. On the other hand, my father's response appears, retrospectively, as prescient as well as understandable. The coming of Lucy, and of American TV, was among the first explicit announcements to a general public still vaguely imagining itself as having been 'British' that Australia was now (as it had in fact been anyway since 1942) hooked into the media network of a different war machine.

My second anecdote follows logically from that, but is set in another world. Ten years later, after a whole cultural revolution in Australia and another war with Americans in Asia, I saw a TV catastrophe one banal Christmas Eve. There we were in Sydney, couch-potatoing away, when the evening was shattered by that sentence which takes different forms in different cultures, but is still perhaps the one sentence always capable of reminding people everywhere within reach of TV of a common and vulnerable humanity – 'We interrupt this transmission for a special news flash'.

Usually, on hearing that, you get an adrenaline rush, you freeze, you wait, you hear what's happened, and then the mechanisms of bodily habituation to crisis take over to see you through the time ahead. This occasion was alarmingly different. The announcer's voice actually stammered: 'er . . . um . . . something's happened to Darwin'. Darwin is the capital of Australia's far north. Most Australians know nothing about it, and live thousands of miles away. It takes days to get into by land or sea, and in a well-entrenched national imaginary it is the 'gateway' to Asia, and, in its remoteness and 'vulnerability', the likely port of a conventional invasion. This has usually been a racist nightmare about the 'yellow peril' sweeping down, but it does also have a basis in flat-map logic. There's no one south of Australia but penguins.

Some people panicked, and waited anxiously for details. But the catastrophe was that there was *no information*. This was not catastrophe *on* TV – like the *Challenger* sequence – but a catastrophe of and *for* TV. There were no pictures, not reports, just *silence* – which had long ceased to be coded as paradisal, as it was in my fable of origin, but was not the very definition of a state of total emergency. The announcer's stammer was devastating. Losing control of all mechanisms of assuring credibility, his palpable personal distress had exposed us, unbelievably, to something like a *truth*.[5] When those of us who could sleep woke up the next day to find everyday life going on as usual, we realized it couldn't have been World War III. But it took another twenty-four hours for 'true' news to be re-established, and to reassure us that Darwin had merely been wiped out by a cyclone. Whereupon we went into the 'natural disaster' genre of TV living, and banality resumed for everyone, except for the victims. But in the aftermath, a question surfaced. Why had such a cyclone-sensitive city not been forewarned? It was a very big cyclone – someone should have seen it coming.

Two rumors did the rounds. One was an oral rumor, or a folk legend. The cyclone took Darwin by surprise because it was a Russian weather warfare experiment that had either gone wrong or – in the more menacing variant – actually found its target. The other rumor made it into writing in the odd newspaper. There had been foreknowledge: indeed, even after the cyclone there was a functioning radio tower and an airstrip which might have sent news out straight away. But these belonged to an American military installation near Darwin, which was not supposed to be there. And in the embarrassment of realizing the scale of disaster to come, a decision had been made by someone somewhere to say nothing, in the hope of averting discovery. If this was true, 'they' needn't have worried. The story was never, to my knowledge, pursued further. We didn't really care. If there had been such an installation, it wasn't newsworthy; true or false, it wasn't catastrophic; true or false, it merged with the routine stories of conspiracy and paranoia in urban everyday life; and, true or false, it was – compared with the Darwin fatality count and the human interest stories to be had from survivors – just too banal to be of interest.

My anecdotes are also banal, in that they mark out a televisual contradiction which is over-familiar as both a theoretical dilemma, and an everyday experience. It is the contradiction between one's pleasure, fascination, thrill, and sense of 'life', even birth, in popular culture, and the deathly shadows of war, invasion, emergency, crisis, and terror that perpetually haunt the networks. Sometimes there seems to be nothing more to say about that 'contradiction', in theory, yet as a phase of collective experience it does keep coming back around. So I want to use these two anecdotes now to frame a comparison between the late work of Baudrillard, and some aspects of 'British' (or Anglo-Australian) cultural studies – two theoretical projects that have had something to say about the problem. I begin with Baudrillard, because 'banality' is a working concept in his lexicon, whereas it is not a significant term for the cultural studies that today increasingly cites him.

In Baudrillard's terms, my anecdotes marked out a historical shift between a period of concern about TV's effects on the real – which is thereby assumed to be distinct from its representation (the *Lucy* moment) – and a time in which TV *generates* the real to the extent that any interruption in its process of doing so is experienced as more catastrophic in the lounge room than a 'real' catastrophe elsewhere. So I have simply defined a shift between a regime of production, and a regime of simulation. This would also correspond to a shift between a more or less real Cold War ethos, where American military presence in your country could be construed as friendly or hostile, but you thought you should have a choice, and that the choice mattered; and a pure war (or, simulated chronic cold war) ethos, in which Russian cyclones or American missiles are completely interchangeable in a local imaginary of terror, and the choice between them is meaningless.

This analysis could be generated from Baudrillard's major thesis in *L'échange symbolique et la mort* (1976). The later Baudrillard would have little further interest in my story about Lucy's voice and domestic squabbles in an Australian country town, but might still be mildly amused by the story of a city disappearing for 36 hours because of a breakdown in communications. However, where I would want to say that this event was for participants a real, if mediated, experience of catastrophe, he could say that it was just a final flicker of real reality. With the subsequent installation of a global surveillance regime through the satellization of the world, the disappearance of Darwin could never occur again. Everything is now already seen and filmed before it actually happens anyway.

So Baudrillard would collapse the 'contradiction' (in itself, an archaic term) that I want to maintain: and he would make each semantic pole of my stories (the everyday and the catastrophic, the exhilarating and the frightful, the emancipatory and the terroristic) invade and contaminate its other in a process of mutual exacerbation. This is a viral, rather than an atomic, model of crisis in everyday life. If for Andreas Huyssen, modernism as an adversary culture constitutes itself in an 'anxiety of contamination' by its Other (mass culture),[6] the Baudrillardian text on (or of) mass culture is constituted by perpetually *intensifying* the contamination of one of any two terms by its other.

So like all pairs of terms in Baudrillard's work, the values 'banality' and 'fatality' chase each other around his pages following the rule of dyadic reversibility. Any one term can be hyperbolically intensified until it turns into its opposite. Superbanality, for example, becomes fatal, and a super-fatality would be banal. It's a very simple but, when well done, dizzying logico-semantic game which makes Baudrillard's books very easy to understand, but any one term most difficult to define. A complication in this case is that 'banality' and 'fatality' chase each other around two books, *De la séduction* (1979) and *Les stratégies fatales* (1983).

One way to elucidate such a system is to imagine a distinction between two sets of two terms – for example, 'fatal charm' and 'banal seduction'. Fatal charm can be seductive in the old sense of an irresistible force, exerted by someone who desires nothing except to play the game in order to capture and to immolate the desire of the other. That's what's fatal about it. Banal seduction, on the other hand, does involve desire: desire for, perhaps, an immovable object to overcome. That's what's fatal for it. Baudrillard's next move is to claim that both of these strategies are finished. The only irresistible force today is that of the moving *object* as it flees and evades the subject. This is the 'force' of the sex-object of the silent zombie-masses, and of femininity (not necessarily detached by Baudrillard from real women, but certainly detached from feminists).

This structure is, I think, a 'fatal' travesty, or a 'seduction' of the terms of Althusserian epistemology and *its* theory of the moving object. In *Les stratégies fatales*, it is rewritten in terms of a theory of global catastrophe. The human species has passed the dead point of history: we are living out the ecstacy of permanent catastrophe, which slows down as it becomes more and more intense (*une catastrophe au ralenti*, slow-motion, or slowing-motion catastrophe), until the supereventfulness of the event approaches the uneventfulness of absolute inertia, and we begin to live everyday catastrophe as an endless dead point, or a perpetual freeze frame.

This is the kind of general scenario produced in Baudrillard's work by the logic of mutual contamination. However, an examination of the local occurrences of the terms 'banal' and 'fatal' in both books suggests that 'banality' is associated, quite clearly and conventionally, with negative aspects of media – over-representation, excessive visibility, information overload, an obscene plenitude of images, a gross platitudinousness of the all-pervasive present.

On the other hand, and even though there is strictly no past and no future in Baudrillard's system, he uses 'fatality' as both a nostalgic and a futuristic term for invoking a classical critical value, *discrimination* (redefined as a senseless, but still rule-governed, principle of selectiveness). 'Fatality' is nostalgic in the sense that it invokes in the text, for the present, an 'aristocratic' ideal of maintaining an elite, arbitrary, and avowedly artificial order. It is futuristic because Baudrillard suggests that in an age of overload, rampant banality, and catastrophe (which have become at this stage equivalents of each other), the last Pascalian wager may be to bet on the return, in the present, of what can only be a simulacrum of the past. When fatal charm can simulate seducing banal seduction, you have a fatal strategy. The animating myth of this return is to be, in opposition to critical philosophies of Difference (which have now become identical), a myth of *Fatum* – that is, Destiny.

So read in one sense, Baudrillard's theory merely calls for an aesthetic order (fatality) to deal with mass cultural anarchy (banality). What makes his appeal more charming than most other tirades about the decay of standards is that it can be read in the opposite sense. The 'order' being called for is radically decadent, super-banal. However, there is a point at which the play stops.

In one of Baudrillard's anecdotes (an enunciative *mise en abyme* of his theory), set in some vague courtly context with the ambience of a mid-eighteenth century French epistolary novel, a man is trying to seduce a woman. She asks, 'Which part of me do you find most seductive?' He replies, 'Your eyes'. Next day, he receives an envelope. Inside, instead of the letter, he finds a bloody eye. Analyzing his own fable, Baudrillard points out that in the obviousness, the literalness of her gesture, the woman has purloined the place of her seducer.

The man is the banal seducer. She, the fatal seducer, sets him a trap with her question as he moves to entrap her. In the platitudinous logic of courtliness, he can only reply 'your eyes' – rather than naming some more vital organ which she might not have been able to post – since the eye is the window of the soul. Baudrillard concludes that the woman's literalness is fatal to the man's banal figuration: she loses an eye, but he loses face. He can never again 'cast an eye' on another woman without thinking literally of the bloody eye that replaced the letter. So Baudrillard's final resolution of the play between banality and fatality is this: a banal theory assumes, like the platitudinous seducer, that the subject is more powerful than the object. A fatal theory knows, like the woman, that the object is always *worse* than the subject (*'je ne suis pas belle, je suis pire . . .'*).

Nonetheless, in making the pun 'she loses an eye, but he loses face', Baudrillard in fact enunciatively reoccupies the place of control of meaning by *de*-literalizing the woman's gesture, and returning it to figuration. Only the pun makes the story work as a fable of seduction, by draining the 'blood' from the eye. Without it, we would merely be reading a horror story (or a feminist moral tale). So it follows that Baudrillard''s figuration is, in fact, 'fatal' to the woman's literality, and to a literal feminist reading of her story that might presumably ensue.

This embedding of an inscription of woman as literalness in a discourse that admires it, but denies it power, is not specific to Baudrillard. It could be compared to Jean-François Lyotard's myth of femininity as a fatal collapse of meta-language, or a bearer of that terrible destiny, that general liquidation of discourse, that Derrida calls 'catastrophe'.[7] I suspect that the problem of woman as literalness (ultimately, as we know, an undefinable concept) could be a more 'fatal' object of study than femininity and metaphor. At any rate, the privilege of 'knowing' the significance of the woman's fatal-banal gesture is securely restored to meta-language, and to the subject of exegesis.

Recent cultural studies offers something completely different. It speaks not of restoring discrimination, but of encouraging cultural democracy. It respects difference, and sees mass culture not as a vast banality-machine, but as raw material made available for a variety of popular practices.

In saying 'it', I am treating a range of quite different texts and arguments as a single entity. This is always unfair to any individual item, but it is a mode of perception endemic to, and possibly valid for, the experience of cultural booms. Sometimes, reading magazines like *New Socialist* or *Marxism Today* from the last couple of years, flipping through *Cultural Studies*, or scanning the pop-theory pile in the bookshop, I get the feeling that somewhere in some English publisher's vault there is a master-disk from which thousands of versions of the same article about pleasure, resistance, and the politics of consumption are being run off under different names with minor variations. Americans and Australians are recycling this basic pop-theory article, too: with the perhaps major variation that English pop-theory still derives at least nominally from a left populism attempting to salvage a sense of life from the catastrophe of Thatcherism. Once cut free from that context, as commodities always are, and recycled in quite different political cultures, the vestigal *critical* force of that populism tends to disappear or mutate.

This imaginary pop-theory article might respond to my television anecdotes by bracketing the bits about war and death as a sign of paranoia about popular culture, by pointing out that it's a mistake to confuse conditions of production with the subsequent effects of images, and by noting that with TV one may always be 'ambivalent'. It would certainly stress, with the Lucy story, the subversive pleasure of the female spectators. (My father could perhaps represent an Enlightenment paternalism of reason trying to make everything cohere in a model of social totality.) With the Darwin story, it would insist on the creativity of the consumer/spectator, and maybe have us distractedly zapping from channel to channel during the catastrophe instead of being passively hooked into the screen, and then resisting the war machine with our local legends and readings. The article would then restate, using a mix of different materials as illustration, the enabling theses of contemporary cultural studies.

In order to move away now from reliance on imaginary bad objects, I'll refer to an excellent real article which gives a summary of these theses – Mica Nava's 'Consumerism and its contradictions'. Among the enabling theses – and they *have* been enabling – are these: consumers are not 'cultural dopes', but active, critical users of mass culture; consumption practices cannot be derived from or reduced to a mirror of production; consumer practice is 'far more than just economic activity: it is also about dreams and consolation, communication and confrontation, image and identity. Like sexuality, it consists of a multiplicity of fragmented and contradictory discourses.'[8]

I'm not now concerned to contest these theses. For the moment, I'll buy the lot. What I'm interested in is firstly, the sheer proliferation of the restatements, and secondly, the emergence in some of them of a *restrictive definition* of the ideal knowing subject of cultural studies.

John Fiske's historical account in 'British cultural studies and television' [reprinted here as Chapter 6] produces one such restatement and restriction. The social terrain of the beginning of his article is occupied by a version of the awesomely complex Althusserian subject-in-ideology, and by a summary of Gramsci on hegemony. Blending these produces a notion of subjectivity as a dynamic field, in which all sorts of permutations are possible at different moments in an endless process of production, contestation, and reproduction of social identities. By the end of the article, the field has been vastly simplified: there are 'the dominant classes' (exerting hegemonic force), and 'the people' (making their own meanings and constructing their own culture 'within, and sometimes against' the culture provided for them) (Fiske, 1987, 286).

Cultural studies for Fiske aims to understand and encourage cultural democracy. One way of understanding the *demos* is '*ethnography*' – finding out what the people say and think about their culture. But the methods cited are 'voxpop' techniques common to journalism and empirical sociology – interviewing, collecting background, analyzing statements made spontaneously by, or solicited from, informants. So the choice of the term 'ethnography' for these practices emphasizes a possible 'ethnic' gap between the cultural student and the culture studied. The 'understanding' and 'encouraging' subject may share some aspects of that culture, but *in the process of interrogation and analysis* is momentarily located outside it. 'The people' is a voice, or a *figure of* a voice, cited in a discourse of exegesis. For example, Fiske cites 'Lucy', a 14-year-old fan of Madonna ('She's tarty and seductive . . . but it looks alright when she does it, you know, what I mean . . .'); and then goes on to translate, and diagnose, what she means: 'Lucy's problems probably stem from her recognition that marriage is a patriarchal institution and, as such, is threatened by Madonna's sexuality' (273).

If this is again a process of embedding in meta-discourse a sample of raw female speech, it is also a perfectly honest approach for any academic analyst of culture to take. It differs from a discourse that simply appeals to 'experience' to validate and universalize its own conclusions. However, such honesty should also require some analysis of the analyst's own investment – some recognition of the double play of transference. (Lucy tells us her pleasure in Madonna: but what is our pleasure in Lucy's?) This kind of recognition is rarely made in populist polemics. What takes its place is firstly a citing of popular voices (the informants), an act of translation and commentary, and then a play of *identification* between the knowing subject of cultural studies, and a collective subject, 'the people'.

In Fiske's text, however, 'the people' have no necessary defining characteristics – except an indomitable capacity to 'negotiate' readings, generate
new interpretations, and remake the materials of culture. This is also, of
course, the function of cultural studies itself (and in Fiske's version, the
study does include a 'semiotic analysis of the text' to explore *how* meanings
are made) (Fiske, 272). So against the hegemonic force of the dominant
classes, 'the people' in fact represent the most creative energies and functions of critical reading. In the end they are not simply the cultural
student's object of study, and his native informants. The people are also
the textually delegated, allegorical emblem of the critic's own activity. Their
ethnos may be constructed as other, but it is used as the ethnographer's
mask.

Once 'the people' are both a source of authority for a text and a figure of
its own critical activity, the populist enterprise is not only circular but (like
most empirical sociology) narcissistic in structure. Theorizing the problems
that ensue is a way to break out of the circuit of repetition. Another is to
project elsewhere a mis-understanding or discouraging Other figure (often
that feminist or Marxist Echo, the blast from the past) to necessitate and
enable more repetition.

The opening chapter of Iain Chambers's *Popular Culture* provides an
example of this, as well as a definition of what counts as 'popular' knowledge that is considerably more restrictive than John Fiske's. Chambers
argues that in looking at popular culture, we should not subject individual
signs and single texts to the 'contemplative stare of official culture'. When
applied to the tactile, transitory, expendable, visceral world of the popular,
contemplation would be a mis-understanding called Vanity. Instead, it is a
practice of 'distracted reception' that really characterizes the subject of
'popular epistemology'. For Chambers, this distraction has consequences
for the practice of writing. Writing can imitate popular culture (life . . .) by,
for example, 'writing through quotations', and refusing to 'explain . . .
references fully'. To explain would be to reimpose the contemplative
stare, and adopt the authority of the 'academic mind'.[9]

Chambers's argument emerges from an interpretation of the history of
subcultural practices, especially in music. I've argued elsewhere my disagreement with his attempt to use that history to generalize about popular
culture in The Present.[10] Here, I want to suggest that an image of the
subject of pop epistemology as casual and 'distracted', obliquely entails a
revival of the figure that Andreas Huyssen, Tania Modleski, and Patrice
Petro have described in various contexts as 'mass culture as woman'.[11]
Petro in particular further points out that the contemplation/distraction
opposition is historically implicated in the construction of the 'female
spectator' as site, and target, of a theorization of modernity by male
intellectuals in Weimar.[12]

There are many versions of a 'distraction' model available in cultural
studies today: there are housewives phasing in and out of TV or flipping
through magazines in laundromats as well as pop intellectuals playing
with quotes. In Chambers's text, which is barely concerned with women
at all, distraction is not presented as a female characteristic. Yet today's
recycling of Weimar's distraction nonetheless has the 'contours', in Petro's

phrase, of a familiar female stereotype. Distracted, absent-minded, insou-
ciant, vague, flighty, skimming from image to image . . . the rush of
associations runs irresistibly towards a figure of mass culture not as
woman but, more specifically, as bimbo.

In the texts Petro analyzes, 'contemplation' (of distraction in the cinema)
is assumed to be the prerogative of male intellectual audiences. In pop
epistemology, a complication is introduced via the procedures of projection
and identification that Elaine Showalter describes in 'Critical cross-dressing'.[13] The knowing subject of popular epistemology no longer contem-
plates 'mass culture' as bimbo, but takes on the assumed mass cultural
characteristics in the writing of his own text. Since the object of projection
and identification in post-subcultural theory tends to be black music and
'style' rather than the European (and literary) feminine, we find an actantial
hero of knowledge emerging in the form of the *white male theorist* as bimbo.

White male theorists today have their problems, and I don't want to
diminish them. I'm not averse to cross-dressing – indeed, the wonderful
American word 'bimbo' was actually suggested to me by Kathleen Wood-
ward when I was struggling to articulate my own contemplative interest in
the Sylvester Stallone of *Rocky* I and II. I think the real problem with the
notion of pop epistemology is not, in this case, the vestigial anti-feminism of
the concept of distraction. The problem is that in anti-academic pop-theory
writing (much of which, like Chambers's book, circulates as textbooks with
exam and essay topics at the end of each chapter), a stylistic enactment of
the 'popular' as distracted, scanning the surface, and short on attention-
span, performs a retrieval, at the level of *enunciative* practice, of the thesis of
'cultural dopes'. In the critique of which – going right back to the early
work of Stuart Hall, not to mention Raymond Williams – the project
cultural studies effectively and rightly began.

One could claim that this interpretation is only possible if one continues
to assume that the academic traditions of 'contemplation' really do define
intelligence, and that to be 'distracted' can therefore only mean being
dopey. I would reply that as long as we accept restating the alternatives
in those terms, that is precisely the assumption we continue to recycle. No
matter which of the terms we validate, the contemplation/distraction,
academic/popular, oppositions can only serve to limit and distort the
possibilities of popular practice.

Furthermore, I think that this return to the postulate of cultural dopism
in the *practice* of writing may be one reason why, beyond the pressure on
individual producers to supply the demand created by booms, pop-theory
is now generating over and over again the same article which never goes
beyond recycling and restating its own basic premises. If a cultural dopism
is being enunciatively performed (and valorized) in a discourse that tries to
contest it, then the argument in fact *cannot* move on, but can only retrieve
its point of departure as 'banality' (a word pop theorists don't normally
use) in the negative sense.

For the thesis of cultural studies as Fiske and Chambers present it runs
perilously close to this kind of formulation: people in modern mediatized
societies are complex and contradictory, mass cultural texts are complex
and contradictory, therefore people using them produce complex and

contradictory culture. To add that this popular culture has critical and resistant elements is tautological – unless one (or a predicated someone, that Other who needs to be told) has a concept of culture so rudimentary that it excludes criticism of and resistance from the practice of everyday life.

Given the completely different values ascribed to mass culture in Baudrillard's work and in pop-theory, it is tempting to make a distracted contrast between them in terms of elitism and populism. However, they are not symmetrical opposites.

Cultural studies posits a 'popular' subject 'supposed to know' in a certain manner, which the subject of populist theory then claims to understand (Fiske) or mimic (Chambers). Baudrillard's elitism, however, is not an elitism of a knowing subject of theory, but an elitism of the *object* – which is forever, and actively, evasive. There is a hint of 'distraction' here, an echo between the problematics of woman and literalness and mass culture as bimbo which deserves further contemplation. A final twist is that for Baudrillard the worst (that is, most effective) elitism of the object can be called, precisely, 'theory'. Theory is understood as an objectified and objectifying (never 'objective') force strategically engaged in an ever more intense process of commodification. Like 'distraction' it is distinguished by the rapidity of its *flight*, rather than by a concentrated pursuit.

Instead of pursuing it, however, I shall come back around to commodification, and the problem of cultural boom.

It is remarkable, given the differences between them and the crisis-ridden society that each in its own way addresses, that neither of the projects I've discussed leaves much place for an unequivocally pained, unambivalently discontented, or *aggresive* theorizing subject. It isn't just negligence. There is an active process going on in both of dis-crediting – by direct dismissal (Baudrillard), or covert inscription as Other (cultural studies) – the voices of grumpy feminists and cranky leftists ('Frankfurt School' can do duty for both). To discredit such voices is, as I understand it, one of the immediate political functions of the current boom in cultural studies (as distinct from the intentionality of projects invested by it). To discredit a voice is something very different from displacing an analysis which has become outdated, or revising a strategy which no longer serves its purpose.

Baudrillard's hostility to the discourses of political radicalism is perfectly clear and brilliantly played out. It is a little too aggressive to accuse cultural studies of playing much the same game. Cultural studies is a humane and optimistic discourse, trying to derive its values from materials and conditions already available to people. On the other hand, it can become an apologetic 'yes, *but* . . .' discourse, that most often proceeds *from* admitting class, racial, and sexual oppression *to* finding the inevitable saving grace – when its theoretical presuppositions should require it at least to do both simultaneously, even 'dialectically'. And in practice the 'but . . .' – that is to say, the argumentative rhetoric – is immediately directed not to the hegemonic force of the 'dominant classes', but to other critical theories (vulgar feminism, the Frankfurt school) inscribed as misunderstanding popular culture.

This may be partly a result of the notions of 'negotiated', 'resistant', and 'oppositional' *readings* that still play such a large part in our analyses. In the end, the aim of analysis becomes to generate one of these, thus repeatedly proving it possible to do so. Since there is little point in re-generating a 'dominant' reading of a text (the features of which are usually pre-supposed by the social theory which frames the reading in the first place), the figure of a misguided but on-side Other is necessary to justify the exercise and guarantee the 'difference' of the reading. I think that two related rhetorical determinants also enable cultural studies to work this way in spite of the intentions of many of us who do it.

The first of these is a tendency towards emotional simplification. To simplify myself, I'd say that where the fatal strategies of Baudrillard keep returning us to his famous Black Hole – a scenario that is so grim, obsessive, and in its enunciative strategies maniacally over-coherent, that instead of speaking, a woman must *tear out her eye* to be heard – the voxpop style of cultural studies is on the contrary offering us the sanitized world of a deodorant commercial where there's always a way to redemption. There's something sad about that, because cultural studies emerged from a real attempt to give voice to much grittier experiences of class, race, and gender.

If emotional simplification is one problem, then there is another that helps to produce the simplification. This 'problem' is one of the enabling theses of cultural studies: that 'consumption' can be treated as a quasi-autonomous reality diverging from another 'reality' called 'production' – which, after Marxism, we are supposed to know quite enough about for the time being. Production 'processes' are well known, but consumption 'practices' remain enigmatic.

There are a number of difficulties with this even as a rough working assumption: for example, consumption (albeit as 'practice') can only be opposed as an equivalent term to 'production' once the concept of *'mode of production'* has been reduced to 'factories making goods, capitalists making profits'. Only in this utterly vestigal economic sense can the practice of consumption be predicated as a 'separate sphere' rather than one of the necessary, complex, variable *phases* of a productive process – which is no more autonomous from, than it is metonymic of, that process. 'Difference', after all, is not 'autonomy'.

More concretely, at a time when it is impossible to determine to what extent, and in which places, 'practices' like program-trading and arbitrage in foreign exchange futures are effects or causes of a catastrophic stock market crash which is immediately reconstituted as banal in media *also* functioning indeterminately as causes and effects in the process, the assumption that production is 'known' and consumption enigmatic is, to say the least, unhelpful. Baudrillard, for all his unrelenting bleakness, is in this respect more effective, more *fatal*, as an analyst of the way the world is working. The kind of explanation from 'production' so cheerfully rejected in cultural studies usually boils down to one based on a model of good old-fashioned, family-company industrialism. You can't derive your analysis of what people make of a record from finding out that capitalists own the factory. You can't deduce our uses of TV from knowing who makes the program and who owns the channels and how they link to other companies and agencies of state.

Indeed, you can't. But in an era of *de*-industrialization and increasing integration of markets and circuits alike, the problem of theorizing relations between production and consumption (or thinking 'production' at all) is considerably more complex than is allowed by a reduction of the effort to do so to anachronistic terms. The computerization of capitalism is also a factor which makes extremely dubious the literary analogies that underpin, all too often unquestioned, the notion of consumer practice: production is like writing, consumption is like reading, therefore we can write our readings of consumption without reference to the author's (capitalism's) intentions. However, unlike the concept of 'writing', the term 'production' in cultural theory has atrophied instead of being re-theorized. These days it is often used as a shorthand term for 'talking economics'. 'Consumption' means talking about sex, art, 'cultural politics', and fun. Before completely relegating the former to the realm of the *déjà vu*, however, it may be as well to consider that in the late twentieth century, after a century of romanticism, modernism, the avant-garde, and psychoanalysis, economics, in fact, may be considerably more enigmatic than sexuality.

Yet in saying this, my own discourse is taking on the haranguing tone of an already-discredited voice. The sense of frustration that some of us who would inscribe our own work as cultural studies feel with the terms of present debate can be disabling. If one is equally uneasy about fatalistic theory on the one hand, and about cheerily 'making the best of things' in the name of a new politics of culture on the other, then it is a poor solution to consent to confine oneself to (and in) the dour position of rebuking both.

In *The Practice of Everyday Life*, Michel de Certeau provides a more positive approach to the politics of theorizing popular culture, and to the particular problems I have discussed.[14] One of the pleasures of this text for me is the range of moods that it admits to a field of study which – rather surprisingly, since 'everyday life' is at issue – often seems to be occupied only by cheerleaders and prophets of doom. So from it I shall borrow – in a contemplative rather than a distracted spirit – two quotations to interrupt my own slide into sermonizing.

The first quotation is in fact from Jacques Sojcher's *La Démarche poétique*. De Certeau cites it after arguing for a double process of mobilizing the 'weighty apparatus' of theories of ordinary language to analyze everyday practices, *and* seeking to restore to those practices their logical and cultural legitimacy. De Certeau insists, however, that in this kind of research, everyday practices will 'alternately exacerbate *and disrupt* our logics. Its regrets are like those of the poet, and like him, it struggles against oblivion'. So I will use this quotation in turn as a response to the terrifying and unrelenting coherence of Baudrillard's fatal strategies. Sojcher:

> And I forgot the elements of chance introduced by circumstances, calm or haste, sun or cold, dawn or dusk, the taste of strawberries or abandonment, the half-understood message, the front page of newspapers, the voice on the telephone,

the most anodyne conversation, the most anonymous man or woman, everything that speaks, makes noise, passes by, touches us lightly, meets us head on. (xvi)

The second quotation comes from a discussion of 'Freud and the ordinary man', and the difficult problems that arise when 'elitist writing uses the "vulgar" [or, I would add, the 'feminine'] speaker as a disguise for a metalanguage about itself'. For de Certeau, a recognition that the 'ordinary' and the 'popular' can act as a mask in analytical discourse does not imply that the study of popular culture is impossible except as recuperation. Instead, it requires a displacement in the practice of knowledge:

> Far from arbitrarily assuming the privilege of speaking in the name of the ordinary (it cannot *be* spoken), or claiming to be in that general place (that would be a false 'mysticism'), or, worse, offering up a hagiographic everydayness for its edifying value, it is a matter of restoring historicity to the movement which leads analytical procedures back to the frontiers, to the point where they are changed, indeed disturbed, by the ironic and mad banality that speaks in 'Everyman' in the sixteenth century, and that has returned in the final stages of Freud's knowledge. . . . (5)

In this way the ordinary, he suggests, 'can reorganize the place from which discourse is produced'. I think that this means being very careful about our enunciative and story-telling strategies – much more careful than much cultural studies (and feminist writing) has been in its mimesis of a popular – or 'feminine' – voice.

In spirit, de Certeau's work is much more in sympathy with the populist, *bricoleur* impulse of cultural studies than with apocalyptic thinking. The motto of his book could be the sentence, 'People have to make do with what they have' (18). Its French title is *Arts de faire*: arts of making, arts of doing, arts of making-do. What is useful in his book as a charm against emotional and theoretical simplification is its perpetual movement *between* what he calls 'polemological' and 'utopian' spaces and practices (15–18).[15]

The basic assumption founding any polemological space is summed up by a quotation in the text from a Maghrebian syndicalist at Billancourt: 'They always fuck us over'. This is a sentence that seems inadmissible in contemporary cultural studies: it defines a space of struggle, and *mendacity* ('the strong always win, and words always deceive'). But at the same time, a utopian space is reproduced in the popular legends of *miracles* that circulate and intensify as social repression becomes more absolute and apparently successful. As an example, de Certeau tells the story of a legendary friar in northeastern Brazil.

I'd cite as an allegory of both a television anecdote about the Sydney Birthday Cake Scandal. 1988 is the celebration of the Australian Bicentenary. But it's really the Bicentenary of Sydney as the original penal colony. 'Australia' is in fact only 87 years old, and so the event is widely understood to be an exercise in the simulation, rather than celebration, of a national history.

A benevolent Sydney real estate baron proposed to build a giant birthday cake above an expressway tunnel in the most famous social wastage-and-devastation zone of the city, so we could know we were having a party. The project was unveiled on a TV current affairs show, and there was an uproar – not only from exponents of good taste against kitsch. The network switchboards were jammed by people pointing out that, above the area that belongs to junkies, runaways, homeless people, and the child as well as adult prostitution trade, a giant cake would invoke a late eighteenth-century voice quite different from that of our first prison governor saying, 'Here we are in Botany Bay'. The voice would be Marie Antoinette's – 'Let them eat cake'. There was nothing casual or distracted about the voxpop observation.

The baron then proposed a public competition, again via TV, to find an alternative design. There were lots of proposals: a few of us wanted to build Kafka's writing machine from 'In the penal colony'. Others proposed an echidna, a water tower, a hypodermic, or a giant condom. The winner was a suburban rotary clothesline: Australia's major contribution to twentieth-century technology, and thus something of a symbol for the current decline in our economy. But in the end, the general verdict was that we'd rather make-do with the cake. As one person said in a voxpop segment, 'At least with the cake, the truth about the party is all now out in the open'. So had the cake been built, it would have been, after all that polemological narrativity, a very political and problematized, utopian popular monument.

No monument materialized, and the story died down. However, it reappeared in a different form when an extravagant Bicentennial Birthday Party was duly held on January 26, 1988. Two and a half million people converged on a few square kilometres of harbor foreshore on a glorious summer's day to watch the ships, to splash about, to eat and drink and fall asleep in the sun during speeches. The largest gathering of Aboriginal people since the original Invasion Day was also held, to protest the proceedings. The party ended with a fabulous display of fireworks, choreographed to music including 'Power and the Passion' by Australia's most polemological rock band, Midnight Oil. The day after this splendid and awful event, a slogan surfaced in the streets and on the walls of the city and in press cartoons: 'Let them eat fireworks'.

De Certeau's insistence on the movement *between* polemological and utopian practices of making-do makes it possible to say that if cultural studies is losing its polemological edge – its capacity to articulate loss, despair, disillusion, anger and thus to learn from failure – Baudrillard's work has not lost its utopianism, but has rather produced a *convergence* between polemological and (nightmare) utopian spaces. But to invoke instead with de Certeau a *'mad and ironic banality'* of the popular that can insinuate itself in our techniques as theorists, and reorganize the place from which our discourse is produced, is immediately to posit an awkward position for theorizing subjects for whom *Everyman* might not serve as well as *I Love Lucy* as a political fable of origin. For me as a feminist, as a distracted media baby, and also, to some extent, as an Australian, a reference to *Everyman* is rather a reminder of the problems of disengaging my own thinking from patriarchal, humanist, and eurocentric cultural norms.

'Banality' is one of a group of words – including 'trivial' and 'mundane' – whose modern history inscribes the disintegration of old ideals about the common people, the common place, the common culture. In medieval French, the 'banal' fields, mills, and ovens were those used communally. It is only in the late eighteenth century that these words begin to accumulate their modern sense of the trite, the platitudinous, and the unoriginal. So it's a banal observation that if banality, like triviality, is an irritant that returns again and again to trouble cultural theory, it is because the very concept is part of the modern history of taste, value, and critique of judgment, that constitutes the polemical field within which cultural studies takes issue with classical aesthetics.

If banality keeps on coming back around in our polemics, it is less because of the residual elitism of individual intellectuals, and populist reaction to it, and more because 'banality' as mythic signifier is always a mask for the question of value, *and* of value-judgment, or 'discrimination'. If I find myself in the contradictory position of wanting to reject the patronizing idea that 'banality' is a useful framing concept to discuss mass media, and yet go on to complain myself of 'banality' in cultural studies, the problem may arise because the critical vocubulary available to people wanting to theorize the discriminations that they make in relation to their own experience of popular culture – without debating the 'validity' of that experience, even less that culture *as a whole* – is still, today, extraordinarily depleted. It seems to me, therefore, that the worst thing one can do in this context is to accuse people trying to develop a critique of popular culture of succumbing to 'elitism' or pessimism.

For there is an extra twist to the history of banality. In the Oxford version of this history, before it goes round through old French to come round in medieval English, it has a twin or double heritage in, on the one hand, old English, *bannan* – to summon, or to curse – and a Germanic *bannan* – to proclaim *under penalty*. So banality is related to banishing, and also to wedding *bans*. In other words, it is a figure inscribing power in an act of *enunciation*. In medieval times, it could mean two things beside 'commonplace'. It could mean, to issue an edict or a summons (usually to war). That was the enunciative privilege of the feudal lord. Or it could mean to proclaim under orders: to line the streets, and cheer, in the manner required by the demand *'Un ban pour le vainqueur!'* To obediently perform a rhythmic applause is the 'banal' enunciative duty of the common people.

This two-sided historical function of banality – lordly pronouncement, mimetic popular performance – is not yet banished from the practice of theorizing the popular today. It's very hard, perhaps impossible, not to make the invoked voice of the popular perform itself obediently in just that medieval way in our writing. However, when the voice of that which academic discourses – including cultural studies, however populist they may be – constitutes *as* popular, begins in turn to theorize its speech, then you have an interesting possibility. That theorization may well go round by way of the procedures that Homi Bhaba has theorized as 'colonial mimicry', for example, but may also come around eventually in a different, and as yet utopian, mode of enunciative practice.[16]

166   *What is cultural studies?*

For this reason, I think that minoritarian theorizing subjects in cultural studies have to work quite hard *not* to become subjects of banality in that old double sense: not to formulate edicts and proclamations, yet to keep theorizing; not to become supermimics in the Baudrillardian sense of becoming, by reversal, the same as that which is mimicked, yet to refuse to subside permanently either into silence or into a posture of reified difference. Through some such effort, pained and disgruntled subjects, who are also joyous and inventive practitioners, can articulate our critique of everyday life.

So as a vocal *spin-off*, perhaps, rather than 'child' of Lucy-television and its complex effects as a 'foreign policy of potential "containment"' in my culture, I come back around, in the end, to Patricia Mellencamp's stress on engaging with the contradictions of Lucy in the situation 'comedy' of *the present*. 'Child' is probably an unfortunate way of thinking about historical relationships: as Sonja Rein has pointed out, one of the difficulties with feminist theorization of television from the 1950s (and also with the imagery of distraction) is that it easily becomes just another way of talking about our mothers – in a mode of regression to an imaginary, if utopian, infancy.[17] Mellencamp's analysis, however, polemologically refuses to 'contain' Lucy in the past, or to a theory of 'subversive' humor, 'resistant' pleasure, alone. In the context of a cultural boom in these propositions, it may well be less fatalistic (if more 'fatal' in Baudrillard's sense, more utopian in de Certeau's) to keep spinning off from her insistence on 'dilemmas which, for me, no modern critical model can resolve' (87).

Notes

1. John Fiske, 'British cultural studies and television', *Channels of Discourse: Television and Contemporary Criticism*, ed. Robert C. Allen (Chapel Hill: University of North Carolina Press 1987), 254–89. Reprinted here as Chapter 6.
2. Judith Williamson, 'The problems of being *popular*', *New Socialist*, September 1986, 14–15.
3. *On the Street*, 21 October 1987.
4. Patricia Mellencamp, 'Situation comedy, feminism and Freud: discourses of Gracie and Lucy', *Studies in Entertainment: Critical Approaches to Mass Culture*, ed. Tania Modleski (Bloomington: Indiana University Press, 1986), 80–95.
5. Cf. Margaret Morse, 'The television news personality and credibility: reflections on the news in transition', *Studies in Entertainment*, 55–79.
6. Andreas Huyssen, *After the Great Divide: Modernism, Mass Culture, Postmodernism* (Bloomington: Indiana University Press, 1986), vii.
7. Jean-François Lyotard, 'One of the things at stake in women's struggles', *SubStance* 20 (1978), 9–17; Jacques Derrida, 'No apocalypse, not now (full speed ahead, seven missiles, seven missives)', *Diacritics* (Summer 1984), 20–31.
8. Mica Nava, 'Consumerism and its contradictions', *Cultural Studies* 1 (2) (May 1987), 204–10. The phrase 'cultural dopes' is from Stuart Hall, 'Notes on deconstructing "the popular"', *People's History and Socialist Theory*, ed. Raphael Samuel (London: Routledge and Kegan Paul, 1981), 227–39.
9. Iain Chambers, *Popular Culture: The Metropolitan Experience* (New York: Methuen, 1986), 12–13.
10. Meaghan Morris, 'At *Henry Parkes* Motel', *Cultural Studies* 2 (1) (1988), 1–47.

11. Andreas Huyssen, 'Mass culture as woman: modernism's other', *After the Great Divide*, 44–62; Tania Modleski, 'Femininity as mas(s)querade: a feminist approach to mass culture', *High Theory/Low Culture*, ed. Colin MacCabe (Manchester: Manchester University Press, 1986), 37–52; Patrice Petro, 'Mass culture and the feminine: the "place" of television in film studies', *Cinema Journal* 25 (3) (Spring 1986), 5–21.
12. Patrice Petro, 'Modernity and mass culture in Weimar: contours of a discourse on sexuality in early theories of perception and representation', *New German Critique* 40 (Winter 1987), 115–46.
13. Elaine Showalter, 'Critical cross-dressing: male feminists and the woman of the year', *Men in Feminism*, ed. Alice Jardine and Paul Smith (New York: Methuen, 1987), 116–32.
14. Michel de Certeau, *The Practice of Everyday Life*, trans. Steven F. Rendall (Berkeley: University of California Press, 1984), xvi.
15. A space for de Certeau is the product of, as well as a potential arena for, a practice. See *The Practice of Everyday Life*, Part III, 'Spatial practices'.
16. Homi K. Bhaba, 'Of mimicry and man: the ambivalence of colonial discourse', *October 28* (Spring 1984), 125–33.
17. Private conversation. One could argue that the topic of punk for the subcultural strand of cultural studies may well perform much the same role.

8

The future of cultural studies

Raymond Williams

I wish here to address the issue of the *future* of Cultural Studies, though not as a way of underestimating its very real current strengths and development – a development which would have been quite impossible, I think, to predict thirty or so years ago when the term was first beginning to get around. Indeed, we should remind ourselves of that unpredictability, as a condition likely to apply also to any projections we might ourselves make, some of which will certainly be as blind. Yet we need to be robust rather than hesitant about this question of the future because our own input into it, our own sense of the directions in which it should go, will constitute a significant part of whatever is made. And moreover the clearing of our minds which might lead to some definition of the considerations that would apply in deciding a direction is both hard and necessary to achieve, precisely because of that uncertainty.

I want to begin with a quite central theoretical point which to me is at the heart of Cultural Studies but which has not always been remembered in it. And this is – to use contemporary terms instead of the rather more informal terms in which it was originally defined – that you cannot understand an intellectual or artistic project without also understanding its formation: that the relation between a project and a formation is always decisive; and that the emphasis of Cultural Studies is precisely that it engages with *both*, rather than specializing itself to one or the other. Indeed it is not concerned with a formation of which some project is an illustrative example, nor with a project which could be related to a formation understood as its context or its background. Project and formation in this sense are different ways of materializing – different ways, then, of describing – what is in fact a *common* disposition of energy and direction. This was, I think, the crucial theoretical invention that was made: the refusal to give priority to either the project or the formation – or, in older terms, the art or the society. The novelty was seeing precisely that there were more basic relations between these otherwise separated areas. There had been plenty of precedents for kinds of study which, having looked at a particular body of intellectual or artistic work related it to what was called its society; just as there was a whole body of work – for example, in history – which described societies and then illustrated them from their characteristic forms of thought and art. What we were then trying to say, and it remains a difficult but, I do believe, central thing to say, is that these concepts – what we would now define as 'project' and 'formation' – are addressing not the relations between two separate entities, 'art' and 'society', but processes which take these different material forms in social formations of a creative or a critical kind, or on the other hand the actual forms of artistic and intellectual work. The importance of this is that if we are serious, we have to apply it to *our own* project, including the project of Cultural Studies. We have to look at what kind of formation it was from which the project of Cultural Studies developed, and then at the changes of formation that produced different definitions of that project. We may then be in a position to understand existing and possible formations which would in themselves be a way of defining certain projects towards the future.

Now that is, in a summary way, a theoretical point; and I'd like to give one or two examples of it. First, not in Cultural Studies but in one of the contributors to it; namely English or Literary Studies. It is very remarkable that in every case the innovations in literary studies occurred outside the formal educational institutions. In the late nineteenth century, when there was in fact no organized teaching of English literature at all, the demand came in two neglected and in a sense repressed areas of the culture of this society. First, in adult education, where people who had been deprived of any continuing educational opportunity were nevertheless readers, and wanted to discuss what they were reading; and, even more specifically, among women who, blocked from the process of higher education, educated themselves repeatedly through reading, and especially through the reading of 'imaginative literature' as the phrase usually has it. Both groups wanted to discuss what they'd read, and to discuss it in a context to which they brought their own situation, their own experience – a demand which was not to be satisfied, it was very soon clear, by what the universities (if they had been doing anything, and some informally were) were prepared to offer, which would have been a certain kind of history or a set of dates, a certain description of periods and forms. The demand, then, was for a discussion of this literature in relation to these life-situations which people were stressing outside the established educational systems, in adult education and in the frustrated further education of women. Hence some of the most remarkable early definitions of what a modern English course might be arose from Oxford Extension lecturers who'd gone out and formed their ideas in relation to this quite new demand. And when this new kind of study of literature – outside traditional philology and mere cataloguing history – finally got into the university, its syllabus was written, for example at Cambridge, almost precisely on the lines which that early phase in the late nineteenth century and early twentieth century had defined. It was said by one of the founders of Cambridge English that the textbook of that period was virtually a definition of their syllabus.

But then look what happened: having got into the university, English studies had within 20 years converted itself into a fairly normal academic course, marginalizing those members of itself who were sustaining the original project. Because by this time what it was doing within the institution was largely reproducing itself, which all academic institutions tend to do: it was reproducing the instructors and the examiners who were reproducing people like themselves. Given the absence of that pressure and that demand from groups who were outside the established educational system, this new discipline turned very much in on itself. It became, with some notable advantages, as always happens, a professional discipline; it moved to higher standards of critical rigour and scholarship; but at the same time the people who understood the original project, like Leavis for example, were marginalized. The curious fact is that they then tried to move outside the university, to set going again this more general project. But because of the formation they were – largely, if one wants to be strict in the usual terms, a group of people from petty-bourgeois families, almost equally resentful of the established polite upper middle class which thought it possessed literature, and of the majority who they felt were not only indifferent to it but hostile and even threatening – they chose a very precise route. They went out, and sent their students out, to the grammar schools to find the exceptional individuals who could then come back to the university and forward this process. What had been taken as their project into the university was not any longer the same project, so they went outside. But because they conceived themselves as this minority institution, seeking to educate a critical minority, it was now a different project and not the general project of the first definition. And so all the people who first read what you could now quite fairly call 'Cultural Studies' from that tendency – from Richards, from Leavis, from *Scrutiny* – who were studying popular culture, popular fiction, advertising, newspapers, and making fruitful analyses of it, found in time that the affiliation of this study to the reproduction of a specific minority within deliberately minority institutions created a problem of belief for them, and also a problem for defining what the project was.

If you then look at the site in which there was a further process of change and in which a different project was defined, it was again in adult education. Indeed, it can hardly be stressed too strongly that Cultural Studies in the sense we now understand it, for all its debts to its Cambridge predecessors, occurred in adult education: in the WEA, in the extramural Extension classes. I've sometimes read accounts of the development of Cultural Studies which characteristically date its various developments from *texts*. We all know the accounts which will line up and date *The Uses of Literacy, The Making of the English Working Class, Culture and Society,* and so on. But, as a matter of fact, already in the late forties, and with notable precedents in army education during the war, and with some precedents – though they were mainly in economics and foreign affairs – even in the thirties, Cultural Studies was extremely active in adult education. It only got into print and gained some kind of general intellectual recognition with these later books. I often feel sad about the many people who were active in that field at that time who didn't publish, but who did as much as any of us did to establish this work. In the late forties people were doing courses in the visual arts, in music, in town planning and the nature of community, the nature of settlement, in film, in press, in advertising, in radio; courses which if they had not taken place in that notably unprivileged sector of education would have been acknowledged much earlier. Only when it reached either the national publishing level or was adopted – with some recoil – in the university, was this work, in the typical ways of this culture, perceived as existing at all. There were people I could tell you about who did as much as any of us in my generation, whose names the people now teaching Cultural Studies would simply not know, and they were doing it in a site which was precisely a chosen alternative to the Leavis group. And it should be stressed that it was a *choice*: it was distinctly as a vocation rather than a profession that people went into adult education – Edward Thompson, Hoggart, myself and many others whose names are not known. It was a renewal of that attempt at a majority democratic education which had been there all through the project, but which kept being sidetracked as elements of it got into institutions which then changed it. Thus there was an initial continuity from the Leavis position of certain analytic procedures which eventually were thoroughly changed, because these people wanted precisely a democratic culture, and did not believe that it could be achieved by the constitution of a Leavisite 'minority' alone. They were nevertheless aware, because this was a very practical and pressed kind of work, that the simplicities of renouncing mass-popular education and democratic culture, when you have to go out and negotiate them on the ground, would not be easily resolved.

I give this example because so often the history of each phase of Cultural Studies has been tracked through *texts*. Such accounts talk about this individual having done this work; this tendency; this school; this movement labelled in this or that way; which looks very tidy as this type of idealist history – a very academicized kind of literary or intellectual history – always is. Yet that is in a sense only the surface of the real development, and is moreover misleading because what is happening each time is that a formation in a given general relationship to its society is taking what you could otherwise trace as a project with certain continuities, and in fact *altering* it, not necessarily for the better. There have been as many reversions as there have been advances; and one of the reversions comes, I think, in the next phase. Because as some of this work began to be recognized intellectually, as it was both in discussion and in periodicals and to some extent in the universities, it was thought to be a much newer thing than it was. If you take my book *Communications* which was commissioned because the National Union of Teachers called a conference on 'Popular Culture and Personal Responsibility' which in fact came out of the 1950s concern about horror comics – the root is as odd as that – I actually made the book, which didn't take long to write, out of the material I had been using in adult classes for fifteen years. Thus the sense of novelty which is easily conveyed by tracing the texts is in fact misleading, since the real formation of the project was already there. But when this began to happen it made a certain significant intellectual difference in the university, though never one which could shift its most central institutions and assumptions.

But then a period of expansion in education occurred which created new sites for precisely this kind of work, and a new kind of formation – one perhaps continuous until today – came into existence. I can still remember my own students getting their first jobs and coming back and saying 'I went to meet the principal as the newly appointed lecturer in Liberal Studies, and I asked him what Liberal Studies was and he said, 'I don't know; I only know I've got to have it'. They were, then, in that unprecedented situation, for most people starting their first job, of being able to write a syllabus, which otherwise you labour and drag yourself for a lifetime to climb towards, and then probably fail to do. They had the option to put down certain ideas, and what they put down, in the majority, in new universities, in polytechnics, in colleges of further education, in some schools even, as this new phase got around, was precisely this area of work which the university was rather warily looking at but keeping well outside its really central and decisive areas. And they were able to do this because the option for Liberal Studies had been so vague; it had been based on nothing much more than the sense – itself based, perhaps, in the lingering cultural distrust of science and technology as too worldy – that people should discover certain of the finer things of life.

In this way, and without any well-established body of work to base itself on, a new formation in these new institutions began to develop, but with certain consequences. First, that precisely as you move into the institutions – as you pass that magic moment when you are writing the syllabus and have to operate it, to examine it; as you are joined by colleagues; as you become a department and as the relations between departments have to be negotiated, as the relative time and resources are given to them – what then takes place is precisely the process which emasculated English at Cambridge. At the very moment when that adventurous syllabus became a syllabus that had to be examined, it ceased to be exciting. And just at the moment when this new work flooded into what were, for all the welcome elements of expansion, still minority institutions – still, moreover, formed with certain academic precedents around departments, about the names of disciplines and so on – then certain key shifts in the project occurred.

Yet there is one other kind of institution which I'd first like to mention which also occurred in just this period – I'm talking of the sixties – and that's the Open University. On this, two crucial points need to be made, as it were, simultaneously. First, that this was an extraordinary attempt in the tradition of that movement towards an open-access democratic culture of an educational kind – not the bureaucratically centralized imposition of a cultural programme which would enlighten the masses but one of a genuinely open and educational kind. At the same time, however, it was a deliberate break with the traditions of its own society in adult education and the Co-operative Guild, in all the local self-educating organizations of working people and others, which had been based precisely on a principle which it could not realize: that intellectual questions arose when you drew up intellectual disciplines that form bodies of knowledge in contact with people's life-situations and life-experiences. Because of course that is exactly what had happened in adult education. Academics took out from their institutions university economics, or university English or university philosophy, and the people wanted to know what it was. This exchange didn't collapse into some simple populism: that these were all silly intellectual questions. Yet these new students insisted (1) that the relation of this to their own situation and experience had to be discussed, and (2) that there were areas in which the discipline itself might be unsatisfactory, and therefore they retained as a crucial principle the right to decide their own syllabus. This process of constant interchange between the discipline and the students, which was there institutionalized, was *deliberately* interrupted by the Open University, a very Wilsonian project in two senses. It was on the one hand this popular access; on the other hand it was inserting a technology over and above the movement of the culture. This project would bring enormous advantage but it lacks to this day that crucial process of interchange and encounter between the people offering the intellectual disciplines and those using them, who have far more than a right to be tested to see if they are following them or if they are being put in a form which is convenient – when in fact they have this more basic right to define the questions. These people were, after all, in a practical position to say 'well, if you tell me that question goes outside your discipline, then bring me someone whose discipline *will* cover it, or bloody well get outside of the discipline and answer it yourself'. It was from this entirely rebellious and untidy situation that the extraordinarily complicated and often muddled convergences of what became Cultural Studies occurred; precisely because people wouldn't accept those boundaries. Yet the Open University, as a major example of a breakthrough beyond a minority institution, had this element in it of a technology inserted over and above the social process of education: it had this characteristic double dimension.

I now come to my controversial point. At just this moment, a body of theory came through which rationalized the situation of this formation on its way to becoming bureaucratized and the home of specialist intellectuals. That is to say, the theories which came – the revival of formalism, the simpler kinds (including Marxist kinds) of structuralism – tended to regard the practical encounters of people in society as having relatively little effect on its general progress, since the main inherent forces of that society were deep in its structures, and – in the simplest forms – the people who operated them were mere 'agents'. This was precisely the encouragement for people not to look at their own formation, not to look at this new and at once encouraging and problematic situation they were in; at the fact that this kind of education was getting through to new kinds of people, and yet that it was still inside minority institutions, or that the institutions exercised the confining bureaucratic pressures of syllabus and examination, which continually pulled these raw questions back to something manageable within their terms. At just that moment – which I hope is still a moment of fruitful tension – there was for a time a quite uncritical acceptance of a set of theories which in a sense rationalized that situation, which said that this was the way the cultural order worked, this was the way in which the ideology distributed its roles and functions. The whole project was then radically diverted by these new forms of idealist theory. Even the quite different work of Gramsci and Benjamin was subsumed within them; and of the powerful early challenge to such Modernist idealisms launched by Bakhtin, Voloshinov and Medvedev, little or nothing was heard. Even (and it was not often) when formations *were* theorized, the main lesson of formational analysis, concerning one's own and other *contemporary* formations, was less emphasized than more safely distanced academic studies.

In its most general bearings, this work remained a kind of intellectual analysis which wanted to change the actual developments of society, but then locally, within the institution, there were all the time those pressures that had changed so much in earlier phases: from other disciplines, from other competitive departments, the need to define your discipline, justify its importance, demonstrate its rigour; and these pressures were precisely the opposite of those of the original project. Now there was indeed a very great gain in this period, as anybody who compares the earlier and later work will see. When I wrote *Communications* we were analyzing newspapers and television programmes, with material strewn over the kitchen floor and ourselves adding up on backs of envelopes, and when I look now at Media Studies departments and see the equipment they have to do the job properly I of course recognize the advances as being marked. Similarly with film studies, we never knew whether the film would (a) arrive, (b) work with that projector, (c) whether in an adult class people wouldn't be so dazed after watching the film that when you asked for discussion you never got a word; now film courses operate in a proper institution, and I've never doubted the advantages of this; just as nobody in the centre of the English Faculty at Cambridge now could believe for a moment that what they do isn't infinitely superior to Leavis's work. I mean, in certain new ways it *is* always more professional, more organized, and properly resourced. On the other hand, there remains the problem of forgetting the real project. As you separate these disciplines out, and say 'Well, it's a vague and baggy monster, Cultural Studies, but we can define it more closely – as media studies, community sociology, popular fiction or popular music', so you create defensible disciplines, and there are people in other departments who can *see* that these are defensible disciplines, that here is properly referenced and presented work. But the question of what is then happening to the project remains. And in a sense the crisis of these last years should remind us of the continuing relation between the project and the formation: the assumption that we were witnessing the unfolding of some structure which was, so to say, inherent – a continuation of some simple line, as in those accounts of the history of Cultural Studies which had shown people gradually, although always with difficulty, overcoming their residual errors and moving on a bit – has been brutally interrupted by the very conscious counter-revolution of these last years.

This is where I come to the question of the future. For what we now have is a situation in which the popular cultural institutions have changed so profoundly through the period in which Cultural Studies has been developed, with relative alterations of importance – for example between broadcasting and print – of a kind that no one would have believed possible in the fifties. We've got new sets of problems both inside the different kinds of study we do, as to which of them really bear on the project, and also the question of considering our own formation in this now very changed situation. I'll take a couple of examples first from the internal process of the subjects themselves, illustrating the contradictory effects of this welcome development but simultaneous institutionalization of Cultural Studies. If you take the question of popular culture, or popular fiction, it has been clearly quite transformed in the 1980s from its situation in the 1950s, not only because people have been more prepared, because of general social and formational changes, to relate directly to popular culture, putting themselves at a very conscious distance from Richards and Leavis in the 1920s and 1930s who saw it only as a menace to literacy – an element which survives, perhaps, although always as uncertainly and ambiguously as ever, in Richard Hoggart's book. But at the same time that earlier tension between two very different traditions and kinds of work can as easily be collapsed as explored. It is necessary and wholly intellectually defensible to analyse serials and soap operas. Yet I do wonder about the courses where at least the teachers – and I would say also the students – have not themselves encountered the problems of the whole development of naturalist and realist drama, of social-problem drama, or of certain kinds of serial form in the nineteenth century; which are elements in the constitution of these precise contemporary forms, so that the tension between that social history of forms and these forms in a contemporary situation, with their partly new and partly old content, partly new and partly old techniques, can be explored with weight on both sides. This can very easily not happen if one is defining the simpler kind of syllabus because the teacher can say 'well, for that you'd have to go to drama', or literature or fiction, 'we're doing popular fiction'. Yet how could you carry through the very important work now being done on detective stories, for instance, without being able to track back to the crime stories of the nineteenth century and grasp the precise social and cultural milieu out of which that form came, so that you are then able to add an extra dimension of analysis to what we now say about the form of the detective story? Or, in the sociological dimension of Cultural Studies, there is the whole problem of the relation between very close-up contemporary work which is crucially necessary to history, and the very complicated interpretations of history which are not to be diminished, in my view, simply to labour history or popular history, because otherwise one isolates a class precisely from the relations which, in a sense, constitute that class. I give these cases as examples of how in the very effort to define a clearer subject, to establish a discipline, to bring order into the work – all of which are laudable ambitions – the real problem of the project as a whole, which is that people's questions are not answered by the existing distribution of the educational curriculum, can be forgotten. And people, when they are free to choose – though they are often not, because of quite natural pressures and determinations and a reasonable ambition to qualify – again and again refuse to limit their questions to the boundaries of the set course. So that the interrelations between disciplines, which are the whole point of the project, have this inherent problem in what is otherwise a valuable process of defining and modelling the subject.

But the more crucial question now is this: that even after the expansion we've had, which was first halted and then turned back by a succession from Callaghan to Thatcher and Joseph, we are facing a situation which is quite different in kind but just as challenging as that which faced any of those people who developed the project in particular circumstances in earlier periods. What we have got now, and what was not available when the studies were getting into the new institutions, is the effective disappearance of those kinds of teenage work which were profound anti-educational pressures at just the time that some of these developments were happening. There were then understandable pressures of money and work against the problems of staying on with that kind of school, that kind of education. We've now got the extraordinary institution of courses which in a sense are deliberately placed beyond the reach of education. We have the effective education of the majority in the age-group of 16 to 18 being removed as far as possible from what are conceived as the old damaging educators. We now encounter a definition of industrial training which would have sounded crude in the 1860s when something very like it was proposed – and we might be glad if it *had* then happened: at least it would have solved one set of problems. It is again being said that people must gain work experience within the forms of the economy to which they must adapt, and as *that* syllabus is written, as that programme of work experience is written, no place at all is envisaged for people like us. I don't mean that individual initiatives don't happen, but rather that a whole substitute educational provision is being made with certain very powerful material incentives, including the possibility of employment. And while the labour movements say of such work experience that it's merely 'cheap labour' or whatever, I say what educators must say – and this is, as a matter of fact, where I see the future of Cultural Studies. Here is a group which – if it is given only what is called 'work experience', but which is actually its introduction to the routines of the foreseen formations of this new industrial capitalism – will be without that dimension of human and social knowledge and critical possibility which again and again has been one of the elements of our project. And if it seems hopeless that people in their own hard-pressed institutions, which of course we have to defend, should be asked to look towards this area which has very consciously, as a matter of political policy, been removed as far as possible from professional educators, I would say this: that there is the prospect, after all, within two, three, four years, of another kind of government; there is the possibility of the renewal of the existing institutions or at least the easing of some of their resource and staffing problems. When that comes, shall we simply cheer that the budgetary crisis is over, the establishment crisis relieved a bit? If we do, then those cheers should only be uttered out of one side of the mouth because if we allow an absolutely crucial area of formative human development to remain deliberately isolated from educators – moreover an area in which what Cultural Studies has to contribute is particularly relevant – then we shall have missed a historic opportunity; just as related opportunities were nearly missed or only partly realized, or to a large extent incorporated and neutralized, in earlier phases. We shall have missed that historic opportunity because we had become, in our very success, institutionalized.

I have deliberately not summarized the whole development of Cultural Studies in terms of the convergence of intellectual disciplines, which is another way of writing this history; an internal and illuminating way, but nevertheless insufficient unless you relate it all the time to the very precise formations and social institutions in which these convergences happened and *had* to happen. For that approach in terms of intellectual history may obscure from us what is, as we enter the coming period, a historic opportunity for a new Cultural Studies formation. And the time to prepare this new initiative, which would indeed be much resisted by many vested and political interests, is precisely *now*. Because it is only when a persuasive, reasoned and practical proposal is put forward to a favourable local authority or government, which would then have you sort through the ways in which you would teach it, that this new work will become more than a resented interruption from what is otherwise taught. If this is thought through now, if we fight for it, even if we fail we shall have done something to justify ourselves before the future. But I don't think we need fail at all; I think that the results will be uneven and scattered, but this is where the challenge now is. If you accept my definition that this is really what Cultural Studies has been about, of taking the best we can in intellectual work and going with it in this very open way to confront people for whom it is not a way of life, for whom it is not in any probability a job, but for whom it is a matter of their own intellectual interest, their own understanding of the pressures on them, pressures of every kind, from the most personal to the most broadly political – if we are prepared to take that kind of work and to revise the syllabus and discipline as best we can, on this site which allows that kind of interchange, then Cultural Studies has a very remarkable future indeed.

9

The circulation of cultural studies

Lawrence Grossberg

Cultural studies is moving rapidly into the mainstream of contemporary intellectual and academic life in the United States. Within the discipline of communications, it seems that cultural studies is no longer merely tolerated as a marginal presence; it is courted and even empowered – within limited parameters – by the discipline's ruling blocs. It is one of the few intellectually marginal and politically oppositional positions to be legitimated and incorporated into the mainstream of this relatively young discipline. And this, to some extent, has made it problematic for those in other still marginalized positions, who see its success as an imperialistic attempt to represent them. At the same time, cultural studies has suddenly appeared in other disciplines including sociology and literary studies but with little sense of its radical challenge to these disciplinary traditions.

The fact that cultural studies increasingly, and in new ways, is being commodified and institutionalized raises a number of disturbing questions (Allor, 1987; Morris, 1988b). As a commodity, it has little identity of its own and is celebrated only for its mobility and its capacity to generate further surplus capital. As an institutional site, it is reinscribed into the academic and disciplinary protocols against which it has always struggled. I would like to address one consequence of the changing place of cultural studies: the more we talk about it, the less clear it is what we are talking about.[1] As cultural studies becomes something of an established position, it loses its specificity. As the term appears with increasing frequency, its relation to a specific British body of work disappears, and it becomes less clear what space we are supposed to be inhabiting.[2]

This dilemma is constructed from two sides. On the one hand, cultural studies has been hijacked by an alliance between the apparent demands of intellectual work (which requires that it be condensed into a position that can be defined and summarized), the exigencies of the distribution of its work (which have functionally erased its history, its internal differences, and its continuous reconstruction through ongoing debates), and its own successes as a politically committed and theoretically sophisticated body of work. This has meant that, too often, a specific exemplar of cultural studies – most commonly, a single position derived from somewhere in the work of the Centre for Contemporary Cultural Studies (whether defined in terms of theory, politics, or collective intellectual work) – is taken to be the defining position or model, the stable representation of the history and terrain of cultural studies. On the other hand, the assimilation of cultural studies into the broader universe of theories of cultural interpretation (e.g. the forums held on cultural studies at the 1988 meeting of the Modern Language Association) simply ends up substituting, metonymically, cultural studies for the more ambiguous notion of critical theory; the result is that cultural studies is entirely dispersed, left without any sense of how its intellectual and political history offers a different way of engaging questions of culture and power.

Those of us working in 'cultural studies' find ourselves caught between the need to define and defend its specificity and the desire to refuse to close off the ongoing history of cultural studies by any such act of definition. This is, it must be said, a very real dilemma that cannot be solved by a simple assertion. It is not a question of 'possessing' cultural studies but of asking why it is that the name has suddenly been taken up by people in different theoretical, political, and disciplinary positions. It is not a question of 'policing' the boundaries but of recognizing that there is a history of intellectual and political practices that is worth struggling over. If there are real stakes in the struggle over namings, then the project of articulating 'cultural studies' involves a refusal to relinquish the gains which a specific intellectual formation (with its own history, contradictions, uneven developments, conflicts, unities, and differences) brings to the study of culture.

The formation of cultural studies. The power and attractiveness of cultural studies depends partly upon three features that often directly contradict the forms of its contemporary appropriation: First, it refuses to construct itself as a finished or singular theoretical position which can freely move across historical and political contexts. The history of cultural studies can be read as the continuous effort to reconstruct itself in the light of changing historical projects and intellectual resources. This does not mean, however, as some would have it, that there are no boundaries on that history, that every theory of culture, or even of culture and politics, represents a viable position within the field of cultural studies. It is not that cultural studies has no identity but rather that its identity is always contested, always multiple, always changing; cultural studies is an historically articulated 'unity-in-difference'.

Second, cultural studies refuses to define its own theoretical adequacy in academic or narrowly epistemological terms. Theory in cultural studies is measured by its relation to, its enablement of, strategic interventions into the specific practices, structures, and struggles characterizing its place in the contemporary world. Cultural studies is propelled by its desire to construct possibilities, both immediate and imaginary, out of its historical circumstances. It has no pretensions to totality or universality; it seeks only to give us a better understanding of where we are so that we can get somewhere else (some place, we hope, that is better – based on more just principles of equality and the distribution of wealth and power), so that we can have a little more control over the history that we are already making. This is not to say that it surrenders the epistemological question; rather it historicizes and politicizes it. A theory's ability to 'cut into the real', to use Benjamin's metaphor, is measured by the political positions and trajectories theory enables in response to the concrete contexts of power it confronts. Just like people in everyday life, cultural studies begins to grapple with and analyze difficult political situations using the resources and experiences at hand; it draws upon and extends theories to enable it to break into experience in new ways. Thus, cultural studies' development is not a series of epistemological ruptures or paradigm shifts (the rationalist illusion) but the ongoing attempt to measure old theories against the emergence of new historical articulations, new cultural events, changes in the tempo and texture of social life, new structures of social relationships and new subjectivities.

Cultural studies refuses to be driven by purely theoretical considerations; its agenda is always constructed by events and discourses that are located, in the first instance, outside of its own theoretical agenda. This anchor in history enables cultural studies to cope with the impossible complexity of its own historical context – a context in which our theories demand more of us than we can reasonably accomplish, in which everything is evidence and evidence is changing more rapidly than we can document.

Third, the form of its interdisciplinary character is built upon the recognition that much of what one requires to understand cultural practices and relations is not, in any obvious sense, cultural. Whatever the effects of cultural production, they are never autonomous facts to be located in, and compared with, other forms of social relationships. Culture exists in complex relations with other practices in the social formation, and these relations determine, enable, and constrain the possibilities of cultural practices. Cultural studies does not attempt to explain everything from the cultural point of view; rather, it attempts to explain culture using whatever resources are intellectually and politically necessary and available, which is determined in part by the form and place of its institutionalization. Consequently, cultural studies has always been a collective activity, although it is often produced by a single author and the forms of its collectivity have varied greatly and can never be defined in advance, outside of any specific historical and institutional context.

If there is no fixed definition of cultural studies, perhaps the terrain on which it operates can at least be identified: cultural studies is concerned with describing and intervening in the ways 'texts' and 'discourses' (i.e. cultural practices) are produced within, inserted into, and operate in the everyday life of human beings and social formations, so as to reproduce, struggle against, and perhaps transform the existing structures of power. That is, if people make history but in conditions not of their own making (Marx), cultural studies explores the ways this process is enacted within and through cultural practices, and the place of these practices within specific historical formations. But such statements are fraught with danger for they suggest that the history of cultural studies, and the differences within it, can be represented as a continuous rephrasing of some original problematic. Cultural studies is then reducible to a particular theory of the relationship between culture and society, or between culture and power, and the history of the formation is seen as the teleological or rational achievement of a more powerful and enlightening theory of the relationship.

I believe that we need to begin with the more troubling recognition that the very questions – the problematic – at the heart of cultural studies are constantly being reshaped and reinflected. Cultural studies is the ongoing effort to define its own local specificity. At any moment, the project of cultural studies involves locating 'culture' by defining the specificity of both cultural struggle and the historical context within and against which such struggles are functioning. It is the historically constructed form, structure, and effectivity of the relationship itself as a terrain of power that defines the site of cultural studies' intervention. In other words, the point of cultural studies is that the relations between culture and society, or between culture and power, are always historically constituted. It follows, then, that cultural studies is not built upon a theory of the specificity of culture (usually defined in terms of signification, ideology, subjectivity, or community); rather, cultural studies examines how specific practices are placed – and their productivity determined – between the social structures of power and the lived realities of everyday life. It is for this reason that current work on postmodernity intersects with cultural studies; it is not a matter of taking up postmodernism as a political and theoretical position but of engaging its description of the nature of contemporary cultural and historical life.

Obviously, any attempt to 'define' cultural studies is immediately caught in a dilemma. There is not one cultural studies position, either synchronically or diachronically; there are always multiple, overlapping, changing projects, commitments and vectors according to which it has continued to rearticulate itself. Cultural studies is constantly renegotiating its identity and repositioning itself within changing intellectual and political maps. Its identity – as well as the significance of any position or concept within cultural studies – can only be defined by an always incomplete history of political engagements and theoretical debates in response to which alternative positions are constantly being taken into account and new positions offered. But the history of cultural studies – the only place in which its specificity (as an emergent set of commitments and projects) can be found – is not a linear or progressive development. Cultural studies has always encompassed multiple positions, and it has always continuously engaged in debates, not only within these differences but also with positions which were never quite a part of cultural studies (although they sometimes were appropriated and rearticulated into it). Cultural studies has always proceeded discontinuously and erratically through a continuing struggle to rearrange and redefine the theoretical differences of the terrain itself in response to specific historical questions and events. Thus, it has often moved onto terrain it will later have to abandon and abandoned terrain it will later have to reoccupy. It has had its share of false starts which have taken it down paths it has had to struggle to escape; it has at times been forced to retrace its own steps and even, occasionally, to leap onto paths it had scarcely imagined. In that sense, cultural studies involves constant theoretical work on already occupied – theoretically and politically – ground.

Thus, practicing cultural studies is not simply a matter of taking up positions offered by various individuals or groups in the British tradition; such appropriations fail to recognize the complex ways in which these various efforts (e.g. the work of the Birmingham Center, or Raymond Williams, or the *Screen* collective) were determined by their place within a specifically British topography and history. Nor is it a matter of erasing the specific formations, trajectories, and histories of the British tradition. Such a 'fetishism of the local' would contradict cultural studies' commitment to explore the complex and changing relations between local contexts and larger (perhaps even global) vectors.

Rearticulating cultural studies. The task confronting us is to work on already occupied ground, to rearticulate cultural studies into specific American contexts and in the process, to transform cultural studies itself.[3] But this would seem to require some sense of the relevant ground, some map of the space we are to occupy and the ways we can take up places within it. I suggest that we can read the mobilities and stabilities of cultural studies, the various forms of its unity-in-difference,[4] as a continuing struggle to articulate a set of commitments which would both differentiate it from other theoretical positions and empower the places from which it seeks to intervene into a political space. I am not claiming that all of these commitments are unique to cultural studies, nor even that they 'originate' within cultural studies. In fact, much of my description will reflect the radical way in which contemporary feminisms have transformed the social, intellectual, and political conditions of cultural studies. I offer my own take (motivated by my own context and project) on the 'tendential lines of force' which have often propelled cultural studies, defined the concepts it has struggled around, and articulated it in ways and directions it could not have foreseen.

Materialism describes human reality in terms of material practices: what people do, how they transform the world. But it is less a matter of intentions than of effects, and it is less a matter of origins than of distribution (i.e. what practices are available to whom, and which are taken up). Materialism does not reduce the world to a collection of bodies, although it does recognize the reality of socially constructed biological bodies. It addresses the world of people in social, cultural, political, technological, and economic relations; it talks about people with ideas, desires, pleasures, and emotions, all of which are defined by the forms and organizations of practices that are available to transform these dimensions of reality. In that sense, ideas are real because they transform realities; they make a difference. But it is often less a matter of the content of ideas than the practices by which ideas are constructed and transformed and placed into the world.

Anti-essentialism describes a contingent history in which nothing is guaranteed in advance, in which no relationship (correspondence) is necessary, in which no identity is intrinsic. Such 'essences' may be historically real, but they are not necessary. What we take for granted, the starting point of whatever story we tell, is always the end point of another story that has yet to be told. History is precisely the ongoing struggle to forge connections, to articulate practices together – linking this text to that meaning, this meaning to that experience, this experience to that political position, producing specific effects and thereby constructing the structures of social and historical life. Articulation describes this ongoing construction of one set of relations out of another: rearticulation always entails disarticulation. It is the continuous struggle to reposition practices within a shifting field of forces, to construct structures, moments in which things appear to be stitched into place, out of or on top of the differences.

I do not mean to suggest that the field is ever entirely open, that we are able to remake history at our whim. We are always constrained by a history we did not make, by the distribution of practices available to us, by the effective force of the multiple histories of articulation (leaving 'traces without an inventory' that are often so tightly bound into place as to appear inevitable), by the multiple and often contradictory logics of those articulations which define the 'tendential forces' of larger historical spaces. Thus, the process of making history is always partly anonymous since we are never in control of the effects of our struggles. But it is carried out by the practices of real individuals and groups, consciously and unconsciously, through activity or inactivity, through victories – which may sometimes have disastrous consequences – or defeats.

It is in this sense that cultural studies is often described as antihumanistic; cultural studies does not deny real people, but it does place them in equally real and overdetermined historical realities. What they are, as individuals and human beings, is thus not intrinsic to them. Our practices produce our identity and our humanity, often behind our backs. In fact, the production of the individual as a social subject is a complex process by which different social positions are produced – there are no necessary correspondences among economic, political, ideological, and social subjects. Individuals must be won or interpellated into these positions or, if you prefer, they have to take them up in specific ways, and these positions can then be articulated to each other (as well as to other structures of meaning and practice) so that a certain cultural or ideological identification appears to pull its subjects into specific political positions. Antihumanism does not deny individuality, subjectivity, experience, or agency; it simply historicizes and politicizes them, their construction, and their relationships. If there is no essential human nature, we are always struggling to produce its boundaries, to constitute an effective (and hence real) human nature, but one which is different in different social formations. In other words, human nature is always real but never universal, singular, or fixed. It is in the history of struggles, of articulation, that history itself is given shape and direction, and that historically constituted relations of power are put into place.

Power operates at every level of human life; it is neither an abstract universal structure nor a subjective experience. It is both limiting and productive: producing differences, shaping relations, structuring identities and hierarchies, but also enabling practices and empowering social subjects. After all, every articulation provides the conditions of possibility for other articulations even as it structures and limits the field. At the level of social life, power involves the historical production of 'economies' – the social production, distribution, and consumption – of different forms of value (e.g. capital, money, meanings, information, representations, identities, desires, emotions, pleasures).[5] It is the specific articulation of social subjects into these circuits of value, circuits which organize social possibilities and differences, that constructs the structured inequalities of social power. While there is no guarantee that different economies trace out the same lines of inequality, the inequalities are rarely random. On the contrary, they circulate around, and are articulated to, systems of social difference which are themselves historically constructed. Moreover, different economies may operate in different ways; we cannot ignore the fact that sometimes the distribution of resources is strategically manipulated through conspiracies, intimidation, misrepresentation, etc. In these complex ways, the social formation is always organized into relations of domination and subordination. The struggle over power, then, involves the struggle to deconstruct and reconstruct correspondences between systems of the unequal distribution of resources and systems of social identities and differences.

Anti-reductionism claims that people and practices are always implicated, in contradictory ways, in hierarchical structures of power. It tells us to avoid assuming either too simple a beginning or too neat an ending to our story. History is never all tied up into a single knot waiting to be unraveled. There is no single structure which stitches all of history into place, the patterns of which are indelibly sewn into the fabric of history. Consequently, power cannot be reduced to any single dimension of value which can be assumed is necessarily and always fundamental. Nor can power be reduced to any single social structure of difference. No single plane of disempowerment, suffering, or oppression has a guaranteed privileged relation to history.

The *conjuncture* defines cultural studies' methodological commitment to specificity. It dictates that we can only deal with, and from within, specific contexts, for it is only there that identities and relations exist effectively. The struggle to articulate a practice is the struggle to construct its context. Structures are real and effective only within a specific context, always defined at a particular level of abstraction. For example, the commodity is a necessary structure of capitalism. But having said that, we must recognize that it operates at such an abstract level – describing many centuries and many national contexts – that it tells us very little about more concrete contexts. If we remain at the high level of abstraction at which Marx wrote *Capital*, the effects of the commodity seem simple and direct. As we move to other levels, attempting to construct 'the concrete', its effects are increasingly delayed, deferred, detoured, hybridized, etc. And the only way to arrive at its actual 'local' effectivity is to recognize (a) how it is articulated by other relations and (b) its specific ability to produce effects – its reach or penetration into the social formation – across time and space. Thus, the practice of cultural studies involves the attempt to construct the specificity of a conjuncture, the appropriateness of which is only given by the intellectual and political project at hand. This, then, is not merely a matter of acknowledging the context, of interpreting texts and taking the context into account. It involves the movement of cultural studies from an interpretive or transactional view to 'a more historical and structural view' (Hall *et al.*, 1978, p. 185).

The *popular* defines a necessary focus and commitment of cultural studies. As a political commitment, it is anti-elitist; it demands that we not separate ourselves entirely from the masses. We are, as it were, part of the people who are always trying to influence their own march through history. This does not assume that 'the people' exists as a reified category always defined by some intrinsic property; 'the people' as an historically constructed social category, a site of struggle articulated by specific inter-pellations (e.g. as nomadic subjects in media culture [Grossberg, 1987] and as the nation in hegemonic struggles [Hall, 1988]). Cultural studies recog-nizes that subordination is, after all, not the same as manipulation, nor total subjection. People live their positions in complex, contradictory, and active ways; they reproduce and resist their subordination; they seek ways of transforming and improving their position according to their own ima-gined possibilities and resources; they live with, within, and against their subordination, attempting to make the best of what they are given, to win a bit more control over their lives, to extend themselves and their resources. This is not to say that they are always struggling, or that when they do, it is always effective or victorious, or even that their victory will be progressive. To say that people are always empowered in some ways by their positions does not require us to equate empowerment with struggle, resistance, or opposition; it merely requires us to recognize the active complexity in which people live their lives. Nor does it require us to deny that sometimes people are manipulated, misled, misinformed, mystified; but we cannot take such passive positionings to be the totality or constitutive nature of the people. We need to recognize that subordination, empowerment, pleasure, resistance, and even struggle refer to complex sets of local effects and that the relations among them are never guaranteed in advance.

Only in this messy terrain can we begin to sort out how people recognize and transform themselves and their world within and through popular cultural practices. Thus, we need to address how specific forms of popular culture, forms which may produce a variety of pleasures and which may empower their audiences in a variety of ways, are themselves struggled over and articulated to larger historically specific political projects. Hence, 'the popular' also defines a focus, for cultural studies' interventions will not succeed if it does not enter onto the terrain of people's own lives in order to offer them new possibilities, and to locate the ways in which 'the people' are themselves constructed through their cultural practices. It is only by entering into the popular – popular languages, cultures, logics, emotions, experiences, moralities, desires, consciousnesses – that we can gain a better sense of the field of forces, that we can see where struggles are actualized and possible, that we can help articulate, nurture, and support them. It is in the popular that we can discover how subordination is lived and resisted, that we can understand the possibilities of subordination and resistance that are opened by and within the structures of domination and which point beyond these structures. It is the popular – as a field of culture and everyday life – that makes available to us the complex field of power in which people live their lives.

The popular – as both commitment and focus – forces us back into a strategic engagement with real people, existing in real relations of power. It is neither our task to condemn them nor to define their utopian aspirations. Cultural studies does not valorize every moment of local and popular activity, nor does it erase its own intellectual labor in order 'to let the subordinate speak'. It does not always and only speak the languages of the masses, but it must refuse the luxury of perpetual self-analysis. Cultural studies is a constant strategic effort to articulate its own local identity – both as intellectual critique and as political intervention – to find a place for itself from which it can struggle to reconstruct the larger spaces of our historical lives.

186 What is cultural studies?

Notes

1. This essay represents my latest effort to think through the specificity of cultural studies; however, it is in many ways better represented as the latest take in an ongoing polylogue, my own statement of a truly collective effort. Thus, I am indebted to many people, and I apologize for not having attempted to document their individual contributions, ideas, and phrases. I can only acknowledge their great help and contribution to this essay: Martin Allor, James Hay, Meaghan Morris, Janice Radway, Andrew Ross, Jennifer Daryl Slack, and Ellen Wartella. In addition, I acknowledge a very real debt to Tony Bennett, John Clarke, and Stuart Hall.
2. Hall (1980) and Johnson (1986–87) are the 'standard' descriptions of cultural studies.
3. See my 1988 work for a critique of the British tradition in the service of an effort to define an American practice of cultural studies responding to the specific political context constructed by the rise of the New Right. Part of the labor of this transformation involves reading one history into another: Cultural studies in the United States has to locate itself within the trajectories of the American Left, including the various urban-immigrant, labor, and agrarian-populist formations, the culturalism of the New Left, the various feminist struggles, and the different intellectually inspired projects of *Monthly Review, Cultural Correspondence,* and *Social Text.* It would have to recognize the specific conjunctural limits of the American Left: the United States never formed an integrated and institutionalized Left which could occupy a place in common sense. I am grateful to Jody Berland for this point.
4. For histories of cultural studies, see my 'in press' article [Grossberg, 1989] and my earlier – and flawed – effort (1983).
5. Certainly, within the British tradition, cultural studies focused on a limited set of these values – specifically meaning, representation, and identity. It is the articulation of these three economies that Hall describes as ideology.

References

ALLOR, M. (1987) 'Projective readings: Cultural studies from here', *Canadian Journal of Political and Social Theory* 11, 134–137.
GROSSBERG, L. (1983) 'Cultural studies revisited and revised'. In Mander, M.S., (ed.), *Communications in Transition* (pp. 39–70). New York: Praeger.
GROSSBERG, L. (1987) 'The in-difference of television', *Screen* 28, 28–46.
GROSSBERG, L. (1988) *It's a Sin: Essays on Postmodernism, Politics, and Culture.* Sydney: Power Publications.
GROSSBERG, L. (in press [1989]) 'The formations of cultural studies: an American in Birmingham', *Strategies* [2, 114–49].
HALL, S. (1980) 'Culture studies and the Centre: some problematics and problems'. In Hall, S., Hobson, D., Lowe, A. and Willis, P. (eds), *Culture, Media, Language* (pp. 15–47). London: Hutchinson.
HALL, S. (1988) *The Hard Road to Renewal: Thatcherism and the Crisis of the Left.* London: Verso.
HALL, S., CRITCHER, C., JEFFERSON, T., CLARKE, J., and ROBERTS, B. (1978) *Policing the Crisis: Mugging, the State and Law and Order.* London: Macmillan.
JOHNSON, R. (1986–1987) 'What is cultural studies anyway?', *Social Text* 6, 38–90. Reprinted here as Chapter 5.
MORRIS, M. (1988) 'Banality in cultural studies'. In Mellencamp, P., (ed.), *The Logics of Television.* Bloomington, IA: Indiana University Press. Reprinted here as Chapter 7.

10

The problem of American cultural studies

Alan O'Connor

This essay raises questions about cultural studies in the United States and contrasts it with cultural studies in Britain. It is argued that cultural studies should be understood as practice, institution, and cultural form. In Britain, the practice is an effort at collective intellectual work – a genuine attempt at a democractic graduate research institute. The typical published form in England is a certain kind of collectively written book. Cultural studies in the United States is discussed with particular reference to the work of Grossberg. A concluding argument is made for research that makes connections with grass roots organizations, including the production of alternative media forms.

Cultural studies in Britain is an intellectual tradition. It is composed of several institutions and formations, and it has a characteristic cultural form and teaching practice. Cultural studies is not a science. It is neither organized about a central problematic (or paradigm), as Althusser argued a science must be (Althusser & Balibar, 1970), nor does it aspire to the almost mathematical goal of semiotics. Neither is it organized as a professional activity of liberal scholarship for its own sake along the lines of the Modern Language Association or other professional associations. The tradition of cultural studies is not one of value-free scholarship but of political commitment. This includes a reflexivity about its own activities that is not exempt from its own kind of scrutiny and analysis.

The founding institution of cultural studies, now the Department of Cultural Studies at the University of Birmingham, has been described many times (Hall, 1980; 1986, p. 59; Tolson, 1986; Women's Studies Group, 1978, pp. 7–17). The intellectual formations – or invisible colleges and their affiliations (Williams 1977b) – of cultural studies is a more difficult issue. It is nonetheless crucial because the model of individual scholarship is particularly inappropriate. In the work of the Birmingham Centre during the 1970s,[1] for example, there are noticeable affiliations with the radical sociology of the National Deviancy Conference (Rock & McIntosh, 1974), the *May Day Manifesto* group (Williams, 1968),[2] the Women's Liberation Movement, and the analysis of *Race Today*, as well as more obvious intellectual debts to Raymond Williams in the early years and later to the Althusser school. There are also important debates with the formations around *Screen* magazine, and later with the formation around *Media, Culture and Society.*[3]

The characteristic cultural form of cultural studies is a certain kind of collectively produced book.[4] This is directly related to the tradition of group work and collective projects developed at the Birmingham Center and continued in the team teaching of the Open University course on popular culture. The best examples of English cultural studies are all of this kind. *Resistance through Rituals* (Hall & Jefferson, 1976). *Women Take Issue* (Women's Studies Group, 1978), *Working Class Culture* (Clarke, Critcher, & Johnson, 1979), and *Policing the Crisis* (Hall, Critcher, Jefferson, Clarke, & Roberts, 1978) are collectively written projects with a direct relation to their conditions of production at a graduate research center and the broader Left political culture in which they are clearly embedded.

Cultural studies in Britain is characterized by the extraordinary diversity and originality of the topics that have been studied. The studies of youth subcultures and television news programs are well known. Equally deserving of attention are studies of masculinity (Tolson, 1977), the image of women (Millum, 1975), ways in which the past is presented in museums (Lumley, 1988), young women at school and work (Griffin, 1985), job training (Finn, 1987), the politics of sport (Whannel, 1984), the history of sexuality (Mort, 1988), Caribbean music (Hebdige, 1987a), gender and expertise (McNeil, 1987), James Bond (Bennett & Woollacott, 1987), dime novels (Denning, 1987b), the history of middle class intellectuals (McNeil, 1987), and how white kids in Birmingham respond to reggae music (Jones, 1988).

Along with the diversity of topics there is a wide range of theoretical approaches and lively debate among them. Cultural studies is not unified around a central theme or problematic but is characterized by a diversity of concrete studies which are theoretically informed. There has been a tendency, in general discussions, to reduce the theoretical diversity of cultural studies to a small number of alternative positions. The actual practice is a tradition of theorizing through concrete and historical studies which must be read in their own terms.

Cultural studies in the United States. The idea of cultural studies is fairly new in the United States. However, a minority tradition of communication scholarship has existed for 10 or 15 years which has made a claim for cultural studies against the behavioral and functionalist paradigms of mainstream communication research.[5] Carey (1977) makes a case for a 'ritual' perspective in which communication is understood as part of the creation and transformation of a shared culture. However, the interpretive approach for which he calls does not address the issue of its own political intentions. It is presented as a humanities subject in the university, beyond politics.

Newcomb (1984; Newcomb & Hirsch, 1983) presents a more text-oriented version which points to the multiple meanings in television and other mass media. Like Carey, Newcomb insists that communication media are not in any way secondary but are an important part of contemporary culture. He rejects abstraction for a notion of the complexity of experiences.

His overall emphasis on the complexity of texts and his existential rejection of the idea of 'mass' communication – because each viewer or reader makes something different of it – is close in some ways to the early work of Williams (1961). Newcomb, however, has little sense of the social or political structure, which appears in his work only as the behaviorist and functionalist social science research that he rejects.

In Grossberg (1983), there is a critique of Carey on the grounds that he ignores issues of power. Whereas Carey and Newcomb understand American media as part of everyday life in the United States, Grossberg argues that communication is the site of symbolic struggles among antagonistic social groups. This is a very important argument indeed.

In his own subsequent work, Grossberg (1983, 1984b) presents the British cultural studies tradition as a series of failed attempts to study the relationships between culture and society. By this account Williams (1961) tried to study this relation with his concept of a 'structure of feeling'. But Grossberg argues, drawing on Althusser, that the concept is flawed because it assumes a holistic unity and excludes social and political conflict. Studies of encoding/decoding in television discourse (Brunsdon and Morley, 1978, Morley, 1980, 1981, 1983) also fail to connect culture (encoding) and society (decoding). Grossberg reads these studies as showing no patterns of response by various social groups and therefore failing in any systematic way to connect structures of television encoding and audience decoding. Hebdige's study of youth subculture (1979) also fails. According to Grossberg, it tries to connect the encodings of the fashion and entertainment industries (culture) with the ways their products are actually used by youth subcultures (society). But Grossberg argues that the concept of subcultural 'style' fails to accomplish this research goal. Since he reads cultural studies in this way as a series of failed attempts to connect culture and society, Grossberg then proposes that the concepts should be abandoned. There is no such thing as culture or society. To replace cultural studies Grossberg (1983, 1984b) proposes a postmodernist research practice in which power and desire are located in concrete anarchist examples.

Grossberg's more recent work is centered around the description of the 'affective economy' of the 'rock music apparatus' (1984a; 1986b) and the 'television apparatus' (1986a). Instead of deconstructing categories such as culture and society, Grossberg now proposes a nonunified theoretical discourse about embodied experience (affect, the body) which in part constructs a field (e.g. different groups of fans include different things as 'rock music') in particular epochs (e.g. the era of nuclear weapons). These and other vectors intersect in different ways. Grossberg stresses a situated diversity of form and experience and rejects the possibility of a unified theory of culture.

His own conceptual suggestions amount to a kind of theoretical *bricolage*. Scattered through these recent writings are the 'nomadic subject' (Deleuze & Guattari, 1977), a 'billboard world' (Jameson, 1984), a 'culture of pessimism' (Benjamin, 1968), 'affect' and 'youth' (from mainstream social psychology and sociology), and a notion of a postmodern experience (Baudrillard, 1983). This weird theoretical apparatus has been criticized by Marcus (1986, p. 78), who says that 'The theory has no support other than its ability to float in the air', and Nugent (1986, p. 82), who points out that Grossberg's use of the word 'hegemony' barely connects with Gramsci's active interest in politics. It may be that this theoretical apparatus best fits Grossberg's interest in rock music in the United States, a topic where cognitive and directly political models seem to be of little use.

A critique of Grossberg. The main problem of Grossberg's influence is that in making his case for postmodernism and more concrete studies of 'cultural apparatuses' he apparently discards most of cultural studies as it has developed in Britain. At conferences in the United States, cultural studies has become synonymous with various types of postmodern theorizing.

There are two factors which encourage this development. The first is the difficulty in the United States of reading the cultural studies style of theorizing through concrete examples when most of the examples are specific to British society. How many students in the United States have read a copy of *Jackie* magazine? How many have seen a *Nationwide* television news show? Also, there are difficulties of obtaining copies of most cultural studies articles and books in the United States. The more general overviews and discussions of theory obviously cross the Atlantic better. This has led to a tendency to falsely unify the field around a small number of articles by Stuart Hall. Given Hall's strong advocacy of collective and committed intellectual work, this is an ironic development.

The second difficulty is the relative isolation of cultural studies scholars in the United States and the relative absence of a Left intellectual tradition. Cultural studies in the United States is being sponsored by scholars who rarely have any connection to existing political and cultural movements and are somewhat surprised that this might even be possible.

Grossberg's selective history of cultural studies is mapped as an alternative paradigm for communication studies. This highly selective presentation concentrates mainly on the early work of Williams, on research using the model of encoding and decoding in television, and on Hebdige's book on subcultures. There is a logic in this selection. Williams is read through a comparison with Dewey's interest in community and communication. Hall's encoding/decoding model is read through the dominant paradigm of American communication studies: the production of media and their active reception by audiences.[6]

The reading of Williams, however, is partial and reductionistic. Grossberg essentially stops at about 1974 and nowhere discusses Williams' major work of communication theory, *Marxism and Literature* (1977b). Grossberg treats Williams as if the notion of a 'structure of feeling' is a rigorous concept which guides all of his work. It is actually a contradictory and *ad hoc* formulation and has only a residual role in Williams's work after the mid-1970s (O'Connor, 1989b, pp. 83–85).[7] Grossberg's reading of Hall has lost the sense of rootedness of communication processes in social reproduction and politics. Hall becomes a theoretician of the superstructure, of communication effectively isolated from material and political limits and pressures.

Grossberg's more recent work employs theoretical vectors which frequently look very similar to ideas he ruled out of court in articles in the early 1980s. For example, his sketch of a postwar 'culture of pessimism' in the United States after the 1950s seems in effect very close in purpose to Williams' sketch (1961) of the structure of feeling of Britain in the 1960s. A wide diversity of books which are somewhat similar to Grossberg's recent position, including Bennett (1982), Bourdieu (1984), and Williams (1977b), are rarely mentioned and for reasons that are completely unclear.

The effect is a somewhat esoteric framework that has little in common with the much more generous boundaries of cultural studies in Britain. What has happened under the rubric of postmodernism is that the sense of culture as practice, form, and institution has been lost. This has resulted in confused thinking about how cultural studies might look as institution, practice, and cultural form in the United States.

Cultural studies in and out of the classroom. It appears to be difficult to reproduce the institutional situation of the Birmingham Center or the Open University in North America, although there is the example of the Center for Twentieth Century Studies at the University of Wisconsin-Milwaukee and the Department of Cultural Studies at Trent University in Canada. Individual instructors in humanities or social science faculties have to work, often in isolation, within their existing institutional framework. In particular, collective work, while possible, is actively discouraged in America's university system.

This does not, however, mean that the activity has to become one of cultural theory rather than the practice of cultural studies. There are some traditions of research in the United States which ought to be continued. One of these is an interest in studying alternative media (Downing, 1984). Another possibility is to critically appropriate the theme of community and media, if this is an important theme in North American culture, sharply criticizing naive notions of 'community' and radicalizing the topic. It would also seem sensible for cultural studies in the United States to develop a strong interest in doing cultural studies in Mexico and the rest of Latin America – especially since the 'communication for development' paradigm is almost completely discredited there, but there is a strong interest there in semiology and the work of Bourdieu. Cultural studies in North America could be very different if a strong feminist presence were there from the start, rather than having to fight against an already established formation. Connections should be made to studies of the cultural and political struggles of black, Latino, Asians, and other minority fractions within the United States.[8]

It may be useful to make one further point in conclusion. Williams (1977a) has said that we live in a world that is in a sense rotten with criticism. A work of theory and criticism is today valued more highly than the actual cultural production upon which it is a commentary. Part of the reason for this in England is the difficulty of doing rather than writing about alternative cultural forms. (Williams' own film projects were effectively blocked, although he did script several television productions.) But this is less the case in the United States with its different organization of radio and television. There is nothing in England that corresponds to the Pacifica group of radio stations or public access television. Cultural studies in the United States will be poorer if it neglects this alternative experience. It surely also would be useful to make the connection with alternative film and television producers whose work deals critically with media issues and is itself an example of an alternative cultural practice. Examples include Lizzie Bordon's film *Born in Flames* (1983) and 'Paper tiger television' (Halleck, 1984). Finally, it is usually possible in American universities for students to learn about cultural forms first hand. Instead of theorizing about encoding and decoding, students can learn by trying to create and find an audience for an alternative television program.[9]

Notes

1. Articles by members of the Birmingham Centre include Hall (1980), Johnson (1979; 1986), Tolson (1986), Lumley and O'Shaughnessy (1985), Connell and Mills (1985), Green (1982), and Sparks (1977). American introductions include Becker (1984), Streeter (1984), and Grossberg (1983). See also the *Journal of Communication Inquiry* special issue on Stuart Hall (1986). Fiske's introductions from an Australian formation (1986; 1987) give more emphasis to his own version of social semiotics and are less politically engaged.
2. Williams was editor of the *May Day Manifesto, 1968*, and the large working group included Thompson, Hall, and others.
3. For these debates, see Chambers *et al.* (1977–78), Coward (1977), Hall (1980), and Johnson (1979). On the history of the *Screen* formation, see MacCabe (1985). Hall (1980) should be understood not as 'cultural theory' but as part of a debate between the political economy arguments of the journal *Media, Culture and Society* and cultural studies in general. This debate, initiated in Collins *et al.* (1986), deserves to be taken much more seriously in the United States.
4. Examples of the collective work from the Birmingham Center include Smith (1975), Hall, Connell, and Curti (1976), Center for Contemporary Cultural Studies (1978; 1981; 1982a; 1982b), Batsleer *et al.* (1985), Women's Studies Group (1978), and English Studies Group (1979). Other books and articles by past members of the Birmingham Center include: Brunsdon and Morley (1978), Morley (1981; 1983; 1986), Brunsdon (1981), Hebdige (1979; 1987a; 1987b), Langan and Schwarz (1985), Millum (1975), Hobson (1982), Willis (1977; 1978), Denning (1987a; 1987b), Bromley (in press), Chambers (1986), Jones (1988), McRobbie (1980; 1984), and McRobbie and McCabe (1981). Although many of these were written after the authors left the Center they are clearly extensions of work done there and evidence of the fruitfulness of group work.
5. This section is indebted to the very helpful response of *CSMC* reviewers of the first draft of this essay.
6. Sparks (1977) does not even mention the encoding/decoding model in his survey of cultural studies. See also Johnson (1979; 1986). Cohen (1980, p. 83) says his interest in subcultures is not a matter of studying decodings of the dominant culture. Cultural studies narrowly interpreted as the study of encoding/decoding is criticized by Corner (1986).
7. See also my 1989a work, *Raymond Williams on Television* and, for an overview, my 1989b work. Elsewhere (1981), I review Hebdige (1979) and Clarke *et al.* (1979).
8. Birmingham Center books on issues of race include Hall *et al.* (1978), Hebdige (1979), Center for Contemporary Cultural Studies (1982a), Gilroy (1987), and Jones (1988).

9. On 'activist' cultural studies, see McRobbie and McCabe (1981) and McRobbie (1982). For activist cultural studies research in the United States, see Kahn and Neumaier (1985), Halleck (1984), Lippard (1984), and Kellner (1985).

References

ALTHUSSER, L. and BALIBAR, E. (1970) *Reading Capital*. London: New Left Books.
BATSLEER, J., DAVIES, T., O'ROURKE, R., and WEEDON, C. (1985) *Rewriting English: Cultural Politics of Gender and Class*. London: Methuen.
BAUDRILLARD, J. (1983) 'The ecstasy of communication'. In Foster, H., (ed.), *The Anti-aesthetic: Essays on Postmodern Culture* (pp. 126–34). Port Townsend, WA: Bay Press.
BECKER, S.L. (1984) 'Marxist approaches to media studies: the British experience'. *Critical Studies in Mass Communication* 1; 81–109.
BENJAMIN, W. (1968) 'Theses on the philosophy of history'. In Arendt, H. (ed.), *Illuminations* (pp. 253–64). New York: Schocken.
BENNETT, T. (1982) *James Bond as Popular Hero*. Birmingham: Open University Press.
BENNETT, T. and WOOLLACOTT, J. (eds), (1987) *Bond and Beyond: The Political Career of a Popular Hero*. New York: Methuen.
BORDON, L. (1983) 'Born in flames.' *Heresies: A Feminist Publication on Art and Politics* 16, 12–16.
BOURDIEU, P. (1984) *Distinction: A Social Critique of the Judgement of Taste* (trans. R. Nice). Cambridge: Harvard University Press.
BROMLEY, R. (in press) *Memory Making: The Representation of the Period 1918–1945 in Contemporary Writings*. London: Routledge and Kegan Paul.
BRUNSDON, C. (1981) " 'Crossroads': notes on soap opera", *Screen* 22(4), 32–37.
BRUNSDON, C. and MORLEY, D. (1978) *Everyday Television: 'Nationwide.'* London: British Film Institute.
CAREY, J.W. (1977) 'Mass communication research and cultural studies: an American view'. In Curran, J., Gurevitch, M. and Woollacott, J. (eds), *Mass Communication and Society* (pp. 409–25). London: Edward Arnold.
Centre for Contemporary Cultural Studies (1978) *On Ideology*. London: Hutchinson.
Centre for Contemporary Cultural Studies (1981) *Unpopular Education: Schooling and Social Democracy since 1944*. London: Hutchinson.
Centre for Contemporary Cultural Studies (1982a) *The Empire Strikes Back: Race and Racism in 70s Britain*. London: Hutchinson.
Centre for Contemporary Cultural Studies (1982b) *Making Histories: Studies in History Writing and Politics*. London: Hutchinson.
CHAMBERS, I. (1986) *Popular Culture: The Metropolitan Experience*. London: Methuen.
CHAMBERS, I., CLARKE, J., CONNELL, I., CURTI, L., HALL, S., and JEFFERSON, T. (1977–78) 'Marxism and culture', *Screen* 18(4), 109–19.
CLARKE, J., CRITCHER, C., and JOHNSON, R. (1979) *Working Class Culture: Studies in History and Theory*. London: Hutchinson.
COHEN, P. (1980) 'Subcultural conflict and working-class community'. In Hall, S., Hobson, D., Lowe, A. and Willis, P. (eds), *Culture, Media, Language: Working Papers in Cultural Studies* (pp. 78–87). London: Hutchinson.
COLLINS, R., CURRAN, J., GARNHAM, N., SCANNELL, P., SCHLESINGER, P., and SPARKS, C. (eds), (1986) *Media, Culture and Society*. London: Sage.
CONNELL, I., and MILLS, A. (1985) 'Text, discourse and mass communication'. In Van Dijk, T.A. (ed.), *Discourse and Communication: New Approaches to the Analysis of Mass Media Discourse and Communication* (pp. 26–43). Berlin: Walter de Gruyter.

CORNER, J. (1986) 'Codes and cultural analysis'. In Collins, R., Curran, N., Garnham, P., Scannell, P., Schlesinger, P. and Sparks, C. (eds), *Media, Culture and Society.* London: Sage.

COWARD, R. (1977) 'Class, 'culture' and the social formation', *Screen* 18(1), 75–105.

DELEUZE, G. and GUATTARI, F. (1977) *Anti-Oedipus: Capitalism and Schizophrenia.* New York: Viking.

DENNING, M. (1987a) *Cover Stories: Narrative and Ideology in the British Spy Thriller.* London: Routledge and Kegan Paul.

DENNING, M. (1987b) *Mechanic Accents: Dime Novels and Working Class Culture in America.* London: Verso.

DOWNING, J. (1984) *Radical Media: The Political Experience of Alternative Communication.* Boston: South End Press.

English Studies Group (1979) 'Thinking the thirties'. In Barker, F., Bernstein, J., Coombes, P., Hulme, P., Musselwhite, D. and Stone, J. (eds), *1936: The Sociology of Literature* (Vol. 2. pp. 1–20). Colchester: University of Essex Press.

FINN, D. (1987) *Training without Jobs: New Deals and Broken Promises.* London: Macmillan.

FISKE, J. (1986) 'Television and popular culture: reflections on British and Australian critical practice', *Critical Studies in Mass Communication* 3, 200–16.

FISKE, J. (1987) 'British cultural studies and television'. In Allen, R.C. (ed.), *Channels of Discourse* (pp. 254–89). Chapel Hill: University of North Carolina Press. Reprinted here as Chapter 6.

GILROY, P. (1987) *There Ain't No Black In The Union Jack.* London: Hutchinson.

GREEN, M. (1982) 'The Centre for Contemporary Cultural Studies'. In Widdowson, P. (ed.), *Re-reading English* (pp. 77–90). London: Methuen. Reprinted here as Chapter 3.

GRIFFIN, C. (1985) *Typical Girls? Young Women Move from School to Work.* London: Routledge and Kegan Paul.

GROSSBERG, L. (1983) 'Cultural studies revisited and revised'. In Mander, M.S. (ed.), *Communication in Transition* (pp. 39–70). New York: Praeger.

GROSSBERG, L. (1984a) 'I'd rather feel bad than not feel anything at all: rock and roll, pleasure and power', *Enclitic* 8, 94–110.

GROSSBERG, L. (1984b) 'Strategies of Marxist cultural interpretation', *Critical Studies in Mass Communication* 1, 392–421.

GROSSBERG, L. (1986a) *The In-Difference of Television or Mapping in TV's Popular (Affective) Economy.* (ERIC report No. 293516.)

GROSSBERG, L. (1986b) 'Is there rock after punk?', *Critical Studies in Mass Communication* 3, 50–74.

HALL, S. (1980) 'Cultural studies: two paradigms', *Media, Culture and Society* 2, 57–72. Reprinted here as Chapter 2.

HALL, S. (1986) 'On postmodernism and articulation: an interview', *Journal of Communication Inquiry* 10(2), 45–60.

HALL, S., CONNELL, I., and CURTI, L. (1976) 'The 'unity' of current affairs programmes'. In Bennett, T., Boyd-Bowman, S., Mercer, C. and Woollacott, J. (eds), *Popular Television and Film* (pp. 88–117). London: British Film Institute.

HALL, S., CRITCHER, C., JEFFERSON, T., CLARKE, J., and ROBERTS, B. (1978) *Policing the Crisis: Mugging, the State and Law and Order.* London: Macmillan.

HALL, S. and JEFFERSON, T. (1976) *Resistance through Rituals: Youth Subcultures in Post-war Britain.* London: Hutchinson.

HALLECK, D. (1984) 'Paper tiger television: smashing the myths of the information industry every week on public access cable', *Media, Culture and Society* 6, 313–18.

HEBDIGE, D. (1979) *Subculture: The Meaning of Style.* London: Methuen.

HEBIDGE, D. (1987a) *Cut 'n' Mix: Culture, Identity and Caribbean Music*. London: Comedia.
HEBIDGE, D. (1987b) *Hiding in the Light*. London: Comedia.
HOBSON, D. (1982) *Crossroads: The Drama of a Soap Opera*. London: Methuen.
JAMESON, F. (1984) 'Postmodernism, or the cultural logic of late capitalism', *New Left Review* 146, 53–92.
JOHNSON, R. (1979) 'Three problematics: elements of a theory of working-class culture'. In Clarke, C., Critcher, C. and Johnson, R. (eds), *Working Class Culture: Studies in History and Theory* (pp. 201–37). London: Hutchinson.
JOHNSON, R. (1986) 'What is cultural studies anyway?', *Social Text* 16, 38–80. Reprinted here as Chapter 5.
JONES, S.C. (1988) *Black Culture, White Youth*. London: Macmillan.
Journal of Communication Inquiry (1986) 10(2). [Special issue on Stuart Hall].
KAHN, D. and NEUMAIER, D. (1985) *Cultures in Contention*. Seattle: The Real Comet Press.
KELLNER, D. (1985) 'Public access television: alternative views'. In Radical Science (ed.), *Making Waves: The Politics of Communications* (pp. 79–92). London: Free Association Books.
LANGAN, M. and SCHWARTZ, B. (eds), (1985) *The Crises in the British State: 1880–1930*. London: Hutchinson.
LIPPARD, L.R. (1984) *Get the Message? A Decade of Art for Social Change*. New York: Dutton.
LUMLEY, B. (1988) *The Museum Time-Machine: Putting Cultures on Display*. London: Routledge.
LUMLEY, B. and O'SHAUGHNESSY, M. (1985) 'Media and cultural studies'. In Baranski, Z.G. and Short, J.R. (eds), *Developing Contemporary Marxism* (pp. 268–92). London: Macmillan.
MACCABE, C. (1985) Class of '68: elements of an intellectual autobiography 1967–81. In *Theoretical Essays: Film, Linguistics, Literature* (pp. 1–32). Manchester: Manchester University Press.
MARCUS, G. (1986) 'Critical Response', *Critical Studies in Mass Communication* 3, 77–81.
MCNEIL, M. (ed.), (1987) *Gender and Expertise*. London: Free Association Books.
MCROBBIE, A. (1980) 'Settling accounts with subcultures', *Screen Education* 34, 37–50.
MCROBBIE, A. (1982) 'The politics of feminist research: between talk, text and action', *Feminist Review* 12, 46–57.
MCROBBIE, A. (1984) 'Dance and social fantasy'. In McRobbie, A. and Nava, M. (eds), *Gender and Generation* (pp. 130–61). London: Macmillan.
MCROBBIE, A. and MCCABE, T. (1981) *Feminism for Girls*. London: Routledge and Kegan Paul.
MILLUM, T. (1975) *Images of Women*. London: Chatto and Windus.
MORLEY, D. (1980) *The 'Nationwide' Audience: Structure and Decoding*. London: British Film Institute.
MORLEY, D. (1981) 'The 'Nationwide' audience: a postscript', *Screen Education* 39, 3–14.
MORLEY, D. (1983) 'Cultural transformations: the politics of resistance'. In Davis, H. and Walton, P. (eds), *Language, Image, Media* (pp. 104–17). Oxford: Basil Blackwell.
MORLEY, D. (1986) *Family Television: Cultural Power and Domestic Leisure*. London: Comedia.
MORT, F. (1988) 'Boys own? Masculinity, style and popular culture'. In Chapman, R. and Rutherford, J. (eds), *Male Order: Unwrapping Masculinity* (pp. 193–244). London: Lawrence and Wishart.

MOSCO, V. and WASKO, J. (eds), (1985) *Popular Culture and Media Events: The Critical Communications Review* (Vol. 3). Norwood, NJ: Ablex.

NEWCOMB, H.M. (1984) 'On the dialogic aspects of mass communication', *Critical Studies in Mass Communication* 1, 34–50.

NEWCOMB, H.M. and HIRSCH, P.M. (1983) 'Television as a cultural forum: implications for research', *Quarterly Review of Film Studies* 8(2), 45–55.

NUGENT, S.L. (1986) 'Critical response', *Critical Studies in Mass Communications* 3, 82–85.

O'CONNOR, A. (1981) 'Cultural studies and common sense', *Canadian Journal of Political and Social Theory* 5, 183–195.

O'CONNOR, A. (ed.), (1989a) *Raymond Williams on Television*. London: Routledge and Kegan Paul.

O'CONNOR, A. (1989b) *Raymond Williams: Writing Culture, Politics*. London: Basil Blackwell.

ROCK, P. and MCINTOSH, M. (1974) *Deviance and Social Control*. London: Tavistock.

SMITH, A.C.H. (1975) *Paper Voices: The Popular Press and Social Change, 1935–1965* (with E. IMMIRZI and T. BLACKWELL). Totawa, NJ: Rowman and Littlefield.

SPARKS, C. (1977) 'The evolution of cultural studies', *Screen Education* 22, 16–30. Reprinted here as Chapter 1.

STREETER, T. (1984) 'An alternative approach to television research: development, in British cultural studies at Birmingham'. In Rowland, W.R. Jr and Watkins, B. (eds), *Interpreting Television: Current Research Perspectives* (pp. 74–97). Beverly Hills: Sage.

TOLSON, A. (1977) *The Limits of Masculinity*. London: Tavistock.

TOLSON, A. (1986) 'Popular culture: practice and institution'. In MacCabe, C. (ed.), *High Theory/Low Culture: Analyzing Popular Television and Film* (pp. 143–55). New York: St Martin's Press.

WHANNEL, G. (1984) *Blowing the Whistle: The Politics of Sport*. London: Pluto.

WILLIAMS, R. (1961) *The Long Revolution*. Harmondsworth: Penguin Books.

WILLIAMS, R. (ed.) (1968) *May Day Manifesto, 1968*. Harmondsworth: Penguin Books.

WILLIAMS, R. (1974) *Television: Technology and Cultural Form*. Glasgow: Fontana.

WILLIAMS, R. (1977a) 'A lecture on realism', *Screen* 18(1), 61–74.

WILLIAMS, R. (1977b) *Marxism and Literature*. Oxford: Oxford University Press.

WILLIS, P. (1977) *Learning to Labour: How Working Class Kids get Working Class Jobs*. London: Saxon House.

WILLIS, P. (1978) *Profane Culture*. London: Routledge and Kegan Paul.

Women's Studies Group (eds), (1978) *Women Take Issue: Aspects of Women's Subordination*. London: Hutchinson.

11

Feminism and cultural studies

Elizabeth Long

British cultural studies is now in the process of redefinition through appropriation. This process appears to be both especially difficult and consequential. Difficult because, as both Grossberg [Chapter 9] and O'Connor [Chapter 10] point out, it is not a sharply bounded or 'single fathered' intellectual lineage. This is a radical heritage, and its political standpoint appears in danger of being compromised by absorption into the American scene as just another paradigm for sale on the market-place of ideas.[1]

I am struck by the ways in which the summary or presentational statements about British cultural studies that have been made in this country have already practiced an exclusion that seems to have marginalized its feminist practitioners, ironically the strand of that tradition that has arguably the best chance of maintaining a critical stance in its appropriation by feminist scholars in America, both because of their connections with a broad social movement and because of the nature of their practices within the academy. This is particularly troubling given the tendency for feminist thought to have a truncated 'circuit' (Escarpit, 1965) of distribution and readership beyond feminist circles, which are often on the margins of 'general' theory and research. It is this lacuna that I address by discussing, first, what British cultural studies feminists have contributed to cultural studies in 'general' and, second, some of the ways feminist British cultural studies have been – and might be – well used by Americans.

The small number of women at the Birmingham Center for Contemporary Cultural Studies began their work mainly in reaction to the invisibility of women in the theoretical and empirical analyses of their male senior colleagues and peers, and their work bears some of what Leslie Roman and Linda Christian-Smith (1988) call a 'reactive' stamp. However, they were responding not only to the absence of women as subjects and as a category – an absence that fueled the early years of feminist critique in the United States – but from within a theoretical, methodological, and institutional position that allowed the simple question 'What about women?' to have large consequences. One methodological and three conceptual arenas seem to have been especially significant both for engendering British feminist contributions to cultural studies and for those Americans who refer back to their work. I discuss each in turn.

First, Birmingham feminists took issue with the valorization of the public sphere that marked the Center's work on subcultural forms and the media. As Angela McRobbie's articles on the study of subcultures pointed out, the focus on spectacular male group behaviors on the street or in other public places tended to address girls only by the terms of derogation common among participants. For the most part, this focus simply made females invisible, since the 'public' bias of subcultural studies marginalized the family and other contexts in which girls might be participating in 'equivalent rituals, response, and negotiations' (McRobbie, 1980; McRobbie & Garber, 1976).

Similarly, Dorothy Hobson and Charlotte Brunsdon challenged media studies that valorized news and public affairs programs over soap operas and other 'female' genres (see also Ang, 1985). Their early identification of the family as an important site for the appropriation of television programming opened the way for innovative investigations of the interpellation of public and private life. In her book *Crossroads* (1982), about a soap opera of the same name, Hobson, for example, discusses how the family context influences both the concentration and perspective that people bring to their viewing, and the ways in which the women viewers 'use' the program to reflect on their own family issues, linking women's sense of 'ownership' of the program not only to its content but to its inclusion in their domestic routine.[2] Such early feminist formulations clearly demanded further theoretical and empirical work, for asserting the importance of women and the domestic sphere did not address the issue of how the structural and ideological boundaries between public and private are historically constituted and hierarchized so as to devalue women, their domestic and market-oriented labor, and the social settings and cultural forms in which they are 'at home'.

If the feminists challenge to the Center's valorization of public life was somewhat inhibited by their refusal to problematize 'the private', they were much clearer about the need to challenge the regnant assumption that social class was the primary or singular mechanism of domination. Yet, all remained convinced of the importance of class as well as gender. So instead of posing these as exclusive claimants for analytic attention (class vs. gender vs. race), the writings of Mica Nava (1984a; 1984b), Erica Carter (1984), McRobbie (1978a; 1978b; 1980; 1982; McRobbie & Garber, 1976), Valerie Amos and Prathiba Parmar (1981; Parmar, 1982), Brunsdon (1981), and Hobson (1981; 1982) manifest a concern with how to integrate class and gender in cultural studies.

I think this work is particularly exciting for two reasons. First, informed by the Center's commitment to keeping a close and dialectical connection between theory and empirical research, these feminist culturalists discuss the intersection of systems of subordination in the lived experience of active and sense-making human beings, rather than as static determinant variables or as purely abstract theoretical categories that must somehow be brought together. In general, work of this kind seems crucial for understanding the complexly contradictory ways in which subjectivity is constructed under late capitalism and for gaining the leverage (both scholarly and political) to understand the often conflicted ways our many-stranded identities are positioned within the existing social order, the first stage of working toward resistance of its imperatives.

Second, especially in their essays about the state and its role in enforcing gendered as well as class relations of domination, Birmingham feminists began to undermine still prevalent assumptions that gender can somehow be equated with a marginal 'woman's sphere' of sexuality and the family. Rather, as essays by Nava (1984a; 1984b) and Barbara Hudson (1984) in *Gender and Generation*, as well as those by Anne Strong (1981), Trisha McCabe (1981; McCabe & Sharon, 1981), and Gill Frith (1981) in *Feminism for Girls*, detail the work of educational and judicial authorities in enforcing what Robert Connell (1987) calls 'hegemonic' masculinity and 'emphasized' femininity in their class-related inflections has consequences that pervade the social order.

This kind of work seems particularly important today, when new wave conservatism is centrally concerned with enforcing a regressive-utopian vision (or visions, since all such policies are differentiated by class and race) of 'traditional' womanhood, of homophobic masculinity, and of sexuality and the family in ways that legitimize other repressive political, military, and economic initiatives.

It is because of the deep connection between sexuality, desire, and the emotional roots of both domination and resistance that articles like McRobbie's 'Dance and social fantasy' (1984) are so important not only for feminists but for all those concerned with modifying the rationalistic bias of Marxism and, indeed, most academic representations of human action. British feminists, like their American counterparts, have pushed their exploration further, theoretically working through their assignment as women to the realm of intuition and sexuality. Worth noting is McRobbie's insistence on mapping out the *social* nature of the construction of female subjectivity, pleasure, and desire – by a discussion of the history of popular dance, its representations in the media, several ethnographic experiences in modern discos, and the relationship of dance to working class family customs and women's life cycles.[3]

Perhaps because of their understanding of the cross-cutting complexities of power relations, the British feminists extended not only the Centre's substantive interests but also their methodological program in regard to producing and disseminating scholarly work. Another McRobbie article (1982) is, again, exemplary of feminist cultural studies discussions about ethnography. In it, she criticizes 'naturalistic' sociology by pointing out that researchers do not lose their social privilege while in the field, which undermines the 'innocence' of the knowledge field encounters generate, as well as the 'transparency' of the process by which data become text.

There is some indication in McRobbie's work, and that of other British feminists who interviewed mainly women, that the relations between women informants and women ethnographers – as well as the Women's Liberation Movement's preoccupation with domination by authoritative talk, disempowerment through silence, and with ways to democratize access to the spoken and written word – informed her insights about ethnographic knowledge. The connection with an oppositional social movement certainly influenced McRobbie and McCabe's attempt to make an innovative political intervention through publishing an 'engaged' feminist collection of essays, *Feminism for Girls* (1981), written by academics, politically involved teachers, and students, and also directed to those students, teachers, and youth workers as well as to scholars. The book is an impressive but awkward attempt to speak beyond the academy, one that founders in the reality of the divergences in interest and vocabulary between these constituencies. In some ways, it stands for certain qualities of the British feminist presence in cultural studies that are both strengths and limits: its theoretical eclecticism, its often informal methodological stance, and its enthusiastic risk-taking in the name of nurturing resistance.

If British cultural studies in general has had something of a blind spot about feminism because of what feminists from various perspectives have called class 'essentialism' or economic or class 'reductionism', mainstream American feminists have until recently manifested a similar blind spot toward British cultural studies (feminist or nonfeminist) because of a tendency toward 'gender essentialism' and an accompanying sympathy toward models drawn from individual psychology that obscure questions of class and race.[4] Even now, it is mainly feminists influenced by Marxism or neo-Marxisms who find this tradition sympathetic. This is admittedly a gross generalization about a many faceted intellectual/political movement – and one I modify later – but, even insofar as it holds, feminists may be the scholars who can best maintain the critical stance of British cultural studies in the United States – for two major reasons.

First, feminist scholarship in America has remained in touch with an oppositional social movement – however embattled or embourgeoisified – and thus has had a genuine (self) interest in critical thinking; domination and subordination are, for the Birmingham thinkers, more than academic categories. Further, while this critical stance is often ambivalent – because of the possibility of some rewards from the status quo – it is always being reconstituted by 'the environing society'. Indeed, as mentioned earlier, much of the thrust of the New Right has been in the arenas of family, sexuality, and the proper 'sphere' for women, as well as in policies, such as the erosion of affirmative action, that make explicit the connection between women's oppression and that of other subordinate social groups. This environing society comprises, as well, the still male-dominated academy; so even intellectual workers find themselves, as women, at odds with the prevailing hierarchies of scholarly value and open to critical thought.[5]

Second, feminist scholarship displays many of the institutional features and work practices argued by both O'Connor and Grossberg to be not only characteristic of the Birmingham Center but constitutive of their radical intellectual politics. For instance, feminists work across disciplines and often in marginal positions in relation to mainstream academic departments or subspecialties. So, feminist reception of British cultural studies has occurred not only in communication but also in education, sociology, women's studies, popular culture, American studies, and rhetoric. The interdisciplinary nature of the feminist response to British cultural studies in America has militated against its simplistic encapsulation within a specific field as one of that field's 'paradigms' (as has been true for feminist scholarship as a whole) and has supported the desire, enacted at Birmingham, to challenge the existing, depoliticizing, disciplinary fragmentation of cultural studies.

There is also a strong tradition of collective work among feminist scholars and an equally strong desire to undercut the hierarchical nature of academic life (although this stands in tension with the desire to amass individual 'intellectual capital'). More often than men, women are apt to have nonstandard careers and thus are more likely to make contributions as graduate students, to need support within inhospitable university environments, and to work out innovative 'spaces' to develop this support. Thus, the feminist scholarly community in America, being composed of 'deviants' who have feminist traditions of anti-hierarchical and democratic processes, finds sympathy with the 'processual' aspects of the British cultural studies tradition and, indeed, has had a history of similar work processes.

The already constituted nature of feminist scholarship in the United States (marginal, interdisciplinary, and collectivist in action or desire) may also explain why such a wide-ranging group of critically oriented feminist scholars has begun to take up British cultural studies as formative of their work. It appears that the political and intellectual scenes were similar enough to engender some parallel developments in critical scholarship in Britain and the United States, so that when American feminists of a critical orientation became aware of British cultural studies they incorporated it very quickly.

This appropriation, however, is relatively recent.[6] So, just as British cultural studies has appeared in the discipline of communication as part of the almost generational paradigmatic 'ferment' of the past few years, its feminist 'wing' has become most influential among a generation of scholars finishing graduate school or in the junior stages of their academic careers. These are women for whom the theoretical advances of a decade ago – such as object relations or Lacanian perspectives, post-structuralism, the Frankfurt School – are taken-for-granted and somewhat constraining aspects of their intellectual background. This is also a group who, in the conservative, jumpy 1980s, is searching for ways to invest political/theoretical energy in analyses that have the critical power to intervene in both the academy and the world outside it, because they are informed by a theoretical tradition that understands them both as sites whose cultural or symbolic practices are also social struggles.

The point here is that American feminist appropriations of British cultural studies challenge both mainstream feminism and mainstream cultural studies less by transforming substantive areas (the study of subcultures, curricula, popular media, etc.), or by a focus on women's popular culture, sexuality, and the family, than by foregrounding a multidimensional understanding of power, domination, and possibilities for resistance.[7] Particularly important contributions are the feminist culturalists' appreciation that people's social identities and allegiances are multivalent and bring them into often contradictory positions in regard to hegemonic discursive practices, and their equally perspicacious understanding of the multiplicity of sites wherein repressive forms of social subordination can be reproduced or can provide opportunities for contestation. To make this point more concrete, I discuss the work of two American women scholars whose projects powerfully integrate these issues.

Tricia Rose's studies of rap music (1989; in press) – the central component of Hip Hop, predominantly black urban youth culture also known for break dancing and graffiti art – argue that it is not a natural outgrowth of oral Afro-American forms but a complex fusion of oral forms, modern notions of individual authorship, and postmodern technology. She also contextualizes rap as a cultural response to the brutal policies of urban renewal in the South Bronx that abandoned a gutted neighborhood to Blacks and Hispanics. Moving from social history to 'close readings' of rap songs and their live performances, she demonstrates that the music incorporates highly self-conscious references to a musical and cultural tradition that is recuperated through reconstitution, as well as artful critiques of dominant social values and their replication in the power relations of the commercialized music industry. Showing how women in Hip Hop are marginalized in mainstream and leftist journalism, Rose analyzes how the songs, videos, and style of women rappers, and fans challenge hegemonic notions of sexuality, courtship, and bodily aesthetics, articulating a community-based feminist perspective within the subculture. Her work urges consideration of the complex interrelationships among gender, race, and class as they are constructed at specific historical junctures in struggles between collectivities of sharply different power, as they are represented by the performances of cultural activists – whether on the streets, at concerts, or in the studio, ambivalently legitimated by the music industry – and as they are framed by diverse wings of the media and the academy.

Leslie Roman's ethnographic and semiotic analyses (1987; 1988; in press) of how middle and working class Punk young women culturally produce their feminine sexualities in the slam dance examine a smaller social 'scene', with equally challenging theoretical and empirical consequences. Addressing three problems within cultural studies – romanticization of 'resistance', 'class essentialism', and 'productivism' – Roman shows how the young women's class-differentiated experiences within the family (often including sexual abuse and family violence), school, and their different opportunities and histories in the work world provided them with very different symbolic and material resources for self-articulation within the subculture. She explores the 'asymmetries in subjectivity' that kept the young women's gender- or class-based alliances from transcending momentary insight and becoming socially transformative. Moreover, her activist and 'dialogic' ethnography illuminates the epistemological ramifications of ethical and political research choices. Roman's work links the most private levels of subjectivity to its multiple sites of structuration, illuminating the complexities of motivation for action, whether defensive or challenging in relation to an equally complex understanding of the landscape of power relations.

This kind of political engagement, methodological innovation, and willingness to use gender as an entry into a more multiplex and less romantic understanding of the constituents of power, subordination, and resistance *in general* demonstrates – as does the work of other feminists using the British tradition to grasp the specificity of contemporary America – that feminism is central for developing the critical potential of cultural studies. Moreover, at a time when hegemonic interests are vested in remapping the relations between public and private, family and work, in redefining dependency and individual responsibility, and in tapping into the well-springs of terror and desire for dubious purposes of pacification and mobilization, the feminist contribution to critical cultural studies will be critical indeed.

Notes

1. My thanks to Michele Farrell, George Lipsitz, Ellen Wartella, and Joe Dumit.
2. Likewise, feminist and other criticisms of Morley's study (1980) of viewer response to the news program *Nationwide* (he constructed artificial audience 'groups' on the basis of occupation, though also attending to gender and race) led to his book *Family Television* (1986), which begins to address how that most domestic of media is incorporated within and constitutive of the relations of familial power and authority.
3. This is, as well, a project vital for feminist scholarship in the United States, and McRobbie often appears in citations as the authorization for a move to undercut the essentialist tendencies that psychoanalysis – as received in America – often seems to encourage vis a vis issues of fantasy, desire, and subjectivity.
4. Different aspects of this discussion have been taken up by scholars as varied as Michele Barrett, Allison Jaggar, Sandra Harding, Heidi Hartmann, Toril Moi, and Leslie Roman.
5. The link of a (at least potentially) broad social movement with other oppressed social groups has tended to keep even liberal American feminist cultural studies work in touch with issues of power, and thus somewhat protected from falling into the two intellectual camps or tendencies that have marked American cultural studies: 'high' and often pessimistic theory vs. celebration (often optimistic, pluralistic, and blind to issues of power) of the popular. See my 1986 work for a fuller discussion of this issue.
6. From an interview with Ellen Wartella (4/30/89). As examples of American work that may not have been directly influenced by British cultural studies but engaged with similar problematics, I would note my own writing on middle class women's reading groups (1986; 1987; in press) and the work by Radway (1984), McCormack (1983), and Tuchman (1978), to name just a few examples from the realms of sociology and literary studies.
7. This quality characterizes scholarship in all three of the categories under which I have grouped some recent American 'cultural studies' publications by feminists. For instance, a fair number of scholars deal primarily with texts. Their work is not only politically informed but also tends to be historically, contextually, or institutionally grounded rather than formalistic (Carter, 1988; Christian-Smith, 1988), to be concerned with the relation between constraints like gender and class, ethnicity, or race, rather than with gender alone (Bright, 1989a; Franco, 1986; Steeves & Smith, 1987), and to be oriented toward the intersection between 'texts' and audiences' cultural practices even when not engaged in empirical studies of cultural usages by specific people (Byards, 1987; Ellsworth, 1988; Lewis, 1987a; 1987b; Silverman, 1986; Taylor, 1989). Another strand of research examines culturally mediated social relations, usually using some combination of

ethnographic, historical, and institutional analysis (Banks & Zimmerman, 1987; Press, in press). Of particular note are Bright's discussion (1986b) of the ethno-aesthetics of masculine identity among Mexican-American low riders, Henderson's work (1989) on the social construction of 'individual' talent at a film school and the undermining effects of that ideology on women's attempts to organize against a male dominated establishment there, Lesko's work (1988) on style, authority, and class among girls at a Catholic high school, Amesly's work (in press) on *Star Trek* culture, and Rakow's work (1988b) on gender and technology in communication. More theoretical or programmatic works (Henderson, 1988; Press, 1987; Rakow, 1986; Schwichtenberg, 1986; 1989; Steeves, 1987) have been particularly useful to me when they understand theory and methodology as cultural practices in themselves. Essays by McCarthy (1988), Smith (1988), Treichler (1986), Treichler and Wartella (1986), Henderson (1987), and Rakow (1989) are especially noteworthy in this regard.

References

AMESTY, C. (in press) 'How to watch *Star Trek*', *Cultural Studies*.

AMOS, V. and PARMAR, P. (1981) 'Resistances and responses: the experiences of black girls in Britain'. In McRobbie, A. and McCabe, T. (eds), *Feminism for girls: An Adventure Story* (pp. 129–52). London: Routledge and Kegan Paul.

ANG, I. (1985) *Watching Dallas: Soap Opera and the Melodramatic Imagination*. London: Methuen.

BANKS, J. and ZIMMERMAN, P. (1987) 'The Mary Kay way: the feminization of a corporate discourse', *Journal of Communication Inquiry* 11(1), 85–99.

BRIGHT, B. (1989a) 'Nade y Nade: language, power and emotion in the poetry of Evangelina Vigil'. Unpublished manuscript.

BRIGHT, B. (1989b) 'Gendered voices in Chicana poetry'. Unpublished manuscript.

BRUNSDON, C. (1981) 'Crossroads: notes on soap opera', *Screen* 22(4), 32–37.

BRUNSDON, C. (1986) *Films for Women*. London: British Film Institute.

BRUNSDON, C. and MORLEY, D. (1978) *Everyday Television: 'Nationwide'* London: British Film Institute.

BYARS, J. (1987) 'Reading feminine discourse: prime-time television in the US', *Communication* 9, 289–304.

CARBY, H. (1982) 'White woman listen! Black feminism and the boundaries of sisterhood'. In Centre for Contemporary Cultural Studies (ed.), *The Empire Strikes Back* (pp. 212–35). London: Hutchinson.

CARTER, E. (1984) 'Alice in consumer wonderland'. In McRobbie, A. and Nava, M. (eds), *Gender and Generation* (pp. 185–214). London: Macmillan.

CARTER, E. (1988) 'Intimate outscapes: problem-page letters and the remaking of the 1950s West German family'. In Roman, L., Christian-Smith, L. and Ellsworth, E. (eds), *Becoming Feminine: The Politics of Popular Culture* (pp. 60–75). London: Falmer Press.

CHRISTIAN-SMITH, L. (1988) 'Romancing the girl: adolescent romance novels and the construction of femininity'. In Roman, L., Christian-Smith, L. and Ellsworth, E. (eds), *Becoming Feminine: The Politics of Popular Culture* (pp. 76–101). London: Falmer Press.

CLIFFORD, J. and MARCUS, G. (eds), (1986) *Writing Culture: The Poetics and Politics of Ethnography*. Berkeley: University of California Press.

CONNELL, R. (1987) *Gender and Power: Society, the Person and Sexual Politics*. Cambridge: Polity Press.

ELLSWORTH, E. (1988) 'Illicit pleasures: feminist spectators and personal best'. In

Roman, L., Christian-Smith, L. and Ellsworth, E. (eds), *Becoming Feminine: The Politics of Popular Culture* (pp. 102–19). London: Falmer Press.

ESCARPIT, R. (1965) *The Sociology of Literature*. Painesville, OH: Lake Erie College Press.

FRANCO, J. (1986) 'The incorporation of women: a comparison of North American and Mexican popular narrative'. In Modleski, T. (ed.), *Studies in Entertainment: Critical Approaches to Mass Culture* (pp. 119–38). Bloomington: Indiana University Press.

FRITH, G. (1981) 'Little women, good wives: is English good for girls?' In McRobbie, A. and McCabe, T. (eds), *Feminism for Girls: An Adventure Story* (pp. 27–49). London: Routledge and Kegan Paul.

GLAZER, N. (1980) 'Overworking the working woman: the double day in a mass magazine'. *Women's Studies International Quarterly* 3, 79–95.

HENDERSON, L. (1987, November) 'Critical ethnography and the duality of structure'. Paper presented at a meeting of the American Studies Association, New York.

HENDERSON, L. (1988, April) 'Picturing women: feminism and popular culture'. Paper presented at a meeting of the Symposium on Women, Language, and Power, Haverford College, Pennsylvania.

HENDERSON, L. (1989, May) 'Interpreting 'talent': local meaning and ethnographic evidence'. Paper presented at a meeting of the International Communication Association, San Francisco.

HOBSON, D. (1981) 'Now that I'm married . . . '. In McRobbie, A. and McCabe, T. (eds), *Feminism for Girls: An Adventure Story* (pp. 101–12). London: Routledge and Kegan Paul.

HOBSON, D. (1982) *'Crossroads': The Drama of a Soap Opera*. London: Methuen.

HUDSON, B. (1984) 'Femininity and adolescence'. In McRobbie, A. and Nava, M. (eds), *Gender and Generation* (pp. 31–53). London: Macmillan.

LESKO, N. (1988) 'The curriculum of the body: lessons from a Catholic high school'. In Roman, L., Christian-Smith, L. and Ellsworth, E. (eds), *Becoming Feminine: The Politics of Popular Culture* (pp. 123–42). London: Falmer Press.

LEWIS, L. (1987a) 'Consumer girl culture: how music video appeals to women', *One Two Three Four: A Rock and Roll Quarterly* 5, 5–15.

LEWIS, L. (1987b) 'Female address in music video', *Journal of Communications Inquiry* 11(1), 73–84.

LONG, E. (1986) 'Women, reading and cultural authority: some implications of the audience perspective in cultural studies', *American Quarterly* 38(4), 591–612.

LONG, E. (1987) 'Reading groups and the crisis of cultural authority', *Cultural Studies* 1(2), 306–27.

LONG, E. (1988) 'The quest for the 'serious': a study in contemporary reading practices'. Unpublished manuscript.

McCABE, T. (1981) 'Schools and careers: for girls who do want to wear the trousers'. In McRobbie, A. and McCabe, T. (eds), *Feminism for Girls: An Adventure Story* (pp. 57–79). London: Routledge and Kegan Paul.

McCABE, T. and SHARON, K. (1981) 'A note on lesbian sexuality'. In McRobbie, A. and McCabe, T. (eds), *Feminism for Girls: An Adventure Story* (pp. 178–86). London: Routledge and Kegan Paul.

McCARTHY, C. (1988) 'Marxist theories of education and the challenge of cultural politics of non-synchrony'. In Roman, L., Christian-Smith, L. and Ellsworth, E. (eds), *Becoming Feminine: The Politics of Popular Culture* (pp. 185–203). London: Falmer Press.

McCORMACK, T. (1983) 'Male conceptions of female audiences: the case of soap operas'. In Wartella, E., Whitney, D.C. and Windahl, S. (eds), *Mass Communication Review Yearbook* (pp. 273–83). Beverly Hills: Sage.

McROBBIE, A. (1978a) *Jackie: An Ideology of Adolescent Feminity*. Birmingham: The Centre for Contemporary Cultural Studies.

McROBBIE, A. (1978b) 'Working class girls and the culture of feminity'. In Women's Studies Group (eds), *Women Take Issue: Aspects of Women's Subordination* (pp. 96–108). London: Hutchinson.

McROBBIE, A. (1980) 'Settling accounts with subcultures: a feminist critique', *Screen Education* 34, 37–49.

McROBBIE, A. (1982) 'The politics of feminist research: between talk, text and action', *Feminist Review* 12, 46–57.

McROBBIE, A. (1984) 'Dance and social fantasy'. In McRobbie, A. and Nava, M. (eds), *Gender and Generation* (pp. 130–61). London: Macmillan.

McROBBIE, A. and GARBER, J. (1976) 'Girls and subcultures'. In Hall, S. and Jefferson, T. (eds), *Resistance through Rituals* (pp. 209–23). London: Hutchinson.

McROBBIE, A. and McCABE, T. (eds), (1981) *Feminism for Girls: An Adventure Story*. London: Routledge and Kegan Paul.

MORLEY, D. (1980) *The 'Nationwide' Audience: Structure and Decoding*. London: British Film Institute.

MORLEY, D. (1986) *Family Television: Cultural Power and Domestic Leisure*. London: Comedia.

NAVA, M. (1984a) 'Drawing the line'. In McRobbie, A. and Nava, M. (eds), *Gender and Generation* (pp. 85–111). London: Macmillan.

NAVA, M. (1984b) 'Youth service provision, social order and the question of girls'. In McRobbie, A. and Nava, M. (eds), *Gender and Generation* (pp. 1–30). London: Macmillan.

PARMAR, P. (1982) 'Gender, race, and class: Asian women in resistance'. In Centre for Contemporary Cultural Studies (ed.), *The Empire Strikes Back* (pp. 236–75). London: Hutchinson.

PRESS, A. (1989) 'The ongoing feminist revolution', *Critical Studies in Mass Communication* 6, 196–202.

PRESS, A. (in press) *Women Watching Television*. Philadelphia: University of Pennsylvania Press.

RADWAY, J. (1984) *Reading the Romance: Women, Patriarchy, and Popular Literature*. Chapel Hill: University of North Carolina Press.

RADWAY, J. (1988) 'The Book-of-the-Month Club and the general reader: on the uses of 'serious' fiction', *Critical Inquiry* 14, 516–38.

RAKOW, L.F. (1986) 'Rethinking gender research in communication', *Journal of Communication* 36(4), 11–26.

RAKOW, L.F. (1988) 'Gendered technology, gendered practice', *Critical Studies in Mass Communication* 5, 57–70.

RAKOW, L.F. (1989) 'Feminist studies: the next stage', *Critical Studies in Mass Communication* 6, 209–15.

ROMAN, L. (1987) 'Punk feminity: the formation of young women's gender identities and class relations in the extramural curriculum within a contemporary subculture'. Unpublished doctoral dissertation, University of Wisconsin, Madison.

ROMAN, L. (1988) 'Intimacy, labour, and class: ideologies of feminine sexuality in the Punk slam dance'. In Roman, L., Christian-Smith, L. and Ellsworth, E. (eds), *Becoming Feminine: The Poltics of Popular Culture* (pp. 143–84). London: Falmer Press.

ROMAN, L. (1989) 'Double exposure: the politics of feminist materialist ethnography'. Unpublished manuscript.

Feminism and cultural studies 207

ROMAN, L. and CHRISTIAN-SMITH, L. (1988) 'Introduction'. In Roman, L., Christian-Smith, L. and Ellsworth, E. (eds), *Becoming Feminine: The Politics of Popular Culture* (pp. 1–34). London: Falmer Press.

ROSE, T. (1989, November) 'Hit the road Sam: black women rappers and sexual differences'. Paper presented at a meeting of the American Studies Association. Toronto, Canada.

ROSE, T. (in press) 'Orality and technology: rap music and Afro-American cultural resistance', *Popular Music and Society* 13(4), Winter, 1989.

SCHWICHTENBERG, C. (1986, June) 'Feminist politics and feminine style: central issues in feminist film theory'. Paper presented at a meeting of the International Communication Association, Chicago.

SCHWICHTENBERG, C. (1989) "The 'mother lode' of feminist research: congruent paradigms in the analysis of beauty culture". In Dervin, B., Grossberg, L., O'Keefe, B. and Wartella, E. (eds), *Re-thinking Communication: Paradigm Exemplars* (Vol. 2 pp. 291–306). Newbury Park, CA: Sage.

SILVERMAN, K. (1986) 'Fragments of a fashionable discourse'. In Modleski, T. (ed.), *Studies in Entertainment: Critical Approaches to Mass Culture* (pp. 139–52). Bloomington: Indiana University Press.

SMITH, D. (1988) 'Femininity as discourse'. In Roman, L., Christian-Smith, L. and Ellsworth, E. (eds), *Becoming Feminine: The Politics of Popular Culture* (pp. 37–59). London: Falmer Press.

STEEVES, H.L. (1987) 'Feminist theories and media studies', *Critical Studies in Mass Communication* 4, 95–135.

STEEVES, H. and SMITH, M. (1987) 'Class and gender in prime-time television entertainment: observations from a socialist feminist perspective', *Journal of Communication Inquiry* 11(1), 43–63.

STRONG, A. (1981) 'Learning to be a girl: girls, schools, and the work of the Sheffield education group'. In McRobbie, A. and McCabe, T. (eds), *Feminism for Girls: An Adventure Story* (pp. 186–98). London: Routledge and Kegan Paul.

TAYLOR, E. (1989) *Prime Time Families: Television Culture and Postwar America.* Berkeley: University of California Press.

TREICHLER, P.A. (1986) 'Teaching feminist theory'. In C. Nelson (ed.), *Theory in the Classroom* (pp. 57–128). Urbana: University of Illinois Press.

TREICHLER, P.A. and WARTELLA, E. (1986) Interventions: feminist theory and communication studies. *Communication* 9, 1–18.

TUCHMAN, G. (1978) 'The symbolic annihilation of women'. In Tuchman, G., Kaplan Daniels, A. and Benet, J. (eds), *Hearth and Home: Images of Women in the Mass Media* (pp. 3–38). New York: Oxford University Press.

12

Discipline and vanish: feminism, the resistance to theory, and the politics of cultural studies

Ellen Rooney

> . . . cultural studies is not one thing; it has never been one thing.
> (Hall, 'Emergence', 11)

Headnote (1990)

In November of 1988, the National Association of Scholars held a conference in New York City. Three hundred academics attended, including such well-known media figures as John Silber, then president of Boston University, later a candidate for governor of Massachusetts, and Jeanne J. Kirkpatrick, a political scientist, formerly of the United Nations. The assembled scholars were exhorted 'to redeem American higher education from intellectual and moral servitude to forces having little to do with the life of the mind or the transmission of knowledge'. These usurping forces, composed of academic 'radicals' engaged in 'oppression studies', apparently threaten the objective pursuit of knowledge with politics. Feminists figured prominently in the convention's apocalyptic narratives of giddily declining standards, 'radical egalitarianism', and 'chilling' demands for political correctness. At the same time, the purveyors of radical scholarship were paradoxically described as frail and timid. As one speaker put it: 'the barbarians are among us. We need to fight them a good long time. Show them you are not afraid[;] they crumble' (Berger, 22). 'Say to the feminists, "What do you mean by separate courses? You have no methodology." When you lose, make them state their agenda to the world. They haven't got the guts to state it, and you'll beat them that way' (Mooney, 11). This imagery conflates an urgent call to arms with the contemptuous and imperial assurance that the 'barbarians' lack the courage to put up much of a fight; it suggests that the campus radical is more fearsome as a lurid spectacle than she proves to be in an honest confrontation.[1]

A few weeks after this rousing affair, in December of 1988, I delivered the following essay as a talk in an MLA program that might be characterized as the NAS's worst nightmare come true. The session was one of five organized by Nancy Armstrong and Richard Ohmann for the Division of Sociological Approaches to

Literature. Over the course of three days, four workshops on 'Third World and Multicultural Studies', 'The Politics of Cultural Studies', 'Practicum: Making a Cultural Studies Program', and 'Feminism and Cultural Studies', and a general forum all addressed the question 'What Should Cultural Studies Be?'[2] The politics, internal and external, of this question was a topic raised in every session. The coordinated series of panels could easily be interpreted as a response to the onslaughts of right-wing critics of the university like William Bennett or the National Association of Scholars. The Chronicle of Higher Education, *for example, reported the MLA sessions under the headline: 'In Face of Growing Success and Conservatives' Attacks, Cultural-Studies Scholars Ponder Future Directions.' Yet this angle of the story can be overstated; thus far, at least, cultural studies has not allowed reactionary ideologues to set the terms of its debates. This has been especially true with regard to the category of the 'political'. Neo-conservatives demand that the allegedly recent politicization of the university be reversed; cultural studies has generally been committed to a heterogeneous and inclusive account of the political and suspicious of efforts to 'return' politics to their 'proper' venue. And yet, as the US cultural studies movement has expanded (mounting more panels and bigger conferences), the question of politics, specifically, the question of what counts as political, has reemerged. As Meaghan Morris suggests in 'Politics now (anxieties of a petty-bourgeois intellectual)', this question often revolves around the relation (or the difference) between 'aesthetic gestures, textual "subversions" [on the one hand, and] political actions'. Morris cautions that 'in a mass-media society with mass-media cultures and mass-media politics, the relationship between signifying (rather than "aesthetic") gestures and political ones may not be so clear cut' (185). In practice, the 'political' anxiety attacks of cultural studies scholars seem both warranted and gestural. Strangely, the rhetoric of clarifying limits echoes the redemptive language of neo-conservative polemic, though of course the cultural studies scholar intends politics rather than intellectual objectivity to be the object of his saving grace; the intertwined imagery of denunciation and dismissiveness also reappears in exhortations to attend to real political acts, not mere texts. At the same time, the politics of cultural studies remains problematic.*

My essay intervenes in this discussion to propose the feminist model of a politics of knowledge production as a possible strategy for cultural studies. I have retained the polemic of my oral presentation in the present text. This seemed especially important as I reworked the talk and discovered (yet again) the problem of the pronoun. In New Orleans in 1988, it seemed fairly clear who 'we' were; in 1990, in differences: A Journal of Feminist Cultural Studies, *the 'we' has shifted and reemerges as one of the stakes in the construction of cultural studies within the university. I am grateful to Richard Ohmann and Nancy Armstrong for including me in the panel; to Elizabeth Weed, Neil Lazarus, and Khachig Tololyan for their helpful comments on the text; and to the Center for the Humanities at Oregon State University for a fellowship that enabled me to pursue these questions.*

My argument begins by articulating feminism as a network of feminist practices. I want to approach the politics of cultural studies through an analysis of the relation between cultural studies, on the one hand, and women's studies, feminist theory, and the women's liberation movement, on the other. The asymmetry of this formulation, in which cultural studies is opposed to women's studies *and* to feminist theory *and* to the women's movement, is an allegory of my argument.[3] The historical and institutional situation of cultural studies in the United States does not yet allow us to name any particular political movement (outside the university) as 'properly' affiliated with cultural studies. This fact makes the second term of the feminist configuration – that is, theory – a crucial weapon for cultural studies as it tries to stake out its political position(s), both within the academy and elsewhere. In my analysis, the question of the politics of cultural studies in the US is inseparable from the question of the theory of cultural studies, where theory is understood primarily as the *practice* of interrogating the production of knowledge. Stuart Hall has suggested that cultural studies can only resist 'the remorseless march of the division of knowledge and the gap between theory and practice' by 'developing a practice in its own right, a practice to bring together theory and practice'. Suggesting that the politics of cultural studies can never be reduced to a 'populist intellectual project', Hall argues that 'the vocation of intellectuals is not simply to turn up at the right demonstrations at the right moment, but also to alienate that advantage which they have had out of the system, to take the whole system of knowledge itself and, in Benjamin's sense, attempt to put it at the service of some other project' ('Emergence', 18). This alienation of advantage requires a theoretical and political reading that forces the system of knowledge out of its 'proper', disciplinary context. As a politics of knowledge production, cultural studies can have far-reaching and radical effects; a theoretical practice that interrogates the disciplinary production of systems of knowledge can ground its progress. On the other hand, if cultural studies collaborates in the resistance to theory, it will quickly be assimilated to the disciplinary structure of the university, which is to say, it will trade its political effects for a proper place among the disciplines.

If we examine cultural studies in light of the example of feminism's triple practice as women's studies, feminist theory, and the women's liberation movement, three topics emerge immediately for consideration. First, the politics of women's studies, especially in relation to students, who constitute one of the most important constituencies scholars and critics address and who may act in the university either as agents of recuperation or of radical critique. Second, the effort to theorize the object of cultural studies, that is the struggle among practitioners to answer the question put by Richard Johnson: 'what is cultural studies anyway?' And, finally, the *form* of the dangers the university's disciplinary logic presents to any oppositional discourse at work within its precincts: what kind of deformations will cultural studies as theory and practice undergo if it succumbs either to the temptations or the bullying of disciplinarity?

The specter that haunts my analysis is the possibility that the institutional emergence of cultural studies in the US will lead to its rapid recuperation by the disciplines as a reactionary discourse.[4] I intend the word 'reactionary' in as literal a sense as possible: the cunning of ideology all but assures that the university will respond to the challenges presented by cultural studies by promoting its own version thereof. This kind of reaction-formation would reinforce the very disciplinary effects that cultural studies even now disrupts. The ideology of free and objective inquiry, of knowledge beyond power, which structures the liberal university and conceals many of its social and political functions, demands that cultural studies be assimilated to a disciplinary logic. To anticipate myself for a moment, I want to suggest that cultural studies molded into a disciplinary format would lead, at a minimum, to the following unhappy results: first, our students (and eventually our faculties) would never need to confront the fundamentally political significance of their own intellectual labor, thus deadening the acute awareness of the politics of knowledge that now characterizes cultural studies; second, our object of study would be redefined as an historical-geopolitical period or as a unit of area studies and thus naturalized as the proper content of a disciplinary domain; finally, cultural studies would abandon its position as a critical reading of the traditional disciplines and of the disciplinary as such (Green, 84; Hall 'Cultural' and 'Emergence'; Johnson, 38–43) and take up its own authoritative niche among the disciplines.

My anticipation of disaster gains urgency from an analogy with the history of American studies. Despite the leftist strains in its past and the important work of many individual scholars (like Janice Radway, Michael Denning, and Mary Jo Buhle), American studies too frequently participates in the resistance to progressive work in the humanities. There are exceptions to this tendency, but the rule holds well enough to make us pause over this institutional history. As a field, American studies has no particular political constituency or valence. Indeed, the disciplinary character of American studies, its institutional status as a discipline, is indistinguishable from that of other disciplinary formations, like English, Philosophy, or Romance Languages.[5] My point here is not to accuse the late, great forefathers of American studies – much less its current practitioners – of some failure of political insight or will, but to disclose the ruses of disciplinary recuperation as they have played themselves out in the history of American studies' life in the university.[6] At the moment, the disciplinary structure of American studies is such that it is *as difficult* to undertake critical work there as it is in any of the traditional disciplines. This is at least partly due to the fact that American studies has been established as a 'period', a well-mapped geo-political and historical domain in which objects of inquiry appear as givens; to be sure, these objects are investigated from various perspectives and even occasionally 'redefined', but they are freighted with the full authority of the disciplinary object. In other words, the problematic of American studies has been naturalized and thus has disappeared as an object of contestation or inquiry (Althusser). We must confront the possibility that cultural studies could repeat the institutional trajectory of American studies.

Institutional context and the history of the disciplines are everything to the analysis I propose. As Stuart Hall suggests, cultural studies is 'an adaptation to its terrain . . . a conjunctural practice' ('Emergence', 11). The prominence I want to assign to theoretical practice is a response to conditions in the US academy. The importance of this caveat cannot be exaggerated. In no sense do I mean to suggest that theory with a capital 'T' serves, by virtue of its apparent self-reflexivity, as an infallible prophylactic against recuperation or as the guarantee of an essentially radical practice in any field. (Countless examples, many from my own 'home' discipline of English, demonstrate the politically conservative or negligible effects of theoretically sophisticated work.) I do not propose that theory-as-self-consciousness will set us free; on the contrary, theoretical practice seems important to me primarily insofar as it discloses degrees of unfreedom, irreducible limits and exclusions, the often harsh terrain. As Bruce Robbins has persuasively argued, theory is neither 'a determinate set of philosophical positions' nor an 'authoritarian ruler' that seeks to dominate practice from without. Rather, theory is itself a practice within a particular *'historical conjuncture'*, that is, an 'event', and Robbins insists that we should define it 'in terms of [the] historical moment' (4, 5–6).

> The public insufficiencies and internal contradictions of the New Criticism, the urgencies of the Vietnam War and the feminist and civil rights movements, changing ethnic and gender proportions of students and teachers along with the pressure for capitalist vocationalizing of the universities, movements of national liberation abroad energizing Lévi-Strauss' critique of Eurocentrism and literary criticism's slow surrender to a global, anthropological view of culture – all were clearly part of the conjuncture, and if it is difficult to assign a specific weight to any one element, to accumulate them is to feel their collective force. Consent to speak around theory's new series of propositions (though not necessarily to assent to them) had emergent social power behind it.(6)

The question of theory is a question of what we can do now, given where we are in the history of the United States and of the US academy, and in the history of cultural studies as an intellectual practice and as a field of work within the university. For the foreseeable future, I believe that a theoretical practice that concentrates on exposing the enabling assumptions and the stakes of intellectual projects is essential to grounding the progressive politics of cultural studies. We require, as Adrienne Rich argues, a theory and a 'politics of location'. Given its present location in the US academy, cultural studies must foreground the conflict of (its) theoretical problematics – within the 'field' of cultural studies and between cultural studies and the disciplines it challenges. This *strategy* enables what Gayatri Spivak has called a persistent critique of the disciplinary production of knowledge all around cultural studies, as well as within its boundaries, a critique that can never elude the question of politics ('In a Word', 126).[7]

To speak very generally, those scholars and critics pursuing cultural studies are united by the desire that their students (and their colleagues, for that matter) see culture, not as a 'canon' or a 'tradition', but as the embodiment and site of antagonistic relations of domination and subordination, that is, as a productive network of power relations. In principle and in practice, it matters relatively little whether students come to this critical position by earning a degree in a cultural studies program or on some disciplinary site. Indeed, many of those who currently practice cultural studies are extremely wary of disciplinarization: 'cultural studies must be inter-disciplinary (and sometimes anti-disciplinary) in its tendency' (Johnson, 42). At the same time, programs are being established willy-nilly (Ohmann 'Thoughts'), and they may be less vulnerable to recuperation if we are prepared to recognize and resist the specific forms of disciplinary recuperation.

Cultural studies in the United States has a political problem insofar as its relationship to a specifically political struggle outside the university is *at best* contested. Practically speaking, women's studies has an enormous advantage over both cultural studies and American studies: its students are often a politically conscious constituency before they enter the field, that is, before they are subjected to the relatively loose 'disciplinary' practices of women's studies. (African American studies has a similar advantage in some settings.) I realize that in many colleges and universities only a significant minority of the students in women's studies courses are also part of the women's movement. But feminist students have a disproportionate weight within the field and within their programs. Frequently, they parallel their work in women's studies with some form of political work, where the political includes cultural activity under the rubric of feminism. The oppositional politics of women's studies is forged as much by these students as it is by the women (and men) teaching in the programs and writing essays and books 'in' women's studies. This practical advantage has theoretical consequences in the form of students' awareness that their political work is intimately linked to their intellectual projects; indeed, this tie to so-called 'real world' politics suggests the ideological interestedness of women's studies, reminding everyone that this 'field' is not ideologically neutral, merely disciplinary.

The simple fact that its youngest scholars are often also activists of some kind does not ensure that women's studies will play a disruptive political role within the university. (There are, of course, dramatic limits to the current politics of women's studies in many places; the feminism of many women's studies' faculties guarantees no particular politics.)[8] Indeed, it runs counter to my entire polemic to suggest that the politics of women's studies is simply parasitic upon the so-called 'real world' politics of women's liberation. Nevertheless, I want to stress the theoretical importance of the political activities of women's studies students outside the university, without idealizing them. This emphasis is not meant to imply that some students (or faculties) have 'authentic' politics that 'naturally' express themselves, while others need prosthetic devices; nor do I mean to suggest that any programatic link between cultural studies as a (political) activity within the university and some particular practice (of cultural politics) outside the university is impossible in the US. My point is simply that its current absence robs cultural studies of one strategy of resistance to disciplinarization and alerts us to the possibility that cultural studies may be peculiarly vulnerable to political neutralization *within the university.*

I place such a strong emphasis on the positioning of students not simply because the existence of programs assumes the existence of students, but because they can so easily be invoked as an alibi for the university's demands (generally presented by a curriculum committee of some kind) for 'discipline'. It is frequently in their name (though often not through their efforts) that disciplinary standards are established, codified, and printed up in course catalogues as requirements. And as this scenario suggests, the critique of the production of disciplinary knowledge is *institutionally specific to the university*. As Gayatri Spivak continually argues, this critique is always a 'made' thing ('In a Word'), requiring painstaking construction and reconstruction, 'with no end in sight' ('Political', 218).

In other words, a critique of the politics of knowledge production is never merely a side-effect of political activity outside the university. The feminist students who choose to major in women's studies *construct* their choice as a political one. I believe this is always true (though I write that phrase with a certain dread). This sense of the politics of the field itself prepares them to work against the disciplines, as feminist theory demands. The creation of women's studies programs entails a specifically feminist critique of the disciplines. This critique is predominantly anti-essentialist and attacks the common-sense view of disciplinary discourse as at least potentially objective in its representation of the real.[9] These interventions insist that the university organizes knowledge politically and that the disciplines themselves are political at every level. Feminist theory *in the academy* is constituted by the discovery that a politicized, theoretical intervention within the disciplines is unavoidable. There follows a rejection both of the figure of the neutral, transparent investigator – the subject of disciplinary knowledge – and of the disciplinary myth of the given object of knowledge, innocently discovered in the world. As Jane Gallop suggests, 'one of the goals of what we so ambiguously call women's studies [might] be to call into question the oppressive effects of an epistemology based on the principle of a clear and nonambiguous distinction between subject and object of knowledge' (15–16).[10] 'Men's studies modified' (Spender) means a recognition of the interested nature of all knowledge, of every construction of an object, and of every inquiring subject's position.

Cultural studies seeks to participate in a similar critique, to 'alienate' the system of knowledge, as Hall puts it ('Emergence', 18). But while women's studies joins its intra-disciplinary critique to a project of feminist theory building that interpellates its subjects as 'feminist', it is not at all clear yet what (or who) the 'subject' of cultural studies will be. At a minimum, cultural studies must pursue an anti-disciplinary practice defined by the repeated, indeed, endless rejection of the logic of the disciplines and of the universal subject of disciplinary inquiry (Johnson, 42; Spivak 'Political' and 'Can the subaltern'; Rooney 'What'). Without such a consistent effort to politicize the subject of inquiry, the insinuating subject of disciplinary knowledge will inevitable reemerge. As Michael Green argues,

> . . . the relation of cultural studies to the other disciplines is . . . one of critique: of their historical construction, of their claims, of their omissions, and particularly of the forms of their separation. At the same time, a critical relationship to the disciplines is also a critical stance to their forms of knowledge production – to the prevalent social relations of research, the labour process of higher education. (84)

This anti-disciplinary practice begins by rejecting the universal subject of disciplinary knowledge; it produces new relations to knowledge and new subjects.

The plural is essential and may remain so indefinitely. The politics of the students initially attracted to cultural studies are obviously heterogeneous, and I use that term not entirely in its honorific sense. (I am thinking here of vague feelings of discontent and resentment which may have so little political focus as to approach the genuinely apolitical.) This amorphous situation cannot be remedied by assigning a particular politico-theoretical model – on the order of the Jameson of *The Political Unconscious*, for example, or 'the Birmingham School'[11] – and demanding that students adopt it, even assuming such a thing were possible. The problem cannot, in other words, be solved by giving students a theory of culture and assuring them that *its* politics are *the* politics of cultural studies. Whatever the limits of political heterogeneity, I do not see any possibility of elaborating a 'line', a unified theory, or even a political center to orient the whole of the enormous and diverse project of cultural studies. Indeed, in the US context, such a unifying project would very likely contribute to the process of disciplinarization that I have been at such pains to oppose. In contrast, to place the political conflict among theoretical problematics at the center of cultural studies programs would be to enable students (and scholars) to confront their own intellectual projects as political from the ground up: choices about subject matter, methodology, theory cannot be made according to any set of invariant principles, but are always an effect of the project one privileges and seeks to pursue. The student of cultural studies is a cultural worker. Within the university, her politics must *begin* with that positionality. In the US academy, a specific form of consciously theoretical discourse is essential to pursuing this point, precisely because it directly contradicts the positivist emphasis of what Margaret Ferguson has called the 'hidden curriculum' of the university (219). I must repeat that this is not because theoretical self-consciousness is innately subversive. Rather, cultural studies discloses theoretical choices as political choices. The visceral antipathy that certain self-nominated defenders of tradition have for theory becomes more explicable in this view. The student-scholar of cultural studies should work from the beginning with what Althusser calls a 'guilty' sense of the political effects of her theoretical and practical choices, beginning with the choice of cultural studies itself (14). This can only happen if students and critics have the theoretical tools to see their own work simultaneously as a tactic of resistance *and* an exercise of power, a process of exposing the concealed investments of disciplinary systems and deliberately re-organizing the pursuit of knowledge as such.

As a discipline, American studies has lost this political sense of position. Despite the efforts of many, many individual practitioners, in most universities, a student's choice of the field of American studies is neither politically nor theoretically discomfiting.[12] Uneasiness is a sign that the myth of the neutral division of reality into appropriate disciplines is under pressure; those fields most vehemently attacked at a National Association of Scholars convention are those cultural studies should emulate. While a women's studies major or graduate program can never escape its resonance as a political choice, and will thus always be available for attack, there is no political weight whatsoever to the choice of American studies as a discipline. It remains to be seen if cultural studies will be constituted as just another major.

'Just another major' is institutional shorthand for disciplinarization, the effort to obscure the position and thus the political investment of the inquirer and to naturalize the object of inquiry. An anti-disciplinary practice (such as women's studies) cannot be disciplined if it insists that the object of knowledge, the content that defines the discipline as such, is always a political fiction and a political choice, never a given. Women's studies struggles constantly to maintain these insights, to avoid 'reverting to the very terms of opposition which feminist theory has sought to undo' (Kamuf, 42),[13] and there is certainly nothing new in arguing that cultural studies ought to be self-conscious about its production of objects. But an emphasis on this *process* itself as an aspect of critical practice needs to be central to our curricula. One disturbing trend in cultural studies is a tendency to discipline programs as the study either of a geo-historical period, 'culture under capital', or of media practices within the culture industry, such as 'Hollywood', 'rock and roll', and 'sport'. At my own institution, one of the sites for cultural studies work is the program in Modern Literature and Society, which effectively excludes cultural materialistic work that situates itself before the French Revolution. In a recent report on 'CS in the US', Richard Ohmann, who has long been an advocate for cultural studies, as well as one of the most cunning and lucid of counter-critics on the left, traces the genesis of cultural studies to the efforts by intellectuals to understand the 'massive cultural transformations' of consumer society, especially the 'role of mass culture in shaping consciousness'; in the course of this analysis, the term 'mass culture' appears in four consecutive sentences, most interestingly in the phrase 'mass cultural studies in the US'.[14] Although nothing could be further from his intention, to reduce cultural studies to the study of mass culture (that is, to a period) is to invite a disciplinary fix that will ultimately displace the politics that Ohmann hopes to foreground. Disciplinary logic presses cultural studies to define its object in just such positivist terms, terms that conceal the contingency of the gesture of definition itself and, with it, its political effects. Women's studies has never permitted itself to be delimited in these terms, and, as a consequence, it is continually (and sometimes bitterly) re-theorizing its project. On the other hand, American studies is defined precisely as a historical and geographical period study.

If cultural studies becomes a new 'period', it will inevitably become a natural object for disinterested inquiry, a discipline. The irony is that this process is encouraged by some cultural studies scholars. Not surprisingly, the drive to fix a subject/object for cultural studies is often accompanied by vehement resistance to the 'textualization' of culture, which is then associated with theory (or 'bad' theory). The respectful hearing accorded recent suggestions that the so-called theoretical era is coming to a close is also related to disdain for 'the ideology of the text', and this disdain too tends to pride itself on political tough-mindedness. This resistance to textuality is announced as an effort to maintain a proper space for political action 'outside the text',[15] but its actual effect is to depoliticize the very significant practices which enable us to engage in any kind of politically motivated intellectual work whatsoever. In the name of politics, politically useful strategies are dismissed. The coincidence of this backlash with growing institutional support for programs in cultural studies suggests that the dominant discourses of the university have perhaps found a way to have their cultural studies and not have it, too. The NAS view of politics as something external to intellectual work itself can slip in unremarked.

Margaret Ferguson reminds us of an old women's studies adage when she argues that radical work in the academy requires that 'changes in the *content* of the curriculum . . . be correlated with changes in the *forms* of instruction' (219). When cultural studies burdens all of its students with the political effects of their intellectual work; when it owns political and intellectual responsibility for the construction of its objects; when it clings to its anti-disciplinary polemic and refuses to cultivate its own garden to the neglect of neighboring fields; then, in this specific and temporarily privileged form as a critique of the disciplinary organization of knowledge, cultural studies *will be* a radical transformation of the forms of instruction, a direct threat to the entire 'hidden curriculum' of the disciplines.

Notes

1. In 'Conservative', Mooney reports one conferee's conclusion: 'They're small in numbers, but so are termites' (11). She also notes the discrepancy between the willingness of 'many conferees [to] describ[e] themselves as conservative – intellectually, politically, or both' – and the official line, which fabulates a silent (and unrepresented) majority: 'We don't intend to be a bunch of right wing scholars pushing for our own beliefs. I think we represent a much larger group out there' (11).
2. The forum, presided over by Ohmann and including presentations by Gayatri Spivak, Janice Radway, Catherine Gallagher, and Richard Johnson, was itself entitled 'What Should Cultural Studies Be?', echoing the title of Johnson's essay, 'What is cultural studies anyway?'
3. I use the word 'opposed' only in the sense of 'in contrast to'. Obviously, women's studies, feminist theory, and the women's liberation movement are not 'opposed' to cultural studies in the sense of being antithetical or in opposition to them. *differences* itself testifies to the existence of 'feminist cultural studies', as do works like *Women Take Issue*, Hook's *Yearning*, Sheridan's *Grafts*, and essays like Hall's 'Cultural' and Johnson's 'What is'.
4. I am specifically concerned here with the dilemmas of cultural studies within the academy; the institutional pressures brought to bear by the peculiar practices and ideologies of the university differ significantly from those that shape cultural workers on other sites, including cultural studies scholars who are not affiliated with universities.
5. This is not to say it is static or even stable; but in this age of the 'crisis' of the humanities, critical interrogation has engulfed every discipline. American studies is often housed in programs and centers rather than in departments, but this is changing slowly, and 20-year-old programs can behave very much like departments. Shumway analyzes the uneven process of disciplinarization in 'Interdisciplinarity'. He notes that a commitment to interdisciplinary work does not necessarily forestall the development of disciplinary structures and effects; he also observes that 'American Studies had never given up th[e] idea

[of interdisciplinarity], and it had never recognized its own disciplinary nature' (20).

6. I am sympathetic to the view that American studies, as a discourse that seemed unavoidably to reflect (and celebrate) American ideology at large, was particularly vulnerable to reactionary recuperation, but I cannot enter too deeply into that argument here. I will argue only that today American studies scholars must struggle *against the grain* of the discipline just as scholars in the so-called traditional disciplines do. The relative rates of success are extremely variable and often depend on 'external' forces. Denning makes a very helpful distinction in his reading of 'American studies as a substitute Marxism'. He contrasts 'American cultural studies' pursued under the sign of American studies with 'marxist work in social or labor history . . . sociology or economics' which deals with the US (373); the former seems to him to be the site of an 'exceptional' resistance to marxism and British cultural studies. For some recent discussions of the ideology of American studies, see: Giroux; Denning; Shumway; Wise.

7. My inclination to worry about this particular matter is part of my own intellectual and political history as a feminist. As a Wesleyan undergraduate on the committee investigating/agitating for the creation of a women's studies program, I was the doubter, anxious to craft a proposal that placed as much power as possible in the hands of students, 'us', at that point. I did not care very much about being able to major in women's studies. I cared about being a feminist and about making that as easy and as radical a practice as possible within the confines of the university, where ease and radical intervention seemed opposed. To make a course of study easy, or rather, how easy to make it – specifically, how easy to make it to major in cultural studies – is for me a crucial question.

8. See Spivak, 'Political', for a discussion of the upward mobility and material rewards that may attend a career as a feminist scholar in the 'first world'.

9. I do not use the term anti-essentialist as code for post-structuralist. The enormous and growing bibliography of the theory and practice of women's studies in a wide range of institutions reveals varied and complex relations to theory and to the problem of the disciplines. While the word 'anti-essentialism' is certainly not universally privileged in these analyses, the emphasis is always on a critique of the production of knowledge itself, not simply on the marginalization or trivialization of women as objects of study. This is true even in those texts that ultimately do call for an effort to think feminist scholarship in disciplinary terms: women's studies 'as a discipline' is always a counter-discipline. An extremely abbreviated list of texts touching on this topic includes Bowles; DuBois; Farnham; Hull; Minnich; Mohanty; Spender; Treichler.

10. See also Bell.

11. Stuart Hall has recently protested the tendency to position the Birmingham Centre as the origin of or an authority on cultural studies: 'there is no such thing as the Birmingham school. To hear 'the Birmingham School' evoked is, for me, to confront a model of alienation in which something one took part in producing returns to greet one as thing, in all its inevitable facticity' ('Emergence', 11). Johnson also insists that 'the research and writing [at Birmingham], has been political, but not in any immediate pragmatic sense. Cultural studies is not a research programme for any particular party or tendency. Still less does it subordinate intellectual energies to any established doctrines' (42).

12. This may not have always been the case. Insofar as American studies represented an alternative to the traditional belles-lettristic view of literature, which privileged English over American texts and elite culture over popular, and

proposed to transgress the boundaries separating history from literary studies, it did disrupt business as usual in those disciplines.

13. See Derrida.
14. See *English* and *Politics* for discussions of topics ranging from 'English 101 and the military industrial complex' to canon formation, teaching mass culture, and 'The function of English at the present time'.
15. The tendency to see cultural studies as a period can easily develop out of a position that discounts theory as ahistorical and lacking in specificity or that opposes 'concrete', 'particular' projects to abstraction; these moves are often correlated with a deep suspicion of categories like 'textuality'. Among contemporary cultural critics tending to this line are Edward Said, Fredric Jameson, and Terry Eagleton. See Rooney, 'Going'; Shumway, 'Transforming'; Robbins.

References

ALTHUSSER, L. and BALIBAR, E. (1970). *Reading Capital*. London: New Left.

BELL, S.G. and ROSENHAN, M.S. (1981). 'A problem in naming: women studies – women's studies?' *Signs: Journal of Women in Culture and Society* 6, 540–42.

BERGER, J. 'Scholars attack campus "radicals".' *New York Times* 15 November 1988: 22.

BOWLES, G. and DUELLI-KLEIN, R. (eds), (1980) *Theories of Women's Studies*. Berkeley: University of California Press.

COUGHLIN, E.K. (1989) 'In face of growing success and conservatives' attacks, cultural studies scholars ponder future directions', *Chronicle of Higher Education* 18 January, 4–5, 12.

DENNING, M. (1986) ' "The special American conditions": Marxism and American studies'. *American Quarterly* 38, 356–80.

DERRIDA, J. (1984) 'Women in the beehive: a seminar with Jacques Derrida', *Subject/objects* 2, 5–19.

DUBOIS, E.C., KELLY, G., KENNEDY, E., KORSMEYER, C. and ROBINSON, L. (1987) *Feminist Scholarship: Kindling in the Groves of Academe*. Urbana: University of Illinois Press.

FARNHAM, C. (1987) *The Impact of Feminist Research in the Academy*. Bloomington: Indiana University Press.

FERGUSON, M. (1988) 'Teaching and/as reproduction', *The Yale Journey of Criticism* 1.2, 213–22.

GALLOP, J. (1985) *Reading Lacan*. Ithaca: Cornell University Press.

GIROUX, H. SHUMWAY, D., SMITH, P. and SOSNOSKI, J. (1984) 'The need for cultural studies: resisting intellectuals and oppositional public spheres', *Dalhousie Review* 64, 472–86.

GREEN, M. (1982) 'The Centre for Contemporary Cultural Studies.' In Widdowson, P. (ed.), *Re-Reading English*. London: Methuen, 77–90. Reprinted here as Chapter 3.

HALL, S. (1980) 'Cultural studies and the Centre: some problematics and problems', *Culture, Media, Language: Working Papers in Cultural Studies, 1972–79*. London: Hutchinson, 15–47.

HALL, S. (1990) 'The emergence of cultural studies and the crisis in the humanities', *October* 53, 11–23.

HOOKS, B. (1990) *Yearning: Race, Gender, and Cultural Politics*. Boston: South End.

HULL, G., BELL-SCOTT, P. and SMITH, B. (eds), (1982) *All the Women are White, All the Blacks Are Men, But Some of Us are Brave: Black Women's Studies*. Old Westbury, NY: Feminist.

JAMESON, F. (1981) *The Political Unconscious: Narrative as a Socially Symbolic Act.* Ithaca: Cornell University Press.

JONHSON, R. 'What is cultural studies anyway?', *Social Text* 16 (1986–87): 38–80. Reprinted here as Chapter 5.

KAMUF, P. (1982) 'Replacing feminist criticism', *Diacritics* 12.2, 42–48.

MINNICH, E., O'BARR, J. and ROSENFELD, R. (eds), (1988) *Reconstructing the Academy: Women's Education and Women's Studies.* Chicago: University of Chicago Press.

MOHANTY, C.T. (1983) 'On difference: the politics of black women's studies', *Women's Studies International Forum* 6, 243–47.

MOONEY, C.J. (1988) 'Conservative scholars call for movement to "reclaim" academy', *Chronicle of Higher Education* 23 November, 11, 13.

MORRIS, M. (1988) 'Politics now (anxieties of a petty bourgeois intellectual).' *The Pirate's Fiancée: Feminism, Reading, Postmodernism.* London: Verso, 173–86.

OHMANN, R. (1976) *English in America: A Radical View of the Profession.* New York: Oxford University Press.

OHMANN, R. (1987) *Politics of Letters.* Middletown: Wesleyan University Press.

OHMAN, R. (forthcoming) 'Thoughts on CS in the US.' *Critical Studies.*

RICH, A. (1986) 'Notes towards a politics of location', *Blood, Bread, and Poetry: Selected Prose, 1979–85.* New York: Norton, 210–31.

ROBBINS, B. (1987–8) 'The politics of theory', *Social Text* 18, 3–18.

ROONEY, E. (1985) 'Going farther: literary theory and the passage to cultural criticism', *Works and Days* 3.1, 51–72.

ROONEY, E. (forthcoming) 'Marks of gender', *Rethinking Marxism.*

ROONEY, E. 'What is to be done.' In Weed (ed.), *op. cit.* 230–39.

SHERIDAN, S. (ed), (¹1988) *Grafts: Feminist Cultural Criticism.* London: Verso.

SHUMWAY, D. 'Interdisciplinarity and authority in American studies.' Unpublished manuscript.

SHUMWAY, D. (1985) 'Transforming literary studies into cultural criticism: the role of interpretation and theory', *Works and Days* 3.1, 79–89.

SPENDER, D. (1981) *Men's Studies Modified: The Impact of Feminism on the Academic Disciplines.* Oxford: Pergamon.

SPIVAK, G.C. (1988) 'Can the subaltern speak?' *Marxism and the Interpretation of Culture.* Ed. Cary Nelson and Lawrence Grossberg. Urbana: University of Illinois Press.

SPIVAK, G.C. (1989) 'In a word. *Interview.*' With Ellen Rooney. *differences: A Journal of Feminist Cultural Studies* 1.2, 124–56.

SPIVAK, G.C. 'The political economy of women as seen by a literary critic', Weed 218–219.

TREICHLER, P.A., KRAMARAE, C. and STAFFORD, B. (eds), (1985) *For Alma Mater: Theory and Practice in Feminist Scholarship.* Urbana: University of Illinois Press.

WEED, E. (ed), (1989) *Coming to Terms: Feminism, Theory, Politics.* New York: Routledge.

WISE, G. (1979) ' "Paradigm dramas" in American studies: a cultural and institutional history of the movement', *American Quarterly* 32, 293–337.

Women's Studies Group of the Centre for Contemporary Cultural Studies, (eds), (1978) *Women Take Issue: Aspects of Women's Subordination.* London: Hutchinson.

13

Pessimism, optimism, pleasure: the future of cultural studies

Duncan Webster

[...] To reduce cultural studies to the study of popular culture narrows its range and places much interesting work outside the scope of my argument, but popular culture has been central to the emergence and development of the discipline, and their relation is at the core of criticisms of trends in contemporary cultural studies. A repeated accusation is that a notion of a democratised culture, a transformed and 'truly popular' culture, has been diluted to become a populist celebration of existing popular forms.

[...] Martin Barker's review of [John] Fiske's *Reading the Popular* and *Understanding Popular Culture* [...] suggests, in the first issue of the *Magazine of Cultural Studies*, that 'the problems with Fiske's version of cultural studies are just those this magazine was born to oppose'. Fiske's books, student textbooks 'cashing in on a new market in America and elsewhere', represent a 'real threat to cultural studies'. The problems found in the books are 'their profound lack of any interest in history; their transmogrification of theory into hollow and mechanical epithets; their congratulatory domestication of culture, and their dulling of all politics of culture under the guise of advocating "semiotic resistance"'. What's more, they're 'bloody dull'. Fiske's work, Barker argues, 'represents all that is going bad in work on popular culture. It is the equivalent of cheering in the face of defeats, warming one's hands in the cold fog of the new conservatism'. It doesn't analyse or challenge the dominant right-wing culture and politics: 'People negotiate their readings – wow!' Barker concludes by saying that if this 'is cultural studies, let's write five books, draw our salaries and go back to bed'.[1]

If the tone and openness of Barker's review are rare, the feeling that something either is going wrong with cultural studies or has already gone wrong is widespread, and overlaps with anxieties expressed elsewhere about the loss of *critical* work. So Ann Gray in a review-essay of studies of TV viewing concentrates on 'the problem of the popular', taking issue with Jane Root's *Open the Box*. Gray worries that while Root challenges a 'left-middle class intellectual elitism', she also seems to suggest that, in this instance, the 'spontaneous' pleasure of *The Price is Right* studio audience is 'natural' and unmediated. There is, therefore, a danger of falling into 'the consumerism notion of popular culture which naturalises the meanings produced by capitalism', of accepting that television gives '"the audience what it wants"'. This isn't seen as a particular flaw of Root's work but as a 'worrying trend': 'by celebrating on the one hand an active audience for popular forms and on the other those popular forms which the audience "enjoy", we appear to be throwing the whole enterprise of a cultural critique out of the window'. A populist polemic against the myth of TV audiences as passive zombies, combined with 'the subjectivity licensed by the postmodern ethos', leads to the loss of some 15 years' hard labour around the *production of meaning* and the ideological and political significance of the cultural. These things do matter'. 'Distance', she argues, is a necessary part of the process of cultural critique if it is 'to go beyond a simple celebration of what is already there'.[2]

So, cultural critique and critical distance versus a populist celebration of the popular. A response from that populist perspective might focus on Gray's quotation marks around *enjoy* and the punitive sound of that '15 years' hard labour', and argue that the popular is not a problem but 'the problem of the popular' is. In this analysis 'pleasure' might well replace 'ideology', but that should be presented not as a depoliticisation of cultural criticism but as a way of addressing not just the pleasures of the audience but also the position of the critic, the conditions of that 'distance' – class, education, 'cultural capital'. I will return to these issues, but it is important to emphasise different variations of this critique-versus-celebration opposition. Two pieces by Paul Willemen are of interest here since they stress that the 'problem' is seen as cultural theory in the last decade, not just specifically cultural studies. In a long piece on 'The Third Cinema question', Willemen offers a critique of current approaches to 'popular culture' and a polemic against 'post' theory.

He characterises such approaches as either 'hypocritically opportunist', as in the 'attempts to validate the most debilitating forms of consumerism, with academics cynically extolling the virtues of the stunted products of cultural as well as political defeat', or as degenerating into 'a comatose repetition of 1970s deconstructivist rituals'. Instead, 'the question to be asked today in Britain is: how to induce people into adopting, critical-socialist ways of thinking'.[3] He continues this argument in a review of John Hill's *Sex, Class and Realism* in the same issue. Hill's book, rather like the Third Cinema, is praised as offering 'the way out of the main impasse currently incapacitating Anglo-Saxon criticism': the 'impossible choice' between deconstruction's claims that films are 'thoroughly plural' and 'the abdication of critical responsibilities in favour of the celebration of existing patterns of consumption'. The latter is seen to stem from a refusal 'to countenance the possibility that vast sections of the population have come to derive pleasure from conservative orientated media discourses'.[4] Note that 'have come to derive', which suggests changes either in popular culture or its audiences which are nowhere analysed.

Socialist film (and cultural) theory of the 1970s, according to Willemen, implied 'an image of what a socialist cultural practice might be, for producers as well as consumers', and 'operated with a socialist ideal ego as something yet to be attained'. He admits that this 'ideal ego' was 'a puritanical one', but argues that since Thatcher, 'large sectors of the apparently left-inclined intelligentsia' have abandoned any kind of goal to work towards. This has been done 'under the guise of criticising the shortcomings of 1970s theory and its puritanical ideal ego which has to work for its gratifications'. Intellectuals in the 1980s no longer argue for 'a socialist cultural practice', since that was relocated in the ways that 'working-class people (and black people, and women, and gays, etc.) made sense of/with the material provided for them by the established media multi-nationals and our existing television regimes'. 'At best', this was seen in terms of resistance; 'at worst (and predominantly) existing patterns of consumption were legitimised and even celebrated'. Based on 'the (innocent?) misuse of certain aspects of 1970s theory', such as 'textual plurality' and a socialist essentialism (if 'oppressed consumers' enjoy popular culture, then it must contain socialist elements), this was 'cloaked in an aggressively populist rhetoric aimed against intellectuals at a time when we need to keep our critical wits more than ever' (117).

'The tragic mistake of many left cultural commentators, and academics is to connive' with the forces of commodification, 'wittingly or not'. Although he sees the 'pleasure question' as important, Willemen sees the role of 'pleasure' in the discussion of popular film and television as helping the 'commodity disguise itself as the ultimate object of enjoyment' (119). Furthermore, these ideas of subversive pleasures depend on 'a capitalist logic which creates and defines the sites of possible contestation. Merely to play around within those spaces with the material offered is to consent to that process of definition, not to challenge it' (118). One problem with Willemen's argument is the striking absence of history from a socialist analysis; deconstruction and populism are transcended rather than located. There is the coincidence of left cultural critics making a 'tragic mistake' and Thatcherism, but the only relation between them is some sense of guilt by association: cynical opportunists betraying socialism ('under the guise of . . . ', 'innocent?', 'wittingly or unwittingly'). There's no discussion of any problems within socialism during a decade of the New Right's hegemony, nor is there any discussion of the problems of funding alternative cultural spaces since the 1970s. Nor is there much analysis of any of the problems within 1980s theory which may have shaped the positions he attacks. His discussion of pleasure not only overlooks work on pleasure and use-value (Terry Lovell's *Consuming Fiction*, for example), it also seems to surrender a great deal. If we give up struggles within spaces defined by capitalist logic, where is left? We return to a traditional picture of the left intellectual as mediator between socialist vanguard and artistic avant-garde. The starting point for a 'socialist critical-cultural practice' appears to be to inform people that their pleasure in popular culture is suspect, then to form them into an orderly crocodile and march them off to a retrospective of Cuban cinema.

Judith Williamson's recent criticisms of cultural studies at least place more of a stress on history. In 'The problems of being popular', she complains that the Left's vocabulary no longer includes words such as 'revolutionary' or 'reactionary', and instead, feminist and left academics are busy discovering 'subversion' in almost any aspect of popular culture. She sees the Left as becoming less and less *critical*, stemming from the Left's 'post-1979 awareness of the Right's successful populism, known to many as "Thatcherism"'. Two readings of this awareness are offered: a 'charitable' one which sees the Left trying to reappropriate 'popular pleasures' from the Right, and a more critical view where politically demoralised socialist academics sink into popular culture out of a mixture of pessimism and boredom. She argues that they should be offering radical and new ways of meeting popular demands and desires instead.[5]

[. . .] The criticisms of cultural studies outlined so far reveal a pattern: a conflict between a socialist criticism and one that is seen as Left-populist, and behind that, at points overlapping with it, some notion of being 'for' or 'against' postmodernism, also a sense of an argument between cultural and political optimism and pessimism. This last opposition connects changes within cultural criticism to the diverse processes of 'rethinking' on the Left in the 1980s. So both Labour and the Communist Party have been accused of a pessimistic capitulation to Thatcherism, taking over the Right's agenda rather than transforming it [. . .]; just as, so the argument goes, cultural studies has capitulated to the existing cultural industries, in order to celebrate the couch potato rather than propose an alternative. [. . .] It might be useful here to turn to some perspectives from outside Britain, to follow the export of British theory but also to get a different viewpoint on these debates.

[. . .] If a typical cultural studies text of the past might be characterised by its strong sense of locality (from Hoggart through to subcultural theory), a text like Lawrence Grossberg's *It's a Sin* is possibly typical of cultural studies now: an American academic discusses contemporary American culture and the history of British cultural studies in front of an Australian audience.

Grossberg's first section on 'The scandal of cultural studies' starts with cultural studies' success in the United States: 'its recent rise has all the ingredients of a made-for-TV movie', but it 'has been installed into the American academy at just the moment when its work – especially in the US – seems to be stalled'.[6] For Grossberg, cultural studies is powerful in so far as it sees theory historically, politically and strategically, but its success threatens to restrict its theoretical mobility. He argues that it is now failing to address links between political struggles and the national popular culture. His critique overlaps with the others outlined above, as he welcomes work on 'the politics of everyday life' (Modleski, Chambers, Fiske), but suggests that 'the everyday' is seen in this work 'as if it were absolutely autonomous, and its practices as if they were always forms of empowerment, resistance and intervention'. This approach 'simply answers too many questions ahead of time'; not only do terms like pleasure or resistance 'refer to complex sets of different effects which have to be specified concretely', but also the relations between them 'are themselves complex and never guaranteed in advance' (13).

However, Grossberg's worries about how effective cultural studies is relate problems in recent work back to its original emergence (Hoggart, Williams and Thompson in the usual shorthand) and its institutionalisation at the Birmingham Centre for Contemporary Cultural Studies. He argues that this initial step skewed cultural studies: 'first, a cultural theory of communication is transformed into a communicational theory of culture; second, the terms of the problematic – culture and society – are bifurcated and disciplinised into literary-textual studies and sociology'. As 'these two theoretical structures are mapped onto each other', cultural studies subsequently focuses on the ideological relationship between the production of meaning and experience' (15).

Thus cultural studies 'is always caught in the twin pulls of textual and sociological research'; reading 'experience off of texts' or reading 'texts through experience' with ideology as 'the ultimate object of research' for both traditions. This leads Grossberg to locate another problem, 'a populist politics based upon the identification of the popular with social position', arguing that this differs from Williams but resembles Thompson's criticism of him, which replaced ways of life with ways of struggle, 'that is, which identified cultural and political positions' (17).

In some ways, then, Grossberg reverses other criticisms of current cultural studies by relating problems with today's models to its initial conception. However, his argument is not that clear about where and when cultural studies stalled. The 'scandal' seems to be both its current political weakness and its initial theorisation as a discipline. By politicising theoretical questions it's possible that he's arguing that despite theoretical problems cultural studies 'worked' until meeting the transformed political and cultural terrain of the 1980s. The changed conditions of cultural analysis are thus both theoretical and historical.

Both theory and historically different conditions have undermined fixed notions of texts (19) and audiences (21). Apart from debates within cultural theory, there's 'the changing spatial and temporal complexity of the cultural terrain itself' (19): new technologies, the expansion of leisure, the difficulty in isolating one area of popular culture – his example is American television (20–21). Grossberg criticises cultural studies for reducing culture to ideology, suggesting that a focus on meaning misses the importance of 'complexly produced affective structures – structures of desire, emotion, pleasure, mood, etc.' (35). This is central to his analysis of the American New Right who have located the 'crisis of America' as 'neither economic nor ideological, but rather affective' (31). His discussion of Reaganism's attempt to produce a new national popular is an interesting analysis, and although I will not be able to discuss his argument, I will return to the postscript of *It's a Sin* to examine Grossberg's suggestions about the future of cultural studies rather than his quarrel with its past.

Grossberg refers to Williamson's 'Problems of being popular' and to Meaghan Morris' 'Banality in cultural studies', probably the two most-cited pieces in the debates about cultural studies now. Morris relocates the debates about cultural studies through an engagement with feminism and postmodernism. The range of her writing (movies, philosophy, art, the everyday), and her own position outside the academy, contribute to a constant awareness of the circulation of 'theory'. She is, for example, as interested in 'the theoretical debates that circulate in and as popular culture as I am in academically situated theoretical work *about* popular culture'. She also points to the 'shuttling' of people and discourses 'between pedagogical institutions and the cultural industries', as part of a process of the dissemination and commodification of ideas. The academy functions within a network of bookshops, TV chat-shows, interviews, reviews, exhibitions, and so on.[7] This stress on mobility across social sites and cultural spaces runs alongside an insistence on specificity, the cultural politics of space and place. 'Things to do with shopping centres', for instance, concerns the specificity of place, the history of particular Australian mall developments, but also addresses the place of the analyst.

The analysis of shopping centres involves 'exploring common sensations, perceptions and emotional states aroused by them', both positive and negative, but also working against those 'in order to make a place from which to speak other than that of the fascinated describer'. The latter can be 'outside' in the role of ethnographer or, 'in a pose which seems to me to amount to much the same thing', supposedly 'inside' as the 'celebrant' of popular culture. The first position belongs to the sociology of consumerism or leisure and the second corresponds to positions in cultural studies. Morris quotes Iain Chambers's argument that recognising 'the democratic "potential" of people's active appropriations of popular culture involves the "wide-eyed presentation of actualities"' that Adorno criticised in Walter Benjamin. Morris relocates this argument over a materialist account of Baudelaire's Paris to the Australian mall. Adorno declared that Benjamin's study was located '"at the crossroads of magic and positivism. That spot is bewitched"', but theory can break the spell. Morris rejects both the 'strategy of "wide-eyed presentation"' and the 'faith in theory as the exorcist'; neither meets 'the critical problems posed by feminism in the analysis of "everday life"'. Feminist cultural studies pays more attention to 'everyday discontent' in shopping, 'anger, frustration, sorrow, irritation, hatred, boredom, fatigue', rather than consumerism as liberating (remember 'shopping for democracy'). Feminism's discontent with the everyday, 'and with wide-eyed definitions of the everyday as "the way things are"', thus 'allows the possibility of rejecting what we see and refusing to take it as "given"'.[8]

Morris comments on the vogue for emphasising the meanings for users/shoppers and the possible resistance inherent in contemporary practices of consumption. Articles return to certain 'exemplary inaugural stories' (punk is her example); 'principles of cultural action – bricolage, cut-up, appropriation, assemblage and so on' are restated. But as 'time passes in shoppingtown, however, it's tempting to wonder how much longer (and for whom) these stories can do the rounds'. After the analyst has hung out at the mall, what happens next? There are two slides: 'from user to consumer to consumption, from persons to structures to processes'; and from 'notions of individual and group "creativity" to cultural "production" to political "resistance"'. Morris quotes a friends parody of this slide a '"the discovery that washing your car on Sunday is a revolutionary event"' (213–14). Pehaps that point needs to be related back to the productionist aesthetics of the 1970s. Washing your car or queuing in Sainsbury's isn't revolutionary, but equally 'baring the device' in independent films didn't cause a rush to the barricades either. Instead, Morris challenges current theorisations of the production/consumption process, arguing that the opposition needs to be rethought and that assumptions that we know about 'production' and 'can move to the other side' are problematic. She suggests that an essay could be written on the slides she identifies; it could, she did – 'Banality in cultural studies'.[9]

Morris starts with her irritation with Baudrillard's use of 'banality' in theorising the media and with trends in the analysis of the popular and the everyday, which 'seems to be criticism that actively strives to achieve "banality"'. She doesn't oppose these positions 'as, say, pessimistic and optimistic approaches to popular culture', which admittedly avoids simplifying these debates but also, I think, misses a chance to historicise them (Baudrillard's relation to Marxism and situationism, for example). The *boom* in cultural studies is placed through the politics of intellectual work as it relates to, and moves in and out of, 'commodity circulation' (15). Recent work, with its ideas of 'cultural democracy', of 'mass culture not as a vast banality machine, but as raw material made available for a variety of popular practices' (19), suggests to Morris that there's an English 'master-disk from which thousands of versions of the same article about pleasure, resistance, and the politics of consumption are being run off under different names with minor variations' (20). Ideas are not just repeated but exported, and an English left populism is decontextualised and 'recycled in quite different political cultures', Australia and America, for example, dulling any oppositional edge along the way (20).

She does not challenge the 'enabling theses' of theories of consumption that consumers are not '"cultural dupes"' (Stuart Hall), but 'active, critical users of mass culture'; that consumption can't be read off from production nor confined to the economic; and that consumption practices, like sexuality, are made up of 'a multiplicity of fragmented and contradictory discourses' (20). Instead she criticises the style and ways in which intellectuals inscribe their relation to the popular. An ethnographic approach cites 'popular voices', translates and comments on their pleasures, then introduces 'a play of *identification* between the knowing subject of cultural studies, and a collective subject "the people"'. In John Fiske's work, for example, Morris suggests that 'the people' are defined as negotiating their readings, reworking and interpreting culture: 'This is also, of course, the function of cultural studies itself'. 'The people' end up not just as 'the cultural student's object of study, and his native informants' but also as 'the textually delegated, allegorical emblem of the critic's own activity'. They are 'both a source of authority for a text and a figure of its own critical

228   *What is cultural studies?*

activity'; the 'populist enterprise' is seen as both circular and narcissistic (20).

Morris then moves on to another strategy, impersonating the popular. Referring to work on 'mass culture as woman', the conflation of stereotypes of feminity with the popular, Morris looks at Iain Chambers's *Popular Culture* as a text which invites this distracted skimming over the surfaces of the popular, and as an example of 'critical cross-dressing' (Elaine Showalter's phrase): 'the *white male theorist* as bimbo' (22). The problem of 'anti-academic pop-theory writing' shaped, she argues, by 'the vestigial anti-feminism of the concept of distraction', is that 'a stylistic enactment of the "popular" as distracted, scanning the surface, and short on attention-span' reproduces, 'at the level of *renunciative* practice', the notion of 'cultural dupes' that cultural studies opposes. Recycling the oppositions of contemplation/distraction, academic/popular, regardless of 'which of the terms we validate', limits critical and popular interventions in a 'return to the postulate of cultural dopism in the *practice* of writing' (22). She argues that cultural studies may have stalled now because its style contradicts its argument, and it can only motivate its repetitions through inscribing an Other ('grumpy feminists and cranky leftists') who needs to be reminded of the complexities of consumption. In her view, discrediting these other voices is 'one of the immediate political functions of the current book in cultural studies' (23).

Morris announces her frustration at the choice in cultural theory between 'cheerleaders and prophets of doom'. She is 'equally uneasy about fatalistic theory on the one hand, and about cheerily "making the best of things"' and calling it cultural studies on the other (24). The problems of recent cultural studies are set out quite brilliantly here, but if that concluding stand-off between fatalists and cheerleaders captures elements of the present impasse, the piece avoids a sense of how this came about. Reintroduce history and those discredited voices get louder; the stand-off is no longer between cheery populists and apocalyptic postmodernists, other voices are heckling from the sidelines, and what they're shouting is: 'What's all this crap, then?' This takes us back to another Morris piece, but also suggests reasons for the populists' caricatures of those who 'misunderstand' popular culture.

In the conclusion to 'Banality in cultural studies', Morris suggests that seeing the need for a discriminating criticism of popular culture as pessimistic or elitist leaves us with a weaker, poorer critical language. I agree, but the associations that a word like 'discrimination' carries are not easily scraped off. If you wanted to locate another impasse within cultural studies, it's easily found in the history of (Left) Leavisite attempts to separate out good and bad popular culture, Marxist judgements of the 'progressive text', and feminist quests for 'positive images', and the depressing narrative of their interchanges. And that's a history of an *engagement* with popular culture, there's also simple dismissal. In 'Politics now' Morris talks of the inscription of politics 'as a perfect *non sequitur*': her example is an immediate response to a lecture by Juliet Mitchell after *Psychoanalysis and Feminism* was published, 'that nightmare voice of the Left, yelling boldly from the back of the room, "*Yeah, Juliet, what about Chile?*"' She adds that this is not a question of 'the gulf between intellectuals and the working class, but a matter of the way that petty-burgeois intellectuals treat each other'.[10]

The conclusion to 'Politics now' introduces a topic often greeted with exactly this kind of dismissal – postmodernism. Using Jameson's analysis of postmodernism as 'the cultural logic of late capitalism', Morris argues that there's a 'practical insistence' that any 'critical political culture' must engage with these debates and take into account that the 'abolition of "critical distance"' makes 'the old tools of ideology-critique' ineffective. A further practical point is that 'in a mass-media society with mass-media cultures and mass-media politics, the relationship between *signifying* . . . gestures and political ones' cannot easily be divided up between the cultural/aesthetic and the political. She argues against a kind of blackmail: a rhetoric of *urgency* which dismisses the 'idle speculation, wild theorising, and lunatic prose'. She argues the opposite: 'things are too urgent now for the Left to be giving up its imagination, or whatever imagination the Left's got left . . . . The very last thing that's useful now is a return (as farce, rather than tragedy) to the notion of one "proper" critical style, one "realistic" approach, one "right" concern' (185–86). Bearing in mind Morris's critique of 'banality' and her warning against prescription, my concluding suggestions for 'the future of cultural studies' are offered as a way of reframing the debates outlined above, rather than an urgent demand for a change of direction.

Pistachio shirts and corsets: intellectuals and the popular

> It's always tempting these days – and especially at the end of long essays – to wheel on Gramsci as a 'hey-presto' man, as the theorist who holds the key to all our current theoretical difficulties.[11]

Echoing in the debates outlined above, there is a longer argument between cultural optimism and pessimism, often also connected to analyses of political possibilities. However, the position that the mass media have a 'progressive potential' currently deformed through existing social and economic relations has been eclipsed by a sense of the 'popular' which locates 'cultural democracy' here and now in the active resistance and negotiations of consumers. One reason for this radical relocation of that ideal from a socialist future to a capitalist present lies in a rejection of the cultural conservatism that intellectuals of the Left and Right have shared. Commenting on the parallels between Debray's *Teachers, Writers, Celebrities* and the work of the Leavises, Francis Mulhern points to the 'tense combination of fatalism and defiance' in both analyses. Debray's study could take as its motto either 'Gramsci's famous borrowing "pessimism of the intelligence, optimism of the will'", or 'the perhaps more lucid Leavisian phrase, "desperate optimism'".[12] Baudrillard's view of the masses turns this inside out – optimistic despair – staying in the terms of cultural conservatism (the masses as zombie consumers) but rejecting critique.

Gramsci's 'famous borrowing' suggests the qualities needed for digging in for a long struggle. Setting aside optimism and pessimism, what of will and intelligence? Where are they located?

[. . .] I want to suggest that, in reaction to 1970s theory, what gets inserted into this pessimism/optimism, intelligence/will couplet is *pleasure*. Pleasure, the blind spot of much past Marxist and feminist analysis, introduces questions of desire, affective investment, fantasy and so on, shifting the focus to consumption rather than production. I think this was a necessary and productive move, but one which has faltered by locating pleasure in audiences (or in a poststructuralist delirious play of textuality), leaving the academic or critic as the secretary or analyst of these pleasures, transcribing, commenting, explaining, but disembodied.

'Pleasure' as poststructuralist *jouissance* or as populist fun inserts the body into cultural studies as a site of resistance, respectively reconstructing the propriety of power or empowering the consumer, but what is often invisible here is the intellectual's own body and power, not just intellectuals' desire but their position in regimes of power-knowledge. I'm basing this on a belief that the 'collapse of critical distance' is not just an epistemological question but a historical and material process, and also on a rejection of current positions: a nostalgia for a panoptical ivory tower, a left variant of that nostalgia, where the intellectual scans the horizon and confidently pronounces on progressive texts and forces, and the populist perspective that Morris uncovered, gazing at the popular in order to celebrate cultural studies' own reflection. What I'm suggesting instead isn't a position so much as a project, maintaining criticism while respatialising 'distance'. Some work on intellectuals and the popular can serve as signposts.

Grossberg adds a postscript to *It's a Sin* as he felt his conclusion was too pessimistic; it left 'little room for that "optimism of the will" which Gramsci thought necessary for political struggle'. He finds that optimism by relating the fanatic, utopian side of American history to the shifting terrain of popular culture, and exploring 'the postmodern gap' between fans, fanatics and ideologues (66). The differences between these have been produced by discourses of power-knowledge and by the drawing of 'distinctions' (Bourdieu). Postmodernity unsettles these differences, but Grossberg takes issue with many versions of 'the postmodern collapse of critical distance and the increasing uncertainty about the authority of intellectual and political voices/positions'. Since this has been articulated as 'an abstract epistemological problem', the answer has been seen as a 'need for reflexivity', defined as 'auto-critique and self-revelation, as a search for more autobiographical and dialogical writing forms' (66). But that move surrenders not just authority but also the possibility of intervention; 'it cannot rearticulate a new structure of authority appropriate to the contemporary context' (67).

Grossberg argues that the collapse of critical distance and 'the crisis of authority' are not epistemological questions 'but a concrete historical dilemma', shaped by the fact that we are a part of the terrain we write about (67). Our authority cannot rest on 'privileged distinctions of taste and distaste', so reflexivity needs to be rethought as the basis for a new form of critique. As fans and critics, 'we can be simultaneously on the terrain but not entirely of it', enabling 'an historically specific form of critical distance' (68). We may have to limit our claims but as 'intellectuals, we have the resources to articulate social possibilities': as 'critical fans', our task is not to define '"proper" cultural tastes' or '"proper" political positions', but to analyse "specific investments'" in the popular and their political possibilities. If 'we are fans, we are not only fans; nor are we only intellectuals' (68). Instead of reconstructing authority, we need 'to rearticulate new forms of authority which allow us to speak as critical fans'. He ends with a vision of a 'politics for and by people who live in the modern world, people who live in the world of popular tastes. An impure politics for pop people!' (69).

Grossberg's account of the contradictory spaces of contemporary popular culture can be complemented by Andrew Ross's *No Respect*, a history of the relation between American intellectuals and popular culture from early responses to mass culture to postmodernism. It's an important study precisely because that 'and' is a terrain of genuine debate and dialogue, linking, for example, arguments within the American Left to debates over modernism and kitsch, focusing on concepts that bridged the intellectual and the popular (hip, camp, and so on), ranging across cultural forms from the Rosenberg letters to pornography, examining the complex interactions between discourses and bodies, class and taste, and widening the definition of the intellectual by drawing on Gramsci and Bourdieu among others. Ross's approach is necessarily dialectical, for a history of popular culture cannot be just a history either of producers or of consumers, it must also be 'a history of intellectuals – in particular, those experts in culture whose traditional business is to define what is popular and what is legitimate'.[13]

Ross offers a 'postmodern picture of multiple and uneven activities, loyalties, obligations, desires and responsibilities' of intellectual work now, suggesting, like Grossberg, a sense of 'impure' political possibilities (230). Both arguments stem from a practical, local rather than apocalyptic, sense of postmodernism's dissolution of boundaries between popular and high cultures, with an awareness that power relations between intellectuals and popular culture do not simply dissolve in that process. Bearing Ross's argument that intellectuals and popular culture need to be thought of together, we can now turn from changes in the position of intellectuals to a transformed culture.

In a review-essay of work on popular culture, Geoffrey Nowell-Smith suggests that the term is now problematic: 'popular cultural forms have moved so far towards centre stage in British cultural life that the separate existence of a distinctive popular culture in an oppositional relation to high culture is now in question.'[14] The idea that 'the leading lights of British rock music would shortly be asked to perform before the Princess of Wales must have seemed a crazy pop-culturalists' dream in 1956, but this is what has happened' (83). Nowell-Smith historicises that shift, first by an interesting comparison between Britain and other European

countries and their relation to American popular culture, then by turning to the late 1950s and the simultaneous emergence of cultural
studies (Williams and Hoggart) and a new popular culture (rock 'n'
roll and commercial television). Despite these changes and the expansion of leisure and popular culture in the 1960s, an assumption
remained that class divisions were reflected in 'differential cultures'. It
was assumed that 'the divide that seemed to exist between popular
cultural forms and those of high culture was a permanent feature of the
modern world', and that this division 'could be mapped sociologically
and made to correspond to divisions in society at large. Two cultures
had to exist, and they had to be the cultures of the dominant and
dominated classes respectively' (82). He argues that this meant that
differences 'between and within cultures' were overlooked. Also, that
this is another instance of the 'pecularities' of British culture, highly
stratified and following 'class stratification more closely than in other
countries' (82). Britain in the 1960s, then, did not provide an appropriate model for analysis of popular culture in other countries, nor do
the critical assumptions of that period work for today's popular culture.

Today, Nowell-Smith argues, the choice is between saying that there is
'one culture (albeit with divisions in it) or several cultures (overlapping and
rubbing up against each other) but no longer that there are two cultures,
high and popular, divided from each other'. He suggests that there is 'one
(multiply divided) culture' with the dominant forms being those 'traditionally designated as popular' (83). He feels that the use of 'popular' can
itself be a distraction outside of an analysis of a form's producers or its
public, and writing from within film studies rather than cultural studies
proper, he uses that distanced engagement to call into question central
assumptions of (popular) cultural studies. Although he seems to approve
of the 'move away from the theoretical high ground into the empirical
flatlands' in the work he reviews, he notes the absence of an 'implicit
theory' of how 'the components of popular culture relate to each other'
(90). He suggests that if the central project of seeing 'culture as a whole' is
set aside, then cultural studies has lost its rationale, and he sees a weakness
in the stress on consumption at the expense of production; 'the most
striking absence' in the study of popular culture is, for him, 'any sense of
artistic production'. When production 'comes in, or rather when it comes
back, then the study of popular culture will have become the study of . . .
culture' (90).

Dick Hebdige argues for a similar shift in both the study of popular
culture and the field itself, in a piece that suggests the radical potential of
'banality' (post-Live Aid events, etc.). If in the 1950s and 1960s the 'artificial
order of the classroom was built against the viral chaos' of the popular,
those popular forms are now legitimate objects of study from schools to
post-graduate research. The central assumption that '"pop/pap" was
culture's Other' maintained a strictly policed frontier between the popular
and a threatened culture ('classical, high, modernist even . . . folk, progressive rock or gritty working class'). 'Popular culture was an animal to be
approached Barbara Woodhouse-style with firm voice and steady hand'.
Now, in the West at least, the map has been redrawn: 'popular culture is no

longer marginal, still less subterranean. Most of the time and for most people it simply *is* culture'. This needs to be recognised within cultural studies, and in a provocative paradox, Hebdige suggests that popular culture now 'may not actually exist anywhere except on the shelves of academic bookshops.[15]

Hebdige suggests that the maps being used by academics, the popular as a knowable terrain crossed by class, race, and gender, are no longer as persuasive as the discourses of identity and desire offered by marketing and advertising practices. He's not suggesting that the consumerism paradise of endless individuation has arrived, nor that class, race and gender are irrelevant, but pointing to the weakness of current cultural studies: 'academics (I count myself among them) armed with semiotics, a truncated account of Gramsci and the remnants of Raymond Williams's culturalism have been staggering around the ruins of the sixties-in-the-eighties accompanied by their publishers trying to revive the fallen giant of the masses'. We return to the stand-off between 'gloomy, decadent Baudrillard' and 'optimistic, enabling cultural studies', but this time offered as a mirroring: Baudrillard 'is progressive British cultural studies back to front'. The way out is to smash that glass 'on to which generations of intellectuals have been projecting so many of their own largely unadmitted anxieties and desires'; to let go 'of our selves and the gravity traditionally accorded to intellectual projects'; to admit that 'disposable culture is *intrinsically* worth studying without trying to justify it by referring the analyses back to "proper" political concerns'; to give up 'speaking on behalf of the whole of humanity' and 'the quest of intellectuals either to merge with the imaginary masses or to triumph in their disappearance'.

While I'm not persuaded that the pop humanism of Live Aid is a great advance on the humanism of the universal intellectual, Hebdige's useful proposals link transformations within popular culture to a rethinking of the position of intellectuals. In a related piece, he again outlines a transfigured social mapped by post-Fordist marketing's vocabulary of desire, aspiration and identity, in order to argue that cultural studies, and the Left in general, must learn from both postmodern scepticism and the alternative definitions of race and national identity within popular culture. This vision of 'new times' escapes a universal mode of postmodernism's 'logic' and the 'old language of the left'. To intervene within this changing world we need 'to abjure certain kinds of authority we might have laid claim to in the past, without losing sight of the longer-term objective, how to articulate a new kind of socialism, how to make socialism, as Raymond Williams might have said, without the masses'.[16]

My claims are more modest but could be summarised as the need to rethink the position of intellectuals; to follow the dissolution of 'popular culture' into 'culture' or 'the popular'; and to link that with the relation between the construction of a national-popular within an international popular culture and changing definitions of national identity. This last point raises the complex relations between 'Englishness' and its production through culture and leisure practices ('heritage', etc.), and the form of the nation-state within a context of multiculturalism, 'Europe', American popular 'cultural imperialism', and the political demands for a transformation of that form. This may provide a way of rethinking audiences and consumption, reframing them with questions of citizenship and the complex relations of power-knowledge that shape discussions of 'taste', 'standards' and 'quality' and which link these terms to the national – British television as the best in the world.

Rethinking the relations between intellectuals, popular culture and (cultural) democracy takes us back to Gramsci, the 'hey-presto' man. Alan O'Shea and Bill Schwarz ask what Gramsci has to offer:

> He had no liking for the Americanised popular culture of his own day, for all the originality of his cultural investigations he was never the slightest bit interested in its modern manifestations like the cinema and radio, he systematically subordinated self to politics, had nothing interesting to say on the symbolic forms of popular cultures or their elements of fantasy, wrote incomprehensibly on psychoanalysis, suffered nervous collapse if subjected too long to the speediness of city life, and so on: a grizzled old Bolshevik about as far removed from the dynamics of contemporary popular cultures as one could possibly imagine.[17]

Such a critique could be extended, they argue, to the way that the study of the popular is institutionalised, specifically the externality of academic discourse and intellectuals when confronting this terrain.

Orwell is introduced here as a figure representing 'almost any explorer of popular culture of the past hundred years or so', sitting on a train, 'insulated from the culture he watches', seeing a woman clearing out a drain. That self-reflexivity, *The Road to Wigan Pier*'s awareness of the social relations implied by this kind of observation and description, is eclipsed as Orwell wriggles free in order to suggest that it's not himself who is 'caught up in all this after all, but *others*, and to 'castigate the deluded, pistachio-shirted intellectuals all around him'. O'Shea and Schwarz find a mirror-image of this move in Iain Chambers's mapping of the 'metropolitan experience', *Popular Culture*. By turning from the academy to the postmodern dazzle of the streets, Chambers 'can make it appear as if all the problems of knowledge and pedagogy lie with others in this bi-polar world: the monochrome guardians of official culture'. Chambers is the pomo Orwell, appearing to 'absolve himself from his own positions: only this time he champions the pistachio-shirts'. But externality, indeed social relations, can't simply be rhetorically shrugged off. O'Shea and Schwarz rightly refuse 'the choice between two planetary discourses – the one academic, totalising and external, the other lived and popular'. They suggest that a return to Gramsci might enable those discourses to be 'more fruitfully, and more justly' integrated. Gramsci's work, historicising both intellectuals and the popular, provides the terms for the critique of Gramsci. If Chambers's 'popular epistemology' does not resolve the problems of externality, 'it may be necessary – wizened, miserable old Bolshevik that he was – to go back to Gramsci, to read him anew, to imagine or invent a Gramsci for our own bleak times' (108–109).

Rosalind Brunt, discussing the 'politics of identity', does just that, arguing for a new image of the political activist. Instead of the activist as 'mole', tunnelling beneath capitalism in order to undermine it, she turns to Gramsci's suggestive metaphor for ' "intellectuals of a new type" ': they should become ' "as it were, the whalebone in the corset" '. Her pleasure in this image stems from its idea of 'revolutionary stiffening and control while also being an intimate, indeed sensuously materialist figure of speech'. It's an image of discipline but support, of literally ' "keeping in touch" ' with the masses, while suggesting a non-vanguardist 'way of working: up front, open and close'.[18]

In the context of cultural studies, the 'whalebone in the corset' is an image that suggests both embracing the popular and shaping it. It may draw on images of 'mass culture as woman', but it also provides a figure for the problems of externality and distance, and suggests ways of linking the two. Madonna's lingerie, and the fierce arguments about the meaning of her embodiment of a female pop and desiring subject, could be seen as deconstructing an opposition between outside and inside, for example. As an image of *transition*, of new ways of relating intellectuals and the popular, it also suggests the ways that cultural studies is now seen as 'sexy' by publishers, as worryingly commodified and populist by critics, and potentially, as a way of rearticulating a critical practice within and outside the popular.

Notes

1. BARKER, M. (1990) *MOCS*, 1 March, pp. 39–40.
2. GRAY, A. (1987) 'Reading the audience', *Screen*, 28. Summer, pp. 27–28, 30.
3. WILLEMEN, P. (1987) 'Notes and reflections', *Framework*, 34, p. 7, 37.
4. WILLEMEN, P. 'Review of *Sex, Class and Realism*', *Framework*, 34, p. 115.
5. WILLIAMSON, J. (1986) 'The problems of being popular', *New Socialist*, 41. September, pp. 14–15; KAPLAN, C. 'The culture crossover', *New Socialist*, 43 (November 1986); DUNCAN WEBSTER, *Looka Yonder! The Imaginary America of Populist Culture* (London, 1988).
6. GROSSBERG, L. (1988) *It's a Sin*. Sydney, p. 8.
7. MORRIS, M. (1988) *The Pirate's Fiancée: Feminism, Reading, Postmodernism.* London, pp. 8, 9, 10.
8. MORRIS, M. (1988) 'Things to do with shopping centres', in Sheridan, S. (ed.), *Grafts: Feminist Cultural Criticism.* London, pp. 196–97.
9. *Ibid.*, p. 214; 'Banality in cultural studies', *Block*, 14 (1988). Reprinted here as Chapter 7.
10. MORRIS, *Pirate's Fiancée*, pp. 180–81.
11. BENNETT, T. (1989) 'Marxism and popular fiction', in Bob Ashley (ed.), *The Study of Popular Fiction: A Source Book*. London, p. 182.
12. MULHERN, F. (1981) 'Introduction to Regis Debray', *Teachers, Writers, Celebrities.* London, p. xii.
13. ROSS, A. (1989) *No Respect: Intellectuals and Popular Culture.* London, p. 5.
14. NOWELL-SMITH, G. (1987) 'Popular culture', *New Formations*, 2. Summer, p. 80.
15. HEBDIGE, D. (1988) 'Banalarama, or can pop save us all?' *New Statesman and Society*, 9 December, pp. 31–32.

16. HEBDIGE, D. (1989) 'After the masses', *Marxism Today*, January, p. 53.
17. O'SHEA, A. and SCHWARZ, B. (1987) 'Reconsidering popular culture', *Screen*, 28, 3. Summer, p. 106.
18. BRUNT, R. (1988) 'Bones in the corset', *Marxism Today*, October, p. 23.

14

Culture and communication: towards an ethnographic critique of media consumption in the transnational media system

Ien Ang

Cultural studies and cultural critique

An intense interest in culture is one of the most significant trends in contemporary communication studies. The term 'culture' is so widely used and its meaning so elusive that its current prominence could obscure the fact that its analysis is being undertaken from a diversity of perspectives and approaches. The emergence of a set of critical-cultural approaches to communication, generally called cultural studies, needs to be distinguished from the less-encompassing social-scientific interest in cultural phenomena displayed within mainstream communication research. More precisely, the perceived convergence of disparate scholarly traditions that is hailed by some observers (e.g. Blumler *et al.*, 1985; Schrøder, 1987; Curran, 1990) should be embraced with caution. Although culture may at first sight be a 'common object of study' (Rosengren, 1988: 10) that can contribute to the further erosion of unproductive divisions between 'mainstream' and 'critical' traditions, the theoretical and methodological, as well as epistemological and political, differences between the two traditions remain impressive and need to be acknowledged as such (Ang, 1989).

In brief, 'culture' in mainstream communication research is generally conceptualized in behavioural and functionalist terms, about which 'objective' knowledge can be accumulated through the testing of generalizable hypotheses by way of conventional social-scientific methods. The cultural indicators projects of Gerbner and associates in the United States and Rosengren and associates in Sweden are the most well known large-scale programmes in this vein. Important as these research projects are, such positivist interest in media culture is, in many respects, at odds with the concerns of cultural studies. In the latter, 'culture' is not simply treated as a discrete object of communication research. It is the contradictory and continuous *social process* of cultural production, circulation and consumption that cultural studies is about, not 'culture' defined as a more or less static, objectified set of ideas, beliefs and behaviours.

This implies a completely different set of working principles: cultural studies is interested in historical and particular meanings rather than in general types of behaviour, process-oriented rather than result-oriented, interpretive rather than explanatory. Most important, what fundamentally divides both traditions is their respective self-conceptions as intellectual discourses: the scientistic ambitions of the one will always be rejected by the other. As an intellectual practice, cultural studies is positively and self-consciously eclectic, critical and deconstructive.[1] It does not seek paradigmatic status, nor does it obey established disciplinary boundaries. Its intellectual loyalties reach beyond the walls of the academe to the critique of current cultural issues in the broadest sense. Cultural studies form what Clifford Geertz (1983) has called a 'blurred genre' of intellectual work: it is at once cultural research and cultural criticism. Ultimately, doing cultural studies does not mean contributing to the accumulation of science for science's sake, the building of an ever more encompassing, solidly constructed, empirically validated stock of 'received knowledge', but participating in an ongoing, open-ended, politically-oriented debate, aimed at evaluating and producing critique on our contemporary cultural condition. In this context, topicality, critical sensibility and sensitivity for the concrete are more important than theoretical professionalism and methodological purity. A French Marxist psychologist told me years ago, quite non-apologetically, 'I don't work hard enough because I read too many newspapers'. In my view, above all else it is this worldly attitude that is required for doing cultural studies.

Media reception as focus of cultural critique

Cultural studies has gained an enormous popularity in the past decade or so. It has become one new hope for scholars who are searching for alternatives, not only to the worn-out paths of the 'dominant paradigm', but also to the increasingly sterile reiterations of classical critical theory (e.g. Hardt, 1989; Real, 1989). The work of the Birmingham Centre for Contemporary Cultural Studies (e.g. Hall *et al.*, 1980) is generally seen as the source of the emerging tradition, but its influence has spread to many critical-intellectual corners in advanced capitalist societies, although, paradoxically enough, less so in continental Europe than in Canada, Australia and, particularly, the United States (Ang and Morley, 1989).

The aim of this article, then, is to sketch out some of the central issues related to media and communication that have preoccupied cultural studies and clarify the lines along which the formulation of cultural critique within this tradition has developed. Some of the themes which I find particularly pertinent for cultural studies to take up in the present period of massive economic, political and technological transformation of our media environment will also be suggested. In the European context, the question of 'national identity' has been particularly prominent in official responses to these changes and the discussion here will focus on this issue. The European case will only be rendered obliquely, however, because European problems are hardly unique (although certainly historically specific) in a world that moves progressively towards global integration, at least at the structural level of political economy. Finally, the importance of an ethnographic approach in assessing the cultural impact of these current developments will be highlighted.

These concerns reflect a personal point of view – a perspective coloured by the politics of my own work, which has centred on ways to conceptualize and understand television audiences. Thus, *Watching Dallas* (1985), in which letters from viewers about the America prime-time soap were analysed, was an attempt to probe the ways in which audiences interpret and give meaning to a popular television text, but its broader political context was the then rampant public outrage about the 'Americanization' of European public broadcasting. In showing how *Dallas* fans were silenced and thus disempowered by a dominant official discourse which categorically rejected such programmes as 'bad mass culture', I had hoped to disarticulate the often assumed conflation between the logic of the commercial and the pleasure of the popular. The aim was to open up the possibility for a less deterministic mode of thinking about these issues: a political stance against the increasing commercialization of broadcasting at the level of policy should not, as so often happens, preclude the recognition, at a cultural level, of the real enjoyment people take in commercially produced media material – a recognition that is sustained by making understandable the textual and socio-cultural paramaters of that pleasure. In other words, I imagined my work to be, among many other things, a form of cultural critique that aimed at unsettling the prevailing and, from a personal viewpoint, counterproductive views on popular television and its audiences.

Of course, the way the book was *received* (and, as a result, its discursive effectiveness) was beyond my control, and is something about which I can say very little here. What is important to emphasize, however, is that while the book came to be seen as an exercise in what is now commonly called 'reception analysis', the ideological and cultural climate in which the book was written played a decisive role in shaping the arguments and interpretations put forward in it.[2] In 1990, a reception analysis of *Dallas* would undoubtedly be inspired by very different political and socio-cultural problematics. (For example, the very success of *Dallas* has dramatically challenged European programming policies, to the point that it has become an accepted model for European productions of television drama [Silj, 1988].)

It may seem immodest to propose my own work to illustrate the value of 'conjuncturalism' in cultural studies, that is, the need to try 'writing at just the right moment in just the right way', as Richard Rorty (1989: 174) has put it and I apologize for this. The justification for it, however, is the fact that reception analysis (that is, the study of audience interpretations and uses of media texts and technologies) has been one of the most prominent developments in recent communication studies, including cultural studies (e.g. Morley, 1980, 1986; Radway, 1984, to name but the classic examples).

In more general terms, reception analysis has intensified our interest in the ways in which people actively and creatively make their own meanings and create their own culture, rather than passively absorb pre-given meanings imposed upon them. As a result, the question of media consumption as itself a locus of active cultural production has acquired a central place in cultural studies. The thrust of the interest has been ethnographic; while most reception studies were limited to analysing the specifics of certain text/audience encounters, the methods used were qualitative (in-depth interviewing and/or participant observation), and the emphasis has been overwhelmingly on the detailed description of how audiences negotiate with media texts and technologies. In this sense, reception analysis could very well be called the ethnography of media audiences.[3]

Numerous concrete studies which were inspired by this trend have been carried out. Australian critic Meaghan Morris (1988: 20) even goes so far as to suggest that 'thousands of versions of the same article about pleasure, resistance, and the politics of consumption are being run off under different names with minor variation'. She goes on to say that while the theses underlying the ethnography of audiences have been extremely enabling for cultural studies (e.g. that consumers are not 'cultural dopes', but critical users of mass culture), she is now worried about 'the sheer proliferation of the restatements', which in her view threaten to lead to 'the emergence . . . of a *restrictive definition* of the ideal knowing subject of cultural studies'.

Translated freely, the problem signalled by Morris is as follows: the perspective of the ethnography of audiences has led to a boom in isolated studies of the ways in which this or that audience group actively produces specific meanings and pleasures out of this or that text, genre or medium. However, while the positivist would be pleased with such an accumulation of empirical verifications (and elaborations) of a central hypothesis, it is not adequate for purposes of cultural critique. On the contrary, self-indulgent 'replications' of the same research 'design' would run the danger of merely producing an ever more absolute formal 'Truth', an empty, abstract and ultimately impotent generalization that could run like this: 'people in modern mediatised societies are complex and contradictory, mass cultural texts are complex and contradictory, therefore people using them produce complex and contradictory culture' (Morris, 1988: 22).

Although audience ethnographies have certainly enhanced and transformed our understanding of the dynamics of media consumption, I do take Morris's concerns to heart. For purposes of cultural critique, validating audience experience, or 'taking the side of the audience' alone is not enough. In this sense, the term reception itself bears some limitations because, stemming from the linear transmission model of communcation, it tempts us to foreground the social-psychological moment of direct contact between media and audience members, and thus to isolate and reify that particular moment as the preferred instance that merits ethnographic examination. A more thoroughly *cultural* approach to reception, however, would not stop at this pseudo-intimate moment of the media/ audience encounter, but should address the differentiated meaning and significance of specific reception patterns in articulating more general social relations of power. The conflict-ridden reception of Salman Rushdie's novel *The Satanic Verses* would be a dramatic case in point here. This case illustrates how the clash between different interpretive communities can form a nodal point where complicated political tensions, ideological dilemmas and economic pressures (e.g. relating to the publishing industry) find their expression in ways which have worldwide consequences. This admittedly extraordinary example suggests the importance of not reducing reception to an essentially psychological process, but to conceptualize it as a deeply politicized, cultural one.[4]

To avoid the 'banality' in cultural studies that Morris points to, then, the ethnographic perspective on audiences needs to be placed in a broader theoretical framework, so that it ceases to be just a sophisticated form of empirical audience research, but becomes part of a more encompassing understanding, both structural and historical, of our contemporary cultural condition. In other words, what we need is not more ethnographic work on discrete audience groups, but on reception as an integral part of popular cultural practices that articulate both 'subjective' and 'objective', both 'micro' and 'macro' processes. That is to say, reception should be seen as one field of 'the complex and contradictory terrain, the multi-dimensional context, within which people live out their everyday lives' (Grossberg, 1988: 25). At the same time, it is in this very living out of their everyday lives that people are inscribed into large-scale, structural and historical relations of power which are not of their own making. This set of theoretical assumptions will be borne in mind in charting a conceptual terrain that can inform such a 'globalization' of the ethnographic pursuit. First, however, I want to place the ethnographic shift within cultural studies in a more specific historical and theoretical perspective.

The power of the popular: beyond ideology and hegemony

The ethnographic thrust in audience studies has functioned as a way of relativizing the gloomy tendency of an older perspective within cultural studies, namely ideological criticism. A distinctive assumption of cultural studies is that the social production and reproduction of sense and meaning involved in the cultural process is not only a matter of signification, but also a matter of power.[5] The intimate connection of signifying practices and the exercise of power is a focal interest of cultural studies. As Grossberg (1983: 46) notes, 'Once we recognize that all of culture refracts reality as well as reproducing it as meaningful, then we are committed as well to examining the interests implicated in particular refractions'. Consequently, ideology was logically placed in the foreground of cultural studies to the point that the cultural and the ideological tended to be collapsed into one another; cultural processes are by definition also ideological in that the way the world is made to appear in a society tends to coincide with the interests of the dominant or powerful classes and groups in that society. The Gramscian concept of hegemony is mostly used to indicate the cultural leadership of the dominant classes in the production of generalized meanings, of 'spontaneous' consent to the prevailing arrangement of social relations – a process, however, that is never finished because hegemony can never be complete. Since the communications media are assumed to play a pivotal role in the continuous struggle over hegemony, cultural studies became preoccupied with the question of how the media helped to produce consensus and manufacture consent (Hall, 1982). This set of assumptions has enabled us to understand the precise textual and institutional mechanisms by which the media function ideologically; how, that is, in processes of institutionalized cultural production particular meanings are encoded into the structure of texts, 'preferred meanings' which tend to support existing economic, political and social power relations.

As a form of cultural critique, this kind of ideological analysis (only a simplified description is given here) is ultimately propelled by a will to demystify, denounce and condemn; it is a deconstructive practice which presupposes that the researcher/critic can take up the marginal position of critical outsider. However, this perspective was soon sided by a countercurrent, which emphasized not top–bottom power, but bottom–top resistance, itself a form of (informal, subordinate) power. The well known work on youth subcultures (e.g. Hall and Jefferson, 1976; Willis, 1977; Hebdige, 1979), but also the emergence of ethnographic approaches to media audiences are part of the same trend. It is a populist reaction which stressed the vitality and energy with which those who are excluded from legitimate, institutional power create a meaningful and liveable world for themselves, using the very stuff offered to them by the dominant culture as raw material and appropriating it in ways that suit their own interests. Hall's (1980) encoding/decoding model opened up the space to examine the way in which the media's preferred meanings could be 'negotiated' or even occasionally subverted in recalcitrant audience readings. John Fiske, the most exuberant ambassador of this position, has pushed it to an extreme in several provocative publications by virtually declaring the audience's independence in the cultural struggle over meaning and pleasure (e.g. Fiske, 1987a, 1987b). In this version of cultural studies the researcher-critic is no longer the critical outsider committed to condemn the oppressive world of mass culture, but a conscious fan, whose political engagement consists in 'encouraging cultural democracy at work' (Fiske, 1987a: 286), by giving voice to and celebrating audience recalcitrance.

As Morris (1988: 23) has remarked, what we have here is a 'humane and optimistic discourse, trying to derive its values from materials and conditions already available to people'. What, however, does it amount to as cultural critique? There is a romanticizing and romanticist tendency in much work that emphasizes (symbolic) resistance in audience reception, which, according to Morris, can all too easily lead to an apologetic '*yes but* . . . ' discourse that downplays the realities of oppression in favour of the representation of a rosy world 'where there's always a way of redemption'. Similar criticisms have been voiced by other critical theorists (e.g. Modleski, 1986; Schudson, 1987; Gripsrud, 1989).

But this kind of 'selling out' is not the inevitable outcome of ethnographic work on media audiences. In this respect, it is unfortunate that the politics of reception analysis has all too often been one-sidedly cast within the terms of a liberal defence of popular culture, just as uses and gratifications research could implicitly or explicitly, in theoretical and political terms, serve as a decontextualized defence of the media status quo by pointing to their 'functions' for the active audience (cf. Elliott, 1974). Similarly, research into how audiences create meanings out of items of popular culture has often been used as an empirical refutation of the elitist argument that mass culture stupefies, numbs the mind, reinforces passivity and so on. There is something truly democratic about this discourse, and I would be the last to want to question the importance of attacking the damaging impact of the high/low culture divide, which still pervasively informs – and limits – diverse cultural and educational policies, for example. However, revalidating the popular alone – by stressing the obvious empirical fact that audiences are active meaning producers and imaginative pleasure seekers – can become a banal form of cultural critique if the popular itself is not seen in a thoroughly social and political context. In other words, audiences may be active in myriad ways in using and interpreting media, but it would be utterly out of perspective to cheerfully equate 'active' with 'powerful', in the sense of 'taking control' at an enduring, structural or institutional level. It is a perfectly reasonable starting point to consider people's active negotiations with media texts and technologies as empowering in the context of their everyday lives (which, of course, is *the* context of media reception), but we must not lose sight of the *marginality* of this power. As de Certeau (1984: xvii) has remarked about the clandestine tactics by which ordinary women and men try to 'make do' in their everyday practices of consumption:

> this cultural activity of the non-producers of culture, an activity that is unsigned, unreadable, and unsymbolized, remains *the only one possible* for all those who nevertheless buy and pay for the showy products through which a productivist economy articulates itself. (Emphasis added)

To be sure, one of the important contributions made by ethnographic studies of reception is exactly the 'signing', 'reading' and 'symbolizing' – the documenting, the putting into tangible discourse – of the fragmented, invisible, marginal tactics by which media audiences symbolically appropriate a world not of their own making. This is no doubt what Fiske meant by encouraging cultural democracy, and he is right. However, if audience ethnography wants to elaborate its critical function, it cannot avoid confronting more fully what sociologists have dubbed the micro/macro problematic: the fact that there are structural limits to the possibilities of cultural democracy *à la* Fiske, that its expression takes place within specific parameters and concrete conditions of existence. In short, we need to return to the problematic of hegemony.

If the euphoria over the vitality of popular culture and its audiences has tended to make the question of hegemony rather unfashionable in some cultural studies circles, it is because the popular came to be seen as an autonomous, positive entity in itself, a repository of bold independence, strength and creativity, a happy space in which people can arguably stay outside of, and resist, the hegemonic field of force. In fact, however, the

relationship between the hegemonic and the popular should not be conceived of in terms of mutual exteriority; the hegemonic can be found within
the very texture of the popular. As Colombian communication theorist
Martín-Barbero (1988: 448) has noted, 'we need to recognize that the
hegemonic does not dominate us from without but rather penetrates us,
and therefore it is not just against it but from within it that we are waging
war'. Therefore, he is wary of a 'political identification of the popular with
an intrinsic, spontaneous resistance with which the subordinate oppose the
hegemonic'. Instead, what should be emphasized is 'the thick texture of
hegemony/subalternity, the interlacing of resistance and submission, and
opposition and complicity' (Martín-Barbero, 1988: 462). The resulting forms
of cultural resistance are not just ways to find redemption, but also a matter
of capitulation; invested in them is not just pleasure, but also pain, anger,
frustration – or sheer despair.

In fact, Martín-Barbero's Latin-American perspective, informed as it is by
the harsh and ugly realities which are a product of the subcontinent's
unequal economic development, profound political instability and day-
to-day social disorder, especially in the explosive urban areas, not only
can help to undermine the Euro- and Americo-centrism of much cultural
studies, but also, more positively, can (re)sensitize us to the messy and
deeply political contradictions which constitute and shape popular practices. In Latin America, the popular is often nostalgically equated with the
indigenous, and this in turn with the primitive and the backward – the
disappearing 'authentic popular' untouched by, and outside of the realm of
modernity. From this perspective, the unruly, crime-ridden, poverty-
stricken culture of the urban popular, concentrated in the *favelas*, the
barrios and other slums, diffuses its subversions from there right into the
hearts of the modern city centres, and could only be conceived of as
contamination of indigenous purity, as an irreconcilable loss of authenticity. Against this vision, Martín-Barbero (1988: 460) proposes to reconcep-
tualize the indigenous as at once 'dominated and yet as the possessors of a
positive existence, capable of development'. In this way, we can begin to
see the urban popular not as inauthentic degeneration but as the truly
contemporary site where powerless groups seek to take control of their
own conditions of existence within the limits imposed by the pressures of
modernity.

In the west, where everyday life is relatively comfortable even for the
least privileged, the struggle for popular survival and self-affirmation
seems to have lost its urgency. However, it is not true that, as Martín-
Barbero (1988: 464) would have it, 'in the United States and Europe . . .
to talk of the popular is to refer solely to massness or to the folklore
museum'. In the developed world, too, the popular remains invested
with intense conflict: this is the case even in such a seemingly innocent
terrain as cultural consumption and media reception. To be sure, Martín-
Barbero's assumption that popular culture is a subordinate culture that
stands in a contradictory relation to dominant culture, is hardly unique
and is well represented in British cultural studies too, particularly as a
result of its Gramscian legacy (e.g. Bennett *et al.*, 1986). However, this
general theoretical assumption has not sufficiently succeeded in informing

concrete analyses of media audiences. Instead, our understanding of
media reception – one of the most prominent practices where the popular
takes shape in today's 'consumer societies' – is still governed by the
unhelpful dichotomies of passive/activity, manipulative/liberating, and
so on. What a critical ethnography of media audiences needs to ferret out,
then, is the unrecognized, unconscious and contradictory effectivity of the
hegemonic within the popular, the relations of power that are inscribed
within the texture of reception practices. The following section sketches
out one of the trajectories along which we can begin to stake out this
terrain.

The hegemonic specified: the transnational media system

To begin with, it is important to develop a concrete sense of the hegemonic
forces that rule the world today. In too much cultural studies writing
understanding of hegemony remains at an abstract theoretical level,
evoked rather than analysed, by alluding to basic concepts such as
'class', 'gender' and 'race'. We need to go beyond these paradigmatic
conceptualizations of hegemony and develop a more specific, concrete,
contextual, in short, a more ethnographic sense of the hegemonic (Marcus, 1986).

A good point to begin with, although briefly, is the rather disturbing
changes that the world media system – arguably an important locus of
hegemonic forces – is undergoing at present. As we move towards the
end of the century the communications industries, as part of the ever
expanding capitalist system, have been in a process of profound economic
and institutional restructure and transformation, which can be characterized by accelerated transnationalization and globalization. We can see this
in the emergence of truly global, decentred corporations in which diverse
media products (film and television, press and publishing, music and
video) are being combined and integrated into overarching communications empires such as those of Bertelsmann, Murdoch, Berlusconi and
Time-Warner. This process is accompanied by an increased pressure
towards the creation of transnational markets and transnational distribution systems (made possible by new communication technologies such as
satellite and cable), transgressing established boundaries and subverting
existing territories – a process which, of course, has profound political
and cultural consequences (Robins, 1989; Morley and Robins, 1990). The
currency of such notions as 'the information revolution' and 'postmodernity' are indicative of the perceived pervasiveness of the changes, and in
our everyday lives we bear direct witness to these changes, through the
turbulent transformation of our media environment, in both technological
(cable, satellite, video) and institutional (new TV channels, dismantling of
public service monopoly) terms.

These historical developments form, in very specific ways, the structural
and global configurations of hegemony within which contemporary practices of media reception and consumption evolve. As we have seen,
ethnographies of media audiences emphasize, and tend to celebrate, the

capability of audience groups to construct their own meanings and thus their own local cultures and identities, even in the face of their virtually complete dependence on the image flows distributed by the transnational culture industries. However, this optimistic celebration of the local can easily be countered by a more pessimistic scenario, pictured by Manuel Castells, who foresees 'the coexistence both of the monopoly of messages by the big networks and of the increasingly narrow codes of local microcultures around their parochial cable TV's' (quoted in Robins, 1989: 151). In other words, would not the vitality and creativity of audiences in creating their own cultures merely amount to paltry mani-festations of, in Castells' words, 'cultural tribalism' within an electronic global village?'

It would be ludicrous, I would argue, to try to find a definitive and unambiguous, general theoreticalal answer to this question – as the theory of cultural imperialism has attempted to do – precisely because there is no way to know in advance which strategies and tactics different peoples in the world will invent to negotiate with the intrusions of global forces in their lives. For the moment, then we can only hope for provisional answers – answers informed by ethographic sensitivity to how structural changes become integrated in specific cultural forms and practices, under specific historical circumstances. Only such a particularistic approach will allow us to avoid premature closures in our understanding and keep us alert to contextual specificities and contradictions.

However, an ethnographic perspective suitable for and sensitive to the peculiarities of our contemporary cultural condition needs to move beyond the restrictive scope delimited by the boundaries of the local, and to develop an awareness of the pertinent asymmetries between production/distribution and consumption, the general and the particular, the global and the local. In other words, ethnography's critical edge does not only have to reside in discovering and validating diversity and difference in an increasingly homogeneous world, as has been suggested by several authors (e.g. Van Maanen, 1988), it can work more ambitiously towards an unravel-ling of the intricate intersections of the diverse and the homogeneous (e.g. Lull, 1989). Furthermore, the ethnographic perspective can help to detail and specify the abstracting, telescopic view invoked by structural analysis of the transnational global system:

> The ethnographic task lies ahead of reshaping our dominant macro-frame-works for the understanding of historical political economy, such as capital-ism, so that they can represent the actual diversity and complexity of local situations for which they try to account in general terms. (Marcus and Fischer, 1986: 88)

In short, one means of examining the way in which the hegemonic and the popular interpenetrate one another is to trace the global in the local and the local in the global. The last section of this article gives an illustration of this trajectory.

Where the global and the local meet: nationality and the struggle for cultural identities

One central issue, in which recognition of the intertwining of global and local developments has particularly strong theoretical and political consequences, is the issue of cultural identity. In the struggles that are fought out around this issue in many parts of the world today, the structural changes brought about by the transnationalization of media flows are often assessed and officially defined in terms of a threat to the autonomy and integrity of 'national identity'. However, such a definition of the problem seems a very limited and limiting one, because it tends to subordinate other, more specific and differential sources for the construction of cultural identity (e.g. those based upon class, locality, gender, generation, ethnicity, religion, politics, etc.) to the hegemonic and seemingly natural one of *nationality*. The defence and preservation of national identity as a privileged foundation for cultural identity is far from a general, self-evidently legitimate political option. After all, nations are themselves artificial, historically constituted politico-cultural units; they are not the natural destiny of pre-given cultures, rather their existence is based upon the construction of a standardized 'national culture' that is a prerequisite to the functioning of a modern industrial state (Gellner, 1983). The desire to keep national identity and national culture wholesome and pristine is not only becoming increasingly unrealistic, but is also, at a more theoretical level, damagingly oblivious to the contradictions that are condensed in the very concept of national identity. Defining national identity in static, essentialist terms – by forging, in a manner of speaking, authoritative checklists of Britishness, Dutchness, Frenchness, and so on – ignores the fact that what counts as part of a national identity is often a site of intense struggle between a plurality of cultural groupings and interests inside a nation, and that therefore national identity is, just like the popular identities in Latin America and elsewhere, fundamentally a dynamic, conflictive, unstable and impure phenomenon.

However, contrary to the subterranean tactics by which informal popular identities are created, the categories of national identity and national culture are invested with formal, discursive legitimacy and are at present still dominantly used as a central foundation for official cultural and media policies. It is this constellation that has been thrown into question by the electronic intrusions of the transnational media system, which does not care about national boundaries, only about boundaries of territory, of transmission and of markets. It is not just a question of 'cultural imperialism', that older term that suggests the unambiguous domination of one dependent culture by a clearly demarcated other. The homogenizing tendencies brought about by the transnational era may be better characterized by the term 'cultural synchronization' (Hamelink, 1983), and it poses quite a different problem as to the politics of cultural identity. The Mexican theorist, Garcia Canclini, has formulated the problem as follows:

> To struggle to make oneself independent of a colonial power in a head-on combat with a geographically defined power is very different from struggling

for one's own identity inside a transnational system which is diffuse, complexly interrelated and interpenetrated. (Quoted in Martín-Barbero, 1988: 452).

In other words, in the increasingly integrated world system there is no such thing as an independent cultural identity; every identity must define and position itself in relation to the cultural frames affirmed by the world system. Ignoring this, which is the case when national identity is treated as a sacrosanct given, not only can lead us to undesirable unintended consequences, but is itself an act of symbolic power, both by defining an abstracted, unified identity for diverse social and cultural groups within a nation, and by fixing, in a rigid fashion, relationships between national 'imagined communities' (Anderson, 1983).

Two more Third World examples can illuminate how a politics of national identity, or one that is propelled in its name, always implies a rearrangement of relations of cultural power, both locally and globally. The examples also point to the kind of concrete situations that ethnographies of reception could take up while holding together both local specificity and global pressures.

In its attempt to foster Malaysian identity, the Malaysian government ruled in 1989 that television commercials were no longer allowed to feature 'pan-Asian' models (and still less Caucasian models or advertisements 'suggesting Western superiority'). Instead, actors should represent Malaysia's main ethnic groups: Malays, Chinese and Indians. Ironically, however, the government had in the early 1980s taken precisely the opposite tack, directing advertising agencies to stop using racially identifiable models, reasoning that using mixed-race actors would be more adequate to promote Malaysian identity (Goldstein, 1989). What we see here is not only that national identity is a matter of selective construction, including some and excluding other elements from it (defining itself as much in terms of what it is not as in what it is), but also the very uncertainty and instability of what the identity is and should be. The inconsistency exemplified in this case glaringly elucidates the precariousness of a cultural politics that depends on the concept of national identity for its rhetoric and assumptions.

The second example describes a more popular case of cultural nationalism. In the Philippines, English, brought by the American colonizers at the turn of the century, has been the official language for nearly 30 years after the nation's independence in 1946. English was the language that served linguistically to unify a country inhabited by peoples who speak more than seventy regional languages and dialects. After the downfall of President Marcos in 1986, however, the country has seen the spectacular and spontaneous (i.e. unplanned) emergence of one of the native languages, Tagalog, as a popular national language. Tagalog, not English, was the language of street rallies and demonstrations and it became an emblem of national self-esteem. Now, most popular TV shows and comic books are in Tagalog, TV newscasts in Tagalog are drawing far larger audiences than those in English, and there is even a 'serious' newspaper in Tagalog, breaking the previous English-language monopoly in this market. Politicians can no longer rely upon delivering their speeches in

English only. (President Aquino's command of the indigenous language is said to have improved tremendously) (Branegan, 1989). If this turn of events would stir some optimism in the hearts of principled nationalists, it also has more contradictory consequences: it may lead, for example, to new, linguistically-based inequalities and social divisions. It is not unlikely that the use and command of English will gradually decline among the less privileged, while the upper and middle classes will continue to speak both languages. After all, on a global scale English is the language that gives access to economic success and social mobility.

These two examples reinforce Schlesinger's (1987: 234) claim that it is important for communication researchers

> not to start with communication and its supposed effects on national identity and culture, but rather to begin by posing the problem of national identity itself, to ask how it might be analyzed and what importance communication practices might have in its constitution.

Furthermore, we can see how the cultural constitution of national identity, as articulated in both official policies and informal popular practices, is a precarious project that can never be isolated from the global, transnational relations in which it takes shape. At a more general level, these cases give us a hint at the multiple contradictions that are at play in any local response to global forces.

There is also an opposite tack to take. While the transnational communications system tends to disrupt existing forms of national identification, it also offers opportunities of new forms of bonding and solidarity, new ways of forging cultural communities. The use of video by groups of migrants all over the world (e.g. Indians, Chinese and Turks) is a telling case. The circulation and consumption of ethnically specific information and entertainment on video serves to construct and maintain cross-national 'electronic communities' of geographically dispersed peoples who would otherwise lose their ties with tradition and its active perpetuation (Gillespie, 1989). Thus, while official, national(ist) policies against further dissemination of the transnational media system seem to be less possible and more ineffectual than ever, social groups inside and between nations seem to have found informal ways to construct their own collective identities within the boundaries of the system that limits and binds us all.

The above cases have not been highlighted out of cross-cultural romanticism, but because things happening in distant places and among other peoples – often reified as an amorphous Third World – may offer us lessons that are relevant to our own situations. For example, European national identities have recently been thoroughly put under pressure by the growing importance of an integrated European media policy, as for example in the EEC's directive for a *Television without Frontiers*. Culturally, this policy, which is an attempt to regulate the otherwise uncontrolled expansion of the transnational media system across Europe, is legitimized by pointing to the need to defend and promote some notional, supranational 'European identity', in which the spectre of separate national identities in Europe will presumably be represented. However, this sweeping pan-Europeanism, which is increasingly becoming a hegemonic force at the level of official politics, contains many contradictions. For one thing, it is clear that there is no agreement about what such a European identity should look like. Thus, the smaller nations (such as the Netherlands, Denmark and Greece) are suspicious about the dominance of the larger nations (France, Germany and Italy), while there is also a clash of visions and interests between nations who define themselves as part of a 'Nordic' European culture and those that represent the 'Latin' culture. Of course, this is not to say that the separate national identities themselves should be seen as harmonious givens to which we could resort as a safe haven (after all, the nations themselves are repositories of conflicting cultural identifications); rather, it is to suggest that the politics of European identity is a matter of cultural power and resistance, not simply a question of cherishing some 'heritage', as official policy discourse would have it.

Troubling in this respect is the way in which such a 'heritage' is artificially forged by the formulation of what is included in and excluded from the configuration of 'Europeanness'. This implies symbolic strategies that are sustained by constructing the image of a unified European culture that needs to be protected from the supposed threat of external, alien cultural influences. In his book *Orientalism*, Edward Said (1978) has already shown how the idea of 'Europe' has benefited from the colonial period onwards from its claimed superiority to the culture of the 'Orient'. This 'heritage' of latent and manifest racism still has troubling effects on ethnic relations in most European countries.

More recently, Europeanists have shown obsessive concern about the supposed threat of cultural 'Americanization' as a consequence of the transnationalization of the media system. This blatantly ignores the fact, however, that American cultural symbols have become an integral part of the way in which millions of European construct their cultural identities. Thus, official policies based upon a totalizing antagonism of 'Europe' against 'America' are necessarily out of touch with everyday life in contemporary Europe. If American popular culture seems so attractive to so many in the world, how do people incorporate it into their activities, fantasies, values and so on? What multifarious and contradictory meanings are attached to images of the 'American way of life' in what specific circumstances? Surely, those meanings cannot be the same in different parts and among different groups and peoples living in Europe or, for that matter, in Latin America or South East Asia, but we know almost nothing about such differences. Against this background, pan-Europeanist discourse should not simply be seen as a counter-hegemonic response to the very real American hegemony in the field of cultural production and distribution, but as itself a hegemonic strategy that tends to marginalize the more elusive popular responses of ordinary Europeans. More specifically, I suggest that the official definition of 'Americanization' as an unambiguous threat should be relativized by looking at the contradictory losses *and* opportunities allowed by it. As Marcus and Fischer (1986: 136) suggest:

the apparent increasing global integration suggests not the elimination of cultural diversity, but rather opportunities for counterposing diverse alternatives that nonetheless share a common world, so that each can be understood better in the other's light.

What I have tried to conjure up, then, is the broad range of creative but contradictory practices which peoples in different parts of the world are inventing today in their everyday dealings with the changing media environment that surrounds them. The often hazardous and unpredictable nature of these practices makes them difficult to examine with too formalized methods: it is an ethnographic approach that can best capture and respect them in their concrete multi-facetedness. Here then lies the critical potential of an ethnography of audiences that evinces global and historical consciousness as well as attention to local detail. In the words of Marcus and Fischer (1986: 116), 'since there are always multiple sides and multiple expressions of possibilities active in any situation, some accommodating, others resistant to dominant cultural trends or interpretations, ethnography as cultural criticism locates alternatives by unearthing these multiple possibilities as they exist in reality'.

Its emphasis on what *is* rather than on what could be makes ethnography a form of cultural critique that is devoid of utopianism. But then we live in particularly non-utopian (or post-utopian) times – which is, of course, precisely one of the central features of the 'postmodern condition' (cf. Lyotard, 1984; Ross, 1988; Rorty, 1989). The *de facto* dissemination of the transnational media system is an irreversible process that cannot be structurally transcended, only negotiated in concrete cultural contexts. In such a situation, a critical perspective that combines a radical empiricism[6] with open-ended theorizing[7] may be one of the best stances we can take up in order to stay alert to the deeply conflictive nature of contemporary cultural relations. It is a form of cultural critique which is articulated by 'pained and disgruntled subjects, who are also joyous and inventive practitioners' (Morris, 1988: 26).

Notes

1. The clearest plea for 'cultural studies' status as a critical and deconstructive intellectual project has been voiced by Stuart Hall (in Grossberg, 1986).
2. The original version of the book was published in Dutch in 1982, when the controversy about *Dallas* was at its height.
3. It is precisely the ethnographic turn in the analysis of media consumption which is appealing for cultural studies, as opposed to more formal and formalizing approaches to reception. From an anthropological point of view, however, the ethnographic method has only been applied in a limited way in the study of media audiences. See Radway (1988).
4. A similar point has been made with regard to reader-response criticism, the literary variant of reception analysis, by Pratt (1986).
5. It is the place of power, conflict and struggle in the process of culture that characterizes the central difference between American cultural studies, of which Carey is a representative, and British cultural studies. The humanist idealism of the American perspective is countered by the grimmer and more cynical

252   *What is cultural studies?*

European perspective, with its eye never diverted from the social costs of any form of order and consensus.
6. Radical empiricism should emphatically be distinguished from vulgar empiricism. While vulgar empiricism has a built-in tendency towards conservatism because it takes 'reality-as-it-is' for granted, radical empiricism questions that taken-for-grantedness precisely because it fully engages itself with the messiness of the world we live in. See Higgins (1986: 120).
7. According to Hall, such open-ended theorizing is necessary in order to keep cultural studies sensitive to historical process. 'It is theorizing in the postmodern context, if you like, in the sense that it does not believe in the finality of a finished theoretical paradigm' (Grossberg, 1986: 60).

References

ANDERSON, B. (1983) *Imagined Communities*. London: Verso.
ANG, I. (1985) *Watching Dallas*. London: Methuen.
ANG, I. (1989) 'Wanted: audiences. On the politics of empirical audience studies', in Seiter, E., Borchers, H., Kreutzner, G. and Warth, E. (eds), *Remote Control: Television, Audiences and Cultural Power*. London and New York: Routledge.
ANG, I. and MORLEY, D. (1989) 'Mayonnaise culture and other European follies'. *Cultural Studies*. 3(2): 133–44.
BENNETT, T., MERCER, C. and WOOLLACOTT, J. (eds), (1986) *Popular Culture and Social Relations*. Milton Keynes: Open University Press.
BLUMLER, J.G., GUREVITCH, M. and KATZ, E. (1985) 'Reaching out: a future for gratifications research', pp. 255–73 in Rosengren, K.E., Wenner, L. and Palmgreen, P. (eds), *Media Gratifications Research: Current Perspectives*. Beverly Hills: Sage.
BRANEGAN, J. (1989) 'Bubbling up from below', *Time*, 21 August.
CERTEAU, M. de (1984) *The Practice of Everyday Life* (translated by Steven Rendall). Berkeley: University of California Press.
ELLIOTT, P. (1974) 'Uses and gratifications research: a critique and a sociological alternative', pp. 249–68 in Blumler, J.G. and Katz, E. (eds), *the Uses of Mass Communications*. Beverly Hills and London: Sage.
FISKE, J. (1987a) 'British cultural studies and television', pp. 254–89 in Allen, R.C. (ed.), *Channels of Discourse*. Chapel Hill and London: University of North Carolina Press. Reprinted here as Chapter 6.
FISKE, J. (1987b) *Television Culture*. London and New York: Methuen.
GEERTZ, C. (1983) *Local Knowledge*. New York: Basic Books.
GELLNER, E. (1983) *Nations and Nationalism*. Oxford: Basil Blackwell.
GILLESPIE, M. (1989) 'Technology and tradition: audiovisual culture among South Asian families in West London', *Cultural Studies* 3(2): 226–39.
GOLDSTEIN, C. (1989) 'The selling of Asia', *Far Eastern Economic Review* 29 June: 60–61.
GRIPSRUD, J. (1989) ' "High culture" revisited', *Cultural Studies* 3(2): 194–207.
GROSSBERG, L. (1983) 'Cultural studies revisited and revised', pp. 39–70 in Mander, M.S. (ed.), *Communications in Transition*, New York: Praeger.
GROSSBERG, L. (ed.) (1986) 'On postmodernism and articulation. An interview with Stuart Hall', *Journal of Communications Inquiry* 10(2): 45–60.
GROSSBERG, L. (1988) *It's A Sin. Essays on Postmodernism, Politics and Culture*. Sydney: Power Publications.
HALL, S. (1980) 'Encoding/decoding', pp. 128–38 in Hall, S., Hobson, D., Lowe, A. and Willis, P. (eds), *Culture, Media, Language*. London: Hutchinson.
HALL, S. (1982) 'The rediscovery of "ideology": return of the repressed in media

studies', pp. 56–90 in Gurevitch, M., Bennett, T. and Woollacott, J. (eds), *Culture, Society, and the Media*. London and New York: Methuen.

HALL, S., HOBSON, D., LOWE, A. and WILLIS, P. (eds), (1980) *Culture, Media, Language*. London: Hutchinson.

HALL, S. and JEFFERSON, T. (eds), (1976) *Resistance through Rituals*. London: Hutchinson.

HAMELINK, C. (1983) *Cultural Autonomy in Global Communications*. New York: Longman.

HARDT, H. (1989) 'The return of the "critical" and the challenge of radical dissent: critical theory, cultural studies, and American mass communication research', pp. 558–600 in Anderson, J. (ed.), *Communication Yearbook 12*. Newbury Park: Sage.

HEBDIGE, D. (1979) *Subculture: The Meaning of Style*. London: Methuen.

HIGGINS, J. (1986) 'Raymond Williams and the problem of ideology', pp. 112–22 in Arac, J. (ed.), *Postmodernism and Politics*. Minneapolis: University of Minnesota Press.

LULL, J. (ed.), (1989) *World Families Watch Television*. Newbury Park: Sage.

LYOTARD, J.F. (1984) *The Postmodern Condition* (trans. Bennington, G. and Massumi, B.). Minneapolis: University of Minnesota Press.

MARCUS, G.E. (1986) 'Contemporary problems of ethnography in the modern world system', pp. 165–93 in Clifford, J. and Marcus, G.E. (eds), *Writing Culture*. Berkeley: University of California Press.

MARCUS, G.E. and FISCHER, M.M.J. (1986) *Anthropology as Cultural Critique*. Chicago and London: The University of Chicago Press.

MARTÍN-BARBERO, J. (1988) 'Communication from culture: the crisis of the national and the emergence of the popular', *Media, Culture and Society* 10(4): 447–65.

MODLESKI, T. (1986) 'Introduction', pp. ix–xix in Modleski, T. (ed.), *Studies in Entertainment*. Bloomington and Indianopolis: Indiana University Press.

MORLEY, D. (1980) *The 'Nationwide' Audience*. London: BFI.

MORLEY, D. (1986) *Family Television: Cultural Power and Domestic Leisure*. London: Comedia.

MORLEY, D. and ROBINS, K. (1990) 'Spaces of identity', *Screen*, 30(1).

MORRIS, M. (1988) 'Banality in cultural studies', *Block* (14): 15–25. Reprinted here as Chapter 7.

PRATT, M.L. (1986) 'Interpretive strategies/strategic interpretations: on Anglo-American reader-response criticism', pp. 26–54 in Arac, J. (ed.), *Postmodernism and Politics*. Minneapolis: University of Minnesota Press.

RADWAY, J. (1984) *Reading the Romance*. Chapel Hill: University of North Carolina Press.

RADWAY, J. (1988) 'Reception study: ethnography and the problems of dispersed audiences and nomadic subjects', *Cultural Studies* 2(3): 359–76.

REAL, M. (1989) *Super Media: A Cultural Studies Approach*. Newbury Park: Sage.

ROBINS, K. (1989) 'Reimagined communities? European image spaces, beyond Fordism', *Cultural Studies* 3(2): 145–65.

RORTY, R. (1989) *Contingency, Irony and Solidarity*. Cambridge: Cambridge University Press.

ROSENGREN, K.E. (1988) *The Study of Media Culture: Ideas, Actions, and Artefact*. Lund Research Papers in the Sociology of Communication. Report No. 10. Lund: University of Lund.

ROSS, A. (ed.), (1988) *Universal Abandon? The Politics of Postmodernism*. Minneapolis: University of Minnesota Press.

SAID, E. (1978) *Orientalism*. New York: Pantheon Books.

SCHLESINGER, P. (1987) 'On national identity: some conceptions and misconceptions criticized', *Social Science Information* 26(2): 219–64.

SCHRØDER, K. (1987) 'Convergence of antagonistic traditions? The case of audience reserach', *European Journal of Communication* 12(1): 7–32.

SCHUDSON, M. (1987) 'The new validation of popular culture: sense and sentimentality in academia', *Critical Studies in Mass Communication* 4(1): 51–68.

SILJ, A. (1988) *East of Dallas. The European Challenge to American Television*. London: BFI.

VAN MAANEN, J. (1988) *Tales of the Field*. Chicago and London: The University of Chicago Press.

WILLIS, P. (1977) *Learning to Labour*. London: Saxon House.

15

Feminism and cultural studies: pasts, presents, futures

Sarah Franklin, Celia Lury and Jackie Stacey

This book [Franklin *et al.*, 1991] is concerned with forms of knowledge, power and politics. In it we are bringing together feminism and cultural studies in a variety of contexts and at different stages of development.[1] Both feminism and cultural studies have complicated and contradictory histories, inside and outside the academy. It would be impossible to map out a comprehensive outline of these developments here, as well as perhaps undesirable to construct such an account, as if there were simply one single, linear or unified history. However, we feel it is important to highlight what we consider to be some of the key issues in these developments which relate both to the chapters in this collection and to the context of the production of this book. In the first section of this introduction we look at some parallels between feminism and cultural studies in terms of these histories. In the next section, we look at the lack of overlap, and explore some more general questions about the feminist analysis of culture. [. . .]

Inside and outside the academy: contested territories

Both women's studies and cultural studies have in common a strong link to radical politics outside the academy, having their academic agendas informed by, or linked to the feminist movement and left politics respectively.[2] The interdisciplinary basis of each subject has produced consistent and important challenges to conventional academic boundaries and power structures. Thus, there has been a shared focus on the analysis of forms of power and oppression, and on the politics of the production of knowledge within the academy, as well as elsewhere in society. In addition, both subjects have attempted to challenge some of the conventions of academic practice, such as introducing collective, rather than individual work, encouraging greater student participation in syllabus construction and opening up spaces for connections to be made between personal experience and theoretical questions. These challenges have recently come under increasing pressure in the context of public spending cut-backs in Britain and the attempt to transform politically educational practice in the name of enterprise under the Thatcher governments.

Feminism and women's studies

Despite the commonalities mentioned above, women's studies and cultural studies have developed unevenly. Women's studies has offered feminism an institutional base in further and adult education over the last ten years; there are now a number of undergraduate and postgraduate courses in women's studies, and most major publishers now have women's studies or gender studies lists,[3] alongside the wide range of publications available from the feminist presses. Many of these achievements have been hard won, and feminists in all areas of education have struggled to get issues of gender inequality on to the syllabus and to keep them there. Struggling against tokenism, the 'add women and stir' approach, co-option and marginalization, feminists have managed to establish a space within educational institutions from which to document, analyze and theorize the position of women in society.

Early interventions by feminists in the academy often involved highlighting the absence of attention to gender within existing theories and debates. As well as challenging existing academic knowledges, feminists have also introduced new issues into the academic arena. Many of these emerged from the women's movement in the 1970s and 1980s, where consciousness raising groups, political campaigns and national and local conferences were important in raising issues based on women's experiences, which were unfamiliar in mainstream political and academic contexts. Concerns such as male violence, sexuality and reproduction were introduced on to academic agendas by feminists convinced that the 'personal was political'. These topics, amongst others, became subjects of study in their own right in sociology, anthropology, history and literature, as well as within women's studies.

Alongside the documenting of women's oppression which occurred across a broad range of disciplines, feminists began to develop generalized theories to explain how and why women are oppressed. These theories have taken very different starting points and produced a highly complex and often competing set of perspectives on the subject of women's subordination. Whilst it is problematic to summarize such a large area of scholarship, because of the dangers of reductionism and exclusion, a few examples are none the less illustrative of the developments in this area. Some feminists have drawn on already existing social theory to formulate generalized accounts of women's oppression; so, for example, feminists have extended existing Marxist theories of the exploitation of labour within capitalism to look at women's position in paid employment. These writers include Beechey (1987), Phizacklea (1983) and Dex (1985). Marxist theory has also been extended to examine areas conventionally outside its remit, such as the sexual division of labour within the households; so, for example, Benston (1970), Seccombe (1974), James and Dalla Costa (1973) all contributed to the domestic labour debate. Other feminists, such as Ferguson (1989), Walby (1986; 1990), Lerner (1986) and O'Brien (1981), believe the basis of women's subordination to be located outside class relations, and have developed theories of patriarchy as a relatively separate system of exploitation. Amongst those who have attempted to introduce entirely new frameworks and concepts to analyze patriarchal society are MacKinnon (1982; 1987; 1989), Daly (1978) and Rich (1977; 1980). Finally, feminists who have emphasized the embeddedness of patriarchal social relations in a matrix of intersecting inequalities, such as racism, heterosexism, imperialism and class division, include Lorde (1984), Spelman (1990), Bunch (1988) and hooks (1984; 1989).

The usefulness of the term patriarchy in explanations of women's oppression has itself been debated within feminism (Rowbotham, 1981; Barrett, 1980; Beechey, 1987), and this in turn, has encouraged a greater specificity in its use. One of the key issues in this debate has been the extent to which women are universally subordinated. Feminists working within anthropology (Ortner, 1974; Rosaldo, 1974; MacCormack, 1980; Strathern, 1980) and history (Leacock, 1981; Lerner, 1986; Riley, 1988; Davidoff and Hall, 1987) have been particularly significant in this debate about the commonality of women's subordination cross-culturally and transhistorically. The analysis of precapitalist societies has been a particularly important source of insight into the question of the extent to which gender inequality can be understood as a product of colonization, imperialism and capital accumulation (Mies, 1986; Leacock, 1981; Ortner and Whitehead, 1981).

Early feminist theory tended to emphasize the commonalities of women's oppression, in order to establish that male domination was systematic and affected all areas of women's lives. Feminists offered analyses of women's subordination, exploitation and objectification at all levels of society. This emphasis on commonality, however, often resulted in the neglect of differences between women. Differences based on ethnic identity, nationality, class and sexuality have been increasingly important within feminist work, leading both to the documentation of experiences (Bryan, Dadzie and Scafe, 1985; Moraga and Anzaldua, 1981; Lorde, 1984; Walker, 1984), and to challenges to theories and concepts within feminism based on limited models of the category 'woman' (Carby, 1982; Parmar, 1982; Riley, 1988; Lugones and Spelman, 1983; Spelman, 1990; Ramazanoglu, 1989). These changes within feminist theory have been influenced by changes within the women's movement more generally, where differences between women have come to be seen as one of the strengths of the feminist movement, in terms of a diversity of both national and international politics (Cole, 1986; Bunch, 1988). These differences between women, however, have also been seen to call into question the collective 'we' of feminism (Ramazanoglu, 1989; hooks, 1984; 1989; Cliff, 1983). The challenge remains, at both a theoretical and political level, for feminists to be able to hold on to certain commonalities in women's position in relation to oppressive patriarchal social structures, without denying the very real differences between women and the resulting specificities in the forms of their oppression.

The questioning of the category 'woman' within feminist theory was not only a result of changes in the women's movement and challenges to the limits of its inclusions. It also drew its impetus from areas of academic theorizing which had a significant impact on feminist thought, namely, poststructuralism and postmodernism (Weedon, 1987; Fraser and Nicholson, 1988; Nicholson, 1990; Diamond and Quinby, 1988; Spivak, 1987). The general engagement with these theories of ideology, subjectivity, discourse and sexual difference was seen by many feminists to offer a more complex understanding of the operations of patriarchal power and the reproduction of inequality. Indeed, the scepticism about the unity of identities, characteristic of these perspectives, produced a questioning of the possibility of a unified and meaningful category 'woman', the subject of so much recent feminist analysis. The influence of psychoanalytic theory in particular, which asserted the disruptive nature of the unconscious to any coherent, unified identity, undermined some of the foundational assumptions of feminist analysis. However, these influences remain relatively marginal within many women's studies courses and research, as well as being theoretical perspectives which many see as incompatible with feminism (for a discussion of this issue, see Wilson (1981), Sayers (1986), Brennan (1989), Mitchell (1975), Gallop (1982) and Rose (1986)). These are contested areas within feminist research, but what remains important is that feminist debates continue to produce more complex understandings of the different forms of women's subordination, patriarchal society and the conditions of its existence and reproduction.

Marxist theory, left politics and cultural studies

Responding to changes in Marxist theory and left politics, cultural studies has been a major site of developments within theories of cultural production, and more recently, cultural consumption. Like women's studies, cultural studies is not a unified body of work, set of practices, or even an easily defined academic subject (Johnson, 1983; see also McNeil and Franklin, 1991). Rather, it has offered a place within higher education, and elsewhere in adult and further education, for traditional disciplines to be challenged, for the kinds of knowledges produced to be questioned and for power relations in educational practices to be transformed.

Cultural studies has been a particularly important site of developments within Marxist theory which attempts to leave behind the limits of economic determinism, and an over-emphasis on the mode of production as the key contradiction within society. This shift has taken place in Marxist theory generally, but cultural studies has been central in the development of analyses which take the cultural dimensions of power and inequality seriously. This is, in part, because cultural studies itself emerged from critical perspectives within several disciplines, including history, literature and sociology. These perspectives challenged the terms of previous theoretical assumptions within those subjects. For example, in the study of literature, Marxist cultural theorists challenged bourgeois notions of the literary, and the limited understandings of 'culture' prevalent in that academic subject. The study of popular cultural forms was introduced on to the syllabus alongside a re-evaluation of the literary canon (indeed, the concept of the canon itself). Cultural studies has provided similar challenges to the academic analysis of history, the state, education and the media (CCCS, 1982; Women's Study Group, 1978) and, in conjunction with Marxist theorists in these fields, produced a substantial body of alternative knowledges and approaches.

Recent developments within cultural studies can be attributed to various influences. One of the most important of these has been the impact of critical theory, particularly the Frankfurt School, poststructuralism, psychoanalysis and postmodernism. Discourse theory, deriving from the work of Foucault, has been a significant strand in poststructuralist theory, challenging traditional understandings of the relationship between knowledge, power and politics. The notion of discourse provided an alternative to the concept of ideology which had been developed within Marxist-influenced cultural studies to explore the cultural aspects of the reproduction of inequality. Through an understanding of discourse as power-knowledge, dispersed in a network of micro-relations, this work criticized monolithic and totalizing notions of causality and determination and challenged assumptions of a linear, progressive history. It also proposed an understanding of the subject produced through the discourses of 'self'-knowledge, developed through the construction of social categories such as madness, discipline and sexuality.

The critical elaboration of psychoanalysis under the influence of poststructuralism, most notably by Jacques Lacan, and the subsequent emergence of what has come to be known as sexual difference theory, associated with journals such as *m/f* and *Screen*, have been another source of important theoretical influences on cultural studies. In particular, a concern with the importance of the unconscious in the formation of identity led to an acknowledgement of both the fragmented nature of subjectivity and the difficulty of maintaining stable, unified identities. Taking the notion of the unconscious seriously meant that the previously unified subject of cultural analysis was called into question; instead, social identities were seen to be complex and heterogeneous. In addition, questions about the role of pleasure, desire and fantasy began to be analyzed more frequently as part of the process of cultural construction of subjects, identities and practices.

Most recently, the emergence of postmodernism as an influential critical perspective (Lyotard, 1984; Baudrillard, 1988; Jameson, 1984; Kroker and Cook, 1986) has challenged the so-called foundationalist underpinnings which had informed previous theory within cultural studies. Postmodernism is associated with a set of questions about the state of knowledge in contemporary society. It poses a challenge both to conventional understandings of the standpoint of the knowing subject (objectivity, neutrality, distance) and the traditional object of knowledge (a separate reality about which the truth can be discovered). These modernist, foundationalist, post-Enlightenment assumptions are challenged by postmodernism, which argues that they are essentialist, falsely universalist and ultimately unsustainable. Unlike poststructuralism, which also raised these issues, postmodernism is associated both with actual contemporary phenomena, such as architectural styles and other representational practices, and with broad changes in the organization of Western consumer culture. These changes are seen to include the break-down of the historical distinction between high and popular culture, the disappearance of what is variously called the depth, content, or referent of signification, and the increasing instability and complexity of contemporary cultural processes.

Another of the main influences transforming cultural studies through the 1980s has been the impact of feminism. *Women Take Issue* (Women's Studies Group, 1978) was an early example of feminist work within cultural studies, both using and attempting to transform Marxist theory. Looking at questions of cultural reproduction as well as production, *Women Take Issue* highlighted the need for cultural studies to engage with the 'personal' dimensions of culture in the political context of a feminist analysis. Since then, the impact of feminism on cultural studies has had an increasing significance. The shift, for example, from interest in issues concerning ideology and hegemony to those concerning identity and subjectivity can, in part, be attributed to feminist interventions, as well as to the influence of psychoanalysis and poststructuralism. Another area of increasing interest within some strands of cultural studies which can be seen as evidence of the impact of feminism is sexuality. However, while work on the construction of sexual identities (Mulvey, 1989; Heath, 1982), the analysis of narratives of romance (Modleski, 1982; Radway, 1987), cultural representations of AIDS (Watney, 1987) and studies of state regulation of sexual 'deviancy' (Weeks, 1981; 1985), addresses sexuality as well as gender, the way in which sexuality has been taken up has been selective, and often has not been integrated with feminist analyses such as those of the patriarchal institution of heterosexuality. Similarly, lesbian and gay issues are only very gradually beginning to be taken seriously within cultural studies.

Theories of ethnicity and analyses of racism have also made an important contribution to shaping developments within cultural studies. *Policing the Crisis* (Hall *et al.*, 1978) stressed the role of racist representations of social problems such as crime in the emergence of a law and order society in Britain in the early 1970s. Following this and other work on the construction and representation of ethnicity and national identity, *The Empire Strikes Back* (CCCS, 1982) criticized the pathologization of race within race relations and sociology, and the racism of some white feminist analyses. It also explored the importance of racist ideologies in both shaping aspects of state regulation in Britain, such as immigration law, and the construction of notions in Britishness and citizenship informing contemporary definitions of national identity. Another area in cultural studies which has been influenced by the study of ethnicity has been the analysis of subcultural practices (Hebdige, 1979; Gilroy, 1987). Earlier models of subculture were challenged and transformed to include an acknowledgement of both the history of ethnic inequality and racism, and the struggles for collective self-representations by black people. However, the impact of debates about and struggles against racism on cultural studies continues to be rather uneven.

Changes within left politics have also had an effect on the kinds of political questions taken seriously within cultural studies. What has been seen as a crisis in left politics had led to a rethinking of political strategies, allegiances and agendas by some on the left. In some circles, this has contributed to a broadening of agendas and a desire for stronger political alliances with other radical forces such as the women's movement, black politics, the green movement and lesbian and gay liberation.

These, then, are some of the principal influences in the development of cultural studies and feminism in the last decade or so. As this account makes clear, there are a number of points of overlap between feminism and cultural studies. Theoretically both are concerned with analyzing the forms and operations of power and inequality, and take as an integral part of such operations the production of knowledge itself. To some extent, each has drawn on critical insights from discourse theory, poststructuralism, psychoanalysis, semiology and deconstructionism. Both have drawn on strands of critical theory which are seen to offer more sophisticated tools for analyzing the reproduction of social inequality, and relations of dominance and subordination at a cultural level. The analytic possibilities opened up by these approaches were seen to strengthen existing theories of power and resistance within both cultural studies and feminism. To some degree, then, overlaps in both areas have produced possible points of convergence between feminism and cultural studies.

The lack of overlap: feminism and cultural analysis

There are, however, also considerable divergences in interest which suggest a rather different ordering of priorities within feminism and cultural studies. Just as many feminists earlier posed critical questions about concepts such as ideology and hegemony, drawing attention to the ways in which they and the traditions of thought which produced them were gender-blind, there is now caution about the use of concepts such as discourse, deconstruction and difference. In addition, although feminism has influenced cultural studies, there are limits to this influence which are important for what they reveal about the uneven interaction between the two fields. Perhaps one of the clearest indicators of the limits to this influence is provided by the lack of interest within cultural studies in the developments in feminist theories of gender inequality discussed earlier; for example, the models of culture employed within cultural studies have remained largely uninformed by feminist theories of patriarchy. This has produced a number of problems for feminists working in cultural studies.

Many of the reasons why the influence of feminism on cultural studies has been limited can be traced back to some of the more general understandings of culture employed within cultural studies. These include the models of culture derived from certain strands of Marxist thought. As discussed earlier, cultural studies was itself both central to, and in some senses a product of, a major set of shifts within Marxist perspectives away from the assumption of a mechanistic economic determinism. Indeed, the influence of feminism has been particularly significant within cultural studies around this issue. On the one hand, for example, the Althusserian framework offered greater attention to the cultural within (or, relative to other) Marxist frameworks, and has informed some of the most influential feminist work in cultural studies (Williamson, 1978; Barrett, 1980; Winship, 1987; Women's Studies Group, 1978). Yet on the other hand, the appropriation and development of these models within cultural studies did little to counter the marginalization of issues of importance to feminism.

Indeed, these theoretical frameworks, which are largely unable to account for sexuality, reproduction and violence, are characterized by quite fundamental conceptual limitations from some feminist points of view. Within the Althusserian framework, for example, the social field is seen to be composed of economic, political and ideological levels. But, the economic level, conceptualized in terms of the forces and relations of production, is seen to determine all other levels in the last instance, and thus retains a privileged significance in the construction of inequality. This limited move away from economic determinism is inadequate for many understandings of gender inequality. Some feminists, for example, have disputed the Marxist conception of the economic, in so far as it is seen to be based on the industrial mode of production associated with capitalism, and to naturalize the sexual division of labour (Firestone, 1974; Delphy, 1984; Mies, 1986). Other feminists (Daly, 1978; MacKinnon, 1987, 1989) have suggested that not only is such an ordering of determination open to question, but that the division of levels is unhelpful for an analysis of gender inequality: how is sexuality, for example, to be understood in relation to these discrete levels of power?

Another powerful model of culture which has been developed in cultural studies has its origins in structuralism. This model has two principal strands, deriving from social anthropology and linguistics. The first of these was introduced into cultural studies through the work of Claude Lévi-Strauss. This version of structuralism takes the exchange of women as the original or founding cultural moment, thus creating an essentialist tautology from a feminist point of view, and providing little hope of ever changing patriarchal society. As has been pointed out (Rubin in Reiter, 1975), by constructing the sexual division of labour and sexual difference as *a priori* constants, structuralism reifies patriarchal dominance as a 'natural fact'. The problem for feminists, therefore, is that this model of culture takes for granted precisely what feminism is most concerned to explain.

The second broad strand of structuralist thought that has been influential within cultural studies is based on the work of Ferdinand de Saussure, who proposed a structural analysis of language as a system of signs. This has since been extended in semiotic, poststructuralist and sexual difference theories to the analysis of other cultural systems, including, for example, fine art (Parker and Pollock, 1981), advertising (Williamson, 1978) and film (Cowie, 1978). From this perspective, meaning is understood to be produced through the play of difference and is relational (produced in relation to other signs) rather than referential (produced by reference to objects existing in the world). The development of these interpretive techniques, in which the analogy of language as a system is extended to culture as a whole, marked a substantial break from the positivist and empirical traditions which had limited much previous cultural theory. However, while structuralism and post-structuralism have been important for feminists in so far as they provided important critiques of some kinds of reductionism and essentialism, and facilitated the analysis of contradictory meanings and identities, their use has often obscured the significance of power relations in the constitution of difference, such as patriarchal forms of domination and subordination.

However, one strand of poststructuralism, developed by feminists working within cultural studies, which has addressed the reproduction of such patriarchal relations, is that which draws upon psychoanalysis in order to provide an account of how difference is fixed as inequality through the acquisition of a gendered identity (Mitchell, 1975; Rose, 1986; Mulvey, 1989). This, in turn, has been challenged by others, who argue that sexual difference is so fundamental to the very terms of psychoanalytic thought (as in the strand of structuralism which derives from Lévi-Strauss), that its use invariably contributes to the naturalization of gender inequality (Rubin in Reiter, 1975).

The poststructuralist tendency in cultural studies outlined above has also been supplemented by the use of literary methods of analysis, such as deconstructionism (Derrida, 1981; Ricoeur, 1986; De Man, 1979), in which cultural processes are analyzed as texts. The advantages for feminists of the bridge between literary analysis and social science constructed in the wake of 'the structuralist challenge' are clearly apparent. The ability, for example, to locate the production, criticism and consumption of literary texts in the context of the non-literary 'texts' of patriarchal social relations opened up an obvious space for more politicized readings of both the literary canon and what had been excluded from it. Likewise, the emphasis on how meanings are encoded into practices of cultural production and consumption opened up a whole range of radical rereadings of traditional subjects in both the humanities and the social sciences.

Nevertheless, this understanding of cultural processes as texts obscures the specificity and significance of different kinds of practices and results in a reductionism which raises problems for feminist analysis. Central issues for feminists, such as the control of women through their bodies, present problems for this textual analogy; some feminists would suggest that the female body cannot be considered simply as a text. Furthermore, such a method may contribute to the problem of objectification, whereby the female body becomes an object of scrutiny and investigation, devoid of subjectivity or personhood. Analyzing gender within the model of culture 'as a language', then, presents specific problems for feminists who have highlighted the objectifying practices (or, the construction of woman as object) within language itself.

There have been other influential frameworks for the study of culture within cultural studies, including, for example, the understanding of culture as 'ways of life' and 'ways of struggle' as developed in the work of Williams (1961, 1965, 1981), Thompson (1968, 1978), Hoggart (1958) and Seabrook (1985, 1988). These have sought to construct new understandings of culture based on working-class experiences and positions. However, whilst they have offered alternative models of culture to the dominant versions, based on bourgeois life and values, they have often excluded the gendered dimensions and specificities of working-class experience (Steedman, 1986).

Ethnographic work within cultural studies, drawing on perspectives from anthropology, has provided one of the main sources of exploration of 'lived cultures'. Working-class culture has been a particular focus of this work within cultural studies, where ethnographic material has been used as evidence of the relationship between dominant culture and subordinate groups. In particular, forms of resistance (Willis, 1978) and the formations of subcultures (Hebdige, 1979; 1988) have been explored in this context. These have also been challenged by feminists within cultural studies, not only for their gender specificity, but also for their lack of acknowledgement of the patriarchal elements of these forms of resistance (Griffin, 1985; McRobbie, 1980).

In this section, then, some of the important models of culture employed within cultural studies have been discussed in terms of the limits, as well as the possibilities, they pose for feminist analysis. The aim has been to show the way in which the frameworks outlined above pose substantial problems for feminists concerned with *patriarchal* culture, and limit the potential influence of feminism upon cultural studies, as well as of cultural studies upon feminism. Thus, while feminists have turned to disciplines such as cultural studies for frameworks to analyze the cultural dimensions of gender inequality, and whilst the work of feminists has been influential in both challenging and reworking these frameworks, there remain substantial difficulties in defining what might be meant by specifically feminist understandings of culture.

Ironically, this is true at a time when cultural issues are seen to be of growing importance to feminism. The power relations of pornography, abortion, male violence, technology and science have increasingly come to be seen not only in terms of social institutions and practices, but also of symbolic meanings, the formation of identities and deeply-rooted belief systems. Even in those areas that appear to be most easily understood in conventional social and economic terms, such as paid work, feminists have begun to uncover the ways in which the construction of gender-appropriate identities and subcultures helps to organize, for example, the hierarchies in internal labour markets and the nature of workplace activities (Cockburn, 1983, 1985; Game and Pringle, 1984; Beechey, 1988; Phillips and Taylor, 1980). Indeed, cultural issues are so central to a wide variety of analyses of women's subordination that it might seem surprising that feminists have not developed general frameworks within which the significance of cultural processes might be more fully realized.

However, to the extent that feminism has long relied on an eclectic combination of frameworks and methods, often extracted from traditional disciplines and reworked to take account of gender, this may require less explanation. Moreover, the fact that some feminists have explicitly resisted overarching models and 'grand' theories, which belong to what has been seen as a masculine tradition, in part explains the lack of attention to a clearer definition of the elements of specifically feminist analyses of culture. Nevertheless, this lack of clarity about what is meant by cultural analysis in the context of feminism has led to some confusion in recent debates. This results both from the implicit or unacknowledged use of models of culture and the explicit naming of a disparate set of analyses as cultural.

One example of the confusion which results from the implicit use of different understandings of culture is provided by the current debate about pornography. Some feminists (Coward, in Betterton, 1987; Merck, in Betterton, 1987) see pornography as a process of signification or representation, ultimately irreducible to, and, to some extent, separate from, social and economic relations. They attempt to demonstrate the continuum between pornographic and other images of women circulating in contemporary culture, arguing for the impossibility of drawing a fixed line between offensive and acceptable images. Pornographic images of women, then, are understood as the extreme articulation of the objectification of women *at the representational level*. The model of culture being drawn upon here is one which assumes that representations have a relative autonomy and are a mediated articulaton of social practices. Other feminists (Dworkin, 1981; Griffin, 1978; MacKinno, 1979) propose an understanding of pornography not as a representational form of patriarchal culture, but as its exemplary moment of expression: pornography reveals to us the truth about what men really think about women. It is seen as an expression of male sexual violence and as an integral part of violent practices against women. Here, culture is seen to parallel directly the social, and is derivative of the misogyny deeply embedded in patriarchal society. Thus, an analysis of pornography forces us to face and to challenge the full extent of misogyny in this society. What is at stake, then, in discussions about whether it is possible to distinguish between pornography and erotica, or in disagreements about the role and relevance of censorship, are not only different understandings of pornography, but also implicit models of culture which are rarely addressed in these debates.

Another important example of feminist work where the models of culture have not been foregrounded is the analysis of gender and objectification. Feminists who have emphasized the objectification of women in terms of commodity fetishism and the circulation of objects within capitalist relations of exchange often draw heavily on Marxist models of culture (Gaines, 1982). Another perspective criticizes the voyeuristic and fetishistic construction of woman in visual images, and uses a psychoanalytic account of the cultural construction of gendered identities to explain and challenge the patriarchal pleasures offered by such processes of objectification (Mulvey, 1989). A third approach develops an analysis of the forms of female objectification through the construction of female sexuality in patriarchal culture, and points towards a feminist methodology which would challenge such objectification (MacKinnon, 1979, 1982, 1987, 1989).

As these debates make clear, attention to the cultural dimensions of gender inequality is not simply about arriving at a sharper understanding, or a more encompassing set of explanations. They are also about the strategies for change and transformation which are at the core of feminist politics. How one defines the power of pornography depends in large part on how one understands much more general processes involved in the cultural construction of meanings, images and identities. This, in turn, has direct implications for how to challenge pornography. Similarly, discussions about the question of whether the processes of objectification imply consent or coercion lead to very different strategies for change or resistance.

In addition to the problem of understandings of culture being present but submerged, as in the current debates over pornography or objectificaton, there is another set of questions which arises out of the explicit use of radically heterogeneous understandings of the cultural. Again, bespeaking the divergent roots and resources of feminist scholarship across a wide range of disciplines, cultural criticism has come to mean a very wide variety of things within feminism. The resulting confusion is perhaps most evident in the description of some American radical feminist work as cultural feminism.[4] The proliferation of understandings of the cultural further contributes to the need to define more clearly the assumptions underpinning frameworks in the analysis of culture, and raises the question of whether there are any commonalities that run through the various uses of 'cultural' as a modifier.

Some feminists working within women's studies have used more explicit models of culture drawn from the disciplines in which they are based. For example, feminist sociological theory tends to analyze the cultural as something distinct from the social, a differentiated sphere which is structured through specific institutions, such as the media, education and religion, and has drawn on a range of methods of analysis to conceptualize the specificity of the cultural in this sense. Alternatively, feminists working within anthropology, in which culture is the traditional object of study, have drawn upon a diverse set of frameworks and methods for cultural analysis. These include detailed ethnographic accounts, crosscultural comparisons, evolutionary and archaeological approaches, and linguistic studies. Culture is also studied within other disciplines, such as psychology, linguistics, literary criticism and history, through frameworks which are formulated in various ways in relation to the primary objective of study. Many of these approaches to the study of culture from the traditional disciplines have been borrowed by feminists in order to investigate the cultural dimensions of gender relations.

The importance of theories of culture to feminism, then, arises from many different sources and for many different reasons. Be it due to the limits of existing models within cultural studies and conventional disciplines, the increasing importance of cultural issues within feminist theory and politics, or the confusion arising out of the use of divergent models of culture within feminist analysis, the need to clarify what might be meant by feminist analyses of culture becomes increasingly important. This concern arises both from the recognition of these problems and the desire to provide a set of terms for an analysis of culture which addresses the specificity of patriarchal power and suggests ways in which to challenge it.

However, the question of what these terms might consist of is only just beginning to be asked. It might, for example, be possible to argue that a feminist cultural analysis would, given the intimate nature of women's subordination, be shaped by an interest in the construction of sexuality, the gendered body and the realm of subjectivity. Yet there are acknowledged problems with reinforcing links between the personal and the feminine which would require the issue of essentialism to be addressed. Debates about the implications of the conceptual distinctions between lived experience, the subjective and subjection, lie at the heart of many current debates within feminism, not the least of which is that concerning the strategic value of the category 'woman', and all of which are concerned to transform the significance of what it is to be a woman.

One of the primary aims in bringing together feminism and cultural studies, is to consider the significance within feminist theory and politics of questions concerning the cultural dimensions of gender inequality and patriarchal power. This introduction has suggested that there are two ways of exploring this significance: to investigate the role of culture in the reproduction of gender inequality; and to ask how an analysis of gender can contribute to an understanding of culture. However, it seems that whilst feminists have gradually built up a complex picture of the operations of patriarchal culture, there has been less of an attempt to systematize generalized theories of these power relations. We have tried to suggest some of the reasons for this, including both the limits to feminist influence within cultural studies and the difficulties of asking what a specifically feminist cultural analysis would look like.

However, the diversity and heterogeneity of contemporary feminist analyses of culture would suggest that such a project, while focused on a common set of themes, is not, and is unlikely ever to be, unified. This is itself indicative of the strength and diversity of contemporary academic and political feminism.

In bringing together feminism and cultural studies we have tried to approach the question of how to develop feminist cultural analysis. This important project can draw much that is of value from work within cultural studies. Yet, it must also take account of the shortcomings and limitations of the models of cultural analysis on offer within cultural studies. In turn, as it has already done, feminist analysis will likely serve as both a resource and a stimulus to cultural studies, in their continuing shared project to challenge the existing conventions of producing and sharing knowledge, and to combine theoretical debate with strategies for change.

Notes

We would like to thank Maureen McNeil for her detailed comments on an earlier version of this Introduction.

1. Whilst 'women's studies' and 'cultural studies' might seem to be more obviously analagous terms, we have chosen to use 'feminism' and 'cultural studies' in order to include developments in feminist theory and politics which have occurred outside the institutional boundaries of women's studies.
2. However, women's studies and cultural studies have rather different relationships to radical politics, given that women's studies emerged as a direct result of the women's movement. Cultural studies, on the other hand, has had a more tenuous and uneven relationship to left politics.
3. The recent shift from women's studies to gender studies has produced considerable debate and controversy. Mary Evans offered a sceptical analysis of the political significance of this shift in her keynote paper at the Women's Studies Network Conference, Coventry Polytechnic, 18 March 1989.
4. The range of American radical feminist work labelled 'cultural feminist' is very broad and thus the term is often confusing. It includes work which attempts to reclaim a 'woman-centred' culture, exemplified in the films of Barbara Hammer, as well as critiques of patriarchal culture and knowledge, such as those developed by Mary Daly.

References

BARRETT, M. (1980) *Women's Oppression Today: Problems in Marxist Feminist Analysis*. London: Verso.
BAUDRILLARD, J. (1988) *Selected Writings*. Cambridge: Polity Press.
BEECHEY, V. (1987) *Unequal Work*. London: Verso.
BEECHEY, V. (1988) 'Rethinking the definition of work: gender and work', in Jenson, J., Hagen, E. and Reddy, C. (eds), *Feminization of the Labour Force: Paradoxes and Promises*. Cambridge: Polity Press.
BENSTON, M. (1970) 'The political economy of housework', in Tanner (ed.), *Voices from Women's Liberation*. New York: Signet.
BETTERTON, R. (ed.), (1987) *Looking On: Images of Femininity in the Visual Arts and Media*. London and New York: Pandora.
BRENNAN, T. (ed.), (1989) *Between Feminism and Psychoanalysis*. London: Routledge.
BRYAN, B., DADZIE, S., and SCAFE, S. (1985) *The Heart of the Race: Black Women's Lives in Britain*. London: Virago.
BUNCH, C. (1988) 'Making common cause: diversity and coalitions', in McEwan, C. and O'Sullivan, S. (eds), *Out the Other Side: Contemporary Lesbian Writing*. London: Virago.
CARBY, H. (1982) 'White women listen! Black feminism and the boundaries of sisterhood', in CCCS, University of Birmingham, *The Empire Strikes Back: Race and Racism in 70s Britain*. London: Hutchinson.
Centre for Contemporary and Cultural Studies (CCCS), University of Birmingham (1982a) *Making Histories: Studies in History – Writing and Politics*. London: Hutchinson.
Centre for Contemporary and Cultural Studies (CCCS), University of Birmingham (1982b) *The Empire Strikes Back: Race and Racism in 70s Britain*. London: Hutchinson.
CLIFF, M. (1983) *Claiming an Identity they Taught us to Despise*. Watertown, MA: Persephone Press.
COCKBURN, C. (1983) *Brothers: Male Dominance and Technological Change*. London: Pluto Press.

COCKBURN, C. (1985) *Machinery of Dominance: Women, Men and Technical Know-How*. London: Pluto Press.

COLE, J.B. (ed.), (1986) *All American Women: Lines that Divide, Ties that Bind*. New York: Macmillan.

COWIE, E. (1978) 'Woman as sign', *m/f*, no. 1, pp. 49–63.

DALY, M. (1978) *Gyn/Ecology: The Metaethics of Radical Feminism*. London: The Women's Press.

DAVIDOFF, H. and HALL, C. (1987) *Family Fortunes: Men and Women of the English Middle Class, 1780–1850*. London: Hutchinson.

DELPHY, C. (1984) *Close to Home: A Materialist Analysis of Women's Oppression*. London: Hutchinson.

DE MAN, P. (1979) *Allegories of Reading: Figural Language in Rousseau, Nietzsche, Rilke, and Proust*. New Haven, CT: Yale University Press.

DERRIDA, J. (1981) *Writing and Difference*. London: Routledge and Kegan Paul.

DEX, S. (1985) *The Sexual Division of Work: Conceptual Revolutions in the Social Sciences*. Brighton: Wheatsheaf.

DIAMOND, I. and QUINBT, L. (eds), (1988) *Feminism and Foucault: Reflections on Resistance*. Boston, MA: Northeastern University Press.

DWORKIN, A. (1981) *Pornography: Men Possessing Women*. London: The Women's Press.

FERGUSON, A. (1989) *Blood at the Root: Motherhood, Sexuality and Male Dominance*. London: Pandora.

FIRESTONE, S. (1974) *The Dialectic of Sex: The Case for Feminist Revolution*. New York: Morrow.

FRASER, N. and NICHOLSON, L. (1988) 'Social criticism without philosophy: an encounter between feminism and postmodernism', *Theory, Culture and Society*, vol. 5, nos 2 and 3, pp. 373–94.

GAINES, J. (1982) 'In the service of ideology: how Betty Grable's legs won the war', *Film Reader*, no. 5, pp. 47–59.

GALLOP, J. (1982) *Feminism and Psychoanalysis: The Daughter's Seduction*. London: Macmillan.

GAME, A. and PRINGLE, R. (1984) *Gender at Work*. London: Pluto Press.

GILROY, P. (1987) *There Ain't No Black in the Union Jack: The Cultural Politics of Race and Nation*. London: Hutchinson.

GRIFFIN, C. (1985) *Typical Girls? Young Women from School to the Job Market*. London: Routledge and Kegan Paul.

GRIFFIN, S. (1978) *Women and Nature: The Roaring Inside Her*. New York: Harper and Row.

HALL, S., CRITCHER, C., JEFFERSON, T., CLARKE, J., and ROBERTS, B. (1978) *Policing the Crisis: Mugging, the State and Law and Order*. London: Macmillan.

HEATH, S. (1982) *The Sexual Fix*. London: Macmillan.

HEBDIGE, D. (1979) *Subculture: The Meaning of Style*. London: Methuen.

HEBDIGE, D. (1988) *Hiding in the Light: On Images and Things*. London: Routledge.

HOGGART, R. (1958) *The Uses of Literacy*. Harmondsworth: Penguin Books.

HOOKS, B. (1984) *Feminist Theory: From Margin to Center*. Boston: MA: South End Press.

HOOKS, B. (1989) *Talking Back: Thinking Feminist, Thinking Black*. Boston, MA: South End Press.

JAMES, S. and DALLA COSTA, M. (1973) *The Power of Women and the Subversion of the Community*. Bristol: Falling Wall Press.

JAMESON, F. (1984) 'Postmodernism, or the cultural logic of late capitalism', *New Left Review* no. 146, pp. 55–92.

JOHNSON, R.J. (1983) 'What is cultural studies anyway?' *Stencilled paper* no. 74.

Birmingham Centre for Contemporary Cultural Studies, University of Birmingham. Reprinted here as Chapter 5.

KROKER, A. and COOK, D. (1986) *The Postmodern Scene: Excremental Culture and Hyper-Aesthetics*. New York: St Martin's Press.

LEACOCK, E. (1981) *Myths of Male Dominance: Collected Articles on Women Cross-Culturally*. New York: Monthly Review Press.

LERNER, G. (1986) *The Creation of Patriarchy*. New York: Oxford University Press.

LORDE, A. (1984) *Sister-Outsider: Essays and Speeches*. Trumansburg, NY: The Crossing Press.

LUGONES, M. and Spelman, E.V. (1983) 'Have we got a theory for you? Feminist theory, cultural imperialism and the demand for "The Woman's Voice"', *Women's Studies International Forum*, vol. 6, no. 6, pp. 573–82.

LYOTARD, J. (1984) *The Postmodern Condition: A Report on Knowledge*. Minneapolis, MN: University of Minnesota Press.

MACCORMACK, C. (1980) 'Nature, culture and gender: a critique', in MacCormack, C. and Strathern, M. (eds), *Nature, Culture and Gender*. Cambridge: Cambridge University Press.

MACKINNON, C. (1979) *The Sexual Harassment of Working Women: A Case of Sex Discrimination*. New Haven, CT: Yale University Press.

MACKINNON, C. (1982) 'Feminism, Marxism, method and the state: an agenda for theory', *Signs*, vol. 7, no. 3, pp. 515–44.

MACKINNON, C. (1987) *Feminism Unmodified: Discourses of Life and Law*. Cambridge, MA: Harvard University Press.

MACKINNON, C. (1989) *Toward a Feminist Theory of the State*. Cambridge, MA: Harvard University Press.

MCROBBIE, A. (1980) 'Settling accounts with sub-cultures: a feminist critique', *Screen Education*, vol. 34, pp. 37–49.

MIES, M. (1986) *Patriarchy and Accumulation on a World Scale: Women in the International Division of Labour*. London: Zed Books.

MITCHELL, J. (1975) *Psychoanalysis and Feminism*. Harmondsworth: Penguin Books.

MODLESKI, T. (1982) *Loving with a Vengeance: Mass-Produced Fantasies for Women*. London: Methuen.

MORAGA, C. and ANZALDUA, G. (eds), (1981) *This Bridge Called My Back: Writings by Radical Women of Color*. New York: Kitchen Table Press.

MULVEY, L. (1989) *Visual and Other Pleasures*. London: Macmillan.

NICHOLSON, L.J. (ed.), (1990) *Feminism/Postmodernism*. London: Routledge.

O'BRIEN, M. (1981) *The Politics of Reproduction*. London: Routledge and Kegan Paul.

ORTNER, S. (1974) 'Is female to male as nature is to culture?' in Rosaldo, M. and Lamphere, L. (eds), *Woman, Culture and Society*. Stanford, CA: Stanford University Press.

ORTNER, B. and WHITEHEAD, H. (eds) (1981) *Sexual Meanings: The Cultural Construction of Gender and Sexuality*. Cambridge: Cambridge University Press.

PARKER, R. and POLLOCK, G. (1981) *Old Mistresses: Women, Art and Ideology*. London: Routledge and Kegan Paul.

PARMAR, P. (1982) 'Gender, race and class: Asian women in resistance', in University of Birmingham, CCCS, *The Empire Strikes Back: Race and Racism in '70s Britain*. London: Hutchinson.

PHILLIPS, A. and TAYLOR, B. (1980) 'Sex and skill: notes towards a feminist economics', *Feminist Review*, no. 6, pp. 79–83.

PHIZACKLEA, A. (1983) *One Way Ticket*. London: Routledge and Kegan Paul.

RADWAY, J.A. (1987) *Reading the Romance: Women, Patriarchy and Popular Literature*. London: Verso.

RAMAZANOGLU, C. (1989) *Feminism and the Contradictions of Oppression*. London: Routledge.

REITER, R.R. (ed.), (1975) *Toward an Anthropology of Women*. New York: Monthly Review Press.

RICH, A. (1977) *Of Woman Born: Motherhood as Experience and Institution*. London: Virago.

RICH, A. (1980) 'Compulsory heterosexuality and lesbian existence', *Signs: Journal of Women in Culture and Society*, vol. 5, no. 4, pp. 631–60.

RICOEUR, P. (1986) *Lectures on Ideology and Utopia*. New York: Columbia University Press.

RILEY, D. (1988) *Am I That Name?: Feminism and the Category of 'Women' in History*. London: Macmillan.

ROELOFS, S. (1988) 'Clause 28', *Spare Rib*, no. 189, pp. 38–41.

ROSALDO, M.Z. (1974) 'Woman, culture and society: a theoretical overview', in Rosaldo, M. and Lamphere, L. (eds), *Woman, Culture and Society*. Stanford, CA: Stanford University Press.

ROWBOTHAM, S. (1981) 'The trouble with "patriarchy"', in Feminist Anthropology Collective (ed.), *No Turning Back: Writings from the Women's Liberation Movement, 1975–1980*. London: The Women's Press.

SAYERS, J. (1986) *Sexual Contradictions: Psychology, Psychoanalysis, and Feminism*. London: Tavistock Publications.

SEABROOK, J. (1985) *Landscapes of Poverty*. Oxford: Basil Blackwell.

SEABROOK, J. (1988) *The Leisure Society*. Oxford: Basil Blackwell.

SECOMBE, W. (1974) 'The housewife and her labour under capitalism', *New Left Review*, no. 83, pp. 3–24.

SPELMAN, E.V. (1990) *Inessential Woman: Problems of Exclusion in Feminist Thought*. London: The Women's Press.

SPIVAK, G.C. (1985) 'Strategies of vigilance', *Block*, no. 5, pp. 5–9.

SPIVAK, G.C. (1987) *In Other Worlds: Essays in Cultural Politics*. London: Methuen.

STEEDMAN, C. (1986) *Landscape for a Good Woman: A Story of Two Lives*. London: Virago.

STRATHERN, M. (1980) 'No nature, no culture', in MacCormack, C. and Strathern, M. (eds), *Nature, Culture and Gender* (Cambridge: Cambridge University Press).

THOMPSON, E.P. (1968) *The Making of the English Working Class*. Harmondsworth: Penguin Books.

THOMPSON, E.P. (1978) *The Poverty of Theory and Other Essays*. London: Merlin Press.

WALBY, S. (1986) *Patriarchy at Work: Patriarchal and Capitalist Relations in Employment*. Oxford: Polity Press.

WALBY, S. (1990) *Theorizing Patriarchy*. Oxford: Basil Blackwell.

WALKER, A. (1984) *In Search of our Mother's Gardens: Womanist Prose*. London: The Women's Press.

WATNEY, S. (1987) *Policing Desire: Pornography, Aids and the Media*. Minneapolis, MN: University of Minnesota Press.

WEEDON, C. (1987) *Feminist Practice and Poststructuralist Theory*. Oxford: Basil Blackwell.

WEEKS, J. (1981) *Sex, Politics and Society: The Regulation of Sexuality Since 1880*. London: Longman.

WEEKS, J. (1985) *Sexuality and its Discontents: Meanings, Myths and Modern Sexualities*. London: Routledge and Kegan Paul.

WILLIAMS, R. (1961) *Culture and Society, 1780–1950*. Harmondsworth: Penguin Books.

WILLIAMS, R. (1965) *The Long Revolution*. Harmondsworth: Penguin Books.

WILLIAMS, R. (1981) *Politics and Letters: Interviews with New Left Review*. London: Verso.

WILLIAMSON, J. (1978) *Decoding Advertisements: Ideology and Meaning in Advertising*. London: Marion Boyars.

WILLIS, P.E. (1978) *Profane Culture*. London: Routledge and Kegan Paul.

WILSON, E. (1981) 'Psychoanalysis: psychic law and order', *Feminist Review* no. 8, pp. 63–78.

WINSHIP, J. (1987) *Inside Women's Magazines*. London: Pandora.

Women's Studies Group, Birmingham Centre for Contemporary Cultural Studies (1978) *Women Take Issue*. London: Hutchinson.

16

Always already cultural studies: academic conferences and a manifesto

Cary Nelson

The Americanization of cultural studies

The rapidly increasing visibility of cultural studies in the United States gives us an opportunity to reflect on and debate its articulation to existing institutions in medias res, before those articulations are fixed for any period of time. As part of that debate, I have argued for some time that people who comment on or claim to be 'doing' cultural studies ought at least to familiarize themselves with the British cultural studies tradition, beginning with Raymond Williams and Richard Hoggart and moving through Birmingham and beyond. Almost nothing in this tradition, one must note at the outset, is simply and unproblematically transferable to the United States. Williams was partly concerned with defining a distinctly British heritage. British subcultural theory, often focused on entire ways of life, is not well suited to describing quite partial identities or mere leisure activities in the United States. The recent anti-essentialist British work on race must in this country confront an often essentialist identity politics. Thus, while anti-essentialist theories of race have the potential to be quite liberating here, we cannot simply adopt them without asking what Americans of different races have gained and lost from essentialism. The interdisciplinary work at Birmingham was often deeply collaborative, a style that has little chance of succeeding in American departments and of surviving the American academic system of rewards. Yet the struggle to shape the field in Britain has lessons we can learn much from, and British cultural studies acheived theoretical advances that are immensely useful in an American context.

That would be part of my answer to a question Jonathan Culler posed, with an air of whimsical hopelessness, at an October 1990, University of Oklahoma conference called 'Crossing the Disciplines: Cultural Studies in the 1990s': 'What is a professor of cultural studies supposed to know?' A professor of cultural studies might, in other words, be expected to know the history of the field. Professors of cultural studies need not agree with or emulate all the imperatives of British cultural studies, but they do have a responsibility to take a position on a tradition whose name they are borrowing. Moreover, people with strong disciplinary training who are now feeling their way toward cultural studies have something to gain from encounters with others who have already made such journeys. Leaving open what it will mean to realize cultural studies in America, British cultural studies nonetheless establishes some of what is at stake in theorizing culture in any historical moment.

After I made a similar argument at a regional Modern Language Association conference in 1988, my friend Vincent Leitch, who ought to know better, stood up in the audience, waving his arms as he scaled some Bunker Hill of the imagination, and declared that he 'thought we had thrown off the yoke of the British 200 years ago'. More recently again, at an Indiana University of Pennsylvania conference on theory and pedagogy in September of 1990 ('The Role of Theory in the Undergraduate Literature Classroom: Curriculum, Pedagogy, Politics'), I heard James Berlin prophesy, with a solemnity nowhere cognizant that he was predicting coals would be brought to Newcastle, that he was simply giving critical theory a new name, that cultural studies would miraculously turn our attention toward 'textuality in all its forms'. The claim was hardly new; indeed, this heralded revolution had already taken place under another name. In November 1990, a panel on cultural studies at the Pacific Coast Philological Association unself-consciously offered two models of cultural studies: as an opportunistic umbrella for English professors who want to study film or the graphic arts, and as a terrain of vague, metonymic sliding among all the competing theories on the contemporary scene. Cultural studies in that context was considered interchangeable with semiotics, the New Historicism, and other recent bodies of theory. And at an October 1990, University of Illinois panel on 'The Frontiers of Eighteenth-Century Studies', John Richetti, preening himself in the manner of a disciplinary cockatoo, announced with satisfaction that 'eighteenth-century people had been doing cultural studies all along'.

I could add other anecdotes. But these are enough to introduce the first points I want to make: Of all the intellectual movements that have swept the humanities in America since the 1970s, none will be taken up so shallowly, so opportunistically, so unreflectively, and so ahistorically as cultural studies. It is becoming the perfect paradigm for a people with no sense of history – born yesterday and born on the make. A concept with a long history of struggle over its definition, a concept born in class consciousness and in critique of the academy, a concept with a skeptical relationship to its own theoretical advances, cultural studies is often for English studies in the United States little more than a way of repackaging what we were already doing. At its worst, anyone who analyzes popular culture in any way whatsoever – or makes the slightest gesture toward contextualizing high cultural texts – can claim to be doing cultural studies. Of course, nothing can prevent the term *cultural studies* from coming to mean something very different in another time and place. But the casual dismissal of its history needs to be seen for what it is – an interested effort to depoliticize a concept whose whole prior history has been preeminently political and oppositional. The depoliticizing of cultural studies will no doubt pay off, making it more palatable at once to granting agencies and to conservative colleagues, administrators, and politicians, but only at the cost of blocking cultural studies from having any critical purchase on this nation's social life.

People interested in theory have often been accused by the right of facile opportunism. But the historical record actually suggests a very different and much more difficult pattern of struggle and mutual transformation for those invested in the major bodies of interpretive theory. Consider the deep personal transformation, the institutional changes, the wholesale reorientation of social understanding that accompanied the feminist revolution and its extension into the academy. Compare the series of times in this century when taking up Marxism has meant a comparable reorientation of one's whole understanding of society. Even a body of theory like psychoanalysis, which in its academic incarnations has avoided many of its imperatives toward personal and institutional change, has entailed a good deal more than adopting a special vocabulary. Even for academics, psychoanalysis has meant accepting a view of human agency that isolates them from their traditionally rationalist colleagues. In Britain and Australia, taking up cultural studies has followed the more radical pattern among these alternatives. But not for most disciplines in the United States.

Thus, one regularly hears graduate students and faculty members talk frankly about 'repackaging' themselves as cultural studies people. The disastrous academic job market, to be sure, along with most of the daily messages consumer capitalism sends out, encourages that sort of anxious cynicism about how one 'markets' one's self. Indeed, the job market in cultural studies – at least in English – gives a pretty good indication of how the discipline is going to take up this new paradigm. In 1989 a graduate student at Illinois – who is a specialist in feminist cultural studies and has a degree in communications – interviewed for cultural studies positions at the Modern Language Association convention. It was quite clear that many departments had not the faintest idea what cultural studies is. It was seen as a way to ask the dean for new money by pointing out an area where departments needed to catch up and a way for interviewers to make a display of ignorance look like canny interrogation: 'So what is all this cultural studies stuff about anyway?' What better way to ask uninformed questions than in the role of job interviewer? Who cares what serious cultural studies job candidates might think? If the answers are confusing or slightly threatening, the candidate will be out of the room in 20 minutes anyway. Some departments in effect conducted fake, exploratory cultural studies searches as a lazy way of finding out between cocktails a little bit about what the young people are up to these days. As the Illinois student found out, it all comes down to the final question: 'But can you fill in when we need someone to do the Milton course?' Meanwhile, the October 1993 *MLA Job Information List* includes such potentially disingenuous ads as those seeking a 'medieval literature/cultural studies' specialist or someone in 'literary and cultural studies before 1800'. Somehow I suspect familiarity with Stuart Hall's work will not be required of candidates for these positions.

At the Oklahoma conference, surprisingly enough, the only plenary speaker who made a full effort to define the project of cultural studies was J. Hillis Miller. Yet Miller, unfortunately, gave no evidence of having read any previous cultural studies work. The field thus presented no challenges, only opportunities. Apparently, the spread of American power and culture across the globe has led some Americans to believe Disneyland is the origin of the world. As someone who respects and admires much of Miller's early work, especially his elegant phenomenological readings of literary texts, I must in this context say that I just do not see its productive relation to the cultural studies tradition. A concern with ethics, central in his recent publications, is not the same as the long cultural studies engagement with left politics. And the internationalization of technology, which was at the center of his Oklahoma talk, 'The work of cultural criticism in the age of digital reproduction', in fact points to the importance of global politics and economics, the global dissemination and localization of cultural power – issues Miller thinks will be swept aside in a McLuhanesque spread of technology creating a common global culture. Indeed, it is only blindness to economics, power, and cultural differences that made it possible for Miller to present as an argument his offensive fantasy that everyone in the world will have a personal computer within a few years. Has he no sense of what life is like in South Central Los Angeles, let alone in Bangladesh or Somalia? I take this as the limit case, false cultural studies as its most ugly – a warrant for privileged American academics who are used to juggling theories to begin making claims about the material world as well, without ever looking at it.

The effect of Miller's appearance at the first plenary session at Oklahoma was to give the program an opening benediction, a benediction warranting a humanized, 'transnational', confidently democratized version of cultural studies as the new American world order. His key role in depoliticizing deconstruction was apparently to be repeated for cultural studies. I think it is relevant to recall that Miller once cosigned a letter (published in the *MLA Newsletter*) warning that an official Modern Language Association position against the undeclared Vietnam war might make all thirty thousand MLA members liable to a charge of treason. I bring this up not to question Miller's position on the war, but because the letter pointed specifically to his insistence on the separation between academic and political life, a separation that cultural studies has sought to overcome. What is at stake here is a definition of the nature, limits, and mission of cultural studies. Both in the letter and in his efforts to limit deconstruction to a depoliticized version of textual analysis, Miller has more than once had something to say about the cultural role of English studies. Those views are very much at odds with the heritage of cultural studies. They may well come to dominate the Americanization of cultural studies, but this is not a process that should proceed unremarked.

In this context, I do not think an uncritical argument for liberal diversity has much value. Welcoming the opening of the cultural studies field need not necessitate abandoning a debate about which enterprises do and do not deserve to use the cultural studies name, about what commitments cultural studies entails. That is not to say I think either the British, or the Americans and Australians and Canadians who have learned from them, can police the field. In fact, I think a more open, generous, democratic – but less critical – model will likely win the day. This much more inclusive vision probably *is* the future of cultural studies in the United States. I am merely trying to offer a challenge to that enterprise, even if it is a challenge likely to be swept aside by events.

At a paper presented at the annual Modern Language Association convention in December 1991, Janice Radway argued that attempts to define cultural studies and police its borders risk turning it into a 'ghostly discipline'. I would argue that cultural studies has always been exactly that – a ghostly discipline with shifting borders and unstable contents – and that it needs to continue being so. It is an ongoing set of traditions, a body of work whose contributors are in dialogue and debate with one another. Attempts to define its aims and limits, regularly overthrown, have been part of its history from the outset. It is also in significant ways antidisciplinary; that is, it responds critically to the exclusive parcelling out of objects of study to individual disciplines, to the way academic disciplines divide up the field of knowledge, and to the social impact of much academic work. To some degree, it puts forward its own contra-disciplinary forms of knowledge. Yet none of these stances comes into being in a universe free of disciplinary histories and constraints. Cultural studies defines its enterprise in part by positioning itself in relation to more traditional disciplines; in the process, it becomes something like a cluster of disciplines under erasure. Its own ghostly disciplinarity unsettles all other humanities and social science disciplines; that ghostly disciplinarity is, thus, a condition to be welcomed rather than feared.

The resistance to *any* effort to define cultural studies – a resistance unique to its Americanization – reflects a widespread and quite warranted dissatisfaction with the constraints of disciplinary knowledge. Especially for students and faculty in reactionary departments, cultural studies seems to offer the only realistic solution to a repressive work environment – literally overthrowing disciplinary knowledge. That cultural studies would then itself be occupied with defining its boundaries and deciding which activities should and should not be included under its umbrella seems a betrayal of the emotional needs cultural studies was counted on to meet. For some people, cultural studies is imagined as a kind of polymorphously free zone for any and all intellectual investments. That some individual or collaborative cultural studies work comes to be more widely recognized or valued than other projects seems in that context a violation of the undifferentiated zone of permission cultural studies was imagined to be. That some people defend their particular practices passionately seems equally suspect.

One can begin to see why some students are distressed at the emergence of cultural studies 'stars' in the field. It suggests a field hierarchized by reputation and achievement in much the way traditional disciplines are. But is there any alternative? Actually, there is, but only one: whole-sale anti-intellectualism. Some ordinarily canny cultural studies scholars are in fact willing to appeal to just that anti-intellectual strain in American cultural studies. Thus Gayatri Spivak was cheered when she opened her Oklahoma talk by disingenuously declaring how relieved she was to be presenting a lecture that was not destined to be immortalized in a book. Would she be even more relieved to have that state of affairs persist for a few years? Similarly, Radway met with applause when she declared at the Modern Language Association convention that the definition of cultural studies should be expanded to include a whole range of political activities. Presumably one could be 'in' cultural studies by virtue of joining campus demonstrations. Obviously, cultural studies allies itself with and helps to theorize political action. Cultural studies writers both inside and outside the academy are often involved in politics and concerned with the con-tribution their work makes to political action. But political action and cultural studies are not interchangeable. It should not be necessary to say this, but apparently it is: Cultural studies is a set of writing practices; it is a discursive, analytic, interpretive tradition.

Although none of the above was acknowledged openly at Oklahoma, these values churned under the surface. This helps explain the absence of references to the history of cultural studies from more than a few of the talks. Actually, the Oklahoma conference did have an implicit but unstated mission. Although some people were invited to participate, most of the papers were given by people who answered an open invitation to submit topics. Essentially everyone who volunteered to give a talk was placed on the program. The result was about 350 papers given in a hundred sessions over three days. So the conference, in effect, said, 'Here is a self-selected group of North Americans who declare themselves to be doing cultural studies. Let's see where they stand'. That is an interesting and potentially important mission, although its value was limited by being undeclared and, thus, never an explicit subject of discussion during the conference itself.

A cultural studies manifesto

From my perspective, a good deal of what was presented at Oklahoma simply did not qualify as cultural studies. Indeed, I felt it reflected the widespread dissolution and depoliticization of cultural studies in the United States. My experience at the Oklahoma and other conferences, my experience in co-organizing 'Cultural Studies Now and in the Future', a conference held at the University of Illinois in April of 1990, and my experience in co-editing *Cultural Studies*, a collection that grew out of that conference (see Grossberg *et al.* 1992) – together with teaching seminars in cultural studies and writing a book that tried to map out a cultural studies model of a literary genre – leads me to believe some generalizations about the cultural studies enterprise can and must be put forward. I think it is important to try to say both what cultural studies is and what it is not. Keeping in mind the well-known series of definitional articles written throughout the history of cultural studies, I would like to do so in the form of a series of numbered points, a first draft of one version of a cultural studies manifesto.

1. Cultural studies is not simply the close analysis of objects other than literary texts. Some English departments would like to believe that their transportable methods of close reading can make them cultural studies departments as soon as they expand the range of cultural objects they habitually study. Indeed, cultural studies is usually sold to English departments as part of the manifest destiny of the discipline. Our skills at close reading need to be extended to other cultural domains, it is often argued, lest these domains be left to the dubious care of student sub-cultures or the imprecise attention of lesser disciplines like speech communication. Similarly, some scholars like the sense of theoretical prestige that an unspecified cultural studies umbrella gives their close readings of non-traditional objects. Indeed, cultural studies often arrives in English departments in the form of an easy alliance between debased textuality and recent theory. But the immanent formal, thematic, or semiotic analysis of films, paintings, songs, romance novels, comic books, or clothing styles does not, in itself, constitute cultural studies. Perhaps that is why one department in 1993 advertised for a cultural studies specialist in 'theory and practice' – to avoid being deluged by writing samples consisting of decontextualized readings of films and popular novels. Of course, it is only in America that cultural studies theory and practice are in danger of being severed from one another.

2. Cultural studies does not, as some people believe, require that every project involve the study of artifacts of popular culture. On the other hand, people with ingrained contempt for popular culture can never fully understand the cultural studies project. In part that is because cultural studies has traditionally been deeply concerned with how all cultural production is sustained and determined by (and in turn influences) the broad terrain of popular common sense. Thus, no properly historicized cultural studies can cut itself off from that sense of 'the popular'.

3. Cultural studies also does not mean that we have to abandon the study of what have been historically identified as the domains of high culture, although it does challenge us to study them in radically new ways. Because every cultural practice has a degree of relative autonomy, every cultural practice potentially merits attention. But we need to recognize that autonomy is not a function of intrinsic merit and that it is never fixed and never more than relative. The notion of relative autonomy, of course, makes it properly impossible to repeat traditional claims that some cultural production transcends history.

4. Cultural studies is not simply the neutral study of semiotic systems, no matter how mobile and flexible those systems are made to be. There can be a semiotic component to cultural studies, but cultural studies and semiotics are not interchangeable. Cultural studies is not

satisfied with mapping sign systems. It is concerned with the struggles over meaning that reshape and define the terrain of culture. It is devoted, among other things, to studying the politics of signification.

5. Cultural studies is committed to studying the production, reception, and varied use of texts, not merely their internal characteristics. This is one of the reasons that cultural studies work is more difficult in periods when the historical record is either fragmentary or highly restrictive in class terms. So long as the difficulties are foregrounded, however, limited but ambitious and important cultural studies projects can be carried out for earlier periods of history.

6. Cultural studies conceives culture relationally. Thus, the analysis of an individual text, discourse, behavior, ritual, style, genre, or subculture does not constitute cultural studies unless the thing analyzed is considered in terms of its competitive, reinforcing, and determining relations with other objects and cultural forces. This task is also, it should be noted, an impossible one to complete in any given instance. But unless the constitutive and dissolving cultural relations are taken as a primary concern, the work is not, properly considered, cultural studies.

    This relational understanding of culture was one of cultural studies' earliest defining goals. Yet just what is meant by the relational study of culture has changed and evolved and abruptly shifted throughout the history of cultural studies, from Williams's efforts to describe culture as a whole way of life to the effort by Hall and others to adapt Antonio Gramsci's notion of a war of position to discursive and political analyses of contemporary Britain. One could, in fact, write the history of cultural studies in terms of how it conceives relationality and puts it into practice.

7. Cultural studies is not a fixed, repeatable methodology that can be learned and thereafter applied to any given cultural domain. It is the social and textual history of varying efforts to take up the problematic of the politics and meaning of culture. Its history mixes founding moments with transformative challenges and disputations. To do cultural studies is to take a place within that history.

8. Taking a place within that history means thinking of one's work in relation to cultural studies work on the politics of race. It means taking seriously the way feminism radically transformed cultural studies in the 1980s. And it means positioning one's work in relation to the long, complex, and often contentious history of cultural studies' engagements with Marxism, from Williams to Hall. To treat that history of engagements with Marxism as irrelevant, as many Americans do, is to abandon cultural studies for a fake practice that merely borrows its name.

9. Cultural studies is concerned with the social and political meaning and effects of its own analyses. It assumes that scholarly writing can and does do meaningful cultural work. To avoid facing this challenge and retreat into academic modesty (asserting that interpretive writing is impotent or irrelevant) or into claims of disinterested scholarship (protesting that political commitments vitiate scholarly objectivity) is

to hide from cultural studies' historical mission. A poststructuralist academic liberalism might lead one to argue that, because the political effects of discourse are indeterminate and unpredictable, scholarship and politics are best kept separate. Cultural studies might counter by arguing that such arguments do not free us from responsibility for the political meaning of scholarly work. Cultural studies typically accepts the notion that scholarship entails an engagement with and commitment to one's own historical context. The choice of what scholarly writing to do involves a decision about what one's most effective cultural and political intervention can be.

10. In much the same way, it must be emphasized that cultural studies does not simply offer students a liberal cornucopia of free choices. Cultural studies seeks to empower students to understand the social and political meaning of what they learn throughout the university. It urges them to reflect on the social meaning of disciplinary work and to decide what kinds of projects the culture needs most. A cultural studies pedagogy, thus, encourages a more critical relationship to cultural and political life. One small but necessary implication is that current debates and social practices need to be far more pervasive elements of many more courses than is now the case. Fields like history and literature that often teach pure period courses need to make detailed and specific analogies to present conditions. It is not enough to establish contexts for and relationships between discourses in earlier periods on the assumption that students will make the contemporary connections and work out the contemporary differences on their own. The Taylorized curriculum needs to be thoroughly undermined with the aim of gaining critical purchase on contemporary life.

11. Cultural studies has a responsibility to continue interrogating and reflecting on its own commitments. In fulfilling this task, however, cultural studies has inevitably had a history that is far from perfect. It needs now to critique its investment in what has been called the left's 'mantra of race, class, and gender', categories that are properly considered both in relation to one another and to the culture as a whole. It needs as well to question its recent fetishizing of 'fandom'. A ritualized, unreflective confession of fandom has become almost a requirement in some American cultural studies circles. Being a fan is not a prerequisite for doing cultural analysis. Invoking fandom without describing or specifying its conditions and its cultural construction has little intellectual value. Being a fan gives potential access to important insights; the challenge is to reflect on fandom and articulate what one learns from it.

12. Cultural studies is not required to approve a struggle for dominance among the disenfranchised. Multiculturalism in America sometimes degenerates into a competitive form of identiy politics in which oppressed and marginalized groups work to sort themselves out into a hierarchy based on their record of historical suffering. Cultural studies is not, however, simply a neutral field in which people can give free reign to their inclinations to play identity politics. Cultural studies is properly an enterprise in which people can explore their

race, ethnicity, or gender and articulate its relations with the larger culture. A properly relational and historical analysis suggests that no one group can claim the ultimate site of oppression. The progressive alliances we now need require us to avoid using previously marginalized identities to suppress debate and criticism. At the other end of the spectrum, multiculturalism restricts itself to an unrealistic, liberal ideal of diversity and difference without conflict. Cultural studies may thus establish alliances with multiculturalism but should resist being absorbed by it. Similarly, if multicultural work is to claim a place within cultural studies, it cannot ignore all the innovative work other cultural studies scholars have done on race, gender, and ethnicity.

13. The historicizing impulse in cultural studies is properly in dialogue with an awareness of the contemporary rearticulation of earlier texts, contexts, and social practices. In literary studies, New Historicism may sometimes succumb to an illusion of being able to address only the earlier historical period being analyzed, but cultural studies properly does not. Being historically and politically here and there – then and now – is part of the continuing, and thus necessarily newly theorized, burden of cultural studies. Nothing we rescue from forgetfulness or distortion stays the same. To study the present or the past is inevitably to rearticulate it to current interests; that is a problem and an opportunity to take up consciously, not to repress or regret. Cultural studies can never be a simple program of recovery; properly speaking, such programs are not cultural studies. Indeed, a conservative tendency to categorize every limited project of cultural recovery as cultural studies usually signals a high cultural contempt for the things being recovered. The tendency, for example, to classify efforts to recover minority literatures as cultural studies sometimes reflects an assumption that these literatures are inherently inferior or that they lack the aesthetic importance of the traditional canon.

14. In its projects of historical and contemporary analysis, cultural studies is often concerned as well with intervening in the present and with encouraging certain possible futures rather than others. Thus, as cultural studies people reflect on the simultaneously undermined and reinforced status of the nation-state in different parts of the world, they are often also concerned with the future status of nationhood. An interest in how high technology has changed our lives may be combined with an effort to shape its future impact. The opportunities that fragmented postmodern identities offer are not only to be studied, but also to be exploited. A study of the multiple meanings of gender in a given moment may lead to reflection on how our lives may be gendered in the future. For many scholars outside cultural studies, such double investments are to be avoided. In cultural studies they can be at the center of the enterprise.

15. Cultural studies accepts the notion that the work of theorizing its enterprise is inescapably grounded in contemporary life and current politics. New social and political realities require fresh reflection and debate on the cultural studies enterprise, no matter what historical

period one is studying. Although it is possible to overstate the phenomenon of a local theorizing grounded in current social realities because such a process involves a rearticulation of previously existing theories, it is nonetheless true that major changes in cultural studies have regularly come from an effort to understand and intervene in new historical conditions. From a cultural studies perspective, then, one never imagines that it is possible to theorize for all times and places. Not only our interpretations but also our theories are produced for the world in which we live.

16. Cultural studies within the academy is inescapably concerned with and critical of the politics of disciplinary knowledge. It is not simply interdisciplinary in the model of liberal diversity and idealized communication. This means that the nontrivial institutionalization of cultural studies within traditional academic disciplines is impossible unless those disciplines dismantle themselves. A first step, for a discipline like English, is to make a commitment to hiring faculty members who do not have degrees from English departments. Otherwise there is little chance that English departments will even admit that literature does not acquire its meaning primarily from its own autonomous traditions, let alone take up the general problematics of culture. Yet while English departments have much to gain from expanding their enterprises to include cultural studies, it is less clear what cultural studies has to gain from being institutionalized in English departments. If it is to be institutionalized at all, cultural studies might be better served by a variety of programs outside traditional departments.

Not every individual cultural studies book or essay can fulfill all the conditions in these 16 points. But a successful cultural studies project should position itself in relation to these concerns. When it does not take them on directly, they should be implicit in the project's interests, terms, and references. These, it seems to me, represent some of the key aims and imperatives growing out of 30 years of cultural work. These points are effectively part of the cultural studies paradigm and part of the cultural studies challenge to the contemporary world. Because they are focused on the ways cultural studies has and is likely to continue to change and develop, they are less rigid than the form of a numbered manifesto may lead some readers to think. Indeed, to take up these points is to write in such a way as to engage in a continual interrogation of what cultural studies is and can be. Thus, I have articulated this manifesto at a level of theoretical generality that does not totalize and synthesize all cultural studies projects. These principles do not attempt to anticipate the specific work of local theorizing. To place oneself in relation to the history of cultural studies is precisely to recognize that the practices of cultural studies are not given in advance. They are always to be rethought, rearticulated to contemporary conditions. That imperative to continuing political renewal and struggle is part of what cultural studies has bequeathed to us.

Cultural studies now and in the future

Such a process of negotiation and debate over what is and is not cultural studies has to take place if cultural studies is to have any intellectual power and political effectiveness. Wider alliances need to be formed, but not every alliance is worth the potential price in dissolution and compromise. Perhaps I sound like a Third Period Stalinist who is not ready to accept the Popular Front coalition of the late 1930s. But we need to remember that the broad, inclusive alliance of the Popular Front had a political mission and a political reason for the compromises it made – the struggle against fascism. Those on the left in America and those committed to progressive projects in humanities departments in universities have a related mission – the struggle against the global inequities inherited from the Reagan-Bush era, the struggle against the New Right's views of American education and American culture, the growing articulation of discomfort and anger over racism and sexism as universities' efforts to become more 'culturally diverse' take hold. It is our task to make American institutions nervous about cultural studies. One boundary worth drawing around the cultural studies alliance is between those who will and those who will not join that struggle. The price of depoliticizing the cultural studies project is not a price we should be willing to pay. If the bargain is that we may have cultural studies so long as we do not criticize the government in our classrooms, we should reject it. Cultural studies does not need to render unto Caesar what Caesar thinks belongs to him.

Caesar, however, is in the midst of having his say in any case. Over the past several years, the phrase *cultural studies* has been taken up by journalists and politicians of the New Right in America as one of a cluster of scare terms – the others include *multiculturalism* and *deconstruction* – that have been articulated together to signal a crisis in higher education and American intellectual life generally. One fair response for cultural studies people would be to work to disarticulate these terms, already effectively welded together in popular common sense. Cultural studies is not multiculturalism and is not deconstruction, we might argue, although cultural studies welcomes some versions of multiculturalism and shares with deconstruction sympathies for the general project of poststructuralism. Unfortunately, it seems likely that the qualifications in the second half of the sentence pretty much undo any useful work the denials in the first half of the sentence might do in the public arena. These are distinctions we need to draw for our students and colleagues, but we are unlikely to be able to do so successfully for the media or the public. These are different intellectual traditions, but their points of partial correspondence are sufficient to convince people they are part of the same general cultural pattern. Our audiences, in other words, will smell a rat. Because we can do little now to resist that moment of recognition, it might be better to welcome it. Cultural studies, in other words, might well set out to *be that rat*.

The creature I have in mind is a largely urban animal who is wary, focussed on local conditions, and willing to eat almost anything – an animal very much like cultural studies. He or she is a political animal attuned to assuring the survival of his or her interests. Now that recent theory as a whole has been accused of being politicized – something many theorists of the seventies and eighties would themselves be hard put to demonstrate – cultural studies can willingly occupy the site of theory as politics. Now that efforts to open up the canon and efforts to expand the cultural reach of academia's field of vision have been scandalized for abandoning the transcendent and eternal standards of Western high culture – something not everyone involved in canon revision or multiculturalism would want to embrace – cultural studies can cheerfully occupy the site of standard-free omnivorousness. Everyone else may choose to respond to the right's assault by filling and backsliding and denying they are now or ever have been political in their aims or interests. Cultural studies can step in and be the very thing the right loves to hate. Indeed, those cultural studies professors who are tenured should do their best to attract the bulk of the criticism about politicized pedagogy and scholarship.

Cultural studies has never meant only one thing, and it is unlikely to mean only one thing in the future. It may, then, be necessary for individuals to adopt different cultural studies identities in different contexts. When strategically useful, they can be deconstructionists or multiculturalists. All the while, however, they should be reiterating that the real villain is cultural studies. That should certainly thin the ranks of cultural studies' fair weather friends. More important, it should focus on a body of work (cultural studies) the political responsibilities and effects the field has traditionally worked to understand.

The time has come when the political meaning of teaching and scholarship can no longer be avoided. Attacks on feminist, minority, multicultural, and theoretical research in the academy are helping to discredit those values and constituencies in the general culture as well. A delegitimated university thus does double duty: It oversees its own increasingly curtailed and embattled mission, while serving as an object lesson that undermines progressive thought throughout the culture. Meanwhile, the heyday of free time for research in the humanities and social sciences has past. It was a spinoff of the cold war, and the cold war has ended. If the New Right in America has its way, the only time available for research will be that funded by industry. If universities give up their role of social critique, only conservative think tanks will remain to fund social critique over the long term. At the same time, access to higher education will be steadily restricted to more wealthy families. Public elementary and secondary education, increasingly vocational, will be reserved for the poor. A divisive struggle for power among minorities will only facilitate that agenda. We need relational analyses of the political meaning of the work all of us do, we need careful disarticulations of the elements the right has joined to win popular consent, and we need unsentimental readings of the possibilities for alliances among those with the most to lose spiritually and economically. That is a task historically appropriate for a politicized cultural studies that devotes itself to the kinds of cultural analysis the society needs.

Note

An earlier version of this essay, entitled 'Always already cultural studies: Two conferences and a manifesto', appeared in the *Journal of the Midwest Modern Language Association*. Used by permission of the Midwest Modern Language Association.

17

The Americanization of cultural studies

Joel Pfister

Recently I attended a conference entitled 'Cultural Studies Now and in the Future', sponsored by the Unit for Criticism and Interpretive Theory at the University of Illinois, Urbana-Champaign, and organized by Cary Nelson and Lawrence Grossberg. During his lecture, Stuart Hall commented critically on the proceedings and warned that cultural studies in the US is in 'a moment of danger'. Shortly after he began to take questions, some members of the audience of several hundred erupted in protest, claiming among other things that the conference positioned them as 'fans' who were meant to support a star-making (or star-polishing) machinery. Some who were infuriated with the event drafted and distributed a manifesto called 'Hypocrisy in cultural studies', which posed the question: 'Is there any point in establishing a radical voice which only duplicates those structures it seeks to displace?'

'Mixed impressions' describes my own take on the conference, and the term also applies, though for different reasons, to my reading of the first book-length overview of cultural studies, Patrick Brantlinger's *Crusoe's Footprints* (1990). In this essay, I hope to work out the implications of some of these impressions and place them in a clear theoretical and historical frame. Thus my aim is to return to and review some key contributions to the British tradition of cultural studies and, by examining the conference, Brantlinger's book, and other sources, to trace the forms that the 'Americanization' of the field seems to be taking. In what follows, I will situate one important school of British cultural studies in its political-intellectual setting; review the conference and *Crusoe's Footprints* as ideological symptoms of the 'Americanization' of British cultural studies [. . .] and close with some thoughts on cultural studies as a social practice, one undertaken by the academic wing of the professional-managerial class in this country.

Unlearning the Old Left: the political work of British CS

In his review of Raymond Williams' *Politics and Letters* (1979), Stuart Hall concluded, 'It is not a book for the religious'. At the Illinois conference, Hall profiled cultural studies in the same way and underscored how crucial it is to keep the field 'open'. Hall learned how open its political project *had* to be in the mid- and late 1970s when feminism and concerns with race and racism *'broke* through the windows' of the Birmingham Center for Contemporary Cultural Studies (CCCS), while he served as its director. The CCCS Women's Studies Group published their anthology *Women Take Issue* (1978) as an 'intervention' which would not only put women on the agenda but force a political-intellectual rethinking of the 'field' and 'object' of cultural studies. Next, *The Empire Strikes Back* (1982) and Paul Gilroy's *There Ain't No Black in the Union Jack* (1985) 'intervened' as 'corrective' to the 'invisiblity of "race"' within cultural studies. Recently Tony Fry has suggested that the class-stratified students and staff of CCCS learned about the dynamics of class within as well as outside their own institution. Thus Richard Johnson, who took over as director when Hall left for the Open University in 1979, had good reason to describe the field not as a doctrinal 'research programme for a particular party or tendency' but rather as a 'political-intellectual stance' made 'possible because the politics which we aim to create is not yet fully formed'.[1]

Yet it is important to underscore that this understanding of British cultural studies as an open, though not pluralistic, project has its roots not in some pretence to 'value-free scholarship' but in what Alan O'Connor has termed 'political commitment'. This is clear from both Hall's opening statement as founding editor of *New Left Review* (*NLR*) in 1960 and his recent contributions to *New Times* (1989), a collection of essays most of which were originally published in *Marxism Today*. 'We are convinced that politics, too narrowly conceived, has been a main cause of the decline of socialism in this country', he wrote in 1960. In arguing that the rebuilding of a cold war socialist movement requires 'cultural and social' as well as 'economic and political' strategic critique, he stressed that the study of 'the cinema or teen-age culture in *New Left Review*' is not for purposes of appearing trendy but must be grasped as indispensable to a knowledge of 'imaginative resistances of people who have to live within capitalism'. Early anthologies published by CCCS under Hall's directorship, such as *Resistance Through Rituals* (1976) and *Policing the Crisis* (1978), joined by Paul Willis's *Learning to Labour* (1977) and Dick Hebdige's *Subculture* (1979), carried on this project.

Hall's stress on *culture* grew out of the pressing need to unlearn some of the assumptions, strategies, and goals of the Old Left: 'There is no law which says that the Labour Movement, like a great inhuman engine, is going to throb its way into socialism.' Under Hall's editorship (1960–61), *NLR* featured articles by contributors such as E.P. Thompson, Raymond Williams, and Richard Hoggart next to advertisements for Left cafés and listings of Left discussion groups around Britain.[2] The New Left's cultural studies was indivisible from the project of regrouping in response to the predicament of socialism within the crisis of cold war capitalism.

British cultural studies is currently rethinking the possibilities of political critique and organization in magazines like *Marxism Today*. Stuart Hall and Martin Jacques' *New Times* collects essays whose object of study is not 'culture' per se (for the interdisciplinary academic challenge it poses) but, more specifically, an epoch of advanced capitalism, a 'post-Fordism' which supercedes what Gramsci labelled 'Fordism'. The strategic question for the contributors is how post-Fordism (of which Thatcherism is a manifestation) has altered 'the world in which the Left has to operate'. 'If "post-Fordism" exists,' writes Hall, much as he did in *NLR* decades before, 'then it is as much a description of cultural as of economic change.' Here, too, Hall makes it clear that cultural study is driven by political necessity: 'Can a socialism of the twenty-first century revive, or even survive, which is wholly cut off from the landscapes of popular pleasures, however contradictory and "commodified" a terrain they represent? Are we thinking dialectically enough?' Dialectical thinking in 'new times' must take for its critique 'cultural and subjective dimensions' and must recognize, for example, not only that gender is constructed and 'deployed politically' in ways which must be delineated but that 'social practices', 'forms of domination', and even the 'politics of the Left' are 'inscribed in and to some extent secured by sexual identity and positioning'. A reluctance to acknowledge and study these intersections, Hall adds, is nothing less than a strategic failure, because without an understanding of them 'we simply do *not* have a language of sufficient explanatory power' which illuminates both 'the institutionalisation of power' and 'the secret sources of resistances to change'.[3] Richard Johnson's statement that British cultural studies is not in any *doctrinal* sense a 'research programme for a particular party' is true, but it underplays the fact that cultural studies' New Left-inspired project has been, historically, 'to create' or recreate a (socialist) politics 'not yet fully formed'.

As Hall and Johnson note in their essays on intellectual developments within CCCS, the Center was drawn early on to E.P. Thompson's *The Making of the English Working-Class* (1963) and Raymond Williams' *The Long Revolution* (1961) (the first New Left) precisely because these works recognized culture as a productive, determining force in its own right and not merely as a reflection or expression of the economic 'base'. But it was the translations of the work of the Frankfurt School, Walter Benjamin, Louis Althusser, and Antonio Gramsci in the 1960s and 1970s (by the second New Left) that refashioned cultural study at CCCS. Althusser's concept of 'overdetermination', for instance, challenged Old Left assumptions about 'totalizing' and 'totality' and the role of culture in causality: 'A social transformation is not a "totality" of the essential type, in which there is simple "identity between levels", with the superstructural levels the mere "epiphenomena" of the objective laws governing "the economic base",' writes Hall. 'It is, rather a unity of a necessarily complex type – an "ensemble" which is always the result of many determinations.' The Althusserian structuralist 'moment' of the 1970s prompted CCCS to retheorize 'culture' as a relatively autonomous *'signifying* practice' and 'not so much the product of "consciousness" as the conscious forms and categories through which historically definite forms of consciousness were produced'. This theoretical perspective was more subtle and comprehensive than the Old Left's explanatory emphasis on what Richard Johnson has termed the 'more brutally-obvious "determinations" – especially mechanisms like competition, monopolistic control, and imperial expansion'. The

New Left challenge to the Old Left sets the context for Hall's recent observation that CCCS always approached Marxism as a problem rather than the solution.[4]

Old Left constructions of 'history', therefore, had to be rehistoricized and its categories retheorized, based on different concepts of totality, determination, and historical subjects. The Old Left labor history (for example, Maurice Dobb and Dona Torr) focus on the category of class and on members of the working-class as the universal subjects of history functioned, as Johnson notes, to classify both 'a sphere of legitimate politics and a "non-political" realm'. This 'history' produced a 'truth' that was both too narrow and unstrategic for New Left cultural studies in the 1970s, for their project had to acknowledge 'new' historical agents (who were not new!).[5]

The influences of Roland Barthes, Althusser, Jacques Lacan, and Gramsci pushed forward a critique of assumptions about access to 'lived experience' in Hoggart's *The Uses of Literacy* (1961), Williams' *The Long Revolution*, Thompson's *Making of the English Working-Class*, and other histories and ethnographies. Thompson's *The Poverty of Theory* (1978) retaliated by polemicizing against Althusser and the *NLR* policy of privileging 'theory' which Thompson felt was seducing the younger Left in Britain away not only from 'lived experience' but from 'lived' political activity. As Hall put it in his exchange with Thompson, 'experience' must be thought of as a *category* rather than an essence to be discovered in 'the people', a category which must be 'interrogated for its complex interweaving of real and ideological elements'. Or as Johnson framed it, 'Concrete social individuals are always already constructed as class-ed, sex-ed, and age-ranked subjects, have already entered into complex cultural forms, already have a complexly formed subjectivity'.

At this same juncture, when history and theory were in danger of being perceived as separate or even antithetical enterprises, the Women's Studies Group and the race and racism group pressed the Center to reevaluate its 'theoreticist' (to use Hall's word) and historicist occlusions. The outcome was a commitment to a more theoretically informed history and historically informed theoretical practice, which was thought through in CCCS anthologies like *Working Class Culture* (1979) and *Making Histories* (1982). 'The reintroduction of history is not a minimal aim', Paul Gilroy noted, envisioning a more complex and inclusive historicizing of 'history': 'Racism rests on the ability to contain blacks in the present.' '[The] term historical,' as Hall observed, 'is taken, simple-mindedly, to refer to the past, but we have attempted rigorously, to break with this disabling, inert definition.'[6]

What is patent about these Birmingham anthologies is their political-intellectual-pedagogical commitment to enabling their readers to think 'dialectically enough'. If cultural studies is at a critical juncture, what Hall termed a 'moment of danger', I wonder if it might not also be the moment to make more of this Birmingham work available to a US audience, as a crucial reminder of the breadth of activity British cultural studies has undertaken. Several US republishing projects in particular would be desirable: (1) collections of Hall's and Johnson's essays, (2) *Culture, Media, Language: Working Papers in Cultural Studies, 1972–79* (1980), along with another volume of selected essays from CCCS anthologies, and (3) an anthology of essays from the cultural studies journal *Screen Education*. But if such publishing projects are ever undertaken, an effort must be made to situate these writings in the particular historical 'conjuncture' (a term I will discuss later) which produced their debates and which their debates sought to transform, rather than reifying them as 'classic' or (even worse) 'authentic' British cultural studies (i.e. the 'real' way to do cultural studies). These debates and advances must be seen just as Cornel West recently profiled Hall: as examples, rather than static models, of 'how to keep political work alive in an age of shrinking possibilities'.[7]

Americanization: towards a post-political cultural studies

At the Illinois conference, Hall raised three points to clarify what the 'moment of danger' is for cultural studies on these shores. First, he pointed out that British cultural studies never underwent a 'moment' of extreme professionalization and institutionalization like the one that is already a determining force in US cultural studies. Second, he expressed concern that if the American academy does to cultural studies what it did to French post-structuralism, then 'it would formalize questions of power' and constitute power solely as a problem of 'textuality'. Hall went on in good Foucauldian fashion to affirm that power is always already lodged in textuality, but the force of his admonition remained. Third, he commented diplomatically on the extraordinary 'fluency' of some of the presenters, hinting that 'fluency' should be a means to an end not an end in itself (more on these observations later).[8]

In 1988, Lawrence Grossberg suggested that the selling (out) of US cultural studies was well advanced, and that its success story has 'all the ingredients of a made-for-tv movie'. Manuscripts eagerly solicited, books pouring off presses, and cultural studies job openings all suggest that the field in the US 'appears to be the latest signifier of what was called "critical theory" in a variety of academic organisations'. Grossberg is an American graduate of CCCS who usually writes about rock music (e.g. 'MTV: swinging on a (postmodern) star', in I. Angus and S. Jhally, *Cultural Politics in Contemporary America*, 1987). He is perhaps the most active promoter of the cultural studies boom in the US. His apprehensions about the future of US cultural studies are voiced in a book entitled *It's a Sin* (1988).

Grossberg's promotion of cultural studies has centered on Stuart Hall and has targeted Communications departments (where cultural studies is more often debated than in English departments). In a recent issue of *Critical Studies in Mass Communications* (*CSMC*), a journal which has become a regular forum for debate over cultural studies, contributors have charged Grossberg himself with the 'sin' of swinging on the (postmodern) cultural studies star. Alan O'Connor – whose new book on Raymond Williams and whose new collection of Williams' writings will be bought and read in the light of this (postmodern) star – characterizes much of Grossberg's (re)construction of cultural studies as a 'postmodernist' 'theoretical bricolage' and claims that Grossberg 'has lost . . . [Stuart

Hall's] sense of the rootedness of communication processes in social reproduction and politics'. For O'Connor, Grossberg's work is of a piece with 'conferences in the United States' which produce cultural studies as 'various types of postmodern theorizing'. Academics 'who rarely have any connection to existing political and cultural movements and are somewhat surprised that this might even be possible' are institutionalizing US cultural studies.[9] What O'Connor misses most in this (postmodern) cultural studies is political commitment.

Grossberg has in fact been attentive to the *specific* ways in which cultural studies might get de-politicized in the US. For example, at the Illinois conference Tony Bennett succinctly caricatured the celebration-of-plea-sure-as-resistance approach to consumers of popular culture as 'sleuthing for subversiveness where one would least expect to find it'. In *It's a Sin*, Grossberg (citing similar critiques by Judith Williamson and Meaghan Morris) concurs: 'The fact that specific cultural practices are pleasurable, even empowering, does not tell us anything about the political valences of such pleasures, or the possibilities of articulating such empowering moments to explicit political positions.' Yet in *CSMC* three Communications scholars recently argued that Grossberg, as well as John Fiske (a British mass media critic who now teaches in the US), textualize and celebrate consumers' responses which are not discernably 'oppositional', or if occasionally 'oppositional', certainly do not translate into 'direct thinking about and behavior in politics'. Todd Gitlin, in an indirect response to their critique, also registers skepticism about a cultural studies which frames 'style' as resistance: 'It is pure sloppiness to conclude that culture or pleasure *is* politics.'[10]

Thus there is a growing uneasiness in Communications departments with a US cultural studies seemingly deracinated from politics in the *narrow* sense. In the British Labour party and Communist party context, Hall stresses that *culture* is a necessary political concern, but in the US, with few viable narrowly political alternatives apparently available, the apprehension is that US cultural studies will turn into a de-politicized 'politics' of the 'cultural'. What Hall and others witnessed in Illinois, in some of the presentations and discussions, seemed to be the production of a *post-political* cultural studies which fogged over the ground of contradictions that makes cultural study imperative. The word 'contradiction' was scarcely uttered in many of the talks.

The conference had many strengths, especially in global emphasis: 'Think globally and act locally', advised Paul Gilroy. Graeme Turner, an Australian, and Tony Bennett, who now teaches in Australia, made it clear that British cultural studies cannot be lifted from its context, universalized, and applied automatically to another national set of conditions and contradictions. Thus there was much evidence in Illinois of an *enabling* cultural studies.

However, the emergence of cultural studies as *interpretive performance* was also apparent and reminiscent of post-structuralist interpretive performances, stylish in the early 1980s. Richard Johnson, in reconceptualizing cultural studies as the historical analysis of forms of subjectivity, has referred to the need for a 'post-post-structuralist' theory of subjectivity. The term 'post-post-structuralist' has been picked up by American academics as a synonym for cultural studies. Cultural studies has much to learn from post-structuralism, not least of all because, as Bruce Robbins has noted, it has dragged 'oppositional discourse into the field of fire' by making visible the 'oppression of older categories like "race" and "woman" and "the people"'. But what many viewed, on occasion, on stage in Illinois was akin to what Stuart Hall had seen at CCCS years before when seminars had become both too big and overly 'theoreticist': discussion 'depended too much on prior knowledge, privileged access to the discourse and a false search for abstractions at a rarefied level'. Hall's political-intellectual response to this circumstance in Illinois was a plea for 'intellectual modesty' and a reminder that cultural studies is 'deadly serious'.[11] What was also obvious was that some (postmodern) stars-in-the-making were indeed 'formalizing questions of power'.

There was something else post-modern about the conference as well: an absence of a sustained engagement with the matter of history. The only panel devoted to the role of history in cultural studies featured Carolyn Steedman and Catherine Hall, and it was held in the evening of the last day.[12] Both panelists wondered about the significance of history being left until a time when about two-thirds of the audience had already departed. Catherine Hall began by voicing criticism of the 'excess of textuality' manifest in some of the conference presentations and pleaded that history not be relegated to the status of backdrop. Her talk, 'Positioning missionaries: history and theory', was an example of how to study a complicated historical 'conjuncture' – Jamaica, 1830s–1850s. In this period, missionaries, discursive constructions of 'Englishness', shifts in domestic ideology, and native Jamaicans intersected in complex ways to produce a new (not unresisted) form of racism. After the presentation, one person asked her to define what was 'cultural studies' in her lecture (besides the 'deconstruction' of Englishness), while another asked where the 'politics' was in her analysis. Such questions betokened, in my view, a post-history 'presentism', a failure to see that history is inseparable from *contemporary* cultural studies. It would be hyperbolic to say that history was a thing of the past at the conference, but after the discussion following the final lectures the thought crossed my mind.

Marx's footsteps to Crusoe's footprints: the liberalization of CS

The wide-ranging bibliography in Patrick Brantlinger's *Crusoe's Footprints: Cultural Studies in Britain and America* will prove useful to anyone who wishes to learn more about this field and some of the debates that animate it. Brantlinger, who has been director of Victorian Studies at Indiana University for many years, has done much reading and research in cultural studies. I find the book to be of greater value as an elaborated bibliographic essay than as a crucial statement on what is at stake in the field. It will also be of interest to readers as a symptom of how cultural studies may be 'Americanized', as it is institutionalized and professionalized by the US academy. Brantlinger's construction of cultural studies is not of the post-political speaking-in-tongues variety I occasionally viewed in Illinois; rather it is fundamentally a liberal packaging of the field. Brantlinger's liberalism can be best seen in his vision of multiculturalism, the humanities-in-crisis, and the English department-in-crisis.

The Crusoe of Brantlinger's title is, I take it, the white, middle-class, male professor who acknowledges that Friday's footprints are his own. The 'main lesson' of cultural studies, Brantlinger tells us, is that 'in order to understand ourselves, the discourses of "the Other" – of all the others – is that which we most urgently need to hear'. And the 'goal of cultural workers' is 'an authentically democratic mass culture uniting people through recognition of and respect for differences'.[13] But Brantlinger should be reminded that there are different kinds of multiculturalism which require sorting out. In 'Schooling in Babylon' (1982), an essay which Brantlinger knows, Hazel Carby's analysis of multicultural policies introduced to 'liberalize' English secondary education in racially mixed communities led her to conclude: 'Multiculturalism has reacted to racism as if it were limited to a struggle over forms of representation – a struggle over images – in an attempt to disguise the social relations of domination in which it is situated and which it reproduces.' Brantlinger's humanist-in-crisis multiculturalism veers toward the 'pluralistic model' of multicultural ideology which, Carby writes, 'implies that racial prejudice and racial discrimination would come to an end through an education in cultural diversity'. The racisms that Catherine Hall analyzes in 'Positioning missionaries' and that Gilroy examines in *There Ain't No Black in the Union Jack* are, however, not simply a matter of attitude which can be remedied by a more 'humanistic' representation of diversity; the racisms they study are embedded in complex economic practices, domestic ideologies, and cultural formations.

Both Stuart Hall and Brantlinger see cultural studies as emerging, in part, from a 'crisis in the humanities'. But if Hall's cultural studies response to this crisis is, at the most fundamental level, a radical effort to explain and act upon the postwar predicament of British socialism in late capitalism, Brantlinger's interest in cultural studies seems more narrowly academic. Brantlinger, sounding a bit like a college promotional brochure, wishes to use cultural studies to make 'the humanities disciplines . . . genuinely human, engaged, and engaging'. The struggle is to make the liberal arts truly liberal: 'The *liberal* arts – the humanities and social sciences, *must* be "liberal" – even "liberating" – or else degenerate into mere hypocrisy of obfuscation.' This is closer to the pedagogical liberalism of William Cain and Gerald Graff (whom Brantlinger cites often in his first chapter) than it is to the politics of Hall. Brantlinger introduces the possibility of 'the revolutionary overthrow of capitalism' but, revealingly, as 'the only conceivable way of solving the ongoing "crisis of the humanities"'.[14] That Branglinger is a supporter of British cultural studies is unquestionable, but that he is often translating it into liberal terms is also clear. If the British constituency of cultural studies in the 1980s was, in part, comprised of readers of *The New Socialist* and *Marxism Today*, who will be the constituency of US cultural studies, and what will they expect? It is likely that *Crusoe's Footprints* will help produce their expectations, and this makes me uneasy.

Cultural studies also appeals to Brantlinger as an interdisciplinary 'critical theory' (which is the name change that Grossberg forecast in *It's a Sin*). Four out of his five chapters begin with literary references. In cultural studies Brantlinger sees the theoretically informed, multicultural English department of the future, where Frederick Douglass's *Narrative* would not '*displace* other great works of American literature' such as *Moby Dick* or *Walden*, but would 'certainly take its place alongside them'. (Friday and Crusoe live happily ever after.) Stuart Hall, then, is a dialectical materialist who analyzes culture because it is politically pressing to do so. Brantlinger is mainly a literary culturalist with an intellectual appreciation for interdisciplinary cultural studies that has a materialist base.

What I find surprising is that this appreciation did not lead him to cite the work of scholars whose work really bridges cultural studies and Victorian Studies, such as Catherine Hall, Nancy Armstrong, Mary Poovey, and Judith Walkowitz. Notwithstanding these omissions and other major ones (e.g. Janet Wolff, Joan Scott, Susan McClary, Stanley Aronowitz, Hal Foster, Douglas Crimp), Brantlinger offers an informative sweep of who's who and who's doing what in cultural studies today.[15] [. . .]

Romanticizing 'intervention': cultural studies by the PMC

I wish to move towards a conclusion by echoing the emphasis of Richard Ohmann in *Politics of Letters* (1987), that those who practice cultural studies in the US academy are members of what Barbara Ehrenreich and John Ehrenreich call the 'professional-managerial class', a class 'whose major function in the social division of labor' is historically 'the reproduction of capitalist culture and capitalist class relations'. It is crucial to think about how constructions and promotions of US cultural studies will be complicit in this process of 'reproduction'. Which brings up the question: if cultural studies is practiced by the PMC, who is it *for*? At the Illinois conference, Cornel West, evidently drawing on Russell Jacoby's much debated *The Last Intellectuals* (1987), observed that the waning of the public sphere functions to displace political debate and cultural critique into the academy.[40] Will a US cultural studies be primarily comprised of debates among academicians? Thus far this seems to be the case.

As lucid and compelling as Stuart Hall's writing can be, it often veers into language familiar only to those with some background in critical theory. A curious and often powerful style of writing has emerged in the academic era of cultural studies: one that can be clear, engaging, conversational, and public, and yet theoretical or technical to the uninitiated when 'conjunctures', 'negotiations', 'interventions', and 'interrogations' are suddenly dropped into sentences with little or not effort to define them and no shift in tone. Despite the praiseworthy let's-not-speak-in-tongues impulse such language signals that the author has no doubt about who is going to be reading her or his writing. With whom are such 'interventions' intervening? Several of my friends (some in the academy) expressed interest in reading this essay to learn about 'cultural studies', but they also asked if they would be able to understand it.

What I shall call the 'discourse of intervention' should be seen as potentially problemtic, particularly in cultural studies on this side of the Atlantic. Words like 'intervention' and 'interrogation' are meant to signify the cultural studies critic's serious 'oppositional' stance towards hegemonic traditions of knowledge production. These two words carry some obvious militaristic and disciplinary connotations: armies intervene and spies are interrogated; police intervene and suspects are interrogated. 'Intervention' and 'interrogation' have given critical theorists in US English departments a powerful self-image and sense of mission. Personally, I am delighted that literary critics in both Britain and the US are 'intervening' in a literary criticism and 'interrogating' a canon that have frequently been misrepresented as having no political agenda. But I am also bothered because this discourse of intervention seems to *romanticize* the critic's academic role as sufficiently 'oppositional'. Critics in the US and those who visit the US are able to command steep fees for lecturing on or writing up their latest thoughts on oppositional practices and interventions. Yet when the implications of this professionalized 'opposition' are thought through, the cultural studies approach suggests that a good deal more must be done than cultural *studies*.

The audience eruption at the Illinois conference made it clear to me that cultural studies is potentially explosive, in part, because those who do take its oppositional critiques seriously come to realize that studying culture in the academy is only one force which potentially contributes to changing culture. During his tenure as director of CCCS, Hall understandably insisted on the importance of 'studying seriously' rather than being 'a good activist' because '[w]hat the movement needed from us as part of their struggles of resistance and transformation . . . was what we had in our heads'.[41] What is needed in the US now is certainly not a postmodern romanticization of the 'political-intellectual' but a greater *historical* understanding of the social, political, and academic conditions within which a discourse of 'intervention' seemed to make sense for those British intellectuals who practiced cultural studies because it was unmistakably one necessary dimension of a *larger intervention* underway. Of course this 'conjunctural' inquiry, should it be undertaken, might also suggest that British cultural studies, faced with grim prospects of social change, has romanticized its own interventionist practices, capabilities, and concrete social achievements.

When I think back to the lists of Left discussion groups and advertisements for Left cafés which abounded in *NLR* during its first two years, I find it telling that, nowadays, there is little discussion of organizing in cultural studies publications and conferences. Much of the PMC cultural studies work I read *does* seem distant from the contradictions and concerns that are written about in *In These Times* and books like Jeremy Brecher and Tim Costello's anthology, *Building Bridges: The Emerging Grassroots Alliance of Labor and Community* (1990). In both 1960 and 1989 Hall was apprehensive about politics being 'too narrowly conceived' by the British Left, and yet American Communications scholars, like Gitlin, when confronted with a very *cultural* style of US cultural studies, caution that 'politics in the strict sense' must not be forgotten. In *Another Tale to Tell* (1990), Fred Pfeil states his intention to contribute together in new ways to reach them', and he regards his writing as one area of his political work.[42] How strategic does a US cultural studies wish to be, and should its 'oppositional' studies be channeled into writing about a collective project in detailed ways? I think that we can interpret the muting of this concern within US cultural studies as one symptom of its PMC 'Americanization'.

In closing, I offer a restatement of my initial point that, as Stuart Hall has urged, a US cultural studies must retain a strategic openness. This openness is neither simplistically pluralistic, nor is it merely an apparent pedagogical openness, layering over implicit or hidden agendas. The best cultural studies work is explicit about its positions and lucid about how its positions are located in debates, thus leaving those who engage with such positions free (as possible) to choose. That dual openness is worth practicing.

Notes

This essay was written while I held a fellowship at the Center for the Humanities at Wesleyan University and a fellowship from the American Council of Learned Societies. I gratefully acknowledge their support. Some of the ideas in this essay were developed in conversation with Michael Denning, Hazel Carby, Paul Gilroy, Khachig Tölölyan, and Sarah Winter.

1. For details about the manifesto, see Scott Heller, 'Protest at cultural-studies meeting sparked by debate over new field', *The Chronicle of Higher Education* XXXVI (May 2, 1990): A10–A11. Stuart Hall, 'Politics and letters', in *Raymond Williams: Critical Perspectives*, ed. Terry Eagleton (Boston: Northeastern University Press, 1989), 66. Raymond Williams, *Politics and Letters: Interviews with New Left Review* (London: Verso, 1979). Stuart Hall recounted these political 'interventions' in CCCS in his conference paper, 'Cultural studies and its theoretical legacies'. Women's Studies Group, eds, *Women Take Issue: Aspects of Women's Subordination* (London: Hutchinson, 1978), 11. CCCS, *The Empire Strikes Back: Race and Racism in 70s Britain* (London: Hutchinson, 1982); Paul Gilroy, *There Ain't No Black in the Union Jack* (London: Hutchinson, 1987), 12. Tony Fry, 'From (sunlight) to sin', in Lawrence Grossberg, Tony Fry, Ann Curthoys, Paul Patton, *It's a Sin: Essays on Postmodernism in Politics and Culture* (Sydney: Power Publications, 1988). Richard Johnson, 'What is cultural studies anyway?' *Social Text* 16 (1986): 42. Reprinted here as Chapter 5.
2. Alan O'Connor, 'The problem of American cultural studies', *Critical Studies in Mass Communications* 6 (1984), 405; reprinted here as Chapter 10. Also see O'Connor's excellent bibliography. Stuart Hall, 'Editorial', *NLR* 1 (January–February 1960): I. Stuart Hall and Martin Jacques, eds, *New Times: The Changing Face of Politics in the 1990s* (London: Lawrence and Wishart, 1989). Stuart Hall and Tony Jefferson, *Resistance Through Rituals: Youth Subcultures in Post-War Britain* (London: Hutchinson, 1976); Stuart Hall, Tony Jefferson, John Clarke, and Brian Roberts, *Policing the Crisis: Mugging, the State and Law and Order* (London: Macmillan, 1978). Paul Willis, *Learning to Labour: How Working Class Kids Get Working Class Jobs* (London: Saxon House, 1977); Dick Hebdige

Subculture: The Meaning of Style (London: Methuen, 1979). Stuart Hall, 'Editorial', 2–3.

3. Stuart Hall and Martin Jacques, 'Introduction', 13; Stuart Hall, 'The meaning of new times', 128, 128–29, 132. Both pieces are in *New Times*.

4. Stuart Hall, 'Marx's theory of the classes', *Class and Class Structure*, ed. Alan Hunt (London: Lawrence and Wishart, 1977), 23. Stuart Hall, 'Cultural studies and the Centre: some problematics and problems', in *Culture, Media, Language: Working Papers in Cultural Studies, 1972–79* (London: Hutchinson and CCCS, 1980), 31. Richard Johnson, 'The story so far: and further transformations?' in *Introduction to Contemporary Cultural Studies*, ed. David Punter (New York: Longman, 1986), 55. Also see Stuart Hall, 'Rethinking the base/superstructure metaphor', in *Class, Hegemony, and Party*, ed. John Bloomfield (London: Lawrence and Wishart, 1976). Stuart Hall commented on Marxism as a problem in his conference paper, 'Cultural studies and its theoretical legacies'.

5. Richard Johnson, 'Culture and the historians', in *Working Class Culture: Studies in history and theory*, ed. John Clarke, Chas Critcher, and Richard Johnson (London: Hutchinson and CCCS, 1979), 63.

6. Phases in the rethinking of 'lived experience' can be seen in CCCS, *On Ideology* (London: Hutchinson, 1978); CCCS, *Working Class Culture*, and Richard Johnson, Gregor McLennan, Bill Schwarz, David Sutton, eds, *Making Histories: Studies in History-Writing and Politics* (London: Hutchinson and CCCS, 1982), E.P. Thompson, *The Poverty of Theory* (New York: Monthly Review Press, 1978); Stuart Hall, 'In defence of theory', in *People's History and Socialist Theory*, ed. Raphael Samuel (London: Routledge and Kegan Paul, 1981), 383; Richard Johnson, 'Histories of culture/theories of ideology: notes on an impasse', in *Ideology and Cultural Production*, ed. Philip Corrigan, Annette Kuhn, Janet Wolff (New York: St Martin's Press, 1979), 75; Gilroy, *There Ain't No Black in the Union Jack*, 12; Hall, 'Cultural studies and the Centre', 41.

7. As Alan O'Connor has pointed out, many cultural studies texts are difficult to procure in the States (published by Hutchinson). Anthologies not listed in *Books in Print 1990–91* are: *The Empire Strikes Back; Culture, Media, Language; Women Take Issue; On Ideology;* Gilroy's *There Ain't No Black in the Union Jack* isn't listed either. Republished anthologies are: *Making Histories* (University of Minnesota); *Resistance through Rituals* (Unwin Hyman); *Working Class Culture* (St Martin's Press); *Policing the Crisis* (Holmes and Meier). O'Connor 'The problem of American cultural studies', 407. Cornel West's conference paper, 'The postmodern crisis of black intellectuals'.

8. Cary Nelson and Lawrence Grossberg also organized a Marxist theory conference in 1983, part of the proceedings of which were published in a book they edited, *Marxism and the Interpretation of Culture* (Urbana and Chicago: University of Illinois Press, 1988). Nelson, Grossberg, and the Unit will also edit and publish selections from the cultural studies papers delivered at the April 1990 conference. For a good example of 'cultural studies' American literary history, see Cary Nelson's *Repression and Recovery: Modern American Poetry and the Politics of Popular Memory 1910–1945* (Madison: University of Wisconsin Press, 1989). Hall, 'Cultural studies and its theoretical Legacies'.

9. Grossberg, 'It's a Sin', in *It's a Sin*, 8. Ian Angus and Sut Jhally, eds, *Cultural Politics in Contemporary America* (New York: Routledge, 1989). An issue of the *Journal of Communication Inquiry* 10 (1986) was devoted to the work of Stuart Hall, who was interviewed: 'On postmodernism and articulation: an interview.' See Lawrence Grossberg, 'Strategies of Marxist cultural interpretation', *CSMC* 1 (1984): 392–421. Alan O'Connor, *Raymond Williams: Writing, Culture, Politics* (London: Basil Blackwell, 1989) and Raymond Williams, *Raymond Williams on*

Television: Selected Writings, ed. Alan O'Connor (London: Routledge, 1989). O'Connor, 'The problem of American cultural studies', 407, 408, 407.

10. Tony Bennett, 'Putting policy into cultural studies', reprinted here as Chapter 19; Grossberg, 'It's a sin', in *It's a Sin*, 3; Mike Budd, Robert M. Entman, Clay Steinman, 'The affirmative character of US cultural studies', *CSMC* 7 (1990): 177–78; Tod Gitlin, 'Who communicates to whom, in what voice and why, about the study of mass communication', *CSMC* 7 (1990): 191–92.

11. Paul Gilroy, 'Cultural studies and ethnic absolutism'; Graeme Turner, ' "It works for me": British cultural studies, Australian culture, and Australian film', reprinted here as Chapter 20; Johnson, 'What is cultural studies anyway?' 63, reprinted here as Chapter 5; Bruce Robbins, 'The politics of theory', *Social Text* 88 (Winter 1987): 11; Hall, 'Cultural studies and the Centre', in *Culture, Media, Language*, 44.

12. Carolyn Steedman, 'Culture, cultural studies and the historians'.

13. Patrick Brantlinger, *Crusoe's Footprints: Cultural Studies in Britain and America* (New York: Routledge, 1990), 3, 198.

14. Hazel Carby, 'Schooling in Babylon', in *The Empire Strikes Back*, 197, 193, 194. Brantlinger, *Crusoe's Footprints*, 163, 11, 73; Stuart Hall, 'The emergence of cultural studies and the crisis of the humanities', *October* 53 (Summer 1990): 11, 12, 22.

15. Brantlinger, *Crusoe's Footprints*, 155.

[. . .]

40. See Richard Ohmann, *Politics of Letters* (Middletown, CT: Wesleyan University Press, 1987) and 'Thoughts on CS in the US', *Critical Studies* (forthcoming). Barbara Ehrenreich and John Ehrenreich, 'The professional-managerial class', 5–45, and 'Rejoinder', 313–34, in *Between Labor and Capital*, ed. Pat Walker (Boston: South End Press, 1979); also see 12. Cornel West, 'The postmodern crisis of the black intellectuals'. For an excellent critique of Russell Jacoby's book see Richard Ohmann, 'Graduate students, professionals, intellectuals', *College English* 52 (March 1990): 247–57.

41. Hall, 'The emergence of cultural studies and the crisis of the humanities', 17, 18.

42. Jeremy Brecher and Tim Costello, eds, *Building Bridges: The Emerging Grassroots Coalition of Labor and Community* (New York: Monthly Review Press, 1990). Fred Pfeil, *Another Tale to Tell*, 9.

18

Black studies, cultural studies: performative acts

Manthia Diawara

One of the most important, and appealing, aspects of cultural studies is its critical, or even polemical, attitude toward every form of theoretical orthodoxy. The term *elabore*, used by Antonio Gramsci to stretch and test the limits of Marxism, captures the sense of critical attitude I have in mind here. Elaboration has become, within cultural studies, a means to make use of some of the approaches and methodologies of poststructuralism while being critical of it as an institutionalized discipline.

Cultural studies often delineate ways of life by elaborating them quite literally, embarrassing and baffling previous theoretical understanding of those forms of life. This ethnographic approach has helped cultural studies ground some of its key concepts in material conditions: for example, uneven development, cultural articulation, positionality, and specificity. Through the 'literal reading of event', cultural studies explicates the material bases and implications of world views we assume, and analyzes identity politics as moments of difference and rupture in the hegemonic status quo described by the discourses of Marxism or psychoanalysis.

I want to follow the evolution of the practice of elaboration from its development by early practitioners at the Center for Contemporary Cultural Studies, University of Birmingham, through its use by London-based black artists and writers to its deployment in the United States, particularly in departments of black studies and in feminist studies. I would like to distinguish what I call the London-based black British cultural studies from the tradition derived from work at the Birmingham Center. In the 1960s and 1970s researchers at the Birmingham Center were mainly interested in the British working class and in an attempt to constitute an unique and alternative British Marxist theory around that subject. They were concerned to generate a British Marxism that would challenge the theoretical work of Louis Althusser, Claude Lévi-Strauss, and the Frankfurt School. In contrast, in the 1980s black filmmakers, artists, photographers and writers were decomposing and restructuring the terms of Britishness using race as the modality through which to read class. Black British cultural studies took as its main subject the elaboration of black Britishness over and against ethnic absolutism in Britain, the construction of a hegemonic blackness by black Americans, and other manifestations of diasporan aesthetics.

London-based black cultural workers found the language specific to their condition of black Britishness by submitting to a critical reading not only the texts of the white left, which often ignored race, but also texts from the black diaspora. Some of the most fascinating moments in Paul Gilroy's *There Ain't No Black in the Union Jack* (1987) involve a critique of the work of George Orwell and Raymond Williams for their English ethnocentrism. In order to carve out a space for blackness in Britain, Gilroy had to denounce Williams and Orwell in a similar way that he denounced British right-wingers such as Enoch Powell for their nostalgic celebration of a mythic, homogeneous way of life of the English working class. Isaac Julien similarly developed his film language through a critical reading of white avant-garde cinema. Julien states that:

> On the left of avant-gardism is pleasure, which the avant-garde itself denies, clinging to the purism of its constructed ethics, measuring itself against a refusal to indulge in narrative or emotions and indeed, in some cases, refusing representation itself, because all these systems of signs are fixed, entrenched in the 'sin or evil' of representation. The high moral tone of this discourse is based on a kind of masochistic self-censorship that relies on the indulgence of a colonial history and a post-colonial history of cinema or white representations based on our black absence. The problematic that surfaces when black film-makers experiment with the idea of black film text and the subjective camera, is that subjectivity implies contradiction. But this is not, in itself, fixed.[1]

Black British cultural workers also engage with the black American culture of the 1960s and 1970s and elaborate it into something energetic and specifically British. Some of the most significant diasporic influences on black British cultural studies have been the works of black Americans such as June Jordan, whose *Civil Wars* (1981) helped young black British thinkers to theorize 'policing' in their own context: Manning Marable, Cedric Robinson, James Baldwin, Toni Cade Bambara, Ntozake Shange, and Toni Morrison. Carribean Influences included C.L.R. James, George Lamming, Wilson Harris, Frantz Fanon, Aime Césaire, Edward Braithwaite, and Derek Walcott, and African influences included Ngugi Wa Thiongo and Ousmane Sembène. But these diasporic texts were articulated with black Britishness to create new approaches that were attentive to the fluidity of identities, class, and sexual politics in the British context.

While the distinction between the 'Birmingham school' – an economic, or class-based cultural studies – and a 'black British school' – a race-, or ethnic identity-based cultural studies may be difficult to maintain in light of the fact that figures such as Stuart Hall, Gilroy, and Dick Hebdige played and continue to play key roles in our understanding of both these strands of thought, it is a useful distinction to consider if we want to understand why in the US academic context there appear to be two different kinds of 'cultural studies' even though both are said to be derived from 'British cultural studies'.

One prevalent strain of cultural studies in the US posits race at its center and uses metaphors of racial construction to bring to light the ways of life

of oppressed groups. It is concerned with issues such as black appropriation of the discourse of modernism, the performative character of the
construction of identity, cross-over texts, cultural ambivalence, and sexism
and homophobia in black communities. Thus, it combines elements of what
we might call 'oppression studies' – historical and sociological work that
has concerned itself with uncovering the various modes of oppression of
black men and women, the black family, etc. – with descriptive and
semiotic study of the ways of life and artifacts of black individuals and
communities. Writers such as bell hooks, Michele Wallace, Marion Riggs,
Wahneema Lubiano, Tommy Lott, Henry Louis Gates Jr, Houston Baker Jr,
Cornel West, Jane Gaines, Cora Caplan, Hazel Carby, and Herman Gray, to
name a few, have entered into dialogue with the strand of black British
cultural studies that focuses on issues of hybridity, essentialism, etc. – for
example, with the work of Paul Gilroy, Kobena Mercer, Sonia Boyce, David
Bailey, Sankofa, and the Black Audio Film Collective. The December 1991
conference 'Black Popular Culture', organized by the Dia Center in New
York City, brought together many of these critics and reasserted the
centrality of the discourse of blackness to cultural studies.

The other cultural studies in the US explicitly links itself to the Birmingham Center for Contemporary Cultural Studies. Taking as one of its
primary projects the description of people's ways of life, it focuses on
cultural practices and texts such as rock music, Hollywood and independent films, and so-called new ethnicities. Practitioners of this form of
cultural studies also describe the impact on culture of, for example, the
medical profession, leisure industries, and corporate control of electronic
media. While these theorists maintain a strong anti-essentialist perspective,
their abstract discourse belies the fact that they have been more influenced
by certain strains of poststructuralism than by recent developments in the
black strand of cultural studies. The conference 'Cultural Studies Now and
in the Future', held at the University of Illinois at Urbana-Champagne April
4–9, 1990, represented not only the best and highest levels of abstraction in
the discourse of this brand of cultural studies, but also its tendency to
evacuate race and gender as primary issues.

This geneology of cultural studies obviously oversimplifies the field; for
example, the forms I have described are not simply in opposition: many
cultural workers cross the boundaries of many of these approaches. The
purpose of constructing a typology is that comparing and analyzing foci of
each form facilitates exposing its advantages as well as its limitations. For
example, British cultural studies theorists have criticized some black cultural workers for essentializing blackness by reifying black ways of life
even as they debunk the ethnic absolutism they associate with Englishness
and black nationalism. This anti-essentialist critique of black cultural work
suggests how an emphasis on identity politics can encourage people to
forego the project of coalition building and actually fragment revolutionary
struggle.

Similarly, contradictions within US cultural studies underline the fact
that the importation of theoretical traditions of the Birmingham Center to
the US must include an engagement with the material condition of culture
in the US. Unfortunately, a good deal of US cultural studies that invokes the

Birmingham tradition disengages theory from its spaces of application. The perspectives of the Birmingham school cannot simply be lifted and applied to the US – where traditions of family, nation and spectatorship, for example, are quite different – without a negotiation and reapplication of the tools of ethnography and analysis in the context of US social and material conditions. In their attempt to replace deconstruction with cultural studies as a new academic discipline, its practitioners have made anti-essentialism their strongest critical tool, and turned their backs on the theoretical and methodological contributions of Marxism, feminism, and black studies. The anti-essentialism of this cultural studies has become an essentialism of its own kind: the reification of discourse.

At the same time, practitioners of the Birmingham school tradition in Britain and of black British cultural studies have much to learn from black studies and feminist studies as they have been developed in the US. Black British writers studying, for example, the implications of postmodern films or theories of global systems might do well to look at work that has been done in such areas as African studies, Asian studies, and Latin American studies before declaring that we are beyond history, development, and recovery. The perspective of British cultural studies researchers on such issues as essentialism and binarism would also be complicated by examination of case studies produced by US feminists and African American scholars on racism, oppression, and exclusion.

The challenge for black Americans is now to engage British cultural studies and to develop cultural work that addresses issues such as the plight of inner city youth as well as what Cornel West calls the 'institutions of caring' in the black community.[2] To effectively analyze the specificity of the black public sphere in the US, black studies must engage both the ethnographic approach of the Birmingham school and the race-centered approach of the black British school. We must ground our cultural studies in material conditions. We cannot wait for Hall or Gilroy or Boyce or Julien to tell us how to do this. On the contrary, we have to elaborate the US context in light of the work of Hall and other British scholars, not find replications of their ethnographies or abstractions. We must read their work in such a way that they do not recognize themselves. Cultural studies in our hands should give new meanings to terms such as hybridity, essentialism, ambivalence, identity politics, and the black community.

Black studies in the US

If the Dia 'Black Popular Culture' conference is any indication, the careful integration of elements from both strands of British cultural studies promises to enable black studies in the US to expand in purview as well as depth, shifting its emphasis from 'oppression studies' to what I call 'performance studies'.

'Oppression studies' has historically done much to uncover and decipher the exclusion of blacks from the inventions, discourses, and emancipatory effects of modernity, and much still needs to be said about this. A great deal of contemporary work seeks to continue this line of study, and is furthermore concerned to respond to the critiques of poststructuralism and cultural studies. In an effort to break down the so-called 'black community', these theorists focus analysis on subgroups delineated through such categories as class, sexuality, gender, etc. The importance of specificity in narratives about descrimination and oppression is undeniable. However the identification of study subjects as 'the black woman', 'the young endangered black male', 'the black gay or lesbian', 'the middle-class black', within the larger political context has posed a danger to black studies. The fragmented perspective of such narratives can exacerbate political divisions in responses to events such as the Mike Tyson trial or the Clarence Thomas/Anita Hill hearings that may call for unity across lines of class, gender, and sexual orientation.

Furthermore, 'oppression studies' need not overshadow the actions of black people that helped to refine the tools of modernity and advance its democratic ideals. Black 'performance studies' would mean study of the ways in which black people, through communicative action, created and continue to create themselves within the American experience. Such an approach would contain several interrelated notions, among them that 'performance' involves an individual or group of people interpreting an existing tradition – reinventing themselves – in front of an audience, or public; and that black agency in the US involves the redefinition of the tools of Americanness. Thus, the notion of 'study' expands not only to include an appreciation of the importance of performative action historically, but to include a performative aspect itself, a reenaction of a text or a style or a culturally specific response in a different medium. At the 'Black Popular Culture' conference, for example, Greg Tate explored a new realism of black urban life by adding his knowledge of jazz, funk, and science fiction to his familiarity with the dramatic, audience-involving traditions of preaching and music within black communities. Such a 'performance' is both political and theoretical: it refers to and draws on existing traditions; represents the actor as occupying a different position in society; and interpellates the audience's response to emerging images of black people.

In the US today young writers, artists, and performers like Trish Rose, Lisa Kennedy, Jaqui Jones, and Tate are interested less in what legal scholar Regina Austin has called cross-over dreams and the narrative of the 'dream deferred' as in the notion of a black public sphere. These cultural workers are heirs of the civil rights movement and the black nationalist movements of the 1960s, but differ significantly in focus and perspective from both. They are different from civil rights intellectuals and activists in that they are not as concerned with forwarding integration and the development of 'oppression studies', which dominated black studies, women's studies, and Chicano studies in the 1970s. Their ideology is also significantly different from the black nationalism in the 1960s which in the context of white supremacism developed strong strains of sexism, racism, and homophobia.

These thinkers are motivated by social and economic changes among black communities occasioned by the combination of post-World War II patterns of migration and urbanization and the civil rights movements. This period saw the growth of an unprecedented mass literacy among blacks, who earlier depended on the church and popular music as their primary arena for cultural and political debate. This broad cultural shift to a new black public sphere set the stage for an environment in which books, fims, the visual arts, and music no longer principally exhibit an interest in the project of integration, or in belonging to the society of the 'good life', which is increasingly recognized as being white. Instead, seeing one's life reflected at the center of books, films, visual arts, and music takes precedence.

Indeed, the shift to the new black public sphere has been accompanied by the evolution of a new version of black nationalism. The traditional exclusionary themes of black nationalism are transformed in the works of writers such as Terry McMillan and filmmakers as diverse as Reginald Hudlin, Spike Lee, Julie Dash, and Charles Burnett into the themes of a black 'good life': elements of black nationalism are reinscribed in contemporary material and cultural conditions to construct a different black version of the American dream. Today black artists, from rap musicians to filmmakers and writers, are deriving fame and success from exploiting the themes of a black public sphere, or as Public Enemy puts it, a 'black planet'. The consumers of art about the black 'good life' society are not only both black and white, but exist internationally. This 'good life' has become the object of interest, and even envy, of Americans of different origins and races.

Civil rights activists feared that black nationalism would enhance ghettoization. But white youth and an international audience have become increasingly fascinated by cultural production that calls itself authentically black. Reasons for this attraction range from the pull of the exotic to the incorporation of liberatory themes into resistance to parent ethnic culture that position themselves as universal. Rap, for example, has moved from the underground toward the center, making it the subject of incorporation by white pop musicians as well as the object of parody by 'Deadheads' and country musicians.

As the work of younger scholars has already shown, cultural studies of the black British variety can make an important intervention in the analysis of the new arts produced about the black good life society. Emphasis on hybridity, cross-over, and the critique of homophobia yields some tools with which to check the regressive consequences of any nationalism. Black British cultural workers have a love and hate relationship with black American culture; this both enables the British to use American culture as raw material for its own critical and artistic endeavors, and prompts the British to criticize American culture for being obsessed with the discourse of race and slavery, for being nationalistic in the worst sense, and for not being reflexive or self-critical. Black British viewers do not identify with the notion of a black good life society, let alone with the consumers of a Spike Lee film.

I submit that a measure of identification with the US black public sphere, its cultural consumers and reproducers, is necessary for the production of engaging texts on the black good life society and its arts. In addition, it is not sufficient to analyze only the art of the black good life society and the consumers of that product. One must understand the forms of life of blacks and whites in the US in order to appreciate the techniques that black artists engage in transforming well-established white meanings.

Conditions of black life in America have resulted in a black American response to modernity that is both innovative and antimodern. Blacks have constantly redefined the meanings imposed on the tools and products of modernization by a linear and often destructive Eurocentrism. For example, the acts of black leaders such as Ida B. Wells, Frederick Douglass, and Martin Luther King Jr served as the background to the rewriting of laws that were written to protect the rights of whites only. At the same time, by being situated at the margins, black people observed the advancement of the most efficient modernity in the world upside down. As a result, black people have provided – and continue to provide – some of the most important critiques of modernity through what might be called techniques of reversability. Take, for example, black people's iconoclastic redirection of instruments used in classical music and army bands, which violated many levels of order to create jazz, the music of modernity.

I suggested earlier that the civil rights movement contributed to mass literacy among black people, but the failure of civil rights' politics of integration has left this mass starved for black-centered books, films, painting, music, etc. At the same time, black nationalism's legacy of emphasis on identity, political struggle, and self-determination cannot be placed in the shadows, for it survives in the structures of the new black public sphere. In fact, many black thinkers have a suspicious attitude toward poststructuralism and postmodernism in part because they interpret the emphasis that these theoretical projects put on decentering the subject politically – as a means to once again undermine the black subject. The historical and ideological discontinuities between those giving voice to the black good life society and their predecessors in the civil rights and black nationalist movements need to be addressed urgently in order for the black public sphere to continue to develop its black-centered perspectives and techniques.

To reproduce itself, the new black public sphere needs both an economic base that provides jobs for young people and definitions and discussions of the culture it is producing daily. US black studies can develop performance studies as a mode of interpolating people in the black cultural sphere, positioning the people of the black good life society as its 'ideal readers'. Such a method of elaboration promises a way to narrate the break with the tenets of the civil rights movement and black nationalism, and move on to higher levels of abstraction along the lines of sexual politics, class, and labor relations.

Notes

1. *Undercut: A Magazine for Independent Video and Filmmakers*, 1988, p. 36.
2. Cornel West, 'Nihilism in Black America', *Dissent* Spring 1991, p. 223.

19

Putting policy into cultural studies

Tony Bennett

There is a calculated ambiguity in my title. For it might seem, in one reading, that I want merely to argue that policy considerations should be accorded a more central place within the concerns of cultural studies. Another reading, however, might suggest that my purpose in proposing that we put 'policy' into 'cultural studies' is to advocate that the latter be displaced by, or transformed into, something else: namely cultural policy studies. Let me, then, lessen the ambiguity a little: my argument does not have the kind of modesty implied by the first reading. But nor is its ambit quite described by the second, and for the good reason that the currency of 'cultural studies' is presently so unsettled that the perspectives I shall advocate could either come to comprise essential components of future work which falls under this heading or, alternatively, require the establishment of a separate field of study with its own nomenclature to distinguish its concerns from those of cultural studies. Which of these proves to be necessary will depend on how the kinds of debates this conference ['Cultural Studies Now and in the Future', University of Illinois, April 1990] was arranged to engage with are conducted and resolved over the next few years.

For the present, however, I see little alternative but to recognize the elasticity of usage that the term 'cultural studies' has acquired. It now functions largely as a term of convenience for a fairly dispersed array of theoretical and political positions which, however widely divergent they might be in other respects, share a commitment to examining cultural practices from the point of view of their intrication with, and within, relations of power.[1] Assuming, then, that how future work in this area might develop is open to bids, I want to advance four claims regarding the conditions that are necessary for any satisfactory form of engagement, both theoretical and practical, with the relations between culture and power. These are: *first*, the need to include policy considerations in the definition of culture in viewing it as a particular field of government; *second*, the need to distinguish different regions of culture within this overall field in terms of the objects, targets, and techniques of government peculiar to them; *third*, the need to identify the political relations specific to different regions of culture so defined and to develop appropriately specific ways of engaging with and within them; and, *fourth*, the need for intellectual work to be conducted in a manner such that, in both its substance and its style, it can be calculated to influence or service the conduct of identifiable agents within the region of culture concerned.

If this is to stake out a possible future for cultural studies, however, it is clearly one that will require a break with many aspects of its past. Rather than mapping out such a possible future in greater detail, therefore, I shall try to identify the kinds of political and theoretical reorientations that I think are called for to redirect cultural studies down the road I have suggested. I shall do so by engaging critically with some of the trajectories – past and present – which have emerged out of British cultural studies with a view to identifying the respects in which they constitute an impediment to the formation of the kinds of positions I have outlined. Focusing particularly on the Gramscian moment of this tradition and the subsequent politics of difference which has flowed out of its engagements with postmodernism, I shall suggest that it now needs to be viewed as deficient in three crucial respects: its definition of culture; its commitment, however qualified, to the theoretical and political terms of reference supplied by the Gramscian concept of hegemony; and its theory of agency.

A brief biographical note might be appropriate at this point inasmuch as, in criticizing these aspects of British cultural studies, I shall be taking to task arguments and positions which have informed some components of my own earlier work. Indeed, what follows is, in some senses, a formalized working through of some of the disentanglings from earlier positions that have accompanied my more recent concern, in establishing an Institute for Cultural Policy Studies at Griffith University, to put 'policy' into 'cultural studies' theoretically, practically, and institutionally.[2] This has, however, been a fully collaborative project and, in that sense, my paper has been collectively authored by the many conversations and debates which have fueled the development of this work.[3]

Culture, policy, government

Let me come first, then, to the question of culture's definition. But let me do so indirectly by considering its bearing on the manner in which questions of cultural politics have typically been posed and conceived within cultural studies. Two main concerns can be distinguished here. In the first, the emphasis falls on modifying the relationship between persons – whether as readers, members of a subculture, or the devotees of a fashion system – and those cultural forms which have borne consequentially on their formation. The key instrument of politics here is criticism and its primary object is to modify the relationship between, for example, text and reader in such a way as to allow the texts in question to serve as the means for a politically transformative practice of the self into which the reader is inducted. Where such practices of the self are supposed to lead, of course, varies in accordance with the specific ways in which they aim to equip or empower the reader culturally. They might lead from the delu-

sions of ideology to true consciousness and hence revolution, or from the
critique of patriarchy to the search for a feminine position in discourse.
Whichever the case, however, such critical politics usually have two things
in common. First, they always map out a direction, chart an itinerary, for
the subject. Second, they produce, as an artifact of their own procedures, a
text that is capable of serving as both a resource and a landscape for the
itinerary they propose. The course which Althusserian Marxism criticism
charts for the reader is thus one plotted across the epistemologized landscape of the literary text. Poised midway between the misrecognition effect
of ideology and scientific knowledge, the literary text is so fashioned as to
assist the subject's transition from ideology to science in providing a means
through which – by constantly measuring the difference between the
literary and the ideological – the reader can scrape away the clouded
visions of ideology and hence embark upon the royal road which leads
to scientific knowledge.[4]

Precisely how such journeys are mapped, and precisely how the field of
texts is laid out to support them, varies with different accounts of the
relations between culture and power. How such relations are viewed also
affects the second kind of cultural politics associated with cultural studies.
This consists in the type of connections that are made between, on the one
hand, the different transformative trajectories for the self that are plotted
through the conduct of critical politics, and, on the other, the kinds of
political subjects or constituencies it is envisaged might be organized and
mobilized in support of specific collective political projects. Although there
is more than one version of the argument, the Gramscian tradition in
cultural studies is thus distinguished by its concern, first, to produce
subjects opposed to the manifold and varied forms of power in which
they find themselves and, second, through its commitment to a politics
of articulation, to organize those subjects – however loosely, precariously,
and provisionally – into a collective political force which acts in opposition
to a power bloc.

Of course, these rough summaries cut more than a corner or two. The
point I want to make, however, concerns the respects in which both kinds
of politics rest upon a view of culture which sees it as, chiefly, the domain of
signifying practices. Moreover, the central tasks of cultural politics are, in
both cases, to be pursued by cultural – in the sense of signifying or
discursive – means: by means of specific technologizations of the text/
reader relationship in the first case and, in the second, via the discursive
organization of a chain of equivalences between different forms of oppression and the struggles against them. And both are, in this respect, liable to
the criticism that they pay insufficient attention to the institutional conditions which regulate different fields of culture. This leads, in turn, to a
tendency to neglect the ways in which such conditions give rise to specific
types of political issues and relations whose particularities need to be taken
into account in the development of appropriately focused and practicable
forms of political engagement.

To argue that institutional and, more broadly, policy and governmental
conditions and processes should be thought of as a constitutive of different
forms and fields of culture, however, requires that the currency of the term

'culture' as it has figured in the main problematics of cultural studies be reviewed. The most important single influence here, of course, has been Raymond Williams's work, especially in the distinction it proposes between culture as 'a particular way of life, whether of a people, a period or a group' and culture, in its more restricted sense, as 'works and practices of intellectual and especially artistic activity' (R. Williams, 1976, p. 80). While the value of this distinction has been enormous, it has tended to distract attention – including, I would say, Williams's own attention – from the fact that he identifies a third modern usage of culture as 'the independent and abstract noun which describes a general process of intellectual, spiritual and aesthetic development' (p. 80). Arguing that this usage first became regular in the late eighteenth century, Williams notes that its currency in this period was not unheralded. Indeed, when illustrating this usage, he dwells most on a late seventeenth-century example from Milton's *The Readie and Easie Way to establish a Free Commonwealth* (1660) in which Milton urges the need to

> spread much more Knowledg and Civility, yea, Religion, through all parts of the Land, by communicating the natural heat of Government and Culture more distributively to all extreme parts, which now lie num and neglected. (cited p. 78)

Here, Williams goes on to observe, we can 'read government and culture in a quite modern sense'. Unfortunately, he does not say what he means by this. Clearly, however, he sees no contradiction in government and culture being placed on the same side of the equation. For, in Milton's passage, culture is neither the object of government nor, assuredly, its subversive opposite; rather, it is its *instrument* and – with residues of its earlier horticultural uses surviving but also qualified by its conception as a social and political process – is to be applied in *the service of government* to all those parts which 'lie num and neglected'. Yet, having noted this usage, Williams almost immediately takes his eye off it as his discussion takes another, more familiar tack as he traces, first, the processes whereby 'culture' and 'civilization' (still working together in the passage from Milton) come to be separated from one another and, subsequently, the contradictory nineteenth-century passage of 'culture' as its usage becomes at once both more restricted (in aesthetics) and more extended (the route from Herder to, ultimately, Williams's own 'whole ways of life').

A good deal of the history of British cultural studies can be written in terms of the ways in which the relations between these two senses of 'culture' have been read and redefined: the use of the extended definition to legitimize and ground the study of subcultures, popular culture, and ways of life; the construction of culture, in this extended sense, as the forcing ground for forms of symbolic opposition to culture in its more restricted dominant and aesthetic forms.[5] However, in spite of the considerable weight placed on it, there has been little critical examination of the methodological assumptions which underlie Williams's genealogical account of these modern uses of 'culture'. Yet there are grounds for caution here. As Ken Ruthven (1989) has carefully argued, much of this aspect of Williams's work remains in the orbit of Cambridge English in its 'conviction that the hidden processes of history are somehow sedimented in a handful of so-called key-words' (p. 112). While, as Ruthven goes on to note, Williams's particular variant of this argument is useful in 'reuniting the diachronic warps undergone by an individual word with the synchronic wefts produced by the company it keeps' (p. 116), it remains the case that Williams offers us more a snapshot of the shifting semantic horizons of words as traced by the lexicographer than an analysis of the conditions regulating their functioning as parts of a field of discourse.

This limitation is underscored by the system of references which organizes the relations between Williams's keywords. For in acknowledging that the history and meaning of each keyword is writable only in terms of its relations to other keywords, these references also make it abundantly clear that Williams's judgment as to the semantic field in which each keyword is to be located is, to a degree, arbitrary; it rests on a choice in favor of some semantic coordinates at the expense of others. For Williams, the history and meaning of 'culture' is thus conceived as being writable in terms of its relations to 'aesthetic', 'art', 'civilization', 'humanity', and 'science'. While not disputing the relevance of these choices, their incompleteness is equally evident: quite different consequences – pointing the analysis toward quite different fields of discourse – would follow from considering 'culture' in relation to 'morals' and 'manners', for instance.

It is, indeed, in not pursuing considerations of this kind that Williams – and, consequently, a good deal of the subsequent definitional discussion within English cultural studies – misses one of the most distinctive aspects of the late eighteenth- and nineteenth-century transformations in which the changing and conflicting semantic destinies of 'culture' are implicated. This consists in the emergence of new fields of social management in which culture is figured forth as both the *object* and the *instrument* of government: its object or target insofar as the term refers to the morals, manners, and ways of life of subordinate social strata; its instrument insofar as it is culture in its more restricted sense – the domain of artistic and intellectual activities – that is to supply the means of a governmental intervention in and regulation of culture as the domain of morals, manners, codes of conduct, etc.

In arguing for the anthropological plentitude of Williams's extended definition of culture versus its aesthetically restrictive sense in defining its object, then, cultural studies has misperceived at least some aspects of the organization of its field of study. Culture is more cogently conceived, I want to suggest, when thought of as a historically specific set of institutionally embedded relations of government in which the forms of thought and conduct of extended populations are targeted for transformation – in part via the extension through the social body of the forms, techniques, and regimens of aesthetic and intellectual culture. As such, its emergence is perhaps best thought of as a part of that process of the increasing governmentalization of social life characteristic of the early modern period which Foucault and others have referred to by the notion of *police*.

While this concept has many aspects, I shall mention only two here. The first consists in the contrast it organizes between feudal and modern forms of power. The former, as Foucault puts it, was concerned only with 'the relations between juridical subjects insofar as they were engaged in juridical relations by birth, status, or personal engagement' (Foucault, 1988, p. 156). *Police*, by contrast, relates to individuals 'not only according to their juridical status but as men, as working, trading, living beings' (p. 156), forming a network of more or less permanent, constantly enlarging and positive mechanisms for intervening within the lives and conditions of existence of both individuals and specific populations. The aim of *police*, to cite Foucault again, 'is the permanently increasing production of something new, which is supposed to foster the citizens's life and the state's strength' (p. 159). Moreover – and this brings me to my second point – culture, in the sense in which I have defined the term, was clearly thought of as integral to the concerns of *police* from the very earliest elaborations of the conception. In Delamare's *Traite de la police* (1705) theater, literature, and entertainment were as much a matter of concern as public health and safety while, in the English context, Patrick Colquhoun, in his *Treatise on the Police of the Metropolis* (1806), advocated forms of cultural regulation which, a half century later, might well have been penned by an advocate of rational recreations:

> And it is no inconsiderable feature in the science of Police to encourage, protect, and controul such as tend to innocent recreation, to preserve the good humour of the Public, and to *give the minds of the People a right bias*. . . . Since recreation is necessary to Civilised Society, all Public Exhibitions should be rendered subservient to the improvement of morals, and to the means of infusing into the mind a love of the Constitution, and a reverance and respect for the Laws. . . . How superior this to the odious practice of besotting themselves in the Alehouses, hatching seditious and treasonable designs, or engaging in pursuits of the vilest profligacy, destructive to health and morals. (cited in Philipp, 1980, p. 175)

Viewed in the light of these considerations, then, culture might be thought of, and its emergence accounted for, in terms analogous to those associated with Donzelot's (1979) conception of the constitution and development of 'the social' as a particular surface of social management. This would involve a theoretical procedure different from those which seek to arrive at some transhistorical construction of the specificity of culture: as a particular level of social formations, for example, or as the domain of signifying practices, or as both lived cultures and textual practices and their interrelations. In their stead it would enjoin the need to think of culture as a historically produced surface of social regulation whose distinctiveness is to be identified and accounted for in terms of (i) the specific types of attributes and forms of conduct that are established as its targets, (ii) the techniques that are proposed for the maintenance or transformation of such attriutes or forms of conduct, (iii) the assembly of such techniques into particular programs of government, and (iv) the inscription of such programs into the operative procedures of specific cultural technologies.

While this is not a task I propose to undertake here, some brief comments on the historical aspects of the arguments and its methodological and political consequences will help contextualize my later arguments. First, then, let me simply stress the historical peculiarity of that process – traceable to the eighteenth century – through which artistic and intellectual practices come to be inscribed into the processes of government. This is not to say that, in the pre-modern period, such practices had no role in the organization of the relations between rulers and ruled. They manifestly did but more by way, for example, of establishing circuits of inter-elite communication from which the vast mass of the populace was both excluded and meant to feel the symbolic weight of that exclusion – as was the case with the various precursors of the public museum – or, if we recall the Elizabethan theater, as a vehicle for publicly staging and broadcasting the lessons of monarchical power. It is only with the Enlightenment and its aftermath that artistic and intellectual practices come to be thought of as instruments capable of being utilized, in a positive and productive manner, to improve specific mental or behavioral attributes of the general population – usually as parts of programs of citizen formation.

Yet it is never in themselves or solely by virtue of their own properties that such practices are integrated into programs of this kind. To so suppose would be to take the structures of culture's advocates – like Coleridge and Arnold – at their word in accepting that art and culture, in their restrictive senses, are intrinsically endowed with improving qualities.[6] Rather, it is by virtue of the ways in which such practices function as components of particular cultural technologies – and, consequently, of the fields of use and effect that are thus established for them – that they are able to be harnessed to particular types or regions of citizen or person formation. Ian Hunter (1988) has offered one of the most fully developed arguments of this kind in his analysis of the processes through which modern literary education has so fashioned the literary text as to allow it to play a facilitative role in the development of capacities of ethical self-monitoring. The argument, however, can be generalized. The civilizing function attributed to the visual arts in the nineteenth century depended directly on that new cultural technology, the public art museum. Of especial importance in this respect was the new contextualization of artistic practices organized by the art museum in offering, as Carol Duncan and Alan Wallach (1980) have put it, a programmed experience in which the visitor is addressed not, as in earlier princely collections, as a subject but 'in the role of an ideal citizen – a member of an idealized "public" and heir to an ideal, civilised past' (pp. 451–52).

If this is a historical argument, however, it is also a methodological one. For it points to the more general consideration that the programmatic, institutional, and governmental conditions in which cultural practices are inscribed – in short, the network of relations that fall under a properly theoretical understanding of policy – have a substantive priority over the semiotic properties of such practices. For it is the 'overdetermination' of such properties by these conditions that establishes, in any particular set of circumstances, the regions of person or citizen formation to which specific types of cultural practice are connected and the manner in which, as parts of developed technologies, they function to achieve specific kinds of effects. It is, therefore, only by according a methodological priority to considerations of this kind – rather than to the more immediately perceptible

314 What is cultural studies?

qualities of texts or lived cultures – that cultural studies can, as Marx suggested we should, appropriate the 'real concrete' in thought.

And what is accorded a substantive and methodological priority should be similarly treated at the level of practical reasoning. Where culture is viewed as primarily the domain of signification, the critique of cultural practices conducted in a manner intended to be both the starting and the end point of cultural politics. If my analysis holds, however, this is not so. The field of policy relations, as I have outlined it, poses political issues an exclusively critical politics cannot address. Equally, one cannot calculate what the politics of a particular type of criticism are without taking into account the field of policy relations in which it is likely to surface and have effects. The key question to ask of any literary work, Walter Benjamin (1973) once argued, is not how it stands *vis-à-vis* the productive relations of its time – does it underwrite them or aspire to their revolutionary overthrow? – but how it stands *within* them (p. 87). To bend this to my own purpose, my contention is that the key questions to pose of any cultural politics are: how does it stand within a particular cultural technology? what difference will its pursuit make to the functioning of that cultural technology? in what new directions will it point it? And to say that is also to begin to think of the possibility of a politics which might take the form of an administrative program, and so to think also of a type of cultural studies that will aim to produce knowledges that can assist in the development of such programs rather than endlessly contrive to organize subjects which exist only as the phantom effects of its own rhetorics.

Beyond hegemony

I shall return to this last matter later. Before doing so, however, I want to relate the points raised so far to my opening remarks regarding the limitations of the Gramscian moment in cultural studies. It will be clear that the general tenor of my argument so far displays a leaning toward Foucauldian forms of analysis.[7] Yet I might have made some of my historical points equally well by drawing on Gramsci's conception of the historical distinctiveness of the educative and moral functions of the bourgeois state. That I have not drawn on a Gramscian lineage in making these arguments, however, is by way of signaling that – undeniably important and productive though the Gramscian moment in cultural studies has been – it has also now to be recognized that there are real limitations to the work that can be done from within the Gramscian tradition.

This is in part because of the ways in which the Gramscian problematic has been warrened out by the various attempts that have been made to establish some form of accommodation between, on the one hand, the Gramscian theory and project of hegemony, and, on the other, aspects of postmodernism and discourse theory. While, in my view, the resulting formulations are often deeply contradictory and, particularly in their libertarian leanings, politically harmful, the kind of theoretical excavations of Gramsci's work undertaken by Ernesto Laclau and Chantal Mouffe make it clear that many of the assumptions which underlie the Gramscian conception of hegemony – the role accorded class as the coordinating center of social and political life – can neither be sustained theoretically nor, anymore, be of much service politically.[8]

There is to my mind, however, a more compelling difficulty associated with the Gramscian problematic: namely, that it commits us to too automatic a politics, one which – since it contends that all cultural activities are bound into a struggle for hegemony – is essentially the same no matter what the region of its application. The Gramscian moment in cultural studies, in consequence, has tended to be institutionally indifferent and, accordingly, has paid insufficient attention to those considerations which, in differentiating cultural technologies one from another, give rise to specific sets of political relations and forms of calculation.

Let me give an example. Much – but not all – of what I have said concerning the relations between culture and government could be loosely accommodated within Gramsci's conception of the modern state as an educator. There are, moreover, many respects in which this perspective usefully illuminates those cultural technologies – I have in mind the public museum – whose formation has been intimately associated with that of modern conceptions of state-people relations. Duncan and Wallach (1980) have thus usefully noted the respects in which, as an instrument for the display of power, the public museum is governed by different principles from those regulating earlier royal collections. For the museum is characterized by its rhetorical incorporation of the public – conceived as a citizenry – into the form of power which the museum itself displays. Whereas the iconographic program of royal collections served to validate the splendor and power of the prince, thus placing the visitor in a relationship of vassalage to a superior power, the public museum inscribes the visitor in a new relation to power in addressing him/her as 'a citizen and therefore a shareholder in the state' (p. 457). The public museum, that is, serves as an instrument for relaying to the citizens of modern democratic polities a power that is re-presented to them as their own.

In thus inscribing the visitor in a relation of complicity with the power it makes manifest, the museum might be regarded as a textbook instance of the relations between people and state Gramsci had in mind when, distinguishing modern forms of hegemony from mere domination, he referred to the rhetorical enlistment of 'the people' in support of programs of moral, cultural, and intellectual leadership.[9] While I have no wish to gainsay these arguments, it is equally important to note their limitations. Here I will focus on two, although both are aspects of the same argument: that however useful it may be, in a general kind of way, to view museums as hegemonic apparatuses, this perspective is no more able to theorize the specific forms of politics peculiar to the museum than it is able to engage practically and productively with the actual agents that are operative within the field of museum politics.

So far as the first matter is concerned, the two types of political demand which have most typically, and most distinctively, been brought to bear on museums derive from two contradictions which have been inscribed in the institutional form of the public museum from the moment of its inception.[10] The first of these contradictions is that between on the one hand, the museum's conception as an instrument for the collective ownership of cultural property charged with the responsibility for making its resources equally and freely available to all who might be counted among its public, and, on the other, the fact that, in actuality, museums have functioned rather as instruments for differentiating populations. While theoretically democratic and open to everyone, that is to say, museums have proved in practice to be a remarkably productive technology for the development of those practices of social distinction whereby, in the nineteenth century, the bourgeoisie and, in the contemporary context, Bourdieu's 'dominated fraction of the dominant class' have sought to display those principles of taste and forms of demeanor which symbolically police the boundary lines between themselves and the unrulier members of the popular classes.[11] It is the tension thus produced between what the museum is in theory and what it is in practice that accounts for the emergence of a politics of access *vis-à-vis* the museum – that is, for the unending and, I would argue, unendable demand that museums develop more democratic profiles of public use and access.

This, clearly, is a political demand peculiar to the public museum. The conditions which make it intelligible and fuel it are lacking in the case of private museums or other exhibitionary institutions. The same is true of what might be called the principle of representational proportionality which governs the political demands placed on representational practices within museums – that the cultures of different groups should be equally represented within the museum, and represented on their own terms or not at all (as with the 'include us out' perspective which governs Aboriginal demands for the restitution of cultural property from Australian museums).[12] This is generated by the contradiction between the space of representation shaped into being in association with the formation of the public museum – one which, in purporting to tell the story of Man, embodied a principle of general human universality – and the fact that, viewed from this perspective, any particular museum display can be regarded as lacking because of the gendered, racist, class, or national patterns of its exclusions and biases. It is in thus having fashioned a representational norm – Man – which cannot be met that the museum itself fuels the incessant critique to which it is subject. For since no actual representation can be judged adequate in relation to this norm, every museum display can be held to be in need in some form of supplementation or other, thus giving rise to an unstoppable representational politics which, in earlier collections not based on a principle of general human universality – royal collections, for example, or cabinets of curiosities – would have been unintelligible.

These are, of course, no more than brief pointers to the kind of light which appropriately focused genealogies of different cultural technologies might throw on the political rationalities which characterize their present constitution and functioning. Nonetheless, enough has been said to sustain my general argument here. For the types of politics suggested by the perspective of hegemony – restructuring the representational practices of the museum to facilitate the emergence of the oppositional subject of a counter-hegemony, for example – offer no means of connecting with those specific institutional and discursive conditions which, subtending the political pressures brought to bear on museums both from within and without, determine the forms of calculation of those agents with an identifiable capacity to influence museum practices.

Talking to the ISAs

This leads me to the final prong of my argument: that if Gramscian perspectives are limited in their capacity to theorize the forms of political conflict and relations specific to the functioning of particular cultural technologies, they are equally limited in the assistance they can lend to the development of practicable forms of politics capable of affecting the actions of agents within those cultural technologies. This, finally then, raises the question of agency I referred to earlier, a question that might usefully be introduced by way of Brecht's remark that it is no use just to write 'the truth'; one has, he argued, 'to write it *for* and *to* somebody, somebody who can do something with it' (Brecht, cited in Slater, 1977). For Brecht, of course, this meant the proletariat. For Gramsci it meant 'the people' conceived as an ensemble of subordinate social forces fused into a provisional unity that is nucleated around the proletariat by means of a politics of articulation whose primary means are rhetorical or discursive. For the post-Gramscian phase in cultural studies, Brecht's 'somebody' would refer to the totality of all subordinate social forces who, *not* nucleated around the proletariat or any other definite social force, rhetorically hegemonize themselves in relation to the equally rhetorically constructed power bloc they suppose themselves to be opposing.

Yet if, as Barry Hindess (1988) has argued, not even social classes can be construed as agents – that is, as he defines them, as entities capable of arriving at decisions and putting them into effect – it is clear that neither the Gramscian nor the post-Gramscian constructions of 'the people' would meet this test either. And one would find neither classes nor 'the people' – or, for that matter, races or genders – active as identifiable agents in the sphere of museum politics. What one *would* find, of course, would be claims to *represent* class or popular interests, claims which might be advanced by a whole range of effective social agents – museum critics, sectional pressure groups like WHAM,[13] committees of management, teams of designers, curators, sometimes even boards of trustees. One would also be able to point to respects in which the calculations of such agents might have classes, or races, or genders as their targets in the sense that they are intended to give rise to actions envisaged as affecting – benignly or malevolently – the conditions of existence of the occupants of specific class, race, or gender positions. Nonetheless, while 'class' and 'the people' and similar constructs undoubtedly have a real existence as both the targets of specific political programs and as representations which inform the suasive strategies of social agents, they cannot themselves be such agents.

This is not, assuredly, to argue against those rhetorical aspects of political processes which seek to promote shared perspectives among the occupants of the same social positions or to organize alliances between the political struggles of different subordinate social groups. Nor is it to argue against forms of political action which target classes, or women, or blacks, or specific combinations of these, in aiming for specific forms of betterment of their life circumstances. What it *is* to argue against are ways of conducting both of these aspects of political processes, and of connecting them to one another, in ways which anticipate – and are envisaged as paving the way for – the production of a unified class, gender, people, or race as a social agent likely to take decisive action in a moment of terminal political fulfillment of a process assigned the task of bringing that agent into being.[14] And it is to do so precisely because of the degree to which such political projects and the constructions which fuel them hinder the development of more specific and immediate forms of political calculation and action likely to improve the social circumstances and possibilities of the constituencies in question. The road which beckons toward the phantom agents of much cultural theory is littered with missed political opportunities.

My purpose in recalling Brecht's pragmatic maxim, then, is to suggest the need for more circumspect and circumstantial calculations about how and where knowledge needs to surface and emerge in order to be consequential. Foucault (1981) has identified his concerns as being with the ways in which we are governed, and govern ourselves, by means of the production and circulation of specific regimes of truth – regimes which organize the relations between knowledge and action in specific ways in different fields of social regulation. To apply Brecht's maxim in the light of this contention and in the light of my earlier argument that the field of culture needs to be thought of as constitutively governmental is to suggest the need for forms of cultural theory and politics that will concern themselves with the production and placing of forms of knowledge – of functioning truths – that can concretely influence the agendas, calculations, and procedures of those entities which can be thought of as agents operating within, or in relation to, the fields of culture concerned.

This might mean many things. It might mean careful and focused work in the service of specific cultural action groups. It might mean intellectual work calculated to make more strategic interventions within the operating procedures and policy agendas of specific cultural institutions. It might mean hard statistical work calculated to make certain problems visible in a manner that will allow them to surface at the level of political debate or to impinge on policy-making processes in ways which facilitate the development of administrative programs capable of addressing them. It might mean providing private corporations with such information. One thing is for sure, however: it will mean talking to and working with what used to be called the ISAs rather than writing them off from the outset and then, in a self-fulfilling prophecy, criticizing them again when they seem to affirm one's direst functionalist predictions.

These are not, I must admit, intoxicating prospects compared with the other clarion calls which might rally us in support of different futures for cultural studies: perhaps a few more years of heady skirmishing with postmodernism before it goes out of style or a little more sleuth-like searching for subversive practices just where you'd least expect to find them. Yet, I am arguing here, it is only by using the kinds of correctives that would come from putting 'policy' into cultural studies that cultural studies may be deflected from precisely those forms of banality which, in some quarters, have already claimed it while also resisting the lure of those debates whose contrived appearance of ineffable complexity makes them a death trap for practical thinking.

Notes

1. I should make it clear that I do not think cultural studies is or ever has been definable as a specifically national tradition or as a school of thought anchored in a particular institutional locale. In particular, it is not possible to make sense of what was, even in the British context, a much more dispersed and varied set of initiatives than myths of origin usually allow for if it is pretended that cultural studies was somehow spawned at Birmingham. Nor can such a geneal- ogy help us understand the range of debates which are now brought under the heading of 'cultural studies'. This term has now to be recognized as largely a convenient label for a whole range of approaches which, however divergent they might be in other respects, share a commitment to examining cultural practices from the point of view of their intrication with, and within, relations of power. This, in turn, accounts for further shared attributes in differentiating the concerns of these approaches from those of aestheticizing, moralizing, or formalist kinds of cultural analysis.

   Viewed in this light, cultural studies comprises less a specific theoretical and political tradition or discipline than a gravitational field in which a number of intellectual traditions have found a provisional *rendez-vous*. It designates an area of debate in which, certain things being taken for granted, the dialogue can be more focused. As such, the only matter of substance at issue in these debates concerns the development of ways of theorizing the relations between culture and power that will be of service to practical engagements with, and within, those relations.

   Now that cultural studies is attracting its historians, thought needs to be given to the type of histories that will best serve this end. So far as accounts of British cultural studies are concerned, it seems likely that, at least for a time, such histories will echo too closely those purely theoretical accounts of cultural studies' formation which trace its shifts from paradigm to paradigm – from culturalism through structuralism to hegemony. (See, for the most influential account of this type, Stuart Hall, 1980; 1992.) Apart from their tendency to a heroic mode of telling which transforms cultural studies into a full subject capable, it seems, of entering into battles on its own behalf, the most signal weakness of such accounts consists in their neglect of the position of cultural studies within the academy. More interesting and more serviceable accounts will be produced only when attention shifts from such histories of thought to concern itself with the institutional conditions of cultural studies, and especially the changing social composition of tertiary students and teachers. For some interesting reflections on the problems and possibilities for a more critical history of cultural studies, see Grossberg (1988).
2. The Institute for Cultural Policy Studies was established in 1987 for the purpose of organizing research, publications, and conference programs capable of play- ing a positive role within the processes of Australian cultural policy formation.

Its work to date has resulted in the development of a variety of collaborative or consultative relationships with a range of local and national governmental or quasi-governmental agencies operative within the spheres of museum, arts, film, language, and education policies.

3. The paper was first presented at an Institute for Cultural Policy Studies seminar and has been revised in the light of the comments made by those who attended this occasion. I am especially grateful to the suggestions made by Peter Anderson, Jennifer Craik, and David Saunders in this regard.

4. For a fuller elaboration of this argument, see Chapter 6 of Bennett (1990).

5. It is necessary, however, to apply a gender as well as a class perspective to the relations between culture in its elite and extended definitions. See, for an especially telling consideration of the gendered aspects of artistic and aesthetic hierarchies, Parker and Pollock (1983).

6. Yet perhaps this is to malign Arnold who, in a passage in *Culture and Anarchy*, clearly envisages that culture must undergo a process of transformation in order to function effectively as an instrument of government when he argues that 'the great men of culture' are those 'who have laboured to divest knowledge of all that was harsh, uncouth, difficult, abstract, professional, exclusive; to humanise it, to make it efficient outside the clique of the cultivated and learned yet still remaining the *best* knowledge and thought of the time, and a true source, therefore, of sweetness and light' (Arnold, 1965, p. 113).

7. Not, however, one without reservations. The tendency to stress the plurality and dispersal of power relations, while a useful corrective to the conception of all power emanating from the state, often leans to a premature dismissal of state theory. The resulting neglect of the respects in which, through the state, attempts are made to coordinate the functioning of different fields of power relations often leads to different fields of governmentality being granted wildly exaggerated degrees of autonomy from one another: the error of moving from the position of no necessary coordination to no coordination at all. Such views are also often at odds with Foucault's (1980) own formulations, and in particular his contention that, although not all power relations may arise from the state, the state 'consists in the codification of a whole number of power relations which render its functioning possible' (p. 122).

8. See Laclau and Mouffe (1985). Where, as in Stuart Hall (1986) and Dick Hebdige (1988), selected aspects of postmodernism are integrated into a Gramscian framework, the resulting incoherences – while of a different political hue from Laclau and Mouffe's libertarianism – are equally serious. I have discussed these elsewhere: see the penultimate chapter of Bennett (1990).

9. I have, indeed, drawn fully on Gramsci in drawing attention to this aspect of the museum's historical specificity. See Bennett (1988a).

10. For a fuller attempt to identify and outline the consequences of the museum's political rationality, see Bennett (1990).

11. See Bourdieu (1984).

12. See Fourmile (1989) for a clear and influential statement of present Aboriginal demands on these matters.

13. Women Heritage and Museums. For details of its work, see G. Porter (1988).

14. My position is, therefore, in contention with Stuart Hall's [1992] view, expressed in his presentation to the conference from which these proceedings derive, that Cultural Studies should commit itself to the production of organic intellectuals in the mode of the 'as if' – that is, as if the social movements, of class, race, or gender existed in the forms that would make the function of organic intellectuals intelligible. This, it seems to me, is a way of relating to 'new times' which makes little concession to their newness since it belies too clearly a wistfulness

for the political logic of old times in its aspiration to conjure back into being full subjects whose fullness is the product, precisely, of the historical process of their begetting. That apart, to attribute such a function to an intellectual project which has and continues to be based primarily in the academy suggests a degree of misrecognition of its relations to the real conditions of its existence that can only be described as ideological.

References

ARNOLD, M. (1965) *Culture and Anarchy* (ed. R.H. Super). Ann Arbor, MI: University of Michigan Press.

BENJAMIN, W. (1973) *Understanding Brecht*. London: New Left Books.

BENNETT, T. (1988a) 'The exhibitionary complex', *New Formations* 4, 73–102.

BENNETT, T. (1988b) 'Ozmosis: looking at Australian popular culture', *Australian Left Review* April/May.

BENNETT, T. (1990) *Outside Literature*. London: Routledge.

BOURDIEU, P. (1984) *Distinction: A Social Critique of the Judgement of Taste*. London: Routledge.

DONZELOT, J. (1979) *The Policing of Families*. London: Hutchinson.

DUNCAN, C. and WALLACH, A. (1980) 'The universal museum', *Art History* 3, 448–69.

FOUCAULT, M. (1980) *Power/Knowledge: Selected Interviews and other Writings: 1972–1977*. New York: Pantheon.

FOUCAULT, M. (1981) 'Questions of method: an interview with Michel Foucault', *I&C* 8, 3–14.

FOURMILE, H. (1989) 'Aboriginal heritage legislation and self-determination', *Australian Cultural Studies* 7:1/2.

GROSSBERG, L. (1988) *It's a Sin*. Sydney: Power Publications.

HALL, S. (1980) 'Cultural studies: two paradigms', *Media, Culture and Society* 2, 57–72. Reprinted here as Chapter 2.

HALL, S. (1986) 'Race, articulation and societies structured in dominance'. In *Sociological Theories: Race and Colonialism*. Paris: UNESCO.

HALL, S. (1992) 'Cultural studies and its theoretical legacies'. In Grossberg *et al.* (eds), *Cultural Studies*. London: Routledge.

HEBDIGE, D. (1988) *Hiding in the Light*. London: Routledge.

HINDESS, B. (1988) Unpublished seminar paper given at the Sociology Department, University of Queensland.

HUNTER, I. (1988) *Culture and Government*. London: Macmillan.

LACLAU, E. and MOUFFE, C. (1985) *Hegemony and Socialist Strategy*. London: Verso.

PARKER, R. and POLLOCK, G. (1983) *Old Mistresses: Women, Art and Ideology*. London: Routledge.

PHILLIP, D. (1980) '"A new engine of power and authority": the institutionalization of law enforcement in England, 1780–1830'. In Gatrell, V.A. (ed.), *Crime and the Law*. London: Europa Publications.

PORTER, G. (1988) 'Putting your house in order: representations of women and domestic life'. In B. Lumley (ed.), *The Museum Time-Machine: Putting Cultures on Display*. London: Routledge.

RUTHVEN, K. (1989) 'Unlocking ideologies: "Key-Words" as a trope', *Southern Review* 25:1.

SLATER, P. (1977) *Origins and Significance of the Frankfurt School*. London: Routledge.

WILLIAMS, R. (1976) *Keywords*. London: Fontana.

20

'It works for me': British cultural studies, Australian cultural studies, Australian film

Graeme Turner

In Australia, as in the USA, the influence of British cultural studies has been profound. Most of us are aware that, as it establishes itself ever more securely within the academy, and as it becomes increasingly comfortable in its relations with the disciplines it originally interrogated, British cultural studies is in danger of becoming a pedagogic rather than a critical or political enterprise. British cultural studies has always fought against such an eventuality, consistently rejecting suggestions that it was a new and discrete discipline, an evolving orthodoxy within the humanities or social sciences. Motivated, at least in part, by a critique of the disciplines, cultural studies has been reluctant to become one. One can understand why cultural studies, having worked so hard to discredit an elderly universalism within the humanities, should be wary of simply appearing to replace it with something a little more robust and youthful.

But there *is* a universalizing momentum building up throught the export and development of British cultural studies, and its installation as an orthodoxy seems almost inevitable. While I believe this highlights a theoretical problem within cultural studies as a whole, in this paper I want to consider some particular questions raised by this movement, questions about the cultural specificity of British cultural studies and its usefulness within other political or national contexts – in this case, Australia.

My starting point is Ken Ruthven's (1989) article on *Keywords*, published in a special issue of the Australian journal, *Southern Review*, in memory of Raymond Williams. In it, Ruthven criticizes the implicit universality of Williams's *Keywords* project, reminding us that 'the very act of identifying' such key words is 'the product of interpretive processes in the service of an ideological position' which is itself historically and culturally specific (p. 118). While Williams himself is unlikely to have denied this, the wide dissemination of Williams's books, and his status as a major intellectual figure in cultures he never visited or probably never thought about, has conferred onto Williams's project an implied universality. Among the consequences of the canonization of Williams's book(s) within Australian literary and cultural studies, Ruthven argues, is the 'ironic' co-operation of *Keywords* 'in the suppression of Australian "difference"'. Only a comparable, but more explicitly motivated, study of Australian 'keywords' might recover that difference.

It seems to me that such arguments are appearing with greater frequency now. Postcolonial theory within literary studies in Australia and elsewhere constitutes itself through its critique of the often unacknowledged national positions from which the theoretical orthodoxies speak; in the USA, similar arguments have caught my attention on a number of occasions in the last year, the most recent being Andrew Ross's (1989) caution about the cultural and political specificity of British cultural studies in *No Respect* (pp. 7, 233). The privileging of class over gender or race in early British cultural studies, the Anglocentricity of much work on (and resulting assumptions about) ideologies of nationalism or the social function of subcultures, have been noted by cultural studies' friends as well as its enemies (e.g. Schwarz, 1989). Cultural studies' continuing relation to the moralist/elitist 'culture and civilization' tradition customarily represented by the ghostly figures of the Leavises, has a genuinely recondite feel in the USA, I am told, although this is less true in Australia where it released a burst of contagion in English departments during the 1960s. Criticism of the subcultures research identified with Hebdige, Chambers, and, to a lesser extent, Paul Willis also raises the question of the relation between cultural theory and the specific historical conditions which produce it. Examples of such criticism have focused on the romantic treatment of urban subcultures and of popular culture in general – a romanticism seen to derive in part from the common experiences researchers recognize in the subjects of their research (see Born, 1987). This problem is not confined to such relatively early work in the tradition. The temptation to identify sufficiently strongly with 'the people' to see within the practices of their everyday lives an intrinsic subversiveness, is a hotly contested feature of a wide range of work in cultural studies now – particularly the work of John Fiske, itself a hybrid of British, Australian, and American theoretical traditions. In all these instances, the critique of what is now a dominant set of theories and practices suggests they are more culture-bound than they themselves acknowledge.

It has been said that one of the distinctive features of the British appropriations of European structuralist and poststructuralist theory is their applied character (Harland, 1987, p. 4); so much of the theoretical labor in this tradition occurs while dealing with particular, if still resonant, research tasks. David Morley's work on television audiences, or Paul Willis's on youth subcultures, are examples. In such applications, the practical value of theoretical principles is made abundantly clear; what is less clear is the difference between the work of theoretical clarification and the subject matter through which it is developed. Key studies in which important theoretical moves are made are often primarily known through their subject matter: Morley's contribution is, as it were, his *Nationwide* studies, not his testing of the encoding/decoding process; Hebdige's work is on punk and reggae rather than a semiotics of cultural style. Serving the twin objectives of producing applied research dealing with specified materials or processes, and the development through this process of a set of theoretical principles or methodological protocols, the research becomes separated from its own history as its relation to its subject matter is naturalized, universalized.

And yet, British cultural studies is also resolutely parochial. The consistently English (rather than Scottish or Welsh, for instance) perspective employed within British cultural studies, most often goes without acknowledgment or apology. Among the many works examining the making of British histories, Patrick Wright's *On Living in an Old Country* (1985) is remarkable for, at least, his explicit acknowledgment of the particular *kind* of national history he is dealing with, and of the specific rather than merely representative ways in which the nation is called up through its histories. Within media studies, one meets the assumption that the structure and textual features of British television are in the same relation to those of the rest of the world as BBC English is to other versions of spoken English: they are the standard around which the rest of the world provides variants. In so many discussions of news or current affairs in the seventies, the inquiry into the signifying practices of the British media is assumed to be an inquiry into the signifying practices of the media in general. At its worst, British media studies incorporates other media systems into the general argument as variants, their constitutive political and social histories ignored in a way that the British context would never be.

What is being described here is, to some extent at least, a simple Anglocentrism. Just as Britain is the only nation not to put its name on its postage stamp – since they invented it, presumably, only the subsequent users need to nominate themselves – there is a consistent pattern of ex-nomination in the applied British cultural studies. It is *Popular Culture: The Metropolitan Experience*, not *English Popular Cultures*; it is *Television: Technology and Cultural Form*, not *Television in Britain*; and so on. British cultural studies speaks unapologetically from the centers of Britain and Europe, both of them locations where the perspective from the margins is rarely considered. Indeed, Eurocentrism has lately begun to deny itself in a novel way, bidding for the ideological purity that comes with subordination, marginalization, without, of course, needing to accept the powerlessness that denies the genuinely subordinated any satisfaction in such a position. David Morley and Ien Ang's (1989) introduction to their issue of *Cultural Studies* employs such a maneuver: 'Europe itself,' they say, now occupies 'a marginal place in the developed world' (p. 133). (Any discourse that can call itself the developed world is far from being marginal.) Within an otherwise worthwhile argument for the recognition of the 'context-dependence' of cultural studies, suggesting that the 'place and relevance' of cultural studies has to 'be related to the specific character of local forms of political and intellectual discourse on culture' (p. 136), Morley and Ang reveal that, from where they stand, some contexts require less attention than others. They report on the export of cultural studies to such farflung places as Canada and Australia, producing unproblematic if 'ironic echoes' of the 'original map of British imperialism's conquests'. In Australia, we are told on the authority of a letter to the pages of *Screen* magazine, Australian cultural studies is complicated by 'strange-new-world factors' such as the 'inordinate number of left academics wandering around Australia, but talking about Birmingham' (Morley and Ang, 1989, p. 136). This tells us rather less than we would like about 'the specific character of local [Australian] forms of political and intellectual discourse on culture' (which, in fact, are not dominated by Birmingham). Many such 'discourses', in fact, are available in published form – even in the source of the imperial 'echo' – for the authors to have consulted themselves. That they didn't bother, makes it clear that there is at least one place which is more marginal than Europe, and that there are limits to cultural studies' sensitivity to difference.[1]

It is this insensitivity to differences betwen, rather than within, cultures which may be the most pervasive disease working away at contemporary practice in cultural studies. Jim Bee's (1989) review of John Fiske's *Television Culture* registers his disquiet, not only at the theory of resistance and pleasure contained within the book, but at its deliberate homogenizing of television texts and audiences across cultural and political borders. While on the one hand *Television Culture* argues against the notion of the homogeneous audience, on the other hand it assumes that '*Miami Vice* will be empowering whenever and wherever people find it pleasurable' (p. 358). The lack of any conjunctural analysis, locating the articulation of formal and symbolic structures within social processes, practices, and institutions, makes *Television Culture* less than typical of contemporary British cultural studies; more representative is its homogenizing account of television which internationalizes it not only as a technology but as a set of social practices of production and reception. Excised from such an account are the very differences cultural studies set out to recover. Music video, in particular, has suffered from an overly textual criticism; its disarticulation from the industries which produce it and the audiences which consume it has turned the form into a second *nouvelle vague* for some critics. At its most worrying, television analysis within the British tradition is in danger of simultaneously championing certain versions of British television production (Channel 4) as the (paradoxical) representatives of 'the people' and of 'minorities' – a view that insists on the maintenance of difference; while also instituting a blithe internationalism which obliterates differences, assuming commonality across cultures and social structures rather than interrogating the means through which that commonality is constructed.

Australian intellectual traditions have been directly affected by their British counterparts since the beginning, so it is not surprising that Australian cultural studies should bear the traces of all this. In Australia, the cultural studies project has had to find space for itself within existing disciplinary boundaries – working within a strong tradition of left-conservative history, for instance, or within the critical and nationalist movements within literary studies, or the new interest in film and media studies which was reinforced by the revival of the national film industry – or look for a home within the eclectic and cautiously multidisciplinary field of Australian studies. Cultural studies' penetration into these areas has been assisted by its theoretical and temporal coincidence with new accounts of 'the national character' in history, literary studies, and film. Consequently, Australian cultural studies has so far concentrated very closely on local texts, institutions, and constitutive discourses while drawing its major theoretical categories and protocols from Europe, particularly from Britain. Internalized through the practice of analysis and argument, this theoretical influence – inserted into the already complex cultural relations between Britain and Australia – has proved particularly productive; but it has also proved to be very difficult to separate off and interrogate. Subsequently, it is only quite recently that I, for one, have felt the pressing need to review the relevance of the assumptions behind the theories and practice of British cultural studies: to ask, if it works for them will it, to quote TV's Hunter, 'work for me'? Often the answer turns out to be 'no'.

To elaborate a little further on this. It is probably unexceptionable to see E.P. Thompson's *The Making of the English Working Class* as one of the constitutive texts in British cultural studies; it opens the way for a new 'history from below' which recovers the stories of social formations, of popular cultural movements, of non-institutional and subordinated groups and places them against the large-scale administrative institutional, and constitutional narratives of traditional histories. This was not merely an empirical retrieval, though; also recovered were the resistant, oppositional politics of these subordinated social movements. White Australian histories – as distinct from imperial or colonial histories – have, in a sense, *always* been histories 'from below': accounts of a subordinated (that is, a colonized) people, and of their construction of social groups and identities within an extremely repressive and authoritarian social and administrative structure. The whole of Australian social history has been reconstructed through a series of determining oppositions which defined an essential Australianness as the subordinated, the repressed, and the resistant: it is a history which throws convicts against the jailers, prospectors against the diggings police, free settlers against squatters, the Digger against the British officers, and so on. Such structural oppositions located the formation of an Australian identity in the battle between the foreign and the local, the boss and the worker, the authorities and their subjects – a battle always lost by the local, the worker, or the subject. This binary pattern, and its characteristic resolution in the suppression of the national character, has been hailed as constitutive not only of an Australian history but also of an Australian cultural identity.

The binary habit dies hard in Australian cultural questions precisely because they are questions about a postcolonial definition of the nation which is directly provoked by the domination of the colonial power. The postcolonial nation does not simply establish its difference. It defines itself against the imperial Order, distinguishing between two mutually exclusive values. The clearer the distinction, the more categoric the construction of Otherness, the clearer the case for national identity. Within Australian history, the Other has mostly been Britain. (This may perhaps explain why so many Australian cultural critics – myself included – have internalized Britain's high culture/low culture split so strongly, felt such an affinity for the anti-Leavisite tradition of British cultural studies, and thus absorbed its assumptions so uncritically.)

Accordingly, then, when the writers of an Australian history make their most successful bid to control the definitions of the Australian character in the 1950s, theirs is not a mission of recovery; rather, it is an act of revelation.

Their version of the Australian is immediately hailed, recognized, and installed as the dominant articulation of the national identity. Russell Ward's *Australian Legend* (1958) inverts the Barthesian process and turns myth into history, its images and ideologies empirically authorized as the definers of the national character. Ward's work of cultural definition revives and confirms, by and large, regressive attributes: sexism, xenophobia, anti-intellectualism, a populist nationalism, a simple identification between urban and rural working classes, and a sentimental egalitarianism that never quite extends to a commitment to democratic principles. In fact, the characteristics of Paul Willis's (1977) subordinated 'counterschool culture' in *Learning to Labor* are strikingly similar to those of Ward's Australian character. There is, however, a crucial, structural, difference: instead of recognizing an embattled and material subordination, Ward celebrates the ideological dominance of a conservative, masculinist, nationalist, anti-authoritarian ethos which honors manual labor, is sceptical of the intellect, and which proudly sees itself as essentially working class. In much of the British work on subcultures, of which Willis's work is representative, and within many of the histories from below, there is an investment in the subcultures examined which celebrates the resistance of the subordinated, the challenges they offer to dominant ideological formations. Attempts to draw similar political significances from within Australian ideological formations are complicated by the fact that it is the *dominant* which mobilizes nationalist mythologies of resistance and subordination. It is all too easy to become complicit with this strategy; as Tony Bennett (1988) has noted in a review of *Myths of Oz*, a book I co-authored, the 'mythologist' can become the 'myth-maker'.

A key difference between Australian and British theoretical practice is relevant here. Within Australian cultural criticism it has become conventional to construct aspects of Australian life as distinctive – not of a class or of a subculture but of the nation. As Tony Bennett, again, has pointed out in his review:

> This foregrounds an important difference between the European contexts from which Fiske, Hodge and Turner derive most of their theories and the Australian situation to and in which they are applied. Definitions of the distinctiveness of English culture, for example, are so massively mortgaged to bourgeois conceptions of the nation that the self-respecting leftwing critic would rarely regard this ground as worth struggling for – although the situation is different in Scotland and Wales. In these cases, as in Australia, the fact that definitions of the national culture are, in part, shaped through the process of their emergence in opposition to the dominance of imported cultures lend such questions a political pertinence which, in other contexts, would be lacking. (1988, p. 34)

The 'national' within Australia is, of course, largely the captive of similarly bourgeois dominant constructions. That is not the whole story, however; the idea of the nation also contains another, more radical, political potential which is probably unthinkable within the British context. The definition of national identity serves slightly different functions for a nation constructing itself out of a colonial past; different from those which it might serve for a nation attempting to recover an imperial past. This does not only apply to

Australia; Laura Mulvey (1986) has acknowledged a similar relevance within Canada:

> The question of Canadian identity is political in the most direct sense of the word, and it brings the political together with the cultural and ideological immediately and inevitably. For the Canada delineated by multinationals, international finance, US economic and political imperialism, national identity is a point of resistance, defining the border fortifications against exterior colonial penetration. Here nationalism can perform the political function familiar in Third World countries. (p. 10)

(The strain in producing such a perception from a European center is visible in the reference to the third world and in the simplification of a unitary Canadian identity.) Australia, of course, offers a less clear-cut case of continuing colonization; the consequence of this, however, is that it is increasingly difficult to understand the ideological alignments around versions of Australian nationalism through their simple identification with either progressive or regressive effects or through their allegiance to the left or right of the political spectrum. Nationalism can be inscribed into an extraordinary range of political and cultural positions.

If Ruthven was to have his *Australian Keywords*, certainly the longest entry would be for the category of 'the nation'. Australia was settled by Europeans when European nationalism was just beginning, and when the partnership between the ideologies of nationalism, production and colonial capitalism, and social democracy were being forged. Colonial and (later) postcolonial Australia found itself locked into a world increasingly defined by competing nationalisms, a world in which difference had to be given a national character. At the turn of the twentieth century, nationalism was a clear ideological choice for many Australian intellectuals although it was a more pragmatic choice for its politicians, intent on removing restrictions on trade between the various colonial centers. Australians faced what Sylvia Lawson (1983) refers to as the colonial paradox:

> To know enough of the metropolitan world, colonials must, in limited ways at least, move and think internationally; to resist it strongly enough for the colony to cease to be colonial and become its own place, they must become nationalists. (p. ix)

The curious thing about Australian nationalism is not only its varied political potential; it is also the narrow range of images and iconography through which it has signified itself: imagery which locates an essential and distinctive national character in the landscape, in the social structures of the bush, and in a masculinist/socialist pioneering ethic.[2] Initially these images 'belonged', as it were, to the left – or at least to the mixture of racism, sexism, xenophobia, nationalism, rural trade unionism, and international socialism which fed into the foundation of the Labour Party at the end of the nineteenth century. Since Federation (1901), however, this same repertoire of images of the nation has operated as movable but indispensable signifiers of any new hegemonic formation. They are now called up by whoever wants to invoke an essential Australian spirit: as an alibi for the appeal to a 'fair go for families' within a Liberal Party election strategy (which actually narrowed the definition of the family to exclude single parents and the unemployed and thus justify a cut in welfare spending); or within a beer commercial incorporating the holy trinity of men, sport, and beer.

These images do not go uncontested, of course, but any discourse which seeks to oppose 'the national' – to install the 'international' or the 'European' or even the 'Asian' – must deal with a colonial history that categorically attributes such discourses to the regimes of the imperial Other. There are strategies around this problem; proponents of an aggressive development capitalism have inserted notions of progress and prosperity into the depiction of the nation by connecting the myths of the pioneers with the signifiers of industrialization. There is a Eurocentric conservative discourse which is vigorously anti-populist, anti-mass culture, anti-nationalis, but which defends its version of 'culture and civilization', much as the British did, through attacks on strategic targets (Australian vernacular writing, television, popular feature films) rather than through a comprehensive cultural and social agenda. Paradoxically, those voices from the conservative right which defend the maintenance of sophisticated standards in the arts and which remind Australians of the values of the European Metropolitan Centers, can find themselves in unison with progressive left-wing intellectuals calling for the protection of the avant-garde or the experimental in all areas of cultural production.[3]

Within any one field of cultural production, cultural analysts are faced with an intricate set of alliances around the idea of the nation – a left historically connected with, but in many cases antipathetic to, a radical populist nationalism, and a right historically antipathetic to nationalism but accommodated to it through a censorious rhetoric which polices 'cultural standards' and which privileges the elite over the popular, the international over the national, the universal over the international. If we move into a specific area, the Australian film and television industry, it is not difficult to demonstrate how substantive and how ideologically complex a role has been played by specific definitions of the nation and thus of the national film industry over the last 20 years, the years of the revival (or, as some would have it, the renaissance) of the local industry.

It is now widely acknowledged that the funding decisions which produced the revival of the Australian film industry in the 1970s were sufficiently coherent to amount to a conservative hegemony. Against the competing claims of other kinds of film genres (such as the radical nationalist 'ocker films'), conservative definitions of Australian cultural standards were defended through the privileging of the period drama, the Euro-colonial history which collapsed distinctions between the colony and its inhabitants in a cultural *bildungsroman*. For the state-funding bodies which almost singlehandedly determined the character of the industry in these early days, film served a semiotic rather than a commercial function – representing the nation at home and overseas. Films which did not represent the nation in acceptable ways were thus of little interest: contemporary and critical films were eschewed, as well as frankly generic films working – however effectively – within a Hollywood tradition. The first *Mad Max* (1979) film, for example, was a casualty of this narrow range of aesthetic and generic preferences.

The problem, as this example no doubt suggests, is that film does not only represent the nation; it also entertains it. Film may be a culture industry, but it *is* an industry and eventually the state determinations of its character were undermined by measures aimed at enhancing its commercial viability. In the early 1980s, changes to the funding structure attracted private, non-government investors to the industry. This produced a boom in film and television production; also the range of styles, subjects and genres broadened significantly. In this instance, private investment proved more flexible, more liberal, and more adventurous than the state-funding bodies – partly, perhaps, because the cultural function of each film was no longer a central consideration in all cases.

From many points of view, however, this expansion was worrying. The industry itself was, and still is, torn between one view which held that private money and mass marketing offered the route to survival, and the alternative view that while this route may spell financial survival it will defeat the cultural objectives of the Australian film industry – of telling Australian stories for Australian audiences. As Dermody and Jacka (1987, pp. 197–98) point out, within the mainstream Australian film industry there are two, almost entirely discrete discourses: Industry 1, as they call it, is socially concerned, searching for an Australian identity, leftish in its politics, middle class, suspicious of the marketplace and thus in favor of government intervention, arty, and committed to combatting cultural imperialism; Industry 2 is more interested in entertainment than national identity, and is generally internationalist, populist, working class, free marketeer, and unperturbed by cultural imperialism. Signs of Australianness are comfortably accommodated within both discourses – Industry 2 has the working-class, pragmatic, anti-aesthetic ideologies of the dominant masculine Australian culture, while Industry 1 is strongly nationalist in its social and aesthetic objectives.[4]

The divisions in the production industry have their counterparts in the wider film culture – the critics, reviewers, and audiences. Again, the local reception of Australian films is shot through with arguments over the cultural function of the national industry. The highbrow establishment critics have been pleased by those films which elided (that is, transcended) their 'Australianness' by working within the conventions of European art film, or those which offered a mythologized, colonialist version of Australian history and culture. There have been fewer and fewer of such films, though; increasingly, those films which achieve popular success and panned by the highbrow reviewers: *Mad Max*, *The Man from Snowy River 1 and 2*, *Crocodile Dundee 1 and 2*, *Young Einstein*, and most recently, *Delinquents*, are all examples of this. What these films represent is a move towards more clearly generic productions; that is, features which are more recognizably within a Hollywood commercial, rather than a European art film, tradition. This development has angered critics on both sides of the nationalist fence, but for reasons which are still contained within nationalist arguments. Genre films, are criticized as a sellout to Hollywood and a retreat from the enterprise of making distinctively Australian films; critics and producers alike see them as regrettable concessions to the lowest common denominator in mass entertainment, bleeding limited funding away from more adventurous, progressive, or avant-garde projects. This may sound like a straightforward high culture/low culture argument but it is not quite that simple. Defending the genre films does not necessarily entail establishing their aesthetic quality. Indeed, for those of us working within cultural studies and film studies in Australia, dealing with the films *at all* requires a degree of subtlety. In criticizing them, one does not want to support the elitism and internationalism of either the right or the left; yet, in supporting them, one does not want simply to recycle the dominant discourses of a strident, chauvinistic nationalism.

One illustrative argument has aggressively defended the move into the mainstream as a necessary and constitutive strategy for the national film industry on nationalist, commercial, *and* textual grounds. Recent work has suggested that while certain Australian films and television miniseries may have taken on American generic conventions, they have given them an Australian inflection.[5] Such an argument differentiates itself from other nationalist positions through its distinctly postcolonial ring, defining the films' strategy as one of appropriation not of accommodation, as if the American genres were being colonized to Australian ends – naturalizing, rather than raucously foregrounding, Australian subjects, locations, and stories. This position has worked to isolate that section of the film culture which is most similar to the British culture and civilization tradition, which deplores the genre films and wonders why we can't just make things like *Brideshead Revisited*. Finally, the argument is representative of Australian cultural studies inscription of a nationalist politics in both the production strategies it supports and the aesthetic ideologies it resists.

We could peel back further layers, but this should be sufficient to indicate the pervasiveness of the idea of the nation, how specific and contested it is as a category, within Australian cultural debates. The differences between the Australian and the British formation hardly need enumerating, but it is these differences which recommend caution in the application of British theoretical influences.

As a means of extending this argument, I want to conclude by recounting an instance where the adoption of European cultural theory to the Australian context has produced a quite remarkable set of propositions. The example emerges from arguments around the problem of Australian content in Australian television and film. In most Western capitalist countries (other than the USA) there are regulatory mechanisms aimed at preserving some proportion of local material on television and, less frequently, in cinemas. In Australia, the local content debates have largely been resolved in favor of a nationalist and paternalist model of cultural stewardship where the jobs of Australian media workers and an Australian cultural 'identity' are protected by a prescribed proportion of Australian content which the networks are required to screen each year. Inscribed into this requirement is a set of aesthetic assumptions which insist that some forms of television production – drama, primarily – are more essential to our national identity than others – such as sport. The requirement is an imposition, of course. Since male sports are so tightly articulated to the discourses of national identity, they appear on TV no matter what; drama, however, its place in the Australian character less assured, survives as a consequence of government intervention. Nevertheless, within a culture subject to successive waves of cultural imperialism – from Britain, the USA, and Japan – the need to keep Australian subjects, ideas, and voices on our screens attracts support from across the political spectrum. The highbrow right sees it as a way of policing standards and insisting that ballet earns higher points than football, while the nationalist left sees it as a means of resisting American cultural domination, of limiting the powers of an institutionally agglomerated but industrially diversified clique of media owners, and of supporting an indigenous popular culture.

However, and notwithstanding the support of this left populism, the Australian content regulations do express a fear of and distaste for popular culture; what they police is not only cultural imperialism but also the excesses of mass culture. It would be easy to see the regulations as an anti-democratic, anti-populist strategy sheltering under the nationalist alibi of an Australianized media. This is just how John Docker sees them in his unpublished monograph, *Popular Culture versus the State: An Argument against Australian Content Regulations for Television.*

What is interesting about Docker's argument and its repercussions, is the strength of its theoretical pedigree – its grounding in European theories of transgression and the popular – and the reception it has met from those who might share his theoretical influences but who have entirely opposite views on their specific application to the issue of state intervention in the Australian media. Docker's argument is built upon relatively conventional notions drawn from the cultural studies of the last few years. His work privileges the audience over the producer of the television text; he deploys Bakhtinian notions of the carnivalesque in order to attribute an intrinsically resistant politics to popular cultural formations; and he allows a high culture/low culture split to dominate the institutional politics he formulates as a simple binary division. Docker's objective is a critique of the elite paternalism of the existing regulatory system in Australia, and a defense of the open market as an alternative. Not surprisingly, the document was incorporated into a FACTS (Federation of Australian Commercial Television Stations) submission to the Australian Broadcasting Tribunal (the chief regulatory body) in support of an argument for the abolition of all Australian content requirements. To many of Docker's peers working in cultural studies in Australia, this was a scandalous sellout, his enlistment only giving aid and comfort to the enemies of the Australian production industry and of the Australian audience.

And yet, Docker's argument too has its nationalist dimension. He collapses the history of the Australian Broadcasting Commission into that of the Reithian BBC, clearly the initial model for its design, as if there were *no* cultural or historical gaps between the two. This enables Docker to generate post-Leavisite anxieties about the kind of high culture ethic which was institutionalized through government intervention in Britain and which, he claims, has been exported without modification to Australia. State intervention thus becomes identified with a specifically British ideological project, and so it seems reasonable to suggest we will better protect the Australian public by rejecting it. Docker is also a populist. Where the state is elite and conservative, the popular is democratic and transgressive, and so the regulation of the cultural economy should be left to the people themselves. The paternalistic supervisory regime instituted by the regulation is, he argues, intrinsically objectionable and actually impedes the open and balanced negotiation that would otherwise occur between the TV networks and the national-populist.

Histories of the Australian media certainly raise empirical doubts about Docker's proposition, and there are many theoretical and political objections to be made as well. I am aware that this libertarian argument is more at home in the USA, which is the agent rather than the victim of the cultural and economic imperialism state intervention is intended to ameliorate; I was caught by the enunciation of such a principle as one of the ground rules for cultural criticism in *No Respect*, for instance. But it is definitely an unconventional view to come from within Australian cultural studies; and, presumably, it would be a bizarre view to come from the left in the deregulated climate of Thatcher's Britain. To see commercial TV as serving a transgressive definition of the popular *and* the commercial ends of the market, without acknowledging their competing interests, is far from being a familiar left position in either country.

However, I would argue that Docker's view is directly licensed by recent theoretical trends within British cultural studies. The recovery of the audience, the new understandings of the strategies of resistance audiences employ, and the invocation of such strategies within definitons of popular culture, have all been important, corrective developments within British cultural studies. Their export to the USA, however, to a context where the notion of the popular occupies a very different place within dominant cultural definitions, seems to have exacerbated an already significant expansion in the cultural optimism such explanations generate – an optimism that is ultimately about capitalism and its toleration of resistance. The appropriation of de Certeau's work, and the development of John Fiske's line on the popular in the last three years, are symptomatic of this developing theoretical asymmetry in favor of resistance and against containment. Seen in this way, Docker might be regarded as a continuation of a theoretical tradition rather than an aberration; it is only the conclusions produced through his theoretical practice which are idiosyncratic.

This paper has been about the cultural specificity of theory, and it is of course itself speaking from a particular position. I have particular concerns about the effects of British cultural studies on Australian cultural studies; I am concerned that its ultimate effect may well be to turn our attention away from where we live in order that we might speak globally – thereby minimizing the differences that got us into this area in the first place. Without doubt, this is part of a larger problem for Australian cultural politics, that of being on the margins of the 'developed world' while being continually drawn towards 'the centre'. As I have argued elsewhere (Turner, 1989), while one does not want to remain marginal, pushing one's way into the center often carries the penalty of the submersion of difference, the denial of contradictions, the glossing over of oppositions. This is also, however, a problem for cultural studies as a whole; after all, the universalizing process I have just described is one cultural studies should be uncovering, not reproducing.

My aim has been to stress the need to acknowledge that even theory has to have some historical location, specific contexts within which it works to particular ends. The dominance of British models is not intrinsically dangerous unless we take it for granted but, so far, I think we have failed to interrogate the nature and effects of that dominance. More comparative work of the kind I have hinted at in this paper might help to make such an interrogation possible: how do we begin to understand, for example, the industrialized cultures of a Westernized Asia – Korea, Taiwan, Hong Kong – with the tools currently available? As long as cultural studies resists the challenge of more comparative studies, there will be little provocation to revise the British models so that they 'work' for the margins as well as the centers. Cultural studies has a lot to gain from the margins, and it should do its best to investigate the ways in which their specific conditions demand the modification of explanations generated elsewhere. At the very least, such an expansion of the cultural studies project provides a hedge against the development of a new universalism.

Notes

1. I should add that the center's claim to marginality is not only advanced from European centers; *Cultural Studies* has also published a piece recently by Cohen (1989) describing the colonization of American popular culture by such European intellectuals as Eco and Baudrillard as a marginalization of American culture.
2. See my *National Fictions: Literature, Film, and the Construction of Australian Narrative* (1986) for discussion of this.
3. *Screen* theory, for instance, found and still finds its strongest proponents amongst Anglocentric, anti-nationalist cosmopolitans, not among the hard-core national- ists of the Labour left.
4. In 1988, the government dealt with these contradictions by installing a new and even more contradictory funding structure. It downgraded the tax concessions which had attracted investors so that they would no longer serve that function; and to compensate they installed a new state-funded institution which would operate as a commercial lending bank to filmmakers – but only to top up budgets already primarily filled with private money. This new institution, the Film Finance Corporation, attempts to speak the language of both Industry 1 and Industry 2: it professes to support only commercial projects but it also accepts the cultural responsibility of supporting distinctively Australian films. It is too soon to tell just which discourse will prevail.
5. E.g. Stuart Cunningham, 'Hollywood genres, Australian movies' (1985). Cun- ningham takes this argument further in 'Textual innovation in the miniseries'.

References

BEE, J. (1989) 'First citizen of the semiotic democracy', *Cultural Studies* 3, 353–59.
BENNETT, T. (1988a) 'Ozmosis: Looking at Australian popular culture', *Australian Left Review* April/May.
BORN, G. (1987) 'Modern music culture: on shock, pop and synthesis', *New Formations* 1, 51–78.
COHEN, E. (1989) 'The "hyperreal" vs. the "really real": if European intellectuals

stop making sense of American culture can we still dance?' *Cultural Studies* 3, 25–37.

CUNNINGHAM, S. (1985) 'Hollywood genres, Australian movies'. In Moran, A. and O'Regan, T. (eds), *An Australian Film Reader.* Sydney: Currency.

DERMODY, S. and JACKA, E. (1987) *The screening of Australia: Volume One – Anatomy of a Film Industry.* Sydney: Currency.

FISKE, J. (1987) *Television Culture.* London: Routledge.

HARLAND, R. (1987) *Superstructuralism.* London: Routledge.

LAWSON, S. (1993) *The Archibald Paradox.* Ringwood: Penguin Books.

MORLEY, D. and ANG, I. (1989) 'Mayonnaise culture and other European follies', *Cultural Studies* 3, 133–44.

MULVEY, L. (1986) 'Magnificent obsession', *Parachute* 42, 12.

ROSS, A. (1989) *No Respect: Intellectuals and Popular Culture.* London: Routledge.

RUTHVEN, K. (1989) 'Unlocking ideologies: "Key-Words" as a trope', *Southern Review* 25:1.

SCHWARZ, B. (1989) 'Popular culture: the long march', *Cultural Studies* 3, 250–54.

TURNER, G. (1986) *National Fictions: Literature, Film, and the Construction of Australian Narrative.* Sydney: Allen and Unwin.

TURNER, G. (1989) 'Dilemmas of cultural critique', *Australian Journal of Communication* 16.

WARD, R. (1958) *The Australian Legend.* Melbourne: Oxford University Press.

WILLIS, P. (1977) *Learning to Labor.* New York: Columbia University Press.

WRIGHT, P. (1985) *On Living in an Old Country.* London: Verso.

21

Race, culture, and communications: looking backward and forward at cultural studies

Stuart Hall

When I first went to the University of Birmingham in 1964 to help Professor Richard Hoggart found the Center for Contemporary Cultural Studies, no such thing as cultural studies yet existed. Of course, the departments of languages, literature, history, and the fine arts in our faculties of arts were dedicated to the preservation of the cultural heritage; though they refused to name let alone to theorize or conceptualize culture, preferring it to, so to speak, seep through by a process of academic osmosis. Social sciences, on the other hand, dealt sometimes with what they were pleased to call the 'cultural system'; but this was a pretty abstract thing, composed of networks of abstract norms and values. There was little of the concern that Richard Hoggart and I had in questions of culture. Our questions about culture – and I won't attempt to provide any kind of comprehensive definition of the term – were concerned with the changing ways of life of societies and groups and the networks of meanings that individuals and groups use to make sense of and to communicate with one another: what Raymond Williams once called whole ways of communicating, which are always whole ways of life; the dirty crossroads where popular culture intersects with the high arts; that place where power cuts across knowledge, or where cultural processes anticipate social change.

These were our concerns. The question was, where to study them? At that time we taught no anthropology at Birmingham and, besides, the English on whom we wished to turn our inquiring, ethnographic gaze had not yet learned to conceive of themselves as 'the natives'. I remember sitting in Richard Hoggart's room discussing what we should call ourselves. 'Institute', he suggested. Well, that sounded suitably grand and austere. But to be honest, the two of us, who constituted at that time the entire faculty and indeed, the students of the enterprise, could not find it in our hearts to take ourselves that seriously. Well, what about 'Center'? Yes, that had a more informal, rallying-point feel to it, and we settled for that. 'Cultural Studies' came much more naturally. It was about as broad as we could make it; thereby we ensured that no department in either the humanities or social sciences who thought that they had already taken care of culture could fail to feel affronted by our presence. In this latter enterprise, at least, we succeeded.

Today cultural studies programs exist everywhere, especially in the United States – there's not a touch of envy about that – where they've come to provide a focal point for interdisciplinary studies and research, and for the development of critical theory. Each program, in each place, as is appropriate, joins together a different range of disciplines in adapting itself to the existing academic and intellectual environment. Cultural studies, wherever it exists, reflects the rapidly shifting ground of thought and knowledge, argument and debate about a society and about its own culture. It is an activity of intellectual self-reflection. It operates both inside and outside the academy. It represents something, indeed, of the weakening of the traditional boundaries among the disciplines and of the growth of forms of interdisciplinary research that don't easily fit, or can't be contained, within the confines of the existing divisions of knowledge. As such, it represents, inevitably, a point of disturbance, a place of necessary tension and change in at least two senses. First, cultural studies constitutes one of the points of tension and change at the frontiers of intellectual and academic life, pushing for new questions, new models, and new ways of study, testing the fine lines between intellectual rigor and social relevance. It is the sort of necessary irritant in the shell of academic life that one hopes will, sometimes in the future, produce new pearls of wisdom.

But, secondly, in thrusting onto the attention of scholarly reflection and critical analysis the hurly-burly of a rapidly changing, discordant, and disorderly world, in insisting that academics sometimes attend to the practical life, where everyday social change exists out there, cultural studies tries in its small way to insist on what I want to call the vocation of the intellectual life. That is to say, cultural studies insists on the necessity to address the central, urgent, and disturbing questions of a society and a culture in the most rigorous intellectual way we have available. Such a vocation is, above all, in my view, one of the principal functions of a university, though university scholars are not always happy to be reminded of it.

Cultural studies was, therefore, in the first place precisely that. In the aftermath of World War II British society and culture were changing very rapidly and fundamentally. Cultural studies provided answers to the long process of Britain's decline as a world superpower. It also investigated the impact of modern mass consumption and modern mass society; the Americanization of our culture; the postwar expansion of the new means of mass communication; the birth of the youth cultures; the exposure of the settled habits and conventions and languages of an old class culture to the disturbing fluidity of new money and new social relationships; the dilution of the United Kingdom's very homogeneous social population by the influx of peoples from the new Commonwealth, the Caribbean, and the Asian subcontinent especially, leading to the formation, at the very heart and center of British cultural life, of Britain's cities, of their social and political existence, of the new black British diasporas of permanent settlement. In this last aspect we could see the old imperial dream, which had been dealt with, so to speak, at arms length and overseas, at last coming home to roost, completing the triangle that had connected Africa, the metropolitan society, and the Caribbean over such a long time. The paradox was that this coming-home-to-roost of the old empire was happening at exactly the moment when Britain was trying to 'cut the umbilical cord' and also at the moment when Britain was experiencing the cultural trauma, as yet in my view uncompleted and unrequited in English life, of the loss of an old imperial identity and role and the difficulty of discovering a new cultural and national identity.

Now, all those sociohistorical changes we could see were profoundly and to the roots transforming English culture: shifting the boundaries that had made the contours of daily existence familiar to people, setting up new disturbances, and letting loose those profound anxieties that always accompany radical social change. In short, a kind of cultural revolution was taking place in front of our eyes. And nobody, that we could see, was studying this revolution seriously. Nobody thought it worthwhile, let alone right and proper, to turn on this dramatically shifting, kaleidoscopic cultural terrain the search light of critical, analytic attention. Well, that was the vocation of cultural studies. That is what cultural studies in Britain was about. It is not my purpose to review its history nor, indeed, to comment on the role of the Centre for Cultural Studies, in which I worked for over fourteen years, in this enterprise. But I would insist on this starting point; I would insist on the tension characteristic in this work, which has marked my own intellectual development and my own intellectual work ever since. That is, the maximum mobilization of all the knowledge, thought, critical rigor, and conceptual theorization one can muster, turned into an act of critical reflection, which is not afraid to speak truth to conventional knowledge, and turned on the most important, most delicate, and invisible of objects: the cultural forms and practices of a society, its cultural life.

Perhaps readers will better understand what I've been saying if I take an example. The one I've chosen is the work I've been involved with in the area of race, culture, and communications. Now, someone from England trying to tell audiences in the United States about race is a little bit like carrying coals to Newcastle, if readers will forgive the simile. And, yet, one of the things that cultural studies has taught me is, indeed, the importance of historical specificity, of the specificity of each cultural configuration and pattern. There may undoubtedly be, and I think there are, general mechanisms in common across the globe that are associated with the practices of racism. But in each society, racism has a specific history that presents itself in specific, particular, and unique ways, and these specificities influence its dynamic and have real effects that differ from one society to another. One thing that cultural studies has taught me is, indeed, not to speak of racism in the singular, but of *racisms* in the plural. Though readers today might find it hard to believe, in the early 1960s when cultural studies began there was apparently no visible, urgent question of race in contemporary English culture at all. Of course, the question of race had permeated the whole history of imperialism and the contacts established over five centuries between Britain and peoples of the world. The history of the rise of Britain as a commercial and global power could not have been told without encountering the fact of race. But it was very largely relegated to the past and those who studied it: those who studied the Atlantic slave trade; those who looked at the family fortunes that had made possible the growing revolution of the eighteenth century; and those who had been involved in studying the antislavery movement, or who were experts in colonial history and administration. It seemed to have no active purchase as a contemporary theme in understanding British twentieth-century culture, which has already been spoken of as 'postcolonial'. The ways in which the colonizing experience had, indeed, threaded itself through the imaginary of the whole culture, what one can only call racism as the cup of tea at the bottom of every English experience, as the unstirred spoonful of sugar in every English child's sweet tooth, as the threads of cotton that kept the cotton mills going, as the cup of cocoa that sweetened the dreams of every English child – these things had been somehow relegated to the past and suppressed as an active cultural question. The way in which the popular culture of English society – from advertising to the music halls, to pageantry, to celebration, to the diamond jubilees, to the heritage industry, to theatrical melodramas, and so forth – had been orchestrated around the theatre, the spectacle of empire had been largely forgotten. The way in which English masculinity, itself, had proved itself, not simply on the playing fields of Eton but in the foothills of Hyderabad or facing down the howling dervishes in the Sudan, or the very English drama of corruption and conscience nicely balanced against one another, continually reenacted face to face with the heart of darkness; well, these things had been effectively liquidated from the culture in an active way. They had been blown away by, what the Prime Minister, Harold MacMillan, was pleased to call, 'the winds of change'.

It was the great migrations of the fifties and sixties from the Caribbean and from the Asian continent and the formation of black communities at the heart of English experience that brought the theme of racism in a new form to life again. And when it emerged, though it assumed many of the forms we had come to understand by the term 'the past', and from other societies, it had also acquired specifically diferent forms. In terms of the way in which the black experience was represented in the culture, in the media, it carried, of course, all the connotations that racism has had elsewhere: of an alien culture and peoples who are less civilized than the native ones; of a people who stand lower in the order of culture because they are somehow lower in the order of nature, defined by race, by color, and sometimes by genetic inheritance. But, in the new forms of racism that emerged in Britain in this period, and that have come to define the field in English culture since, these earlier forms have been powerfully transformed by what people normally call a new form of 'cultural racism'. That is to say, the differences in culture, in ways of life, in systems of belief, in ethnic identity and tradition, now matter more than anything that can be traced to specifically genetic or biological forms of racism. And what one sees here is the fact, the existence of racism contracting new relationships with a particular form, a defensive and besieged form, of argument around not 'who are the blacks?' but 'who are the English?' This question went right to the heart and center of English culture.

And I can give readers an example of what I'm calling cultural racism. Two years ago the white parents of a school in Dewsbury in Yorkshire withdrew their children from a predominantly black state school. One reason they gave for doing so was that they wanted their children to have a Christian education. They then added that they were not, as it happens, Christian believers at all; they simply regarded Christianity as an essential part of the English cultural heritage. They regarded the Anglican Church as part of the English way of life, rather like roast beef and Yorkshire pudding.

Now, how to study the many different ways in which these new manifestations of race, ethnicity, and racism were figured and represented in the mass media was one of the problems that confronted us in the Centre for Cultural Studies: how to bring to light the deeper historical traces of race in English culture. What were available to us were principally the models developed in communication studies elsewhere, borrowed from societies that had confronted these problems much earlier than we had. And cultural studies, as we appropriate then and now, devoured them. We were alerted to the nature of racial stereotyping, to the negative imagery of race and ethnicity in the mass media, to the absence of accounts of the black experience as a central part of the English story, to the repetition in the mass media of a very simplified and truncated way of representing black history, life, and culture. These provided us with certain methods of analysis and study that were of immense importance to us in the early phase. So, the point that I want to make comes across in the way in which my own understanding of and work on the questions of race and racism have been subsequently transformed by developments within the field of cultural studies itself. I am only able to hint at this transformation here, but it is something that I want to do in order to return to my central point below.

I note a shift, for example, in the way in which we understand how the media construct and represent race. The earlier approach led us to ask questions about the accuracy of media representations. We wanted to know if the media were simply distorting, like a distorting mirror held up to a reality that existed outside of itself. But what cultural studies has helped me to understand is that the media play a part in the formation, in the constitution, of the things that they reflect. It is not that there is a world outside, 'out there', which exists free of the discourses of representation. What is 'out there' is, in part, constituted by how it is represented. The reality of race in any society is, to coin a phrase, 'media-mediated'. And distortions and simplifications of experience, which are certainly there, and above all, *absences* – we had to develop a methodology that taught us to attend, not only to what people said about race but, in England the great society of the understatement, to what people could *not* say about race. It was the silences that told us something; it was what wasn't there. It was what was invisible, what couldn't be put into frame, what was apparently unsayable that we needed to attend to. If you want to ask, 'what can content analysis teach you?' well, one of the questions you have to ask is, 'what about the people who appear to have no content at all – who are just pure form, just pure, invisible form?' You can count lexical items if they're there; but you need a different approach if you really want, as it were, to read a society and its culture symptomatically.

And that is, indeed, what we had to try to begin to learn to do in face of the logics of racism, which worked, we were to discover, rather more like Freud's dreamwork than like anything else. We found that racism expresses itself through displacement, through denial, through the capacity to say two contradictory things at the same time, the surface imagery speaking of an unspeakable content, the repressed content of a culture. Every time I watch a popular television narrative, like *Hill Street Blues* or *Miami Vice*, with its twinning and coupling of racial masculinities at the center of its story, I have to pinch myself to remind myself that these narratives are not a somewhat distorted reflection of the real state of race relations in American cities. These narratives function much more, as Claude Lévi-Strauss tells us, as myths do. They are myths that represent in narrative form the resolution of things that cannot be resolved in real life. What they tell us is about the 'dream life' of a culture. But to gain a privileged access to the dream life of a culture, we had better know how to unlock the complex ways in which narrative plays across real life.

Once we look at any of these popular narratives which constantly, in the imagination of a society, construct the place, the identities, the experience, the histories of the different peoples who live within it, then we are instantly aware of the complexity of the nature of racism itself. Of course, one aspect of racism is, certainly, that it occupies a world of manichean opposites: them and us, primitive and civilized, light and dark, a black and white symbolic universe. But, once you have analyzed or identified this simple logic, it seems all too simple. You can fight it. But you can't spend a lifetime studying it; it is almost too obvious to spend any more time on. It is kind of a waste of time to add another book about a world that absolutely insists on dividing everything it says into good and bad. My conviction now would be completely different from the conclusion of one graduate student who had come to the Center to study popular narratives of race. After two years, she said, 'It's just so (forgive me) bloody obvious. There's nothing more to say. Once I've said it's a racist text what do Chapter 5, and Chapter 6, and Chapter 7 do, just say the same thing over again?' I would now give her very different advice from that which I gave her then.

Contrary to the superficial evidence, there is nothing simple about the structure and the dynamics of racism. My conviction now is that we are only at the beginning of a proper understanding of its structures and mechanisms. And, that is the case because its apparent simplicities and rigidities are the things that are important, symptomatically, about it. It is racism's very rigidity that is the clue to its complexity. Its capacity to punctuate the universe into two great opposites masks something else; it masks the complexes of feelings and attitudes, beliefs and conceptions, that are always refusing to be so neatly stabilized and fixed. The great divisions of racism as a structure of knowledge and representation are also, it now seems to me, a deep system of defense. They are the outworks, the trenches, the defensive positions around something that refuses to be tamed and contained by this system of representation. All that symbolic and narrative energy and work is directed to secure us 'over here' and them 'over there', to fix each in its appointed species place. It is a way of marking how deeply our histories actually intertwine and interpenetrate; how necessary 'the Other' is to our own sense of identity; how even the dominant, colonizing, imperializing power only knows who and what it is and can only experience the pleasure of its own power of domination in and through the construction of the Other. The two are the two sides of the same coin. And the Other is not *out there*, but *in here*. It is not outside, but inside.

This is the very profound insight of one of the most startling, staggering, important books in this field, Franz Fanon's *Black Skin, White Masks*: 'The movement, the attitudes, the glances of the Other fix me here, in the sense in which a chemical solution is fixed by a dye. I was indignant, I demanded an explanation, nothing happened, I burst apart and now the fragments have been put together by another self.' We can see in this quotation that in addition to the mechanisms of directed violence and aggression, which are characteristic of racial stereotyping, are those other things: the mechanisms of splitting, of projection, of defense, and of denial. We come to understand the attempt to suppress and control, through the symbolic economy of a culture, everything that is different; the danger, the threat, that difference represents; the attempt to refuse, to repress, to fix, to know everything about 'the different' so that one can control it; the attempt to make what is different an object of the exercise of power; the attempt to symbolically expel it to the far side of the universe. And, then, we understand the surreptitious return where that which has been expelled keeps coming back home, to trouble the dreams of those who thought, a moment ago, that they were safe.

The violence, aggression, and hatred implicit in racist representation is not to be denied. But we understand very little, as yet, about its double-sided nature, its deep ambivalances. Just as so often in the cultures of the West the representation of women has appeared in its split form – the good/bad girl, the good and the bad mother, madonna and whore – so the representations of Blacks keep, at different times, exhibiting this split, double structure. Devoted, dependent, childlike, the Blacks are simultaneously unreliable, unpredictable, and undependable; capable of turning nasty or plotting treachery as soon as you turn your back. And despite being the object of an infinite benevolence, they are, inexplicably in a society predicated on freedom, given to escaping from us along the freedom trail. Or, in a society that calls itself Christian, they are given to singing songs about the promised land. They just won't be where they ought to be.

And side by side with those representations is a discourse that cannot seem to represent nobility or natural dignity or physical grace without summoning up the black primitive. For example, in modern advertising, the tropics, which are in fact savaged by debt and ravaged by hunger and malnutrition, have become the privileged signifier of the erotic, of good times, of pleasure, of playing away. The period of nobility of any aging chief or of the natives' rhythmic force simultaneously express a nostalgia, a desire in civilized society for an innocence, an erotic power of the body that has been apparently lost to so-called civilized societies. At the same time, these images represent a fear at the heart of civilization itself of being overrun by the recurrence of a dark savagery.

This double syntax of racism – never one thing without the other – is something that we can associate with old images in the mass media; but the problem about the mass media is that old movies keep being made. And so, the old types and the doubleness and the old ambivalence keep turning up on tomorrow's television screen. Today's restless native hordes are still alive and well and living as guerrilla armies and freedom fighters in the Angolan or Namibian bush. Blacks are still the most frightening, as well as the most well-dressed, crooks and policemen in any New York cop series. They are the necessary fleet-footed, crazy-talking, hip undermen who connect Starsky and Hutch to the drug-saturated ghetto. How else would they know where to go? The scheming villains and their giant-sized bully boys of the adventure novel have spilled out into everything that now passes for what we call adventure. The sexually available, half-caste slave girl is still alive and kicking, smoldering away on some exotic television set or on the cover of some paperback, though she is, no doubt, simultaneously also the center of a very special covetous aspiration and admiration, in a sequined gown, supported by a white chorus line.

Primitivism, savagery, guile, unreliability are always just below the surface, just waiting to bite. They can still be identified in the faces of black political leaders or ghetto vigilantes around the world, cunningly plotting the overthrow of civilization. The old country (white version) is often the subject of the nostalgic documentaries on English television: prewar Malaysia, Sri Lanka, old Rhodesia, the South African veldt where hitherto reliable servants, as is only to be expected, plot treason in the outback and steal away to join ZAPU or the ANC in the bush. Tribal men in green khaki.

If you go to analyze racism today in its complex structures and dynamics, one question, one principle above all, emerges as a lesson for us. It is the fear – the terrifying, internal fear – of living with *difference*. This fear arises as the consequence of the fatal coupling of difference and power. And, in that sense, the work that cultural studies has to do is to mobilize everything that it can find in terms of intellectual resources in order to understand what keeps making the lives we live, and the societies we live in, profoundly and deeply antihumane in their capacity to live with difference. Cultural studies' message is a message for academics and intellectuals but, fortunately, for many other people as well. In that sense, I have tried to hold together in my own intellectual life, on one hand, the conviction and passion and the devotion to objective interpretation, to analysis, to rigorous analysis and understanding, to the passion to find out, and to the production of knowledge that we did not know before. But, on the other hand, I am convinced that no intellectual worth his or her salt, and no university that wants to hold up its head in the face of the twenty-first century, can afford to turn dispassionate eyes away from the problems of race and ethnicity that beset our world.

This article is a revised text of a convocation address that I presented in February 1989 on the occasion of having had conferred upon me an honorary degree from the University of Massachusetts in Amherst. I am particularly grateful to the Department of Communication and to Professor Sut Jhally for providing me, on this occasion and in the past, invitations to visit the University.

22

Australian cultural studies

John Frow and Meaghan Morris

I

During the past few years the word 'culture' has come to be used by Australians in a sense that seems far removed from anything to do with artistic and literary texts. When Australian Labor Party Senator Stephen Loosley declares that 'resetting industrial policy is really a matter of reshaping cultural attitudes', he is not defining culture as a domain of aesthetic pleasure, as a set of masterpieces, or even as an expression of national identity. Nor is he speaking in economic terms of culture as a major industry which (the Sydney *Daily Telegraph Mirror* assures us) 'fills Aussie tills'.[1] He is referring to a complex of social customs, values and expectations which affect our ways of working. So, too, was Rupert Murdoch in an interview screened on ABC-TV in 1990. Just as the worst company crashes in Australian history ended an era of financial mismanagement and entrepreneurial crime, the Melbourne host of the ABC current affairs program *7.30 Report* asked Mr Murdoch what 'we' should do to save our economy. Mr Murdoch replied perfunctorily, 'Oh, you know: change the culture'.

Unlike Senator Loosley, Murdoch expected us to 'know' that he was quoting a formula of the neo-liberal rhetoric now broadly shared in Australia (as elsewhere) by bureaucrats, politicians, economists, journalists and financiers as well as union and corporate eladers, namely: economic problems need 'cultural' solutions. Culture in this sense is not just a topic for specialised debate by an esoteric caste of interpreters ('critics'). On the contrary: 'changing the culture' is a shorthand but *expansive* way of challenging the conduct of other people's everyday working lives – whether within the framework of a single company ('changing the culture is not a quick process in something as old and as large as ARC', says a chief executive of Australia's main producer of concrete reinforcing steel); of an industry (a marketing expert offers a paper on 'Changing culture for service: how to effect a change to the service culture in shopping centres'); or an entire national economy ('Professor Hughes said Australians had relied on the "lucky country" attitude for too long. . . . "We have got to cultivate an export culture" ').[2]

In other words, culture itself is imagined as a plastic medium which politically powerful social elites may rework and remould at will. For these economic critics of Australian life, changing the culture primarily means that 'fewer workers must produce more for less'. But this program has social implications. It means changing the minutiae of behaviour ('work practices') at the workplace, and thus the texture and organisation of home and family life; it means inducing workers to invest more actively in the corporate ethos; it can mean improving race and gender relations in the interests of achieving an 'international outlook'; it means sharpening class consciousness by making competitiveness, 'inequality of outcomes' and, therefore, poverty, more acceptable to Australians.

Aesthetic implications follow. 'Changing the culture' means questioning the value of some of the canonical myths of modern Australian history – egalitarianism, mateship, upward mobility for 'all' – along with the ethical images of pleasure, personal development and social worth that circulate in our society. Despite appearances, the neo-liberal critique of culture cannot neatly be disentangled from 'artistic and literary' concerns. By the end of the 1980s it had even prompted a media debate about Australian national identity: 'We are', said Peter Robinson, 'nearly all of us, bludgers. That is the reason the country is in a mess and it will not get out of that mess until the national bludging culture has been reversed.'[3]

Shorn of its subordination of all other goals to that of economic productivity, and without the *moralism* that characterises neo-liberal rhetoric, this usage turns out to be strikingly close to one dimension of the way the word is used in contemporary Australian cultural studies. In this context, too, culture is thought of as directly bound up with work and its organisation; with relations of power and gender in the workplace and the home; with the pleasures and the pressures of consumption; with the complex relations of class and kith and kin through which a sense of self is formed; and with the fantasies and desires through which social relations are carried and actively shaped. In short, 'culture' is a term that can designate, in Raymond Williams' phrase, the 'whole way of life' of a social group as it is structured by representation and by power.[4] It is not a detached domain for playing games of social distinction and 'good' taste. It is a network of representations – texts, images, talk, codes of behaviour, and the narrative structures organising these – which shapes every aspect of social life.

II

But to say that the concept of culture refers to the existence of social groups – their formation, their maintenance, their definition against other groups, the constant process of their re-formation – is to raise difficult questions about the kinds of unity that groups lay claim to. At what level, we must ask, does the concept of culture operate – that of the nation-state and/or of a 'national' culture? That of class, gender, race, sexuality, age, ethnicity?

The answer is that it may operate at any of these levels, and that they do not slot neatly into each other.

Australian cultural studies, it seems to us, has been acutely aware of the danger of positing imaginary social unities as the explanatory basis for its accounts of cultural texts. Its constant impetus is to think of cultures as processes which divide as much as they bring together, and to be suspicious of those totalising notions of culture which assume that there is always, at the end of cultural processes, the achievement of a whole and coherent 'society' or 'community'.

One reason for this may be that Australia moved very rapidly in the late 1960s and early 1970s from attributing to itself a unitary culture and tradition, and indeed conceiving these as directly based in its cultural and even racial inheritance from Britain, to a recognition at the level of official government policy of the diversity of its ethnic make-up (based to a substantial degree on massive postwar migration from southern Europe and elsewhere); the new policy of multiculturalism sought to recognise cultural diversity within, and as the basis of, a more differentiated mode of national cohesion.[5] At roughly the same time Australia moved – again, for good and for bad, at the level of official government doctrine – away from its assimilationist and paternalist policies towards Aboriginal people.[6] What followed was in many ways of little practical difference, as both state and federal governments failed to legislate land rights and self-government for Aborigines. The symbolic step nevertheless had its own force. It defined Aboriginal people rather than government institutions as the ones to decide on their future, and it thereby created its own demand for political empowerment.

The policy of multiculturalism is a compromise formation, and it works well in part because the centrifugal pressures on Australian national unity are relatively weak (there is no profound linguistic split, as there is in Canada for instance, and white settler culture is still comfortably installed as the dominant and unmarked term). The policy is imperfect in both its political and its philosophical dimensions: it is always possible for the category of culture with which it operates to remain at the decorative level of folkloric ethnic markers detached from substructures of real and agonistic difference; conversely, it tends to reproduce imaginary identities at the level of the ethnic 'community' and thereby to screen differentiations and contradictions *within* the community (those of class and gender, for example); it depends upon covering over an asymmetry between migrant and indigenous groups (as though both could have the same historical and structural relation to settler society); and it depends, above all, on a final moment of absorption of difference back into unity at the level of language and national identity.

Within its limits, nevertheless, multiculturalism in Australia has been a relatively successful policy, acting as a working model for a conception of culture ideally based on difference and the recognition of otherness, rather than on cultural and social identity. This history of 'policy' forms part of the context for the essays in Section I of this book [Frow and Morris, 1993], 'Representation Wars', all of which explore the *consequences* of assuming a concept of social identity as mobile, differential and provisional (that is, identity as figure rather than as essence) – and all of which work critically on problems defining the *limits* of multiculturalism as a doctrine of conflict management.

Sneja Gunew's essay on '"Wongar's" *Walg*', for example, considers the unnegotiable status (for this doctrine) of a novel 'authored' by an immigrant Serbian man under an Aboriginal name, and fictively narrated by an Aboriginal woman. Here, the ideology of authorial identity creates a problem of inauthentic difference which can only be resolved by an (impossible) interdiction that seeks to erase the text: '"Wongar" may neither speak nor write.' Conversely, Eric Michaels discusses the elaborate '*mise en discours*' by which Aboriginal Australian art was promoted in the speculative global market (and the postmodernism boom) of the late 1980s. Suggesting that contemporary Warlpiri 'creative and authorial practices' render fraudulent any aesthetic of the Warlpiri 'product' – which raises issues of cultural *authority*, not authenticity, and which derives its value from conditions of struggle with colonialism and racism – Michaels demands that Warlpiri paintings be judged in terms of their complex processes of production and circulation: 'the contradictions of this system resist resolution.'

Vijay Mishra and Bob Hodge argue that aesthetic postmodernism in fact works broadly to mask an 'unmanageable' plethora of asymmetries between settler and non-settler, white and non-white, colonies. As a 'justifying' discourse that incorporates settler cultures in the temporal framework of a unified 'postcolonialism', it reduces the postcolonial to a 'liberal Australian version of multiculturalism'. In her essay on the high-level diplomatic dispute between Australia and Malaysia over the ABC-TV series *Embassy*, Suvendrini Perera examines an instance of crisis in such postmodern conflict-masking. While specifying her own concerns with issues of authority in a 'mesh of cultural economies', Perera's essay also makes explicit the *regional*-historical context (and the flagrant contradictions) in which multiculturalism tries to 'manage' racism in Australia without risking the political legitimacy of White settler concepts of nationhood, challenging the cultural security of the ethnic ('Anglo-Celtic') status quo[7] – or endangering the governmental economic aim of furthering trade with other Asian-Pacific countries.

III

The essays in the opening section are not theoretically congruent, or politically continuous, with each other, nor with the other essays in the book; there are incompatibilities, divergences and edges of disagreement as well as resonances between them (compare, for example, Perera on *Embassy* with Stuart Cunningham on Australian mini-series; Mishra and Hodge on postcolonial literatures with John Hartley on 'invisible fictions' of audience, and global regimes of TV pleasure; Michaels with Adrian Martin on aesthetics; Noel Sanders with Ross Gibson on the cultural construction of landscape; or Tony Bennett with Meaghan Morris on locality tourism). We have, however, used this first section to *frame* as well as to introduce the

Reader, because we think that the pressingly political questions of differential representation raised by these essays have strongly inflected most
Australian work in cultural studies. Perera's essay lends its title to the
section ('Representation Wars') because her analysis of the fears, desires,
and conflicts provoked as well as expressed by *Embassy's* 'charged', fantas-
matic Orientalism also helps to clarify two crucial aspects of the context in
which, we would argue, Australian work is carried out.

Both aspects 'mesh', in complicated ways, with multiculturalism as well
as with each other. One can briefly be described by noting a by-product of
policy debates about the social and cultural dimensions of Australia's
increasing economic integration with Japan (our major trading partner)
and other east Asian countries: the wide circulation in the media of
competing narratives – whether dreams or nightmares, fantasies or fears
– about 'becoming part of "Asia"'.[8] After the 1970s, it became commonplace for proponents of *economic* 'Asianisation' publicly to criticise those
features of our cultural life (xenophobia and parochialism for some, 'free
speech' for others) political organisation (the monarchy for some; 'union
power' for others) and historical tradition (racism for some, human rights
and 'individualism' for others) which can be held to act as obstacles to
promoting Australian interests, and 'credibility', with governments and
business in the region. In this period, too, articulated racist hostility to
'Asian immigration' moved from the mainstream to the still vociferous
margins of policy debate; 'business migration from Asia' became a governmental object of desire, and militant Social Darwinism gave way to a
flexible Orientalism in foreign affairs.

Again, this shift away from an ideology of purity and identity (and from
a 'closed' to an 'open' economy) has been rapid; only in 1965 were the
words 'White Australia' removed from the Australian Labor Party plat-
form. One of its effects has been to undermine the rhetorical force of older
nationalist appeals to 'authenticity' and 'tradition' in the field of *public*
debate; powerful sectors of both the state and capital in Australia have
good reasons to fund their own critiques of 'essentialism'.[9] Another has
been to make available an official discourse of 'nationality' which openly
promotes a constructive, not an organic, concept of Australian culture, and
a pragmatic, even enterprising approach to the uses of historical representation; for this discourse, both 'culture' and 'history' can be valued more as
practices responsible for shaping a prosperous national future than as ways
of conserving a 'heritage' from the past. When Prime Minister Keating
declared in 1992 that the Pacific War and the Kokoda Track are more
appropriate than World War I and Gallipoli as a myth of origins for
contemporary Australia, what semioticians call the 'productivity' of discourse was officially taken for granted – and the practice of history *formally*
defined as a powerful adjunct to trade.

This may be one reason why Australian work in cultural studies has
generally been less concerned to debate the pros and cons of 'essentialism'
as a philosophical stance than to examine the *political* conflicts at stake, in
concrete contexts and for particular groups of people, between differing
stories of community or nation, and to articulate the *historical* struggles
occurring in the gaps between competing narrative programs (of 'prosper-

ity', for example), and the complex social experiences that these aspire to organise. A geo-economic insistence on *location* ('becoming part of Asia') is not, in itself, a new development in the public rhetoric of Australian cultural life, and in this volume the essays by Perera, Mishra and Hodge, Turner, Gibson, Morris, Sanders and Stern explore ways in which old colonial genres and 'structures of feeling' (in Raymond Williams's phrase[10]) continue to shape the social meanings of events in the landscapes produced by economic internationalisation.

At the same time, some writers suggest, Australia may well be caught up in a long-term historical process of 'becoming a nation' in these conditions of ethnic diversity, state multiculturalism and economic internationalism: if so, this is a process in which critical intellectuals perhaps inevitably take part. Dating the current phase of 'nationing' to the 1960s (the period in which Donald Horne published *The Lucky Country*, and another time of lively talk about Australia's 'Asian' location), Tony Bennett explores some of the strategies currently deployed in the formation of a national past; Graeme Turner observes the use of an anti-colonial rhetoric to obscure the responsibility of a series of national governments for the social and environmental effects of nuclear testing; while Stuart Cunningham values the historical mini-series that flourished on TV in the 1980s for taking seriously 'the radical historiographical dictum that "the past is only interesting politically because of something which touches us in the present"' – praising the agenda-setting pedagogy of *Cowra Breakout* and *Vietnam* for their 'multiperspectival', elliptical dramaturgy of major events in Australian history.

The importance of the media in shaping debates about location and nationality in Australia highlights the second contextual feature of cultural studies that we want to emphasise. If 'representation wars' are occurring everywhere in part because of the social uptake of communications technology,[11] many Australians are now receiving a plethora of differing local, regional, 'global' and, for the first time, *national* representations of their own and others' lives. In an important essay published elsewhere, Tom O'Regan argues that it was not until the 1980s – with the introduction of satellite networking and complex changes in federal government broadcasting regulations as well as in media markets – that a 'space-binding', 'nationalising' emphasis could fully emerge in the once strongly state-oriented Australian media system. Paradoxically, he suggests, this emphasis favours 'decontextualised' ways of thinking about self, politics and identity while simultaneously fostering a more national *and* international 'mind-set', confirming as well as disconfirming state boundaries and regional autonomies, and 'encouraging the further development of corridors of information'.[12]

The pressure of these contradictory movements may help to explain the remarkable explicitness of public debate in Australia about power, propriety and representation (who has, and who should have, the power to represent whom; how; and under which conditions). If new national frames of reference are, in fact, emerging just as local, regional and global flows of information are redrawing cultural and political boundaries, then the complex issue of *control* over image production, circulation and consumption becomes enmeshed (as Perera points out) in a whole range of political, economic, legal and diplomatic concerns. At the same time, the technological and geo-economic conditions forcing the question of 'what is involved in the representation of another culture, especially when it is seen by members of that culture' on to the government and thence the *media* agenda are precisely those conditions which make it impossible for 'control' to be fully assured from any given point in the system – or for every dispute to be 'managed' within the national framework of Australian democratic multiculturalism.

Moreover, Australia also has a long history of colonial sensitivity about 'the Australian image' abroad, and a solid record of using public resources to shape the representation of our history and ways of life through state-funded image production. In an article on the furore created by the British-produced ABC-TV series *Sylvania Waters* in 1992, Graeme Turner has pointed out that the reception of this 'documentary' about the everyday lives of the Donaher family was a lot like the outrage which greeted *The adventures of Barry McKenzie* in 1972 and, to a lesser extent, *Crocodile Dundee* in 1986.[13] Like the 'ocker' films of 20 years ago, *Sylvania Waters* provoked heated ethical debates about aesthetic responsibility, genre, and Australian social reality: are many of us *really* like that? are the Donahers' values widely shared? what will people overseas think? should 'ordinary Australians' be allowed to express their racism and homophobia on TV? are British producers entitled to sensationalise the lives of real Australians to flatter British consumers? was the portrayal of Noeline sexist? or class-prejudiced? should soap opera be promoted as 'reality television'? is 'reality TV' ever *real*? Like *Crocodile Dundee*, *Sylvania Waters* also aroused economic anxiety about its impact in Australia (is it a bad sign that most viewers admired the poorest members of the family?) and in other countries (what effect will this have on tourism, immigration, or foreign trade?).

The intertwining of ethical and 'image' concerns with political conflicts in a vulnerable *tourist* economy is a recurring theme of this book; as tourism has vastly expanded in scale and in importance to the Australian economy, so public debate has intensified about the social costs and environmental effects of tourist culture.[14] An important influence on Australian discussions of the politics of representation, however, has come from the work of Aboriginal people directly *confronting* these costs and effects. Historically used as targets for the technological practices, 'nationing' experiments and ethnocidal image campaigns of white Australian society,[15] Aboriginal groups have recently used the media to wage a 'war' of their own to protect their languages and ways of life; to increase their economic independence by developing their own artistic and tourist ventures; to bring political pressure to bear on federal and state governments sensitive to embarrassment and reactive to 'credibility'; to educate public opinion in Australia; to demand positive, informed coverage of Aboriginal activities, and more control over Aboriginal images; and, by these means, to further their political struggle for self-determination.[16]

While there is always controversy about the practical results of this kind of 'symbolic' politics, Aboriginal media practices have at the very least challenged (and, we would argue, altered) the terms on which issues of race, colonialism, cultural value, national identity and history, land ownership and environmental ethics are publicly discussed in Australia – which is to say, they have powerfully affected our political and intellectual life. So have feminist campaigns around images of women, and so, too, have the efforts of migrant groups to change the representational 'norm' of an Anglo-Celtic Australia. In this context, it is not simply a conceit of cultural studies to claim that people can contest and transform the meanings circulated by the culture industries of a media society. On the contrary, the fact that people actually *do* this is a given of contemporary politics, and one determinant of the social context in which cultural studies is practised.

In our view, the most innovative Australian work has therefore been more interested in developing the *implications* of particular forms of symbolic action, and the *consequences* of particular moments of cultural practice, than in proving the case for doing so against older theories of culture. It is not that Australian cultural studies (as we see it) is in any way hostile to 'theory'; theoretical work can also be considered a form of cultural practice. It is merely that the doctrinal disputes which have marked and perhaps enabled the emergence of cultural studies elsewhere – disputes between humanism and formalism, formalism and Marxism, Frankfurt School Marxism and post-structuralism, deconstruction and new historicism, 'textualism' and ethnography – have not long remained the *focus* of debate in Australia, where they are often resolved in practice by a kind of rigorous *mixing* (see the essays by Helen Grace, Virginia Nightingale and Tom O'Regan).

There are many complex institutional reasons for this: the humanities academy is small, state funded, and relatively poor; the publishing industry is embattled; many academics can and do engage in several spheres of public life; few of the theoretical traditions so hotly debated internationally in recent years have played a strong or an inhibiting role in Australian intellectual history.[17] The point here, however, is simply that Australian cultural studies has not only been a *response* to the political and social movements of the past three decades (this much can be said of cultural studies as a project in general), but has also derived many of its themes, its research priorities, its polemics and, in some ways, its theoretical emphases and privileged working methods, from an *engagement* with those movements – and the 'worldly, historical frames' (to borrow a phrase from Said and Perera) in which they operate.

IV

The first set of determinations that we want to posit as acting on Australian cultural studies, then, has to do with its involvement in and its confrontation with the intensities of a 'national' culture and a 'national' politics. A second set of determinations – although this separation is no more than a conceptual artifice – has to do with the emergent logic of the discipline (or the antidiscipline) of cultural studies itself, as it struggles to define its object, the *form* of its relation to its object, and the theoretical stakes of its practice.

At the beginning of his essay on the gift, Marcel Mauss writes:

> In these 'early' societies, social phenomena are not discrete; each phenomenon
> contains all the threads of which the social fabric is composed. In these total
> social phenomena, as we propose to call them, all kinds of institutions find
> simultaneous expression: religious, legal, moral, and economic. In addition, the
> phenomena have their aesthetic aspect and they reveal morphological types.[18]

For cultural studies, we suggest, a similar concentration of social relations
is thought to occur in the pressure points of complex modern societies, but
without the microcosmic expressiveness that Mauss finds in 'archaic' social
structures; rather, social relations are dispersed through these points,
composing their complexity but permitting no read-off of a social totality.
Instead of the 'total social phenomenon', the corresponding concept for
cultural studies is perhaps that of the 'site' (the point of intersection and of
negotiation of radically different kinds of determination and semiosis),
while 'expression' is displaced by the concept of 'event' (a moment of
practice that crystallises diverse temporal and social trajectories).

Thus a shopping mall – to take a banal but central example – offers no
quintessential insight into the organisation of an epoch or a culture (it is not
an emblem or an essence of the postmodern condition or of consumer
capitalism); it is a place where many different things happen, and where
many different kinds of social relations are played out. It is, of course, the
end point of numerous chains of production and transportation of goods,
as well as of the marketing systems that channel them to consumers (and of
the financial structures that underlie all this). These chains belong to
regional and national as well as to global circuits (the 'gourmet' aisle in
the supermarket or the shelves of a delicatessen make visible the global
nature of the capitalist marketplace, and may evoke something of the
history of its formation, while the produce section may – or may not – be
quite local in its reach. In each case the forms of packaging and presentation – 'exotic' or 'fresh', for example – will carry particular ideologies and
particular aesthetic strategies). In another of its dimensions, the mall is an
architectural construct, designed in accordance with an international format (anchored strategically by one or two large stores, with a particular
disposition of parking and pedestrian traffic, a particular mix of boutiques,
of services, of facilities . . .); it constructs (or perhaps fails to construct) a
particular existence and image of community, and works in calculated
ways to display the rewards and pleasures that follow upon work (or,
again, that fail to). It sets up a normative distinction between men's and
women's interactions with this space, and between adults', children's, and
teenagers' uses. It distinguishes sharply, of course, between its affluent
clientele (the proper subjects of its community) and those who are less
welcome – some of them, like schoolkids, it may tolerate; others, like
vagrants and drunks, it will not. The aesthetic organisation of the mall
has to do with the gratification of desire and the organisation of bodies of
space; it's a sensual, subtly coercive kind of space.

But it is also a space that is put to use, that is diverted to ends other than
those foreseen by its architects and managers and guards. This is perhaps
the most familiar lesson of cultural studies: that structures are always

structures-in-use, and that uses cannot be contained in advance. The semiotic space of the shopping mall is a conflictual space, where meanings are negotiated and projected through quite different formations of fantasy and need. This is to suggest a certain freedom, a function perhaps merely of the complexity of these interactions; but, knowing how readily the appearance of freedom can itself be a ruse of power, a cultural studies critic is likely to be wary of positing any transcendental value for this ability to use public space.

In order to get at these disparate structures that meet in and flow through a complex site like a shopping mall, the theorist (because this is never simply a *descriptive* activity) will have of necessity to draw upon, and to cross, the discourses of a number of different disciplines (and again, this cross-disciplinary perspective is characteristic of the working methods of cultural studies). These might include:

- several rather different forms of economic discourse: some relatively technical ways of discussing mall management, commodity supply and demand, and regional patterns of employment; and a more theoretical discourse about commodity production and circulation;

- an aesthetic discourse, relating particularly to architecture, but also to advertising and display; a discourse of musicology, or socio-musicology, to talk about the workings of Muzak or of live performance; and a higher level discourse to deal with the interrelation between aesthetics and economics;

- a discourse of politics, both of the 'mundane' kind that refers to zoning permits and struggles over property values, and a micrological discourse concerned with the politics of bodies in space; the first of these might draw in turn upon the discourses of the law and of town planning; the latter upon a Foucauldian account of corporeal discipline, or upon symbolic interactionism or ethnomethodology, or upon urban geography;

- a discourse about gender (itself necessarily a mixed discourse) to analyse the organisation of gender relations by a mythologised spatial structure, by the gender-specific targeting of consumer desire, by the structure of employment, by childcare provision or its absence, and so on;

- an ethnographic discourse, to get at the particularity of responses to and uses of the mall, to understand it as lived experience (or lived textuality, to use a more precise phrase);

- a discourse of history, capable of talking about changes in the organisation of consumption, perhaps in terms of the 'postmodern' or 'post-Fordist' centrality of consumption to a reorganised capitalist system; and of theorising the changing modes of organisation of community and of the public sphere;

- a discourse perhaps more specific to cultural studies that understands the mall as an intricate textual construct, and understands shopping as a form of popular culture directly interrelated with other cultural forms and with an economy of representations and practices that make up a 'way of life';

- possibly governing the use of some of these other discourses, a policy discourse, serving either the managers of and investors in shopping malls, or local government, or perhaps community groups with an interest in reshaping the forms of community structured by the mall;

- finally, some mix of sociology, semiotics, and philosophy which one might draw on to talk about the position(s) from which such an analysis can be enunciated: to come to terms with the odd duality that splits the critic into participant and observer, practitioner and reflexive intellectual, on the basis of the privilege given by the possession of cultural capital and a relation of some kind to the institutions of knowledge that make such reflexivity possible.

It is perhaps this 'self-situating' and *limiting* moment of analysis that most clearly distinguishes work in cultural studies from some other modes of analysis on which its practitioners may draw. Unlike much empirical work in positivist social science, cultural studies tends to incorporate in its object of study a critical account of its own motivating questions – and thus of the institutional frameworks and disciplinary rules by which its research imperatives are formed. At the same time, cultural studies is not a form of that 'multi'-disciplinarity which dreams of producing an exhaustive knowledge map, and it does not posit (unlike some totalising forms of Marxism) a transcendental space from which knowledges could be synthesised and a 'general' theory achieved.[19]

On the contrary, work in cultural studies accepts its partiality, in both senses of the term: it is openly incomplete, and it is partisan in its insistence on the political dimensions of knowledge. For this reason, the 'splitting' of critical practice between diverse and often conflicting social functions does not give rise, in cultural studies, to a discourse of intellectual *alienation*. While there is no consensus about the politics of intellectual work among the critics represented in this book (still less for cultural studies imagined 'as a whole'), the intellectual project of cultural studies is always at some level marked, we would argue, by a discourse of social *involvement*.

V

The point of this discussion of an imaginary object, the shopping mall, is to give a sense not only of the working methods of cultural studies but of their rationale. Cultural studies often operates in what looks like an eccentric way, starting with the particular, the detail, the scrap of ordinary or banal existence, and then working to unpack the density of relations and of intersecting social domains that inform it. Rather than being interested in television or architecture or pinball machines in themselves – as industrial or aesthetic structures – it tends to be interested in the way such apparatuses work as points of concentration of social meaning, as 'media' (literally), the carriers of all the complex and conflictual practices of sociality.

To say that the shopping mall is organised by a range of diverse and overlapping systems (economic, aesthetic, demographic, regulatory, spatial . . .) and can be the object of very different discourses, none of which has a privileged relation to its object, is to say that it is subject to very different kinds of *reading*, and that there is no principle of totality that can bring these readings into a coherent complementarity. To cast it in terms of reading is then to suggest a relation between the specialised readings of the various disciplines of knowledge and the 'folk' readings performed by the users of the site (readings which are bound up with the 'things to do' in shopping centres rather than being detached analytic exercises – but which are also themselves, however, pleasurable and interesting 'things to do'). This, too, is a characteristic move in cultural studies: a relativising and democratising move which seeks to ensure that talk about an object is not closed off on the assumption that we know everything there is to know about it; and to ensure that the rationality of any discourse to the full range of others is kept constantly in view.

Another way of talking about all this might be to say that it has to do with the way we understand the concept of *genre*. The mixing of discourses and genres in much work in cultural studies has to do with its methodological impurity, perhaps with a certain fruitful insecurity about its legitimacy as a discipline, but perhaps too with the way it conceives its object as being relational (a network of connections) rather than substantial. Anne Freadman puts it this way:

> With the professionalisation of the social sciences and of the humanities, we put ourselves at risk of writing and reading with carefully administered 'methods' that can only be called mono-generic . . . if I am right, that the conditions of sociality are best described as the occupation of, and enablement by, heterogeneous ranges of generic practices, then mono-generic strategies of interpretation will always miss the mark.[20]

The concept of 'sociality' here carries that active, processual sense that cultural studies gives to the concept of culture, and the two are directly related: both have to do with the *practice* (rather than the implementation) of structures of meaning – genres or codes, for example – and with the construction of social space out of the weaving together, the crisscrossing, of such practices (there are clear analogies with the way ethnomethodology understands the construction and maintenance of the social).

There is a precise sense in which cultural studies uses the concept of *text* as its fundamental model. However, in the working out of this metaphor (at its most abstract, that of the marking or tracing of pure relationality), the concept of text undergoes a mutation. Rather than designating a place where meanings are constructed in a single level of inscription (writing, speech, film, dress . . .), it works as an interleaving of 'levels'. If a shopping mall is conceived on the model of textuality, then this 'text' involves practices, institutional structures and the complex forms of agency they entail, legal, political, and financial conditions of existence, and particular flows of power and knowledge, as well as a particular multilayered semantic organisation; it is an ontologically mixed entity, and one for which there can be no provileged or 'correct' form of reading. It is this, more than anything else, that forces cultural studies' attention to the diversity of audiences for or users of the structures of textuality it analyses – that is, to the open-ended social life of texts – and that forces it, thereby, to question the authority or finality of its own readings.

At the same time, this 'text' exists only within a network of *intertextual* relations (the textual networks of commodity culture, let's say, of architecture, of formations of community, of postmodern spatiality). The concept of text in cultural studies is more rich, more complex, more differentiated, and altogether more tricky than it is in the traditional interpretive disciplines (which is not to say that some of these disciplines may not in practice work with a similar conception of textuality). Thus when Tony Bennett writes about the development for tourism of The Rocks in Sydney, the textual object he reads is not, or not only, a physical place but the sets of local struggles and of clashing representations that go to make up the complex temporality of this site, and that link it both to other such sites of historical recuperation, and to a history of discourses about the national past. Similarly, the object of Noel Sanders's reading of the Azaria Chamberlain case is not the 'facts' of the matter (whatever they might have been) but the gossip, jokes, folk etymologies, journalistic innuendo, narrative patterns, and the various official discourses, through all of which 'the Azaria affair' in its full mythological richness was formed.

VI

The conception of culture that, we argue, increasingly informs the discipline of cultural studies – culture not as organic expression of a community, nor as an autonomous sphere of aesthetic forms, but as a contested and conflictual set of practices of representation bound up with the processes of formation and re-formation of social groups – depends upon a theoretical paradox, since it necessarily presupposes an opposition (between culture and society, between representations and reality) which is the condition of its existence but which it must constantly work to undo. Both the undoing of these oppositions, and the failure ever completely to resolve the tension between them, are constitutive of work in cultural studies. If representations are dissolved into the real (if they are thought only to reflect or to re-present, in a secondary way and either more or less accurately, a reality which has an autonomous existence and against which the representation can thus be measured) then the sense of the ways in which the real is textually constructed (as story, as desire, as repetition) gets lost. Conversely, if the real is nothing more than the sum of its representations ('nothing but texts' as the caricature goes) then the sense of *urgency* to the cultural studies project gets lost.

The concerns of this project are not epistemological, however, but have to do with the social processes by which the categories of the real and of group existence are formed. (The word 'social' here means at once semiotic and political, in the sense of involving relations of power. Foucault's concept of power/knowledge is one influential way of thinking this intertwining of meaning and social relationality; the linguistic concept of enunciation is another.[21]) When Ross Gibson and Lesley Stern, in this volume, meditate upon the mode of being of an Australian landscape or cityscape, they apprehend it, as a matter of principle, by means of its constitution through particular apparatuses of signification. There is no brute reality prior to this process of constitution (which is always, however, both a multi-layered and dispersed process, and one which happens in time – which is to say, in history). Landscape – a term that can so quickly become metaphysical – is understood as a social practice of place.

The concept of culture is an imporant one for many other disciplines, notably perhaps for cultural anthropology and the sociology of culture. What, we might ask, is special or different about its use in cultural studies? One answer may be – nothing; and it may be, too, that cultural studies shouldn't be described as a 'discipline'. (It's perhaps too young and unformed to have the strong sense of boundaries required of a discipline; it's also shaped – although this is a different issue – by its rebellion against disciplinarity itself.) Nevertheless, those who work in cultural studies tend to have strong opinions about what distinguishes their work from other fields of enquiry, and it might be useful briefly to explore both the differences and the overlap with these other fields.

The most obvious difference is in the object of study. Whereas anthropology is defined by its relation to an 'allochronic' Other[22] – an Other defined as such by its sociocultural difference within a quite different structure of time, and especially by what's understood as a qualitative difference in social organisation – cultural studies takes as its object the ordinary culture (two very loaded words, but let them stand for the moment) of its own society. Certainly there are movements towards such an orientation in contemporary anthropology, but often – for example, in ethnographic studies of rural or working-class communities or of the homeless – this continues to reproduce the same structure of otherness (of an exoticism now caught within the home society). Cultural studies is sometimes caught in this trap too – treating subcultures, for example, as an exotic or subversive other within the dominant culture – but its *impulse* is towards studying the diverse forms of cultural organisation without recourse to such exoticisation.

There are also differences in methodological orientation. Although cultural studies has adopted (often naively) many of the techniques of fieldwork observation and description developed by ethnography (see Virginia Nightingale's essay in this volume), its focus on complex industrialised societies means that other methodologies may in many instances be more appropriate: in particular because vast archives of written and electronic texts are available to it – because, that is, information about cultural codes and practices can be obtained in many other forms than discussion with an informant and participant observation; and because the writer is a member of the culture that is being studied. Cultural studies tends, as a consequence, to make much greater use of techniques of textual analysis; to make use of a greater diversity of sources; to make a more eclectic use of methodologies; and, once again, to work with a more complex problematic of the relation between the writer and the culture being studied (that is, with an *intensification* of the anthropological problem of the tension between personal and political distance and personal and political involvement).

In relation to the sociology of culture, cultural studies has certainly learned from its use of statistical survey techniques. The interest of cultural studies, however, tends to lie much more in the lived effects and formations of culture, and questions of the distribution of competency, preference and access are usually made secondary to this concern. But the difference between the two disciplines is more likely one of focus than of kind; and the same holds true of the overlapping relationship between cultural studies and social history.[23] One can observe, finally, an overlap with literary studies to the (limited) extent that the latter has retheorised its object in recent years to cover the analysis of social relations of textuality rather than texts or textual systems in themselves. It's worth noting (since our selection includes several essays that deal with 'high' cultural texts) that cultural studies is not restricted to the study of popular culture, and certainly has little in common with folkloric studies (including the 'folkloric' orientation to mass media studies). Rather, as Grossberg, Nelson and Treichler write:

> Cultural studies does not require us to repudiate elite cultural forms – or simply to acknowledge, with Bourdieu, that distinctions between elite and popular cultural forms are themselves the products of relations of power. Rather, cultural studies requires us to identify the operation of specific practices, of how they continuously reinscribe the line between legitimate and popular culture, and of what they accomplish in specific contexts.[24]

The concern of cultural studies is with the constitution and working of systems of relations rather than with the domains formed by these processes. Hence a further characteristic concern of cultural studies (one it shares with much post-structuralist thought): a concern with boundaries and limits, and especially with the fuzziness of such edges and the consequent impurity of genres and disciplines. For example, John Hartley suggests, in his study of broadcast TV as a 'paedocratic' regime, that it is possible 'to see in impurities not a problem but a fundamental criterion for cultural studies', and he defends an international television criticism on the grounds that 'neither television nor nations can be understood . . . except in relational terms'; Tom O'Regan rearticulates the vexed question of the relationship between cultural criticism and cultural policy by considering both as 'porous systems'; and Helen Grace examines the increasingly fluid relations between value and utility, art and commerce, aesthetics and logic, 'play' and 'war', now being produced in the 'serious business' of contemporary management culture.

The effect of this concern is not to dissolve analysis into an all-encompassing description ('cultural studies' as 'studying culture'), but rather to foreground the question of the relation *between* the description of textual/cultural networks and the position of enunciation from which that description is possible. This question is, again, at once *semiotic* (it has to do with the organisation and enablement of textuality by structures of genre) and *political* (it has to do with the social relations of textuality: that is, with the relative positioning of speakers and their discursive construction as the carriers of a certain social identity and authority). It follows that an interest in the concrete conditions and particular instances in which conflicts of authority and problems of authorship are negotiated (or not negotiated), and settled (or unsettled), is not confined to studies which are explicitly concerned with cross-cultural conflict and postcolonial struggle. Here, it is also crucial to McKenzie Wark's study of the cultural politics practised in Australia by Midnight Oil, to Adrian Martin's reflections on the uses of the 'name' of popular culture, and to the essays by Virginia Nightingale, Meaghan Morris and Tom O'Regan on the disciplinary metaphors under-pinning cultural studies.

VII

Genealogies are as misleading for intellectual work as they are for studying personal behaviour: they can tell us nothing about where we are going, or should go, or might want to go. The standard genealogy for Australian cultural studies is British: rather than looking, say, to the North American work of Harold Innis and James Carey on space and communication, or to the 'suburbia' debate amongst Australian social critics in the 1960s,[25] a filiation is set up with the influential enterprise of 'British Cultural Studies' that took shape in the late 1950s as a challenge to hierarchical distinctions between the public and the private, the major and the minor, the 'great' and the 'everyday', as these regulated the field of culture (and the discipline of English) in Britain.

According to the usual narrative, British Cultural Studies begins with the so-called 'scholarship' generation of scholars formed, as Graeme Turner elsewhere explains, by 'the expansion of educationsl opportunities within Britain after the war, and the spread of adult education as a means of postwar reconstruction as well as an arm of the welfare state'.[26] Children of the working class like Richard Hoggart and Raymond Williams saw their task as one of validating the culture of the common people over and against the canonical values of British high cultural elitism, pitting the study of 'culture and society' (the title of Williams' most famous book) against Matthew Arnold's defence of 'culture and civilization'. Where the latter had fostered a nostalgia for pre-industrial English *folk* culture, the new intellectuals examined and affirmed the 'authentic' *popular* culture of the industrial working class. But, as Turner points out, this phase of educational modernisation also corresponded to the postwar expansion of 'industrial' *mass* culture – often North American in source or inspiration. Early critical responses to this 'inauthentic' development (and to working-class enthusiasm for it) were ambiguous, or negative: wedged between the 'folk' and the 'mass', the 'popular' became an increasingly unstable and contested object of study. Some echoes can be traced between British cultural studies in this period, and the nationally inflected but often ambivalent work on Australian popular culture by such diverse critics as A.A. Phillips, Ian Turner and Russell Ward.

Cultural studies emerged as a program in Britain with the work of the Birmingham Centre for Contemporary Cultural Studies (founded in 1964).

During the 1970s and early 1980s, and under the influence of younger scholars who had grown up at home in mass-mediated popular culture, the study of working-class life evolved into 'subcultures' theory, with its interests in pop music, fashion and television on the one hand, and in the politics of race and (a little less so) gender on the other.[27] In this phase, too, there was an acceptance, even a celebration of the Americanisation of Britain as a further way of contesting English 'high' (now also, for some, 'white male') cultural hegemony. In Australia, some of John Docker's work on cultural elites shares the assumptions of this strand of cultural studies.[28]

In theoretical terms, these developments correspond to an increasing insistence on notions of agency in cultural theory. This means studying not how people *are* in a passively inherited culture ('tradition') but what we *do* with the cultural commodities that we encounter and use in daily life ('practice') and thus what we *make* as 'culture'. Inflected by post-structuralist theories of reading as well as by empirical audience research, this shift enabled a redefinition of popular culture not as a stratum (the 'low' one) of aesthetic practice but as a social 'zone of contestation', in Stuart Hall's famous phrase[29] – the ground in and over which different interests struggle for hegemony. *Myths of Oz* by John Fiske, Bob Hodge and Graeme Turner applies this principle to the study of Australian life.[30] It can be argued, however, that later work was more concerned to struggle over popular culture in universities than to explore its constitutive conflicts. In the mid to late 1980s, theories of consumption (defined as an appropriation of cultural meanings rather than the acquisition of goods) came to dominate the field at the height of the economic boom. In the recent work of John Fiske, popular culture is celebrated as a utopian principle of unlimited pleasure production.[31]

Looking back at the Birmingham project, Hall has said that 'there is no doubt in my mind that we were trying to find an institutional practice in cultural studies that might produce an organic intellectual'.[32] Derived from the work of Antonio Gramsci, the notion of an organic (as opposed to traditional) intellectual is now widely used to describe those able to express the knowledges, needs and interests of an emergent class or 'historic movement', in Hall's terms. Instead of representing the interests of socially dominant forces in the name of a mythical 'general public', the organic intellectual will, as McKenzie Wark puts it with reference to Peter Garrett, '[use] his position in a particular set of social relations . . . in order to give voice to his constituency'. For Hall as for Gramsci, organic intellectuals work on two fronts: they must be at the forefront of current theoretical work (they need to 'know more' than traditional intellectuals do), but they must also find ways to share their knowledge with people who are not professional intellectuals.

This model of cultural studies has been criticised on several grounds. Hall himself notes that Gramsci expected the organic intellectual's work to be 'clinched' by a revolutionary party; since there was no such party in 1970s Britain, the organic model defined a 'hope'. Tony Bennett then argues that the whole idea involves a misrecognition of cultural studies' relations to its real conditions of existence, which were and continue to be primarily academic.[33]

Perhaps an extreme form of this misrecognition occurs in work declaring that popular cultural pleasure has socially 'critical' effects. A focus on the active uses made of cultural texts can beg the question of whose uses are being taken as exemplary, and even the laudable attempt to bracket the analyst's theoretically informed criteria of valuation in favour of an ethnographic reconstruction of the value system of a particular group has the consequence that in some sense the analyst's own values are being disavowed and are therefore partly *uncontrolled*. This may mean, to be more precise, that the values of that group – always an analytic construct – may act as a kind of alibi, a fiction into which the analyst's own values are projected in a screened form; and this possibility raises that whole complex set of political issues to do with the propensity of intellectuals to speak 'on behalf of' those who lack a voice in cultural and social debate.[34]

In Australian conditions, however, Bennett's judgment may be too harsh. Wark's essay on Midnight Oil suggests that the organic model may still usefully be applied to non-academic forms of intellectual cultural work. Furthermore, the modest notion of constituency can obviate the need for conjuring up those phantom 'emergent' subjects of history and encourage us to pay more attention to the actual practices developed by real intellectuals in Australia – that is, in a small society with relatively limited institutional resources and with flexible traditions (not to mention mateship networks) allowing a good deal of mobility between institutions. We suspect that a history of cultural studies in Australia would find that the 1960s and 1970s adult education influence (notably in the Workers' Educational Association) both nourished and perpetuated a strong but informal intellectual culture of autodidactic and amateur practice which shaped the values of many who later became, with the expansion of the educational system, professional intellectuals.[35] Our own first encounters with a 'culture and society' approach in the late 1960s came not from reading Raymond Williams but from attending WEA summer schools on film run at Newport Beach in Sydney by John Flaus.

Flaus works as a teacher in university and adult education contexts, as a critic who uses radio as fluently as he writes for magazines, and as an actor in a variety of media from experimental film to TV drama and commercials. If we substitute Wark's notion of constituency for the grand Marxist dream of historic force, we can say that Flaus (like Sylvia Lawson) helped to create a constituency for the project of cultural studies as well as to train a generation of film and media critics. Yet his work, along with the socially mixed but intensely familial urban subculture and the small journal networks[36] which sustained it (both of which were historically deep-rooted in the inner-city life of Sydney and Melbourne) has been erased from those Australian accounts of cultural studies which take their bearings from the British tradition – and then pose problems of application.

Coinciding with the belated professionalisation of media studies in Australia in the late 1970s as well as with the arrival of British cultural studies as a serious academic force, this erasure introduces a distortion, in our view, into current debates. It is one thing to argue that British cultural studies always was primarily academic. It is quite another to assume that if an Australian practice wasn't or isn't primarily academic then it can't be cultural studies – or that it fails to understand what its real situation would have been if it were British. To do this is to ignore the conditions in which Australians have actually worked. This in turn renders invisible the social basis of the partly academic but primarily constituency-oriented work of journalist-critics like Philip Brophy, Ross Gibson, Sylvia Lawson, Adrian Martin and McKenzie Wark,[37] or indeed of policy-oriented intellectuals like Elizabeth Jacka.[38] As the essays in this volume by Stuart Cunningham and Adrian Martin may suggest, the popular media in Australia should perhaps also be thought of as forming a 'porous system' (in Tom O'Regan's phrase) – open on occasion (and to good or bad effect) to exchanging ideas, rhetoric and research images, as well as personnel, with cultural criticism and public policy.

Other genealogies and other kinds of intellectual practice, we suggest, have been at least as important to the development of cultural studies in Australia as the official line of descent. We have no space here for a detailed account, but let us briefly mention Foucault's work. Two texts have been particularly influential: the theoretical model developed in *The Archaeology of Knowledge* opened the way to a more extended and institutionally anchored model of discursivity than was available in other, language- and text-centred notions of discourse; and the first volume of *The History of Sexuality* seemed to offer a much more complex micro-sociological mapping of social power than did other intellectual traditions such as Marxism, as well as overlapping with the rather different ways of conceptualising the construction of sexuality that were prevalent in feminism (especially the psychoanalytic model).

We should also mention the strong influence of Baudrillard, especially for art and media debates, in the early 1980s: his work seemed, for a while, to offer an understanding of the transformations in the structure of 'reality' brought about by the industrialisation, and thus the massive proliferation, of sign-production;[39] and, as Eric Michaels notes, his theory of simulation was read as promising a way to rethink 'the contradictions of colonialism and creativity' in an 'import' economy increasingly geared towards generating cultural images and events for tourist consumption (see the essays by Bennett, Gibson, Morris and Stern). More recently, the writings of Henri Lefebvre and Michel de Certeau have begun to feed into the way cultural studies theorises the structure and practice of everyday life; and Bourdieu's sociology of culture has begun to provide a strong counter-tradition to the culture-and-society line that descends from Raymond Williams.[40]

The list of inputs into this emerging discipline could be extended almost indefinitely; it is perhaps the mark of the newness of a discipline that, lacking an established methodology and even a well-defined object, it draws eclectically and energetically upon a variety of theoretical sources as it seeks to define its own specificity. The influence of phenomenology and ethnomethodology can certainly be traced in its refusal to privilege the interpretations of 'expert' readers and its concern with the experiential dimension of everyday life. The understanding of culture as a site of contestation, which had its roots in Gramscian and post-Gramscian theories of hegemony,[41] has been more recently inflected by postcolonial theory, which gives a more ambivalent and complex account both of the flow of power and of the projective identifications and identities of actors in situations of cultural struggle.

Perhaps more fundamental and more lasting than any other single intellectual influence has been feminism and the feminist understanding of the politics of the everyday and of 'personal' life. In Australia as elsewhere, a critique of culture (and of theories of culture) was already crucial to the 'second wave' movement of Women's Liberation in the early 1970s, and this was reflected in such publications as *Mejane* and *Refractory Girl*. While it would be difficult to try to characterise either the 'effects' on cultural studies of such a complex and diverse social movement, or the affinities (and disjunctions) between work in cultural studies and the now vast literatures of women's studies, gay and lesbian studies, and feminist theory, we can point to two of the *consequences* that have followed for Australian cultural studies from the influence of particular currents in Australian feminism.

One is a tendency to think of 'the self' as a site of *social* creativity, rather than simply as a medium of individual expression. Many Australian feminists have always taken the slogan 'the personal is political' to mean that the resources of the state must be captured and used in the interests of transforming women's lives by increasing their access to social equity and power ('changing the culture'). As a result, work on cultural policy is now able to refer for a precedent (though it does not always do so) to a record of significant achievement by Australian feminist bureaucrats.[42] The other consequence is a tendency to assume that a politics of the everyday and of personal life will always involve a confrontation with the workings of class, racism, and colonialism in Australia as well as with sex and gender – and hence a labour of *historical* understanding. Ann Curthoys argued in 1970 that we 'must analyze why public life has been considered to be the focus of history, and why public life has been so thoroughly occupied by men';[43] if cultural studies continues this line of questioning in an expanded framework today, it finds a precedent in the work of Australian feminist historians.

Notes

1. Stephen Loosley, 'Step towards real changes', (Sydney) *Sunday Telegraph* 17 March 1991; 'Culture fills Aussie tills', (Sydney) *Daily Telegraph Mirror* 11 October 1990.
2. 'Swan Steels ARC for competition', *Sunday Telegraph* 26 November, 1989; Advertisement, Shopping Centres Conference, *Australian Financial Review* 13 August 1992; 'Poor performance "shooting Aust in the head"', *Australian Financial Review* 26 October 1989.
3. Peter Robinson, 'Fair go, we're all bludgers', *Sun Herald* 18 June, 1989.
4. Raymond Williams, *The Long Revolution* (Chatto and Windus, London, 1961).
5. On the history of this policy, see Stephen Castles, Mary Kalantzis, Bill Cope and Michael Morrissey, *Mistaken Identity: Multiculturalism and the Demise of Nationalism in Australia* (Pluto Press, Sydney, 1988).
6. See Roberta B. Sykes, *Black Majority* (Hudson Publishing, Hawthorn, 1989).

7. See Ghassan Hage, 'Racism, multiculturalism and the gulf war', *Arena* 96 (1991), pp. 8–13.
8. See M.T. Daly and M.I. Logan, *The Brittle Rim: Finance, Business and the Pacific Region* (Penguin Books, Ringwood, 1989); Abe David and Ted Wheelwright, *The Third Wave: Australia and Asian Capitalism* (Left Book Club Cooperative Ltd, Sutherland, 1989).
9. On Australian cultural nationalist formations, see Graeme Turner, '"It works for me": British cultural studies, Australian cultural studies, Australian film', in Lawrence Grossberg, Cary Nelson and Paula Treichler (eds), *Cultural Studies* (Routledge, New York and London, 1992, pp. 640–53) (reprinted here as Chapter 20); cf *National Fictions: Literature, Film and the Construction of Australian Narrative* (Allen and Unwin, Sydney, 1986).
10. See Raymond Williams, *Politics and Letters* (New Left Books, London, 1979).
11. For a theory of this phenomenon in the US context, see Joseph Meyrowitz, *No Sense of Place: The Impact of Electronic Media on Social Behavior* (Oxford University Press, New York and Oxford, 1985).
12. Tom O'Regan, 'Towards a high communication policy', *Continuum* 2, 1 (1988–89), pp. 135–58; cf the revised version of this article in *Media Information Australia* 58 (1990), pp. 111–24.
13. Graeme Turner, 'Suburbia vérité', *Australian Left Review* 144 (October 1992), pp. 37–39.
14. See Jennifer Craik, *Resorting to Tourism: Cultural Policies for Tourist Development in Australia* (Allen and Unwin, Sydney, 1991).
15. For an account of a recent image campaign against Aboriginal people, see Steve Mickler, 'Visions of disorder: Aboriginal people and youth crime reporting'; *Cultural Studies* 6, 3 (1992), pp. 322–36; cf *Gambling on the First Race: A Comment on Racism and Talk-Back Radio – 6PR, the TAB and the WA Government*, report commissioned and published by the Louis St John Memorial Trust Fund, Centre for Research in Culture and Communication, Murdoch University, Perth 1992.
16. On these issues, see *Artlink* 10, 1–2 (1990) [*Contemporary Australian Aboriginal Art*]; *Continuum* 3,2 (1990) [*Communication and tradition: Essays after Eric Michaels*]; Sue Cramer (ed.), *Postmodernism: A Consideration of the Appropriation of Aboriginal Imagery* (Institute of Modern Art, Brisbane, 1989); Henrietta Fourmile, 'Aboriginal heritage legislation and self-determination', *Australian–Canadian Studies* 7, 1–2 (1989), pp. 45–61; Adrian Marrie, 'Museums and Aborigines: a case study in internal colonialism', *Australian-Canadian Studies* 7, 1–2 (1989), pp. 63–80; Eric Michaels, *The Aboriginal Invention of Television in Central Australia 1982–1986*, Australian Institute of Aboriginal studies, 1986; Eric Michaels, *For a Cultural Future: Francis Jupurrurla Makes TV at Yuendumu*, Artspace, Sydney, 1987; John Mundine, 'Aboriginal art in Australia today', *Third Text* 6 (1989); 'Aboritinal art in the public eye', special supplement to *Art Monthly Australia*, 56 (1992–93), pp. 3–48.
17. On the problems that 'importing' these debates can create in Australian conditions, see Graeme Turner, 'Dilemmas of a cultural critic: Australian cultural studies today', *Australian Journal of Communication* 16 (1989), pp. 1–12.
18. Marcel Mauss, *The Gift: Forms and Functions of Exchange in Archaic Societies* (trans. Ian Cunnison) (Cohen and West, London, 1970, p. 1).
19. On this debate, see Meaghan Morris, 'The man in the mirror: David Harvey's "condition" of postmodernity', in Mike Featherstone (ed.), *Cultural Theory and Cultural Change* (Sage Publications, London, 1992), reprinted in *Continental Shift: Globalisation and Culture*, Elizabeth Jacka (ed.) (Local Consumption Publications, Sydney forthcoming 1993).
20. Anne Freadman, 'The vagabond arts', in *In the Place of French: Essays in and*

around French studies in Honour of Michael Spencer (Boombana Publications, Mt Nebo, 1992, p. 280).

21. On Foucault, see Graeme Burchell, Colin Gordon and Peter Miller, *The Foucault Effect: Studies in Governmentality* (Harvester Wheatsheaf, London and Sydney, 1991); John Frow, 'Some versions of Foucault', *Meanjin* 47, 1 (1988), pp. 144–56, and *Meanjin* 47, 2 (1988), pp. 353–65; Meaghan Morris and Paul Patton (eds), and *Michel Foucault: Power, Truth, Strategy* (Feral Publications, Sydney, 1979).

    On enunciation, see Ross Chambers, *Room for Maneuver: Reading Oppositional Narrative* (University of Chicago Press, Chicago and London, 1991); Anne Freadman and Meaghan Morris, 'Import rhetoric: "semiotics in/and Australia"', in *The Foreign Bodies Papers*, Peter Botsman, Chris Burns and Peter Hutchings (eds) (Local Consumption Publications, Sydney, 1981); Sneja Gunew, Anne Freadman and Meaghan Morris, 'Forum: feminism and interpretation theory' *Southern Review*, 6, I (March 1983), pp. 149–73; Tom O'Regan, 'Some reflections on the "policy moment"', *Meanjin* 51, 3 (1992), pp. 517–32.

22. See Johannes Fabian, *Time and the Other: How Anthropology Makes its Object* (Columbia University Press, New York, 1983).

23. See Julian Thomas, 'History with and without film', *Meanjin* 48, 2 (1989), pp. 419–27; Tony Bennett, Colin Mercer, Pat Buckridge and David Carter (eds), *Celebration of a Nation* (Allen and Unwin, Sydney, 1992).

24. Lawrence Grossberg, Cary Nelson and Paula Treichler, 'Introduction' *Cultural Studies*, op cit. (note 9), p. 13.

25. On North America, see James Carey, *Communication as Culture: Essays on Media and Society* (Unwin Hyman, London and Sydney, 1989); and Arthur Kroker, *Technology and the Canadian Mind: Innis, McLuhan, Grant* (New World Perspectives, Montreal, 1984).

    For Australia, see Robin Boyd, *The Australian Ugliness*, Penguin Books, Ringwood, 1963; Ronald Conway, *The Great Australian Stupor: An Interpretation of the Australian Way of Life* (Sun Books, Melbourne, 1971); Donald Horne, *The Lucky Country* (Penguin Books, Ringwood, 1964); Craig McGregor, *Profile of Australia* (Hodder and Stoughton, London, 1966) and *People, Politics and Pop* (Ure Smith, Sydney, 1968).

26. Graeme Turner, *British Cultural Studies: An Introduction* (Unwin Hyman, Boston and Sydney, 1990, p. 44).

27. See, for example, Stuart Hall and Tony Jefferson, *Resistance through rituals: Youth Subcultures in Post-War Britain* (Hutchinson, London, 1976); Angela McRobbie, 'Settling accounts with subcultures: a feminist critique', in *Culture, Ideology and Social Process: A Reader*, T. Bennett, G. Martin, C. Mercer and J. Woollacott (eds) (Batsford Academic and Education, London, 1981, pp. 113–23); Paul Gilroy, *There Ain't No Black in the Union Jack: The Cultural Politics of Race and Nation* (Hutchinson, London, 1987).

28. John Docker, 'Popular culture versus the state: an argument against Australian content regulations for television', *Media Information Australia* 59 (February 1991), pp. 7–26; cf *Australian Cultural Elites: Intellectual Traditions in Sydney and Melbourne* (Angus and Robertson, Sydney, 1974).

29. Stuart Hall, 'Notes on deconstructing "the popular"', in Raphael Samuel (ed.), *People's History and Socialist Theory* (Routledge and Kegan Paul, London, 1981).

30. John Fiske, Bob Hodge and Graeme Turner, *Myths of Oz: Reading Australian Popular Culture* (Allen and Unwin, Sydney, 1987).

31. John Fiske, *Reading the Popular* and *Understanding Popular Culture* (Unwin Hyman, Boston and Sydney, 1989). See also John Frow, 'The concept of the popular', *New Formations* 18 (1992), pp. 25–38.

32. Stuart Hall, 'Cultural studies and its theoretical legacies', in Grossberg, Nelson and Treichler, *Cultural Studies, op cit.* (note 9), p. 281.

33. Tony Bennett, 'Putting policy into cultural studies', in Grossberg, Nelson and Treichler, *Cultural Studies, op cit.* (note 9), p. 34.

34. On these issues, see John Frow, 'Michel de Certeau and the practice of representation', *Cultural Studies* 5, 1 (1991), pp. 52–60, and Meaghan Morris, 'Banality in cultural studies' in Patricia Mellencamp (ed.), *Logics of Television* (Indiana University Press, Bloomington, 1990, pp. 14–43) (reprinted here as Chapter 7).

35. On 'amateurism' and/or small journal culture in Australia, see George Alexander, 'Introduction: on editorial strategies', in *Language, Sexuality and Subversion*, Paul Foss and Meaghan Morris (eds) (Feral Publications, Sydney 1978); John Forbes, 'Aspects of contemporary Australian poetry', in *The Foreign Bodies Papers*, Peter Botsman, Chris Burns and Peter Hutchings (eds) (Local Consumption Publications, Sydney, 1981); Adrian Martin, 'S.O.S.', *Continuum* 5, 2 (1992).

36. Many small journals and magazines have published work in cultural studies since the 1970s. Alongside regular outlets like *Continuum, Meanjin* and the *Local Consumption* series, we would include the following (not all of which are extant): *Age Monthly Review, Agenda, ALR [Australian Left Review], Antithesis, Arena, Art & Text, Australian Feminist Studies, Australian Cultural History, Australian Journal of Communication, Australian Journal of Cultural Studies, Binocular, Cinema Papers, Culture and Policy, Filmnews, Frogger, GLP, Hecate, Intervention, Island Magazine, Media Information Australia, Metro, NMA [New Music Articles], On The Beach, Paper Burns, Praxis M, Photofile, Social Analysis, Social Semiotics, Southern Review, STUFF, STUFFING, Tension, The Third Degree, Transition, Typereader, The Virgin Press, West, Westerly, Working Papers in Sex, Science and Culture* [later *Working Papers*].

37. See Ross Gibson, *South of the West: Postcolonialism and the Narrative Construction of Australia* (Indiana University Press, Bloomington, 1992); Adrian Martin, *Phantasms*, McPhee Gribble, Melbourne (forthcoming 1993); McKenzie Wark, *Logic Bombs: Living with Global Media Events* (Indiana University Press, Bloomington forthcoming 1994). For reprints of Philip Brophy's magazine work, see *Restuff 1: Horror–Gore–Exploitation* (1988), *2: Rock & Pop Culture* (1988), *3: Media–Theory–Technology* (Stuff Publications, Northcote, 1991).

    An influential account of the importance of journalism to Australian cultural history is Sylvia Lawson, *The Archibald Paradox: A Strange Case of Authorship* (Allen Lane/Penguin Books, London and Ringwood, 1983); cf Lawson's 'Pieces of a cultural geography', *The Age Monthly Review*, February 1987, pp. 10–13.

38. See Stuart Cunningham and Elizabeth Jacka, 'Cultural studies in the light of the policy process: a curate's egg?' in *Australian Cultural Studies Conference 1990: Proceedings*, Deborah Chambers and Hart Cohen (eds) (Faculty of Humanities and Social Sciences, University of Western Sydney, 1991, pp. 26–56).

39. See André Frankovits (ed.), *Seduced and Abandoned: The Baudrillard Scene* (Stonemoss Publications, Sydney, 1984).

40. For an early use of Bourdieu to analyse Australian culture, see Tim Rowse, *Australian Liberalism and National Character*, Kibble Books, Malmsbury, 1978; cf Rowse's *Arguing the Arts: The Funding of the Arts in Australia*, Penguin Books, Ringwood, 1985. See also John Frow, 'Accounting for tastes: some problems in Bourdieu's sociology of culture', *Cultural Studies* 1, 1 (1987), pp. 59–73.

41. See Tony Bennett, 'Introduction: popular culture and "the turn to Gramsci"', in *Popular Culture and Social Relations*, Tony Bennett, Colin Mercer and Janet Woollacott (eds) (Open University Press, Milton Keynes, 1986, pp. xi–xix).

42. See Hester Eisenstein, *Gender Shock: Practising Feminism on Two Continents* (Allen and Unwin, Sydney, 1991); Suzanne Franzway, Dianne Court and R.W. Connell, *Staking a Claim: Feminism, Bureaucracy and the State* (Allen and Unwin, Sydney, 1989); Marian Sawer, *Sisters in Suits: Women in Public Policy* (Allen and Unwin, Sydney, 1990); Sophie Watson (ed.), *Playing the state: Australian Feminist Interventions* (Allen and Unwin, Sydney, 1990); Anna Yeatman, *Bureaucrats, Technocrats, Femocrats: Essays on the Contemporary Australian State* (Allen and Unwin, Sydney, 1990).
43. Ann Curthoys, 'Women's liberation and the writing of history', in *For and Against Feminism* (Allen and Unwin, Sydney, 1988, p. 4).

Bibliography

ADORNO, T.W. (1941) 'On popular music', *Studies in Philosophy and Social Science*, IX (1).

ADORNO, T.W. (1978) 'The sociology of knowledge and its consciousness' in Arato, A. and Gebhardt, E. (eds), *op cit.*

ADORNO, T.W. (1991) *The Cultural Industry: Selected Essays on Mass Culture* (ed., with intro., J.M. Bernstein). London: Routledge.

ADORNO, T.W. and HORKHEIMER, M. (1979) *Dialectic of Enlightenment.* London: Verso.

AGGER, B. (1992) *Cultural Studies as Cultural Theory.* London: Falmer Press.

ALLEN, R. (ed.), (1992) *Channels of Discourse, Reassembled.* London: Routledge.

ALTHUSSER, L. (1966) *For Marx.* London: Penguin Books.

ALTHUSSER, L. (1971) *'Lenin and Philosophy' and Other Essays.* London: New Left Books.

ALTHUSSER, L. and BALIBAR, E. (1970) *Reading Capital.* London: New Left Books.

ALVARADO, M. and THOMPSON, J. (eds), (1990) *The Media Reader.* London: British Film Institute.

ANDERSON, B. (1983) *Imagined Communities.* London: Verso.

ANDERSON, P. (1969) 'Components of the national culture'. In Cockburn, A. and Blackburn, R. (eds), *Student Power*, London: Penguin Books.

ANG, I. (1985) *Watching Dallas: Soap Opera and the Melodramatic Imagination.* London: Methuen.

ANG, I. (1988) 'Feminist desire and female pleasure', *Camera Obscura* 16, 179–90.

ANG, I. (1990) *Desperately Seeking the Audience.* London: Routledge.

ANG, I. (1991) *Watching Television.* London: Routledge.

ANG, I. (1995) *Living Room Wars.* London: Routledge.

ANGUS, I. and JHALLY, S. (eds), (1989) *Cultural Politics in Contemporary America.* New York and London: Routledge.

APPIGNANESI, L. (1986) *Postmodernism.* London: ICA.

ARATO, A. and GEBHARDT, E. (eds), (1978) *The Essential Frankfurt School Reader.* Oxford: Blackwell.

ARNOLD, M. (1932) *Culture and Anarchy.* London: Cambridge University Press.

BAEHR, H. and DYER, G. (eds), (1987) *Boxed In: Women and Television.* New York: Pandora.

BAILEY, P. (ed.), (1986) *Music Hall: The Business of Pleasure.* Milton Keynes: Open University Press.

BAKHTIN, M. (1981) *The Dialogic Imagination.* Austin, TX: University of Texas Press.

BAKHTIN, M. (1984) *Rabelais and His World*. Bloomington. IN: Indiana University Press.

BALDICK, C. (1983) *The Social Mission of English Criticism*. Oxford: Clarendon Press.

BALSAMO, A. (1991) 'Feminism and cultural studies', *Journal of the Midwest Modern Language Association* 24, 50–73.

BALSAMO, A. and TREICHLER, P.A. (1990) 'Feminist cultural studies: questions for the 1990s', *Women and Language* 13, 3–6.

BARKER, M. (1989) *Comics: Ideology, Power and the Critics*. Manchester: Manchester University Press.

BARKER, M. (1990) 'Review', *Magazine of Cultural Studies* 1.

BARKER, M. and BEEZER, A. (1992) *Reading into Cultural Studies*. London: Routledge.

BARKER, P. (1993) *Michael Foucault*. Hemel Hempstead: Harvester Wheatsheaf.

BARRETT, M. (1980) *Women's Oppression Today: Problems in Marxist Feminist Analysis*. London: Verso.

BARRETT, M., CORRIGAN, P., KUHN, A. and WOLFF, J. (eds), (1979) *Ideology and Cultural Production*. London: Croom Helm.

BARTHES, R. (1972) *Mythologies*. London: Jonathan Cape.

BARTHES, R. (1975) *The Pleasure of the Text*. New York: Hill and Wang.

BARTHES, R. (1977) *Image–Music–Text*. London: Routledge.

BATRA, N.D. (ed.), (1987) *The Hour of Television: Critical Approaches*. Metuchen, NJ: Scarecrow Press.

BAUDRILLARD, J. (1988) *Selected Writings* (ed. M. Poster). Cambridge: Polity Press.

BEE, J. (1989) 'First citizen of the semiotic democracy', *Cultural Studies* 3, 353–59.

BENJAMIN, W. (1969) *Illuminations*. New York: Schocken Books.

BENNETT, T. (1980) 'Popular culture: a "teaching object"', *Screen Education* 34 17–30.

BENNETT, T. (1988) 'Ozmosis: Looking at Australian popular culture', *Australian Left Review*, April/May.

BENNETT, T. (1990a) *Outside Literature*. London: Routledge.

BENNETT, T. (ed.), (1990b) *Popular Fiction*. London: Routledge.

BENNETT, T., BOYD-BOWMAN, S., MERCER, C. and WOOLLACOTT, J. (eds), (1981a) *Popular Television and Film*. London: BFI Publishing in association with the Open University Press.

BENNETT, T., MARTIN, G., MERCER, C. and WOOLLACOTT, J. (1981b) *Culture, Ideology and Social Process*. London: Batsford Academic and Educational in association with the Open University Press.

BENNETT, T., MERCER, C. and WOOLLACOTT, J. (1986) *Popular Culture and Social Relations*. Milton Keynes: Open University Press.

BENNETT, T. and WOOLLACOTT, J. (1987) *Bond and Beyond: The Political Career of a Popular Hero*. London: Macmillan Education.

BERLAND, J. (1988) 'Locating listening: popular music, technological space, Canadian mediation', *Cultural Studies* 2, 343–58.

BEST, S. and KELLNER, D. (1991) *Postmodern Theory*. London: Macmillan.

BETTERTON, R. (ed.), (1987) *Looking On: Images of Femininity in the Visual Arts and Media*. London: Pandora.

BHABHA, H. (1983) 'The other question – the stereotype and colonial discourse', *Screen* 24, 18–36.

BOIME, A. (1990) *The Art of Exclusion: Representing Blacks in the Nineteenth Century*. London: Thames and Hudson.

BORN, G. (1987) 'Modern music culture: on shock, pop and synthesis', *New Formations* 1, 51–78.

BOURDIEU, P. (1977) *Outline of a Theory of Practice*. Cambridge: Cambridge University Press.

BOURDIEU, P. (1986) *Distinction: A Social Critique of the Judgement of Taste* (trans. R. Nice). Cambridge, MA: Harvard University Press.

BOURDIEU, P. (1993) *The Field of Cultural Production*. Cambridge: Polity Press.

BOYNE, R. and RATTANSI, A. (eds), (1990) *Postmodernism and Society*. London: Macmillan.

BRAKE, M. (1985) *Comparative Youth Culture*. London: Routledge and Kegan Paul.

BRAMSON, L. (1961) *The Political Context of Sociology*. Princeton, NJ: Princeton University Press.

BRANTLINGER, P. (1990) *Crusoe's Footsteps: Cultural Studies in Britain and America*. New York: Routledge.

BRUNSDON, C. (1981) 'Crossroads: notes on soap opera', *Screen* 22, 32–37.

BRUNSDON, C. (1991) 'Pedagogies of the feminine: feminist teaching and women's genres', *Screen* 32, 364–81.

BRUNSDON, C. and MORLEY, D. (1978) *Everyday Television: 'Nationwide'*. London: British Film Institute.

BUCKINGHAM, D. (1987) *Public Secrets: 'EastEnders' and its Audience*. London: British Film Institute.

BUDD, M., ENTMAN, R. and STEINMAN, C. (1990) 'The affirmative character of US cultural studies', *Critical Studies in Mass Communication* 7, 169–84.

CALLINICOS, A. (1985) 'Postmodernism, post-structuralism and post-Marxism?' *Theory, Culture and Society* 2, 85–102.

CANCLINI, N. (1988) 'Culture and power: the state of research', *Media, Culture and Society* 10, 467–97.

CAREY, J. (1989) *Communication as Culture: Essays on Media and Society*. Boston, MA: Unwin Hyman.

CARTER, E. *et al.* (1994) *Reading the Popular: Theories of Politics and Culture*. London: Verso.

Centre for Contemporary Cultural Studies (1982) *The Empire Strikes Back*. London: Hutchinson.

CHAM, M. and ANDRADE-WATKINS, C. (eds), (1988) *Blackframes: Critical Perspectives on Black Independent Cinema*. Cambridge, MA: MIT Press.

CHAMBERS, I. (1985) *Urban Rhythms: Pop Music and Popular Culture*. London: Macmillan.

CHAMBERS, I. (1986) *Popular Culture: The Metropolitan Experience*. New York: Methuen.

CHAMBERS, I. (1990) *Border Dialogues: Journeys in Postmodernity*. New York: Routledge.

CHAMBERS, I., CLARKE, J., CONNELL, I., CURTI, L., HALL, S. and JEFFERSON, T. (1977) 'Marxism and culture' (reply to Rosalind Coward), *Screen* 18, 109–19.

CHANDLER, R. (1942) 'Letter to Alfred Knopf' in MacShane, F. (ed.), (1981) *Selected Letters*, New York: Columbia University Press.

CLARKE, J. (1991) *New Times and Old Enemies: Essays on Cultural Studies and America*. London: HarperCollins Academic.

CLARKE, J. and CRITCHER, C. (1985) *The Devil Makes Work: Leisure in Capitalist Britain*. London: Macmillan.

CLARKE, J., CRITCHER, C. and JOHNSON, R. (1979) *Working Class Culture: Studies in History and Theory*. New York: St Martin's Press.

CLARKE, J. *et al.* (1976) 'Subculture, Cultures and Classes' in Hall, S. and Jefferson, T. (eds) *op. cit.*

COHEN, E. (1989) 'The "hyperreal" vs. the "really real": if European intellectuals stop making sense of American culture can we still dance?' *Cultural Studies* 3, 25–37.

COLLINS, J. (1989) *Uncomon Cultures: Popular Culture and Post-modernism*. London: Routledge.

CONNER, S. (1989) *Postmodern Culture: An Introduction to Theories of the Contemporary*. Oxford: Blackwell.

COOK, P. (ed.), (1985) *The Cinema Book*. London: British Film Institute.

COWARD, R. (1977) 'Class, "culture" and the social formation', *Screen* 18, 75–105.

COWARD, R. (1984) *Female Desire*. London: Paladin.

COWARD, R. and ELLIS, J. (1977) *Language and Maternalism: Development in Semiology and the Theory of the Subject*. London: Routledge and Kegan Paul.

CRANE, D. (1992) *The Production of Culture*. London: Sage.

CREED, B. (1987) 'From here to modernity: feminism and postmodernism', *Screen* 28, 47–67.

CUNNINGHAM, H. (1980) *Leisure in the Industrial Revolution*. London: Croom Helm.

CURRAN, J. (1990) 'The "new revisionism" in mass communications research', *European Journal of Communication*, 5.

CURRAN, J. and GUREVITCH, M. (eds), (1991) *Mass Media and Society*. London: Edward Arnold.

CURRAN, J., GUREVITCH, M. and WOOLLACOTT, J. (eds), (1977) *Mass Communication and Society*. London: Arnold.

CURTI, L. (1992) 'What is real and what is not: female fabulations in cultural analysis'. In Grossberg, L. *et al.* (eds), *op cit*.

DAVIS, H. and WALTON, P. (eds), (1983) *Language, Image, Media*. London: Blackwell.

DAY, G. (ed.), (1990) *Readings in Popular Culture*. London: Macmillan.

DE CERTEAU, M. (1984) *The Practice of Everyday Life*. Berkeley, CA: University of California Press.

DE LAURETIS, T. (1984) *Alice Doesn't*. Bloomington, IN: Indiana University Press.

DE LAURETIS, T. (ed.), (1986) *Feminist Studies/Critical Studies*. Bloomington, IN: Indiana University Press.

DE LAURETIS, T. (1987) *Technologies of Gender: Essays on Theory, Film, and Fiction*. Bloomington, IN: Indiana University Press.

DERRIDA, J. (1976) *Of Grammatology* (trans. G. Spivak). Baltimore, MD: Johns Hopkins University Press.

DOCHERTY, T. (1992) *Postmodernism: A Reader*. Hemel Hempstead: Harvester Wheatsheaf.

DOCKER, J. (1994) *Postmodernism and Popular Culture: A Cultural History*. Cambridge: Cambridge University Press.

DORFMAN, A. and MATTELART, A. (1975) *How to Read Donald Duck*. New York: International General.

DOYLE, B. (1989) *English and Englishness*. London: Routledge.

DREYFUS, H.L. and RABINOW, P. (1983) *Michel Foucault: Beyond Structuralism and Hermeneutics* (2nd edn, with an afterword by and an interview with Michel Foucault). Chicago, IL: University of Chicago Press.

DURING, S. (1992) *Foucault and Literature*. London: Routledge.

DURING, S. (ed.), (1993) *The Cultural Studies Reader*. London: Routledge.

DYER, R. (1979) *Stars*. London: British Film Institute.

DYER, R. (1986) *Heavenly Bodies: Film Stars and Society*. New York: St. Martin's Press.

DYER, R., GERAGHTY, C., JORDAN, M., LOVELL, T., PATERSON, R. and STEWART, J. (1981) *Coronation Street*. London: British Film Institute.

EASTHOPE, A. (1986) *What a Man's Gotta Do: The Masculine Myth in Popular Culture*. London: Paladin.

EASTHOPE, A. (1991a) *British Post-Structuralism*. London: Routledge.

EASTHOPE, A. (1991b) *Literary into Cultural Studies*. London: Routledge.

EASTHOPE, A. and MCGOWAN, K. (eds), (1992) *A Critical and Cultural Theory Reader*. Milton Keynes: Open University Press.

ECO, U. (1979) *The Role of the Reader: Explorations in the Semiotics of Texts*. Bloomington, IN, and London: Indiana University Press.

ELLIS, J. (1982) *Visible Fictions*. London: Routledge and Kegan Paul.

FEATHERSTONE, M. (1991) *Consumer Culture and Postmodernism*. London: Sage.

FISKE, J. (1982) *Introduction to Communication Studies*. London: Methuen.

FISKE, J. (1983) 'The discourses of TV quiz shows or school + luck = success + sex', *Central States Speech Journal* 34, 139–50.

FISKE, J. (1984) 'Popularity and ideology: a structuralist reading of Dr Who'. In Rowland, W. and Watkins, B. (eds), *Interpreting Television: Current Research Perspectives*, Beverly Hills, CA: Sage.

FISKE, J. (1985) 'Television: a multilevel classroom resource', *Australian Journal of Screen Theory* 17/18, 106–25.

FISKE, J. (1986a) 'Television and popular culture: reflections on British and Australian critical practice', *Critical Studies in Mass Communication* 3, 200–16.

FISKE, J. (1986b) 'Television: polysemy and popularity', *Critical Studies in Mass Communication* 3, 391–408.

FISKE, J. (1986c) 'MTV: post structrual post modern', *Journal of Communication Inquiry* 10, 74–79.

FISKE, J. (1987a) *Television Culture*. New York: Routledge.

FISKE, J. (1987b) 'British cultural studies and television'. In Allen, R. (ed.), *Channels of Discourse: Television and Contemporary Criticism*, Chapel Hill, NC: University of North Carolina Press.

FISKE, J. (1989a) *Understanding Popular Culture*. Boston, MA: Unwin Hyman.

FISKE, J. (1989b) *Reading the Popular*. Boston, MA: Unwin Hyman.

FISKE, J. (1990) 'Ethnosemiotics: some personal and theoretical reflections', *Cultural Studies* 4, 85–99.

FISKE, J. (1993) *Power Plays, Power Works*. London: Verso.

FISKE, J. (1994) *Media Matters*. Minneapolis, MN: University of Minnesota Press.

FISKE, J. and HARTLEY, J. (1978) *Reading Television*. London: Methuen.

FISKE, J., HODGE, B. and TURNER, G. (1987) *Myths of Oz: Reading Australian Popular Culture*. Sydney, London and Boston, MA: Allen and Unwin.

FORGACS, D. (1989) 'Gramsci and Marxism in Britain', *New Left Review* 176, 70–90.

FOSTER, H. (1983) *Post-modern Culture*. London: Pluto Press.

FOUCAULT, M. (1978) *The History of Sexuality. Volume One: An Introduction* (trans. R. HURLEY). New York: Pantheon.

FOUCAULT, M. (1980) *Power/Knowledge: Selected Interviews and Other Writings 1972–77*. New York: Pantheon.

FOUCAULT, M. (1988) *Politics, Philosophy, Culture: Interviews and Other Writings 1977–1984*. London: Routledge.

FRANKLIN, S. et al. (eds), (1991) *Off-Centre: Feminism and Cultural Studies*. London: HarperCollins.

FRITH, S. (1988) *Music for Pleasure: Essays in the Sociology of Pop*. New York: Routledge.

FRITH, S. and GOODWIN, A. (eds), (1990) *On Record Rock, Pop and the Written Word*. New York: Pantheon.

FRITH, S., GOODWIN, A., and GROSSBERG, L. (eds), (1991) *Sound and Vision: The Music Television Reader*. Boston, MA: Unwin Hyman.

FROW, J. (1990) 'Accounting for tastes: some problems in Bourdieu's sociology of culture', *Cultural Studies* 1, 59–73.

FROW, J. (1991) 'M. de Certeau and the practice of representation', *Cultural Studies* 5, 52–60.

FROW, J. and MORRIS, M. (1993) *Australian Cultural Studies: A Reader*. St Leonards: Allen and Unwin.

GALLOP, J. (1985) *Reading Lacan*. Ithaca, NY: Cornell University Press.

GAMMAN, L. and MARSHMENT, M. (eds), (1988) *The Female Gaze: Women as Viewers of Popular Culture*. London: Verso.

GARNHAM, N. and WILLIAMS, R. (1980) 'Pierre Bourdieu and the sociology of culture: an introduction', *Media, Culture and Society* 2, 209–23.

GERAGHTY, C. (1991) *Women and Soap Opera*. Cambridge: Polity Press.

GIROUX, H. (1994) *Distrubing Pleasures*. London: Routledge.

GIROUX, H., SHUMWAY, D., SMITH, P. and SOSNOSKI, J. (1984) 'The need for cultural studies: resisting intellectuals and oppositional public spheres', *Dalhousie Review* 64, 472–86.

GIROUX, H. and SIMON, R. (eds), (1989) *Popular Culture, Schooling, and Everyday Life*. New York: Bergin and Garvey Press.

GILROY, P. (1987) *Their Ain't No Black In The Union Jack*. London: Hutchinson.

GILROY, P. (1993a) *The Black Atlantic: Modernity and Double Consciousness*. London: Verso.

GILROY, P. (1993b) *Small Acts: Thoughts on the Politics of Black Culture*. London: Serpent's Trail.

GITLIN, T. (1983) *Inside Prime Time*. New York: Pantheon.

GLEDHILL, D. (ed.), (1987) *Home is Where the Heart Is: Studies in Melodrama and the Woman's Film*. London: British Film Institute.

GODELIER, M. (1970) 'Structure and contradiction in "Capital"'. In Lane, M. (ed.), *Structuralism: A Reader*, London: Jonathan Cape.

GOODWIN, A. (1991) 'Popular music and post-modern theory', *Cultural Studies* 5, 174–203.

GRAMSCI, A. (1971) *Selections from the Prison Notebook* (ed. and trans. Q. Hoare and G. Nowell-Smith). London: Lawrence and Wishart.

GRAMSCI, A. (1985) *Selection from Cultural Writings* (ed. D. Forgacs and G. Nowell-Smith). London: Lawrence and Wishart.

GRAY, A. and McGUIGAN, J. (eds), (1993) *Studying Culture: An Introductory Reader*. London: Arnold.

GREER, G. (1971) *The Female Eunuch*. London: Paladin.

GROSSBERG, L. (1986a) 'History, politics and postmodernism: Stuart Hall and cultural studies', *Journal of Communication Inquiry* 10, 61–77.

GROSSBERG, L. (1986b) 'Teaching the popular'. In Nelson, C. (ed.) *Theory in the Classroom*, Urbana, IL: University of Illinois Press.

GROSSBERG, L. (1986c) 'Is there rock after punk?' *Critical Studies in Mass Communication* 3.

GROSSBERG, L. (1987) 'The in-difference of television', *Screen* 2, 28–45.

GROSSBERG, L. (1988) 'Wandering audiences, nomadic critics', *Cultural Studies* 2, 377–91.

GROSSBERG, L., (1989a) 'The formations of cultural studies: an American in Birmingham', *Strategies* 2, 114–49.

GROSSBERG, L. (1989b) 'The circulation of cultural studies', *Critical Studies in Mass Communication* 6, 413–20.

GROSSBERG, L. (1992) *We Gotta Get Out of this Place: Popular Conservatism and Postmodern Culture*. London: Routledge.

GROSSBERG, L. (1988) with FRY, T., CURTHOYS, A. and PATTON, P. (1988) *It's a Sin: Essays on Postmodernism, Politics, and Culture.* Sydney: Power Publications.

GROSSBERG, L. *et al.* (eds), (1992) *Cultural Studies.* London: Routledge.

GUREVITCH, M., BENNETT, T., CURRAN, J. and WOOLLACOTT, J. (eds), (1982) *Culture, Society and the Media.* London: Methuen.

HALL, S. (1977) 'Culture, the media and the "ideological effect"'. In J. Curran *et al.* (eds), *op. cit.*

HALL, S. (1980a) 'Cultural studies: two paradigms', *Media, Culture and Society* 2, 57–72. Also (1986) in Collins, R. *et al.* (eds), *Media Culture and Society: A Critical Reader,* London: Sage.

HALL, S. (1980b) 'Cultural studies and the Centre: some problematics and problems'. In Hall, S. *et al.* (eds), *op. cit.*

HALL, S. (1980c) 'Encoding and decoding'. In Hall, S. *et al.* (eds), *op. cit.*

HALL, S. (1981) 'Notes on deconstructing "the popular"' in Samuel, R. (ed.), *op. cit.*

HALL, S. (1982) 'The rediscovery of "ideology": return of the repressed in media studies'. In Gurevitch, M. *et al.* (eds), *op. cit.*

HALL, S. (1983) 'The problem of ideology – Marxism without guarantees'. In Matthews, B. (ed.), *Marx 100 Years On,* London: Lawrence and Wishart.

HALL, S. (1985) 'Signification, representation, ideology: Althusser and the post-structuralist debates', *Critical Studies in Mass Communication* 2, 91–114.

HALL, S. (1986) 'On postmodernism and articulation: an interview with Stuart Hall', *Journal of Communication Inquiry* 10.

HALL, S. (1987) 'Minimal selves'. In *The Real Me: Postmodernism and the Question of Identity,* London: ICA.

HALL, S. (1990a) 'The emergence of cultural studies and the crisis of the humanities', *October* 53, 11–90.

HALL, S. (1990b) 'Cultural identity and diaspora'. In Rutherford, J. (ed.), *op. cit.*

HALL, S. (1992) 'Cultural studies and its theoretical legacies'. In Grossberg, L. *et al.* (eds), *op. cit.*

HALL, S., CRITCHER, C., JEFFERSON, T., CLARKE, J. and ROBERTS, B. (1979) *Policing the Crisis: Mugging, the State and Law and Order.* London: Macmillan.

HALL, S., HOBSON, D., LOWE, A. and WILLIS, P. (1980) *Culture, Media, Language.* London: Hutchinson.

HALL, S. and JEFFERSON, T. (eds), (1976) *Resistance through Rituals: Youth Sub-cultures in Post-war Britain.* London: Hutchinson.

HALL, S. and WHANNEL, P. (1964) *The Popular Arts.* London: Pantheon Books.

HARRIS, D. (1992) *From Class Struggle to the Politics of Pleasure: The Effects of Gramscianism on Cultural Studies.* London: Routledge.

HARVEY, D. (1989) *The Condition of Postmodernity.* Oxford: Blackwell.

HAWKES, T. (1977) *Structuralism and Semiotics.* Berkeley, CA: University of California Press.

HEBDIGE, D. (1979) *Subculture: The Meaning of Style.* New York: Routledge.

HEBDIGE, D. (1986) 'Postmodernism and "The Other Side"', *Journal of Communication Inquiry* 10, 78–97.

HEBDIGE, D. (1987) *Cut 'n' Mix.* London: Comedia.

HEBDIGE, D. (1988) *Hiding in the Light: On Images and Things.* London: Routledge.

HELD, D. (1980) *Introduction to Critical Theory: Horkheimer to Habermas.* London: Hutchinson.

HIRSCHKOP, K. and SHEPHERD, D. (eds), (1989) *Bakhtin and Cultural Theory.* Manchester: Manchester University Press.

HOBSON, D. (1982) *Crossroads – The Drama of a Soap Opera.* London: Methuen.

HOGGART, R. (1957; rpt 1990) *The Uses of Literacy.* Harmondsworth: Penguin.

HOGGART, R. (1972) *On Culture and Communication*. New York: Oxford University Press.

HORKHEIMER, M. (1941) 'Art and mass culture', *Studies in Philosophy and Social Science* IX, (2).

HORKHEIMER, M. and ADORNO, T.W. (1972) *Dialectic Enlightenment* (trans. J. Cumming). New York: Herder and Herder.

HUYSSEN, A. (1986a) *After the Great Divide: Modernism, Mass Culture and Postmodernism*. London: Macmillan.

HUYSSEN, A. (1986b) 'Mass culture as woman: modernism's other'. In Huysen, A., *op. cit.*

Institute of Contemporary Arts (1987) *Identity: The Real Me*. London: ICA.

INGLIS, F. (1975) 'Culture and cant', *Universities Quarterly* 29.

INGLIS, F. (1993) *Cultural Studies*. Oxford: Blackwell.

JAMESON, F. (1981) *The Political Unconscious: Narrative as a Socially Symbolic Act*. Ithaca, NY: Cornell University Press.

JAMESON, F. (1984) 'Postmodernism, or the cultural logic of late capitalism', *New Left Review* 165, 53–92.

JEFFORDS, S. (1989) *The Remasculinization of America*. Bloomington, IL and Indianapolis. IN: Indiana University Press.

JENKS, C. (1993) *Culture*. London: Routledge.

JHALLY, S. (1987) *The Codes of Advertising: Fetishism and the Political Economy of Meaning in the Consumer Society*. London: Frances Pinter.

JOHNSON, R. (1987) 'What is cultural studies anyway?', *Social Text* 6, 38–90.

JONES, S. (1988) *Black Culture, White Youth*. London: Macmillan.

JORDAN, G. and WEEDON, C. (1994) *Cultural Politics*. Oxford: Blackwell.

KAPLAN, C. (1986) *Sea Changes: Culture and Feminism*. London: Verso.

KAPLAN, E.A. (ed.) (1983) *Regarding Television – Critical Approaches: An Anthology*. American Film Institute Monograph Series, Vol. 2. Frederick, MD: University Publications of America.

KAPLAN, E.A. (1986) 'History, spectatorship, and gender address in music television', *Journal of Communication Inquiry* 10, 3–14.

KAPLAN, E.A. (1987) *Rocking Around the Clock: Music Television, Postmodernism, and Consumer Culture*. New York: Methuen.

KAPLAN, E.A. (1988) *Postmodernism and its Discontents: Theories, Practices*. New York: Verso.

KAPLAN, E.A. (1992) 'Feminist Criticism and Television' in Allen, R. (ed.), *op cit*.

KELLNER, D. (1995) *Media Culture*. London and New York: Routledge.

KLEIN, M. (ed.), (1994) *An American Half Century: Postwar Culture and Politics in the USA*. London: Pluto Press.

LACLAU, E. (1977) *Politics and Ideology in Marxist Theory*. London: New Left Books.

LACLAU, E. (1990) 'Populist rupture and discourse', *Screen Education* 34, Spring.

LAING, D. (1985) 'Music video – industrial product, cultural form', *Screen* 26, 78–83.

LAING, S. (1986) *Representations of Working-Class Life, 1959–64*. London: Macmillan.

LAPLANCHE, J. and PONTALIS, J.B. (1973) *The Language of Psychoanalysis*. New York: Norton.

LATIMER, D. (1984) 'Jameson and postmodernism', *New Left Review* 148, 116–28.

LAZERE, D. (ed.), (1987) *American Media and Mass Culture*. Berkeley, CA: University of California Press.

LEAVIS, F.R. (1930) *Mass Civilisation and Minority Culture*. Cambridge: Minority Press.

LEAVIS, F.R. and THOMPSON, D. (1933) *Culture and Environment*. London: Chatto and Windus.

LEFEBVRE, H. (1984) *Everyday Life in the Modern World* (trans. Rabinovitch, S.). New Brunswick, NJ: Transaction Books.

LEFEBVRE, H. (1991) *Critique of Everyday Life* (Vol. 1). London: Verso.

LEVINE, L. (1988) *Highbrow/Lowbrow: The Emergence of Cultural Hierarchy in America.* Cambridge, MA: Harvard University Press.

LEVINE, S. (1972) 'Art values, institutions and culture', *American Quarterly* 24, 131–65.

LÉVI-STRAUSS, C. (1963) *Structural Anthropology.* New York: Basic Books.

LEWIS, L. (1990) *Gender, Politics, and MTV: Voicing the Difference.* Philadelphia, PA: Temple University Press.

LEWIS, L. (ed.), (1992) *The Adoring Audience: Fan Culture and Popular Media.* London: Routledge.

LONG, E. (1987) 'Reading groups and the postmodern crisis of cultural authority', *Cultural Studies* 1.

LONGHURST, D. (ed.), (1989) *Gender, Genre and Narrative Pleasure.* London: Unwin Hyman.

LOUVRE, A. and WALSH, J. (eds), (1988) *Tell Me Lies About Vietnam.* Milton Keynes: Open University Press.

LOVELL, T. (1983) *Pictures of Reality.* London: British Film Institute.

LYOTARD, J.-F. (1986) *The Postmodern Condition: A Report on Knowledge.* Manchester: Manchester University Press.

MacCABE, C. (ed.), (1986) *High Theory/Low Culture: Analysing Popular Television and Film.* Manchester: Manchester University Press.

MacDONALD, D. (1953) 'A theory of mass culture', *Diogenes* 3, 1–17.

MACHEREY, P. (1978) *A Theory of Literary Production.* London: Routledge and Kegan Paul.

McGUIGAN, J. (1992) *Cultural Populism.* London: Routledge.

McROBBIE, A. (1980) 'Settling accounts with subcultures', *Screen Education*, 34.

McROBBIE, A. (1982) 'The politics of feminist research: between talk, text and action', *Feminist Review*, 12.

McROBBIE, A. (1986) 'Postmodernism and popular culture'. In *Postmodernism, ICA Documents* 4, London: ICA.

McROBBIE, A. (1991a) 'New times in cultural studies', *New Formations* Spring, 1–17.

McROBBIE, A. (1991b) 'Moving cultural studies on – post-modernism and beyond', *Magazine of Cultural Studies* 4, 18–22.

McROBBIE, A. (1992) 'Post-Marxism and cultural studies: a post-script'. In Grossberg, L. *et al.* (eds), *op. cit.*

McROBBIE, A. (1994) *Postmodernism and Popular Culture.* London: Routledge.

McROBBIE, A. and NAVA, M. (eds), (1984) *Gender and Generation.* London: Macmillan.

MARCUS, G. (1989) *Lipstick Traces: A Secret History of the Twentieth Century.* Cambridge, MA: Harvard University Press.

MARX, K. (1976) *Preface and Introduction to 'A Critique of Political Economy'.* Peking: Foreign Languages Press.

MARX, K. and ENGELS, F. (1970) *The German Ideology.* London: Lawrence and Wishart.

MARX, K. and ENGELS, F. (1977) *Selected Letters.* Peking: Foreign Languages Press.

MASTERMAN, L. (ed.), (1984) *Television Mythologies: Stars, Shows and Signs.* London: Comedia/UK Media Press.

MELLANCAMP, P. (ed.), (1990) *The Logics of Television.* Bloomington, IA: Indiana University Press.

MERCER, C. (1988) 'Entertainment, or the policing of virtue', *New Formations* 4, 41–71.

MERCER, K. (1988) 'Diaspora culture and the dialogic imagination'. In Cham, W. and Andrade-Watkins, C. (eds), *op. cit.*

MERCER, K. (1990) 'Welcome to the jungle: identity and diversity in postmodern politics'. In Rutherford, J. (ed.) *op. cit.*

MIDDLETON, R. (1990) *Studying Popular Music.* Milton Keynes: Open University Press.

MILNER, A. (1991) *Contemporary Cultural Studies.* Sydney: Allen and Unwin.

MODLESKI, T. (1984) *Loving with a Vengeance.* London: Methuen.

MODLESKI, T. (1986a) 'Femininity as mas(s)querade: a feminist approach to mass culture'. In McCabe, C. (ed.) *op. cit.*

MODLESKI, T. (ed.), (1986b) *Studies in Entertainment: Critical Approaches to Mass Culture.* Bloomington, IN: Indiana University Press.

MOHANTY, C. (1988) 'Under western eyes: feminist scholarship and colonial discourses', *Feminist Review* 30, 60–88.

MORLEY, D. (1980) *The 'Nationwide' Audience: Structure and Decoding.* London: British Film Institute.

MORLEY, D. (1986) *Family Television: Cultural Power and Domestic Leisure.* London: Comedia.

MORLEY, D. and CHEN, K.-H. (eds), (1996) *Stuart Hall: Critical Dialogues in Cultural Studies.* London: Routledge.

MORRIS, M. (1988a) 'At Henry Parkes Motel', *Cultural Studies* 2, 1–47.

MORRIS, M. (1988b) *The Pirate's Financée.* London: Verso.

MORRIS, M. (1990) 'Banality in cultural studies'. In P. Mellencamp (ed.), *op. cit.*, and (1988) *Block 14* Autumn; (1988) *Discourse* 10, 3–29.

MUKERJI, C. and SCHUDSON, M. (1991) *Rethinking Popular Culture: Contemporary Perspectives in Cultural Studies.* Berkeley, CA: University of California Press.

MULVEY, L. (1989) *Visual and Other Pleasures.* London: Macmillan.

NAREMORE, J. and BRANTLINGER, P. (eds), (1991) *Modernity and Mass Culture.* Bloomington, IL and Indianapolis, IN: Indiana University Press.

NAVA, M. (1987) 'Consumerism and its Contradictions', *Cultural Studies* 1, 2.

NEAL, S. (1980) *Genre.* London: British Film Institute.

NELSON, C. and GROSSBERG, L. (eds), (1988) *Marxism and the Interpretation of Culture.* Urbana, IL: University of Illinois Press.

NELSON, C. *et al.* (1992) 'Cultural studies: an introduction'. In Grossberg, L. *et al.* (eds), *op. cit.*

NICHOLSON, L.J. (ed.), (1990) *Feminism/Postmodernism.* New York: Routledge.

O'CONNOR, A. (1989) 'The problem of American cultural studies', *Critical Studies in Mass Communication* 6, 405–13.

Open University (1982) *Popular Culture (U203).* Milton Keynes: Open University Press.

O'SHEA, M. and SCHWARZ, B. (1987) 'Reconsidering popular culture', *Screen* 28, 104–109.

PALMER, J. (1991) *Potboilers: Methods, Concepts and Case studies in Popular Fiction.* London: Routledge.

PARMAR, P. (1990) 'Black feminism: the politics of articulation'. In Rutherford, J. (ed.), *op. cit.*

PAWLING, C. (ed.), (1984) *Popular Fiction and Social Change.* London: Macmillan.

PENLEY, C. (ed.), (1988) *Feminism and Film Theory.* New York and London: Routledge/BFI Publishing.

PRIBRAM, E.D. (ed.), (1988) *Female Spectators: Looking at Film and Television.* New York and London: Verso.

PUNTER, D. (ed.), (1986) *Introduction to Contemporary Cultural Studies.* London: Longman.

RADWAY, J. (1984) *Reading the Romance: Women, Patriarchy, and Popular Literature.* Chapel Hill, NC: University of North Carolina Press; (1987) London: Verso.

RADWAY, J. (1986a) 'Reading is not eating: mass culture, analytical method, and political practice', *Communication* 9, 93–123.

RADWAY, J. (1986b) 'Identifying ideological seams: mass culture, analytical method, and political practice', *Communication* 9, 93–123.

RADWAY, J. (1988) 'Reception study: ethnography and the problems of dispersed audiences and nomadic subjects', *Cultural Studies* 2, 359–67.

RADWAY, J. (1990) 'The scandal of the middlebrow: the Book-of-the-Month Club, class fracture, and cultural authority', *South Atlantic Quarterly* Fall, 703–704.

RAKOW, L.F. (1986) 'Feminist approaches to popular culture: giving patriarchy its due', *Communication* 9, 19–41.

RANSOME, P. (1992) *Antonio Gramsci: A New Introduction.* Hemel Hempstead: Harvester Wheatsheaf.

REGAN, S. (1993) *Raymond Williams.* Hemel Hempstead: Harvester Wheatsheaf.

ROBBINS, D. (1991) *The Work of Pierre Bourdieu.* Milton Keynes: Open University Press.

ROMAN, L.G. *et al.* (1988) *Becoming Feminine: The Politics of Popular Culture.* London: Falmer Press.

ROSENBERG, B. and WHITE, D.W. (eds), (1957) *Mass culture: The Popular Arts in America.* New York: Macmillan.

ROSS, A. (ed.), (1988) *Universal Abandon? The Politics of Post-modernism.* Minneapolis, MN: University of Minnesota Press.

ROSS, A. (1989) *No Respect: Intellectuals and Popular Culture.* London: Routledge.

RUTHERFORD, J. (ed.), (1990) *Identity, Community, Culture, Difference.* London: Lawrence and Wishart.

RYAN, M. and KELLNER, D. (1988) *Camera Politica: The Politics and Ideology of Contemporary Hollywood Film.* Bloomington, IL: Indiana University Press.

RYLANCE, R. (1993) *Roland Barthes.* Hemel Hempstead: Harvester Wheatsehaf.

SAID, E. (1978) *Orientalism.* New York: Random House; (1985) Harmondsworth: Penguin Books.

SAMSON, A. (1992) *F.R. Leavis.* Hemel Hempstead: Harvester Wheatsheaf.

SAMUEL, R. (ed.), (1981) *People's History and Socialist Theory.* London: Routledge and Kegan Paul.

SARUP, M. (1993) *An Introductory Guide to Post-Structuralism and Postmodernism* (2nd edn). Hemel Hempstead: Harverster Wheatsheaf.

SCHUDSON, M. (1987) 'The new validation of popular culture: sense and sentimentality in academia', *Critical Studies in Mass Communication* 4, 51–68.

SCHWARZ, B. (1985) 'Gramsci goes to Disneyland: postmodernism and the popular', *Anglistica* (Naples) 28.

SCHWARZ, B. (1989) 'Popular culture: the long march', *Culture Studies* 3, 250–54.

SCHWARZ, B. (1994) 'Where is Cultural studies?' *Cultural Studies* 8,

SEITER, E., BORCHERS, H., KREUTZNER, G. and WARTH, E.-M. (eds), (1989) *Remote Control: Television, Audiences, and Cultural Power.* London: Routledge.

SHERIDAN, A. (1980) *Michel Foucault: The Will to Truth.* London: Tavistock.

SHIACH, M. (1989) *Discourse on Popular Culture.* Cambridge: Polity Press.

SHIACH, M. (1991) 'Feminism and popular culture', *Critical Quarterly* 33, 37–45.

SILVERMAN, K. (1983) *The Subject of Semiotics.* New York and Oxford: Oxford University Press.

SIM, S. (ed.), (1995) *The A–Z Guide to Modern Literary and Cultural Theorists.* Hemel Hempstead: Harvester Wheatsheaf.

SLATER, P. (1977) *Origin and Significance of the Frankfurt School.* London: Routledge.

SONTAG, S. (1966) *Against Interpretation.* New York: Deli.

SONTAG, S. (1982) *A Susan Sontag Reader*. New York: Farrar, Straus and Giroux.

SPIGEL, L. (1988) 'Installing the television set: popular discourses on television and domestic space, 1948–1955', *Camera Obscura* 16, 11–46.

SPIVAK, G.C. (1987) *In Other Worlds: Essays in Cultural Politics*. London and New York: Methuen.

STALLYBRASS, P. and WHITE, A. (1986) *The Politics and Poetics of Transgression*. London: Methuen.

STEDMAN JONES, G. (1973–74) 'Working-class culture and working-class politics in London, 1870–1900: notes on the remaking of a working class', *Journal of Social History* 7, 461–508.

STEPHANSON, A. (1987) 'Regarding postmodernism – a conversation with Fredric Jameson', *Social Text* 17, 29–54.

STOREY, J. (1993) *An Introductory Guide to Cultural Theory and Popular Culture*. Hemel Hempstead: Harvester Wheatsheaf.

STOREY, J. (ed.), (1994) *Cultural Theory and Popular Culture: A Reader*. Hemel Hempstead: Harvester Wheatsheaf.

STOREY, J. (1996) *Cultural Studies and the Study of Popular Culture*. Edinburgh: Edinburgh University Press.

STRINATI, D. (1992) 'Postmodernism and popular culture', *Sociology Review* April.

STRINATI, D. (1995) *An Introduction to Theories of Popular Culture*. London: Routledge.

TASKER, Y. (1991) *Feminist Crime Writing: The Politics of Genre*. Sheffield: Pavic.

TAYLOR, H. (1989) *Scarlett's Women*. London: Virago.

THOMPSON, E.P. (1961) 'Review of *The Long Revolution*', *New Left Review* 9, 24–33.

THOMPSON, E.P. (1963; rpt 1966) *The Making of the English Working Class*. New York: Vintage.

THOMPSON, E.P. (1978) *The Poverty of theory and Other Essays*. London: Merlin Press.

THWAITES, T., DAVIS, L. and MULES, W. (1994) *Tools for Cultural Studies: An Introduction*. South Melbourne: Macmillan.

TRAUBE, E. (1992) *Dreaming Identities: Class, Gender, and generation in 1980s Hollywood Movies*. Boulder, CO: Westview Press.

TULLOCH, J. and ALVARDO, M. (1983) *'Doctor Who': The Unfolding Text*. London: Macmillan.

TURNER, G. (1991) *British Cultural Studies: An Introduction*. Boston, MA: Unwin Hyman.

URRY, J. (1990) *The Tourist Gaze: Leisure and Travel in Contemporary Societies*. London: Sage.

VOLOSINOV, V.N. (1973) *Marxism and the Philosophy of Language*. London: Seminar Press.

WAITES, B., BENNETT, T. and MARTIN, G. (eds), (1982) *Popular Culture Past and Present*. London: Croom Helm/Open University Press.

WALSH, J. (ed.), (1995) *The Gulf War Did Not Happen*. Aldershot: Arena.

WEBSTER, D. (1988) *Looka Yonder: The Imaginary America of Popular Culture*. London: Comedia/Routledge.

WEBSTER, D. (1990) 'Pessimism, optimism, pleasure: the future of cultural studies', *News From Nowhere* 8.

WEEDON, C. (1987) *Feminist Practice and Poststructuralist Theory*. Oxford: Blackwell.

WHITE, M. (1992) 'Ideological analysis and television'. In Allen, R. (ed.), *op. cit.*

WILLIAMS, P. (1993) *Colonial Discourse and Post-Colonial Theory: A Reader*. Hemel Hempstead: Harvester Wheatsheaf.

WILLIAMS, R. (1958) *Culture and Society 1780–1950*. London: Chatto and Windus; (1963) Harmondsworth: Penguin Books.

WILLIAMS, R. (1961; rpt 1965) *The Long Revolution*. London: Penguin Books.
WILLIAMS, R. (1975) *Television: Technology and Cultural Form*. New York: Schocken Books.
WILLIAMS, R. (1976) *Keywords*. London: Fontana. (Second edition, 1983.)
WILLIAMS, R. (1977) *Marxism and Literature*. Oxford: Oxford University Press.
WILLIAMS, R. (1979) *Politics and Letters*. London: Verso.
WILLIAMS, R. (1981) *Culture*. London: Fontana.
WILLIAMS, R. (1989) *The Politics of Modernism: Against the New Conformists*. London: Verso.
WILLIAMSON, J. (1978) *Decoding Advertisements: Ideology and Meaning in Advertising*. London: Marion Boyars.
WILLIAMSON, J. (1986a) 'The problems of being popular', *New Socialist* September, 14–15.
WILLIAMSON, J. (1986b) *Consuming Passions: The Dynamics of Popular Culture*. London and New York: Marion Boyers.
WILLIS, P. (1977) *Learning to Labour: How Working Class Kids get Working Class Jobs*. Farnborough: Saxon House.
WILLIS, P. (1978) *Profane Cultures*. London: Routledge and Kegan Paul.
WILLIS, P. (1990) *Common Culture*. Milton Keynes: Open University Press.
WINSHIP, J. (1987) *Inside Women's Magazines*. London: Pandora.
WOLMARK, J. (1993) *Aliens and Others: Science Fiction, Feminism and Postmodernism*. Hemel Hempstead: Harvester Wheatsheaf.
Women's Studies Group, Centre for Contemporary Cultural Studies (1978) *Women Take Issue: Aspects of Women's Subordination*. London: Hutchinson.

Index

Adorno, T.W. 92, 93, 226
adult education 169, 170, 171, 172
African-American studies 12, 213
Agger, B. 59
Althusser, L. 20, 22, 23, 39, 40, 41, 45, 57, 77, 115, 117, 118, 121, 124, 187, 189, 211, 215, 289, 290, 300
American Studies 211, 213, 215, 216
Amos, V. 198
Ang, I. 7, 9, 324
Another Tale to Tell 297
Archeology of Knowledge, The 362
Armstrong, N. 208, 209, 295
Arnold, M. 15, 313, 359
Aronowitz, S. 295
audience/audience studies 2, 9, 127, 128, 132, 143, 222, 234, 239, 240, 241, 242, 243, 244, 245, 251, 323, 333, 355
Austin, R. 304

Bailey, D. 302
Baker, Jr. H. 302
Bakhtin, M. 126, 173
Baldwin, J. 301
Bambara, T. 301
Barker, M. 7, 221
Barthes, R. 84, 96, 98, 102, 290
'Base and Superstructure in Marxist Cultural Analysis' 36
base/superstructure metaphor 9, 35, 36, 37, 38, 40, 46, 48, 117, 289
Baudrillard, J. 147, 153, 154, 155, 156, 160, 161, 164, 166, 227, 229, 233, 362
Bee, J. 325
Beechey, V. 256
Beezer, A. 7
Bell, D. 68

Benjamin, W. 92, 93, 173, 180, 210, 226, 289, 314
Bennett, T. 3, 5, 96, 142, 199, 292, 327, 347, 349, 356, 360, 361, 362
Bennett, W. 209
Benston, M. 256
Berelson, B. 61
Bernstein, B. 54, 100
Bhaba, H. 165
Birmingham Centre for Contemporary Cultural Studies 5, 7, 8, 11, 12, 14, 16, 20, 24, 25, 26, 33, 49, 55, 57, 59, 65, 83, 92, 97, 98, 99, 106, 115, 148, 179, 182, 187, 191, 197, 198, 199, 200, 201, 215, 225, 238, 273, 288, 289, 290, 291, 293, 296, 300, 302, 303, 336, 338, 340, 359, 360
black Audio Film Collective 302
Black Skin, White Masks 342
Blake, W. 51
Bordon, L. 192
Bourdieu, P. 64, 67, 191, 230, 231, 316, 358, 362
Boyce, S. 302, 303
Braithwaite, H. 301
Brantlinger, P. 287, 293, 294, 295
Brecht, B. 93, 94, 99, 102, 317, 318
Brennon, T. 288
Brophy, P. 362
Brunsdon, C. 128, 198
Brunt, R. 235
Buhle, M. 211
Bunch, C. 257
Burke, K. 64, 67
Burnett, C. 305

Cain, W. 294
Canclini, G. 247
Capital 43, 80, 81, 184
capitalism 17, 18, 19, 20, 23, 24, 27, 38, 42, 43,

production in use 4, 9
psychoanalysis 46, 95, 98, 118, 128, 162, 258,
    259, 260, 261, 263, 265, 275, 300, 362
Psychoanalysis and Feminism 229

race 3, 8, 10, 13, 76, 89, 106, 116, 125, 127, 128,
    139, 144, 161, 198, 199, 200, 202, 233, 245,
    260, 273, 280, 281, 282, 288, 290, 293, 300,
    301, 302, 316, 317, 318, 323, 338, 339, 340,
    341, 345, 350, 360
Race Today 187
racism 12, 76, 77, 105, 250, 257, 260, 284, 288,
    290, 293, 294, 303, 304, 339, 340, 341, 342,
    343, 347, 348, 350, 363
Radway, J. 211, 277, 278
Reading Capital 40
Reading the Popular 221
Reaganism 225
reception analysis 239, 240, 242
Rein, S. 166
reproduction 9, 70, 260
Resistance Through Rituals 21, 23, 188, 288
Rich, A. 212, 257
Richards, I.A. 170, 175
Richardson, K. 128
Richetti, J. 274
Riesman, D. 64
Riggs, M. 302
Road to Wigan Pier, The 234
Robbins, B. 212, 293
Robinson, C. 301
Robinson, P. 345
Roman, L. 197, 202
Rooney, E. 12
Root, J. 221, 222
Rorty, R. 63, 67, 239
Rose, T. 202, 258, 304
Rosengren, K. 237
Ross, A. 231, 323
Rushdi, S. 241
Ruskin, J. 16
Ruthven, K. 310, 311, 322, 328

Said, E. 250, 351
Sanders, N., 347, 349, 356
Saussure, F. de 39, 262
Sayers, J. 258
Seabrook, J. 264
Secombe, W. 256
Schlesinger, P. 249
Schwarz, B. 234
Scott, J. 295
Screen/Screen theory 99, 100, 115, 128, 182,
    259, 291, 324
Sembene, O. 301
semiology-semiotics 39, 46, 91, 94, 95, 96, 98,
    99, 101, 107, 108, 127, 128, 132, 137, 140,
    158, 187, 191, 202, 221, 233, 261, 262, 274,
    279, 302, 323, 358

Sex, Class and Realism 222
Shange, N. 301
Showalter, E. 159, 228
Silber, J. 208
Sojcher, J. 162
Southern Review 322
Sparks, C. 1
Spelman, E. 257
Spender, D. 214
Spivak, G. 212, 214, 278
Steedman, C. 293
Stern, L. 349, 357, 362
Strong, A. 199
Structuralism 4, 36, 39, 40, 41, 42, 43, 44, 46,
    47, 48, 53, 65, 66, 69, 81, 86, 94, 95, 98,
    100, 103, 104, 106, 115, 116, 127, 128, 132,
    173, 262, 263, 289, 323
'structure of feeling' 34, 35, 38, 69, 189, 190,
    349
'Subcultural Conflict and Working Class
    Community' 21
Subculture 288
subcultures/subcultural theory 21, 22, 23, 26,
    53, 65, 158, 189, 190, 197, 198, 201, 202,
    222, 242, 260, 264, 273, 310, 323, 327, 359
subjective forms 83, 86, 91, 95, 97, 98, 106
subjects/subjectivity 23, 46, 70, 77, 80, 81, 82,
    83, 86, 95, 96, 98, 99, 100, 101, 102, 103,
    104, 116, 118, 119, 120, 121, 122, 124, 128,
    131, 133, 135, 136, 137, 258, 259, 260, 263,
    267, 290, 292, 301, 306

Tate, G. 304
Television Culture 325
Television, Technology and Cultural Form 324
texts/textuality 2, 53, 83, 85, 94, 96, 97, 98, 99,
    107, 130, 143, 180, 263, 355, 356
Thatcherism/Thatcher, M. 49, 92, 175, 223,
    224, 256, 289, 333
There Ain't No Black in the Union Jack 8, 288,
    294, 301
Thiongo, N.W. 301
Thompson, E.P. 32, 33, 36, 37, 38, 51, 65, 66,
    86, 90, 171, 225, 264, 288, 289, 290, 326
Tololyan, K. 209
Tolson, A. 25
Torr, D., 290
Travesia 60
Treichler, P. 358
Tripp, D. 128
Turner, G. 11, 292, 327, 349, 350, 359, 360
Turner, I. 359

Understanding Popular Culture 221
Unpopular Education 92, 93, 97
Uses of Literacy, The, 14, 32, 50, 53, 170, 290

Vietnam War 16, 67, 124, 212, 276
Volosinov, V.N. 4, 100, 127, 173